KJV

Standard
LESSON COMMENTARY®

Edited by
Ronald L. Nickelson

KING JAMES
VERSION

Jonathan Underwood,
Senior Editor

Volume 60

Standard®
PUBLISHING

Cincinnati, Ohio

IN THIS VOLUME

Scripture taken from the *King James Version*.

Lessons based on International Sunday School Lessons © 2009 by the Lesson Committee.

INDEX OF PRINTED TEXTS

The printed texts for 2012–2013 are arranged here in the order in which they appear in the Bible.

DVD-ROM AVAILABLE

The *Standard Lesson Commentary*® is available in an electronic format in special editions of this volume. The DVD contains the full text of the King James *Standard Lesson Commentary* and *The NIV® Standard Lesson Commentary* powered by Bible Explorer® from WORDsearch™ Bible Software, additional study helps, and a collection of presentation helps that can be projected or reproduced as handouts. Order 020510212 (KJV) or 020520212 (NIV). Some 200 additional books and resources are available by FREE download from www.wordsearchbible.com/freebooks.

For questions regarding the installation, registration, or activation of the DVD, contact WORDsearch Customer Service at (800) 888-9898 or (512) 832-2125, Mon–Fri, 9 AM to 10 PM; or Sat, 10 AM to 5 PM (Central Time). For problems with the DVD, contact WORDsearch Technical Support at (512) 835-6900, Mon–Fri, 9 AM to 5:30 PM (Central Time) or by e-mail at Support@WORDsearchBible.com.

Logos users! You can purchase the *Standard Lesson eCommentary* as a direct download from www.logos.com/standard. This is a separate purchase from the print edition.

CUMULATIVE INDEX

A cumulative index for Scripture passages used in the STANDARD LESSON COMMENTARY
for September 2010—August 2013 is provided below.

HOW TO SAY IT

Abraham *Ay*-bruh-ham.
Adramyttium Ad-ruh-*mitt*-ee-um.
agape *(Greek)* uh-*gah*-pay.
Ahasuerus Uh-haz-you-*ee*-rus.
Ahava Uh-*hay*-vuh.
Ahaz *Ay*-haz.
Alexandrians Al-ex-*an*-dree-unz.
Amaziah Am-uh-*zye*-uh.
Ammonites *Am*-un-ites.
Amos *Ay*-mus.
Ananias An-uh-*nye*-us.
Antiochus Epiphanes An-*tie*-oh-kus
   Ih-*piff*-a-neez.
apocalypse uh-*pock*-uh-lips.
apocalyptic uh-*pah*-kuh-*lip*-tik.
Apocrypha Uh-*paw*-kruh-fuh.
apologetics uh-*pah*-luh-**jeh**-tiks.
apostasy uh-*pahs*-tuh-see.
Aram *Air*-um.
Archippus Ar-*kip*-us.
Aristarchus Air-iss-*tar*-cuss.
Artaxerxes Are-tuh-*zerk*-seez.
Artemis *Ar*-teh-miss.
Asaph *Ay*-saff.
Asia *Ay*-zha.
Assyria Uh-*sear*-ee-uh.
Assyrian Uh-*sear*-e-un.
Augustine *Aw*-gus-teen
   or Aw-*gus*-tin.
Azarael *Az*-air-el or Ah-*zay*-ree-ul.
Azariah Az-uh-*rye*-uh.

Baal *Bay*-ul.
Babylon *Bab*-uh-lun.
Babylonian Bab-ih-*low*-nee-un.
Barbarian Bar-*bare*-ee-un.
Barnabas *Bar*-nuh-bus.
Belshazzar Bel-*shazz*-er.
Bethany *Beth*-uh-nee.
Bethlehem *Beth*-lih-hem.
Binnui *Bin*-you-eye.
Bithynia Bih-*thin*-ee-uh.

Caesar Augustus *See*-zer Aw-*gus*-tus.
Caesarea Sess-uh-*ree*-uh.
Caligula Kuh-*lig*-you-luh.
Canaan *Kay*-nun.
Cappadocia Kap-uh-*doe*-shuh.
Chaldeans Kal-*dee*-unz.

Chaldees *Kal*-deez.
cherubims *chair*-uh-bims.
Cilicia Sih-*lish*-i-uh.
Cleopas *Clee*-uh-pass.
Cleophas *Klee*-o-fus.
Colosse Ko-*lahss*-ee.
Colossians Kuh-*losh*-unz.
concision kun-*sih*-zhun.
concupiscence kon-*cue*-puh-sense.
Constantine **Kahns**-tun-*teen.*
Corinth *Kor*-inth.
Corinthians Ko-*rin*-thee-unz
   (*th* as in *thin*).
Crete Creet.
Cyrenaica Sir-uh-**nay**-ih-kuh.
Cyrenians Sigh-*ree*-nee-unz.
Cyrus *Sigh*-russ.

Damascus Duh-*mass*-kus.
Darius Duh-*rye*-us.
Deuteronomy Due-ter-*ahn*-uh-me.
diaspora dee-*as*-puh-ruh.
Diocletian Dye-uh-*klee*-shun.
Donatus *Don*-uh-tuss.

Ebal *Ee*-bull.
Ecclesiastes Ik-*leez*-ee-*as*-teez.
Egyptian Ee-*jip*-shun.
Elamites *Ee*-luh-mites.
Elijah Ee-*lye*-juh.
Elim *Ee*-lim.
Emmaus Em-*may*-us.
Enoch *E*-nock.
Epaphras *Ep*-uh-frass.
Epaphroditus Ee-*paf*-ro-**dye**-tus.
Ephesians Ee-*fee*-zhunz.
Ephesus *Ef*-uh-sus.
Ephraim *Ee*-fray-im.
eschatology ess-kuh-*tah*-luh-gee.
Esdras *Ez*-druss.
Ethanim *Eth*-uh-nim.
Ethiopian E-thee-o-*pee*-un (*th* as
   in *thin*).
Eucharist *You*-kuh-rust.
eunuch *you*-nick.
Euphrates You-*fray*-teez.
Eurydice You-*rih*-dih-see.

Felix *Fee*-licks.

Festus *Fes*-tus.

Galatia Guh-*lay*-shuh.
Galatians Guh-*lay*-shunz.
Galilaeans Gal-uh-*lee*-unz.
Gamaliel Guh-*may*-lih-ul
   or Guh-*may*-lee-al.
genealogy jee-nee-*ah*-luh-jee.
Gentiles *Jen*-tiles.
Gerizim *Gair*-ih-zeem
   or Guh-*rye*-zim.
Gethsemane Geth-*sem*-uh-nee
   (G as in *get*).
Gihon *Gye*-hahn.
Gilalai *Gill*-ah-lie (*G* as in *get*).
Grecians *Gree*-shunz.

Habakkuk Huh-*back*-kuk.
Hagar *Hay*-gar.
Haggai *Hag*-eye or *Hag*-ay-eye.
Hanani Huh-*nay*-nye.
Hashabiah Hash-uh-*bye*-uh.
Hebrews *Hee*-brews.
Henadad *Hen*-uh-dad.
heresies *hair*-uh-seez.
heretic *hair*-ih-tik.
Herod Agrippa *Hair*-ud Uh-*grip*-puh.
Herodotus Heh-*rod*-uh-tus.
Hezekiah Hez-ih-*kye*-uh.
Hierapolis Hi-er-*ap*-o-lis.
Hodaviah Hoe-duh-**vie**-uh.
Horeb *Ho*-reb.
Hosea Ho-*zay*-uh.
Hoshaiah Hoe-*shay*-yuh.

Isaac *Eye*-zuk.
Isaiah Eye-*zay*-uh.
Ishmael *Ish*-may-el.

Jebusite *Jeb*-yuh-site.
Jechonias Jek-o-**nye**-us.
Jehoiachin Jeh-*hoy*-uh-kin.
Jeshua *Jesh*-you-uh.
Jonah *Jo*-nuh.
Josephus Jo-*see*-fus.
Jozabad *Jaws*-ah-bad.
Jozadak *Joz*-uh-dak.
Judaea or Judea Joo-*dee*-v
Judah *Joo*-duh.

Judaism *Joo*-duh-izz-um
   or *Joo*-day-izz-um.
Judaizers **Joo**-duh-*ize*-ers.
Judas Iscariot *Joo*-dus Iss-*care*-ee-ut.
Julius Caesar *Joo*-lee-us *See*-zer.

Kadmiel *Cad*-mih-el.
Keturah Keh-*too*-ruh.
Ketuvim *(Hebrew)* *Ket*-you-vim.

Lamentations Lam-en-*tay*-shunz.
Laodicea Lay-*odd*-uh-**see**-uh.
lasciviousness luh-*sih*-vee-us-nuss.
Levites *Lee*-vites.
levitical leh-*vit*-ih-kul.
Libertines *Lib*-er-teens.
Lucian *Loo*-shun.
Lysimachus Lie-*sih*-meh-kus.

Maai May-*a*-eye.
Maccabees *Mack*-uh-bees.
Macedon *Mah*-suh-dun.
Macedonian Mass-eh-*doe*-nee-un.
Magdalene *Mag*-duh-leen
   or Mag-duh-*lee*-nee.
Maranatha *(Aramaic)* Mah-ruh-
   nay-thuh.
martyrdom *mar*-ter-dum.
Mattaniah Mat-uh-*nye*-uh.
Medes Meeds.
Mediterranean Med-uh-tuh-**ray**-
   nee-un.
Medo-Persia *Mee*-doe *Per*-zhuh.
Melchizedek Mel-*kiz*-eh-dek.
Melita *Mel*-i-tuh.
Meremoth *Mair*-ee-moth.
Mesopotamia Mes-uh-puh-**tay**-
   me-uh.
Messiah Meh-*sigh*-uh.
messianic mess-ee-*an*-ick.
Michaiah My-*kay*-uh.
Milalai Mih-ah-*lay*-eye.
Moabites *Mo*-ub-ites.
Moses *Mo*-zes or *Mo*-zez.

Nazareth *Naz*-uh-reth.
Nebuchadnezzar *Neb*-yuh-kud-
   nez-er.
Nehemiah *Nee*-huh-**my**-uh.
Nethaneel Nih-*than*-e-el
   (*th* as in *thin*).
Nethinims *Neth*-ih-nims.
Netopha *Nee*-*toe*-fuh.

Nevi'im *(Hebrew)* *Neh*-vih-im.
Nineveh *Nin*-uh-vuh.
Noadiah No-uh-**die**-uh.
Noah *No*-uh.
Nymphas *Nim*-fuss.

Olivet *Ol*-ih-vet.
omniscient ahm-*nish*-unt.
Onesimus O-*ness*-ih-muss.
Orpheus *Or*-fyus or *Or*-fee-us.

Pamphylia Pam-*fill*-ee-uh.
Parousia *(Greek)* Par-*oo*-see-uh.
Parthians *Par*-thee-unz
   (*th* as in *thin*).
patriarch *pay*-tree-ark.
patriarchs *pay*-tree-arks.
Pentecost *Pent*-ih-kost.
Persia *Per*-zhuh.
Pharisee *Fair*-ih-see.
Pharisees *Fair*-ih-seez.
Philemon Fih-*lee*-mun or
   Fye-*lee*-mun.
Philippi Fih-*lip*-pie or *Fil*-ih-pie.
Philippians Fih-*lip*-ee-unz.
Phinehas *Fin*-ee-us.
Phoenician Fuh-*nish*-un.
Phrygia *Frij*-e-uh.
Pontus *Pon*-tuss.
proselytes *prahss*-uh-lights.
Ptolemy *Tahl*-uh-me.
Publius *Pub*-lih-us.

Qumran Koom-*rahn*.

rabbi *rab*-eye.
Rahab *Ray*-hab.

Sadducee *Sad*-you-see.
Salamis *Sal*-uh-mis.
Samaria Suh-*mare*-ee-uh.
Samaritans Suh-*mare*-uh-tunz.
Samosata Suh-*mah*-suh-tah.
Sanhedrin *San*-huh-drun
   or San-*heed*-run.
Sapphira Suh-*fye*-ruh.
Scythian *Sith*-ee-un.
Sebaste Seh-*bas*-tee.
seder *say*-der.
Selah *(Hebrew)* *See*-luh.
Seleucus Suh-*loo*-kuss.
Septuagint Sep-*too*-ih-jent.
Seraiah Se-*ray*-yuh or Se-*rye*-uh.

seraphims *sair*-uh-fims.
shalom *(Hebrew)* shah-*lome*.
Shealtiel She-*al*-tee-el.
Shemaiah She-*may*-yuh
   or Shee-*my*-uh.
Sherebiah Sher-ee-**bye**-uh.
Shetharboznai She-thar-**boz**-nye.
Silas *Sigh*-luss.
Sinai *Sigh*-nye or *Sigh*-nay-eye.
Sion *Zi*-un.
Sodom *Sod*-um.
Susa *Soo*-suh.
Sychar *Sigh*-kar.
synagogue *sin*-uh-gog.
syncretism *sin*-kreh-*tih*-zum.
Syria *Sear*-ee-uh.

tabernacle **tah**-burr-*nah*-kul.
Tarsus *Tar*-sus.
Tatnai *Tat*-nye or *Tat*-eh-nye.
Tertullian Tur-*tull*-yun.
Theodosius Thee-uh-**doe**-shus.
theophany thee-*ah*-fuh-nee
   (*th* as in *thin*).
Thermopylae Thur-*muh*-puh-lee.
Thessalonians Thess-uh-**lo**-nee-unz
   (*th* as in *thin*).
Thessalonica Thess-uh-lo-**nye**-kuh
   (*th* as in *thin*).
Tiberias Tie-*beer*-ee-us.
Tiglath-pileser *Tig*-lath-pih-*lee*-zer.
Tigris *Tie*-griss.
Tishri *Tish*-ree.
Tobiah Toe-*bye*-uh.
Torah *(Hebrew)* *Tor*-uh.
traditores *(Latin)* trad-ih-*tor*-ez.
Tychicus *Tick*-ih-cuss.
Tyre Tire.

Ulai *You*-lye or *You*-luh-eye.
Ur Er.
Uzziah Uh-*zye*-uh.

victuals *vih*-tulz.

Xerxes *Zerk*-seez.

Yahweh *(Hebrew)* *Yah*-weh.

Zechariah Zek-uh-**rye**-uh.
Zephaniah Zef-uh-*nye*-uh.
Zerubbabel Zeh-*rub*-uh-bul.
Zion *Zi*-un.

A LIVING FAITH

Special Features

Lessons

Unit 1: What Is Faith?

Unit 2: Who Understands Faith?

Unit 3: Where Does Faith Take Us?

QUARTERLY QUIZ

Use these questions as a pretest or as a review. The answers are on page iv of This Quarter in the Word.

Lesson 1

1. No more _____ for willful sins remains after receiving knowledge of the truth. *Hebrews 10:26*

2. It is a fearful thing to fall into the hands of the living God. T/F. *Hebrews 10:31*

Lesson 2

1. Which Old Testament man was taken by God without experiencing death? (Moses, Abraham, Enoch?) *Hebrews 11:5*

2. The psalmist explains why he is afraid during cataclysmic events. T/F. *Psalm 46:2, 3*

Lesson 3

1. Experiencing the Lord's discipline provides assurance that He loves us. T/F. *Hebrews 12:6*

2. The discipline of the Lord is meant to result in what? (spiritual hardness, righteousness, new testings?) *Hebrews 12:11*

Lesson 4

1. The blood of Jesus is more effective than the blood of which Old Testament murder victim? (Abel, Jonathan, Absalom?) *Hebrews 12:24*

2. "God is a consuming _____." *Hebrews 12:29*

Lesson 5

1. When we show hospitality to strangers, we may be entertaining _____. *Hebrews 13:2*

2. Sacrificing one's body is always a noble act of love. T/F. *1 Corinthians 13:3*

Lesson 6

1. Stephen performed great wonders and miracles. T/F. *Acts 6:8*

2. Solomon built a house for God, not David. T/F. *Acts 7:45-47*

Lesson 7

1. Stephen said those who rejected his message were uncircumcised in _____ and _____. *Acts 7:51*

2. Just before dying, Stephen had a vision of whom? (David, Moses, Jesus?) *Acts 7:55*

Lesson 8

1. The believers in Samaria did not receive the Holy Spirit until Andrew came. T/F. *Acts 8:14-17*

2. Peter rebuked Simon the sorcerer because he continued to bewitch people. T/F. *Acts 8:18-20*

Lesson 9

1. The Ethiopian whom Philip met was in charge of what for his queen? (her treasury, her army, her foreign relations?) *Acts 8:27*

2. Philip used a passage from Ezekiel to teach the Ethiopian about Jesus. T/F. *Acts 8:30, 35*

Lesson 10

1. Festus claimed Paul's learning had made him what? (arrogant, cynical, mad?) *Acts 26:24*

2. Both Agrippa and Festus believed Paul didn't deserve to die. T/F. *Acts 26:30, 31*

Lesson 11

1. The soldiers nearly killed the prisoners on the ship for fear they would _____. *Acts 27:42*

2. None of the 276 passengers died as a result of the shipwreck on Melita. T/F. *Acts 27:37, 44*

Lesson 12

1. Paul survived the bite of a what while on the island? (spider, viper, tiger?) *Acts 28:3-5*

2. Paul healed the father of Publius while on the island. T/F. *Acts 28:7, 8*

Lesson 13

1. Paul's teaching in Rome was accepted by all who heard him. T/F. *Acts 28:24*

2. How long was Paul in Rome awaiting trial? (three weeks, six months, two years?) *Acts 28:30*

3. Paul was kept in a jail cell while he was in Rome. T/F. *Acts 28:16, 30*

QUARTER AT A GLANCE

by Mark S. Krause

BASEBALL FANS were stunned in 1973 when the New York Mets staged an improbable, late-season run. The team was in last place in its division with a month to go, but they turned a corner and won the National League Pennant. Central to this success was pitcher Tug McGraw, who kept telling teammates, reporters, and fans, "Ya gotta believe!"

McGraw touched on a fundamental human attribute: our ability to have faith that things will turn out a certain way when circumstances indicate otherwise. Faith for the Christian, however, is infinitely sharper since it involves God.

Unit 1: What Is Faith?

Our first unit considers the grand panorama of biblical faith as presented in Hebrews. These lessons address the necessity of faith, examples of faith, and the practicing of faith in the community of the church.

The final lesson in this unit shows a side of faith that is sometimes missed: active faith as undergirding actions of love. This lesson begins in Hebrews and then moves to the Bible's great treatise on love, namely 1 Corinthians 13. There Paul packages faith, hope, and love as essential, ageless qualities for Christians, but he insists that faith without love is without lasting value.

Unit 2: Who Understands Faith?

The Bible offers many examples of folks whose faith in God influenced the outcomes of their lives. By the world's standards, these heroes of faith may seem foolish, for their faith-based lives often led to hardship. Stephen's faith, for example, led to his death as the first martyr of the church. What Stephen's opponents viewed as the end of a problem turned out to be an impetus for the spread of the gospel. Stephen's brief, shining faith-moment has served as an inspiration for Christians for centuries. Stephen understood faith!

Two men in the book of Acts offer a stark contrast with one another when it comes to faith. One, Simon the sorcerer, saw faith and its spiritual treasures as commodities to be exploited economically, and he was condemned for trying to do so. The other, an Ethiopian visiting Israel, responded quickly, enthusiastically, and sincerely to the message of faith as explained by Philip. We need both examples, do we not?

Unit 3: Where Does Faith Take Us?

Paul was a man whose secure career path was radically redirected when he was confronted by the risen Christ. Paul's faith in Christ transformed him from the great persecutor of the church to the church's great preacher. His faith led to a life of unsettling events, including being put on trial for his life before a king and a Roman governor. That was followed by his providential survival of a terrifying shipwreck on a remote island.

As this unit concludes, we will leave Paul in Rome under house arrest, awaiting trial before the most powerful man in his world: the emperor of Rome. We cannot help but see God's hand in the paths where Paul's faith adventure took him!

Ya gotta believe! Our faith is our confidence about future realities and outcomes. Nothing

> *Ya gotta believe—in Jesus!*

good happens without someone first believing that it will happen. Even so, faith in one's own abilities is subject to failure. The "Ya gotta believe!" faith of the 1973 New York Mets took them to the World Series, but there they lost.

The Christian life is grounded in faith in God, not faith in self. May our study this quarter bring about a deeper faith and a richer relationship with our Lord. *Ya gotta believe—in Jesus!*

GET THE SETTING

by Tom Thatcher

THIS QUARTER'S LESSONS draw on passages that explore the nature of faith. The first-century Jewish Christians faced harsh challenges to their faith commitment. These Christians have much to teach us.

Pressure from Jewish Authorities

The Jewish authorities viewed Christianity as a heretical sect, sometimes using force to punish Christians or limit their influence. Christian Jews were subject to various forms of pressure from fellow Jews, depending on the temperament of the local Jewish leadership. Jewish attacks on early Christians generally took one of four forms.

First, Jewish mobs might take the law into their own hands (see Acts 7:54-60; 14:19). Mob persecution that resulted in death was a real but somewhat rare threat. The Roman authorities reserved for themselves the right to impose capital punishment (John 18:31), and most Jews did not view Christians as worthy of death.

Second, Jewish leaders could order Christian teachers to be flogged. Rabbinic law refers to beatings of this kind as "lashes of rebellion," stressing the fact that this punishment was meted out to those who refused to submit to the synagogue authorities. Paul received 39 lashes at least five times (2 Corinthians 11:24). The rabbis viewed beatings in excess of 40 lashes to be cruel, so they limited the number to 39 to avoid accidental violations due to a miscount.

Third, Jews could lobby local Roman authorities to arrest Christian leaders for disturbing the peace, thereby forcing the believers to leave town (Acts 16:39). While Jews generally did not enjoy legal status as citizens of the Roman empire, they often represented a powerful economic block and could leverage Roman authorities to support their interests. Mobs of Jews would sometimes appear at public hearings to pressure judges to decide in their favor (example: Acts 17:5-9).

Fourth, synagogue leaders could place Jewish Christians "under the ban," thereby excluding them from religious, social, and economic contact with other Jews (John 12:42). The nature of the ban was sharpened in the mid-80s by the addition of the "Curse on the Heretics" prayer to the synagogue liturgy. This public prayer drew attention to those seen to have aberrant beliefs.

Pressure from Roman Authorities

Rome did not tolerate religious innovation, and new sects were banned unless/until formally approved by the state. Judaism was an "approved" religion, and Christians who were not affiliated with synagogues could be targets of Roman persecution. This was particularly so in areas where the Jewish or pagan communities lobbied against them (Acts 17:5-9; 19:23-41).

As time moved on, Christians might suffer public humiliation, imprisonment, and seizure of property at the hands of Rome. They could be asked to demonstrate publicly their loyalty to the state by making offerings to images of the emperor. Those who refused could suffer torture or death under suspicion of treason.

Reactions to Pressure

Faith in Christ could carry serious consequences! Some believers paid the ultimate price of their lives. Others abandoned homes and fled to other regions. Against this backdrop, the authors of Acts and Hebrews urge believers to remain true to their calling, even in the face of death. The earliest Christians well understood what it meant to "count the cost" (see Luke 14:25-33). Do we?

THIS QUARTER IN THE WORD

Answers to the Quarterly Quiz on page 2

Lesson 1—1. sacrifice. 2. true. Lesson 2—1. Enoch. 2. false. Lesson 3—1. true. 2. righteousness. Lesson 4—1. Abel. 2. fire. Lesson 5—1. angels. 2. false. Lesson 6—1. true. 2. true. Lesson 7—1. hearts and ears. 2. Jesus. Lesson 8—1. false. 2. false. Lesson 9—1. her treasury. 2. false. Lesson 10—1. mad. 2. true. Lesson 11—1. escape. 2. true. Lesson 12—1. viper. 2. true. Lesson 13—1. false. 2. two years. 3. false.

Lesson Cycle Chart

International Sunday School Lesson Cycle, September 2010—August 2016

Year	Fall Quarter (Sep, Oct, Nov)	Winter Quarter (Dec, Jan, Feb)	Spring Quarter (Mar, Apr, May)	Summer Quarter (Jun, Jul, Aug)
2010-2011	The Inescapable God (Exodus, Psalms)	Assuring Hope (Isaiah, Matthew, Mark)	We Worship God (Matthew, Mark, Philippians, 1 & 2 Timothy, Jude, Revelation)	God Instructs His People (Joshua, Judges, Ruth)
2011-2012	Tradition and Wisdom (Proverbs, Ecclesiastes, Song of Solomon, Matthew)	God Establishes a Faithful People (Genesis, Exodus, Luke, Galatians)	God's Creative Word (John)	God Calls for Justice (Pentateuch, History, Psalms, Prophets)
2012-2013	A Living Faith (Psalms, Acts, 1 Corinthians, Hebrews)	Jesus Is Lord (John, Ephesians, Philippians, Colossians)	Undying Hope (Daniel, Luke, Acts, 1 & 2 Thessalonians, 1 & 2 Peter)	God's People Worship (Isaiah, Ezra, Nehemiah)
2013-2014	First Things (Genesis, Exodus, Psalms)	Jesus and the Just Reign of God (Luke, James)	Jesus' Fulfillment of Scripture (Pentateuch, 2 Samuel, Psalms, Prophets, Gospels, Acts, Revelation)	The People of God Set Priorities (Haggai, Zechariah, 1 & 2 Corinthians)
2014-2015	Sustaining Hope (Psalms, Job, Isaiah, Jeremiah, Ezekiel, Habakkuk)	Acts of Worship (Psalms, Matthew, Luke, John, Ephesians, Hebrews, James)	The Spirit Comes (Mark, John, Acts, 1 Corinthians, 1, 2, & 3 John)	God's Prophets Demand Justice (Isaiah, Jeremiah, Ezekiel, Amos, Micah, Zechariah, Malachi)
2015-2016	The Christian Community Comes Alive (Acts)	Sacred Gifts and Holy Gatherings (Pentateuch, Song of Solomon, Hosea, Micah, Gospels)	The Gift of Faith (Mark, Luke)	Toward a New Creation (Genesis, Psalms, Zephaniah, Romans)

"God"	"Hope"	"Worship"	"Community"	"Tradition"	"Faith"	"Creation"	"Justice"

"HERE'S A QUESTION . . ."

Teacher Tips by Brent L. Amato

I HAVE OBSERVED over 35 years of teaching and studying teachers that the most popular teaching method is lecture. Yet often it is the least effective method. Since, in Howard Hendricks words, "It's not what's taught, but what is caught," how do you go about determining if your students are connecting with you and learning from your teaching? Questions are part of the answer!

Before we dig into the *what, which,* and *how* of questions, keep in mind that there are two overarching questions that every lesson must answer. The first is *So what?* Nothing may be "caught" unless learners see relevancy! The second question is *Now what?* This will help the students move toward an obedient response to the lesson. Without it, nothing might change!

What Is Communicated

What can questions communicate to your students about you? First of all, they show that your focus is on the students. Learners understand that you came to class with them on your mind. How often we teachers get consumed by our teaching and our lesson! Your questions can communicate to your students that they're important, and they count for more than attendance. They show you're sincerely glad they came, and maybe even that they are appreciated.

On a particular morning, a student may want nothing more than for someone to pay attention to him or her in a positive way. Questions are an effective way to draw out the less vocal, energize the disinterested, direct the disruptive, and affirm all the students you teach.

Which Questions to Use and Not Use

Some questions are more effective than others. Less effective questions are closed (requiring only a yes/no or brief answer), overly complex, vague, "leading" (based on a hidden or not so hidden agenda of the teacher), confusing, or insignificant (detracting from the main idea of the lesson). Such questions may stifle the learning process.

Well-designed questions stimulate thought, with no "pat" answers. Better questions often are application-oriented; that is the direction taken by the five discussion questions you see in each lesson of this commentary. Good questions take time to develop, so they should be prepared in advance.

How They Help

Questions were a large part of Jesus' teaching style. What can we learn from Him? Jesus, the master teacher, used questions to determine desires (John 5:6), stimulate thinking (Luke 9:25), restore a relationship (John 21:15-17), challenge customs (Matthew 15:3), and encourage faith (Mark 4:40). Are you doing this in your classroom with the questions you use?

Jesus also used sequential questions to clarify attitudes and convictions. Consider these: "Whom do men say that I the Son of man am? . . . But whom say ye that I am?" (Matthew 16:13, 15). These simple yet profound questions helped the disciples move beyond public opinion to personal confession.

Further Questions

But I'm sure you still have questions about questions. How do "declarations of truth" fit with questions? You need both. How long should you wait in silence for an answer to your question? For adults, 60 seconds (maintaining eye contact and restating the question, if necessary). If there is no answer to your question, should you answer it? Try not to. Can you answer a question with a question? Why not? Should you always allow time for questions? Yes.

If there are no further questions, start preparing to ask some good ones. Then watch what happens to your relationships with your students, to class interaction, and to "what is caught"!

FAITH CALLS FOR PERSEVERANCE

DEVOTIONAL READING: Romans 5:1-5
BACKGROUND SCRIPTURE: Hebrews 10

HEBREWS 10:19-31

19 Having therefore, brethren, boldness to enter into the holiest by the blood of Jesus,

20 By a new and living way, which he hath consecrated for us, through the veil, that is to say, his flesh;

21 And having an high priest over the house of God;

22 Let us draw near with a true heart in full assurance of faith, having our hearts sprinkled from an evil conscience, and our bodies washed with pure water.

23 Let us hold fast the profession of our faith without wavering; (for he is faithful that promised;)

24 And let us consider one another to provoke unto love and to good works:

25 Not forsaking the assembling of ourselves together, as the manner of some is; but exhorting one another: and so much the more, as ye see the day approaching.

26 For if we sin wilfully after that we have received the knowledge of the truth, there remaineth no more sacrifice for sins,

27 But a certain fearful looking for of judgment and fiery indignation, which shall devour the adversaries.

28 He that despised Moses' law died without mercy under two or three witnesses:

29 Of how much sorer punishment, suppose ye, shall he be thought worthy, who hath trodden under foot the Son of God, and hath counted the blood of the covenant, wherewith he was sanctified, an unholy thing, and hath done despite unto the Spirit of grace?

30 For we know him that hath said, Vengeance belongeth unto me, I will recompense, saith the Lord. And again, The Lord shall judge his people.

31 It is a fearful thing to fall into the hands of the living God.

KEY VERSE

Let us hold fast the profession of our faith without wavering; (for he is faithful that promised).

—Hebrews 10:23

Photo: Ryan McVay / Lifesize / Thinkstock

A LIVING FAITH

Unit 1: What Is Faith?

LESSONS 1–5

LESSON AIMS

After participating in this lesson, each student will be able to:

1. Recite from memory the four imperatives that begin "let us" in the text.

2. Explain the consequences for those who fail to persevere in their faith.

3. Suggest a new way his or her church can build up the faith of its members.

LESSON OUTLINE

Introduction

A. Hellfire and Brimstone?

The American colonial preacher Jonathan Edwards (1703–1758) is best known for his sermon "Sinners in the Hands of an Angry God." In this sermon, Edwards rides the theme of God's anger and the judgment that awaits sinners. Edwards preached this: "The wrath of God burns against them, their damnation [doesn't] slumber, the pit is prepared, the fire made ready, the furnace is now hot, ready to receive them."

Many assume that Edwards used Hebrews 10:31 (part of today's lesson text) as the basis for this sermon. This is not quite the case, however, for that verse says, "It is a fearful thing to fall into the hands of the *living* God," not *"angry* God." Edwards imported the image of the Lord as the God of wrath from the Old Testament and mixed it with the Bible's picture of God as judge to create his terrifying picture.

Edwards did not always preach like this, but he defined a style of preaching sometimes known as *hellfire and brimstone.* These are sermons that emphasize the horrible fate awaiting unbelievers. While this style of preaching was once common, even popular, it has declined in favor of more positive messages about God's love and forgiveness. To preach only about the wrath of God-as-judge is to preach something less than the full gospel.

Yet there is a solid biblical basis for preaching about the threat of God's judgment. In both the Old and New Testaments, God is pictured as the ultimate judge (examples: Psalm 50:6; Ecclesiastes 3:17; Hebrews 12:23). The New Testament also pictures the Son of God, Jesus Christ, in this role (see Acts 10:42; 17:31). Today's lesson will look at a passage in the book of Hebrews that helps us understand the reality of God's judgment and how we can be saved from this through faith.

B. Lesson Background

The book of Hebrews is not always given a place of importance in the teaching and preaching of the church. Many prefer to focus on the stories of Jesus as found in the Gospels, the magnificent doctrine of Paul's letters, and/or the mysterious

    Faith Calls for Perseverance

images of the book of Revelation. But Hebrews is filled with descriptions of Christ that are unique, and we dare not neglect these. Here we see the role of the Son of God in creation (Hebrews 1:1, 2). Jesus is described as the "captain" of our salvation (2:10). Christ serves as both our eternal high priest (10:21) and our eternal sacrifice for sins (9:26).

The book of Hebrews is tied to the Old Testament. It quotes the Old Testament more than 30 times, sometimes at considerable length. This is done not merely to reinforce a point the author is making, but to dig into these older Scriptures and find what they have to say about Jesus and the new covenant. In particular, the author is concerned to show that the priests of Israel, their temple, and their sacrifices were all pointers to Jesus.

I. Faith's Boldness
(Hebrews 10:19-25)
A. Basis (vv. 19-21)

19, 20. Having therefore, brethren, boldness to enter into the holiest by the blood of Jesus, by a new and living way, which he hath consecrated for us, through the veil, that is to say, his flesh.

The phrase *the holiest* refers to the innermost chamber of the Jewish tabernacle or temple. This is sometimes called "the holy of holies," although that exact phrase does not appear in the Bible (compare Exodus 26:33; Hebrews 9:3). This chamber was the intended location for the ark of the covenant; it was a place traditionally entered once a year by the high priest of Israel on the Day of Atonement. It was believed that this place was where a human being had a yearly appointment to meet God directly (compare Luke 1:8, 9).

However, the author of Hebrews is not speaking of an earthly holy of holies, but of a perfect place. We may understand this along the lines of John's vision of the temple in Heaven, opened to reveal a heavenly ark of the covenant (or "ark of his testament," Revelation 11:19).

In the earthly temple in Jerusalem and the movable tabernacle that preceded it, the holy of holies was protected by a large veil or curtain (Exodus 26:31-33). There is now no need for such a barrier between God and humans (compare Mark 15:38).

The author wants his readers to know that they now have access to this most intimate of places, full access to God himself.

How is this? We now have access because of the work of Jesus Christ, through *his flesh.* This refers to the incarnation of our Lord in the person of Jesus of Nazareth (see Hebrews 2:9). God bridged the gap between sinful humanity and our holy God when He took on human form. Through Jesus, we have come to know our Father in Heaven in a way we never could before (see John 1:18).

Thus, we should remember that while the book of Hebrews speaks in abstract and figurative ways, its message is grounded in the historical reality of the incarnation: the birth, death, burial, and resurrection of Jesus as the Son of God. Later, the author reveals his intimate knowledge of this history by saying that Jesus was crucified outside the gate of the city of Jerusalem (Hebrews 13:12). This is a detail not recorded in the Gospels.

21. And having an high priest over the house of God.

We remember from Old Testament history that Jewish priests came from the tribe of Levi (Deuteronomy 17:9, 18; 18:1; etc.). That's where we get the phrase *levitical priesthood.* Hebrews 7:14 acknowledges, however, that Jesus' genealogy does not include lineage from the priestly tribe of Levi. Even so, the author already has made a careful argument that shows Jesus possessing a superior claim to high priesthood, for He is a priest like Melchizedek. That man is a mysterious figure from Genesis, and he predates the Jewish, levitical priesthood (see Hebrews 6:20; compare Genesis 14:18).

The priesthood of Melchizedek is superior for two reasons. First, it was acknowledged by Abraham, the ancestor of Levi (Hebrews 7:4). Second, it has an eternal character, without beginning or end (7:3). This fits Jesus, for He has conquered death and can therefore be an eternal high priest (7:16).

In describing Jesus as the eternal *high priest over the house of God,* the author does not mean that Jesus is over a physical building, such as the temple in Jerusalem. Rather, this refers to the spiritual house of God, which is made up of the believers—the church (compare Ephesians 2:21, 22).

Don't like traditional Christianity? No problem —just create your own religion! Or if that's too much work, several existing religions offer easy access to "spirituality." One particular Web site offers tips for "success" for those who choose the path that the site promotes. There you can become a high priest or priestess easily. No need to bother with less prestigious positions!

Grabbing for prestige, position, and power seems to be part of human nature (Mark 10:35-37). Having prestige handed to us seems attractive. Earning prestige in a do-it-yourself format is pridefully satisfying. But Christianity has no place for such attitudes (Mark 10:42-45). Christianity is not a do-it-yourself religion, but a God-has-done-it-himself religion. God has done it through Jesus, who is now "high priest over the house of God."

This sets Christianity apart. We have one great high priest who has done the work necessary for our salvation. Christian faith recognizes our inability to save ourselves. Do-it-yourself paths to spirituality can lead only to a "trying hard, never sure" uneasiness. Only in Jesus are we sure of our salvation. —C. R. B.

B. Benefits (vv. 22, 23)

22. Let us draw near with a true heart in full assurance of faith, having our hearts sprinkled from an evil conscience, and our bodies washed with pure water.

We move to an image of a temple pilgrim entering for worship. The sprinkling is a reference to the use of sacrificial blood to sprinkle both the people and the implements of the temple to purge them from impurity (see Exodus 24:6-8; 29:16-21; Hebrews 9:18-22). The Christian believer has no need for this ceremony of physical blood spattering, for he or she has been given the purifying effects of the atoning blood of Jesus, shed on the cross. This is the perfect and eternal "blood of the testament" (Hebrews 9:20; compare Luke 22:20).

We also approach our worship with washed bodies. From an Old Testament perspective, this is a reference to the ritual cleansing a pilgrim takes before entering the Jerusalem temple (compare Ezekiel 36:25). From a New Testament perspec-

tive, the author may be using the image of Christian baptism (compare 1 Peter 3:21). Baptism is pictured elsewhere as a symbolic washing of the person who has come to faith (see Acts 22:16). It is more likely, however, that we are being given a bigger picture of which baptism is a part. That bigger picture is that the ultimate cleansing of a believer is a spiritual cleansing, a sanctification through the gift of the Holy Spirit (see 1 Corinthians 6:11).

Coming into the presence of God is to be done with the heart properly prepared. It must be a *true heart,* the opposite of a false, hypocritical heart. And it must be a heart with *full assurance of faith.* This expression is parallel to the *true heart.* The emphasis in the Greek text is not on the *assurance* part, but on the *full* part. Our hearts are fully true, completely trusting and believing. We have every reason for this confident approach to God, for we have the perfect high priest who has taken care of the sin that once separated us from our Creator.

> *What Do You Think?*
> What hinders you from entering God's presence "in full assurance"? How do you overcome problems in this regard?
> *Talking Points for Your Discussion*
> ▪ Issues of doubt (James 1:6-8)
> ▪ Issues of presumption (Job 38:2; 40:1)
> ▪ Issues of despair (Lamentations 3:42-44)
> ▪ Issues of rebellion (Proverbs 28:9)

23. Let us hold fast the profession of our faith without wavering; (for he is faithful that promised;)

The work of Jesus, which allows our access to God, gives us reason to *hold fast . . . without wavering.* These words undoubtedly speak personally to the original readers, who may be thinking of abandoning the Christian faith to return to the Jewish synagogue. These words speak today to Christians enduring periods of discouragement.

In the final analysis, it is not our circumstances or the actions of others that determine whether we remain faithful. We can remain faithful because God is faithful. We are like the survivors of the horrors of the destruction of Jerusalem in 586 BC who could sing, "Great is thy faithfulness!" (Lamentations 3:23). The Lord God always keeps His promises. We can depend on this as much today as when these words were written many centuries ago.

C. Sharing (vv. 24, 25)

24. And let us consider one another to provoke unto love and to good works.

We now see what should happen if one is holding fast to an assured faith: believers are to influence one another in attitude and action. Our lives should stimulate love among our Christian brothers and sisters. This attitude of love should work itself out in acts of good works and loving deeds as a natural expression of our salvation.

In other words, the Christian faith should make an observable difference in the lives of believers. This echoes the teaching of James, who says that faith without works is dead (James 2:17, 26). If loving works are not evident in the life of a Christian, then there is a problem with this person's faith. Loving works should be the natural result of trust in our loving God (compare 1 John 3:18).

25. Not forsaking the assembling of ourselves together, as the manner of some is; but exhorting one another: and so much the more, as ye see the day approaching.

HOW TO SAY IT

Deuteronomy	Due-ter-*ahn*-uh-me.
genealogy	jee-nee-*ah*-luh-jee.
Hebrews	*Hee*-brews.
Levi	*Lee*-vye.
levitical	leh-*vit*-ih-kul.
Melchizedek	Mel-*kiz*-eh-dek.
Nazareth	*Naz*-uh-reth.

This is one of the most quoted verses in Hebrews, often used to encourage Christians to attend church services on a weekly basis. Following immediately after the author's encouragement for love and good works in verse 24, we can understand that participation in the weekly fellowship of a church body is a way to practice such things.

The author is not exhorting his readers to be regular in attendance for their own benefit so much as for the benefit of other believers. We need each other. The author's world is hostile to Christianity, and ours is not much changed. We function as the body of Christ as the Lord intends when we assemble in the name of Jesus to worship, fellowship, and learn (see Acts 2:42). The fact that the readers *see the day approaching*—most likely a reference to Judgment Day—adds a sense of urgency.

II. Faith's Determination
(Hebrews 10:26-31)
A. Stop Sinning (vv. 26, 27)

26. For if we sin wilfully after that we have received the knowledge of the truth, there remaineth no more sacrifice for sins.

The text addresses the all-too-common issue of ongoing sin in the life of the believer. If taken out of context, the verse seems to say that (1) if we have made a Christian commitment and (2) we make a knowingly sinful choice, then (3) we fall into a state of *no more sacrifice for sins* (unforgiveness).

First, let us admit that great heroes of the faith can have sin issues after their conversion. In a famous episode, Paul had to confront Peter for his hypocrisy in rejecting fellowship with Gentile believers (Galatians 2:11). It would seem that this was a willful choice by Peter, a sinful action that required his repentance.

Visual for Lesson 1. *Keep this map posted throughout the quarter to give your learners a geographical perspective on the lessons.*

Second, the Bible teaches that we can be forgiven for sins, even those committed intentionally, if we confess them and ask for forgiveness (see 1 John 1:9; compare Psalm 51:2-4). The area of danger is when we harbor a lack of repentance for our sins. It is one thing to sin willfully and then repent; it is quite another to sin defiantly and refuse to repent.

Third, we should put the phrase *no more sacrifice for sins* in the larger context of what the author has already taught. There is one, final, ultimate sacrifice for sins: the sacrifice of Jesus through His death on the cross (see Hebrews 2:17; 9:26). We delude ourselves if we think we can abandon Christian faith and find some other way to take care of our sins. The sacrifice of Jesus is the only sufficient way to cancel our sins; there is no other.

❧ DIVINE SACRIFICE ❧

Human sacrifice has been practiced by various cultures throughout history. When Spanish explorers reached the New World, they documented numerous cases of this practice among the Aztecs. The victims, usually prisoners of war, were offered to "the gods" for various reasons. For example, the blood flowing from the wounds of a sacrificial victim was thought to represent the life-giving rains of spring that would cause crops to grow.

Critics of the Christian faith sometimes argue that the story of Christ's crucifixion falls in the same category of primitive superstition that the Aztecs embraced. To be sure, Jesus was a "human sacrifice," but any comparison that stops there is superficial. Jesus offered himself willingly. He was indeed human, but He was also God's Son. He was God's once-for-all-time offering to pay the penalty of human sin. His sacrifice was part of God's plan from the beginning. Now that we have this knowledge, what will we do with it?

—C. R. B.

27. But a certain fearful looking for of judgment and fiery indignation, which shall devour the adversaries.

The author points out the results of rejecting the sacrifice of Jesus for our sins. If we believe we can find an easier and more viable alternative, we are wrong. The one who rejects Christ has only the promise of judgment and punishment in his or her future. The ultimate justice of God will not be thwarted by unbelievers *(the adversaries)*. This should be adequate motivation to take the problem of sin seriously.

What Do You Think?

How does culture downplay the seriousness of sin? How do you resist cultural influences in this regard?

Talking Points for Your Discussion

- Exodus 23:2
- Psalm 94:7
- Isaiah 5:20
- Mark 7:9-12

B. Respond to Grace (vv. 28, 29)

28. He that despised Moses' law died without mercy under two or three witnesses.

Drawing on the Jewish roots of his readers, the author reminds them of the harsh judgment under the Law of Moses (see Deuteronomy 17:6, 7). The Old Testament gives many examples of the necessary deaths of those whose sin was a threat to the purity and integrity of the nation of Israel, God's covenant people. (For a rather extensive list of offenses that called for death, see Leviticus 20:9-16.) The importance of the verse before us is established next.

Faith Calls for Perseverance

29. Of how much sorer punishment, suppose ye, shall he be thought worthy, who hath trodden under foot the Son of God, and hath counted the blood of the covenant, wherewith he was sanctified, an unholy thing, and hath done despite unto the Spirit of grace?

The author pushes hard for the reader to understand the seriousness of what he is saying. If certain sinners were judged harshly under the Law of Moses, the judgment of those who have rejected the sacrificial death of Jesus will be even harsher. Not only do unbelievers reject the salvation offered through Christ, they also reject the sanctifying power of the Holy Spirit, *the Spirit of grace.*

Hath done despite translates an unusually strong Greek verb to express the author's outrage at how ungrateful unbelievers react to God's work in Christ. The idea is that of a deep, deliberate insult (see Hebrews 6:4-6).

What Do You Think?
What are some ways that people walk all over Jesus today? How should we react when we see this happening?
Talking Points for Your Discussion
- Governmental laws
- Employment policies
- Commercialism
- Media portrayals

C. Avoid Judgment (vv. 30, 31)

30, 31. For we know him that hath said, Vengeance belongeth unto me, I will recompense, saith the Lord. And again, The Lord shall judge his people. It is a fearful thing to fall into the hands of the living God.

The author quotes Deuteronomy 32:35, 36 (compare Romans 12:19). No Christian believer should fear God's condemning judgment because Jesus Christ has delivered us from what we deserve. Jesus was not sent into the world as a judge, but as a Savior (see John 3:16, 17).

Yet we should remember that the promises of judgment on sinful people are sure. If we reject Jesus, there is nothing to keep us from receiving our deserved judgment at *the hands of the living*

God. Having a clever lawyer or trying to plea bargain won't help. God's final judgment will result in a verdict of eternal life or eternal death. Only if we have Jesus as our advocate will we receive the verdict of life (see 1 John 2:1, 2).

Conclusion
A. Secure in Faith

In uncertain times, people naturally want assurances of security. We want to know that our jobs will continue, that our marriages will be successful, and that our retirement plans will be adequate. We experience anxiety when a job terminates, a marriage ends, or retirement savings evaporate. The Christian is subject to the uncertainties of life just as anyone else. Our faith in Christ will not necessarily protect us from financial ruin or personal tragedy. However, our faith in Christ gives us the assurance that our future is in the hands of a loving God.

Because of Jesus' atoning death, we are not subject to God's condemnation and wrath (see 1 Peter 2:24). This is the life of freedom God has given us. It is a life by which we can spur our fellow believers to love one another and to practice our loving faith through good and helpful deeds for others. The one who is securely in the arms of the loving God lives this kind of life.

B. Prayer

Holy God, may the fact that we have been forgiven never cause us to take sin lightly. May we never miss an opportunity to express love through our actions. May we never doubt our salvation through our great high priest, Jesus; amen.

C. Thought to Remember

Know where real security lies.

VISUALS FOR THESE LESSONS

The visual pictured in each lesson (example: page 14) is a small reproduction of a large, full-color poster included in the *Adult Resources* packet for the Fall Quarter. That packet also contains the very useful *Presentation Helps* on a CD for teacher use. Order No. 020019212 from your supplier.

INVOLVEMENT LEARNING

Some of the activities below are also found in the helpful student book, Adult Bible Class.
Don't forget to download the free reproducible page from www.standardlesson.com to enhance your lesson!

Into the Lesson

Form groups of three to six. Provide each group a poster board, a marker pen, and hymnals and/or song books of contemporary Christian music. Display the word *Perseverance* in large letters. Say, "Christian music not only is used as praise and worship, but also is used to teach. Find lines from Christian songs that teach or encourage perseverance in the Christian life. List those phrases on the poster board." Provide an example if your learners need to have their thinking jump-started.

Make the transition to Bible study by saying, "Perseverance is the encouragement that comes from today's study. We will discover wonderful encouragements for a bold faith and a new appreciation for God's grace."

Into the Word

Activity 1: Distribute a two-column handout titled *Faith Calls for Perseverance.* The header of the first column will read "Old Testament Imagery"; the header of the second column will read "Interpretation or Application." List the following verse numbers (referring to Hebrews 10) down the left-hand side of the page: verse 19; verse 20; verse 21; verse 22a; verse 22b. Have learners discover one or more Old Testament images for each. (If learners need a hint, mention Exodus 24, 26, 29, and Deuteronomy 18.) Then discuss and list what the author of Hebrews is teaching Christians through that imagery. (This activity and the next one may be completed individually, in small groups, or as a whole class.)

Activity 2: Distribute a handout titled *A Bold Faith . . . What to Do and Not to Do.* List the following verse numbers (referring to Hebrews 10) down the left-hand side of the page: verse 22; verse 23; verse 24; verse 25a; verse 25b. Ask learners to explore these references to discover what they are to do or not do through their bold faith. When finished, review the "Let us . . ." words in these verses. Ask, "What are things we are challenged to do? What are we challenged *not* to do?"

Activity 3: Review Hebrews 10:26-31 and ask the following discussion questions. 1. How should we interpret "no more sacrifice for sins" in verse 26? (You may need to deliver a mini-lecture using the lesson commentary notes to clarify this text.) 2. What are some of the words or phrases in verses 27-31 that describe the harsh judgment of God on sinners from the Law of Moses? 3. How and why do Christians have the wonderful security of "full assurance of faith" of verse 22?

Option: Have learners complete the "Perseverance and Faith's Power" activity on the reproducible page, which you can download.

Into Life

Church Planning Team(s): This activity may be done in the small groups created at the beginning of the lesson or can be completed as an entire class. Small groups can use poster boards to list the ideas; otherwise, jot responses on the board. **Part A:** Brainstorm two lesson themes that will encourage perseverance through the use of small groups or Sunday school classes. **Part B:** Brainstorm things to include in a worship service that revolve around the concept of perseverance. **Part C:** Brainstorm program ideas for encouraging people one-on-one to persevere in their faith. What teacher or mentor training would be needed?

After completing the activity, ask, "Which of these ideas do you think are appropriate for presenting to our church's leadership?" Make notes of responses. If enthusiasm is high, appoint a class member to take the posters home, summarize the ideas receiving the most support, and present them to the appropriate member(s) of your church's leadership team.

Option: Use the "Perseverance Poem" activity from the downloadable reproducible page. If time is short, distribute this as a take-home activity.

FAITH GIVES ASSURANCE

DEVOTIONAL READING: Psalm 27:1-6

BACKGROUND SCRIPTURE: Hebrews 11; Psalm 46

HEBREWS 11:1-6

1 Now faith is the substance of things hoped for, the evidence of things not seen.

2 For by it the elders obtained a good report.

3 Through faith we understand that the worlds were framed by the word of God, so that things which are seen were not made of things which do appear.

4 By faith Abel offered unto God a more excellent sacrifice than Cain, by which he obtained witness that he was righteous, God testifying of his gifts: and by it he being dead yet speaketh.

5 By faith Enoch was translated that he should not see death; and was not found, because God had translated him: for before his translation he had this testimony, that he pleased God.

6 But without faith it is impossible to please him: for he that cometh to God must believe that he is, and that he is a rewarder of them that diligently seek him.

PSALM 46

1 God is our refuge and strength, a very present help in trouble.

2 Therefore will not we fear, though the earth be removed, and though the mountains be carried into the midst of the sea;

3 Though the waters thereof roar and be troubled, though the mountains shake with the swelling thereof. Selah.

4 There is a river, the streams whereof shall make glad the city of God, the holy place of the tabernacles of the most High.

5 God is in the midst of her; she shall not be moved: God shall help her, and that right early.

6 The heathen raged, the kingdoms were moved: he uttered his voice, the earth melted.

7 The LORD of hosts is with us; the God of Jacob is our refuge. Selah.

8 Come, behold the works of the LORD, what desolations he hath made in the earth.

9 He maketh wars to cease unto the end of the earth; he breaketh the bow, and cutteth the spear in sunder; he burneth the chariot in the fire.

10 Be still, and know that I am God: I will be exalted among the heathen, I will be exalted in the earth.

11 The LORD of hosts is with us; the God of Jacob is our refuge. Selah.

KEY VERSE

Now faith is the substance of things hoped for, the evidence of things not seen. —**Hebrews 11:1**

A LIVING FAITH

Unit 1: What Is Faith?

LESSONS 1–5

LESSON AIMS

After participating in this lesson, each student will be able to:

1. Paraphrase three or four definitions or descriptions of faith from today's text.

2. Describe the relationship between faith and assurance.

3. Write a personal psalm of praise for the assurance of his or her faith in God's provision.

LESSON OUTLINE

Introduction

A. Attacks on Faith

The church I serve is near one of the world's great universities. That university is a mammoth institution, having nearly 40,000 students. There are dozens of similar schools in North America.

Many students come to these universities from a strong background in the church. Some of these young adults are outside a "safe" Christian environment for the first time. They encounter students of other, non-Christian faiths. They are confronted by the strident atheism of some students. But, most dangerously, they end up in classes taught by professors who seem determined to demolish what they see as simplemindedness when it comes to faith. The rules of academic freedom allow for relentless questioning and even ridicule of Christian values and beliefs.

For young Christians navigating college, graduating with an intact faith requires a transition. They must move beyond a "dependent faith," which is based on what they perceive a parent or preacher believes. They must grapple with the great issues of belief to emerge with an independent, personal faith. Only then will they have a faith that will last a lifetime.

The author of Hebrews was aware that faith is always one generation from extinction. This week's lesson looks at examples of faith from the past and give us insights into a deep, abiding, biblical faith for our future.

B. Lesson Background

The book of Hebrews is a carefully crafted argument that shows the superiority of the Christian faith over the Old Testament structure from which it comes. The author never makes his argument in a belittling way; he always shows great respect for the earlier Scriptures. The result is a crescendo that reaches its height in chapter 11.

That chapter sometimes is called "Faith's Hall of Fame." There the author offers an interesting list of faithful individuals from Israel's history: Abel, Enoch, Noah, Abraham, Isaac, Jacob, Joseph, Moses, and Rahab are prominent. The author summarizes these faithful folk as "so great a cloud of witnesses" (Hebrews 12:1), as if they hover over the church by their testimony of faith.

Psalm 46 has been chosen for this lesson as an appropriate Old Testament counterpart to Hebrews 11. We might see it as a "Hall of Fame" for the faithful too, but in this case there is only one member: the Lord God of Israel. Together, these two passages of Scripture help us understand the enduring nature of true faith in God.

I. Faith That Pleases God
(HEBREWS 11:1-6)

We may be surprised to learn that the word *faith* occurs more often in Hebrews than in any other New Testament book. Furthermore, *faith* occurs more in Hebrews 11 than in any other chapter in the New Testament—24 times, which is about 10 percent of the total New Testament occurrences. If we want to understand Christian faith, then Hebrews 11 is a primary resource.

A. Description (vv. 1-3)

1. Now faith is the substance of things hoped for, the evidence of things not seen.

The verse before us has often been seen as presenting a biblical description of faith. This description has two parts. First, *faith is the substance of things hoped for*. Thus faith is future-looking. We don't hope for things in the past, but for things in the present and the future. Faith is the essence of hope. If we have no faith, then we have no basis for hope. We believe the things we learn about God are true, that His promises are sure, and this belief gives us hope for the future.

HOW TO SAY IT

Abraham	*Ay*-bruh-ham.
Canaan	*Kay*-nun.
Enoch	*E*-nock.
Gihon	*Gye*-hahn.
Isaac	*Eye*-zuk.
Moses	*Mo*-zes or *Mo*-zez.
Noah	*No*-uh.
Rahab	*Ray*-hab.
Selah (Hebrew)	*See*-luh.

Second, faith is *the evidence of things not seen*. Some have taken this to mean that faith can extend no further than reliable evidence. Historical evidence is surely important to our faith; most important is the reliable, testimonial evidence that Jesus rose from the dead. But the author is not trying to put faith strictly in a box framed by evidence. For him, faith is personal and active, as the rest of Hebrews 11 makes clear. Faith is a trusting hope in God and His promises, even though we do not see God, and the promises are in the future. We have faith in the person of God, and our faith brings forth obedient actions according to His will. This understanding of faith is demonstrated by the many stories of faithful people who make up the bulk of Hebrews 11.

> **What Do You Think?**
> How does your faith enable you to face the future with confidence?
> *Talking Points for Your Discussion*
> - In times of illness
> - In times of lack
> - In times of spiritual stumbling
> - When a loved one sins

2. For by it the elders obtained a good report.

By *the elders* the author of Hebrews means the ancestors of the faith whose lives are recorded in the Old Testament. The author is convinced that the Old Testament has much to teach us about faith. As important as anything is the conclusion that these ancestors *obtained a good report* because of their faith. The word used here is a form of the verb meaning "to witness" or "to give testimony." The good report itself is from God. God gives His positive witness to the effective faith of these men and women.

This idea—that it is by faith we are justified in God's sight rather than by actions—is reflected elsewhere in the New Testament. For example, a key verse for Paul is Genesis 15:6, where "[Abraham] believed in the Lord; and he counted it to him for righteousness." This verse is a focus for Paul in Romans 4:1-5 and Galatians 3:6 (compare James 2:23).

Automobile makers know that "style sells." Think of all the gadgets included on cars today. Bluetooth® connectivity and plug-ins for MP3 players are standard. Electronic touch controls abound.

A high-tech wonder may "get you there in style," but we wonder if the primary function of the automobile—to "get you there"—is being forgotten as people come to view their cars as mobile entertainment centers. A similar challenge presents itself in the church. Worship connects us to God. Worship that is enhanced by technology can be very appealing, while worship without the technology can seem to be a relic of a bygone era. But when does the technology become the focus rather than the assistant?

Hebrews 11 can help us keep our bearings. Our faith has ancient roots. It is a faith passed down through the centuries. Even without any technology at all, our faith is not out-of-date. —C. R. B.

3. Through faith we understand that the worlds were framed by the word of God, so that things which are seen were not made of things which do appear.

The author now fills out his definition of faith by giving an example. Our understanding of the existence of the universe is a matter of faith. A profound question is, "Why is there something and not nothing?" As one philosopher said, the sense of the universe must lie outside the universe. The universe is not, and will never be, self-explanatory.

The Christian's understanding of the origins of the universe is based on faith that the Creator God designed and made the worlds through His powerful word (see John 1:1-3). Those who deny the existence of a Creator God prefer a materialistic explanation. But science will never be able to prove or disprove that God created the universe, for it is a matter for faith.

B. Results (vv. 4, 5)

4. By faith Abel offered unto God a more excellent sacrifice than Cain, by which he obtained witness that he was righteous, God testifying of his gifts: and by it he being dead yet speaketh.

Jesus spoke of "righteous Abel" (Matthew 23:35). What made this rather obscure Old Testament figure "righteous"? We have the answer here, for the author uses Abel as the a model for faith. Abel was not righteous because he died unjustly due to his brother's anger. Rather, Abel was righteous because he trusted God and gave Him a sacrifice of the very best of his flocks (Genesis 4:4). He believed in God, and this resulted in action. It was tragic that Cain's jealousy resulted in Abel's death, but Abel would have been considered righteous even if his life had not been cut short. His testimony of faith endures today.

5. By faith Enoch was translated that he should not see death; and was not found, because God had translated him: for before his translation he had this testimony, that he pleased God.

The author's second faith hero, Enoch, is also from the book of Genesis. Very little is said of Enoch there, so the author gives us a fuller analysis. Enoch was a man who "walked with God" (Genesis 5:22). This indicates a very close relationship with the Lord, a faith relationship. One day Enoch was gone, taken by God, which is the sense of *translated* (5:24). We do not know if there were witnesses to this event, but those who knew Enoch believed this was an act of God.

The fact that Enoch did *not see death* testifies to his faithfulness. His pattern of faithfulness fits with the example of others from the Old Testament. It still serves as an example for us today.

> *What Do You Think?*
> What would people have to see in your life to conclude that you "walk with God"?
> *Talking Points for Your Discussion*
> - Attitudes that match those of the Bible's heroes of faith
> - Behaviors that match those of the Bible's heroes of faith
> - Behaviors tailored to modern culture

C. Reward (v. 6)

6. But without faith it is impossible to please him: for he that cometh to God must believe

Faith Gives Assurance

that he is, and that he is a rewarder of them that diligently seek him.

Before proceeding with more Old Testament faith examples, the author gives another description of faith. This one is a more dynamic, working description. The examples of Abel and Enoch show that God is pleased by our faith as it is lived out in obedience to Him. Faith is not confined to a dictionary definition; it is demonstrated in the lives of the faithful.

Two things must undergird the life of a person of faith. First, we must believe that God exists. We cannot have a faith relationship with God if we do not acknowledge His existence. An atheist may have some type of faith in certain things, but it is nothing like the faith being presented here.

Second, we must accept certain things about God. One such thing is *that He is a rewarder*. This pictures a personal God, a God with standards and expectations. Earnest attempts to do God's will do not go unnoticed (example: Acts 10:4). They will be rewarded. While we cannot earn God's favor, He does care that we are living to serve Him and please Him. As we move to a consideration of Psalm 46, we learn other things about our personal God.

II. Faith That Recognizes God

(Psalm 46:1-11)

The superscription to this psalm attributes it to "the sons of Korah." Descendants of Korah seem to be important pioneers in the worship in the temple in Jerusalem (see 1 Chronicles 9:19; 2 Chronicles 20:19).

A. No Fear (vv. 1-3)

1. God is our refuge and strength, a very present help in trouble.

The psalmist begins his great statement of faith by highlighting three attributes of God. First, God is a *refuge*. This word pictures a place of safety, a protected shelter. It is used in everyday conversation to refer to something that provides protection from the weather (see Isaiah 4:6). *God is our . . . strength* has the sense of unquestioned authority. This is the kind of power you want to have

Visual for Lesson 2. *Point to this visual as you ask the discussion question associated with Psalm 46:1, below.*

on your side. It is strength through righteousness (see Psalm 99:4). Third, God as a *present help in trouble* gives the picture of something more than abstract ideas of assistance. God never leaves us and is ready to help us at all times.

What Do You Think?

How have you applied the truth that God is "a very present help in trouble" to a personal crisis? How did things turn out?

Talking Points for Your Discussion
- Job loss
- Health crisis
- Loss of a loved one
- Prodigal child

2, 3. Therefore will not we fear, though the earth be removed, and though the mountains be carried into the midst of the sea; though the waters thereof roar and be troubled, though the mountains shake with the swelling thereof. Selah.

Having affirmed God as refuge, strength, and help, the psalmist gives examples where these things are needed. He tells of terrible natural disasters, but he is speaking figuratively also. His God is a tower of strength in times of personal disaster (see Proverbs 18:10). God is our refuge and strength when our personal world is shaken, when we are flooded with misery and hardship. We do not stand alone in these times, so we need not fear. God is greater and more powerful than anything that threatens or bedevils us. Faith in God dispels fear (compare Mark 4:40).

Scholars do not know the meaning of *Selah*. But it seems to be used to indicate logical breaks in the flow of thought.

The classic hymn "Be Still, My Soul" (above) gives poetic expression to the words of Psalm 46. It was reportedly a favorite hymn of Eric Liddell, who won the men's 400-meter event—in record time—at the 1924 Summer Olympics. The story of Liddell's commitment of faith was dramatized in the Oscar-winning 1981 film *Chariots of Fire*.

Liddell had been born in China to Scottish missionaries. After the Olympics, he returned to China as a missionary himself in 1925. While there, he was imprisoned by the invading Japanese army during World War II. He reportedly taught this favorite hymn to his fellow prisoners. He died in the prison camp of a brain tumor in 1945.

Regardless of the storms of life, Liddell found his soul comforted by God. So can we.   —C. R. B.

B. No Defeat (vv. 4-7)

4. There is a river, the streams whereof shall make glad the city of God, the holy place of the tabernacles of the most High.

Cities in the ancient world are sited with three requirements in mind: availability of water, defensibility, and access to trade routes. Two of the three are stressed here.

A city under siege won't survive long without a supply of water within the city walls. The *city of God* in the Old Testament is usually understood as Jerusalem, but there is no river flowing by or through this mountaintop city. Its source of water is the Gihon, a spring on the eastern side of the city. Jerusalem depends on water from this spring and its system of pools and cisterns with stored water (see 2 Chronicles 32:30; 33:14). The picture of a river flowing through the city is one of great plenty and blessing, truly a cause to be glad (compare Ezekiel 47:1-12; Revelation 22:1, 2). The psalmist compares this bounty with the presence of God in the city.

A city's defensible position is enhanced by elevation, since this puts an attacking army at a disadvantage. The psalmist speaks of the presence of *God . . . the most High,* and you can't get any more elevation than that! The presence of *the tabernacles* confirms God's availability.

5. God is in the midst of her; she shall not be moved: God shall help her, and that right early.

While a reliable river is wonderful, to have God in the city is the ultimate in provision. Having God's presence in our lives has similar, confident results: gladness and security. Faith says that God's help will come in a timely manner.

6. The heathen raged, the kingdoms were moved: he uttered his voice, the earth melted.

The heathen are the nations other than Israel, what the New Testament calls *Gentiles.* They are enemies of God and therefore enemies of Israel, God's people (see Psalm 2:1-4). For these foreign nations to be *moved* means they will be defeated in battle. The author expresses this in big terms. Just as the Lord created the earth by speaking (Genesis 1:9, 10), His mighty voice can also destroy the earth. With this in mind, the people of Israel find ultimate security in God's protection.

What Do You Think?
As our culture continues to be "moved" in unholy directions, how do you keep yourself from being "moved" spiritually along with it?
Talking Points for Your Discussion
- Regarding faddish or faulty thinking (Acts 17:21; Colossians 2:8)
- Regarding pointless controversies (1 Timothy 1:4)
- Regarding profane people (2 Timothy 3:1-5)
- Regarding old behaviors (1 Peter 4:3, 4)

---

7. The LORD of hosts is with us; the God of Jacob is our refuge. Selah.

The phrase *the Lord of hosts* occurs roughly 250 times in the Old Testament. It means "Lord of armies" or "master of the heavenly armies." This is a military expression to indicate the invincible power of the God of Israel. If God is moved to intervene in Israel's wars, His army of angels can crush any foe (compare Matthew 26:53). The psalmist's faith in God's power gives him the confidence to envision the Lord himself as Israel's refuge. The water and walls of Jerusalem may eventually fail (and they do), but God will never be defeated.

C. No Peer (vv. 8-11)

8, 9. Come, behold the works of the LORD, what desolations he hath made in the earth. He maketh wars to cease unto the end of the earth; he breaketh the bow, and cutteth the spear in sunder; he burneth the chariot in the fire.

The *desolations* in mind here are the ruins of a defeated army after a battle. On the battlefield can be broken bows and spears as well as burning chariots. Not mentioned but undoubtedly in mind are the many corpses lying about.

Israel can look back on her history to the many times when God's hand was evident in military successes. These include the destruction of the Egyptian army in the Red Sea and the conquest of Jericho and other cities as the Israelites occupied the land of Canaan. Those opposing God come to a bad end. This is a lesson learned very painfully by Israel herself when she abandons her covenant with the Lord. The result: exile in foreign lands.

10. Be still, and know that I am God: I will be exalted among the heathen, I will be exalted in the earth.

The psalmist now moves beyond the nation of Israel to the Lord himself. In the end, God always *will be exalted*—recognized as having the highest possible position.

Our response is to *be still* in our understanding of the power and provision of God. Being still and quiet is an act of faith. Sometimes, waiting and trusting is how faith must work in our lives. The frantic busyness of our lives will push God aside quickly. Faith grows when we have an awareness of God's protective presence, and this will be found in times of quiet contemplation and prayer.

What Do You Think?

What are some things that distract people from "being still" before God? How do we address these areas?

Talking Points for Your Discussion

- 1 Kings 19:1-18
- Psalm 73:2, 3
- Matthew 13:22
- Luke 10:38-42
- 1 Timothy 5:13

11. The LORD of hosts is with us; the God of Jacob is our refuge. Selah.

The final verse repeats verse 7. It is a bold statement of the Lord as the commander of invincible armies and as an impregnable fortress. This is the center of faith. Our God has the power and mercy to see us through any trial of life.

Conclusion
A. Faith and Worship

We often think of faith as a private matter, a deeply personal relationship between God and us. Yet the Bible has a very public view of faith, as today's texts reveal. When we join with other Christians in songs of worship, we are expressing our collective hope and trust in God. When we read Scripture in worship, we are highlighting the great truths that undergird our faith. When we pray together in worship, we are sharing a common trust that God is listening.

Unity in faith builds faith. If we neglect our worship together, we neglect our common faith. There is "one faith" (Ephesians 4:5), and that is the faith in God through Jesus that all Christians share. May we be faithful in worship and worship in faith.

B. Prayer

Lord God, be our strong refuge in trials that test our faith. May our trust in You grow each day throughout our lives. In Jesus' name; amen.

C. Thought to Remember

Faith is our permanent relationship with God.

INVOLVEMENT LEARNING

Some of the activities below are also found in the helpful student book, Adult Bible Class.
Don't forget to download the free reproducible page from www.standardlesson.com to enhance your lesson!

Into the Lesson

Form small groups of two to four for several projects throughout today's lesson. Put the following units of text on eight index cards, one unit per card: *Now faith / is the / substance of / things / hoped for, / the evidence / of things / not seen.* Scramble the cards and place them in an envelope. Create enough sets of eight cards for each small group to have a set. On the outside of each envelope, write one of the letters *A, B,* or *C* as a reference for a later activity. If you create more than three envelopes, use one or more of those three letters again. Distribute envelopes.

After the first team unscrambles the verse from Hebrews 11:1, display a poster with that verse for the remainder of today's study. Make the transition to Bible study by saying, "Faith is often difficult for Christians to define. It is even more challenging to live by. Yet those who do so can discover a remarkable peace for their lives."

Into the Word

Ask the teams to look at the outside of their envelopes, where they will find either *A, B,* or *C.* The teams will do the task corresponding to instructions on handouts you will distribute. (One or more of the assignments will be duplicated if you have more than three teams.) You will need a copy of the hymn "A Mighty Fortress Is Our God" for Team C.

Team A: Paraphrase Hebrews 11:1 and 11:6. The paraphrase should help describe faith. Be ready to tell how or why Abel and Enoch are good examples of faith.

Team B: Give an example of someone you know who has discovered the truth of Psalm 46:1, 11 as he or she experienced extreme difficulty in life (do not use real names). What are some of the blessings of Psalm 46:10, and how can we practice this "be still" discipline? Using all of Psalm 46, what encouragement would you share with a person who has been laid off? How do you do this without being flippant or Pollyannaish?

Team C: Examine the words of the hymn "A Mighty Fortress Is Our God," which is based on Psalm 46. Read this psalm and find lines in the hymn that portray faith. Discuss how each is significant for life today. Be ready to share one of those lines and its application with the class.

Allow one group from each team to report its findings to the class. Allow groups that had duplicated assignments (if any) to share additional information as they wish.

Alternative: Instead of the above, download the reproducible page and have learners complete the "Learning Faith" and the "Expressing Gratitude" activities in small groups or as a whole class. Do not write the letters *A, B,* and *C* on the envelopes of the Into the Lesson activity.

Into Life

Pose this question to the class as a whole: "Realizing that faith is always one generation from extinction, what are some ways we can pass faith to succeeding generations that will help them become lifelong believers?" Jot responses on the board.

Write a Prayer: Ask each learner to write a three-part prayer. Stress that this will be kept personal —you will not collect the prayers or ask anyone to read them aloud.

First, the prayer should thank God for the assurance He offers through today's texts. After the class has had a few minutes to write, say that the second part is a confession of weak faith. Third, ask learners to express a commitment to practice one or more faith disciplines, citing one of "Faith's Hall of Fame" individuals as a model.

Alternative: If you did the three-teams activity in the Into the Word segment, use the "Expressing Gratitude" activity on the reproducible page, which you can download, in place of the "Write a Prayer" activity above.

FAITH EMPOWERS ENDURANCE

DEVOTIONAL READING: James 5:7-11
BACKGROUND SCRIPTURE: Hebrews 12:1-13

HEBREWS 12:1-11

1 Wherefore seeing we also are compassed about with so great a cloud of witnesses, let us lay aside every weight, and the sin which doth so easily beset us, and let us run with patience the race that is set before us,

2 Looking unto Jesus the author and finisher of our faith; who for the joy that was set before him endured the cross, despising the shame, and is set down at the right hand of the throne of God.

3 For consider him that endured such contradiction of sinners against himself, lest ye be wearied and faint in your minds.

4 Ye have not yet resisted unto blood, striving against sin.

5 And ye have forgotten the exhortation which speaketh unto you as unto children, My son, despise not thou the chastening of the Lord, nor faint when thou art rebuked of him:

6 For whom the Lord loveth he chasteneth, and scourgeth every son whom he receiveth.

7 If ye endure chastening, God dealeth with you as with sons; for what son is he whom the father chasteneth not?

8 But if ye be without chastisement, whereof all are partakers, then are ye bastards, and not sons.

9 Furthermore we have had fathers of our flesh which corrected us, and we gave them reverence: shall we not much rather be in subjection unto the Father of spirits, and live?

10 For they verily for a few days chastened us after their own pleasure; but he for our profit, that we might be partakers of his holiness.

11 Now no chastening for the present seemeth to be joyous, but grievous: nevertheless afterward it yieldeth the peaceable fruit of righteousness unto them which are exercised thereby.

KEY VERSES

Let us run with patience the race that is set before us, looking unto Jesus the author and finisher of our faith. —**Hebrews 12:1, 2**

A LIVING FAITH

Unit 1: What Is Faith?

LESSON AIMS

After participating in this lesson, each student will be able to:

1. Summarize the parental model and the athlete model of discipline.

2. Explain why discipline is important to the Christian life.

3. Write a prayer of thanks for God's discipline.

LESSON OUTLINE

  A. No More Discipline?
  B. Lesson Background
I. Running with Endurance (HEBREWS 12:1-3)
  A. Traveling Light (v. 1)
    Home Field Advantage?
  B. Finishing Strong (vv. 2, 3)
II. Growing by Correction (HEBREWS 12:4-8)
  A. What Happens (vv. 4-6)
  B. Why It Happens (vv. 7, 8)
III. Flourishing from Discipline (HEBREWS 12:9-11)
  A. Profiting from Obedience (vv. 9, 10)
    A Loving Father's Discipline
  B. Training for Righteousness (v. 11)
Conclusion
  A. Training While Running
  B. Prayer
  C. Thought to Remember

Introduction

A. No More Discipline?

Children both need and resist discipline. Some among us know of times when misbehaving children are disciplined quite harshly. When this is combined with parental rage or drunkenness, the result can be tragic. A small child might be brutalized by a parent, suffering permanent injury or even death as a result.

This has led some to propose that corporal punishment be rejected altogether. So the pendulum swings the other way—some say too far, with the result being inadequate or nonexistent discipline. This seems to be the case for children where parental attempts at discipline is only verbal in nature. We witness young children who have long since learned to ignore their parents' words. As a result, the children do as they please.

We are greatly comforted by the idea that God is our Father (see Matthew 6:9). We are encouraged to believe that our heavenly Father is our protector and provider. We are not always as keen on the idea that our heavenly Father should be our discipliner and corrector. We are always ready to receive blessings from God, but not as eager to receive corrective discipline. This week's lesson looks at a key passage of Scripture for understanding that we should both expect and humbly receive discipline from our Father in Heaven.

B. Lesson Background

The first 10 chapters of Hebrews lays out a strong case for understanding Jesus Christ as the fulfillment of the prophecies and expectations of the Old Testament. The author of Hebrews holds the Old Testament in very high regard. But for him the Christian system, which centers on the person of the risen Christ, is the superior way. Jesus is seen as the perfect, eternal high priest and the perfect, eternal sacrifice for human sins. Hebrews 11 (last week's lesson) reminds us of the many faithful men and women of the Old Testament era who could only look forward to the salvation effected through Jesus Christ.

Beginning with chapter 12, the author of Hebrews becomes more focused on practical matters. It has been said that Hebrews begins like a treatise, proceeds like a sermon, and ends like a letter. In chapters 12 and 13 we get this more personal feel of a letter. Here the author is writing to folks he knows, with an awareness of specific issues that are troubling their church or churches.

We are far removed from the cultural setting of the churches of the first century. Most of us are not dealing with the relationship between the Jewish system and the Christian system. We have few people in our churches of Jewish background who would be tempted to abandon the church and return to the synagogue (the problem that seems to be the driving force behind the writing of Hebrews). But, as always, the words of Scripture are timeless in their application to our lives. The historical setting may have changed, but these passages of Hebrews have an amazingly contemporary ring when we consider them in depth.

I. Running with Endurance
(Hebrews 12:1-3)
A. Traveling Light (v. 1)

1. Wherefore seeing we also are compassed about with so great a cloud of witnesses, let us lay aside every weight, and the sin which doth so easily beset us, and let us run with patience the race that is set before us.

The *great a cloud of witnesses* is made up of the faithful men and women of chapter 11. When we review that chapter, we realize that these are the ones who acted in faith even though it may have cost them dearly. Obedient faith in God is not always easy. Remaining faithful requires endurance and sacrifice. Just as the author's list includes people who died for their faithfulness (like Abel), so his readers must be willing to make sacrifices in their quest to remain faithful.

The author is not specific here regarding what this includes, but he uses the figure of a *weight* and

HOW TO SAY IT

Josephus	Jo-*see*-fus.
martyrdom	*mar*-ter-dum.
synagogue	*sin*-uh-gog.

the general category of *sin*. We can readily understand the conflict between sin and faithful living, for yielding to sin is the opposite of living by faith. The weights, for their part, are the relationships and commitments we may have that deter us from faithful obedience. For the original readers, these weights may be their continuing ties to the Jewish synagogue, a familiar place of comfort and safety. But if their love for the synagogue and its people draws them away from Christ, then those ties must be severed.

The life of the Christian is compared with a footrace (see also 1 Corinthians 9:24). No competitor wants to carry extra baggage for such an event because traveling light gives the best chance for success. The Greek word the author uses for *race* comes across in English as our word *agony*. This is not a pleasant little jog in the park. It is a lifelong run, slogging through nasty weather and over rough terrain. The apostle Paul uses this same term in a boxing illustration to describe the struggle of the Christian life as the "good fight [agony] of faith" (1 Timothy 6:12; see also 2 Timothy 4:7).

What Do You Think?
Apart from things that Scripture spells out as sin, what are some real and potential hindrances to our Christian "run"? How do we address these?
Talking Points for Your Discussion
- Things that demand intangibles of time and energy
- Things that demand tangibles of money and other resources
- "The good thing is the enemy to the best thing"
- Romans 14:23b

❧ *Home Field Advantage?* ❧

Researchers have found evidence to support the existence of a home field advantage in sports. It seems that home teams win between 55 and 70 percent of the time, depending on the sport being played (*Journal of Sports Behavior,* June 1, 2007). The home field advantage has been found to be particularly significant in football games played in domed stadiums. There, crowd noise can be amplified to the point that the players on the visiting team's offensive unit cannot hear the signals as they are being called.

As we labor for Christ, it often seems that the devil has the home field advantage since he is "the prince of this world" (John 12:31; 14:30; 16:11). Those opposed to Christianity try to shout it down with their humanistic philosophies (Ephesians 2:2; Colossians 2:8). But it is we who have the decisive advantage: Christ has overcome the world (John 16:33). We also have "a cloud of witnesses" to cheer us on (Hebrews 12:1).

The crowd in the stadium can't win the game for a team that is out of shape, unprepared, or distracted. The fact that a great cloud of witnesses is on our side in the spiritual struggles of life does not relieve us of responsibility. We must give diligence to run the best race possible.   —C. R. B.

B. Finishing Strong (vv. 2, 3)

2. Looking unto Jesus the author and finisher of our faith; who for the joy that was set before him endured the cross, despising the shame, and is set down at the right hand of the throne of God.

Hebrews continues the description of the faithful life as a race by applying it to Jesus himself. The writer pictures the finish line as *the joy that was set before* Jesus. This calls to mind the great satisfaction a runner feels when completing a grueling race. Jesus did not drop out at the halfway point. He was a *finisher*. Another word describes Jesus in this life-race: *author*. An author is someone who originates a work. Jesus sets the course for us to live by the example of His life.

Three aspects of Jesus' race-life are mentioned. First, the fact that He *endured the cross* compares Jesus with a runner who continues the race despite great physical pain. Distance runners will testify that every part of their bodies is in agony as they near the finish line. Their feet have blisters. Their lungs are burning. Their muscles are screaming. Yet successful runners endure these pains to finish the race.

Second, Jesus did not let *the shame* of His road to the cross keep Him from finishing. The cross in the first century signifies the shameful way in which

criminals are executed. Paul spoke of this in what he calls the stumbling block of the cross (1 Corinthians 1:23). The scandal is the idea that the Son of God would be killed in a manner reserved for vile lawbreakers. Yet while Jesus was aware of the manner of His death long before His final journey to Jerusalem, He did not try to avoid it (see Matthew 20:19).

Third, Jesus reached His goal. His final place is to be seated at God's right hand, sharing in His judgment throne (see Revelation 5:13). We can almost picture this as the winners' platform, where the medals are awarded. Jesus received the highest award imaginable: to sit at God's right hand in Heaven (see Acts 2:33).

What Do You Think?
What motivates you to stay faithful through hard days?
Talking Points for Your Discussion
- Recalling specific Scriptures
- Recalling specific examples of faithful believers
- Recalling past deliverances

3. For consider him that endured such contradiction of sinners against himself, lest ye be wearied and faint in your minds.

The painful yet faithful life-race of Jesus is held up as an encouragement for the readers, especially those who are ready to call it quits. Jesus not only endured pain but also the *contradiction of sinners* —the hostility of evil people. Hebrews calls the readers to persevere even though they may be very weary of this continuing hostility. Perseverance happens only when we keep our spiritual eyes focused on the goal: eternal life in fellowship with Jesus (1 Thessalonians 4:17).

II. Growing by Correction
(HEBREWS 12:4-8)
A. What Happens (vv. 4-6)

4. Ye have not yet resisted unto blood, striving against sin.

The author now shifts away from the comparison between Jesus and his readers to point out

Faith Empowers Endurance

a contrast: they *have not yet resisted unto blood.* If Hebrews is intended for a church or churches in or around Jerusalem (as many believe), then there are several memories of martyrdom. Stephen (Acts 7:59) and James the brother of John (12:1, 2) were put to death in the city. The Jewish historian Josephus tells us that James the half-brother of Jesus was put to death by his Jewish opponents in Jerusalem about AD 62, although we do not know whether Hebrews was written before or after this date.

Those reading the message of Hebrews in the first century obviously are not dead. The author is not saying that their sufferings for the faith have been minor, but that they still do not compare with Jesus or others who have been faithful unto death in their *striving against sin* (see Revelation 2:10).

5, 6. And ye have forgotten the exhortation which speaketh unto you as unto children, My son, despise not thou the chastening of the Lord, nor faint when thou art rebuked of him: for whom the Lord loveth he chasteneth, and scourgeth every son whom he receiveth.

To this point, the author has used the Old Testament in several ways to help the reader understand the person and role of Jesus in the Christian system. Now he uses Scripture to illustrate the nature of God's discipline for believers, specifically Proverbs 3:11, 12.

In Proverbs, the *chastening of the Lord* is presented in the context of a father who corrects his son. The good father recognizes the goal of chastening: encouragement for the child not to repeat disobedience. Good parents discipline their children because they want them to learn correct and godly behavior. In this light, chastening, even if severe, is motivated by the best interests of the child. From a biblical perspective, the loving parents are those who discipline their children consistently. A parent who avoids or ignores the responsibility of discipline is not acting from love, but from selfishness, laziness, or apathy.

We should not be surprised, then, that our loving Father disciplines us (Deuteronomy 8:5; 2 Samuel 7:14). This is *not* to say that every bad thing that happens in our lives is punishing dis-

Visual for Lesson 3. *Use this visual as a discussion starter for the question "In what ways is the Christian life like and unlike a footrace?"*

cipline from the Lord. If we were punished every time we disobeyed God, our lives would be miserable indeed! It *is* to say that hardship may be for our benefit in the long run as we become stronger and more disciplined in our walk with Jesus.

B. Why It Happens (vv. 7, 8)

7. If ye endure chastening, God dealeth with you as with sons; for what son is he whom the father chasteneth not?

If God's chastening is a sign of God's loving concern, then we should see it as a sign that God is truly our Father. God is not a distant Father who visits only occasionally to bestow gifts and pleasures. God is an active, ever-present Father who watches over us continually.

Some Christians have amazing stories of how God's chastening has worked out in their lives. What seemed only incredibly painful at the time comes to be seen, perhaps years later, as the Lord's chastening for the recipient's benefit. Perhaps the prophet Jonah eventually came to view his time in the belly of a sea creature in this light. God works all things together for good (Romans 8:28), even though we may not understand chastening while we are undergoing it.

8. But if ye be without chastisement, whereof all are partakers, then are ye bastards, and not sons.

The author gives a warning to those who seek to avoid suffering for the faith. We should question our relationship with God if we never undergo the Lord's chastening. A good father will discipline his children; God will do so as well. Anyone who does not have this type of relationship with the heavenly Father should question his or her legitimacy as God's child. To try to free ourselves from the guiding hand of God is to reject Him as our heavenly Father.

> **What Do You Think?**
> While discipline is beneficial, how can we grow in Christ in ways that do not involve "trips to the spiritual woodshed"?
> *Talking Points for Your Discussion*
> - Experience (learning from our own mistakes) vs. Wisdom (learning from the mistakes of others)
> - Deuteronomy 11:18-20
> - Psalm 119:11

III. Flourishing from Discipline
(Hebrews 12:9-11)

A. Profiting from Obedience (vv. 9, 10)

9. Furthermore we have had fathers of our flesh which corrected us, and we gave them reverence: shall we not much rather be in subjection unto the Father of spirits, and live?

The wise child understands the discipline of a godly father as an act of love. Such a child therefore gains respect for the parent who is consistent and timely in corrective discipline. There will always be strong-willed children who chafe under even mild discipline and respond with sullen anger. But this is not the outcome normally expected (see Proverbs 15:20). The discipline we receive from the Lord should not result in resentment on our part. Instead, it should help us love and respect God even more, for we are being shown that He cares for us.

10. For they verily for a few days chastened us after their own pleasure; but he for our profit, that we might be partakers of his holiness.

In speaking of parents who punish children for *their own pleasure,* the author is not referring to sadistic parents who gain enjoyment from beating their children. Rather, the idea is that of parents

who discipline as best they know how. Such discipline is both imperfect and limited. Parents make mistakes, and their role as disciplinarians does not extend throughout a child's life. Adult children are no longer subject to the direct discipline of a parent, and this is all the more true if a parent dies.

By contrast, the discipline of God is always perfect, and it extends throughout our lives. This is amazing to consider, but it means that the 90-year-old Christian veteran is just as much subject to God's discipline as the teenager who has become a believer only recently (although the senior saint may not need as much discipline as the teen). God's fathership is an eternal promise, not a temporary situation.

> **What Do You Think?**
> In what ways have you experienced God's comfort or recognized His love *during* a time of trial/discipline?
> *Talking Points for Your Discussion*
> - Psalm 23:4
> - Romans 5:3-5
> - 2 Corinthians 2:6, 7

❧ *A Loving Father's Discipline* ❧

"Just wait until your father gets home!" If you were a child in the day when father went off to work and mother stayed at home to mind the children, you are probably familiar with those words. Disciplinary action could be expected. Of course, mother could also discipline us when sufficiently provoked.

As we look back on our childhood, we realize that our parents did not always discipline us in the most appropriate way. When father arrived home tired at the end of the workday, he may not have been alert to the distinction between willful misconduct and "normal" childish behavior. He just wanted to relax! So sometimes he may have overreacted in his frustration with us. But blessed is the child whose parents love him or her enough to discipline even given the occasional overreaction!

God is perfect in His loving discipline. He never over- or underreacts. God's loving discipline would be defective if we are not disciplined when we need it. Perhaps that's a reason why Christians suffer just as much or more than unbelievers.   —C. R. B.

B. Training for Righteousness (v. 11)

11. Now no chastening for the present seemeth to be joyous, but grievous: nevertheless afterward it yieldeth the peaceable fruit of righteousness unto them which are exercised thereby.

The author sums up this section by pointing out that we can endure great hardships in our Christian journey if we take the long view of faithful living. The Christian life is not a quick sprint; it is a long-distance run to the end of our lives. We understand this better when we view past periods of pain with the clearer vision of hindsight.

We gain strength by enduring trials. We are rewarded with *the peaceable fruit of righteousness* along the way (compare James 3:17, 18). As we follow the course of Christ—a path of sometimes painful obedience—we become more like Him and more submitted to His will. We seek to reflect the words of Paul, who at the end of his life was able to say that he had finished his life-race and had remained faithful (2 Timothy 4:7).

What Do You Think?
How has God used past stresses and chastenings to align you with His will and ways?
How do you distinguish between the typical stresses of life and the chastenings that God imposes?

Talking Points for Your Discussion
▪ Financial stress or chastening
▪ Family stress or chastening
▪ Occupational stress or chastening

Conclusion

A. Training While Running

General George S. Patton (1885–1945) was an excellent athlete in his college days, competing in the 1912 Stockholm Olympics pentathlon event. The physical training of his youth did more than build up Patton's body. It also instilled great discipline in his life. Part of Patton's success as an army commander in World War II was based on the

strict, even harsh discipline he demanded of his troops. Patton summarized his view of discipline when he said, "You have to make the mind run the body. Never let the body tell the mind what to do. The body will always give up. It is always tired in the morning, noon, and night. But the body is never tired if the mind is not tired."

Any athlete who aspires to run a marathon understands that discipline is required. No one is able simply to get up off the couch and run 26.2 miles without preparation! Those who are preparing for their first marathon begin with much shorter distances to build up endurance and muscle tone. This requires mental discipline, as Patton well knew. When the alarm clock rings, the body wants to roll over and sleep the extra hour that has been set aside for a morning run. Discipline, at its heart, is a spiritual and mental matter.

When we become Christians, we begin the race of faith immediately. We are in training and running the race at the same time. We may run slowly at first. We may falter because of sin. This is not the kind of race, however, where we are trying to beat the others who are running alongside us. Our only objective is to finish.

As we run, remembering three things will help defeat discouragement. First, we are not blazing a new trail. The pathway of faithful living has already been marked by Jesus; this racecourse has been followed by millions of believers since. Second, we are not alone in this race. God is with us, even disciplining us along the way, so that we will grow in faith and endurance. We are running in the fellowship of the church, brothers and sisters in the faith who are following the same trail. Third, we have a great goal set before us, a prize at the finish line. That prize is to be with Christ forever.

B. Prayer

God our Father, as we discipline ourselves for the race, may we accept Your discipline as children who love and respect You. We pray this in the name of Jesus, the one who finished His task with perfect faithfulness; amen.

C. Thought to Remember

Accept God's correction as evidence of His love.

Involvement Learning

Some of the activities below are also found in the helpful student book, Adult Bible Class.
Don't forget to download the free reproducible page from www.standardlesson.com to enhance your lesson!

Into the Lesson

Option 1: Invite a runner or a track coach to give a five-minute talk highlighting the preparations and disciplines needed for successful distance running. Ask him or her to be sure to highlight the importance of endurance and focusing on the goal. The speaker should bring visual aids, such as lightweight shoes and athletic clothing.

After the presentation, say, "Today's text focuses on the disciplines necessary to live the Christian life as God would have us. It uses two illustrations. One illustration comes from a father's loving discipline. The other illustration is of the endurance runner. Both illustrations are very encouraging."

Option 2: Distribute index cards. Ask learners to list the most difficult and important life goals they have tried or are trying to achieve. Then ask them to share one of those goals with a class partner and describe some of the disciplines needed to accomplish that goal. Make the transition to Bible study by saying, "Some of you may have mentioned faithful Christian living as a life goal. Today's study has two illustrations on how to accomplish that."

Into the Word

Form study teams of no more than five learners each. Give each team one of the three assignments below, along with a sheet of poster board and a marker. (Larger classes may have more than one team working on a task.)

Team 1: Read Hebrews 12:1-3. List the expressed and implied disciplines needed for completing the Christian life-race. Write these on the runner's footprints, tape them to the poster board, and be ready to explain to the class how or why each of these is significant in the Christian life. (Teacher: give this team 10 cutouts of footprints in a color that contrasts with the poster board.)

Team 2: Read Hebrews 12:4-11. Create an acrostic of the word *CHASTEN,* using key words or phrases from this text. Be ready to explain why each word or phrase is significant for shaping the Christian's faithful life. Begin or conclude your presentation by telling the class why you think God's chastening is important and beneficial. (Teacher: give this team a poster board with the word *CHASTEN* listed vertically. If your class uses more than one Bible translation, explain that the *King James Version* uses *chasten* while other versions use *discipline.*)

Team 3: Read Hebrews 12:1-11. Create two columns on your poster board with the headings "Costs of Discipleship" and "Rewards of Discipleship." List key words and phrases from the text under each column; be ready to explain their significance to the class. (Teacher: give this team a poster board and a marker.)

Alternative: Have learners complete instead the "Illustrating Discipline(s)" activity from the reproducible page, which you can download. The activity may be completed as an entire class, as small study groups, or as study pairs.

Into Life

Use the same teams for the following assignments, or form new teams to match learner skills and interests with the tasks of the assignments. *Team 1:* Prepare a skit illustrating endurance in the Christian life. Use the metaphor of the race that the class explored. *Team 2:* Write a prayer of thanksgiving for God's chastening. *Team 3:* Identify deceased members of your church who are now part of the "cloud of witnesses." Be ready to tell why you think the faithful lives of these individuals still serve as examples of faithful Christian living and endurance.

Alternative: If you think your class would benefit from a time of deeper interpersonal sharing, have learners complete the "Life's Hurdles" exercise on the reproducible page, which you can download. Ask for volunteers to discuss their personal hurdles.

Faith Empowers Endurance

FAITH INSPIRES GRATITUDE

DEVOTIONAL READING: 2 Thessalonians 1:1-7
BACKGROUND SCRIPTURE: Hebrews 12:14-29

HEBREWS 12:18-29

18 For ye are not come unto the mount that might be touched, and that burned with fire, nor unto blackness, and darkness, and tempest,

19 And the sound of a trumpet, and the voice of words; which voice they that heard intreated that the word should not be spoken to them any more:

20 (For they could not endure that which was commanded, And if so much as a beast touch the mountain, it shall be stoned, or thrust through with a dart:

21 And so terrible was the sight, that Moses said, I exceedingly fear and quake:)

22 But ye are come unto mount Sion, and unto the city of the living God, the heavenly Jerusalem, and to an innumerable company of angels,

23 To the general assembly and church of the firstborn, which are written in heaven, and to God the Judge of all, and to the spirits of just men made perfect,

24 And to Jesus the mediator of the new covenant, and to the blood of sprinkling, that speaketh better things than that of Abel.

25 See that ye refuse not him that speaketh. For if they escaped not who refused him that spake on earth, much more shall not we escape, if we turn away from him that speaketh from heaven:

26 Whose voice then shook the earth: but now he hath promised, saying, Yet once more I shake not the earth only, but also heaven.

27 And this word, Yet once more, signifieth the removing of those things that are shaken, as of things that are made, that those things which cannot be shaken may remain.

28 Wherefore we receiving a kingdom which cannot be moved, let us have grace, whereby we may serve God acceptably with reverence and godly fear:

29 For our God is a consuming fire.

Period of Time

KEY VERSE

Wherefore we receiving a kingdom which cannot be moved, let us have grace, whereby we may serve God acceptably with reverence and godly fear. —**Hebrews 12:28**

A Living Faith

Unit 1: What Is Faith?

LESSONS 1–5

LESSON AIMS

After participating in this lesson, each student will be able to:

1. Explain the metaphor of coming to Mount Zion (Sion).

2. Compare and contrast Moses' approach to Mount Sinai with the Christian's approach to Mount Zion.

3. Tell how he or she expresses reverence and awe (or "fear") in worship.

LESSON OUTLINE

Introduction

A. Earthquakes

Have you ever been in an earthquake? It can be terrifying; our confidence in the idea of "solid ground" may be, well, shaken. Seemingly well-constructed buildings may be damaged beyond repair. Earthquakes can change our reality.

We find evidence of earthquakes throughout recorded history. The prophet Amos, for example, dates his book as having taken place two years before "the earthquake" (Amos 1:1; compare Zechariah 14:5). Which earthquake was this? We don't know for sure, but it was such a mighty event in the day of Amos that he could simply call it "the earthquake." Everyone knew what he was talking about at the time.

People in ancient times understood earthquakes as being under divine control. Some religions even had an earthquake god. The prophet Isaiah pictured a visitation of the Lord God of Israel as coming with earthquakes (Isaiah 29:6). Even today, some people interpret earthquake disasters as signs of God's wrath.

If earthquakes are dramatic evidences of God's power, how should we understand a complete *lack* of temblors? In other words, how should we understand a situation where people are infallibly protected from earthquake harm? Only God can create such a situation. This is envisaged by the author of Hebrews in today's lesson.

B. Lesson Background

Mountains play important roles in the Bible narratives. Noah's ark came to rest in a mountain range (Genesis 8:4). Abraham nearly sacrificed his son Isaac on a mountain (Genesis 22:2). Joshua led a ceremony of covenant renewal between Mount Gerizim and Mount Ebal (Joshua 8:33). Satan took Jesus to the summit of a high mountain to show Him all the kingdoms of the world (Matthew 4:8). It was from the vantage point of a mountaintop that John saw the new Jerusalem descend from Heaven (Revelation 21:10).

Today's lesson features two mountains: Mount Sinai (also called Mount Horeb) and Mount Sion (also spelled "Zion"). Mount Sinai played an

Faith Inspires Gratitude

important role in the life of Moses. Here Moses saw the burning bush and received his commission from the Lord (Exodus 3). After escaping from Egypt, the people of Israel were led to this same mountain in the wilderness of Sinai. There they received their law and covenant from the Lord.

We should remember that that was both a glorious and a terrifying time for Moses and the newly freed Israelites. To touch the mountain meant death (Exodus 19:12). There were "thunders and lightnings" accompanied by "a thick cloud" covering the mountain (19:16a). The piercing, frightening sound of a trumpet was heard (19:16b). The presence of the Lord caused the mountain to shake violently, although we do not know if the people of Israel felt this as an earthquake or simply observed the shaking mountain (19:18). All of this served to help the people understand that God was present and dealing with their nation through Moses.

Sion (or Zion) was an ancient name for the mountaintop fortress of the Jebusite people. David took this place to be his capital city in about 1000 BC (2 Samuel 5:7). Tradition identifies this with Mount Moriah (see 2 Chronicles 3:1). Later, Zion became a more general term for Jerusalem (see Psalm 48:1, 2). It was here that David instructed his son Solomon to build a permanent sanctuary for the Lord, the first Jerusalem temple (1 Kings 5:3-5). Because Jerusalem was the temple city, Zion became a symbolic way of referring to the eternal city of God and His people, the new or heavenly Jerusalem (see Revelation 3:12; compare Galatians 4:25, 26).

HOW TO SAY IT

Amos	*Ay*-mus.
Ebal	*Ee*-bull.
Eyjafjallajökull	*Ay*-yah-fyah-lah-*yoh*-kuul.
Gerizim	*Gair*-ih-zeem or Guh-*rye*-zim.
Haggai	*Hag*-eye or *Hag*-ay-eye.
Horeb	*Ho*-reb.
Jebusite	*Jeb*-yuh-site.
Sinai	*Sigh*-nye or *Sigh*-nay-eye.
Sion or Zion	*Zi*-un.
synagogue	*sin*-uh-gog.

I. Mountain of Terror
(Hebrews 12:18-21)
A. Frightful Phenomena (vv. 18, 19)

18. For ye are not come unto the mount that might be touched, and that burned with fire, nor unto blackness, and darkness, and tempest.

The author's contrast between Mount Sinai and Mount Zion begins with a description of Sinai. The author is aware of the prohibition against touching the mountain during the time of God's presence there (Exodus 19:12). Thus his comment *that might be touched* does not mean the people were encouraged to touch it. Instead this is his way of saying that this mountain was a physical, touchable feature of geography. It appeared fiery yet dark and gloomy, having a stormy wind buffeting it on a continual basis (see Deuteronomy 4:11).

19. And the sound of a trumpet, and the voice of words; which voice they that heard intreated that the word should not be spoken to them any more.

The physical appearance of the mountain was only part of the experience for the people of Israel. Their hearing was also involved. They not only heard what sounded like a mighty trumpet (Exodus 19:16), but a speaking voice that terrified them. This was the voice of the Lord (Deuteronomy 5:22, 23). The terror caused by hearing this voice caused the people to beg that God not speak in their hearing any more for fear of death (Exodus 20:19; Deuteronomy 5:24-26).

B. Dreadful Decrees (v. 20)

20. (For they could not endure that which was commanded, And if so much as a beast touch the mountain, it shall be stoned, or thrust through with a dart.

Part of the people's terror came from the absolute prohibition against having physical contact with the mountain. It is difficult to understand why anyone would have wanted to touch the mountain because of its terrifying appearance and sound. But if someone did, then that person had to be put to death—no exceptions (see Exodus 19:12, 13). Even animals were subject to death if they wandered into the forbidden zone. This prohibition applied to children too, so parents had to be extra vigilant. Fortunately, the warning seems to have worked, for we have no record of deaths because of contact with the mountain.

C. Fearful Scene (v. 21)

21. And so terrible was the sight, that Moses said, I exceedingly fear and quake:).

The author assumes that the reader is familiar with the story of the giving of the law to Israel. This included the horrible scene witnessed by Moses of the people deserting the covenant with the Lord by worshipping an idol, a golden calf. It was then that Moses himself feared the wrath of God upon the people (Deuteronomy 9:19).

The author uses this picture of Mount Sinai as a vivid way of describing the old covenant. While the covenant made through Moses was a good thing for its day, it proved inadequate in the areas of an eternal priesthood (Hebrews 7:23, 24) and an eternal sacrifice for sins (7:27). Now the author shows that this older covenant was founded in fear, presenting God as unapproachable. This prepares the way for one of the most inspiring parts of the book of Hebrews: the presentation of the new covenant as the contrast with this mountain of terror.

> **What Do You Think?**
> Which aspects of the old covenant are you most thankful to have been superseded by the new covenant? Why?
> *Talking Points for Your Discussion*
> - Issues of law and grace
> - Issues of priesthood
> - Issues of sacrifice
> - Other issues

❧ *Appropriate Fear* ❧

Eyjafjallajökull is the nearly unpronounceable name of the volcano in Iceland that shut down air travel across Europe in April 2010. Airlines canceled as many as 17,000 flights per day for nearly a week, stranding countless passengers. Clouds of volcanic ash are hazardous to airplanes and can cause jet engines to fail. The danger was real: a British Airways jet flew into such a cloud at 37,000 feet over Indonesia in 1982, and all four engines stalled. Fortunately, the crew was able to restart the engines before it was too late. The caution of April 2010 was prudent!

Since Moses and the Israelites had no advanced technology, they were immune to any danger in that regard concerning Mount Sinai. However, they could see plainly the physical danger of going near the mountain, and God gave them additional vocal warning as well.

The terrifying appearance of Sinai was a testimony to God's majestic and fearsome power. Hebrews 4:16 encourages us to "come boldly unto the throne of grace, that we may obtain mercy, and find grace to help in time of need." But that does not mean we treat God casually. Do we fear volcanoes more than we fear God?   —C. R. B.

II. Mountain of Hope
(Hebrews 12:22-24)
A. Perfect City (v. 22a)

22a. But ye are come unto mount Sion, and unto the city of the living God, the heavenly Jerusalem.

The new covenant enjoyed by Christians does not focus on the terrifying circumstances of the giving of the law at Mount Sinai. Instead, we look to the perfect, spiritual city that is described in three ways here.

The first description is the name *mount Sion*. The authors of the Bible frequently use this designation to describe the location of Jerusalem (see the Lesson Background). The second description tells us this is not a place from the past, but is the *city of the living God*. The fact that we are pointed to something beyond the physical reality of a hilltop in central Palestine is explained by the third description: *heavenly Jerusalem*.

Our hope lies not in the past of Mount Sinai, but in the present and the future of this heavenly Jerusalem (Revelation 21:2). We are in covenant with God, who reigns from Heaven. We cannot touch this mountain, but not because it is a forbidden rock. Rather, this is a spiritual place, where we relate to God in a perfect and eternal way, far beyond the dramatic visitation of God on Sinai.

Faith Inspires Gratitude

B. Perfect Residents (vv. 22b, 23)

22b, 23a. And to an innumerable company of angels, to the general assembly.

The number of angels present at Mount Sinai during God's temporary residence there is not stressed (Acts 7:32; Hebrews 2:2). By contrast, the heavenly city of God is inhabited by *an innumerable company of angels*. The numerical word used here is the source of our English word *myriad*. It has the sense of "uncountable." It would be akin to the English slang terms *zillions*. In Revelation 5:11, the angels in Heaven are described as being 10,000 times 10,000. Anyway you understand it, it is more angels than we can imagine. *The general assembly* probably refers to the angels being gathered for worship, although it may indicate the entire host of Heaven.

23b. And church of the firstborn, which are written in heaven.

It is not just angels in this heavenly Jerusalem, however, for we as Christians have citizenship there too. We are members of the *church of the firstborn,* the church of Jesus Christ, who is the firstborn from the dead (see Colossians 1:18; Revelation 1:5; compare Hebrews 1:6).

Our citizenship in the city of God is permanent by virtue of having our names written there. This is very much like the images of the book of Revelation that speak of having names written in the book of life. Only those who have their names in this book are allowed into the eternal city (see Revelation 21:27; compare Luke 10:20). This refers to the assurance of salvation we have through faith in Christ. We have the right to be residents in Heaven through our relationship with Him.

23c. And to God the Judge of all, and to the spirits of just men made perfect.

The central resident of the heavenly Jerusalem is God himself. The author describes God as the ultimate judge (compare Genesis 18:25; Psalm 50:6). This would be as terrifying as approaching Mount Sinai except for the author's description of another group, the *spirits of just men made perfect*. Presumably, these are believers who have gone before us in death. They have not perfected themselves, but have been *made perfect* and are therefore suitable for residence in God's city. We may picture them as waiting for us, anticipating the reunion of all God's righteous ones in His new Jerusalem (compare Hebrews 11:40). This too gives us hope for the future in God's glorious city.

❧ A DELIGHTFUL HOPE ❧

Artists have struggled throughout the centuries to depict the glories of the heavenly city. Whether by means of paint, the stone and stained glass of church architecture, or computer graphics, we must presume that no earthly attempt will ever capture the wonders of that city fully. Does that mean that such attempts are wastes of time? By no means! These are worthwhile endeavors when they lift our thoughts to God and help us anticipate being with Him in that heavenly city.

The author of Hebrews intends to do just that with his word picture. He tells us of the love of God, who through the new covenant in Christ's blood has provided a way for us to become citizens of that marvelous place. As we marvel at the artistic depictions of the heavenly city, we remind ourselves that it's going to be even better than we can imagine. —C. R. B.

C. Perfect Covenant (v. 24)

24. And to Jesus the mediator of the new covenant, and to the blood of sprinkling, that speaketh better things than that of Abel.

The author returns to the central theme of the book: the atoning work of Jesus inaugurates a new and better covenant (Hebrews 7:22; 8:6; 9:15). *The blood of sprinkling* is reminiscent of the blood sprinkled on the people of Israel by Moses at the inauguration of the old covenant (Exodus 24:8;

compare 1 Peter 1:2). No covenant can be properly inaugurated without the shedding of blood (Hebrews 9:18). The thing that makes the Christian covenant superior is that it is founded on the eternal, once-for-all-time sacrifice of Jesus and the shedding of His innocent blood (Hebrew 9:14).

There is another blood analogy going on here as well: the comparison with the blood of Abel. After his murder by Cain, Abel's blood cried out from the ground (Genesis 4:10; compare Hebrews 11:4, last week's lesson). Abel's blood reeks of the sinful deed of Cain. Christ's blood, by contrast, carries the promise of pardon and peace. There can be no forgiveness without blood being shed (Hebrews 9:22).

III. Consuming Fire
(Hebrews 12:25-29)
A. Heavenly Voice (vv. 25, 26)

25. See that ye refuse not him that speaketh. For if they escaped not who refused him that spake on earth, much more shall not we escape, if we turn away from him that speaketh from heaven.

As the author approaches the end of this letter, he returns to a point he made near the beginning: there is no escape for those who reject the gospel (Hebrews 2:3). This is the message of salvation spoken by Jesus and passed on by the apostolic witnesses. This is the sound teaching of the church, that Jesus died for our sins (2:17) and therefore brings salvation to those who believe in Him.

We are reminded again of the terrifying experience of the people of Israel at Sinai. There the voice of God was so overwhelming that the people begged that it cease (Hebrews 12:19, above). The point here is that since the gospel is surely the voice of God, then there is no escape for those who reject it. There undoubtedly is a personal plea here from the author, a warning for those Jewish Christian readers who are considering abandoning Christ and church to return to the synagogue.

This message holds true for us today. If we imagine there is another way to be saved other than through faith in Christ, we will not escape either. If we abandon the faith, we have "trodden under foot the Son of God" (Hebrews 10:29) and are liable for judgment. Let us remember that without the atoning blood of Jesus "It is a fearful thing to fall into the hands of the living God" (10:31).

What Do You Think?
In sharing your faith, do you stress more the *rewards* of knowing God or the *consequences* of neglecting His invitation? Which made more of an impact on you when you heard the gospel? Why?
Talking Points for Your Discussion
- Advantages of stressing one or the other
- Situations that call for a particular emphasis
- Dangers of overstressing one or the other

26. Whose voice then shook the earth: but now he hath promised, saying, Yet once more I shake not the earth only, but also heaven.

Although the dreadful experience of Mount Sinai is in the past, the voice of God has not passed away. This is the voice of judgment, a word that will shake both the earth and the heavens (compare Judges 5:4; Psalm 68:8; Haggai 2:6). Just as there is no escape from God, there is nothing that is not subject to the power of His voice. To ignore or disobey it is utter folly.

B. Eternal Word (v. 27)

27. And this word, Yet once more, signifieth the removing of those things that are shaken, as of things that are made, that those things which cannot be shaken may remain.

The author uses a well-known understanding of the Word of God: while other things fade and pass away, the Word of God is eternal. See Isaiah 40:6-8 (quoted in 1 Peter 1:23-25).

What Do You Think?
How can the "shaking" of unreliable things provide an opportunity for Christian witness?
Talking Points for Your Discussion
- Regarding financial structures
- Regarding issues of national security
- Regarding health issues
- Regarding personal freedoms

Faith Inspires Gratitude

C. Unshakable Kingdom (vv. 28, 29)

28a. Wherefore we receiving a kingdom which cannot be moved.

The author has presented God's Son as a king who is granted a kingdom (Hebrews 1:8). Now we are given a vibrant way of understanding this kingdom: it *cannot be moved.* This is earthquake language. The kingdom of God is exempt from any such force. Christians are part of an impregnable, infallible, indestructible, everlasting kingdom.

28b, 29. Let us have grace, whereby we may serve God acceptably with reverence and godly fear: for our God is a consuming fire.

We do not leave this study without a reminder that the God of Mount Sinai is the same as the God of Mount Sion. God is still the all-powerful judge, *a consuming fire* (Deuteronomy 4:24; 9:3; Isaiah 33:14). The God of the old covenant is the same as the God of the eternal kingdom of grace.

We are given directives to help us have a proper relationship with God. We are to *have grace,* an attitude of gratitude and submission. This should be reflected in the way we serve God. The idea of serving in this context has the sense of "worship." How should we worship God? We do so *with reverence and godly fear.* This was the attitude of Jesus, even in the midst of great suffering (see Hebrews 5:7). We no longer fear the consequences for our sin because of the forgiveness we have through Christ. Yet we should never lose our fear of the Lord God Almighty. The church of Jesus Christ must be a God-fearing church if it is to be blessed by the Lord (Acts 9:31).

> *What Do You Think?*
> What helps you most to "serve God acceptably with reverence and godly fear"?
> *Talking Points for Your Discussion*
> ▪ Recalling specific songs
> ▪ Recalling specific Scripture passages
> ▪ Recalling how God has worked in your life
> ▪ Recalling examples of faithful believers
> ▪ Putting faith into action
> ▪ "What comes into our minds when we think about God is the most important thing about us."
> —A. W. Tozer

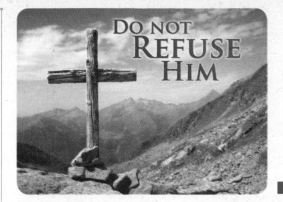

Visual for Lesson 4. *Start a discussion by pointing to this visual as you ask "Why is a 'maybe later' response the same as refusing Jesus?"*

Conclusion

A. Citizens of Heaven

The church I serve may have citizens from many different nations attending on any given weekend. On a recent Sunday, we had citizens of Korea, China, Mexico, the Philippines, Iran, Canada, Malaysia, Great Britain, and Singapore present. Despite cultural, ethnic, and language differences, we were united as we worshipped the same God, the God of the Bible. We may carry different earthly passports, but we are citizens of Heaven (Philippians 3:20). We are united in Christ, our common Savior, Lord, and King.

The church, as imperfect as it may seem in this age, is the congregation of those gathered to Mount Sion, the fellowship of those who have been saved through faith in Christ. Our heavenly citizenship has already begun.

B. Prayer

We love Your kingdom, Lord. May we take comfort in our citizenship in Your holy city, the fellowship of the saved in Christ. May our great reverence for You never be diminished, but grow stronger as we worship You in spirit and truth. We pray these things in the name of Jesus; amen.

C. Thought to Remember

We are citizens of a kingdom that cannot be shaken.

INVOLVEMENT LEARNING

Some of the activities below are also found in the helpful student book, Adult Bible Class.
Don't forget to download the free reproducible page from www.standardlesson.com to enhance your lesson!

Into the Lesson

Place in chairs copies of the "Exploring the Mountains" crossword puzzle from the reproducible page, which you can download. Learners can begin working on this as they arrive.

Say, "We usually think of earthquakes in terms of the destruction they cause. Perhaps we also should think about human reactions to earthquakes. How do people react to earthquakes that are in progress? I'd like everyone to stand and strike a pose that you think shows how people respond physically to earthquakes." (Have a camera ready—you may have a great photo for your classroom bulletin board!)

Continue: "Many of you struck poses that depict fear or fleeing. Earthquakes are fearsome events. The question today is, 'What can earthquakes teach us about our relationship with God and our worship of God?' Our text has the answers."

Into the Word

Display two large visual sketches of mountains, one mountain in each sketch. Label one of the mountains *Sinai, Mountain of Terror.* Label the other *Sion, Mountain of Hope.* Say, "We are going to compare and contrast the two mountains presented in today's text. The first mountain, Sinai, is used by Hebrews as an illustration of the old covenant. The second mountain, Sion, symbolizes the new covenant."

Ask class members to recall the setting, significant events, and reaction of the Israelites regarding Mount Sinai (sometimes called "Horeb") when Moses led them there. In addition to using today's text of Hebrews 12:18-21, some learners may research Exodus 19; Deuteronomy 4:10-14; 9:7-21 for additional descriptions. Jot the brainstorming comments on the face of the first poster.

Before calling for comments regarding Mount Sion, explain the background for the name of this mountain and the Old Testament events surrounding it as described in the last paragraph of the Lesson Background. Then ask learners to scan Hebrews 12:22-24 for word pictures of the mountain and what happened there. Also ask learners to look at Revelation 21 and 22. Jot discoveries on the poster board.

Before reading Hebrews 12:25-29 to the class, ask learners to watch for clues as to why the author contrasts the two mountains. After the reading, ask these discussion questions: 1. By telling us what *not* to do in verse 25, what is the author implying that we *should* do or accept? 2. What point is the author making by contrasting the kingdom of God with the shaking of the mountain? 3. How should worship "with reverence and godly fear" (v. 28) manifest itself in our daily lives?

Answers will serve as a transition to the next segment.

Into Life

Say, "We are going to design a worship service that will focus on teaching people how to worship with 'reverence and godly fear.' We will need to plan five elements: a beginning of the service that emphasizes the theme, a drama, song selection [have song books or hymnals available for reference], a communion thought, and a sermon outline. The primary Scripture will be today's key verse, Hebrews 12:28." Display one poster board for each of the five categories to record ideas.

This activity may be done as a whole class or by five small groups or study pairs. If doing this in groups or pairs, each of the five should design one of the elements. If doing the activity as a whole class, leave the introduction or beginning of the service as the last portion to plan.

After the worship planning is completed, conclude with a prayer that you have written in advance. This prayer should touch important elements of the lesson, especially the need to worship God with reverence and fear.

FAITH INSTILLS LOVE

DEVOTIONAL READING: John 13:31-35
BACKGROUND SCRIPTURE: Hebrews 13; 1 Corinthians 13

HEBREWS 13:1-3, 6

1 Let brotherly love continue.

2 Be not forgetful to entertain strangers: for thereby some have entertained angels unawares.

3 Remember them that are in bonds, as bound with them; and them which suffer adversity, as being yourselves also in the body.

. . . .

6 So that we may boldly say, The Lord is my helper, and I will not fear what man shall do unto me.

1 CORINTHIANS 13

1 Though I speak with the tongues of men and of angels, and have not charity, I am become as sounding brass, or a tinkling cymbal.

2 And though I have the gift of prophecy, and understand all mysteries, and all knowledge; and though I have all faith, so that I could remove mountains, and have not charity, I am nothing.

3 And though I bestow all my goods to feed the poor, and though I give my body to be burned, and have not charity, it profiteth me nothing.

4 Charity suffereth long, and is kind; charity envieth not; charity vaunteth not itself, is not puffed up,

5 Doth not behave itself unseemly, seeketh not her own, is not easily provoked, thinketh no evil;

6 Rejoiceth not in iniquity, but rejoiceth in the truth;

7 Beareth all things, believeth all things, hopeth all things, endureth all things.

8 Charity never faileth: but whether there be prophecies, they shall fail; whether there be tongues, they shall cease; whether there be knowledge, it shall vanish away.

9 For we know in part, and we prophesy in part.

10 But when that which is perfect is come, then that which is in part shall be done away.

11 When I was a child, I spake as a child, I understood as a child, I thought as a child: but when I became a man, I put away childish things.

12 For now we see through a glass, darkly; but then face to face: now I know in part; but then shall I know even as also I am known.

13 And now abideth faith, hope, charity, these three; but the greatest of these is charity.

KEY VERSE

Now abideth faith, hope, charity, these three; but the greatest of these is charity. —1 Corinthians 13:13

A LIVING FAITH

Unit 1: What Is Faith?

LESSONS 1–5

LESSON AIMS

After participating in this lesson, each student will be able to:

1. Tell how today's text describes and illustrates the love believers ought to show toward others.

2. Brainstorm ways to "entertain strangers" in a Christian sense.

3. Commit to putting into practice at least one of the ideas suggested to "entertain strangers."

LESSON OUTLINE

Introduction

A. A World of Confused Love

Were you ever busted for PDA? This is not a criminal infraction, but a school rule against *public display of affection*. School officials realize that teenagers may become boyfriend-girlfriend, but they also understand that the expression of such a relationship in a physical way in the public setting of a school is inappropriate. The need to forbid PDA is a symptom of the larger problem our young people face in trying to understand love.

Confusion when it comes to love is magnified by the messages we receive in popular media. We are constantly led to believe that love is primarily romantic attraction, and that this leads inevitably to sexual activity. Having been fed this false message relentlessly for the last five decades, is it any wonder that media-savvy young people are confused when it comes to love?

Our understanding of love should begin and end with God himself, our loving Father. We are able to love because God "first loved us" (1 John 4:19). Love is not a human innovation. It is a gift of God, part of our created nature. Although popular culture has distorted the concept of love, we may recover the concept of God-based love if we study His Word and live out its teachings. Today's lesson looks at love from God's perspective in the final chapter of Hebrews and in 1 Corinthians 13, one of the best-known chapters in the New Testament.

B. Lesson Background

Central to the Christian understanding of God is that He is a loving God. This becomes "real" for us when we have a personal relationship with Him. God is not a dispassionate Creator. The Lord God as revealed by Jesus is one who loves us in a personal way. God's love is not based on our loveliness or deservedness. It flows from the deepest part of God's nature in a manner we can observe and enjoy but not fully explain.

The perfect expression of God's love is the sending of His Son to be our Savior (John 3:16). He comes to save us while we are in rebellion as His sinful enemies (Romans 5:8-10). There is nothing more central to the Christian faith than understanding the cross as an act of unselfish, gracious love for all men and women.

An intended result of God's expression of love for us is the creation of a community of loving people. Christians are to be loving persons in imitation of their loving Father. The church is to be characterized by genuine, active concern for fellow members and for the community in which they live. Our lesson looks at this from two vantage points.

I. Love as Action
(Hebrews 13:1-3, 6)

The book of Hebrews offers us practical instruction on how the loving community of the church should function.

A. Three Opportunities (vv. 1-3)
1. Let brotherly love continue.

The section begins with a universal command for the readers to persist in *brotherly love*. This is the Greek word *philadelphia*, famously used by William Penn to name his city in Pennsylvania, the city of "brotherly love." Concern for one another is, at the core, motivated by the love of God (see 1 Thessalonians 4:9). The apostle Peter speaks of person-to-person love as springing from the deepest recesses of the human heart (1 Peter 1:22), just as God's love for us is from His innermost nature. We are next offered three concrete examples of how brotherly love can be demonstrated.

2. Be not forgetful to entertain strangers: for thereby some have entertained angels unawares.

First, brotherly love is demonstrated by showing hospitality. Strangers include, at least, fellow Christians. Travelers moving from city to city in the ancient world have few options for accommodations. Lodging is usually found in private

HOW TO SAY IT

agape *(Greek)*	uh-*gah*-pay.
Corinthians	Ko-*rin*-thee-unz (*th* as in *thin*).
Galatians	Guh-*lay*-shunz.
philanthropy	fih-*lan*-thruh-pea.
Sodom	*Sod*-um.

homes. The early church is known for caring for those who are on the move. Since this can become tiresome, a reminder is needed to ensure ongoing hospitality (see 1 Peter 4:9; 3 John 5-8).

The fact that *some have entertained angels unawares* evokes the story of Lot in the city of Sodom. Lot opened his home to strangers whom he encountered at the city gate (Genesis 19:1-3). These strangers were angels sent by the Lord, but Lot did not realize this when he extended hospitality. The point is that it's not necessary to have full information before we offer kindness to a stranger. Such is the nature of brotherly love.

> *What Do You Think?*
> How can our church as a whole do a better job at "entertaining strangers"?
> *Talking Points for Your Discussion*
> - Within the context of Sunday worship
> - Outside the context of Sunday worship

3a. Remember them that are in bonds, as bound with them.

The second example concerns those *in bonds,* meaning in jail or prison. There is a need for ministry to the millions of incarcerated men and women in our world (Matthew 25:36; Hebrews 10:34). This should be especially true with regard to fellow believers who are imprisoned (compare "especially unto them who are of the household of faith" of Galatians 6:10).

To *remember them* means to provide food and other necessities not provided by the prison system of the first century. The Romans do not incarcerate people to serve lengthy prison sentences as punishment. To be in jail is to await trial for corporal punishment, including execution. To provide for the imprisoned may include visiting for prayer and encouragement.

❧ *Prison Ministry* ❧

Robbie Robinson's 5-year-old son died in a house fire. Robbie attended the funeral in handcuffs and shackles. At the time of the funeral, Robbie was serving his second prison term. The first had been for assault, the second for dealing drugs. When given the opportunity to speak at the funeral, Robbie told those gathered about how, through the ministry of Prison Fellowship, he had found the peace that Christ gives. He asked forgiveness from those present whom he had hurt.

When Robbie was released in March 2005, Christians helped him find a transitional home, a church to attend, and an opportunity for a job. He married his girlfriend. He began serving in the church, mentoring young people who were at risk as he had been before Christ changed his life.

The strength of ministries such as Prison Fellowship is not primarily in the organizations. Rather, it is in the individual Christians who take to heart the admonition of today's text.   —C. R. B.

3b. And them which suffer adversity, as being yourselves also in the body.

The third example is ministry to those who *suffer adversity*. This may refer back to the imprisoned, but seems to have a broader application to those within the church who are going through a trying season of life. We should offer help as if we ourselves are suffering. The church is to stand ready to minister to households visited by death, unemployment, illness, and other difficult circumstances.

What Do You Think?
Where do your strengths lie in ministering to the hurting? Where can you improve?
Talking Points for Your Discussion
- Listening skills (Job 2:11-13; 16:1-5)
- Availability (1 Corinthians 16:7)
- "I've been there" (Exodus 23:9)
- Credibility through a consistent lifestyle (Matthew 23:3; Titus 2:7)
- Other

B. One Foundation (v. 6)

6. So that we may boldly say, The Lord is my helper, and I will not fear what man shall do unto me.

The author continues giving practical instructions in verses 4 and 5 (not in today's text), calling for purity in marriage and warning against greed. He sums all this up in the verse before us by quoting Psalm 118:6. Because of the Lord's lov-

ing care, Christians need not fear hardship caused by other people.

II. Love as Life
(1 CORINTHIANS 13:1-13)

First Corinthians 13 comes after Paul has dealt with several troublesome matters within the Corinthian church. These primarily are personal matters in the sense of conflicts and lack of accountability for actions. Chapter 13 caps this discussion with God's method of resolving intrachurch problems: love as the controlling ethic.

A. False Substitutes (vv. 1-3)

1. Though I speak with the tongues of men and of angels, and have not charity, I am become as sounding brass, or a tinkling cymbal.

Most Christians have heard the word *agape*. This is a Greek word, and the *King James Version* translates it as *charity* throughout this chapter. This translation accurately portrays the giving nature of the love Paul is describing.

However, the word *charity* has gained some associations over the centuries that Paul does not intend. Perhaps we think of the Salvation Army or World Vision when we think of charities. Paul does not have this organizational sense in mind, and he does not limit charitable acts to the homeless or the hungry. Paul is speaking of love/charity that is an active, unselfish concern for others, particularly for fellow believers (compare Galatians 6:10). We note that this same word *agape* is translated "love" in 1 Thessalonians 1:3.

Paul begins by describing impressive acts. But if these are lacking in love, they are worthless. The gift of tongues is a concern for the church at Corinth (see 1 Corinthians 12:10), and Paul later gives instructions to bring order to their use (14:13, 27). But on a deeper level, Paul challenges the motives behind using this gift in public: if not motivated out of love for others, it is merely show, just noise.

2. And though I have the gift of prophecy, and understand all mysteries, and all knowledge; and though I have all faith, so that I could remove mountains, and have not charity, I am nothing.

Exercises of prophecy and faith also are potentially loveless acts. As with the gift of tongues, Paul later gives instructions on how the gift of prophecy should be used. Prophecy is giving a direct word of God in an intelligible manner (1 Corinthians 14:23-26). The church's prophets may understand all mysteries and combine this with all knowledge. But the results of exercising the gift of prophecy can be less than positive if this is done without loving motivation.

Paul also speaks of the misuse of faith (compare Romans 12:6, where prophecy and faith are linked). Great things may be accomplished through the power of faith (Matthew 17:20). Yet if love/charity is absent, then the person who claims faith is *nothing*. Faith should have tangible results. But if there is no selfless love behind it, faith will lead to boasting, something Paul abhors (see 1 Corinthians 3:21).

> **What Do You Think?**
> What are some warning signs that our motivation for serving someone is something other than love? What do you do when those warning signs start to pop up?
> *Talking Points for Your Discussion*
> - John 12:4-6
> - 2 Timothy 3:1-7
> - James 2:1-4

3. And though I bestow all my goods to feed the poor, and though I give my body to be burned, and have not charity, it profiteth me nothing.

Paul now gives two extreme examples of acts that are outwardly impressive. First, one may impoverish himself or herself for the benefit of the poor. This is not just giving for the relief of the poor, but actually giving everything away so that you become poor yourself. This would seem to be an act of great generosity and faith, but if charity/love is not the driving reason, then it has no lasting value.

To give one's *body to be burned* is probably Paul's way of describing one who becomes a martyr. Even this, however, may be motivated by self-serving attitudes of wanting to be remembered well. Unless one lays down one's life because of love, there can be no positive legacy (see John 15:13).

❧ MOTIVE ❧

In the summer of 2010, Bill Gates and Warren Buffett, two of the richest men in America, challenged dozens of the world's richest families and individuals to open their wallets to help others. Forty promised to give at least half of their fortunes to charitable causes. Estimates by *Forbes* magazine suggest the result will be at least $125 billion given to charity.

Most of Paul's readers were poor. But rich or poor, God's Word requires us to be charitable toward others (1 John 3:17, 18). Furthermore, giving must be properly motivated. Showy giving that is not motivated by love is an empty gesture; Jesus had strong words in this regard (see Matthew 6:1-4).

We may hope that the 40 billionaires are motivated sincerely by a love of God. If not that, we may hope that their giving is at least a sincere effort in philanthropy ("love for humanity"; see comments on Acts 28:2 in Lesson 12). But ultimately we can control only the motivation of our own giving. See Mark 12:41-44 and 2 Corinthians 8:1–9:15 for additional guidelines.—C. R. B.

B. Trustworthy Marks (vv. 4-7)

4. Charity suffereth long, and is kind; charity envieth not; charity vaunteth not itself, is not puffed up.

Paul now stresses two things love "does" and three things it "does not." On the positive side, *charity suffereth long*—love takes time, and it takes the time necessary. It also *is kind*—it is gentle and caring.

On the negative side, *charity envieth not*—it doesn't jealously guard relationships or personal turf. Love *vaunteth not itself*—this is in keeping with the impressive acts in verses 1-3, which fail if done without love. We may accomplish great things, but not to give ourselves bragging rights. Closely tied to this is Paul's admonition that love *is not puffed up*. This is a condemnation of prideful arrogance we see all too often in the talented and accomplished people of our world.

5, 6a. Doth not behave itself unseemly, seeketh not her own, is not easily provoked, thinketh no evil; rejoiceth not in iniquity.

Five more things that love "does not" now follow. To *behave . . . unseemly* speaks to improper conduct. The only other time the Greek word used here occurs in the New Testament is in 1 Corinthians 7:36. There it is translated "behaveth . . . uncomely" in reference to conduct toward the opposite sex.

Second, the loving person is not a self-advancing egotist. Third, the loving person maintains control of his or her emotional reactions. Paul himself "was stirred" on the occasion noted in Acts 17:16, where the same Greek word translated here as *provoked* is used. The motive behind his provocation had the best intent of his audience at heart, however.

Fourth, the person controlled by love will not dwell on evil. This speaks to grudge-keeping, a popular pastime even today. God says "their sins and iniquities will I remember no more" (Hebrews 10:17). He is our model! Fifth, love takes no pleasure from iniquity. To rejoice in wickedness is itself wicked (see Proverbs 2:14; Jeremiah 11:15).

6b. But rejoiceth in the truth.

Those who love God should love truth, for God will oppose those who oppose the truth (see Romans 1:18-25). God is true and truthful (John 3:33; Romans 3:4). The impulse to lie is self-serving, and therefore opposed to loving truth.

7. Beareth all things, believeth all things, hopeth all things, endureth all things.

Paul ends this section with four quick, universal statements about love. These behaviors (the first and fourth) and attitudes (the second and third) hold true in any circumstance—*all things*. The first and the fourth have the sense of endur-

ance; the loving person does not give up on what is right. Between these bookends we see the mental outlooks of belief and hope that are essential.

Altogether, these four say that the person controlled by love will demonstrate staying power in relationships. Paul is the model in this regard: "We . . . suffer all things, lest we should hinder the gospel of Christ" (1 Corinthians 9:12b).

C. Perpetual Nature (vv. 8-12)

8. Charity never faileth: but whether there be prophecies, they shall fail; whether there be tongues, they shall cease; whether there be knowledge, it shall vanish away.

Paul repeats some of his earlier thoughts about the loving person, but with a twist. Now he contrasts the enduring nature of love with the temporary nature of prophecies, tongues, and knowledge. Love is an eternal quality, being based on the nature of God himself (1 John 4:7, 16). When we practice genuine acts of love, we are acting as God himself acts. Thus we tie our motivations to the eternal.

Charity never faileth is a memorable phrase. Very literally, it means something like "love will never fall down." Love is always on the job.

9, 10. For we know in part, and we prophesy in part. But when that which is perfect is come, then that which is in part shall be done away.

Paul stresses the incomplete nature of even such impressive acts as prophecy. The one who has knowledge doesn't have full knowledge; the one able to prophesy can reveal only what the Lord reveals to him or her—and the Lord doesn't reveal everything. We are finite beings with no claim on eternity except through the Lord.

Paul illustrates this by looking to a time when *that which is perfect is come.* What this is exactly has been the subject of much study. We can see that it is not something humans accomplish, but something that comes to us. Some believe it refers to the completed New Testament, which is still unfinished as Paul is writing to the Corinthians. Under this idea, partial knowledge and prophecies are completed when the New Testament is finished. Others believe *that which is perfect* refers to the second coming of Christ, when He returns to vanquish sin and bring His people home in a state

Faith Instills Love

of perfection. Before we get lost in such debates, we should keep in mind Paul's main point: many things are temporary, but love is eternal.

11. When I was a child, I spake as a child, I understood as a child, I thought as a child: but when I became a man, I put away childish things.

Learning to love is part of the process of maturing in Christ. The squabbles of the church and between Christians can seem very childish. Without love, we operate with the self-centered perspective that characterizes children. A mark of spiritual maturity is when one begins to take a larger view. That view is one of loving others consistently, even those who oppose and bedevil us.

> **What Do You Think?**
> What are some "childish things" that adults tend to hold on to? How can we put these things away? What will happen if we fail to do so?
> *Talking Points for Your Discussion*
> - 1 Corinthians 3:1-3; 14:20
> - 2 Corinthians 12:20
> - Philippians 4:2
> - James 4:1-3

12. For now we see through a glass, darkly; but then face to face: now I know in part; but then shall I know even as also I am known.

The *glass* is a mirror. Mirrors in Paul's day are made of polished metal, and even the best ones offer imperfect reflections. Paul's word-picture tells us that even our best efforts at living the life of love will fall short, for our perspective is limited. This is what it means to *know in part*. There is a future time *(then)* when we will see without distortion. When is this time? We refer back to the debate noted for verses 9, 10, above.

D. Superlative Quality (v. 13)

13. And now abideth faith, hope, charity, these three; but the greatest of these is charity.

Paul ends the chapter by noting three enduring qualities of the Christian life. We live by faith, trusting God in all things. We live by hope, anticipating the blessings of God for the future. Most of all, though, we live by love. Paul refers to these

Visual for Lesson 5

Point to this visual as you ask "How do we pass this truth on to the next generation?"

same three qualities in 1 Thessalonians 1:3, commending the readers for their "work of faith," "labour of love," and "patience of hope."

Conclusion
A. Lifelong Loving

Our world is full of people looking for love. This is natural, for God created us to be objects of His love. Yet many are looking in all the wrong places. Because of this misguided quest, people are frustrated and even become jaded to the whole topic of love. Betrayal leads to disappointment.

This lesson teaches the correct attitudes and actions of love. We can love selflessly because we have faith in God and hope for the future. We can love consistently because we know that God's love for us is eternal and will never fail. And we can love fearlessly, because our love springs from our relationship with God, not from any expectation of having our love returned by another person.

B. Prayer

Lord, You have shown us the depth of Your love by giving Your only Son to be our Savior. May our churches be refuges of love, full of people who show love in attitudes and actions. We pray this in the name of Jesus, who died for us; amen.

C. Thought to Remember

Be an active agent of God's love.

INVOLVEMENT LEARNING

Some of the activities below are also found in the helpful student book, Adult Bible Class.
Don't forget to download the free reproducible page from www.standardlesson.com to enhance your lesson!

Into the Lesson

Bring to class three pictures, one each of an elementary-aged child, an older teen, and a midlife adult. The three pictures need to be large enough to be seen by learners as you walk among them. Ask, "How does a child express love?" Allow discussion, then hold up the picture of the older teen and ask, "How does a teenager express love?" Allow discussion, then show the picture of the adult and ask, "How does an adult express love?"

After the discussion say, "The ways love is expressed change (or should change) as one becomes more mature and experienced in life. That is true whether expressing love to friends, spouse, church family, parents, or children. Today, we will explore criteria to measure the maturity of one's expressions of love."

Into the Word

Distribute handouts titled *Learning Love*. Put on the handouts the five tasks below. Ask learners to complete the tasks with a partner: *1. Love as action:* consult Hebrews 13:1-3 to discover at least two opportunities for showing love. Give an example from your own experience on how to do so. *2. False substitutes for love:* use 1 Corinthians 13:1-3 to discover five acts that may be impressive, but are worthless without love. Discuss motives other than *love* that a person might have for doing such things. *3. Marks of love:* use 1 Corinthians 13:4-7 to find two things love *is* and eight things love *is not*. Then discuss why the four universal statements about love in verse 7 are true. *4. Love's enduring quality:* consult 1 Corinthians 13:8-12 to discover why love has an eternal quality while other things are temporary. How do verses 11, 12 picture the maturity process as it relates to love? *5. Superlative quality of love:* use 1 Corinthians 13:13 to discuss why love (charity) is greater than either faith or hope. Tell of a personal act of love you have witnessed and the outcome of it.

Use 1 Thessalonians 1:3 and 5:8 to enhance your discussion.

After pairs complete their work, ask for volunteers to share discoveries and conclusions. *Option:* Complete this activity as a whole class rather than in pairs. *Alternative:* Instead of the above, have pairs complete the "Love Is, Love Is Not" activity on the reproducible page, which you can download.

Into Life

Recruit in advance some learners to perform one or more of the following skits (no longer than four minutes each). Skits will demonstrate two of the characteristics of love.

Skit 1. The setting: "Susan" and "Mary" are talking about their children. Whenever Susan tries to say something about her child, Mary interrupts with a story about her own child that seems intended to "top" what Susan is saying. Susan uses this situation to demonstrate how love is patient and kind.

Skit 2. The setting: two couples are having dinner together. One husband has just received notice of a promotion. The other husband has just received word he is to be laid off from his job. The actors in the skit will demonstrate how love is not envious or boastful, always persevering.

Skit 3. The setting: a preacher visits a young man who is in jail for stealing the preacher's car. The young man is surprised to see him and doesn't understand why he has come. The minister shows how love perseveres and does not keep a record of wrongs.

After each skit, ask, "What does this scene teach us about love?" Allow free discussion.

Additional or alternative activity: Distribute copies of the "Love Is Personal" exercise from the reproducible page, which you can download. Depending on the time available and the nature of your class, this can be discussed in study pairs, small groups, or as a whole class.

STEPHEN DEFENDS HIS FAITH

DEVOTIONAL READING: Proverbs 8:1-11
BACKGROUND SCRIPTURE: Acts 6:1–7:53

ACTS 6:8-15

8 And Stephen, full of faith and power, did great wonders and miracles among the people.

9 Then there arose certain of the synagogue, which is called the synagogue of the Libertines, and Cyrenians, and Alexandrians, and of them of Cilicia and of Asia, disputing with Stephen.

10 And they were not able to resist the wisdom and the spirit by which he spake.

11 Then they suborned men, which said, We have heard him speak blasphemous words against Moses, and against God.

12 And they stirred up the people, and the elders, and the scribes, and came upon him, and caught him, and brought him to the council,

13 And set up false witnesses, which said, This man ceaseth not to speak blasphemous words against this holy place, and the law:

14 For we have heard him say, that this Jesus of Nazareth shall destroy this place, and shall change the customs which Moses delivered us.

15 And all that sat in the council, looking stedfastly on him, saw his face as it had been the face of an angel.

ACTS 7:1, 2A, 22, 44A, 45B-49

1 Then said the high priest, Are these things so?

2a And he said, Men, brethren, and fathers, hearken.

. . . .

22 And Moses was learned in all the wisdom of the Egyptians, and was mighty in words and in deeds.

. . . .

44a Our fathers had the tabernacle of witness in the wilderness, . . .

45b . . . unto the days of David;

46 Who found favour before God, and desired to find a tabernacle for the God of Jacob.

47 But Solomon built him an house.

48 Howbeit the most High dwelleth not in temples made with hands; as saith the prophet,

49 Heaven is my throne, and earth is my footstool: what house will ye build me? saith the Lord: or what is the place of my rest?

KEY VERSE

Stephen, full of faith and power, did great wonders and miracles among the people. —**Acts 6:8**

A Living Faith

Unit 2: Who Understands Faith?

LESSONS 6–9

LESSON AIMS

After participating in this lesson, each student will be able to:

1. List the charges against Stephen and explain how his speech in Acts 7 responded to those charges.

2. Tell why the temple figures prominently in both the charges against Stephen and in his response.

3. Write a statement of faith that addresses some vital concern of today's culture.

LESSON OUTLINE

Introduction
  A. "May God Help Me"
  B. Lesson Background
 I. Stephen on Trial (Acts 6:8–7:2a)
  A. Boldness (vv. 8-10)
  B. Desperation (vv. 11-14)
  C. Defense (6:15–7:2a)
 II. Truth About Moses (Acts 7:22)
  Is Education a Bad Thing?
 III. Truth About the Temple (Acts 7:44a, 45b-49)
  A. Made by Humans (vv. 44a, 45b-47)
  B. God's True Home (vv. 48, 49)
  Where God Really Wants to Live
Conclusion
  A. The Death of Cheap Grace
  B. Prayer
  C. Thought to Remember

Introduction

A. "May God Help Me"

Pope Leo X declared Martin Luther a heretic in the year 1520 in reaction to Luther's now famous "95 theses." This was a series of talking points that condemned abuses by the church. Luther contended that the church was leading people away from God's truth, and he demanded a return to biblical principles.

Pope Leo sought to silence Luther. Emperor Charles V called Luther to a church council to answer for his teachings. At that council, Luther apologized for the harsh tone of some of his statements, but he said he could not retract their content. One translation has him concluding, "Unless I am convinced by the testimony of the Scriptures or by clear reason . . . I am bound by the Scriptures I have quoted and my conscience is captive to the Word of God. I cannot and will not recant anything, since it is neither safe nor right to go against conscience. May God help me."

The emperor declared Luther an outlaw as a result. This forced Luther to go into hiding for over a year to avoid arrest and execution. Luther's bold testimony serves as a powerful example of a person willing to speak the truth even when it could cost him his life. Luther was not the first to risk his life in such a manner, however.

B. Lesson Background

For the past several weeks, we've focused on the book of Hebrews to define *faith* and to consider ways that faith can empower the Christian life. For the next eight weeks, we'll turn to the book of Acts for illustrations of ways that God uses faithful people.

Our next two studies highlight the ministry of Stephen, who is widely remembered as the first Christian martyr. Stephen probably was a *Hellenist,* meaning a Jewish person who lived outside of Palestine and spoke the Greek language. Stephen seems to have migrated to Judea and, while there, was converted to Christianity by the preaching of the apostles.

We first see Stephen mentioned in his ministry of benevolence in Acts 6. Believers were sharing

Stephen Defends His Faith

resources in a time of need, and this benevolent care extended to widows. The Hellenists (Grecians) complained that their widows were not receiving a fair share, and the apostles invited the church to select seven men to oversee the distribution of aid. One of these was Stephen (Acts 6:5).

I. Stephen on Trial
(ACTS 6:8–7:2a)

Stephen and Philip (two of the seven of Acts 6:3-5) end up being prominent evangelists. Our lessons this month focus on their ministries in that regard.

A. Boldness (vv. 8-10)

8. And Stephen, full of faith and power, did great wonders and miracles among the people.

Luke (the author of Acts) introduces Stephen in Acts 6:5 as "a man full of faith and of the Holy Ghost" to explain why he was chosen as one of the seven mentioned in the Lesson Background. The fact that Stephen is able to do *great wonders and miracles* is evidence of empowerment by the Holy Spirit. The miracles Stephen performs most likely include healings and prophecies. Miraculous works are performed in the name of Jesus to verify the truth of the gospel message.

9. Then there arose certain of the synagogue, which is called the synagogue of the Libertines,

HOW TO SAY IT

Alexandrians	Al-ex-*an*-dree-unz.
Cilicia	Sih-*lish*-i-uh.
Cyrenaica	Sir-uh-*nay*-ih-kuh.
Cyrenians	Sigh-*ree*-nee-unz.
Dietrich Bonhoffer	*Dee*-trik *Bon*-hoffer.
Gamaliel	Guh-*may*-lih-ul or
	Guh-*may*-lee-al.
Grecians	*Gree*-shunz.
heretic	*hair*-ih-tik.
Libertines	*Lib*-er-teens.
medieval	me-*dee*-vul.
Sanhedrin	*San*-huh-drun or
	San-*heed*-run.
tabernacle	*tah*-burr-*nah*-kul.

and Cyrenians, and Alexandrians, and of them of Cilicia and of Asia, disputing with Stephen.

There is a difference of opinion regarding how many identifiable groups of opponents, in terms of numbers of synagogues, are in view here. The strongest view is that there is only one: it is *the synagogue of the Libertines,* which consists of Jews from the other four places noted. The Libertines are former slaves. These liberated Jews have migrated from various places to Jerusalem, where they have established their own synagogue.

Some of these Jews are from Cyrene, which is the capital of the Roman province of Cyrenaica in North Africa (modern Libya; compare Acts 2:10; 11:20; 13:1). Alexandria is a large city in Egypt and home to a substantial Jewish population; the city is renowned as a center of learning (compare Acts 18:24). Cilicia is a Roman province in what is now southeastern Turkey. The province of Asia is a significant population center in southwestern Turkey. It includes the cities mentioned in Revelation 1 and 2.

As a side note, we recall that Cilicia includes the city of Tarsus (Acts 21:39), which is the hometown of Saul (later renamed Paul). He has come to Jerusalem to study under the great rabbi Gamaliel (22:3). We will see Saul's part in the opposition to Stephen in next week's lesson.

10. And they were not able to resist the wisdom and the spirit by which he spake.

Guided by the Spirit's wisdom and verifying the message with works of power, Stephen cannot be stopped. This is a fulfillment of Jesus' prediction in Luke 21:15.

B. Desperation (vv. 11-14)

11. Then they suborned men, which said, We have heard him speak blasphemous words against Moses, and against God.

Suborned men indicates bribery. Thus false evidence is introduced against Stephen (compare 1 Kings 21:1-14; Matthew 26:59).

There are two charges, but they are closely related. To speak *blasphemous words against Moses* means to advocate that Jews not follow the Law of Moses. To speak *against God* reflects a charge that Stephen is speaking against the temple (see

v. 13, below). Teaching against the law or the temple is tantamount to blasphemy, which calls for the death penalty (Leviticus 24:14, 16, 23).

12. And they stirred up the people, and the elders, and the scribes, and came upon him, and caught him, and brought him to the council.

Unable to defeat Stephen in debate, Stephen's opponents forcibly turn him over to *the council*. This is the Sanhedrin, the Jewish ruling body that had declared Jesus worthy of death. The Romans allow this council to pass judgment on religious and social concerns for Jews. This authority includes the right to inflict certain punishments, which include expulsion from the synagogue (John 9:22) and public beatings. Shortly before the incident we are examining now, the Sanhedrin had ordered some apostles to be flogged (Acts 5:17-40). Stephen must realize that he is in for a similar fate—or worse.

> **What Do You Think?**
> What is it about the gospel that stirs up the most hostility? Why is this? How does this vary from setting to setting?
> *Talking Points for Your Discussion*
> - Claims of exclusivity
> - Claims about the reality of sin
> - Claims about the nature of truth
> - Other

13, 14. And set up false witnesses, which said, This man ceaseth not to speak blasphemous words against this holy place, and the law: for we have heard him say, that this Jesus of Nazareth shall destroy this place, and shall change the customs which Moses delivered us.

These verses repeat the two charges mentioned in verse 11, with more detail. Since blasphemy carries the death sentence (see comments on v. 11, above), the implication is that some want Stephen silenced permanently (compare Jeremiah 26:11).

While it is impossible to know what Stephen actually has said that provides grounds for the accusations, verse 14 echoes themes from Jesus' teaching. Perhaps Stephen has quoted Christ's words in the course of his own preaching. The claim *Jesus of Nazareth shall destroy this place*

echoes the accusation that Jesus had threatened to tear down the temple and replace it with a new one (Mark 14:57, 58; compare John 2:19-21). Many Jews understand any challenge to the temple as blasphemy against God himself.

The charge that *Jesus of Nazareth . . . shall change the customs which Moses delivered us* perhaps means that Stephen has been promoting Jesus' teachings about the Sabbath, contact with unclean people and things, kosher food laws, etc. Jesus had aroused the ire of the Pharisees by violating their understanding of the Sabbath (see Luke 6:1-11). Jesus had no qualms about associating with unclean people (see Luke 5:27-32; 7:36-50; 19:1-10). He even went so far as to declare all foods to be clean (the meaning of "purging all meats" in Mark 7:19).

The Pharisees see all these as violations of the Law of Moses. Stephen's proclamation of Christ easily stirs up memories of Jesus' controversial teachings and actions. These provide ready fuel for the fire of controversy.

C. Defense (6:15–7:2a)

15. And all that sat in the council, looking stedfastly on him, saw his face as it had been the face of an angel.

Commentators often note parallels between the trials of Jesus and Stephen. Both are falsely accused of blasphemy (Luke 22:66-71). Jesus said nothing when false witnesses spoke against Him before the Sanhedrin (Mark 14:55-61; compare Matthew 27:14), and Stephen apparently does not respond as his enemies rehearse their charges. Neither Jesus nor Stephen yield to the arguments of the Jewish authorities. Ironically, Saul, who is on the side of those authorities at this point (Acts 8:1), will later find himself on the receiving end of the same charges that Stephen now faces (21:28; 25:8).

The note that Stephen's face resembles that *of an angel* causes many students to see an allusion to Exodus 34:29-35. That passage describes Moses' face as shining with a bright light as he comes down from Mount Sinai. The author may mean that Stephen's face, like that of Moses, bears the glow of God's presence. In any case, the author wishes to stress that God is with Stephen during his time of trial. The Spirit will empower Stephen

Stephen Defends His Faith

to witness on Christ's behalf (compare Luke 12:11, 12). We recall that *angel* is the normal Greek word for "messenger." Stephen is about to speak as a messenger of God's truth.

> **What Do You Think?**
> How do people know that you belong to Christ? What "marks" you most in that regard?
> *Talking Points for Your Discussion*
> - Speech patterns (James 1:26)
> - Spending priorities (James 4:3)
> - Behavior (Romans 13:13)
> - Business practices (1 Timothy 6:10)
> - Other

7:1, 2a. Then said the high priest, Are these things so? And he said, Men, brethren, and fathers, hearken.

We have reached Stephen's moment of decision. The charges have been presented, and the high priest now asks him to confirm or deny what the witnesses have said. Stephen is faced with a choice: (1) compromise and recant or (2) restate his beliefs boldly in the face of opposition. The speech that follows makes Stephen's decision plain.

> **What Do You Think?**
> What should you do when falsely accused? How does the nature of your response (or lack of response) depend on context?
> *Talking Points for Your Discussion*
> - Situations calling for no response (1 Samuel 10:27; Matthew 26:63; 27:14)
> - Situations calling for denial of the accusation (Nehemiah 6:5-8; Acts 26)
> - Situations calling for push back (Jeremiah 26:11-15; Acts 23:6-10)

II. Truth About Moses
(ACTS 7:22)

In Acts 7:2b–21 (not in today's text), Stephen summarizes the history of the Israelites from the time of Abraham's call (about 2092 BC) to the birth of Moses (about 1525 BC). Stephen knows history! What follows is Stephen's response to the charge that he has spoken against the Law of Moses.

22. And Moses was learned in all the wisdom of the Egyptians, and was mighty in words and in deeds.

This verse summarizes Stephen's knowledge of and respect for Moses. The fact that *Moses was learned in all the wisdom of the Egyptians* is a commentary on Exodus 2:10. The fact that Moses was *mighty in words and in deeds* is Stephen's acknowledgment of God's presence with that great leader. Clearly, the charge that Stephen blasphemes Moses is without foundation.

> **What Do You Think?**
> How important is it to study what the world believes? How can we do this without compromising our identity in Christ?
> *Talking Points for Your Discussion*
> - Jeremiah 10:1-5
> - Daniel 1:3-5
> - Acts 17:18-34
> - 1 Corinthians 10:20
> - Colossians 2:8

❧ IS EDUCATION A BAD THING? ❧

A young preacher announced his plans to go to graduate school (seminary). He wanted to prepare himself better for ministry. An elder in the church where he was preaching warned him, "Don't go getting so much education that they ruin you as a preacher." The young man went anyway and had an exemplary lifetime ministry as a missionary.

Educated people are sometimes called "pointy-headed intellectuals," "eggheads," etc. In the Christian realm, some who hold this bias believe that learning will cause loss of faith. To be sure, some who earn advanced degrees do forsake biblical truth. But less education is no guarantee of a correct understanding of the Bible. Some cults attract followers on the basis of the personal dynamism of an unlearned leader.

Moses' case demonstrates that education is not necessarily a detriment either to a proper understanding of God's message or to serving God faithfully. Moses had "all the wisdom of the Egyptians," but was also "mighty in words and in deeds." It wasn't a case of either/or. —C. R. B.

Visual for Lessons 6 & 10. *Point to this visual as you ask "How do we harmonize this imperative with the statements in Ecclesiastes 3:7b and Amos 5:13?"*

III. Truth About the Temple
(Acts 7:44a, 45b-49)

Acts 7:23-43 (not in today's text) is largely Stephen's summary of the time line from Moses' killing of an Egyptian (Exodus 2:11, 12) to the golden calf incident at Mount Sinai (Exodus 32). Stephen adds a prediction of the Babylonian exile from Amos 5:25-27 for good measure.

A. Made by Humans (vv. 44a, 45b-47)

44a. Our fathers had the tabernacle of witness in the wilderness.

Stephen now addresses the second charge against him, the one involving blasphemy against the temple. The portable tabernacle was the forerunner of the temple. After the Israelites left Egypt, God gave Moses a blueprint for the tabernacle as the place of worship (Exodus 25:9, 40). Levites could transport this with them on their way to the promised land (Numbers 1:50-53).

Again we see Stephen's impressive command of the history of his people. He clearly has no intent to offer an "I acted in ignorance" defense!

45b, 46. Unto the days of David; who found favour before God, and desired to find a tabernacle for the God of Jacob.

While Moses (and God) may have viewed the tabernacle as a temporary measure, it ended up serving as the official focus of Israelite worship for several centuries, *unto the days of David*. That king established Jerusalem as the capital of Israel and moved the ark of the covenant (the central feature of the tabernacle) to that city (see 2 Samuel 5, 6). Even so, David eventually began to feel uneasy that he himself was living in a royal palace while God was worshipped in a tent (2 Samuel 7:1-3). David wanted to change that situation.

47. But Solomon built him an house.

God appreciated the spirit of David's desire to build a temple (1 Kings 8:17, 18). But that task fell to one of David's heirs (2 Samuel 7:12, 13), namely Solomon (1 Kings 6).

B. God's True Home (vv. 48, 49)

48. Howbeit the most High dwelleth not in temples made with hands; as saith the prophet.

The idea that the temple is God's "home" or "residence" on earth in a loose sense may be supported by 1 Chronicles 28:2; 2 Chronicles 6:2; 7:2; and Psalm 132:7. Even so, Stephen punctuates his rehearsal of the temple's history with a bold claim: *the most High dwelleth not in temples made with hands*. Logic dictates that God, who is far above the limitations of the physical universe, cannot be confined to a finite space.

Stephen's observation seems so obvious to us that it may be difficult to imagine how brash it sounds to the Sanhedrin. In the ancient world, religion is largely a geographical affair, with various people groups worshipping their ancestral gods in local holy places and tribal shrines. Similarly, the Jews of Stephen's time limit the worship of God to the temple in Jerusalem. This idea suggests that God "lives" on Mount Zion and that He somehow "belongs" to the Jewish people alone.

> **What Do You Think?**
> In what ways do some people try to "box in" God today? How can we recognize and avoid this danger?
>
> *Talking Points for Your Discussion*
> - Identifying "Christian nations"
> - Practicing "Surely, God would . . ." or "Surely, God would not . . ." thinking
> - Adopting a pick-and-choose system of doctrine
> - Other

Stephen implies that God actually lives everywhere and belongs to no one—He is the God of all people. This premise is foundational to Philip's later ministry in Samaria (Acts 8) and to Paul's missions to the Gentiles: if God is everywhere, then anyone can come to Him through Christ, regardless of ethnicity or nationality (see Acts 17:24). What *the prophet* has to say about all this is the subject of the next verse.

❧ WHERE GOD REALLY WANTS TO LIVE ❧

In 1973, author-illustrator David Macaulay published *Cathedral* for children. But the book also fascinated many adults. Macaulay's pen-and-ink drawings illustrated the manner in which a hypothetical thirteenth-century French cathedral was built.

The book eventually became the basis for a PBS television special. The continuing fascination with cathedrals is seen in the fact that PBS aired a new documentary in October 2010 entitled *Building the Great Cathedrals*. This NOVA program described how millions of pounds of stone and decades of construction resulted in some of the most inspiring architecture ever.

The temple of which Stephen spoke was also a magnificent building, without doubt the most amazing structure in the Jerusalem of his day. Yet a few decades later it would lie in ruins (Mark 13:1, 2). The medieval cathedrals of Europe are "in ruins" in the sense that they stand as decaying museums of the dying faith of post-Christian Europe. God has ways of reminding us that He is not content to live in even the finest buildings made with human hands. He lives in the hearts of those who have accepted His Son.   —C. R. B.

49. Heaven is my throne, and earth is my footstool: what house will ye build me? saith the Lord: or what is the place of my rest?

Realizing that the Sanhedrin may question his claims about the temple, Stephen defends himself by referring to Scripture. "The prophet" of verse 48 above is Isaiah. Stephen now quotes from Isaiah 66:1, 2, where that prophet says that God has rejected the Israelites because they do not submit to Him—their worship is not matched by a life-style of obedience. The simple fact of bringing offerings to the temple does not guarantee that the Israelites are right with God. What difference does it make whether people worship in this or that holy place if they do not honor God's Word?

Conclusion
A. The Death of Cheap Grace

Dietrich Bonhoffer (1906–1945) was a brilliant German theologian and minister, having earned his doctorate at age 21. He found himself deeply opposed to the Nazis, who had come to power in 1933. Within a year he had organized the underground "Confessing Church," which refused to cooperate with the state church of Germany due to its relationship with the Nazi government.

Bonhoffer left Germany in 1939 to take a teaching position in New York City. He soon began to feel ashamed at his unwillingness to stay and fight for truth. So he returned to his homeland on the last ship to sail from the U.S. to Germany before the start of World War II. Bonhoffer eventually was arrested, sent first to prison and then to two concentration camps, and executed just three weeks before allied forces captured Berlin.

Along with his legacy as a martyr, Bonhoffer is famous for his attack on "cheap grace"—the notion that it is possible to be a Christian simply by consent and not by action. Bonhoffer's "costly grace" approach called believers to imitate Christ's willingness to stand for truth. Stephen did not take a "cheap grace" approach. For him, God's truth had to be defended at all cost. Stephen's responses to the charges of blasphemy reveal no sense of backtracking, no sense of "What I really meant when I said _____ was _____." The result of Stephen's strategy is the subject of next week's lesson.

B. Prayer

Father, we know that You have called us to stand up for what is right, but many times it's difficult to do so. Please give us the courage to stand for truth. In Christ's name, amen.

C. Thought to Remember

Take a stand for truth.

INVOLVEMENT LEARNING

Some of the activities below are also found in the helpful student book, Adult Bible Class.
Don't forget to download the free reproducible page from www.standardlesson.com to enhance your lesson!

Into the Lesson

Place in chairs copies of the "Searching for a Testimony of Faith" activity from the reproducible page, which you can download. Learners can begin working on this as they arrive.

Write the word *TESTIMONY* on the board. Ask, "What do you think of when you hear this word?" Jot responses on the board. Expect much of the discussion to revolve around testimony in a religious sense, as in one's personal testimony of Christian faith. If no one mentions the legal sense, ask, "What about *testimony* as in *testify* in a legal context—in other words, testifying in court?"

Make the transition to Bible study by saying, "Regardless of what position we hold on the death penalty, I'm sure each of us would be horrified if that penalty was inflicted because of a witness's lies and false testimony. That's the situation in our study today. Yet in this circumstance we find one of history's great demonstrations of speaking the truth with courage."

Into the Word

Create teams for a modern reenactment of the trial of Stephen before the Jewish Sanhedrin. The preparations and enacting of this activity will potentially take a considerable amount of time. Therefore, tell the teams to prepare quickly. You may wish to recruit teams in advance.

The judicial team will consist of four actors to play the parts of high priest, a prosecutor, a witness to bring false testimony, and an expert witness on Jewish law. Give each a photocopy of today's lesson commentary. Each character will bring out certain elements of what happened in Stephen's trial according to the Scripture. The high priest will read the charges that can be gleaned from Acts 6:11-14, will moderate the trial, and will call Stephen to give his defense (7:1). The prosecutor will call the witness to testify and will cross-examine the defense's witness(es). The prosecution's witness

will be the expert on Jewish law; what this witness says and does will reflect Acts 6:9-14.

The defense team will need at least three actors to play the parts of Stephen, one or more character witnesses for Stephen, and a defense attorney. The character witness(es) will use their "sanctified imagination" to counteract the false testimony of Acts 6:9-14. The defense attorney will call Stephen to testify on his own behalf per Acts 7:2, 22, 44-49. The attorney also will deliver a summary of Stephen's defense.

The trial will still be under way (no verdict yet reached) as attention shifts to *the television reporting team*. This team can consist of two actors who compare Stephen's predicament with those of Martin Luther and Dietrich Bonhoffer per the Introduction and Conclusion, respectively, of the commentary. This team will tell how those two serve as examples of defending God's truth at all cost.

Into Life

Distribute handouts with the following discussion questions to the three teams. *The judicial team:* Identify two modern-day examples of people who use slander or misdirection toward Christian principles in today's culture. Suggest some proper ways for Christians to respond. *The defense team:* Identify people who have exhibited courage by taking a stand for Christian principles. You should have one or two from general world history and one or two from the twenty-first century. Explain the issues and the testimony of these models of faith. *The reporting team:* Identify issues or problems in today's world that need to be confronted by Christians. Write a "statement of faith" about one such issue. You may write a simple sentence or use "bullet points" to identify your position.

To conclude, distribute copies of the "A Faith That Passes Tests" activity from the reproducible page, which you can download. Have learners complete this in study pairs.

STEPHEN IS FAITHFUL TO DEATH

DEVOTIONAL READING: Ephesians 6:13-20
BACKGROUND SCRIPTURE: Acts 7:1–8:1

ACTS 7:51-60

51 Ye stiffnecked and uncircumcised in heart and ears, ye do always resist the Holy Ghost: as your fathers did, so do ye.

52 Which of the prophets have not your fathers persecuted? and they have slain them which shewed before of the coming of the Just One; of whom ye have been now the betrayers and murderers:

53 Who have received the law by the disposition of angels, and have not kept it.

54 When they heard these things, they were cut to the heart, and they gnashed on him with their teeth.

55 But he, being full of the Holy Ghost, looked up stedfastly into heaven, and saw the glory of God, and Jesus standing on the right hand of God,

56 And said, Behold, I see the heavens opened, and the Son of man standing on the right hand of God.

57 Then they cried out with a loud voice, and stopped their ears, and ran upon him with one accord,

58 And cast him out of the city, and stoned him: and the witnesses laid down their clothes at a young man's feet, whose name was Saul.

59 And they stoned Stephen, calling upon God, and saying, Lord Jesus, receive my spirit.

60 And he kneeled down, and cried with a loud voice, Lord, lay not this sin to their charge. And when he had said this, he fell asleep.

ACTS 8:1

1 And Saul was consenting unto his death. And at that time there was a great persecution against the church which was at Jerusalem; and they were all scattered abroad throughout the regions of Judaea and Samaria, except the apostles.

KEY VERSE

They stoned Stephen, calling upon God, and saying, Lord Jesus, receive my spirit. —**Acts 7:59**

A LIVING FAITH

Unit 2: Who Understands Faith?

LESSONS 6–9

LESSON AIMS

After participating in this lesson, each student will be able to:

1. Explain the circumstances of Stephen's death.

2. Compare and contrast the rage that resulted in the murder of Stephen with adverse reactions to the preaching of the gospel today.

3. Write a prayer that asks for courage in the face of opposition.

LESSON OUTLINE

Introduction

A. Modern Martyrs

On September 21, 2009, a group of armed men gathered outside the home of Manuel Camacho in San Jose del Guaviare, Colombia. The gunmen were members of The Revolutionary Armed Forces of Colombia (FARC), a Marxist group that has been waging a guerilla war against the Colombian government since 1964.

Camacho was a minister working with a church in the village of Chopal, an area controlled by the FARC. He had been told that his congregation must dissolve. Defying these threats, Camacho continued to minister. He participated in a public revival meeting at which several FARC members accepted Christ. Camacho apparently believed that FARC had finally accepted his efforts and that the gunmen had come to discuss the terms under which he could continue his work.

When Camacho stepped outside, however, he was shot five times. According to one report, his son and his wife dragged the dead body beneath a tree. The son said, "Don't worry; Dad died for Christ and now he is with Christ."

Martyrdom is more common today than ever. One study claims that some 70 million Christians have died for their faith since the first century AD, and that about two-thirds of these were killed in the twentieth century alone. Christians who live in areas dominated by totalitarian governments and religious extremists face daily the threat of persecution. Such persecution takes the forms of exclusion from social and economic life, violence, and murder. For many believers, confessing Christ comes with serious consequences. This should cause us to ask whether we too would be willing to suffer for our faith.

B. Lesson Background

Last week's lesson introduced us to Stephen. The Lesson Background of that study is therefore the same and need not be repeated here. We can offer the additional note that although Stephen ended up being the first martyr after the establishment of the church, he followed in the footsteps of Old Testament martyrs (see Luke 11:51).

Sadly, martyrdom seems to have been not uncommon between the times of the Old and New Testaments. The collection of books known as *The Apocrypha* records many of these. The account of the torture and murder of seven brothers in 4 Maccabees is particularly gruesome. Thus has the history of God's people unfolded and continues to unfold (Revelation 17:6).

We pick up where last week's lesson left off. Stephen had been brought before the Sanhedrin on charges of speaking against Moses and God. The charges are further defined in Acts 6:13, 14, where *against Moses* means against "the law . . . the customs which Moses delivered" and *against God* means "against this holy place" (the temple). Stephen's defense revealed his thorough familiarity with biblical history. As today's lesson picks up, Stephen has shifted from defense to countercharges.

I. Countercharges
(ACTS 7:51-54)
A. Wrong Attitude (v. 51)

51. Ye stiffnecked and uncircumcised in heart and ears, ye do always resist the Holy Ghost: as your fathers did, so do ye.

Stephen's defense (Acts 7:2-50) has relied on facts from history and doctrine. His countercharges move to application: the Jewish leaders refuse to listen to God's truth. Stephen highlights the seriousness of their sin by using several word pictures that describe their resistant attitude.

HOW TO SAY IT

Apocrypha	Uh-*paw*-krih-fuh.
Cilicia	Sih-*lish*-i-uh.
Judaea or Judea	Joo-*dee*-uh.
Maccabees	*Mack*-uh-bees.
Manuel Camacho	Mahn-*well* Cah-*mahn*-cho.
Pentecost	*Pent*-ih-kost.
Pharisees	*Fair*-ih-seez.
Samaria	Suh-*mare*-ee-uh.
San Jose del Guaviare	Sahn Ho-*say* del Gwah-vee-*ar*-ay (rolling the "r")
Tertullian	Tur-*tull*-yun.

The word *stiffnecked* conveys the image of an animal that refuses to submit to a yoke or bridle. Both God and Moses had used this term to describe the Israelites (see Exodus 32:9; 33:3-5; 34:9). To be *uncircumcised in heart and ears* compares the resistant Jews with pagans (see Romans 2:28, 29). Stephen is referring to an attitude. To be uncircumcised in heart represents having wrong feelings and will (Leviticus 26:41; Jeremiah 9:26), while to be uncircumcised in ears indicates having an unwillingness to listen to truth (Jeremiah 6:10).

Because Jesus, Stephen, and the prophets before them spoke by the Holy Spirit, a refusal to listen amounts to a rejection of God himself (Isaiah 63:10). In saying *as your fathers did, so do ye*, Stephen associates his current audience with the ancient Israelites he has described in Acts 7:23-43. Clearly, Stephen is now speaking as a prosecutor, not as a defendant.

> *What Do You Think?*
> Under what circumstances, if any, should our response to the enemies of Christ include characterizations and labels such as "stiffnecked" and "uncircumcised"? What are the dangers of such an approach?
> *Talking Points for Your Discussion*
> - Proverbs 15:1
> - Matthew 12:34; 15:14
> - 1 Peter 3:15
> - Jude 12, 13
> - Stephen's divine insight

B. Wrong Actions (vv. 52, 53)

52. Which of the prophets have not your fathers persecuted? and they have slain them which shewed before of the coming of the Just One; of whom ye have been now the betrayers and murderers.

Stephen asserts that his opponents follow the footsteps of the ancient Israelites who rejected God's prophets. This echoes Jesus' condemnation of the Pharisees in Luke 11:47-51. Further, the Jews have rejected *the Just One*—Jesus—and had him murdered. Thus, the Jewish leaders are guilty

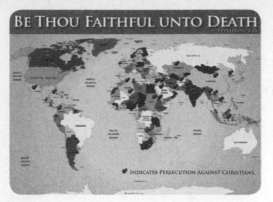

BE THOU FAITHFUL UNTO DEATH
— REVELATION 2:16

● INDICATES PERSECUTION AGAINST CHRISTIANS

Visual for Lesson 7. *Point to this visual to start a discussion on martyrdom today. Have one of your learners be prepared to offer statistics.*

both of rejecting the prophets and of killing the one of whom the prophets spoke—Christ.

53. Who have received the law by the disposition of angels, and have not kept it.

Stephen adds yet another charge to the list: his accusers claim that he has spoken against the Law of Moses, but in fact it is they who do not keep that law. The reference to angels reflects the fact that God spoke to Moses through an angel when giving the law (see Acts 7:38; compare Exodus 3:2; Galatians 3:19); this ties in with the Jewish belief that God uses angels in this manner because God cannot be seen by humans (Exodus 33:20).

In what sense, though, have the members of the Sanhedrin not kept the law? Stephen is not referring to sins of the flesh, but rather to the more basic fact that the Jewish leaders refuse to submit to God's truth. The Law of Moses points to the coming of Christ, whom the Jewish leaders willfully rejected. Their faithlessness, in turn, has led them to break two of the Ten Commandments: bearing false witness against Jesus and securing His murder at the hands of the Romans. Such crimes surely represent the highest form of sin imaginable.

C. Angry Reaction (v. 54)

54. When they heard these things, they were cut to the heart, and they gnashed on him with their teeth.

Stephen's sharp accusations provoke a sharp response. Language similar to *cut to the heart* appears at Acts 2:37. There the Pentecost crowds, convicted by Peter's explanation of their responsibility for Christ's death, ask, "What shall we do?" That response was driven by a sense of shame and guilt. But that is not the nature of the response here! The members of the Sanhedrin are not convicted, but infuriated (compare John 9:34).

Notably, Luke (the author of Acts) has not recorded any response by Stephen's audience before this moment. Some commentators conclude from this that the Sanhedrin is initially impressed by Stephen's discussion of Jewish history and perhaps are favorably inclined by his remarks on Moses and the temple. They become angry only when he accuses them personally of hard-heartedness.

It seems more likely, however, that Luke simply wishes to indicate that Stephen has reached the point of no return. Realizing that speaking the truth will likely cost him his life, Stephen continues to press his point as he sees that the members of the Sanhedrin are not responding positively. We see increasing hostility on their part as we trace their reactions from Acts 4:1-22 to 5:27-42 to 7:54-58.

❧ DEALING WITH HISTORY ❧

"History is more or less bunk. It's tradition. We don't want tradition. We want to live in the present, and the only history that is worth [anything] is the history we made today." So said Henry Ford in an interview printed in the *Chicago Tribune* on May 25, 1916. Ford's opinion sounds a lot like the complaint of many students who are required to study history. It also seems to be the attitude of culture in general. The sad result of such an attitude is that "Those who cannot remember the past are condemned to repeat it" (George Santayana).

But those who study history intently have problems of their own. One problem is to be guilty of a selective use of historical evidence to see things in a biased way. This seems to be the point behind Jesus' criticism in Matthew 23:30. It also seems to be the point of Stephen's criticism of the Sanhedrin.

As Stephen's criticism unfolded, the members of the Sanhedrin had a choice to make. They could either (1) admit that their understanding of the historical predictions of Christ was flawed and that it had been a mistake to reject Jesus, or (2) they could condemn Stephen for his own reading of history and Scripture. The choice they made is a matter of, well, history. —C. R. B.

II. Vision
(ACTS 7:55, 56)
A. What Stephen Sees (v. 55)
55. But he, being full of the Holy Ghost, looked up stedfastly into Heaven, and saw the glory of God, and Jesus standing on the right hand of God.

Accused of violating the customs of Moses, Stephen, like Moses, is privileged to see God's glory (Exodus 33:18-23). In the ancient world as today, *the right hand* is a place of special honor (see Matthew 26:64; Ephesians 1:20; Colossians 3:1; Hebrews 1:3). This imagery is drawn from Psalm 110, which the New Testament cites often as a messianic prophecy.

Psalm 110:1 envisions the newly crowned king sitting at the right hand of God while the Lord places Israel's enemies under His feet. The verse before us varies from that by depicting Jesus *standing* at God's right hand. Two major theories, neither exclusive of the other, have been advanced to explain the wording. One idea proposes that Jesus is rising from His throne to welcome Stephen into Heaven. Another idea is that the description of Jesus standing follows the theme of Luke 12:8: Jesus is rising to testify before God on Stephen's behalf, just as Stephen has testified of Christ before opponents. Either way, Jesus' standing serves to encourage and affirm Stephen in his boldness.

What Do You Think?
Though we may not see Christ as Stephen did, how can we know He hears us and is with us as we boldly stand up for Him?
Talking Points for Your Discussion
- In light of past experiences
- In light of encouragement of fellow Christians
- In terms of inner peace
- In terms of biblical promises

B. What Stephen Says (v. 56)
56. And said, Behold, I see the heavens opened, and the Son of man standing on the right hand of God.

Stephen now verbalizes what he sees in verse 55. Even if Stephen somehow believes that his speech can clear him of the charges of attacking the law and the temple, he can scarcely think that this statement about Christ will secure his release. Notably, Stephen has largely avoided direct statements about Christ to this point. Now Stephen associates Christ with God himself, a confession that he must know will not help his case before the Sanhedrin. Jesus himself had been convicted of blasphemy before this group for associating himself with God (Matthew 26:64, 65; Luke 22:69-71). One can only be impressed with Stephen's courage in the face of deadly opposition.

❧ NEAR-DEATH EXPERIENCES ❧

We've all heard of *near-death experiences* (NDEs). We're not talking about the last-second avoidance of an accident that might have taken one's life. Rather, the phrase refers to a person who may have been clinically dead—as in cardiac arrest, for example—but who has been resuscitated. NDE is what a person remembers happening while being in the state of near or clinical death.

Those who relate their NDEs may speak of being in a state of bliss, being in a brilliantly white room, hearing beautiful music, and/or seeing a loved one beckoning him or her to come on over to "the other side." Some think these experiences are hallucinations; others accept them as evidence of life after death. Millions of people claim to have had NDEs.

Stephen was "near death," but not in the sense we are talking about since the stones were yet to be cast at him. Nevertheless, he was able to fix his gaze on the risen Jesus as death approached. The sense of blessedness that he experienced prepared him for the ordeal that was to take his life. We should not expect to experience a vision as Stephen did as our own deaths approach. But our last thought while on planet Earth should be about Jesus. After all, He is the first one we'll be thinking about as we cross over into His presence! —C. R. B.

III. Death
(ACTS 7:57-60)
A. Mob's Action (vv. 57, 58)

57, 58. Then they cried out with a loud voice, and stopped their ears, and ran upon him with one accord, and cast him out of the city, and stoned him: and the witnesses laid down their clothes at a young man's feet, whose name was Saul.

Covering the ears symbolizes the Sanhedrin's belief that Stephen has just spoken blasphemy. The Jews do not have legal authority to impose capital punishment—the Romans reserve this right for themselves (John 18:31). Yet Stephen's death is more the result of an impulsive mob action than that of an official proceeding. In their rage, the Jewish authorities believe that Stephen's blasphemy deserves immediate and deadly consequences.

What Do You Think?
What are some ways that Christians may think they are doing God's will when in fact they could be fighting against Him?
Talking Points for Your Discussion
- With regard to politics
- With regard to product boycotts
- With regard to certain kinds of church outreach activities

Obviously, this is a low point in the storyline. But at this low point the author (Luke) suddenly introduces a new character: Saul. The note that Stephen's executioners lay their clothes at Saul's feet may imply that Saul has an official role in the proceedings. Saul is in Jerusalem to study under the great rabbi Gamaliel (Acts 5:34; 22:3), although Saul is originally from the city of Tarsus in Cilicia (21:39). The location of his hometown suggests the possibility that Saul associates with "the Libertines" (freed slaves) of last week's lesson since they too are "of Cilicia" (6:9). But the fact that Saul was "free born" (22:28) casts doubt on this idea.

While Stephen's speech obviously does not have much if any immediate impact on Saul, the arguments about the law and the temple will become foundational to Saul's (Paul's) own ministry. He also will have a vision of the risen Christ (Acts 9:1-8). Like Stephen, Saul (as Paul) also will defend himself against charges involving the law and the temple (25:8). Also like Stephen, he will affirm that God "dwelleth not in temples made with hands" (17:24). Stephen's speech thus will be echoed in ways that he does not live to see. Saul's memory of this day will not fade (22:20).

We can note in passing that there are two references to Saul's age in the New Testament. Here he is *young,* while in Philemon 9 he (as Paul) is *aged.* The designation *young* can indicate an age between 24 and 40, according to the use of that word at the time.

B. Stephen's Reaction (vv. 59, 60)

59, 60. And they stoned Stephen, calling upon God, and saying, Lord Jesus, receive my spirit. And he kneeled down, and cried with a loud voice, Lord, lay not this sin to their charge. And when he had said this, he fell asleep.

Last week's lesson noted that Stephen's trial before the Sanhedrin resembles Jesus' trial before the same group at key points. Similarly here, two parallels between Stephen's death and Jesus' death are seen. First, both pray on behalf of those who are killing them (compare Luke 23:34). Stephen wants the mob to know that they are doing something wrong. But he also wants them to know that God can forgive them if they accept the truth.

Second, both Stephen and Jesus commit their spirits to God as they die (compare Luke 23:46). Stephen's final words express confidence that he has done nothing wrong. He believes that God will vindicate and reward his suffering.

What Do You Think?
How can Christians be more effective in praying for and interacting with enemies of the gospel?
Talking Points for Your Discussion
- Exodus 8:9, 28
- Proverbs 24:17
- Jeremiah 7:16; 11:14; 14:11
- Matthew 5:43-48
- Romans 12:20, 21
- 1 Thessalonians 5:15

IV. Legacy

(ACTS 8:1)

8:1. And Saul was consenting unto his death. And at that time there was a great persecution against the church which was at Jerusalem; and they were all scattered abroad throughout the regions of Judaea and Samaria, except the apostles.

Stephen's trial sparks a period of persecution. This persecution forces many Christians to leave Jerusalem; they preach the gospel as they go. The preaching eventually reaches Jews (Acts 11:19), Samaritans (8:4, 5), and Gentiles/Greeks (11:20) *throughout the regions of Judaea and Samaria*. At this point, the persecution seems to be localized *against the church which was at Jerusalem*. Thus by remaining in the city the apostles are choosing to stay where the situation is most dangerous.

Stephen's willingness to die for his faith ends up affecting the world in ways he could not have imagined. About AD 197, some 165 years after Stephen's death, the Christian writer Tertullian will observe that "the blood of the martyrs is the seed of the church." Indeed.

> **What Do You Think?**
> Do Christians cheapen the word *persecution* by the ways they speak of "being persecuted" today? Why, or why not?
> *Talking Points for Your Discussion*
> - "Blame shifting" as a result of self-inflicted distress
> - "Victim mentality"
> - "Chip on the shoulder" attitude
> - General pressures of a secular culture to marginalize the church

Conclusion

A. Higher Cause

In 1943, John Basilone was one of the most well-known and highly respected men in America. Basilone had dropped out of high school to join the U.S. Army before the outbreak of World War II in Europe. He reenlisted with the Marines in 1940. In October of 1942, he was sent to Guadalcanal with the First Marine Division, which was charged with capturing the island from the Japanese. Basilone became famous for an incident in which his small unit held off an enemy regiment of 3,000; his display of courage earned him the Congressional Medal of Honor, the U.S. military's highest award for bravery.

Following this victory, the military decided to use Basilone's heroic reputation on the home front. So he returned to begin a whirlwind national tour as a "poster child" for the sale of war bonds. Over time, however, Basilone became uneasy with his privileged life. He felt convicted that he should return to combat. The Marine Corps eventually granted his request. Basilone ended up at the Battle of Iwo Jima. Exhibiting great courage under fire, he was killed in action on February 19, 1945.

Reflecting on John Basilone's story, we may wonder if he felt regret as he lay dying, wishing that he had remained in the U.S. to live the life of a cherished war hero. We may have a similar question about Stephen. As the stones began to strike him, did he wish that he had continued to "serve tables" (Acts 6:2), leaving the preaching to others? It is difficult to imagine that he did. Just as John Basilone was driven by a sense of a higher cause that led him to reject the easy way, Stephen doubtless realized the dangers inherent in preaching Christ, knowing that he was choosing a path of suffering.

Stephen's suffering was not in vain. His death resulted in the spread of the gospel. Stephen's sense of a higher cause empowered him to act against self-interest. As a result, he is a model of courage in the face of opposition.

B. Prayer

Father, we are thankful for the example of Stephen, who was willing to risk everything to serve You. Grant us the strength to follow his example, even when the outcome seems dangerous or uncertain. Help us to be faithful always to our Lord and Savior, in whose name we pray; amen.

C. Thought to Remember

"The opposite of courage . . . is not cowardice, it is conformity." —Rollo May (1909–1994)

INVOLVEMENT LEARNING

Some of the activities below are also found in the helpful student book, Adult Bible Class.
Don't forget to download the free reproducible page from www.standardlesson.com to enhance your lesson!

Into the Lesson

Read or summarize for the class the story of Manuel Camacho from the Introduction. Follow by noting the statistics and overview of martyrdom that follow that story. *Option:* expand this segment by giving further examples and trends of martyrdom from *The Voice of the Martyrs* Web site (www.persecution.com).

Make a transition to Bible study by saying, "Sadly, martyrdom is nothing new. It happened in both Old and New Testament times. Today's study is about the first martyrdom after the founding of the church."

Into the Word

Early in the week, select a person to be interviewed as "Stephen." For advance preparation, give him a copy of today's lesson commentary and the questions below. Begin the interview by announcing this to your class: "As you all know, this is now the year AD 3012, according to the way we used to calculate years when we were back on planet Earth. Since we have been in Heaven now for so many centuries, I thought we could have this class reunion and invite a special guest. Here he is—Stephen, the church's first martyr!" (Lead the class in applause as "Stephen" enters.)

1. "Stephen, thank you for coming to our class reunion. We'd like to hear your perspective on your martyrdom. First of all, why did you pray for your attackers as the stones were falling on you?"

2. "Let's go back to your sermon. It was a long one, the longest recorded in the book of Acts. One of the things that got you in trouble was when you accused your listeners of being 'uncircumcised in heart and ears.' Would you please explain that?"

3. "Stephen, you also accused the Jews of resisting the Holy Spirit as their forefathers had done. In what ways was this true?"

4. "Just before the stoning you had a vision. Tell us about it. Why was it important?"

5. "When you were dying, a young man named Saul witnessed and supported this event. Did you have any clue at that time about how he would change his position and become a missionary for Jesus?" (A brief answer is fine for this question.)

6. "One last question, Stephen. Your trial sparked a period of persecution for the church. But there were blessings mixed in with that persecution. What were some of the blessings that might not have come about had there not been persecution?"

Thank "Stephen" for agreeing to come as he departs.

Into Life

Ask a "scribe" to be ready to write on the board responses to the following brainstorming activity. Say, "Persecution comes to Christians in many forms. Let's list a few of the ways we may see or feel persecution because of our beliefs." *Option:* Ask a "prosecutor" to stand up front to contradict the ideas that are presented. He or she can begin each disagreement by saying, "That's not really persecution. You just think it is because . . ."

Alternative: Distribute copies of the "Identifying Persecution and Opposition" from the reproducible page, which you can download. Have learners use this to complete their brainstorming in small groups.

After the discussion has run its course, ask, "Can you cite specific instances of martyrdom for Christ's sake in today's world or in recent years? You may have read of circumstances in missionary letters, or you may have seen martyrs portrayed in documentary films." *Option:* If Internet access and video projection are available in your learning space, show your learners some stories and pictures on the *The Voice of the Martyrs* Web site.

Wrap up by having learners complete the acrostic activity "My Prayer for Courage and Faithfulness" from the reproducible page.

Stephen Is Faithful to Death

SIMON WANTS TO BUY POWER

DEVOTIONAL READING: 1 Corinthians 1:18-25
BACKGROUND SCRIPTURE: Acts 8:2-25

ACTS 8:9-25

9 But there was a certain man, called Simon, which beforetime in the same city used sorcery, and bewitched the people of Samaria, giving out that himself was some great one:

10 To whom they all gave heed, from the least to the greatest, saying, This man is the great power of God.

11 And to him they had regard, because that of long time he had bewitched them with sorceries.

12 But when they believed Philip preaching the things concerning the kingdom of God, and the name of Jesus Christ, they were baptized, both men and women.

13 Then Simon himself believed also: and when he was baptized, he continued with Philip, and wondered, beholding the miracles and signs which were done.

14 Now when the apostles which were at Jerusalem heard that Samaria had received the word of God, they sent unto them Peter and John:

15 Who, when they were come down, prayed for them, that they might receive the Holy Ghost:

16 (For as yet he was fallen upon none of them: only they were baptized in the name of the Lord Jesus.)

17 Then laid they their hands on them, and they received the Holy Ghost.

18 And when Simon saw that through laying on of the apostles' hands the Holy Ghost was given, he offered them money,

19 Saying, Give me also this power, that on whomsoever I lay hands, he may receive the Holy Ghost.

20 But Peter said unto him, Thy money perish with thee, because thou hast thought that the gift of God may be purchased with money.

21 Thou hast neither part nor lot in this matter: for thy heart is not right in the sight of God.

22 Repent therefore of this thy wickedness, and pray God, if perhaps the thought of thine heart may be forgiven thee.

23 For I perceive that thou art in the gall of bitterness, and in the bond of iniquity.

24 Then answered Simon, and said, Pray ye to the Lord for me, that none of these things which ye have spoken come upon me.

25 And they, when they had testified and preached the word of the Lord, returned to Jerusalem, and preached the gospel in many villages of the Samaritans.

KEY VERSE

When Simon saw that through laying on of the apostles' hands the Holy Ghost was given, he offered them money. —Acts 8:18

A Living Faith

LESSON AIMS

After participating in this lesson, each student will be able to:

1. List key points of the interactions of Simon with Philip, Peter, and John.

2. Brainstorm ways to prevent old ways, habits, and temptations from causing new believers to stumble.

3. Form support teams for group members to help one another resist temptation.

LESSON OUTLINE

Introduction

A. People Who Would Be God

Caligula was the Roman emperor who ruled from AD 37 to 41. Beginning in AD 40, he often presented himself in public dressed as a god, demanding that people worship him. In several temples he had the head of the god-statue broken off and replaced with a likeness of his own head. Caligula was a man who wanted to be God.

Caligula was not alone. King Darius decreed that he alone was to be prayed to for 30 days (Daniel 6:6-9). Alexander the Great (356–323 BC) demanded that conquered nations venerate him as a god. The fall of the human race was precipitated when Adam and Eve fell for the temptation to "be as gods, knowing good and evil" (Genesis 3:5).

In this lesson we will meet one more person in this less-than-illustrious line who would be god-like. His name was Simon.

B. Lesson Background

Following the death of Stephen, the first Christian martyr, a fierce persecution arose against the church in Jerusalem (last week's lesson). While the apostles stayed in the Holy City, other believers scattered to cities throughout Judea and Samaria. They preached the good news of Jesus everywhere they went (see Acts 8:1-4).

Philip, one of Stephen's original coworkers in the work of feeding needy widows (Acts 6:1-5), went to "the city of Samaria" (8:5) and began proclaiming Jesus. Some students think this city was Sychar, per John 4:5; others think it was Sebaste. We do not know for sure.

Philip found surprising acceptance with the Samaritans. It was surprising because the history of bad blood between Samaritans and Jews was well known. The two peoples refused to have anything to do with each other (John 4:9). Even so, Samaritans are usually seen in a good light in the New Testament. A Samaritan woman and her townspeople accepted Jesus as "the Saviour of the world" (John 4:42). The stories of the good Samaritan and the grateful leper (Luke 10:30-37; 17:11-16) also cast Samaritans in a positive light. Only the Samaritans' inhospitality in Luke 9:51-56 is

Simon Wants to Buy Power

less than admirable. As our lesson opens, crowds of people in Samaria have listened to Philip's preaching and have rejoiced at his miracles (Acts 8:5-8).

I. Wrong Faith
(ACTS 8:9-11)
A. Leader (v. 9)

9. But there was a certain man, called Simon, which beforetime in the same city used sorcery, and bewitched the people of Samaria, giving out that himself was some great one.

John 4:20-25 indicates that the Samaritans worship the God of Israel in their own way, and they expect the Messiah. But here we see that sorcery and superstition are also present. When people embrace such folly, they naturally leave themselves open to be exploited by charlatans. One such imposter is *a certain man, called Simon.*

The kind of sorcery or magic that Simon practices may involve the use of incantations, potions, and good-luck amulets. Superstitious people believe that such things will bring good fortune and can also be used to make bad things happen to enemies. Simon somehow tricks people into thinking he has access to supernatural power. In their eyes, this makes him *some great one.*

When the people believe Simon, they are choosing the wrong object for their faith. The Old Testament forbids the practice of sorcery (Leviticus 19:26; Deuteronomy 18:9-14; Jeremiah 27:9). Indeed, those who practice sorcery or witchcraft are to be executed (Exodus 22:18).

HOW TO SAY IT

Ananias	An-uh-*nye*-us.
Caligula	Kuh-*lig*-you-luh.
Darius	Duh-*rye*-us.
Grecians	*Gree*-shunz.
Pentecost	*Pent*-ih-kost.
Samaria	Suh-*mare*-ee-uh.
Samaritans	Suh-*mare*-uh-tunz.
Sapphira	Suh-*fye*-ruh.
Sebaste	Seh-*bas*-tee.
Sychar	*Sigh*-kar.
syncretism	*sin*-krih-*tih*-zem.

What Do You Think?
How can we be on the alert to the danger of being "bewitched" by an ungodly person or unholy idea today?
Talking Points for Your Discussion
- Genesis 3:1-5
- Proverbs 14:12; 16:25
- Romans 16:18
- 2 Corinthians 11:14
- Colossians 2:8
- 2 Timothy 3:6

❦ SUPERSTITION ❦

Athletes are notorious for their superstitious practices. Baseball players think spitting in their hands before picking up the bat brings good luck. Basketball players wipe the soles of their shoes. Hockey players avoid leaving their hockey sticks lying crossed.

Superstition is part of every culture, even societies considered modern and rational. It's not hard to see how it develops. Things go our way, and we try to remember exactly what we did so we can do it again the same way, hoping for repeated good results. Over time we develop a set of rituals that becomes so ingrained that we continue them regardless of the result. Sometimes a person like Simon takes advantage of people's superstitious nature.

Traditional ways of doing things can become, in effect, superstitions. "We've always done it this way" is a refrain that can kill the spiritual life of a church. We tend to hold on to our familiar and comfortable rituals. On the other hand, a knee-jerk aversion to all things traditional can represent an irrational belief that "newer" always means "better." Are there any such superstitions that need to be set aside in your church?   —A. W.

B. Followers (vv. 10, 11)

10. To whom they all gave heed, from the least to the greatest, saying, This man is the great power of God.

Simon has been making a tremendous impact on the people of Samaria. *From the least to the greatest,* they all listen eagerly to whatever he says. In so doing, they reach the wrong conclusion: that he *is the great power of God.*

We should note that the Samaritans do not credit Simon's apparent power to a pagan god. Rather, it seems that the people of Samaria are ready to combine Simon's sorcery with what they know about the true God. The result is a jumble of truth and error, which we call *syncretism.* We can also note that Barnabas and Paul are celebrated as gods in Acts 14:11-13, but they immediately reject that acclamation (14:14-18). There is no indication here, however, that Simon rejects the conclusion that he *is the great power of God.*

11. And to him they had regard, because that of long time he had bewitched them with sorceries.

Scripture does not indicate whether Simon actually has access to some kind of supernatural demonic power (compare Exodus 8:16-19; Acts 16:16-18), or if he merely deceives people by sleight of hand. Either way, it is dangerous, foolish, and sinful for the people to listen to him as a spokesman for God. But they have been doing so for a long time.

II. Right Faith

(ACTS 8:12-17)

A. Samaritans' Response (v. 12)

12. But when they believed Philip preaching the things concerning the kingdom of God, and the name of Jesus Christ, they were baptized, both men and women.

At Philip's command, demons are cast out and the sick people are healed (Acts 8:6, 7). The fact that the people now listen eagerly to what Philip is *preaching . . . concerning the kingdom of God, and the name of Jesus Christ* likely results from the fact that the miraculous signs they now see are superior to anything they have seen from Simon.

Some Samaritans had met Jesus personally before His crucifixion (John 4). Now the Samaritans hear the entirety of the gospel message. Philip's appeal is apparently the same as that of Peter on the Day of Pentecost, for when the people believe they are baptized (see Acts 2:38).

B. Simon's Response (v. 13)

13. Then Simon himself believed also: and when he was baptized, he continued with Philip, and wondered, beholding the miracles and signs which were done.

Simon is also impressed with the *miracles and signs* that Philip performs. Even Simon can see that the miracles and signs done through Philip are genuine. Simon's belief indicates that he knows his own miracles to be either fake or inferior. Joining many others, Simon therefore believes the gospel message and is baptized. Miracles and signs are important in confirming the truth of the gospel as it spreads in the first century (John 10:25, 38; 14:11; 20:30, 31).

What Do You Think?

How have you seen God work in ways that either created or strengthened someone's faith?

Talking Points for Your Discussion

- Through God's Word
- In observing creation
- In healing
- In timely provision of needs
- In comfort during a time of stress

C. Apostles' Reaction (vv. 14-17)

14. Now when the apostles which were at Jerusalem heard that Samaria had received the word of God, they sent unto them Peter and John.

Soon enough, the apostles back in Jerusalem (Acts 8:1) hear about the evangelistic success in Samaria. The gospel is now spreading from Jerusalem into "all Judaea, and in Samaria" as Jesus commanded (1:8).

At the same time, a problem also presents itself. The Samaritans are known for practicing their own, corrupted form of Judaism (John 4:22). Will they now begin to practice a corrupted form of Christianity? Perhaps it is this question that motivates the apostles to send two of their number, Peter and John, from Jerusalem to Samaria to see what is happening. The apostles have the responsibility to see that the first-century church adheres to the truth (Acts 2:42).

Simon Wants to Buy Power

15. Who, when they were come down, prayed for them, that they might receive the Holy Ghost.

When Peter and John arrive in Samaria, they undoubtedly rejoice to see the new faith of the believers there. But they apparently also realize that something is missing. Therefore, the two apostles pray so that the people will *receive the Holy Ghost.*

This language about receiving the Holy Spirit is surprising because earlier in Acts the preaching of Peter connects the receiving of the Holy Spirit with baptism (Acts 2:38). At this point, the Samaritans have both believed and have been baptized. Their conversion looks authentic. So why have they not yet received the Holy Spirit?

The next verse begins an explanation. Before we move on, however, we should notice that receiving the Spirit is connected here with prayer. Prayer is linked elsewhere with the authentic conversion of a person to Christ (see Acts 9:11; 10:2).

16. (For as yet he was fallen upon none of them: only they were baptized in the name of the Lord Jesus.)

To take the word *only* to mean that the Samaritans have not received the Holy Spirit because they have been baptized improperly creates a problem since their baptism *in the name of the Lord Jesus* matches the plea "be baptized . . . in the name of Jesus Christ" in Acts 2:38. We must read the next verse to discover the reason for the absence of the Holy Spirit to this point.

17. Then laid they their hands on them, and they received the Holy Ghost.

Apparently, the Samaritans have not *received the Holy Ghost* because their baptisms have not been accompanied by a laying on of hands by the apostles. When that is accomplished, the Samaritans do indeed receive the Holy Spirit.

But why is the laying on of the apostles' hands required for receiving the Holy Spirit in this case while there is no mention of the same thing on the Day of Pentecost? One theory is that the Holy Spirit's coming is unpredictable; thus in the case of the Samaritans (and the Ephesians in Acts 19:1-6), the laying on of an apostle's hands is necessary for unknown reasons.

Another idea says that the key lies in the religious and cultural differences between Samaritans and Jews. Perhaps the Samaritans are willing to give Philip a fair hearing if he is a Hellenistic Jew (one of "the Grecians" in Acts 6:1, 5) rather than one of the Palestinian Jews ("the Hebrews" in 6:1) that the Samaritans despise. Under this theory, the Samaritans accept Philip's message, but they also need to see that "salvation is of the Jews" (John 4:22). This requires Peter and John—two "pure blood" Palestinian Jews—to come and lay hands for receiving the Spirit. Thus God in His wisdom provides both (1) a messenger whom the Samaritans will heed (namely, Philip) and (2) a way for the Samaritans to see where salvation truly lies.

Another theory proposes that the laying on of the apostles' hands isn't for the indwelling of the Holy Spirit that all Christians receive, but is for bestowal of certain spiritual gifts (Romans 1:11). This theory is tied to what Simon sees and how he reacts in Acts 8:18-24 (below). When he sees the result of the laying on of the apostles' hands, he wants to purchase the same power. It's not that he wants the Holy Spirit to dwell within him (so the theory goes), but rather he wants the ability to lay hands on people and have them receive the visible signs of the Spirit's presence in terms of miraculous spiritual gifts. Thus when the text says that the Samaritans "only" have been baptized (v. 16), the meaning under this theory is that they cannot receive the miraculous gifts from the Spirit without the laying on of the apostles' hands.

The latter theory has a lot going for it. But whichever theory is best, our text highlights the unique role of the apostles. Their function as representatives of Christ is crucial in many settings.

III. Misguided Faith

(ACTS 8:18-25)

A. Simon's Request (vv. 18, 19)

18. And when Simon saw that through laying on of the apostles' hands the Holy Ghost was given, he offered them money.

Now the beautiful scene is spoiled. Simon the sorcerer has not given up his love for power. He wants in on the action. He apparently thinks that the apostles will respond to a bribe as others do.

19. Saying, Give me also this power, that on whomsoever I lay hands, he may receive the Holy Ghost.

Simon sees great possibilities in being able to confer the power of the Holy Spirit on others. His importance in Samaria will be greater than ever if he can just have the same ability as the apostles. Sadly, Simon does not understand the real significance of God's Spirit in a person's life. All that catches his eye is the spectacle: the miracles and signs that the Holy Spirit produces.

> *What Do You Think?*
> What are some ways that people seek to misuse the power of God today? How do we help them overcome this tendency?
> *Talking Points for Your Discussion*
> ▪ For financial gain (1 Timothy 6:5)
> ▪ To dominate others (Luke 22:24-26)
> ▪ To call attention to themselves (Matthew 6:5)
> ▪ Other

❧ PLAYING WITH A BASKETBALL ❧

I broke my ankle in junior high. I like to say I broke it playing basketball. It sounds better that way—people imagine me slam-dunking or dribbling or . . . well . . . that's all the basketball words I know. Truth is, I've never been much of an athlete. Actually, I broke my leg playing *with* a basketball. My geeky friends and I were taking turns holding the ball between our feet trying to toss it into the air with no hands. I tripped over the ball, landed sideways on my leg, and heard a sickening "pop."

Using athletic equipment the wrong way is ineffective at best, life-threatening at worst. To an infinitely greater degree, the same is true of spiritual power. Some people dabble in the occult, not understanding the reality and malevolence of demons. Others borrow ideas from a variety of faiths to create a spiritual stew that gives them a false sense of security. As the story of Simon illustrates, some even imagine they can manipulate the genuine spiritual power of God.

Do we ever try to manipulate God by "making bargains" with Him in a crisis? Do we secretly feel that God should reward us for the good we do? In the end, are we playing by God's rules or just playing with God?   —A. W.

B. Peter's Rebuke (vv. 20-23)

20. But Peter said unto him, Thy money perish with thee, because thou hast thought that the gift of God may be purchased with money.

Peter rejects Simon's offer harshly. There have always been people who think that religion can be a means of personal gain (see Acts 19:23-27; 1 Timothy 6:5), and Simon seems to be that sort of person. His very name eventually becomes the word for the buying and selling of church offices: *simony*.

21. Thou hast neither part nor lot in this matter: for thy heart is not right in the sight of God.

The fact that Simon has *neither part nor lot in this matter* offers a couple of possible interpretations. First, it can mean that Simon has no part in the Christian faith whatsoever; thus he is a total outsider, with no hope of salvation. This interpretation is unlikely in light of what verse 22 says. Second, and more likely, Peter means that Simon has no share in conferring the Holy Spirit to others. Christianity involves having a new heart, something Simon yet lacks (compare Ezekiel 18:31; 36:26).

22. Repent therefore of this thy wickedness, and pray God, if perhaps the thought of thine heart may be forgiven thee.

There is only one solution for Simon: he must repent. A total change of attitude is necessary. As an indication of genuine repentance, he should pray to God for forgiveness. Sin begins in the heart (see Luke 6:45). Perhaps Simon's sin will be forgiven because God is gracious (see 1 John 1:9).

What Do You Think?
How can we help new Christians keep from falling back into former patterns of life? What should we do if it happens anyway?

Talking Points for Your Discussion
- 1 Corinthians 8
- 2 Corinthians 2:5-11
- Galatians 6:1
- 1 Thessalonians 5:14

23. For I perceive that thou art in the gall of bitterness, and in the bond of iniquity.

Bitterness has no place in the Christian life (Ephesians 4:31; Hebrews 12:15). Christ died to set us free from iniquity (Hebrews 8:12; 2 Timothy 2:19). To remain in iniquity is to reject truth (1 Corinthians 13:6; 2 Thessalonians 2:12). Even so, Simon does not receive the harsh penalty of Ananias and Sapphira (Acts 5:1-10) or of the sorcerer Bar-jesus (Acts 13:6-11).

C. Final Result (vv. 24, 25)

24. Then answered Simon, and said, Pray ye to the Lord for me, that none of these things which ye have spoken come upon me.

The text doesn't tell us if Simon does indeed pray for himself. But he definitely asks Peter to pray on his behalf. Does Simon fear that his own prayer might not be sufficient? Is he truly repentant, or is he merely afraid he will perish as Peter warns? In the end, it is God, who knows the heart, who will be the judge of Simon's fate.

25. And they, when they had testified and preached the word of the Lord, returned to Jerusalem, and preached the gospel in many villages of the Samaritans.

With the unpleasant episode involving Simon finished, Peter and John continue their evangelistic work. If "the city of Samaria" in Acts 8:5 is Sychar, then the trip from Jerusalem and back is at least 50 miles. A walking pace therefore means a trip of four days' duration minimum. The trip is undoubtedly longer given the fact that the apostles preach *the gospel in many villages of the Samaritans.* God has opened the door of faith to the Samaritans, and there is a great harvest of souls.

Conclusion
A. Using God or Being Used by God?

The research paper "Preachers Who Are Not Believers" by Daniel C. Dennett and Linda LaScola (March 15, 2010) tells of ministers who are secret atheists. They once believed in God, perhaps, but now continue in their positions only as a means to make a living. There is some degree of this attitude in many others. What of the politician who mainly attends church for public approval? What of those who believe in God only if He acts as they think He "should"? There are many who would try to use God.

And then there are people whom God would use. They are the ones who believe in Jesus with all their hearts and put His kingdom first. They respond eagerly to God's direction. They may not be the smartest, the most attractive, or the most successful in a worldly sense. But they are the most sincere and the most available. They do not seek God's power for their own advancement; they seek to let God's power enable them to serve.

B. Prayer

Father, forgive us if we have sought to exploit Your kingdom selfishly. Help us to cherish the presence of Your Spirit. In Jesus' name; amen.

C. Thought to Remember
Examine your heart for wrong motives.

Visual for Lesson 8. *Point to this visual as you ask "What is your reaction to the statement 'the best things in life are free'?" Jot answers on the board.*

INVOLVEMENT LEARNING

Some of the activities below are also found in the helpful student book, Adult Bible Class.
Don't forget to download the free reproducible page from www.standardlesson.com to enhance your lesson!

Into the Lesson

Option 1: Invite someone with sleight-of-hand skills to perform several "magic tricks" for the class. (One of these should be a trick for which your performer is willing to reveal how the illusion works.) After the tricks, ask the class, "Are these tricks actual demonstrations of supernatural power or are they illusions?" Then ask your performer to reveal how one of the illusions works.

After you thank your performer, say to the class, "There are always tricksters who are after power or money. Their illusions may take the form of falsified financial documents, fancy double-talk, etc. Perhaps some of them are able to tap into demonic supernatural power. The first-century church also had to contend with those who tried to grab power using wrong motives and means. Today we will look at one such instance."

Option 2: Form small groups. Ask learners to brainstorm within their groups examples of abuses of power in another part of the world. (Restricting ideas to "another part of the world" should help keep the discussion from becoming political.) After a few minutes, ask each group to share one or two examples with the class. Then say, "Grabbing and abusing power seems to be part of human nature. Even so, God wants us to be people of influence. Today's study will help us identify proper and improper motives in that regard."

Into the Word

Early in the week, recruit three people to make a presentation revealing the thoughts of Simon in today's lesson. Make three large name tags: one will say *Simon;* the other two will say *Simon's Thoughts.* The person playing Simon will say nothing; he will only make facial and body expressions reflecting his thoughts as given by the other two actors. The other two actors are to speak Simon's thoughts prior to his asking for the power of the Holy Spirit. The thoughts should include his pride

in his skills, his love for a crowd that follows him, his influence over people of power, his yearning for new magical skills, and his reflections when seeing power in Peter and John. The actors must remember that Simon had believed and been baptized.

After reading today's printed text, introduce the presentation team by saying, "I wonder what Simon was thinking. Why did he become a believer? What tempted him to ask for this new power? We have a team who will give us some insight into Simon's thoughts and possible motives." [This is the cue to begin the presentation.]

After the presentation, ask the following discussion questions: 1. What is the significance of this event taking place in Samaria (see Acts 1:8, last week's lesson)? 2. What was the Samaritan response to the gospel, and why was it significant (Acts 8:12)? 3. What do verses 20-23 teach us about power, motives, and temptation?

Alternative: Instead of using these discussion questions, distribute copies of the "Guided and Misguided Faith" activity from the reproducible page, which you can download. Have learners complete this exercise in small groups.

Into Life

Distribute copies of the "Desire for Power" activity from the reproducible page. Form learners into small groups and ask them to use the activity to relate desire for power to contemporary situations. After discussion, switch from these "negative" considerations to a "positive" tone by saying, "Let's create a personality profile of a Christian who displays authentic desire for the Holy Spirit's power to influence people. What is that person like?" If done as a whole-class exercise, have a "scribe" jot answers on the board.

Form prayer teams of three or four. Ask for a person on each team to pray for pure motives of service within (1) your church leadership and (2) the members of the prayer team.

PHILIP BAPTIZES A MAN FROM ETHIOPIA

DEVOTIONAL READING: Isaiah 56:1-8
BACKGROUND SCRIPTURE: Acts 8:26-39

ACTS 8:26-39

26 And the angel of the Lord spake unto Philip, saying, Arise, and go toward the south unto the way that goeth down from Jerusalem unto Gaza, which is desert.

27 And he arose and went: and, behold, a man of Ethiopia, an eunuch of great authority under Candace queen of the Ethiopians, who had the charge of all her treasure, and had come to Jerusalem for to worship,

28 Was returning, and sitting in his chariot read Esaias the prophet.

29 Then the Spirit said unto Philip, Go near, and join thyself to this chariot.

30 And Philip ran thither to him, and heard him read the prophet Esaias, and said, Understandest thou what thou readest?

31 And he said, How can I, except some man should guide me? And he desired Philip that he would come up and sit with him.

32 The place of the scripture which he read was this, He was led as a sheep to the slaughter; and like a lamb dumb before his shearer, so opened he not his mouth:

33 In his humiliation his judgment was taken away: and who shall declare his generation? for his life is taken from the earth.

34 And the eunuch answered Philip, and said, I pray thee, of whom speaketh the prophet this? of himself, or of some other man?

35 Then Philip opened his mouth, and began at the same scripture, and preached unto him Jesus.

36 And as they went on their way, they came unto a certain water: and the eunuch said, See, here is water; what doth hinder me to be baptized?

37 And Philip said, If thou believest with all thine heart, thou mayest. And he answered and said, I believe that Jesus Christ is the Son of God.

38 And he commanded the chariot to stand still: and they went down both into the water, both Philip and the eunuch; and he baptized him.

39 And when they were come up out of the water, the Spirit of the Lord caught away Philip, that the eunuch saw him no more: and he went on his way rejoicing.

KEY VERSE

As they went on their way, they came unto a certain water: and the eunuch said, See, here is water; what doth hinder me to be baptized? —**Acts 8:36**

A LIVING FAITH

Unit 2: Who Understands Faith?
LESSONS 6–9

LESSON AIMS

After participating in this lesson, each student will be able to:

1. Tell how the Ethiopian eunuch came to know the Lord Jesus.

2. Explain how Philip's example in sharing Christ with the eunuch can be followed by evangelists today.

3. Join (or launch) the personal evangelism ministry in his or her congregation.

LESSON OUTLINE

Introduction
A. Get the Word Out

A tornado is coming—take cover! The river is rising—head for high ground! An escaped convict is on the loose—watch out! Whenever there is imminent danger, the authorities will try to get the word out. They will use television and radio announcements; they will send police cars with loudspeakers into the streets. More recently, reverse 911 phone calls are made to every home and cell phone. The technology may change from generation to generation, but the demands of the emergency are the same: by whatever means possible, the people must be told how they can be saved.

The same thing is true about the greatest danger of all: the peril of losing eternal life. God has gone to great lengths to sound the warning and to provide information about the rescue available through His Son. But what good does it do for Jesus to die on the cross if no one knows about it? How can people turn to Him for deliverance if they have never heard about Him? And how will they hear unless God's people tell them (Romans 10:13-15)?

The incident of Philip and the Ethiopian eunuch is a clear example of God's initiative in getting the word out. Even though the promised Messiah had already died for him, the Ethiopian was not aware of that fact.

B. Lesson Background

Thousands of Jews returned to Jerusalem after the time of exile in Babylon ended, but many scattered to places all across the Mediterranean world. They set up synagogues wherever they settled and translated the Hebrew Old Testament into Greek. As a result, they brought knowledge of God to the Gentiles.

Some Gentiles became believers when they learned about the one true God. A few became full converts to Judaism by submitting to the rite of circumcision (compare Exodus 12:48). Others became only "proselytes of the gate." Either way, these were people who wanted to honor God and learn more about Him (see Acts 2:10; 6:5; 13:26, 43; 17:4, 17). This explains why a court official of

Philip Baptizes a Man from Ethiopia

Ethiopia made a journey all the way to Jerusalem —hundreds of miles each way—to worship God.

I. God's Appointment
(ACTS 8:26-29)
A. Angel's Command (v. 26)

26. And the angel of the Lord spake unto Philip, saying, Arise, and go toward the south unto the way that goeth down from Jerusalem unto Gaza, which is desert.

Philip has preached the gospel in Samaria, and the first converts outside of Jerusalem have been welcomed into the church (Acts 8:5-25). Now the circle of believers is about to be expanded a bit wider. Again, Philip is the spokesman.

God's mission will take Philip to a dry, desolate area—a rather unlikely spot for successful evangelism! Philip had traveled north to go from Jerusalem to Samaria. Now *the angel of the Lord* directs him in a different direction (the word *down* in Acts 8:5 and here indicates going to a lower elevation, not a compass bearing). Gaza is a city about 48 miles southwest of Jerusalem. But Philip is not instructed to go to the city of Gaza itself—only to the road that goes *from Jerusalem unto Gaza.*

What Do You Think?
What are some "desert places" where God has sent you? How did you handle the call? How did things turn out?

Talking Points for Your Discussion
- A move away from family and friends
- A change in jobs
- A neighbor who is hard to love
- Other

❧ DESIRING THE DESERT? ❧

The angel of the Lord didn't sugarcoat the message to Philip: he was to go into a desert region. No explanation necessary. And without a question, Philip simply went.

Many of us don't find it that simple. When my dad felt God was calling him to ministry, the rest of the family didn't share his vision. As a result, we endured years of wrenching strife as he struggled to clarify his calling. This childhood experience made me fear that if I became a Christian, God would call me to do terrible things . . . like going to Bible college or to some foreign mission field!

God doesn't demand that we take premature steps, however. Philip was already committed fully as an evangelist. He was experienced, ready to be deployed whenever and wherever he might be called. At my immature level of faith, God patiently worked with me until I actually *wanted* to be involved in ministry. One night, I sheepishly came to Him in prayer and said, "God, You remember how I said I never wanted to go to Bible college or be a missionary? Well, I kind of want to do those things now if that's OK with You."

Maybe to you the idea of God's call to ministry seems like a call to a barren desert. Keep in mind, however, that someone's eternity may be at stake. When you realize that, the "desert" will be the place of your heart's desire.   —A. W.

B. Devout Man (vv. 27, 28)

27. And he arose and went: and, behold, a man of Ethiopia, an eunuch of great authority under Candace queen of the Ethiopians, who had the charge of all her treasure, and had come to Jerusalem for to worship.

Philip obediently leaves his work in Samaria and begins the two- or three-day trip to a special spot on the desert road. Meanwhile, *a man of Ethiopia* (ancient Cush, the nation south of Egypt), is also traveling that road. He has *come to Jerusalem for to worship,* which indicates that he is a believer in the God of Israel.

What Do You Think?
What was the greatest difficulty you ever had to overcome in order to worship God? How did things turn out?

Talking Points for Your Discussion
- In accepting a change in worship styles
- In traveling a great distance, as the eunuch did
- In attending a worship service that was cross-cultural
- In worshipping alongside someone who held different doctrinal viewpoints

---

This man is a eunuch of great authority under the Ethiopian queen Candace. It is common in Mideastern and oriental countries of the time to emasculate men and place them in charge of the royal harem or in charge of the royal treasury. While the meaning of the word *eunuch* eventually expands to include court officials of any kind, it normally retains its literal sense in the Bible (compare 2 Kings 20:18; Esther 2:15; Matthew 19:12).

Several "firsts" (or "probable firsts") occur as the gospel reaches the Ethiopian eunuch in today's account. Racially, the man likely is African and black. Religiously, he probably is a proselyte to Judaism at some level (see the Lesson Background). Socially and sexually, he is considered an outsider by Jewish society and Old Testament law (see Deuteronomy 23:1).

28. Was returning, and sitting in his chariot read Esaias the prophet.

As the man is on his way back to Ethiopia, he is reading in his chariot. People today are known to drive and read text-messages at the same time—unfortunately! But since this man is "of great authority" (v. 27, above), he probably has the luxury of having a chauffeur do the driving. The fact that the Ethiopian eunuch has a scroll from which he can read *Esaias the prophet* (also known as *Isaiah*) is a further indication of wealth; it is quite a luxury to possess one's own copy of Scripture in the first century!

The book of Isaiah is an appropriate and providential choice for the Ethiopian. More than any other Old Testament book, Isaiah foresaw a day when all nations would come streaming to Jerusalem to acknowledge the true God (see Isaiah

HOW TO SAY IT

Caesarea	Sess-uh-*ree*-uh.
Ethiopian	E-thee-*o*-pee-un (*th* as in *thin*).
eunuch	*you*-nick.
Gentiles	*Jen*-tiles.
Mediterranean	*Med*-uh-tuh-*ray*-nee-un.
proselytes	*prahss*-uh-lights.
Samaria	Suh-*mare*-ee-uh.
Septuagint	Sep-*too*-ih-jent.
synagogues	*sin*-uh-gogs.

49:6-12; 60:1-14), including residents of Ethiopia ("Cush" in 11:11). In the days of the Messiah, the Holy One of Israel is to be honored by all nations, and salvation will come to the ends of the earth.

We also note that the eunuch may be drawn to the book of Isaiah for a personal reason. The book has a specific promise that in the messianic era God will accept eunuchs who keep His Sabbaths and do what is pleasing to Him (Isaiah 56:3-5). For this particular individual, that is good news indeed.

C. Spirit's Instructions (v. 29)

29. Then the Spirit said unto Philip, Go near, and join thyself to this chariot.

The angel of the Lord initially sends Philip down to the desert road (v. 26, above). Now God's own Spirit brings Philip the next instruction.

Philip can find many reasons to resist the call to teach this man. Wasn't Philip already having a successful ministry in Samaria? Why leave a ministry that is reaching many to accept a ministry to only one man, who may or may not respond positively? Doesn't the man seem an unlikely prospect, a person who just won't "fit in" with the rest of the new church? And what traveler wants to be hassled by someone trying to convert him?

We note that in the angel's instructions of Acts 8:26 there is no information given to Philip that his new ministry will be to just one individual. If the angel had given Philip that information, Philip might have resisted. But God knows the bigger picture when we don't. God also has ways of overcoming human resistance and reasoning (compare Acts 10:28, 29).

There seems to be a sense of urgency in the Spirit's instructions to *Go near, and join thyself to this chariot.* The chariot is moving. If Philip hesitates, the Ethiopian may move out of reach.

II. Philip's Message

(ACTS 8:30-35)

A. Offer and Invitation (vv. 30, 31)

30. And Philip ran thither to him, and heard him read the prophet Esaias, and said, Understandest thou what thou readest?

Philip Baptizes a Man from Ethiopia

Philip obeys the Spirit's call, and he has to run to catch the moving chariot. As he gets close, he hears the eunuch reading aloud, and this gives Philip the opening he needs. It is a bit bold, perhaps, to speak as Philip does to a total stranger, but he is on God's mission. Philip has to find a way to initiate the conversation.

31. And he said, How can I, except some man should guide me? And he desired Philip that he would come up and sit with him.

There are times in life when people are more open to receiving the gospel than at other times. The Holy Spirit knows when those times are, and He will guide us to reach people at opportune moments. That's what we see here as the Ethiopian eunuch responds in a friendly, self-deprecating sort of way.

Rather than trying to hide his ignorance, this devout and earnest man is eager to learn what Philip can teach him. The man knows it will do him no good to pretend to know what he does not know. So he urges Philip to join him in the chariot, and they talk as they travel toward Gaza together.

Visual for
Lesson 9

Point to this visual as you introduce the discussion question associated with Acts 8:31.

> **What Do You Think?**
> How do we make ourselves available for spiritual conversations without being pushy?
> *Talking Points for Your Discussion*
> - Job 2:11-13
> - Acts 16:13
> - Acts 17:17
> - 1 Corinthians 9:11-23
> - 2 Corinthians 11:9
> - Other

B. Prophecy and Puzzlement (vv. 32, 33)

32. The place of the scripture which he read was this, He was led as a sheep to the slaughter; and like a lamb dumb before his shearer, so opened he not his mouth.

The place of the scripture that the Ethiopian is reading is known to us as Isaiah 53:7, 8. If you compare the wording of that passage in the Old Testament with what is quoted here, you will notice some differences. This is because the Ethiopian is not reading from the original Hebrew, but from the Greek version known as the Septuagint, which was translated a few centuries before Christ.

In either version, that passage offers a surprising picture of a coming Savior: someone will come to take the iniquities of God's people on himself. In so doing, that person brings peace and healing by his own wounds (see Isaiah 53:2-6). Specifically, this "someone" will be *led as a sheep to the slaughter.* Helpless, defenseless, and vulnerable, this individual will be led out to die! And not only will this man be like a helpless sheep, He will also be like a speechless lamb about to be sheared.

33. In his humiliation his judgment was taken away: and who shall declare his generation? for his life is taken from the earth.

For a man to be treated no better than a slaughtered sheep seems inhuman. The fact that *his judgment was taken away* indicates that he is denied a fair trial. The rhetorical question *who shall declare his generation?* indicates that the victim leaves no children; no one will speak of His descendants because the generations of His family tree end with Him. As he loses His life, His lineage ceases. End of story—a sad, tragic story.

From this side of the cross, however, these words are beautifully symbolic and expressive. We can see exactly how they apply to Jesus as He quietly submitted to the abuse of men and bore the sins of the world on His shoulders. But to the Ethiopian, who apparently does not know of Jesus, nothing about the ancient prophecy makes much sense.

How has your reaction to the story of the suffering and death of Christ changed as you have moved through the seasons of life? How do we keep the story ever new?

Talking Points for Your Discussion
- In your teenage years
- As a young adult
- As an older adult

C. Fulfillment and Jesus (vv. 34, 35)

34. And the eunuch answered Philip, and said, I pray thee, of whom speaketh the prophet this? of himself, or of some other man?

The eunuch is not reading the passage merely for entertainment (contrast Ezekiel 33:22). The man is actually studying the passage, trying to understand. Is Isaiah talking about himself, as another in a long line of prophets who are rejected and killed (see Acts 7:52)? Or is Isaiah speaking *of some other man*? Either way, it is difficult for the eunuch to see how any good can come from such mistreatment of a man of God.

35. Then Philip opened his mouth, and began at the same scripture, and preached unto him Jesus.

The Ethiopian is open to the truth, so Philip seizes the opportunity to teach him. An important technique in sharing the gospel is to "begin where the other person is." That's exactly what Philip does as his response starts *at the same scripture* that the man is reading. This is Philip's launching pad to speak about Jesus, the Son of God.

III. Eunuch's Decision
(ACTS 8:36-39)
A. Eager Response (vv. 36, 37)

36. And as they went on their way, they came unto a certain water: and the eunuch said, See, here is water; what doth hinder me to be baptized?

Even in that dry, rocky countryside, there are several streams and oases between Jerusalem and Gaza. The fact that the eunuch inquires about

the possibility of baptism means that Philip has already mentioned the topic—that's the only way the man can know about it. Thus we conclude that Philip must have declared the whole gospel message to the eunuch by this point (compare Matthew 28:19). What has happened in Jerusalem and Samaria is now happening to a man of Ethiopia—when he believes, he is baptized (see Acts 2:38; 8:12). The gospel is spreading to the whole world.

❧ RELUCTANT BAPTISMS ❧

Historians mark AD 988 as the official birthday of the Russian Orthodox Church. As part of a diplomatic alliance, Prince Vladimir I of Kiev converted from paganism, married a Christian princess, and promised to baptize his people. He had the statues of pagan gods destroyed. Then he ordered all residents of Kiev to meet at the river for baptism or else become the "prince's enemies." Similar scenes were repeated across the country.

People are baptized reluctantly even today. Sometimes in an eagerness for conversions, evangelists use emotional tactics to pressure people into receiving baptism. Some people are baptized to please family members. I met one preteen at a church camp who had been baptized twice—once because his mother told him to and again because his mother said he was too young the first time!

We see no reluctance or pressure in today's text. Philip simply explained the Scripture and let the Ethiopian draw his own conclusions. The result? The Ethiopian requested baptism when he was ready. He went on his way rejoicing because his salvation was real, not just a ritual.   —A. W.

37. And Philip said, If thou believest with all thine heart, thou mayest. And he answered and said, I believe that Jesus Christ is the Son of God.

The earliest Greek manuscripts do not include this verse. Thus verse 37 is not included in most newer translations of the Bible, except as a footnote. What the verse says, however, certainly conforms with the rest of what Scripture teaches. Just like any other man or woman on earth, the eunuch is eligible to accept Christ as his Savior. This does not mean he qualifies by his status or his works; he qualifies by believing in Jesus with all his heart. Jesus said that people should confess Him publicly (see Matthew 10:32), just as Simon Peter did (see Matthew 16:16). Paul will later promise salvation to those who confess "Jesus is Lord" and who believe that God raised Him from the dead (see Romans 10:9, 10). Because the eunuch believes, he is glad to confess his faith openly.

B. Joyful Baptism (vv. 38, 39)

38. And he commanded the chariot to stand still: and they went down both into the water, both Philip and the eunuch; and he baptized him.

In whatever body of water is available, the eunuch is buried with his Lord in the likeness of his death and raised to walk a new life (see Romans 6:2-4). There is something beautiful about this simple scene. There is no need of a fancy church building or an ornate baptistery. All that is needed besides the water is simple, trusting faith. It is with such faith that the eunuch makes his personal response to the gospel.

39. And when they were come up out of the water, the Spirit of the Lord caught away Philip, that the eunuch saw him no more: and he went on his way rejoicing.

No doubt Philip and the eunuch could spend much more time together, gladly investigating the Scriptures. But as they come *up out of the water,* it is time for Philip to move on. The angel of the Lord has sent him to this place; now *the Spirit of the Lord* takes him away. Philip is to continue preaching the gospel, eventually settling in Caesarea (Acts 8:40). The next mention of him in Acts is some 20 years later in this same city, where "Philip the evangelist, which was one of the Seven" has four daughters who prophesy (21:8, 9).

Even though the eunuch does not see Philip again, the all-important message has been delivered successfully. The queen's official resumes his long journey back to Ethiopia, but this time he has in his soul a joy unlike any other. Now he knows that the Lamb of God has died even for his sins.

Conclusion

A. Long-awaited Deliverance

The story of Philip and the Ethiopian eunuch did not begin on a desert road winding its way down toward Gaza. Rather, it began in a garden where the serpent led the parents of the human race into sin. Although Adam and Eve were expelled from paradise, God had a plan to deliver humanity from the penalty and power of sin.

God chose Abraham and made a chosen people through that man's descendants. God spoke to them through Moses and the prophets, leading them forward to the time of redemption. Moses promised that the Lord would raise up a prophet like himself (Deuteronomy 18:15). Job knew that his Redeemer would one day stand on the earth (Job 19:25). David knew that his own descendant would sit on the throne of an everlasting kingdom (2 Samuel 7:13), yet he wrote a haunting psalm predicting that descendant's crucifixion (Psalm 22). Isaiah rejoiced to see a day when, "Unto us a child is born" (Isaiah 9:6), even though that child would become the suffering servant of Isaiah 53.

The unified theme of the Old Testament is the coming Messiah. It is His story—a story thousands of years in the making—that ultimately reached the Ethiopian eunuch. The deliverance had been long awaited, and it was gladly received.

B. Prayer

Lord, we praise You for making Your salvation available to all. Send us on our own road to Gaza to meet someone who needs to hear about Jesus. In His name; amen.

C. Thought to Remember

The gospel is for everyone.

INVOLVEMENT LEARNING

Some of the activities below are also found in the helpful student book, Adult Bible Class.
Don't forget to download the free reproducible page from www.standardlesson.com to enhance your lesson!

Into the Lesson

Option 1. Invite someone who has administered numerous baptisms to share experiences with your class. Provide your guest speaker the following interview questions ahead of time. 1. Whom did you recently baptize? 2. What did you teach this individual before the baptism? 3. What emotions and thoughts do you experience when you baptize? 4. What happens in terms of follow-up? 5. What makes cross-cultural baptisms different from same-culture baptisms, if anything?

After thanking the guest say, "Today we will experience the joy of a unique conversion experience. From this experience we will discover the wonders of touching others with the gospel."

Option 2. Write the word *Diversity* at the top of the board. Ask learners to brainstorm illustrations of diversity within your congregation. They may cite national, racial, or age diversity. Jot responses on the board. Then ask, "Does this listing reflect the diversity of our neighborhood?" Make the transition to Bible study by saying, "It is often a challenge for Christians to reach across various lines to influence others for Christ. Today's example will give us insight regarding this calling."

Into the Word

In no more than three minutes, summarize for the class the information in the Lesson Background and the commentary on verses 27, 28. Your focus will be on how Gentile believers had come in contact with Jews and their Scriptures before the coming of Christ. Then read (or have read) the printed text for the class.

Form study teams of three to five; assign your more "musically inclined" learners to Team 2. Give each team a photocopy of the lesson commentary for assigned portions of the text, a poster board, and a marker. Also distribute handouts of the following assignments. *Team 1:* Review today's printed text. Then list characteristics and personal qualities of Philip and the Ethiopian man that made this encounter an evangelistic success. Be ready to share discoveries with the class. *Team 2:* Focus on the prophecy cited in verses 32, 33. Interpret what is written by setting these thoughts to music. Use a tune familiar to the entire group. Be ready to sing your creation for the class. *Team 3:* Review the baptism of the Ethiopian. Compare what you see with Acts 2:38; Romans 6:2-4; Colossians 2:11, 12; 1 Peter 3:21. Draw up a summary of what these Scriptures taken together teach about baptism. *Team 4:* Review the conversion of the man from Ethiopia. List lessons we can learn from this encounter about sharing Christ that can be followed today.

Alternative: Have teams complete instead the "Who, What, When, Where, and Why?" exercise from the reproducible page, which you can download. This alternative is preferred if you wish all teams to study the entirety of today's text rather than segments.

Into Life

Ask, "What are some modern challenges or obstacles to churches and/or individuals in reaching people of other races or cultures?" Ask a scribe to jot ideas on the board. After several proposals, say, "Let's get creative. Working with your previous teammates, create ideas or strategies for our church to reach those of other cultures or races. Make a list of your ideas."

After a few minutes, have groups share the results of their work. Ask, "Which ideas seem most feasible for our church? What would be your top choices?" Record all ideas, and circle those that learners recommend as top choices. Tell the group that you plan to share their ideas with your church leaders for consideration. To move from abstract ideas to personal commitment, have learners complete the "Who and How?" thought bubbles on the reproducible page, which you can download.

Philip Baptizes a Man from Ethiopia

PAUL TESTIFIES BEFORE KING AGRIPPA

DEVOTIONAL READING: Acts 23:1-11
BACKGROUND SCRIPTURE: Acts 25, 26

ACTS 26:19-32

19 Whereupon, O king Agrippa, I was not disobedient unto the heavenly vision:

20 But shewed first unto them of Damascus, and at Jerusalem, and throughout all the coasts of Judaea, and then to the Gentiles, that they should repent and turn to God, and do works meet for repentance.

21 For these causes the Jews caught me in the temple, and went about to kill me.

22 Having therefore obtained help of God, I continue unto this day, witnessing both to small and great, saying none other things than those which the prophets and Moses did say should come:

23 That Christ should suffer, and that he should be the first that should rise from the dead, and should shew light unto the people, and to the Gentiles.

24 And as he thus spake for himself, Festus said with a loud voice, Paul, thou art beside thyself; much learning doth make thee mad.

25 But he said, I am not mad, most noble Festus; but speak forth the words of truth and soberness.

26 For the king knoweth of these things, before whom also I speak freely: for I am persuaded that none of these things are hidden from him; for this thing was not done in a corner.

27 King Agrippa, believest thou the prophets? I know that thou believest.

28 Then Agrippa said unto Paul, Almost thou persuadest me to be a Christian.

29 And Paul said, I would to God, that not only thou, but also all that hear me this day, were both almost, and altogether such as I am, except these bonds.

30 And when he had thus spoken, the king rose up, and the governor, and Bernice, and they that sat with them:

31 And when they were gone aside, they talked between themselves, saying, This man doeth nothing worthy of death or of bonds.

32 Then said Agrippa unto Festus, This man might have been set at liberty, if he had not appealed unto Caesar.

KEY VERSE

[Paul] said, I am not mad, most noble Festus; but speak forth the words of truth and soberness.

—Acts 26:25

Photo: Thomas Northcut / Photodisc / Thinkstock

A LIVING FAITH

Unit 3: Where Does Faith Take Us?

LESSON AIMS

After participating in this lesson, each student will be able to:

1. Summarize Paul's evangelistic appeal to Agrippa.

2. Compare and contrast Paul's exercise of his ministry with that of modern missionaries.

3. Commit to praying for one or more missionaries (those supported by his or her church, if that is known) by name over the next few months.

LESSON OUTLINE

Introduction

A. A Good Reputation—With Whom?

How important is a good reputation? In one of Shakespeare's plays, a character exclaims, "O, I have lost my reputation! I have lost the immortal part of myself, and what remains is bestial" (*Othello*, Act 2, Scene 3). Most would say a good reputation is important, but just how important?

For the person of faith, obedience to God is always more important than a good reputation with others. Human reputation is based on limited information, but God knows all. Human opinion can vacillate, but God's judgment is unvarying. In the end, human reputation counts for little, but God's estimation counts for everything.

The first-century church had a problem with its reputation. Worshipping a man crucified as an insurrectionist, upsetting the social order by inviting people of all backgrounds to adopt their faith, Christians were regarded as foolish, insane, or even dangerous. In the book of Acts, the story of Paul-the-prisoner addresses this issue. Yes, Paul was indeed a prisoner of Rome. But, says Acts, he was imprisoned not because he was a genuine evildoer, but because he so faithfully testified to the good news of Jesus. Many dismissed him and his message. But because he had seen the risen Jesus and had heard the voice of God, Paul could do nothing other than give voice to the truth of the gospel.

B. Lesson Background

Paul, formerly known as Saul, is the focus of the second half of the book of Acts. The one who approved of Stephen's murder (Acts 8:1, see Lesson 7) was changed forever on the road to Damascus (9:1-9). Converted from opposition to Jesus, Paul traveled throughout Asia Minor and Greece to preach the good news of Jesus and to establish churches.

Having returned to Jerusalem, Paul was arrested by the Romans after a disturbance in the temple (Acts 21:27-33; 23:26-30). Paul had to wait in prison for months. He was questioned in hearings to establish charges on which he could be tried. But there is more to Paul's imprisonment than meets the eye. God used Paul's imprisonment to protect him from those trying to kill him (23:12-24). To avoid trial in Jerusalem, Paul appealed to be heard by the emperor in Rome (25:11), as was his right as a Roman citizen. That legal maneuver became the means by which God not only foiled Paul's opponents but also enabled Paul to testify in Rome, as God had promised (23:11).

So Festus, the Roman governor of Judea from about AD 58 to 62, was obliged to send Paul to Rome. But Festus needed charges to send with him (Acts 25:23-27). Thus, Paul appeared before Festus again, this time joined by King Herod Agrippa II, great-grandson of the infamous King Herod who ruled at the time of Jesus' birth. Agrippa was a reliable advisor to the Romans on Jewish affairs, knowing the Jewish Scriptures well (26:3).

Paul began his speech before this tribunal by recounting his early life as a faithful Jew. A strict Pharisee, Paul was so opposed to the followers of Jesus that he traveled to Damascus to arrest them (Acts 26:2-12). But on the way he saw the risen Jesus, who commanded him to testify to people of all nations (26:13-18). And so we come to the conclusion of Paul's speech, which is our text.

I. Paul's Obedient Life
(ACTS 26:19-23)
A. Vision Received (v. 19)

19. Whereupon, O king Agrippa, I was not disobedient unto the heavenly vision.

Paul has previously described his life as thoroughly devoted to serving the God of Israel. When someone who wants nothing more than to obey God receives a vision that comes from God, what can he do but obey it?

HOW TO SAY IT

Damascus	Duh-*mass*-kus.
Festus	*Fes*-tus.
Gentiles	*Jen*-tiles.
Herod Agrippa	*Hair*-ud Uh-*grip*-puh.
Judea or Judaea	Joo-*dee*-uh.
Messiah	Meh-*sigh*-uh.
Nazareth	*Naz*-uh-reth.
Pharisee	*Fair*-ih-see.

In framing his story this way, Paul makes an important point. He does not follow Jesus because he wants to upset the traditions of his people or disturb the civil order. Rather, he follows Jesus because Jesus' appearance to him has convinced him that Jesus is the divine Son of God, risen from the dead. Because Jesus specifically has sent Paul to preach, Paul, as one striving to obey God, can do nothing less than obey that divine commission.

> **What Do You Think?**
> Whose "faith story" has made you bolder in your witness? Why?
> *Talking Points for Your Discussion*
> - A friend
> - A missionary
> - A Christian leader
> - Other

B. Repentance Preached (v. 20)

20. But shewed first unto them of Damascus, and at Jerusalem, and throughout all the coasts of Judaea, and then to the Gentiles, that they should repent and turn to God, and do works meet for repentance.

Paul now summarizes his career as a preacher of the gospel. It began in Damascus. What was first his destination for arresting followers of Jesus became his first forum for declaring that Jesus is Lord (Acts 9:20-22).

Not mentioned here is Paul's trip to Arabia (see Galatians 1:17, 18). After a few years, he decided to go to Jerusalem. Paul (who was still Saul at the time) was not welcomed by believers in Jerusalem at first. They were uncertain that he was a true disciple (Acts 9:26). But commended by Barnabas, he became a powerful advocate for the gospel in Israel's holy city (9:27, 28). The *coasts of Judaea* refers to the Jewish territory outside Jerusalem; we can infer that Paul took his message to the surrounding regions while in Jerusalem.

Finally, Paul mentions preaching *to the Gentiles,* that is, non-Jews. God had promised that one day He would make himself known to the Gentiles and bring His blessing to them (Genesis 22:18; Isaiah 42:6, 7). Paul intends for his audience to understand that his preaching to the Gentiles has not been a cause of dissension, but is part of God's plan. Anyone who longs to see God's promises fulfilled should rejoice that pagan nations are coming to know the true God through Paul's ministry.

We see that emphasis in the way Paul describes his preaching. Its aim is to provoke the pagan nations to *repent and turn to God,* to abandon a life of rebellion against their Creator. Their repentance will then produce works—actions that express obedience and submission to God.

Paul's preaching provoked violent opposition in both Damascus and Jerusalem (Acts 9:23, 29). But Paul insists that the message of the gospel is nothing dangerous. In fact, it turns the rebellious nations back to submission to their Creator, ready to do His will. If Paul is controversial, then he is so because so many are unwilling to turn back to the one who made them.

❧ *PAUL'S GPS* ❧

My wife gave me a global positioning system (GPS) device for my last birthday. It's amazing how this tiny computer is able to determine my precise location, calculate the quickest route, display a map, and sound a warning when a turn is coming up. If I miss the turn (a frequent occurrence), the computer calculates a new route within seconds to get me back on track. Imagine my surprise one day when I took a wrong turn and heard the GPS say, "I don't know where we are. I'm scared!"

Perhaps the apostle Paul would have been fascinated with this technological marvel, but I also think he would have found it unnecessary. The Holy Spirit guided him and kept him focused on the goal of calling people to repentance and faith in Christ Jesus. Sometimes he ended up in (to him) unexpected places. But wherever he was, Paul never lost sight of the ultimate prize to which God was calling him (Philippians 3:14).

We have access to the same Spirit. Follow Him. He always knows where we are, and He's never scared!
—A. W.

C. Violence Threatened (v. 21)

21. For these causes the Jews caught me in the temple, and went about to kill me.

Everything that makes Paul controversial came to a climax when he was taken *in the temple* (Acts 21:30). To demonstrate to skeptics that he remained observant of the Law of Moses, Paul had gone to the temple to pay for the sacrifices of some Jewish Christians who had completed a sacred vow (21:23, 24). But once there, Paul was falsely accused of bringing Gentiles into the temple (21:28, 29). Only intervention by Roman authorities kept the mob from killing Paul (21:31, 32).

By noting the circumstances of his arrest, Paul turns the tables on his accusers. He is proclaiming the fulfillment of God's promises, but his opponents seized him in God's temple because of that proclamation. If anyone is unfaithful to the God of Israel, if anyone is responsible for civil disorder, it is not Paul, but his enemies.

D. Message Outlined (vv. 22, 23)

22. Having therefore obtained help of God, I continue unto this day, witnessing both to small and great, saying none other things than those which the prophets and Moses did say should come.

Paul continues to talk about faithfulness: his to God and especially God's to him. Through Paul's missionary travels and hardships, God has assisted and protected him, even through his current imprisonment. Paul's preaching has not been aimed at impressing the powerful or at stirring up the vulnerable. He has preached to all, from slaves to kings. All stand equal in their need for God's mercy. Paul's message has not denied or deviated from the Jewish Scriptures. Rather, his message has announced the fulfillment of all the law and the prophets. Paul is no rebel or rabble-rouser. He is an obedient servant of Almighty God.

What Do You Think?
Under what circumstances, if any, should Christians promote their faith in ways that defy or challenge the governing power structures?
Talking Points for Your Discussion
▪ Acts 4:19; 5:29
▪ Romans 13:1-7
▪ 1 Peter 2:13-17

23. That Christ should suffer, and that he should be the first that should rise from the dead, and should shew light unto the people, and to the Gentiles.

Paul now shares the very heart of the gospel message. Jesus' life, death, and resurrection are the climax of everything that God has done since creation. In Jesus' death, God took sinners' punishment on himself. In Jesus' resurrection, God began to fulfill His promise to renew His creation, offering eternal life to all. Everyone who belongs to Him will experience the fulfillment of His promises when He raises them from the dead.

By this means, God is taking back the entire world as His domain. The good news of Jesus is *light unto the people,* meaning the people of Israel. While we tend to focus on the many among the people of Israel who do not respond positively to the good news of Jesus, we may forget the many who do. Nearly every leader of the earliest church is Jewish, including Paul himself. Thousands of Jews become followers of Jesus (Acts 21:20). As far as Paul is concerned, he simply cannot remain faithful to God as a Jew if he does not submit to the authority of the promised Messiah whom God has sent—Jesus of Nazareth.

Jesus' light is not just for Israel but for the Gentiles as well (Isaiah 42:6; 49:6). God's promise is to use Israel as His means of reclaiming rebellious humanity. The book of Acts shows the fulfillment of that promise. Who, then, is being true to the God of Israel—Paul or those who seek to kill him? Paul wants Agrippa to recognize where real faithfulness to God is to be found.

❧ *Spiderweb Speech* ❧

"Honey, you won't believe what happened to Ashley . . . I stopped for gas on the way to pick her up at preschool . . . by the way, the 'check engine' light is still on . . . but at the gas station I ran into Wendy . . . you remember her, she married Dave, who I used to date before I met you . . . so she said she had just been to the preschool and Ashley was crying, and at first I didn't think it was serious because you know how she is sometimes . . ."

Sound familiar? Some people talk like they're spinning spiderwebs, jumping erratically from

topic to topic. If you wait around long enough, the conversation starts to get back around to the central point—if you can remember what it was.

This is similar to the approach many of us take when sharing our faith with others. We talk vaguely about lifestyle issues, discuss church programs, debate the topic of evolution, discuss the ethics of abortion, and maybe dabble in some end-times speculation. But do we ever get to the main point? Paul focused his ministry clearly on Jesus Christ, His death and resurrection. Do we do that, or do we spin spiderwebs? —A. W.

II. Paul's Bold Message
(Acts 26:24-27)

A. Interruption by Festus (v. 24)

24. And as he thus spake for himself, Festus said with a loud voice, Paul, thou art beside thyself; much learning doth make thee mad.

The Roman Governor Festus now breaks in, expressing utter disbelief in what Paul is saying. It is no accident that Festus interrupts just as Paul mentions resurrection from the dead. In Paul's time, only Jews believe that God will one day raise the dead. For non-Jews like Festus, the idea is absurd (compare Acts 17:32), just as it is for many today. After all, dead people stay dead!

So Festus declares that Paul has lost his mind. The only way Festus can explain how anyone can believe in something so absurd as resurrection is to conclude that Paul is insane. Surely it is madness that has driven Paul to travel the world announcing that a man who was crucified by the Romans has risen from the dead.

But Festus's explanation is problematic: Paul does not really act like an insane person. He acts like a learned person. So in desperation, Festus grabs at the one as an explanation for the other: Paul's knowledge of Israel's Scriptures, so evident in his proclamation, has driven him insane. Of course, Paul's behavior has been anything but insane. It has been focused, dedicated, resolute. Festus's "insanity defense" for Paul does little to explain what makes Paul tick. Festus's dilemma confronts everyone who considers the gospel. Is it insane to believe that God raised Jesus from the dead?

B. Response from Paul (v. 25)

25. But he said, I am not mad, most noble Festus; but speak forth the words of truth and soberness.

Deliberately and sanely, Paul denies Festus's allegation. Still addressing Festus respectfully despite the insult, Paul asserts that his message reflects both *truth and soberness*. It reflects truth because it is fully in accord with what Paul and others have witnessed: that God raised Jesus from the dead. *Soberness* is the opposite of insanity; it is behavior that reflects self-control, wisdom, sound judgment.

C. Appeal to Agrippa (vv. 26, 27)

26. For the king knoweth of these things, before whom also I speak freely: for I am persuaded that none of these things are hidden from him; for this thing was not done in a corner.

Paul now shifts his address from Governor Festus to King Agrippa. The king is present as an expert in Jewish religious affairs, so Paul appeals to his expertise. Agrippa certainly knows about the Christian movement, which is about 30 years old at this point and has thousands of adherents within the historic territories of Israel.

The controversy about the gospel is the most important issue within Judaism of that time. Surely none of this has escaped Agrippa's attention! The gospel is not based on secret events or private revelations, but on the things that God has done in full view. Paul's boldness is not madness; it is the necessary consequence of what God had done publicly in Jesus (compare John 18:20).

27. King Agrippa, believest thou the prophets? I know that thou believest.

Agrippa has knowledge of the facts of Christianity. But if he is to respond to Paul's message, he must attach significance to those facts. Therein lies Paul's challenge to him: to live up to his claim to be a faithful believer in the promises of Israel.

Like other members of the Herod family, Agrippa probably has asserted his faithfulness to God in private while living publicly like any pagan king. But if Agrippa believes that the prophets promised God's blessing, and if Agrippa knows about the resurrected Jesus, then it is time to act on that belief and knowledge.

What Do You Think?

How should Christian politicians bring their faith convictions into their jobs as governors, senators, etc., if at all?

Talking Points for Your Discussion
- When casting votes in the legislature or signing legislation
- When criticizing or questioning an opponent
- When campaigning for office
- When asked a question about their faith story

III. A King's Perplexed Response
(ACTS 26:28-32)

A. Impressed but Unconvinced (v. 28)

28. Then Agrippa said unto Paul, Almost thou persuadest me to be a Christian.

But King Agrippa is not willing to take the step of faith. The *King James Version* understands a phrase in the original language to mean *almost,* in which case Agrippa is saying that he is not quite ready to make a commitment. Another idea, however, proposes that the phrase translated *almost* signifies "a short period of time." If that is the sense, then Agrippa is asking, "Do you, Paul, think you can persuade me to make such a huge commitment in a little bit of time?"

But time is not the real obstacle. Agrippa knows that the Christian faith is controversial, rejected by the most powerful leaders of Judaism, and a matter of concern to many Roman officials. If Agrippa were to commit to faith in the gospel, then he would endanger his powerful position. For Paul, however, the only real security is to be identified with Jesus Christ, whose power is supreme.

What Do You Think?

What are some obstacles to faith that don't involve the truthfulness of the Christian message? How do we help unbelievers overcome those obstacles?

Talking Points for Your Discussion
- Family obstacles (Luke 14:26)
- Workplace/career obstacles (Luke 18:18-30)
- Other

The word *Christian* means "belonging to Christ" and aptly describes a follower of Jesus. But in its three New Testament uses, it seems to be quoted from its use by outsiders (here; Acts 11:26; 1 Peter 4:16). What opponents may intend as an insult the followers of Jesus accept as honorable. The word identifies us with our king.

B. Impassioned but Unsuccessful (v. 29)

29. And Paul said, I would to God, that not only thou, but also all that hear me this day, were both almost, and altogether such as I am, except these bonds.

Paul expresses the deep conviction of his life. The solemn *I would to God* means that this is Paul's wish or prayer directed to God. As Paul speaks to two rulers, one a pagan and the other seemingly a Jewish worshipper of the true God, Paul displays the characteristic of his ministry: bold proclamation of the gospel to all people—high and low, Jew and Gentile (Acts 9:15). Paul, the prisoner of Christ, is the truly free man. Agrippa, enslaved to his position and power, is the man truly bound.

> **What Do You Think?**
> How does Paul's witness before Festus and Agrippa compare and contrast with Peter's denial in Mark 14:66-72?
> *Talking Points for Your Discussion*
> - What each had to gain and lose
> - The impact of their personal experiences
> - Their convictions about Scripture

C. Innocent but Imprisoned (vv. 30-32)

30. And when he had thus spoken, the king rose up, and the governor, and Bernice, and they that sat with them.

This ends the public hearing. Festus the governor will now confer with Agrippa. Bernice is Agrippa's sister, present for the hearing (Acts 25:23).

31, 32. And when they were gone aside, they talked between themselves, saying, This man doeth nothing worthy of death or of bonds. Then said Agrippa unto Festus, This man might have been set at liberty, if he had not appealed unto Caesar.

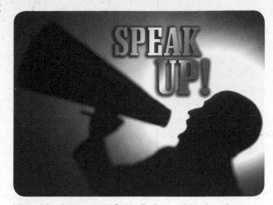

Visual for Lessons 6 & 10. *Point to this visual as you introduce the discussion question associated with either Acts 26:22 or 26:27.*

Neither ruler is persuaded to become a believer, but neither do they conclude that Paul is a criminal (compare Acts 23:29). All that keeps Paul a prisoner is his appeal to Caesar (25:11). In the judgment of skeptical King Agrippa, with Governor Festus agreeing, Paul is an innocent man.

Conclusion

A. Free in Spite of Circumstances

Even unbelieving magistrates who had their own agendas could see that Paul was no criminal. But beyond Paul's innocence was another truth: as a follower of Jesus, he was experiencing something like Jesus had. Paul was imprisoned because of his bold proclamation of the gospel. Speaking about the crucified Jesus made Paul a prisoner of the very government that had carried out the crucifixion.

Faithfulness will put us at odds with many around us. It will lose us some of what the world holds dear. But when our faith costs us, we are richest. When our faith makes us a prisoner, we are most free.

B. Prayer

Lord Jesus, may we be as captivated with You as was Paul, and so may we like him be bold witnesses for You. In Jesus' name; amen!

C. Thought to Remember

Recognize where true freedom lies.

INVOLVEMENT LEARNING

Some of the activities below are also found in the helpful student book, Adult Bible Class.
Don't forget to download the free reproducible page from www.standardlesson.com to enhance your lesson!

Into the Lesson

Place in chairs copies of the "Standing Before Kings" activity from the reproducible page, which you can download. Learners can begin working on this as they arrive.

Read aloud the last names of the current (as of this writing) justices of the U.S. Supreme Court: Roberts, Alito, Breyer, Ginsburg, Kagan, Kennedy, Scalia, Sotomayor, Thomas. Ask, "Who are these people?" After the correct answer say, "Most of us are at least somewhat familiar with how a legal appeal process works. For a Roman citizen, the most supreme court in the New Testament era was none other than the Roman emperor himself. Roman citizens had the right of appeal to him. In today's text, Paul is working his way through the appeal process on his way to Rome to argue his case before that ruler."

Into the Word

Have three good oral readers stand before your group to read the parts of Paul, Porcius Festus, and Herod Agrippa from today's text. Prepare very large name tags to be worn around their necks as identifiers. The reading will proceed as follows: Paul reads verses 19-23; Festus reads (loudly) verse 24b; Paul reads verses 25-27; Agrippa reads verse 28b; Paul reads verse 29; Festus (to Agrippa) reads verse 31b; Agrippa (to Festus) reads verse 32b.

Give each reader a script of the segments to promote smoothness of the back-and-forth readings; make sure to exclude from the script the parts of the text that read "but he said," etc. *Option:* Have a fourth person representing Bernice stand alongside the three readers. She will be silent, but will make skeptical facial expressions.

After the readings, say, "You noticed that Paul made a series of 'I statements' in his defense before King Agrippa and Governor Festus. These are simple affirmations of truth about himself, his life, and his ministry." Give each learner a copy of today's text, Acts 26:19-32 (you can photocopy this from page 81). Say, "Take a couple of minutes and underline the explicit 'I statements.' These are places where Paul affirms 'I was,' 'I am,' etc. You should find eight of these." (Answers: *I was not disobedient* [v. 19]; *I continue unto this day* [v. 22]; *I am not mad* [v. 25]; *I speak freely* [v. 26]; *I am persuaded* [v. 26]; *I know* [v. 27]; *I would to God* [v. 29]; *such as I am* [v. 29].) You may have some learners who also discover a few places where the personal pronoun *I* is not explicitly present, but is clearly implied; an example is *but [I] speak forth* [v. 25]).

After discussing the significance of Paul's "I statements," have learners find Paul's "thou (you) statements." There are only three: two in verse 27 (one of which is part of a question, not a statement) and one in verse 29. Brainstorm this question: "Why are there so many more 'I statements' than 'thou statements'?" Jot suggestions on the board; allow free discussion.

Into Life

Say, "Paul's 'I statements' offer us a way to evaluate our own commitment to Christ. Let's do some of that right now." Distribute handouts titled *Personal Evaluation;* include the following entries and a self-rating scale from 1 (seldom) to 5 (always). 1. I speak of repentance and turning to God whenever possible and appropriate. 2. I sense God's presence and help in fulfilling my obligation to witness. 3. I am ready always to testify "both to small and great." 4. I speak what is reasonable and historically accurate. 5. I pray that Christ's message will be received.

Allow learners to complete the self-evaluations privately. Ask for volunteers to share areas where they are weakest, but don't put anyone on the spot. After discussion, distribute copies of the "Sitting with Commoners" activity from the reproducible page. Discuss in small groups. This can be a take-home activity if time is short.

PAUL SURVIVES A SHIPWRECK

DEVOTIONAL READING: Romans 1:13-17

BACKGROUND SCRIPTURE: Acts 27

ACTS 27:1, 2, 33-44

1 And when it was determined that we should sail into Italy, they delivered Paul and certain other prisoners unto one named Julius, a centurion of Augustus' band.

2 And entering into a ship of Adramyttium, we launched, meaning to sail by the coasts of Asia; one Aristarchus, a Macedonian of Thessalonica, being with us.

. . . .

33 And while the day was coming on, Paul besought them all to take meat, saying, This day is the fourteenth day that ye have tarried and continued fasting, having taken nothing.

34 Wherefore I pray you to take some meat: for this is for your health: for there shall not an hair fall from the head of any of you.

35 And when he had thus spoken, he took bread, and gave thanks to God in presence of them all: and when he had broken it, he began to eat.

36 Then were they all of good cheer, and they also took some meat.

37 And we were in all in the ship two hundred threescore and sixteen souls.

38 And when they had eaten enough, they lightened the ship, and cast out the wheat into the sea.

39 And when it was day, they knew not the land: but they discovered a certain creek with a shore, into the which they were minded, if it were possible, to thrust in the ship.

40 And when they had taken up the anchors, they committed themselves unto the sea, and loosed the rudder bands, and hoised up the mainsail to the wind, and made toward shore.

41 And falling into a place where two seas met, they ran the ship aground; and the forepart stuck fast, and remained unmoveable, but the hinder part was broken with the violence of the waves.

42 And the soldiers' counsel was to kill the prisoners, lest any of them should swim out, and escape.

43 But the centurion, willing to save Paul, kept them from their purpose; and commanded that they which could swim should cast themselves first into the sea, and get to land:

44 And the rest, some on boards, and some on broken pieces of the ship. And so it came to pass, that they escaped all safe to land.

KEY VERSE

And so it came to pass, that they escaped all safe to land. —Acts 27:44

A LIVING FAITH

Unit 3: Where Does Faith Take Us?

LESSONS 10–13

LESSON AIMS

After participating in this lesson, each student will be able to:

1. Narrate the key events of Paul's shipwreck and survival.

2. Tell how Paul's faith sustained him and gave him influence over others on the ship in the midst of crisis.

3. Make a commitment to trust God even in times of crisis.

LESSON OUTLINE

Introduction

A. When You Least Expect It . . .

Do you like surprises? It depends on what kind of surprise, does it not? We like the surprise of finding money in the back of a drawer or discovering that our friends have thrown us a surprise birthday party. We do not like the surprise of learning that we have a serious illness or that a friend has passed away.

Sometimes the surprise is not in what happens, but in what it turns out to mean. A person might get the unhappy surprise of losing a job. But later that person may realize that the job loss led to something better. The first surprise may seem much different with a new perspective.

Today's text is about an event that was a surprise for some. But thanks to God's action, it was a surprise that turned out much differently from what anyone—except Paul—expected.

B. Lesson Background

Our text continues the story of Paul's imprisonment from last week's lesson. Having stood before Governor Festus, Paul was judged innocent of any crime. Paul nevertheless had to be sent to Rome for a hearing with the emperor, for which Paul had appealed (Acts 25:12; 26:32). That trip involved a sea voyage across the Mediterranean.

Sea travel in the ancient world was very dangerous. Even before the episode in today's lesson occurred, Paul reported that he had been shipwrecked three times (2 Corinthians 11:25). Ships of the day were small and dependent on the uncertain winds; navigation was crude and unreliable in bad weather. But the enticement to travel fast is always strong. Thus the decision was made for a sea voyage to Rome rather than an overland trip.

I. Sailing into Danger

(ACTS 27:1, 2)

As the account begins, Paul is every bit the prisoner, the least important man on the sailing vessel. By the end, Paul will effectively be in command. How that transformation takes place and what it means is the message of the text.

A. Destination (v. 1)

1. And when it was determined that we should sail into Italy, they delivered Paul and certain other prisoners unto one named Julius, a centurion of Augustus' band.

Paul is one of several prisoners under guard for delivery to Rome. These are in the custody of a Roman centurion, a leader with responsibility for as many as a few hundred soldiers. This centurion is a member of what is likely a distinguished cohort, since it is named for the famous emperor Caesar Augustus. Clearly, the military commander is the man in charge. Paul, by contrast, is at the bottom of the organizational chart. Or so it seems.

The forthcoming journey will be one of more than 1,300 miles as the crow flies. But ships do not sail as crows fly. To make the journey, the ship will take an irregular path to keep the coast in view for safety, making port whenever possible.

B. Departure (v. 2)

2. And entering into a ship of Adramyttium, we launched, meaning to sail by the coasts of Asia; one Aristarchus, a Macedonian of Thessalonica, being with us.

The journey starts in Caesarea (Acts 25:13), on the eastern coast of the Mediterranean Sea. Paul's ship will sail north along the coastline, then west along the southern coast of Asia Minor (modern Turkey). From the southwestern tip of Asia Minor, the journey will turn southwest toward Crete. The commander books passage for his prisoners on a ship whose home port is far away, for Adramyttium is on the northwest coast of Asia Minor.

HOW TO SAY IT

Adramyttium	Ad-ruh-*mitt*-ee-um.
Aristarchus	Air-iss-*tar*-cuss.
Caesar Augustus	*See*-zer Aw-*gus*-tus.
Caesarea	Sess-uh-*ree*-uh.
Emmaus	Em-*may*-us.
Festus	*Fes*-tus.
Macedonian	Mass-eh-*doe*-nee-un.
Mediterranean	*Med*-uh-tuh-**ray**-nee-un.
Thessalonica	*Thess*-uh-lo-**nye**-kuh (*th* as in *thin*).

We also learn that Paul is accompanied by friends. Aristarchus is likely one of Paul's converts from his preaching in Thessalonica (Acts 17:1-8; 19:29; 20:4). Also with Paul is Luke, the author of Acts, identified by the use of *us*. Of course, Paul is not alone in another sense: God is with him as well. God will assure the fulfillment of His promise that Paul will testify in Rome (Acts 23:11).

> *What Do You Think?*
> On what types of "journeys" is it especially useful to be accompanied by fellow believers? Why?
> *Talking Points for Your Discussion*
> - "Wilderness" journeys (retreats, etc.)
> - Short-term mission trips
> - Evangelistic calling
> - Other

II. Preparing for Landfall
(ACTS 27:33-40)

Paul's situation becomes dire in Acts 27:3-32 (not in today's text). Paul's first ship arrives safely in the southwest of Asia Minor. There the centurion books passage on a ship bound for Italy for the second leg of the journey. The journey becomes more difficult and dangerous as the ship faces contrary winds as it sails across the open sea to Crete.

Winter is approaching as the ship reaches Crete. Paul warns the centurion and the ship's officers that they will face the loss of the ship and the lives it carries if they sail farther (Acts 27:10). But less concerned with a warning from a mere prisoner than with getting to a suitable harbor for winter, those in charge decide to take one more short journey to another port in Crete. Quickly the ship is taken up in a violent storm. Driven by ferocious winds for 14 days, the crew takes desperate measures but still despairs of surviving.

In the midst of this crisis, Paul offers a message of assurance: God has sent an angel to him, reminding him of God's promise that Paul will reach Rome. An added promise is that none on the ship will be harmed, although they will run aground. As the situation unfolds, the sailors realize that the ship is nearing land as dawn approaches. They are in a perilous state. What should they do?

A. Evaluating the Situation (v. 33)

33. And while the day was coming on, Paul besought them all to take meat, saying, This day is the fourteenth day that ye have tarried and continued fasting, having taken nothing.

Having rightly warned of the danger that the ship now faces, Paul has earned respect from the ship's company. As he speaks, they have reason to listen. He urges all to have something to eat. The stress of the storm and the threat of death has prevented the ship's company from eating. But under God's guidance, Paul knows that they will soon need energy. Taking food will be an act of confidence in God's promise to save them and of thanksgiving for what God provides at all times.

B. Promising Protection (v. 34)

34. Wherefore I pray you to take some meat: for this is for your health: for there shall not an hair fall from the head of any of you.

Food, Paul says, will be important for everyone's survival. But the Greek word translated *health* points to something more. This word is commonly translated *salvation* in the New Testament. While it does not have the meaning of eternal salvation here, it does refer to the way that God is about to save the ship's crew and passengers from death in the sea.

Paul's affirmation *for there shall not an hair fall from the head of any of you* has its basis in the Old Testament (see 1 Samuel 14:45; 2 Samuel 14:11). It reminds us of Jesus' assurance of God's protection for His messengers (Luke 12:7). It is not chance or fate that will bring the crew and passengers to safety, but God himself. This deliverance will ultimately point everyone to the most important realization: that God offers salvation from something even more awful than death by shipwreck.

C. Pronouncing Blessing (v. 35)

35. And when he had thus spoken, he took bread, and gave thanks to God in presence of them all: and when he had broken it, he began to eat.

Paul, even though he is a lowly prisoner on the ship, now acts as host at the meal he encourages all to eat. The description reminds us of Jesus'

actions in feeding the multitude in the wilderness (Luke 9:16, 17), at the Last Supper (22:19), and in Emmaus after His resurrection (24:30). This is not an observance of the Lord's Supper, but it is still a meal with sacred significance. Paul invites the ship's passengers and crew to receive the food as God's gift, just as they are about to receive God's gift of an amazing deliverance from danger.

> **What Do You Think?**
> What are some ways we can or should pray when in the midst of a crisis?
> *Talking Points for Your Discussion*
> ▪ Economic (unemployment, etc.)
> ▪ Natural disaster
> ▪ Satanic influences
> ▪ Other

D. Receiving Encouragement (vv. 36, 37)

36. Then were they all of good cheer, and they also took some meat.

Paul's unusual invitation is accepted by all. They not only eat, but are heartened by his assurance. We see the ship's company accepting the notion that there is something unusual about the prisoner Paul, something to be taken very seriously.

> **What Do You Think?**
> What was a time when the way someone coped with a crisis served as a witness to help strengthen your faith?
> *Talking Points for Your Discussion*
> ▪ A church leader
> ▪ A neighbor
> ▪ A politician
> ▪ A young person

37. And we were in all in the ship two hundred threescore and sixteen souls.

The ship's company of 276 is considerable. Out of so many, how can not even one be lost if the ship runs aground in this terrible storm? Only God's protection can bring such an outcome. Out of so many, what is it that distinguishes Paul so that he has such extraordinary command of the situation? Only God's power.

E. Lightening the Load (v. 38)

38. And when they had eaten enough, they lightened the ship, and cast out the wheat into the sea.

The sailors have thrown things overboard throughout the storm to lighten the ship. They do this so that the ship will sail higher in the rough waters and not be swamped. The tackle (the ship's equipment, Acts 27:19) went first. But to this point, the occupants of the boat have kept their food. Even though they have not been eating it until now, it is necessary for survival. Now they jettison the remaining food supply, trusting Paul's assurance that they are about to reach land while losing the ship (27:22).

❧ *FLOTSAM OR JETSAM?* ❧

Flotsam and *jetsam* are technical words used to describe the legal status of goods that are found floating in the sea or that have washed ashore. *Flotsam* refers to goods that result from a shipwreck, but were not thrown overboard intentionally; since the original owner did not jettison the goods voluntarily, he or she still has legal rights to them. Thus anyone who finds flotsam cannot consider it "finders keepers."

Jetsam, on the other hand, refers to goods purposely jettisoned from a ship. Because the goods were thrown overboard intentionally, the owner of the goods forfeits rights of ownership to them.

At some point, each of us finds our Christian faithfulness threatened by some of the baggage of life (see Hebrews 12:1). When that happens, we must realize that such baggage will become either flotsam or jetsam—our choice. If we fail to deal with that baggage, it will become flotsam as a result of shipwrecked faith. The wise person realizes, however, that some baggage *must* be jettisoned for faithfulness to survive the storms of this world. The choice to jettison involves surrendering rights to ownership to that baggage—we don't even want it back. Are we willing to "throw overboard" things that may lead to spiritual death? —J. B. N.

F. Heading for Shore (vv. 39, 40)

39. And when it was day, they knew not the land: but they discovered a certain creek with

Visual for Lesson 11. *Use the modern images in three of these panels to start a discussion regarding ways that God keeps us safe in Him today.*

a shore, into the which they were minded, if it were possible, to thrust in the ship.

The immediately preceding events take place at night. With daylight, the crew sights land, but they do not recognize the shoreline. Expecting to be run aground as Paul has warned, they look for a place where the ship's passengers might make it safely to shore.

The crew spots an appropriate beach, which is the sense of the phrase *a certain creek with a shore.* A beach has a gentle slope to the sea floor. This will allow the ship to run aground without being smashed at once by impact with a steep underwater slope. Survivors can then make their way to land. Thus the crew decides to point the ship toward the beach, allow it to run aground, and then, with "every man for himself," swim for shore.

40. And when they had taken up the anchors, they committed themselves unto the sea, and loosed the rudder bands, and hoised up the mainsail to the wind, and made toward shore.

This verse represents the sailors' final steps in their desperate attempt to run the ship aground. First, they discard the anchors, which no longer serve the purpose they had in Acts 27:29. In the original language of the text, the expression translated *taken up the anchors* indicates throwing those items overboard.

The phrase *loosed the rudder bands* indicates that the rudder previously was tied down. This probably was done the night before to prevent the rudder's destruction by pounding waves. Now the rudder is needed for steering the ship to shore.

Finally, the sailors lift a sail into place. This lets the storm's strong winds carry the ship to the shore. It is an all-or-nothing move, but the sailors and their officers seem to be convinced that Paul's assurances are credible. After all, he had warned them of the storm before it happened. Paul's confidence during the storm's most desperate moments suggests that he has more than his own power to rely on.

III. Delivered Through Peril

(Acts 27:41-44)

We now reach a point of transition between sea and land, between peril and deliverance.

A. Running Aground (v. 41)

41. And falling into a place where two seas met, they ran the ship aground; and the forepart stuck fast, and remained unmoveable, but the hinder part was broken with the violence of the waves.

The ship now runs aground as Paul had predicted (Acts 27:26). The point of impact described as the meeting of *two seas* is a very literal rendering of a Greek word that refers to the higher sea bottom between two deeper pools. Today we refer to such a place as *a sandbar*.

With the front (bow) of the ship buried in the sand, the waves continue to beat against the back (stern) of the ship. Normally, such an impact would force the ship forward. But stuck in the sand as the ship is, the waves break the ship's stern to pieces. Now is the time to abandon ship and make for shore.

❧ Pride as Sandbar ❧

Ships buffeted by strong winds and waves on the open sea normally survive because they can give way to the forces exerted against them. However, if the ship becomes immobile—such as being stuck on a sandbar—there is no "give," and the pounding of the sea can be a very destructive force. This was the situation Paul's ship experienced.

Figuratively speaking, the same thing can happen to people. I have a friend who is a great guy, but he sometimes has the tendency to take an audacious position, speaking without careful thought. When questioned, even in a humorous tone, he may dig in and defend his position even when it becomes clear that the position is ridiculous. Once he has stated a position, he is unwilling to give it up. Other friends in our group then have a great deal of fun lampooning his position and his irrational defense of it.

Perhaps we can call this problem "getting stuck on the sandbar of pride." How common it is that pride precedes our fall as pride does not allow us to give way to the forces of reason!   —J. B. N.

B. Planning to Kill (v. 42)

42. And the soldiers' counsel was to kill the prisoners, lest any of them should swim out, and escape.

Roman soldiers are subject to severe punishment, even death, for failure to keep their prisoners in custody. Thus the soldiers decide to put the prisoners to death on the spot rather than risk their escape. Such a move is far too familiar to subjects of the Roman Empire, though it is exactly what they expect soldiers to do under the circumstances.

Paul has come thus far safely through the storm, just as he has come safely through the plots of his enemies in Jerusalem and the threats of his opponents throughout his missionary travels. Will this now be his end?

C. Escaping Safely (vv. 43, 44)

43. But the centurion, willing to save Paul, kept them from their purpose; and commanded that they which could swim should cast themselves first into the sea, and get to land.

Against conventional wisdom, the centurion orders the soldiers not to follow through in killing the prisoners. He has one reason: respect for Paul. Paul had warned of the storm before it happened, and he assured the ship's company of safety as the storm raged. The centurion must see that some divine power is at work in Paul. The commander does not want to enrage that power by harming the power's spokesman.

The centurion also prevents the deaths of the other prisoners. Paul has pledged that all will make it to safety (Acts 27:22); the centurion is determined to allow Paul's assurance to be fulfilled. So the centurion orders all—prisoners, soldiers, and sailors alike—to make for shore however they can. Those able to swim are to go first, to be followed by those who will make their way more slowly.

We now begin to see the full impact of Paul's influence. He began the journey as a prisoner, but now he, in effect, commands the centurion. Of course, this owes to something more than the power of Paul's personality. God has been at work, leading Paul safely to Rome and demonstrating divine power in the process.

> **What Do You Think?**
> What was a time when your behavior as a believer influenced the behavior of an unbeliever in a crisis? How did things turn out?
> *Talking Points for Your Discussion*
> - Positive effects
> - Negative effects

This part of the story offers certain parallels to Paul's imprisonment in Philippi. On that occasion and this, God does much more than simply deliver Paul from danger. He demonstrates His power to save in all respects (Acts 16:25-34).

44. And the rest, some on boards, and some on broken pieces of the ship. And so it came to pass, that they escaped all safe to land.

Those who cannot swim are ordered to use whatever buoyant materials they can find to aid their escape. Certainly, the wrecked ship provides plenty of such material!

The account of the fateful journey and shipwreck ends with a simple statement that all do indeed make it safely to land. Throughout the ordeal, Paul has affirmed that God has given him the warnings and the assurances. All that Paul has said, all that he has attributed to God, has happened. So the simple statement *they escaped all safe to land* is profound. It is a statement of God's power and faithfulness to fulfill His promises to save. If God can save a shipload of people from a storm, He can also save a sinner from eternal death.

> **What Do You Think?**
> What procedures or methods have you seen God use to deliver people from "the storms of life" today? How have these increased your faith?
> *Talking Points for Your Discussion*
> - God's working through the forces of nature
> - God's working through other people
> - Other

Conclusion

A. Protected Through, Not From

When Acts was written, many held Christianity in low esteem. Its message seemed absurd. It challenged the foundational beliefs of society. Christianity's leaders had been arrested, and some executed. It was spoken against everywhere. Paul's story as prisoner and victim of a shipwreck could reinforce that negative judgment. After all, if God were truly with Paul, then He surely would have protected him from imprisonment, let alone shipwreck, right?

What the telling of this story reveals is something very different, however. God was with Paul, not to protect him *from* imprisonment and shipwreck, but to protect him *through* those trials. God's strength is made perfect in weakness (2 Corinthians 12:9). Those who belong to Christ belong to Him by the power of the cross. God's people live in Christ and by Christ's power through episodes of suffering that are reminiscent of Christ's. Just as God triumphed in Jesus' resurrection, so He does in Paul's deliverance from shipwreck.

When Christians come through hard times by the power of God, they witness His triumph. A Christian's life is not easy, but it is victorious, thanks to the protection of our victorious God.

B. Prayer

Great God, we commit ourselves to Your protection. We thank You for every provision You give to allow Your victory to be made visible in us. In the name of the victorious Jesus; amen.

C. Thought to Remember

God is with us in storms.

INVOLVEMENT LEARNING

Some of the activities below are also found in the helpful student book, Adult Bible Class.
Don't forget to download the free reproducible page from www.standardlesson.com to enhance your lesson!

Into the Lesson

Display a map of the Mediterranean area during the time of Paul's travels; if such a map is not available, sketch one on the board. Recruit someone to deliver the following monologue as "Luke's story," written from Luke's perspective as a companion on Paul's journey to Rome, according to Acts 27:1-39.

"Aristarchus and I were 'along for the sail.' But it was no pleasure cruise of the Greek isles! We traveled close to two thousand miles on ships designed more for cargo than for people. Julius the centurion, the commander in charge, was at times a bit stubborn, but also kind. Certainly the winds were not so kind. Saltwater spray and rolling decks took their toll as we were swept along.

"Instead of packing it in for the winter when we should have, those in charge opted to press farther, contrary to Paul's warning of danger. A gentle wind seemed to whisper, 'Come! Come! I will see you safely to port.' It lied. A storm roared, 'Who dares to try my seas at this time of year? Only a fool!' We were battered for two uncertain weeks, scared for our lives every hour, day and night. Finally, Paul spoke the Spirit's comforting word: 'Eat. You will need strength to survive a shipwreck, but survive you will. My God has revealed it.' At morning's light, we saw the most beautiful thing: land! Praise God!"

Into the Word

Ask learners to look at Acts 27:1, 2, 33-44 (today's text) and decide how each of the following expressions relate to it. Wait for responses as you introduce each one. 1. "Rome or bust!"; 2. "not quite first-class accommodations"; 3. "too busy to eat"; 4. "no hair stylist needed"; 5. "a model of manners"; 6. "a good time for prayer"; 7. "casting bread upon the waters"; 8. "sink or swim . . . or float!"

Anticipated responses: 1. The trip was headed to Italy, more specifically to Rome. 2. Paul and others were transported as prisoners. 3. Everyone was so busy trying to stay alive for 14 terrible days that they did not eat properly, or at all. 4. Paul indicated not a hair on their heads would be lost, if they obeyed. 5. Paul "hosted" the meal as he encouraged everyone. 6. Paul demonstrated Christian faith as he prayed before the food was eaten. 7. After eating, the store of grain was thrown overboard. 8. Those who could swim swam; others grabbed pieces of the ship's wood and drifted ashore.

Next, distribute copies of the "Crisis Management" activity from the reproducible page, which you can download. Have learners work on this in small groups.

State: "False accusations and threats had put Paul into the hands of ungodly men. The resulting trip across the Mediterranean was therefore not of Paul's doing. He was subject to the will of others on board ship. His life and those of his companions were at risk. How did he react and act?" Expect learners to note his decisive but submissive nature, his kindness to all, and his use of prayer to calm and challenge. As this discussion winds down, do one of the following two options.

Into Life

Option 1: Distribute copies of the "I Told You So!" activity from the reproducible page. Have learners complete this in pairs or groups of three.

Option 2: Ask, "How do you respond when the foolishness or malevolence of others puts you at risk?" Consider these stimulus situations: 1. Your company's leadership makes foolish decisions, putting your company on the brink of failure. This could result in the loss of your job. 2. An emotionally unstable person sets fire to your house and causes major damage. 3. A jealous acquaintance spreads untrue rumors of marital infidelity on the part of your spouse, creating an atmosphere of suspicion.

Paul Survives a Shipwreck

PAUL MINISTERS ON MELITA

To Give Help
sewel/servant
INo conccact with
scipported by

2 whocorete

DEVOTIONAL READING: Ezekiel 34:11-16
BACKGROUND SCRIPTURE: Acts 28:1-10

ACTS 28:1-10

1 And when they were escaped, then they knew that the island was called Melita.

2 And the barbarous people shewed us no little kindness: for they kindled a fire, and received us every one, because of the present rain, and because of the cold.

3 And when Paul had gathered a bundle of sticks, and laid them on the fire, there came a viper out of the heat, and fastened on his hand.

4 And when the barbarians saw the venomous beast hang on his hand, they said among themselves, No doubt this man is a murderer, whom, though he hath escaped the sea, yet vengeance suffereth not to live.

5 And he shook off the beast into the fire, and felt no harm.

6 Howbeit they looked when he should have swollen,

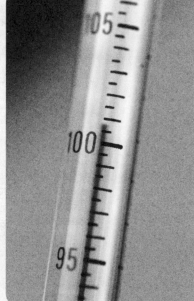

or fallen down dead suddenly: but after they had looked a great while, and saw no harm come to him, they changed their minds, and said that he was a god.

7 In the same quarters were possessions of the chief man of the island, whose name was Publius; who received us, and lodged us three days courteously.

8 And it came to pass, that the father of Publius lay sick of a fever and of a bloody flux: to whom Paul entered in, and prayed, and laid his hands on him, and healed him.

9 So when this was done, others also, which had diseases in the island, came, and were healed:

10 Who also honoured us with many honours; and when we departed, they laded us with such things as were necessary.

KEY VERSE

It came to pass, that the father of Publius lay sick of a fever and of a bloody flux: to whom Paul entered in, and prayed, and laid his hands on him, and healed him. —**Acts 28:8**

A Living Faith

Unit 3: Where Does Faith Take Us?

LESSONS 10–13

LESSON AIMS

After participating in this lesson, each student will be able to:

1. Tell some of Paul's activities on Melita.

2. Describe how adversity resulted in the advancement of God's kingdom on Melita.

3. Make a list of ways believers today can take advantage of adversity to advance the gospel.

LESSON OUTLINE

Introduction

A. Castaway: What Does It Mean?

People are fascinated by stories about castaways marooned on islands. *Robinson Crusoe* is considered a classic in this regard almost 300 years after it was written. American TV audiences in the 1960s watched the comedy *Gilligan's Island,* which depicted the experience in a deliberately unrealistic way. The 2000 movie *Cast Away* offered a serious depiction of the experience. More recently, global TV audiences tuned in to *Lost,* a complex tale about survivors on a mysterious island.

So which of these stories tells what it is really like to be a castaway? Probably none! But we do not need much imagination to put ourselves into the experience. Even the hardiest individual would find it a challenge to live as a castaway.

Today's text is one of the earliest accounts of castaways. It tells of events immediately after one of Paul's shipwrecks, as Paul and his shipmates found themselves on an unfamiliar island. To be sure, they were not castaways in the fullest sense of that word since they quickly were welcomed by the island's inhabitants. But the potential hardships and uncertainties were real.

B. Lesson Background

Last week's lesson focused on the details of Paul's sea journey to Rome, especially with regard to the storm that led to shipwreck. Thus the background for that lesson is the same as this one.

The new factor in today's lesson is an island called *Melita* in the *King James Version.* The island's modern name is *Malta.* It is a rocky island of about 120 square miles, located in the Mediterranean Sea. It is about 58 miles south of Sicily and some 500 miles west of Crete, from which Paul's ship had last set sail. While there is some uncertainty that the island named in the text is indeed the same as modern Malta, most of what we know about Malta fits the details of the story well.

Modern Malta, like many Mediterranean islands, is a popular tourist destination. Simply to mention a Mediterranean island today is to suggest an idyllic paradise. But the outlook in Paul's time was much different. Islands like Malta were isolated, far from the benefits of civilization. People did not vacation in such places. In fact, these places were often where the imperial government exiled enemies and prisoners (see Revelation 1:9).

Among pagans in Paul's time, a shipwreck was commonly understood as a sign of the gods' displeasure. Likewise for Bible-believing Jews, being the victim of a storm might appear to be a sign of God's wrath. After all, Jonah had famously been the victim of a storm that God sent. Was this the case for Paul, who emerged from the shipwreck to find himself on a remote island? Was the whole story of Paul's imprisonment, leading to this disastrous climax, an indication that Paul was God's enemy? What adversity meant for Paul lies at the very center of this story.

I. Warm Welcome
(ACTS 28:1, 2)
A. Island Refuge (v. 1)

1. And when they were escaped, then they knew that the island was called Melita.

The sailors had not recognized the land to which they fled from the storm (Acts 27:39, last week's lesson). Now they learn—probably as they communicate with the natives who find them on the beach—that they are on the island of Melita.

At this point, we should not mistake what the text is emphasizing. The term translated *were escaped* implies not just that Paul and the others managed their unlikely survival, but that someone —God, of course—has brought them safely through a perilous situation. We remember that Paul is safe because of God's action, not cursed because of hardships. Now the question is what will happen in this isolated place where the survivors find themselves.

HOW TO SAY IT

Barnabas	*Bar*-nuh-bus.
Crete	Creet.
Mediterranean	*Med*-uh-tuh-*ray*-nee-un (strong accent on *ray*).
Melita	*Mel*-i-tuh.
Publius	*Pub*-lih-us.

B. Native Hospitality (v. 2)

2. And the barbarous people shewed us no little kindness: for they kindled a fire, and received us every one, because of the present rain, and because of the cold.

The word *barbarous* does not mean that the inhabitants of the island are savages. Rather, it only implies that they do not speak the common Greek language and so are not the beneficiaries of Greco-Roman civilization. The word used to describe the kindness of the people comes across from Greek literally as our English word *philanthropy*. This implies that the response is generous and open-handed. The place may be isolated, but its natives prove hospitable to their unexpected visitors.

> *What Do You Think?*
> What was a time when you saw unbelievers act in a way that could serve as an example for believers to emulate? What did you learn from the experience?
> *Talking Points for Your Discussion*
> - In an emergency
> - In a nonemergency situation involving a one-time need
> - In a nonemergency situation involving an ongoing need

The first order of business is to build a fire. The storm, the time in the sea, and the continuing rain put the survivors in danger of hypothermia and death, thus the need for warmth. We recall that the tally of *us every one* is 276 (Acts 27:37). For the natives to be willing to help so many people is indeed generous! God is providing for Paul throughout his hardships, giving him just what he needs at just the time he needs it.

II. Deadly Situation
(ACTS 28:3-6)
A. Snake Attack (v. 3)

3. And when Paul had gathered a bundle of sticks, and laid them on the fire, there came a viper out of the heat, and fastened on his hand.

What happens next is notable, not just for the event itself, but especially for the way it is understood by the local people. It will begin to shape their view of Paul and his message.

Despite being one of the cold, wet, exhausted people for whom the fire is being built, Paul joins in the task of gathering wood for the fire. This demonstration of unselfish service is not the main focus however. A snake apparently has been asleep among the pieces of wood being gathered by Paul. As the cold-blooded creature is warmed when Paul puts the wood on the fire, it becomes active. Doubtlessly frightened, it latches onto Paul's hand.

The snake is referred to with a word translated *viper.* The term often (but not always) refers to venomous snakes. That point is controversial in this text, as there do not seem to be any venomous snakes on Malta today. It may be the case that venomous snakes were present in ancient times but died out later. But in this text what is important is not whether the snake is truly venomous, but how the bystanders perceive the snake and its significance.

B. Death Watch (vv. 4, 5)

4. And when the barbarians saw the venomous beast hang on his hand, they said among themselves, No doubt this man is a murderer, whom, though he hath escaped the sea, yet vengeance suffereth not to live.

A different Greek word is now used to identify the "viper" of verse 3 (above) as a *venomous beast.* The single word that is translated *venomous beast* is very common in the New Testament, being translated as "wild beast(s)" or simply "beast(s)" everywhere else (example: Acts 28:5, next). The idea that the snake is *venomous* thus apparently comes from the expectations of the local people.

As the event unfolds, the people begin to interpret the scene according to their view of the world. Many ancient peoples interpret unusual events as omens—signs indicating some unseen reality or some impending event (compare Jeremiah 10:2). In their understanding of the world as being governed by various gods with various realms of power, ancient pagans look for signs of the gods' will and actions. Thus the sudden, unexpected appearance of a snake is easily interpreted as a powerful omen.

These natives know that Paul had been aboard the ship as a prisoner. In the typical pagan view, the ship's fate in the storm can readily be seen as an omen of a god's disfavor on one of its passengers (compare Jonah 1). If the prisoner Paul is a murderer or other notorious criminal, then he may be the object of a god's anger.

The bystanders refer to the god they have in mind as *vengeance* (the modern English equivalent is *justice*). They believe in a god—or more likely a goddess—who governs the affairs of good and evil, bringing vengeful punishment through life's circumstances on those who do evil, thereby establishing a form of justice.

But ancient pagan deities are not thought to be almighty. The belief is that sometimes a god's actions can be foiled by clever humans or by other gods. In the view of the locals, Paul has escaped the hands of the goddess Vengeance by surviving the shipwreck. But now Vengeance has sent another avenger, a deadly snake, to slay the evildoer. The phrase *vengeance suffereth not to live* indicates that the local people believe that the goddess sentences Paul to death, and so she sends a snake to finish what the storm did not. This is the first conclusion of the bystanders, but it will not be their final answer. Their familiar interpretation of adversity is about to be modified.

5. And he shook off the beast into the fire, and felt no harm.

Paul's action when bitten by the snake is natural and instinctive: he shakes it off immediately. We assume that Paul then continues doing what he has been doing as he suffers *no harm.*

C. Attitude Change (v. 6)

6. Howbeit they looked when he should have swollen, or fallen down dead suddenly: but after they had looked a great while, and saw no harm come to him, they changed their minds, and said that he was a god.

We can imagine the bystanders waiting expectantly, anticipating with each passing moment that something bad will happen to Paul. But after *a great while,* they are forced to the conclusion that they have been wrong in their previous assumptions. Yet despite the errors of their conclusions in verse 4, the bystanders still believe that they know what all these events mean.

Their new conclusion is no less wrong: that because Paul suffers no harm from the snakebite, then he must be a god himself. Pagans of this time widely believe that the gods sometimes assume human form temporarily. In another instance, people witnessing Paul's healing of a lame man similarly concluded that Paul and Barnabas were gods, but Paul immediately corrected them (Acts 14:8-16). While the text before us does not mention him doing so here, we can be sure that Paul addresses the crowd's amazement, not just to correct their wrong belief about himself, but to introduce them to the true God whose power is at work in him.

What seem to be disasters for Paul are thus turning out quite differently. His shipwreck on a remote island leads to an eager welcome. Bitten by what seems to be a deadly snake, he proceeds unharmed. Each adverse event leads to something that provokes those around him to wonder what power is at work in Paul's life. Through the difficult circumstances that come into Paul's life, God provides repeated demonstrations of His power at work in the good news that Paul preaches.

Visual for Lesson 12. *Point to this visual as you ask the first discussion question that is associated with Acts 28:9.*

shore: *the same quarters* are the territories nearby. These are the possessions of the leading personage of Melita, a man named Publius.

To have landholdings indicates that he is highly influential on the island. The informal designation *chief man of the island* reinforces the picture of Melita as an out-of-the-way, loosely governed place. That Publius welcomes Paul and his friends as guests in his home shows that Paul has gained a good reputation on the island.

B. Healing His Father (v. 8)

8. And it came to pass, that the father of Publius lay sick of a fever and of a bloody flux: to whom Paul entered in, and prayed, and laid his hands on him, and healed him.

As the story continues, so do the adverse circumstances. But now the adversity is not Paul's but another's: Publius's father is ill with fever and severe intestinal distress, or dysentery *(bloody flux)*. Such conditions are common in the ancient world, given rudimentary sanitation.

Paul's actions have made clear that the islanders at the beach were mistaken about his being a god. The fact that Paul prays to God on behalf of Publius's father means that Paul is not exercising a power of his own, but is calling on God to exercise His almighty power. Laying hands on the afflicted man is a posture of prayer for God's blessing on this individual. All of Paul's actions show that the power at work belongs entirely to God, not to Paul

What Do You Think?

What was a time when you saw the circumstances and behavior of a believer modify the attitude of an unbeliever, for better or for worse? What lesson did you draw?

Talking Points for Your Discussion
- In the workplace or at school
- At church
- During a recreational activity
- Other

III. More Evidence
(ACTS 28:7, 8)
A. Staying with the Chief Man (v. 7)

7. In the same quarters were possessions of the chief man of the island, whose name was Publius; who received us, and lodged us three days courteously.

The setting for what happens next is the region near where Paul and his shipmates arrived on himself. The result is that the man is healed. God does not simply protect His servant Paul in his own adversity, but also empowers him to minister to others in their adversity.

❧ THE PERSONAL TOUCH ❧

The words *handiwork, handcrafted,* and *handmade* convey the idea of quality workmanship characterized by a personal touch. The phrase *mass produced,* by contrast, doesn't convey that same idea! "The personal touch" is important in so many areas. A nurse's touch can calm a patient. Sweethearts hold hands. A parent conveys comfort in holding a child during a time of distress.

Is it any wonder, then, that the touch of the hand carries religious significance? The process of consecration or ordination to ministry includes laying on of hands in New Testament times (1 Timothy 4:14) and often does so yet today. We still extend "the right hands of fellowship" (Galatians 2:9). Perhaps it was not strictly necessary for Paul to place his hands on Publius's father in order to heal him. But Paul apparently thought it was important to do so. Hands are the instruments we use to make a special connection with another person.

It is safe to assume that the father of Publius never forgot the personal touch of Paul. Remember: We are God's hands to touch lives in His work. A "mass produced Christianity" is a contradiction in terms. Who will feel the touch of God through your efforts today?   —J. B. N.

IV. Grateful Response
(ACTS 28:9, 10)
A. People Healed (v. 9)

9. So when this was done, others also, which had diseases in the island, came, and were healed.

When Jesus or one of His followers healed a person, word spread throughout the region. As a result, people brought their sick to the healer for similar help (Luke 4:40; 5:15; Acts 5:15, 16; 8:7, 8; 19:11, 12). Why God heals in some instances and not in others remains a mystery to the faithful. But in this episode, we can see the larger effect.

What Do You Think?
 What are some things our church is doing (or could do) to give people a chance to see our faith in action?
Talking Points for Your Discussion
 ▪ Meeting one-time local needs
 ▪ Meeting ongoing local needs
 ▪ Responding to emergencies or disasters

First with Publius's father, then with the larger number of other afflicted people, God makes His power visible. The most important outcome, however, is not that the sick are healed, but that the gospel now can receive a credible hearing. God's power at work in Paul has overwhelmed the people of Melita. Their worldview is overturned!

What Do You Think?
 What are some ways that hardship might confirm or challenge someone's worldview? How can we use such times as avenues to spread the gospel?
Talking Points for Your Discussion
 ▪ Physical suffering
 ▪ Economic hardship
 ▪ Estrangement or alienation
 ▪ Hardship caused by the actions of others

B. Honor Given (v. 10)

10. Who also honoured us with many honours; and when we departed, they laded us with such things as were necessary.

In response to the healings, the man who was first thought to be a murderer is now venerated along with his companions. That the people bestow *many honours* implies a particularly strong response of esteem. This esteem is more than words and handshakes as the people generously provide for the destitute shipwreck survivors as they depart.

Paul and his friends had washed up on shore with nothing. They now leave Melita well supplied by the populace, who give in gratitude and respect: The Maltese knew nothing of the true God when Paul arrived, let alone knowing anything about what God has provided through Jesus

Christ. Now they have an introduction. God in His providence certainly will bring more messengers to them in the future.

What Do You Think?
How did observing believers help you make your own decision to follow Jesus?
Talking Points for Your Discussion
- The witness of a family member
- The witness of a complete stranger
- The witness of a coworker
- The witness of a preacher

❧ THINGS NECESSARY ❧

What comes to mind when you read "they laded us with such things as were necessary"? Recently, we were visiting friends in another city, and we went with them to a pet store to get something for their dog. I found it hard to believe all the stuff that is available for pets! Many Americans spend more money annually on a pet than people in Third World countries spend for a household. In the autumn, I receive flyers in the mail advertising Halloween costumes, party favors, and similar stuff. Many of the costumes are for adults and cost as much as I would pay for a suit. The amount of disposable income Americans have is stunning.

When I was little, my family had few of the modern conveniences that are expected in households today. We got along without telephone, television, microwave ovens, air conditioning, even indoor plumbing. Today, social services would probably take children away from such a home. Things that were considered luxuries a few decades ago are now considered essential—think of power steering in our cars, cell phones, etc.

Yet if life came down to the bare essentials, how much of all this would we really think to be "necessary"? After Paul arrived in Rome, he wrote, "I know both how to be abased, and I know how to abound: every where and in all things I am instructed both to be full and to be hungry, both to abound and to suffer need" (Philippians 4:12). Perhaps that Scripture would be good to meditate on the next time we are tempted to bewail the lack of something we think is "necessary." —J. B. N.

Conclusion

A. God's Power at Work

We are all familiar with adversity. We may never have been shipwrecked, though some of us have probably been through circumstances just as harrowing. In the middle of those painful circumstances, we may wonder whether God will do anything to demonstrate His power in us. We may hope for something as dramatic as what God did with Paul.

Such dramatic deliverances do not always come, however. But we can be sure that God is no less at work in quieter ways. Remembering that the drama of Paul's experiences on Melita came after long months of imprisonment and two weeks of desperation at sea reminds us that God's ways and timing are not always as direct and immediate as we want for ourselves. But clearly or subtly, quickly or slowly, He brings glory to himself as His power works through the people who belong to Him.

Central to today's passage is what Paul's hardships meant. They were in no way signs of God's disfavor on him. Rather, they became occasions for God to demonstrate His power among His people. The God we serve is the God of the cross, who brings salvation to the world by taking the world's adversity on himself in the person of Jesus Christ. He calls His people to bring the good news of the gospel to all people, despite—and even through—difficult circumstances.

When we face tough times, we can and should call out to God for deliverance. But let us not forget also to offer ourselves to God as His servants in adversity. Let us ask God to use us in adversity as His witnesses, demonstrating His almighty power to a world that needs Him desperately.

B. Prayer

Almighty God, please teach us to rely on Your power when times are hard. We offer ourselves to You in both joy and pain so that Your power can be manifested in the earthen vessels of our lives. In the name of Jesus, who died for us; amen.

C. Thought to Remember

Expect God to work through adversity.

INVOLVEMENT LEARNING

Some of the activities below are also found in the helpful student book, Adult Bible Class.
Don't forget to download the free reproducible page from www.standardlesson.com to enhance your lesson!

Into the Lesson

Place in chairs the "Fallen . . . but He *Can* Get Up!" activity from the reproducible page, which you can download. Learners can work on this as they arrive.

As class begins, have this interjection on display: *HOW UNCIVILIZED!* Ask, "What comes to mind when you see this denunciation?" Let learners respond freely, anticipating that some will suggest wild, crude, even cruel behaviors. Then note: "The people of Melita (Malta) were outside the mainstream of Greco-Roman cultured civilization. But they certainly did not act uncivilized. Today's text pictures their extraordinary kindnesses as part of the tapestry of Paul's ministry on that island."

Into the Word

Say, "We're going to read the text through once, then have a closed-book True/False quiz. Ready? Listen carefully!" Have Acts 28:1-10 read. Provide paper and pencil for the quiz. Read the following (or you can put them on a handout).

1. Once the shipwreck victims came to shore, they found out the name of the island. 2. The island residents were at first very suspicious of the visitors. 3. Paul and the others immediately sprawled on the beach to dry out and warm up in the sun. 4. Paul, exhausted, watched the others gather wood for a bonfire. 5. God punished the centurion for his laziness by sending a snake to bite him. 6. The islanders thought Paul's misfortune was because he was some kind of criminal. 7. Paul reacted angrily and violently when the snake bit him. 8. At one point, the islanders thought Paul was a god. 9. The island's most important leader welcomed Paul and his companions into his home. 10. The fact that the father of the island's chief official was sick offered Paul an opportunity to show God's power. 11. While on the island, Paul's ministry included many acts of compassionate healing. 12. After salvaging provisions from their wrecked ship, Paul's group sailed once more toward Rome.

Answers: 1-T, verse 1; 2-F, verse 2; 3-F, verses 2, 3 ; 4-F, verse 3; 5-F, verse 3; 6-T, verse 4; 7-F, verse 5; 8-T, verse 6; 9-T, verse 7; 10-T, verse 8; 11-T, verse 9; 12-F, verse 10.

Say, "When Paul suffered no ill effect from the snakebite, the islanders thought him to be a deity. Actually, he was demonstrating the nature of the one true God. What do you see in Paul's behavior on Malta that reflects that nature?" Though learners may suggest other ideas, the following are certainly part of the answer: (1) Paul shows loving concern for his fellow travelers—good deeds for the physical welfare of others always reflect God's nature; (2) Paul's healing of the father of Publius demonstrates the power of God and His compassion; (3) Paul's patience and persistence as many came to be healed reflects God's patience.

Into Life

Say, "Paul always seemed to be able to use difficult circumstances as opportunities for revealing the power of God and the good news of the gospel. What occasions come to mind when I say that?" Allow discussion. Certainly, readers will recall recently studied events such as Paul's appearance before Festus and Agrippa and last week's prayer and admonitions at the end of the two-week storm. Be sure attention is given to the events of today's study, as the shipwreck and being stranded in the middle of nowhere still provide occasions of healing and, no doubt, preaching.

As the discussion winds down, ask for examples of modern missionaries who also have used difficult circumstances to advance the gospel. These two discussions will set the stage for learners to think of ways to do likewise. Promote this final discussion by distributing copies of the "The Christian Meets Adversity" activity from the reproducible page, which you can download.

PAUL EVANGELIZES
IN ROME

DEVOTIONAL READING: Deuteronomy 4:32-40
BACKGROUND SCRIPTURE: Acts 28:11-31

ACTS 28:16, 17, 23-31

16 And when we came to Rome, the centurion delivered the prisoners to the captain of the guard: but Paul was suffered to dwell by himself with a soldier that kept him.

17 And it came to pass, that after three days Paul called the chief of the Jews together: and when they were come together, he said unto them, Men and brethren, though I have committed nothing against the people, or customs of our fathers, yet was I delivered prisoner from Jerusalem into the hands of the Romans.

· ·

23 And when they had appointed him a day, there came many to him into his lodging; to whom he expounded and testified the kingdom of God, persuading them concerning Jesus, both out of the law of Moses, and out of the prophets, from morning till evening.

24 And some believed the things which were spoken, and some believed not.

25 And when they agreed not among themselves, they departed, after that Paul had spoken one word, Well spake the Holy Ghost by Esaias the prophet unto our fathers,

26 Saying, Go unto this people, and say, Hearing ye shall hear, and shall not understand; and seeing ye shall see, and not perceive:

27 For the heart of this people is waxed gross, and their ears are dull of hearing, and their eyes have they closed; lest they should see with their eyes, and hear with their ears, and understand with their heart, and should be converted, and I should heal them.

28 Be it known therefore unto you, that the salvation of God is sent unto the Gentiles, and that they will hear it.

29 And when he had said these words, the Jews departed, and had great reasoning among themselves.

30 And Paul dwelt two whole years in his own hired house, and received all that came in unto him,

31 Preaching the kingdom of God, and teaching those things which concern the Lord Jesus Christ, with all confidence, no man forbidding him.

KEY VERSE

Be it known therefore unto you, that the salvation of God is sent unto the Gentiles, and that they will hear it. —**Acts 28:28**

A Living Faith

LESSONS 10–13

LESSON AIMS

After participating in this lesson, each student will be able to:

1. Tell how Paul ministered to others during his first imprisonment in Rome.

2. Explain why God's Word causes division among people, as it did when Paul preached it.

3. Discuss when divisions among people are the result of rejecting God's Word and when it results from improper teaching of God's Word—and how to know the difference.

LESSON OUTLINE

Introduction

A. Learning from Losses

Some time ago, a high school girls' basketball team refused to appear for the second half of its game. The reason was that they were already more than 50 points behind and did not want to face further humiliation. Certainly we can all identify with that feeling. No one likes to lose. Even though we identify graciousness in defeat as a sign of good sportsmanship, we all know that winning is more fun than losing.

In some games, the rules specifically allow a person who is behind to call it quits. A chess player can choose to resign, conceding the game to the opponent. However, chess teachers recommend that young players not resign. The saying is, "No one ever learned anything by resigning." In athletics, politics, and business, many would give similar advice: it is important to learn as much as we can from losses, so don't give up. A defeat (or seeming defeat) now may lead to a greater victory later.

As followers of Jesus, we want nothing more than for everyone to know Him as we do. But the harsh reality is that many who hear the gospel reject it. To us, that seems like defeat—not just ours, but God's as well. Today's text is about just such a situation. Paul, the great missionary of first-century Christianity, had arrived in Rome, the capital of the greatest empire of ancient times. He was in chains, which makes the casual observer think of his presence there as a defeat. Our text invites us to look closely at that issue.

B. Lesson Background

Today's text concludes three key layers of biblical narrative. First, it is the conclusion of the apostle Paul's story in Acts, especially the story of his imprisonment. Paul's imprisonment had to have been a shock to early Christians, a scandal that threatened to discredit Christianity. After all, how could God be with Paul if He allowed that apostle to be taken prisoner and tried by Rome?

Second, this story concludes the account of the first-century church in the book of Acts. The church was opposed by powerful forces, especially

Jewish religious leaders. That fact raises a question: Who truly speaks for God—the established religious leaders or the followers of Jesus?

Third, this story concludes Luke's account of God's activity in Jesus and His first-century followers. Luke wrote both the Gospel that bears his name and the book of Acts; these are designed to be a two-volume work (see Acts 1:1, 2). From the beginning of Jesus' ministry, He had demonstrated power and authority that belongs to God alone. He was believed by some, but rejected by many. Like Jesus, the church experiences both the acceptance of the message and its rejection. The books of Luke and Acts aim to help readers understand what that rejection means.

I. Arrival in Rome
(ACTS 28:16, 17)
A. Quarters (v. 16)

16. And when we came to Rome, the centurion delivered the prisoners to the captain of the guard: but Paul was suffered to dwell by himself with a soldier that kept him.

As today's text opens, Paul is under house arrest in Rome. There he awaits his hearing before the Roman emperor, for which he had appealed months before (Acts 25:11). A prisoner might have to wait as long as two years for such a hearing, waiting for the accusers to arrive.

The Romans treat Paul with a respect not given to the other prisoners who made the voyage with him. Only Paul is *suffered to dwell by himself.* This arrangement is entirely beneficial to Paul: the word *suffered* here simply means "allowed" and in no way implies a negative experience for Paul. He is allowed to rent private quarters (Acts 28:30) and

HOW TO SAY IT

Abraham	*Ay-*bruh-ham.
Caesar	*See-*zer.
diaspora	dee-*as-*puh-ruh.
Gentiles	*Jen-*tiles.
Isaiah	Eye-*zay-*uh.
Messiah	Meh-*sigh-*uh.
Niemöller	*Nee-*muhl-uhr.

live there under guard, receiving as many guests as he chooses.

As Paul's imprisonment in Rome begins, we see that it is no ordinary imprisonment. Although the book of Acts does not mention it, Paul uses this time to write letters to churches he has established. It is likely that he writes Ephesians, Philippians, Colossians, and Philemon while in custody in Rome, about AD 63.

What Do You Think?

What are some ways a Christian with limited opportunity or means can still help advance the gospel?

Talking Points for Your Discussion

- A shut-in
- A person on a fixed or temporary income
- A person caring for an elderly parent
- Other

B. Visitors (v. 17)

17. And it came to pass, that after three days Paul called the chief of the Jews together: and when they were come together, he said unto them, Men and brethren, though I have committed nothing against the people, or customs of our fathers, yet was I delivered prisoner from Jerusalem into the hands of the Romans.

Throughout his missionary journeys, Paul begins his preaching with a Jewish audience wherever one is to be found. He is himself a Jew, so he has a natural connection with his kinsmen. Paul calls the gospel God's power for salvation "to the Jew first, and also to the Greek" (Romans 1:16). Paul likely sees his pattern of preaching "to the Jew first" as befitting God's promise to send Israel a great kinsman-redeemer who will not only bless Israel, but ultimately all the nations.

So Paul follows the same pattern of preaching while he is in Rome. Rome's population includes a considerable number of Jews. From the close of the Old Testament forward, Jewish people scatter throughout the lands that eventually comprise the Roman Empire. The term *diaspora,* meaning "scattering," is commonly used to refer to these Jewish expatriates.

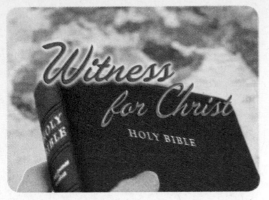

Visual for Lesson 13. *Point to this visual as you ask learners to make lists of things that promote and hinder our Christian witness. Discuss.*

Paul asks for and receives a visit from the leading Jews of Rome: *chief* here means "first" and refers to a group of several prominent people. Paul explains to them the circumstances that have led to his imprisonment. Falsely accused of undermining Israel's laws and traditions (Acts 24:12, 13; 25:8), Paul in fact has been preaching that Israel's most sacred hope is fulfilled in Jesus.

❦ *UNJUST IMPRISONMENTS* ❦

Martin Niemöller (1892–1984) was a German naval officer in the First World War. He rose through the ranks to command his own U-boat (submarine). For his naval exploits, he was awarded the Iron Cross First Class. He resigned his commission after the war and went into the ministry of the Lutheran churches in Germany.

An ardent nationalist, Niemöller initially supported the Nazis as Hitler came to power in 1933. When the Nazi ideology became obvious, Niemöller helped form the "Confessing Church" in opposition (see the conclusion to Lesson 6). He was arrested in 1937 as a result, ending up first in jail then in concentration camps until 1945.

Niemöller could say, with Paul, that he had never done anything against his people. Nevertheless, he joined countless others who ended up being punished unfairly for promoting Christian ideals. Persecution of Christians to the point of martyrdom still exists today. How will this fact affect your prayer life this week?   —J. B. N.

II. Meeting with Jewish Leaders
(ACTS 28:23, 24)
A. Gospel Presentation (v. 23)

23. And when they had appointed him a day, there came many to him into his lodging; to whom he expounded and testified the kingdom of God, persuading them concerning Jesus, both out of the law of Moses, and out of the prophets, from morning till evening.

In verses 18-20 (not in today's text), Paul continues his summary of the reason for his imprisonment. Although judged *not guilty* by Roman officials, it is his appeal to Caesar that has brought him to this point. The Jewish leaders respond that they want to hear more. They have heard of the Christian movement but know it only from negative reports (vv. 21, 22).

So Paul and the Jewish leaders set an appointment for discussion on a later day. When that day comes, the leaders bring with them a larger group of interested Roman Jews. While Acts does not give us Paul's speech, we can infer from the summary here that it is similar to the testimony in earlier speeches in Acts when Paul interacts with Jews.

The Jewish people know their Scriptures well, and they live in anticipation of God's fulfilling the promise of a Messiah. Thus it is natural for Paul to draw heavily on *both . . . the law of Moses, and . . . the prophets* in his explanation. This is not the approach Paul took in preaching to pagan philosophers of Acts 17:16-34. Paul tailors his approach to his audience.

Paul's message is about *the kingdom of God*. This is a key phrase in the New Testament. It refers to the fulfillment of God's promise to rule over the world so that His will is done "in earth, as it is in heaven" (Matthew 6:10). Jesus is the king of God's kingdom, exercising divine power in His miracles, asserting divine authority in His teaching, and finally ascending to rule at God's right hand. Jesus had fulfilled God's promise by His death, resurrection, and ascension.

These truths, Paul asserts, fulfill everything that God has promised in Israel's Scriptures. God promised to bless all the nations through Abraham's seed (Genesis 22:18), to send a prophet who

Paul Evangelizes in Rome

speaks to God face-to-face (Deuteronomy 18:18, 19; 34:10-12), and to rule through a king who will build God's true house (1 Chronicles 17:11-14). The result will be the defeat of evil kingdoms that rule this present age, establishing God's righteous, eternal rule (Daniel 7:13, 14).

These promises, woven throughout Scripture, are now fulfilled in Jesus. He is the seed of Abraham who blesses the nations (Acts 3:25), the prophet like Moses who speaks to God face-to-face (3:22, 23), the great son of David who rules forever (2:29-35), the Son of Man who establishes God's righteousness (7:56).

The debate is vigorous, lasting *from morning till evening.* Clearly, the message of Jesus is no less controversial in Rome than it is elsewhere.

B. Mixed Reception (v. 24)

24. And some believed the things which were spoken, and some believed not.

As always, Paul's aim in his presentation is not so much to defend himself as it is to persuade his listeners to put their faith in Jesus. His aim is fulfilled with some, as part of his audience departs believing the gospel.

But another part of the audience does not believe. The audience is divided sharply. Such is the case across the two-volume storyline of Luke and Acts. Meeting Jesus personally, some believe enthusiastically (Luke 5:18-20) while others bitterly reject Him (Luke 5:21). Thousands believe when the apostles preach the gospel message (Acts 4:4), but the Jewish leaders reject the message and persecute the church (Acts 4:1-3). The same is true throughout Paul's own ministry: in city after city, some believe while others reject the message and persecute the messengers (Acts 17:4, 5).

III. Responding to Rejection
(ACTS 28:25-29)

A. What Is Happening (vv. 25, 26)

25. And when they agreed not among themselves, they departed, after that Paul had spoken one word, Well spake the Holy Ghost by Esaias the prophet unto our fathers.

Paul reacts to the division that the gospel again provokes by introducing a quotation from Isaiah 6:9, 10. Jesus used this passage to explain the division that He himself had provoked (Luke 8:10). Generations before, Isaiah (Esaias) had warned his own audience of the consequences of rejecting God's message. The same consequences now face Paul's audience.

26. Saying, Go unto this people, and say, Hearing ye shall hear, and shall not understand; and seeing ye shall see, and not perceive.

Isaiah records God's warning about the rejection that his message was to receive. God predicted misunderstanding and disbelief while clearly implying that He truly desires repentance. God and messenger are faithful in delivering the message that contains both the promise of salvation and the warning of judgment. In hearing God's message, some will harden themselves against it.

B. Why It Is Happening (v. 27)

27. For the heart of this people is waxed gross, and their ears are dull of hearing, and their eyes have they closed; lest they should see with their eyes, and hear with their ears, and understand with their heart, and should be converted, and I should heal them.

Ultimately, people's failure to believe is not the failure of the message or of the messenger, let alone of God. It is, rather, the hearer's own failure. The text pictures every part of the listener as insensitive. The heart is the figurative seat of the will; it has become unresponsive, the meaning of *waxed gross.* Likewise, the ears and eyes are closed off from the truth (compare Acts 7:57). Were it otherwise, the hearers would believe and so receive salvation, a figurative healing from God.

All this is stated with supreme irony, as if God wants no part in saving His people. But that irony is clear, for why would God give a message of salvation if He does not want it to be believed? In the end, the irony emphasizes how foolish it is to reject God's offer.

Of course, not everyone in Isaiah's day failed to believe. But Isaiah focused on those who did not believe in a last-ditch appeal for them to repent. The same is true of Paul's quotation of Isaiah. He aims to touch the hearts of the unpersuaded by using a familiar, sacred text to warn them.

> ### What Do You Think?
> What things in our culture tend to clog people's ears to the message of the gospel? How do we break through these barriers?
>
> *Talking Points for Your Discussion*
> - Ezekiel 33:30-32
> - Matthew 13:22
> - John 6:60-66
> - John 11:48
> - John 12:42, 43

C. Where It Leads (vv. 28, 29)

28. Be it known therefore unto you, that the salvation of God is sent unto the Gentiles, and that they will hear it.

Concluding, Paul implies that those who reject the gospel may think that they have thereby thwarted its progress. Not so! God will continue to send His saving Word to all people, so that all people can have the chance to hear and respond.

> ### What Do You Think?
> What are some things people do that hinder the spread of the gospel today? How do we recognize and counteract these influences?
>
> *Talking Points for Your Discussion*
> - Intentional hindrances by unbelievers
> - Unintentional hindrances by believers

Several details of Paul's words contribute to this message. One is the word that is translated *salvation* from original language. Though the concept of salvation is very common in the New Testament, the Greek word here is found only three times in this particular form in the New Testament (see Luke 2:30; 3:6). In all three instances, God's promise to bring salvation to all nations is emphasized. Thus Paul is reminding his Jewish audience of a key promise of God: when God fulfills His promises, it is not just Israel that benefits. The whole world is offered salvation.

Paul responded to a divided Jewish audience with a similar warning twice before (Acts 13:46; 18:6). In both cases, he also announced that he was turning to the Gentiles, yet he never stopped preaching to Jews. His words are a provocation—that "outsiders" will be included in God's salvation while many of those to whom it is first sent will be left out (compare Matthew 21:31).

Christians sometimes read these passages as indicating that the Jews as a whole reject the gospel while non-Jews (Gentiles) are inherently more receptive. This is far from the truth. Virtually all the prominent leaders of the first-century church are Jews. Israel as a whole does not reject Jesus. But certainly Israel is divided in its response to Jesus.

God's message always provokes division (Luke 12:51-53). Still, God is taking back His world through the gospel despite the rejection. Even though some reject the gospel, God's purpose to have a people for himself is nevertheless fulfilled in those who do believe.

29. And when he had said these words, the Jews departed, and had great reasoning among themselves.

This verse does not appear in the earliest Greek manuscripts of Acts. Even so, it depicts what is undoubtedly the case: a divided Jewish company vigorously discussing the merits of Paul's message as they depart.

❧ HOW FAR DO YOU LISTEN? ❧

The Jews stopped listening when Paul said God would send the gospel to the Gentiles. The same thing happened earlier at the temple. The Jews there shouted Paul down when he said he was sent to the Gentiles (Acts 22:21, 22). Both audiences stopped listening when they were offended. Don't we all do that at times? I have known of people who walked out during a sermon when the preacher started talking about their pet sins. Anger started, and listening stopped.

People stop listening for reasons other than anger. I read an article by a mother who had been talking with her son about a difficulty at school. The son mentioned numerous incidents of the teacher's nagging him. The mother was about to call the principal and complain about the teacher when the son said, "And then I realized I really wasn't paying attention, just like the teacher said."

What causes you to pay less attention to the Bible than you should? Do its words offend you? Do you allow less important things to distract you? Just how far do you listen?   —J. B. N.

IV. Preaching to All
(ACTS 28:30, 31)
A. Duration (v. 30)

30. And Paul dwelt two whole years in his own hired house, and received all that came in unto him.

Though lasting *two whole years*, Paul's imprisonment is not much of a limitation. He is allowed to receive visitors, with whom he can share the gospel freely. Paul's teaching of everyone who comes to see him results in a gospel witness to "all the palace" (Philippians 1:13) and "Caesar's household" (4:22). We can imagine that those assigned to guard Paul in his quarters had no idea what they would receive from the one they guarded!

> **What Do You Think?**
> What can we do to make people want to come to us to hear the gospel?
> *Talking Points for Your Discussion*
> - In the workplace
> - At school
> - Among relatives

Two years may be the legal limit that the Emperor's court will wait for Paul's accusers to appear and make their case. Their failure to appear

may mean that Paul is released in about AD 63. If this is so, Paul is certainly arrested again later, to be executed in AD 67 or 68 (2 Timothy 4:6-18). Some think that Paul is tried and executed at the end of the imprisonment of today's text. Either way, the author of Acts does not tell us. The author emphasizes other issues instead. Our primary attention needs to be on those.

B. Message (v. 31)

31. Preaching the kingdom of God, and teaching those things which concern the Lord Jesus Christ, with all confidence, no man forbidding him.

Confidence or boldness of gospel preaching appears repeatedly in Acts, emphasizing the courage that the Holy Spirit supplies to believers (see Acts 4:13, 29, 31; 9:27; 13:46; 14:3; 18:26; 19:8). At the end of the story, Paul the prisoner continues to display this same power. The final expression *No man forbidding him* is also the last word in the book of Acts. We hardly expect a prisoner to be described as unhindered, but that is Paul's actual condition. His imprisonment is but another means by which he preaches the gospel.

Conclusion
A. Never Lose Hope

There has never been a time when people received God's Word easily. We should not be surprised when, like Paul, we see the gospel message rejected. But neither should we lose hope. The rejection of the gospel does not surprise God. He warns us to expect it. Despite that rejection, God fulfills His purpose among those who *do* receive His Word. As with Paul, God's Spirit empowers each of us to be bold in our testimony despite rejection and hardships.

B. Prayer

Lord, help us testify even when Your message is rejected. We know Your will is still accomplished among those who believe. In Jesus' name; amen.

C. Thought to Remember

Rejection doesn't mean failure.

INVOLVEMENT LEARNING

Some of the activities below are also found in the helpful student book, Adult Bible Class.
Don't forget to download the free reproducible page from www.standardlesson.com to enhance your lesson!

Into the Lesson

As each learner arrives, hand him or her a small card designed to resemble a boarding pass with this wording: *"Faith Express"; Departure: Today; Destination: _____; Arrival: As Planned (and Unplanned).* As you distribute the boarding passes, say, "Here's the ticket you will need today!"

As class begins, note that this concluding unit of lessons asks, "Where does faith take us?" Relate that question to the last three studies and today's study. Stress: "We may never stand before an important official to speak for our Lord; we may never endure a life-threatening experience at sea; we may never end up on an isolated island. But our faith surely will take us to challenging places! Today's study pictures the way Paul met the challenges and presents that same possibility for us."

Into the Word

Read aloud Acts 28:16, 17, 23-31 or have your learners read it. Then distribute copies of the "Some Believe and Some Don't" activity from the reproducible page, which you can download. Ask learners to take about three minutes to fill out the "Paul in Rome" column, but leave the "Today" column uncompleted. After learners finish, form them into groups of three to have them compare and contrast their responses. After no more than eight minutes, discuss results as a whole class. The ensuing discussion may be lively!

Next, point out that in Acts 28:20, a verse not included in today's printed text, Paul uses two important phrases: "the hope of Israel" and "bound with this chain." Ask, "What does he mean by the phrase *hope of Israel*?" (This, of course, is the grand theme of the Old Testament: that God will provide a new and better King David, the Messiah.)

Prepare in advance about 20 strips of paper measuring about 1" x 8"; if possible, have these cut from silvery-gray paper. (Two ordinary sheets of 8½" x 11" paper can be cut into this approximate number.) Show everyone that you are writing the words *hope* and *chain* on one strip.

Say, "There's something about these two words that seem to conflict; they don't seem to go together." Have an associate standing by to take the strip and tape it into a loop that will be the first link in a chain. Now ask the class to read through the verses of the text and look for other ideas (either words or phrases) that don't seem to go together. As each pair is suggested, write them onto a strip and have your associate make it into a loop while connecting it to the previous one, forming a lengthening chain.

Possible discoveries are verse 17, "have committed nothing" yet "delivered [as a] prisoner"; verse 26a, "hear" and "not understand"; verse 26b, "seeing" and "not perceive." Hold up the completed chain and ask, "In what ways are these tensions still with us today?" Allow discussion.

Into Life

Have learners return to the "Some Believe and Some Don't" activity and fill out the "Today" column. After a few minutes ask, "Why is it true that when the word is preached and taught today, some believe and some don't?" The wording of the activity will provide discussion starters.

Also ask, "At what point is the Christian free to stop teaching when the message is rejected?" Make sure to deal with Mark 6:11 and Acts 18:6 in the ensuing discussion. Also stress that rejection of the gospel by any given unbeliever may call for a great deal of discernment in the way we approach that person again at a later date. Make the point that Paul's persistence in the worst of circumstances is the model for us. Rejection doesn't make the message untrue.

As learners depart, distribute copies of the "Where Does Faith Take You?" activity from the reproducible page as a take-home exercise.

JESUS IS
LORD

Special Features

Lessons

Unit 1: Victory in Jesus

Unit 2: Exalting Christ

Unit 3: Imitating Jesus

QUARTERLY QUIZ

Use these questions as a pretest or as a review. The answers are on page iv of This Quarter in the Word.

Lesson 1

1. In Christ, the mystery of God's _____ has been made known. *Ephesians 1:9*

2. Paul promises that believers have been "sealed" with the Holy Spirit. T/F. *Ephesians 1:13*

Lesson 2

1. As a "wall breaker," Christ serves as our what? (prophet, hope, peace?) *Ephesians 2:14*

2. Regarding the foundation of the church, Christ is the chief ____ ____. *Ephesians 2:20*

Lesson 3

1. Paul encourages the Ephesians to maintain the _____ of the Spirit. *Ephesians 4:3*

2. As we work in ministry, we are to edify the body of Christ. T/F. *Ephesians 4:12*

Lesson 4

1. The Gospel of John teaches us that all things were created by the Word of God. T/F. *John 1:1-3*

2. Paul describes things done in secret as what? (good, shameful, mysterious?) *Ephesians 5:12*

Lesson 5

1. Paul contrasts being Spirit-filled with being what? (drunk, asleep, bored?) *Ephesians 5:18*

2. As husbands love their wives, they should hate themselves. T/F. *Ephesians 5:28*

Lesson 6

1. While some preached Christ out of good will, others did so out of what wrong motivation? (greed, fear, envy?) *Philippians 1:15*

2. No one wanted to cause Paul trouble while he was a prisoner in Rome. T/F. *Philippians 1:16*

Lesson 7

1. Paul told the Philippians that Christ becoming human meant He took on what role? (king, servant, prophet?) *Philippians 2:7*

2. At the name of Jesus, every knee should _____. *Philippians 2:10*

Lesson 8

1. Paul was from the tribe of _____. *Philippians 3:5*

2. Paul's life before becoming a Christian was marked by serious violations of the Jewish laws. T/F. *Philippians 3:6*

Lesson 9

1. Paul kept pressing toward the _____ for the prize in his calling in Christ. *Philippians 3:14*

2. Paul warned of those whose god was their belly. T/F. *Philippians 3:19*

Lesson 10

1. Christ is the firstborn from the what? (mountain, Sanhedrin, dead?) *Colossians 1:18*

2. The fullness of God is to be found in Christ. T/F. *Colossians 1:19*

Lesson 11

1. Having received Christ, we are to do what in Him? (walk, run, shut our eyes?) *Colossians 2:6*

2. According to Paul, all circumcision involves cutting by human hands. T/F. *Colossians 2:11*

Lesson 12

1. Paul identifies *covetousness* with what? (cursing, idolatry, just being lazy?) *Colossians 3:5*

2. Paul advises Christians not to be too quick to forgive each other because they might be tricked. T/F. *Colossians 3:13*

Lesson 13

1. Our speech should be as if seasoned with what? (pepper, coriander, salt?) *Colossians 4:6*

2. Luke, one of Paul's companions, was of what profession? (physician, tentmaker, rabbi?) *Colossians 4:14*

QUARTER AT A GLANCE

by Jon Weatherly

WE LIKE to have an accustomed order to our lives, don't we? But upside-down events happen. Job loss, illness, family conflict, disappointment with others, grief—these life-scramblers are just that. How do we make sense of a scrambled life? Is anyone really in charge when life seems out of kilter?

That question confronted first-century Christians when the apostle Paul was jailed. It's easy to picture believers questioning what that meant. Paul was God's spokesman. Had God abandoned him? Were the opponents of Christianity right after all?

This quarter's lessons are taken from letters that Paul wrote while in prison. Each addresses the question raised by Paul's imprisonment: *Who is in charge when life is scrambled?* For Paul, the answer was clear: despite appearances, Jesus Christ is Lord of all.

Unit 1: Victory in Jesus

Paul's letter to the Ephesians portrays Jesus as Lord in cosmic terms. Before God created the world, His plan was for Christ to gather God's people, the church (Lesson 1). That means that the church, with all its ups and downs, is the true temple of God, where God's Spirit dwells (Lesson 2).

Thus we are to live in unity, pursuing God's purpose and overcoming our differences (Lesson 3). Christmas reminds us that because Christ is the eternal Word of God who gives light, we are compelled to live in His truth and light (Lesson 4). As Christ gave himself for us, His followers are to submit to one another (Lesson 5).

Unit 2: Exalting Christ

That matter of positioning ourselves as servants of others is crucial—and difficult. Paul devotes much of his letter to the Philippians to this topic. His own imprisonment is a shining example. It seems like a humiliation and loss for him, but it really means the advancement of the gospel (Les-

son 6). That seems like an upside-down way of looking at the world, but it is based on the truth that the divine Christ humbled himself to give His life in death by crucifixion (Lesson 7). That makes every other claim of importance to be of no importance at all: Christ is everything (Lesson 8). So the real aim in life is to pursue humble service like Christ's, with a zeal that ignores every competing claim for our allegiance (Lesson 9).

Unit 3: Imitating Jesus

Competing claims can be attractive, however. Paul's letter to the Colossians reminds readers to reject add-ons or substitutes for the lordship of Christ. He is the supreme God who died and arose to make us His (Lesson 10). He has given us every blessing that God has promised, gifts greater than anything available elsewhere (Lesson 11). So the person who knows Him will not just *believe* differently but *live* differently—with the mercy and love that Christ has shown (Lesson 12). That will make for a life focused and disciplined in hab-

> **Despite appearances, Jesus Christ is Lord of all.**

its and relationships, even when life seems to be scrambled (Lesson 13).

Seeing Life As It Is?

When life is "normal," we may think that conventional wisdom is all we need. When the conventional order falls apart, in our desperation we have nowhere to turn but to Christ. So in the end, maybe we have our best opportunity to see life as it is when life seems to be scrambled.

This quarter challenges us to live with Christ on the throne all the time, whether life comes to us normal or scrambled. Can we see through our circumstances to glimpse His glory?

GET THE SETTING

by Mark S. Krause

TODAY'S RELIGIOUS landscape is bewildering. That fact was no less true for the time of the New Testament. As the apostle Paul traveled and spread the gospel, he encountered many different religious beliefs. Consider two examples from the book of Acts.

Wider View

On Paul's first missionary trip, he and Barnabas went to Cyprus. This was home for Barnabas, so we know there was a Jewish presence on that island (Acts 4:36). But what are we to think of the man they met named Barjesus? We are told that he was a Jew, but also a sorcerer and a false prophet (13:6). We don't normally think of Jewish people practicing black magic! This is an uncomfortable mix of religions for us (as it probably was for Paul).

A second example is found on Paul's second missionary journey where he ended up alone in the famous city of Athens. We think of Athens as the great center of Greek philosophy, but the ancient Greeks did not distinguish between philosophy and religion, so Athens was also one of the great religious centers of the world. Paul's "spirit was stirred in him, when he saw the city wholly given to idolatry" (Acts 17:16). He had been brought up as a good Jewish boy to hate idols, and there he was in a place of his worst nightmares!

Three Cities

This quarter's lessons are drawn from Paul's letters to the churches in Ephesus, Philippi, and Colosse. These were all Gentile, Greek-speaking cities, and they shared similar religious assumptions. The Gentiles of these places all believed there were many gods and goddesses who were actively involved in their lives. People thought that these gods and goddesses could be appeased by worship in their temples and shrines, by giving offerings to their priests and priestesses, and by making and fulfilling vows offered to them for special blessings.

Worship of the goddess Artemis—called Diana by the Romans—dominated the city of Ephesus, given the presence of the massive temple named for her (Acts 19:27; that's her picture below). Practi-

tioners of "curious arts" (sorcery and divination; 19:19) permeated Ephesus. A mass conversion of these practitioners resulted in their burning books of their craft estimated to be worth 50,000 silver coins, giving a hint of their huge influence in the city and area.

Philippi, for its part, had been settled by Roman army veterans, which made it less Greek than Ephesus or Athens. These men had been all over the Roman world and undoubtedly brought many religious beliefs back with them. While in this city, Paul was confronted by a slave girl who was used by her masters to give prophecies for cash (Acts 16:16). This girl was not a comedy sideshow, but a business based on people accepting the girl's words as coming from a deity.

Colosse was not a major city, so we do not know as much about its religions, but Paul's letter gives us insights. He warns the Colossians about empty philosophy (Colossians 2:8). He also refers to the religious practice of the worship of angelic beings and a fascination with visions (2:18).

Then and Now

The religious stew of the ancient world is in many respects not far removed from what we find today. But whether in the first century or the twenty-first, the consistent, life-giving message of the gospel is greater than any false faith.

THIS QUARTER IN THE WORD

Answers to the Quarterly Quiz on page 114

Lesson 1—1. will. 2. true. Lesson 2—1. peace. 2. corner stone. Lesson 3—1. unity. 2. true. Lesson 4—1. true. 2. shameful. Lesson 5—1. drunk. 2. false. Lesson 6—1. envy. 2. false. Lesson 7—1. servant. 2. bow. Lesson 8—1. Benjamin. 2. false. Lesson 9—1. mark. 2. true. Lesson 10—1. dead. 2. true. Lesson 11—1. walk. 2. false. Lesson 12—1. idolatry. 2. false. Lesson 13—1. salt. 2. physician.

Black Sea

Thrace

Philippi

Aegean
Sea

Mysia

Asia

Achaia

Hierapolis

Ephesus   Laodicea

Colosse

Pisidia

Mediterranean Sea

Crete

**Churches Addressed in
Paul's Prison Epistles**

0   30   60   90   120

"A Time to Laugh"

Teacher Tips by Brent L. Amato

DO YOUR students laugh in your classroom? While teaching is a serious business, it should also be fun! Teachers should strive to create an environment most conducive to learning, and I believe humor helps prime the pump for an effective learning experience.

I'm struck by the sparse attention given to the topic of humor in teacher training resources, and yet it can be a powerful tool. The ability to laugh is part of our created nature (Genesis 21:6), so why shouldn't we laugh in the classroom? Laughter is woven into the fabric of life (Ecclesiastes 3:4), so why shouldn't it be part of our teaching?

At this point, I know what some of you are thinking: "I am not a humorous person." "I don't know what's funny." "I'll bomb." To you I say, *Be encouraged!* Everyone has a sense of humor; some are just a bit more hidden than others.

The How

Here are some tips to consider in developing humor in your teaching:

1. Don't be afraid to move out of your comfort zone. The Holy Spirit prepares your heart to teach, and He also prepares the hearts of your students to learn. This preparation doesn't exclude the use of humor as a teaching aid.

2. Seize the moment! Some humor will just come naturally, like when you make a mistake or something unexpected or silly happens during the lesson.

3. Study the art of humor as practiced by others. Watch and learn from teachers and speakers who make their audiences laugh. Good resources are available by Christians noted for their humor. Some examples are Charles Swindoll (author of *Laugh Again*), Barbara Johnson, and Patsy Clairmont. You can also find books written for public speakers that have funny stories for many topics.

4. While you're doing #3, tailor your humor to who *you* are. Don't try to mimic others.

5. Make humor part of your lesson plan. Actually script it in.

6. Practice on a spouse or friend. Every well-planned performance has a dress rehearsal.

7. Use humor that is tied to the lesson. You are not there to be a stand-up comedian, cracking jokes just to get a response or to warm up an audience. Humor, like every other part of your lesson, should have the objective of leading your students to an important truth.

8. Avoid humor that is critical of others. I have found that self-deprecating humor is always safe.

9. Use silly, bizarre visual aids. The Into the Lesson segments of these lessons sometimes include ideas along this line.

10. Include humorous role-play activities. Many of your students are natural "hams" when in the spotlight.

11. To the extent possible, find humor in biblical situations. One example is the case of Sarah, a barren wife learning she would have a baby (Genesis 18). Another is the situation of Balaam and the talking donkey (Numbers 22).

12. Pay attention to current events and news stories that are humorous. You may be able to weave these into your lesson.

The Why

Everyone needs to laugh. Teachers need to laugh. Smiling will always make you more attractive to your students. One manifestation of spiritual health is joy, reflected in part by laughter. Students need to laugh. They not only need minds sharpened with truth, but hearts lifted and lightened by laughter. Your students may remember the fun that they had with you as much as the truth that you taught them.

So don't let a class go by without bringing some smiles and laughter. At those times you will most assuredly have the attention of your students; then teach them!

BLESSED IN CHRIST

DEVOTIONAL READING: Psalm 33:8-12
BACKGROUND SCRIPTURE: Ephesians 1

EPHESIANS 1:3-14

3 Blessed be the God and Father of our Lord Jesus Christ, who hath blessed us with all spiritual blessings in heavenly places in Christ:

4 According as he hath chosen us in him before the foundation of the world, that we should be holy and without blame before him in love:

5 Having predestinated us unto the adoption of children by Jesus Christ to himself, according to the good pleasure of his will,

6 To the praise of the glory of his grace, wherein he hath made us accepted in the beloved.

7 In whom we have redemption through his blood, the forgiveness of sins, according to the riches of his grace;

8 Wherein he hath abounded toward us in all wisdom and prudence;

9 Having made known unto us the mystery of his will, according to his good pleasure which he hath purposed in himself:

10 That in the dispensation of the fulness of times he might gather together in one all things in Christ, both which are in heaven, and which are on earth; even in him:

11 In whom also we have obtained an inheritance, being predestinated according to the purpose of him who worketh all things after the counsel of his own will:

12 That we should be to the praise of his glory, who first trusted in Christ.

13 In whom ye also trusted, after that ye heard the word of truth, the gospel of your salvation: in whom also after that ye believed, ye were sealed with that holy Spirit of promise,

14 Which is the earnest of our inheritance until the redemption of the purchased possession, unto the praise of his glory.

KEY VERSES

[God] predestinated us unto the adoption of children by Jesus Christ to himself, according to the good pleasure of his will, to the praise of the glory of his grace, wherein he hath made us accepted in the beloved.

—**Ephesians 1:5, 6**

JESUS IS LORD

Unit 1: Victory in Jesus
LESSONS 1–5

LESSON AIMS

After participating in this lesson, each student will be able to:

1. List some of the spiritual blessings that Paul mentions in today's text.

2. Compare and contrast physical adoption with spiritual adoption.

3. State one area of his or her life that should change in light of adoption in Christ, and make a plan to do so.

LESSON OUTLINE

Introduction

A. Adoption, Ancient and Modern

The practice of adoption goes back thousands of years. Properly motivated, adoption is an act of grace toward orphans or children whose parents are unable to care for them.

In the Roman world of Paul's day, there was another important consideration when it came to adoption: a father who had no sons might adopt one to be his heir. This allowed the father's assets to be distributed according to his will and for his family line and name to continue.

A high-profile example of this was the practice begun by Caesar Augustus for a Roman emperor to select a person suitable to be his heir (and therefore the next emperor). Tiberius, the emperor at the time of Jesus' crucifixion (Luke 3:1), was the adopted stepson of Augustus. Tiberius became the heir- and emperor-apparent when he was adopted by Caesar Augustus.

This was the background when Paul wrote of Christians being adopted by God. As adopted sons and daughters, we become heirs of promises and privileges we could not earn and do not deserve. Through God's grace, we become "joint-heirs with Christ" (Romans 8:17).

B. Lesson Background

Paul's letter to the Ephesian Christians has traditionally been seen as one of his four Prison Epistles (the other three being Philippians, Colossians, and Philemon). This is because of references to the author's being a prisoner (Ephesians 3:1; 4:1) or being in bonds (6:20). Paul was jailed more than once (see 2 Corinthians 11:23), and we cannot be certain which imprisonment was the setting for these letters. The likely scenario is the situation described at the end of the book of Acts. This gives a date for the writing of Ephesians of about AD 63.

The city of Ephesus and its church are important in the pages of the New Testament. Paul briefly visited that city at the end of his second missionary journey, promising to return later (Acts 18:18-21). This he did on the third missionary journey, spending three years in and around this city (19:10;

20:31; AD 54–57), resulting in the longest "located ministry" we know of for the apostle.

Ephesus was a leading city of the Roman Empire. It was a large administrative center, perhaps 200,000 in population. Its Jewish population was substantial (some estimate more than 10,000) with many synagogues. Ephesus was a bustling seaport at the time, the point of contact for trade from the eastern and the western parts of the empire. Its harbor eventually filled with silt and became unusable, however, so the site was abandoned within a few hundred years. Ephesus was home to the Temple of Diana (Artemis), one of the so-called "seven wonders of the ancient world" (Acts 19:35).

I. The Father Adopts Us
(EPHESIANS 1:3-6)
A. Blessed (v. 3)

3. Blessed be the God and Father of our Lord Jesus Christ, who hath blessed us with all spiritual blessings in heavenly places in Christ.

The entirety of this week's lesson text is actually a single, complex sentence in the Greek. The main verb for the 12 verses of our lesson is found right here at the beginning: *blessed be.* This makes these 12 verses a prayer of blessing to God. This prayer is worthy of careful study, for it contains deep insights into the nature of God.

Paul's presentation of God as the *Father of our Lord Jesus Christ* echoes what Jesus himself said about God when He instructed His disciples to pray to God as "our Father" (Matthew 6:9). The Jews of Paul's day have many ways to describe

HOW TO SAY IT

Artemis	*Ar*-teh-miss.
Caesar Augustus	*See*-zer Aw-*gus*-tus.
Ephesians	Ee-*fee*-zhunz.
Ephesus	*Ef*-uh-sus.
Pentecost	*Pent*-ih-kost.
synagogues	*sin*-uh-gogs.
Thessalonians	*Thess*-uh-*lo*-nee-unz (*th* as in *thin*).
Tiberias	Tie-*beer*-ee-us.

God, but this one is not found very often. In the Old Testament, God is king, God is Creator, God is almighty, God is eternal. But God as Father? That seems too familiar, too intimate. Yet this is an understanding of God that runs throughout the teachings of Jesus (examples: Matthew 23:9; John 4:23).

Paul himself employs this understanding of God as Father (see Romans 1:7; 8:15; 1 Corinthians 8:6). Here, Paul lifts up an important characteristic of a good father: one who blesses his children. In this Paul sees God as more than the Father of Jesus alone, but the Father of many sons and daughters. The blessings are heavenly, spiritual in nature, provided to those who are *in Christ* (also Ephesians 2:6).

> **What Do You Think?**
> How should knowing that you have "all spiritual blessings" affect your daily life?
> *Talking Points for Your Discussion*
> - During difficult times "in the valley"
> - During good times "on the mountaintop"
> - Psalm 73:23-26

B. Chosen (vv. 4, 5)

4. According as he hath chosen us in him before the foundation of the world, that we should be holy and without blame before him in love.

We will see the word *adoption* specifically in verse 5 (next), but the verse before us leads into it. Adoption is not a random process since prospective parents have a choice in selecting a child for adoption. We are reminded of this in Paul's statement that God *hath chosen us.*

As we might expect from our eternal, ageless God, this is not a recent choice, but was accomplished *before the foundation of the world* (compare 2 Thessalonians 2:13). God in His foreknowledge has known from eternity past who will turn to Him (1 Peter 1:2). It is on that basis that He has chosen us to be in fellowship with Him.

Our status changes as a result. We become *holy* (set apart in a godly way) and *without blame* (having our sins forgiven). We gain these attributes because of God's efforts through Christ. Our salvation is God's work, not ours.

5. Having predestinated us unto the adoption of children by Jesus Christ to himself, according to the good pleasure of his will.

This verse speaks of a very difficult concept: the connection of God's choosing us with predestination. Some scholars believe this means that everyone's status was decided by God before anyone was born. However, we should not fall into *fatalism*—the belief that free will does not exist, that we can make no choices that influence the outcome. God has chosen us by His grace; we must choose Him through our faith (John 1:12).

The emphasis here is not on predestination, but on adoption. This act of loving mercy is described as coming from *the good pleasure of his will*. Our adoption into the family of God is not done grudgingly or under compulsion. God's desire is for us to be reconciled to Him, to be included among His people. This is based on the work of Jesus Christ. Inclusion into God's family is a marvelous demonstration of God's love (see 1 John 3:1).

C. Accepted (v. 6)

6. To the praise of the glory of his grace, wherein he hath made us accepted in the beloved.

We may not fully understand God's reasons for loving us in such a gracious way, but we can respond by praising Him and giving Him the glory that is due to Him. Our adoption as sons and daughters of the great Father God who created the universe gives no cause for smugness or pride. Instead, it should give us daily pause to remember how blessed we are and how this blessing is undeserved.

This blessed acceptance cannot be separated from the grand act of love that characterizes God's work in Jesus Christ. He is referred to here as *the beloved* (compare Matthew 3:17). Christ is the Son of God in a unique way, but God's love is extended to all who believe and are adopted as sons and daughters in Christ (John 1:12; Galatians 3:26). Our adoption results in full acceptance as children of God, with all the rights of an heir (Galatians 4:7).

II. The Son Redeems Us
(EPHESIANS 1:7-12)

A. Through Blood (vv. 7, 8)

7. In whom we have redemption through his blood, the forgiveness of sins, according to the riches of his grace.

Paul now shifts from extolling our adoption to a fuller explanation of how this is accomplished. Within the context of the work of Christ, Paul lifts up the parallel thoughts of *redemption* and *forgiveness*. Both words can be applied to the slavery practices of Paul's day. *Redemption* means to be "bought back," as a slave might be repurchased. *Forgiveness* means "letting go" and can refer to the release of a slave. If we put these ideas together, we might paraphrase by saying, "We are bought back and released from the slavery of sin by His blood" (compare Colossians 1:14, 20).

> *What Do You Think?*
> How does the realization that your sins are forgiven result in your sinning less and less?
> *Talking Points for Your Discussion*
> ▪ In your thought life
> ▪ In your actions
> ▪ Romans 7:15-20

The word translated *sins* is translated *trespasses* in Jesus' explanation of the Lord's Prayer (Matthew 6:14, 15). The idea behind the word is "to stray from the correct path while traveling." We are reminded of the common biblical depiction of life as a journey made up of choices (see Deuteronomy 30:15-17). Through the blood of Jesus, we have the means to be delivered from wrong choices and be put back on the path of God's choosing. The *riches of his grace* (also Ephesians 2:7) are truly marvelous!

❧ *RE-BUYING* ❧

It's maddening to have to pay for something that's already yours. Once my wife lost her passport while traveling in Eastern Europe. Fortunately, a family got in touch with her to say they had found it; unfortunately, they expected a reward of $200 to return it. Expenditures for car repairs can make us feel like we're paying to keep what we already own. The list goes on.

We keep in mind, however, that the frustration we experience in this regard is nothing compared with the searing pain God went through to buy us back from slavery to sin. We should never take His sacrifice lightly.

God's investment in us doesn't stop once we have been redeemed. The result is (or should be) a daily friendship with Him, healing in our relationships with others, a harvest of spiritual fruit, etc. There are difficulties and pain in this growth process, but the basic question of who owns us is fully settled—a joyful thing indeed!   —A. W.

8. Wherein he hath abounded toward us in all wisdom and prudence.

All wisdom and prudence describes God's way of dealing with His wayward children. In the Bible, *wisdom* has the sense of knowing the difference between right and wrong and making the choice to do the right thing (Proverbs 1:10). God, of course, is always wise, for it is inconceivable that He would make wrong choices. At the same time, we are wise when we follow God's paths in loving obedience (Proverbs 3:6).

Closely connected to *wisdom* is *prudence*. In this context, it refers to correct thinking. As with wisdom, God's thinking is always perfect and right, and His opinion of us is not to be questioned. As we are in the mind of God, so we are. Paul characterizes this expression of God's wisdom and prudent thinking as being abundant. The idea is that of a vessel overflowing, unable to contain all the grace and mercy coming from God to us (compare Psalm 23:5, 6). We are blessed by God's direction of our lives, and we walk in godly wisdom as a result.

B. For a Purpose (vv. 9, 10)

9. Having made known unto us the mystery of his will, according to his good pleasure which he hath purposed in himself.

In the Bible, there are various ways that God makes His will known to humans. One is the pattern of prophecy and fulfillment, with the intention of God's being disclosed before the

Visual for
Lesson 1

Point to this visual as you introduce the discussion question associated with verse 3 (page 123).

event. Another pattern is that of a mystery being revealed, something initially hidden from human understanding, but now being shown (Ephesians 3:9). We understand God as a self-revealing God, for we cannot unravel the deep things of God by our own deep thinking. We know only those things that God chooses to reveal to us. In this case, Paul sees the previously concealed mystery as the purpose God had in the redeeming mission of His Son, Jesus (Romans 16:25).

10. That in the dispensation of the fulness of times he might gather together in one all things in Christ, both which are in heaven, and which are on earth; even in him.

God's purpose includes the restoration and unity of all of creation, rescued from the ravaging effects of sin. A key part of this is the reunification of humanity, which is divided into hostile groups. The barrier between Jews and Gentiles is broken down through Christ (Ephesians 2:14); these groups can be brought together in Christ according to God's will and purpose (3:4-6).

All this is according to God's plan, for it takes place at the proper moment in history: the *fulness of times* (see Galatians 4:4). This recognizes that the work of Christ has made the unity of humanity possible, but also that this unity is not fully accomplished at the time Paul writes. It has yet to be accomplished fully today; we continue to await the time when all of creation will be in submission to the universal reign of Christ (see Hebrews 2:8).

C. For an Inheritance (vv. 11, 12)

11, 12. In whom also we have obtained an inheritance, being predestinated according to the purpose of him who worketh all things after the counsel of his own will: that we should be to the praise of his glory, who first trusted in Christ.

In summing up the redeeming work of the Son, Paul repeats the themes of (1) God's eternal choice of us according to His will, (2) God's timely revealing of His purpose to save His lost children, and (3) the proper response of giving praise and glory to God by the redeemed. Paul frames this in the language of inheritance. It is our adoption that results in the inheritance. We do not inherit money or property, though, but the spiritual treasures of God (Ephesians 1:18). This is the inheritance for those who believe in Christ.

III. The Spirit Seals Us
(EPHESIANS 1:13, 14)
A. For Promise (v. 13)

13. In whom ye also trusted, after that ye heard the word of truth, the gospel of your salvation: in whom also after that ye believed, ye were sealed with that holy Spirit of promise.

Our inheritance as adopted sons and daughters of God is spiritual in nature (see 1 Corinthians 15:50). Paul describes this in dramatic language. After we accept *the word of truth, the gospel,* we are in line for a marvelous inheritance. We do not wait to begin to enjoy the blessings of this inheritance, for we are sealed by God through the gift of the Holy Spirit (Ephesians 4:30). Government officials affix wax seals to documents to indicate their authenticity and authority. Paul uses this image to help us understand the nature of the gift of God's Spirit to the believer. We thereby learn four things about the Holy Spirit, three here and one in verse 14 (below).

First, the seal of the Holy Spirit marks us spiritually as God's children and therefore God's heirs (see Revelation 7:3). We cannot fully understand this since we have very limited insight into the spiritual world. But we can conclude that spiritual beings, both malevolent or benevolent, recognize this spiritual marking and what it signifies.

Second, Paul pictures this spiritual sealing as a promise. This reminds us of Peter's words on the Day of Pentecost, where the outpouring of the Holy Spirit is understood as a fulfillment of the prophecy of the prophet Joel (see Acts 2:16-18). The presence of the Holy Spirit in the life of the Christian believer is part of the predetermined plan of God.

Third, Paul pictures this gift of the Holy Spirit as being bestowed after faith. While the Holy Spirit may have a role in drawing people to faith, the Spirit's presence in the heart is a gift promised to believers (Acts 2:38, 39). This is in line with Paul's portrayal of believers becoming the adopted heirs of the promises of God.

Completing the paperwork for an international adoption is a grueling process. The prospective parents must assemble birth certificates, medical affidavits, financial statements, etc. The family doctor and social worker must include copies of their licenses. Every signature must be notarized, and the county courthouse must verify the authenticity of the notary stamps. The county seal is "apostilled" at the state capital, a fancy way of describing another level of certification. The whole portfolio then goes overseas to be translated, with a new series of stamps added to verify the translation.

Now imagine if it were possible instead for just one person of great authority to look at the portfolio and put one stamp on the whole thing to approve the adoption. No one in his or her right mind would want to do it the old way!

We need not seek earthly "stamps of approval" to validate our worth. God himself has already placed His seal of adoption on us. We may see people who do great acts of service in pursuit of recognition, who consume self-help books to improve themselves, and who keep adding certifications to their résumés for professional advantage. We are mindful, however, that God's seal makes all earthly stamps of approval just that.   —A. W.

B. For Praise (v. 14)

14. Which is the earnest of our inheritance until the redemption of the purchased possession, unto the praise of his glory.

Fourth, the gift of the Holy Spirit is not our full inheritance, but is *the earnest of our inheritance.* The key word *earnest* is a legal term that refers to a down payment in a transaction. The idea is that of a "first installment" (compare 2 Corinthians 1:22). The future holds not only the final defeat of sin and its effects, but also spiritual fulfillment and completion. There is more to come, a time of final redemption of those who have been sealed with God's Spirit.

Paul finishes this long, complex sentence (which began in v. 3) with an observation regarding praise. Praise of God is our recognition of His mighty works and person. When Paul says that God acts for *the praise of his glory,* he is not imply-ing that God somehow needs human approval. Humans should praise God because it is good and proper, and this is part of our created nature. The ability to praise and worship God freely and properly is indeed a part of our inheritance and a manifestation of the Holy Spirit in our lives.

Conclusion
A. Living in Christ

The concept of being "in Christ" is found in various forms 11 times in Ephesians 1 (verses 1, 3, 4, 6, 7, 9, 10, 11, 12, and twice in 13). Being "in Christ" means our existence is tied up with our risen Savior. We believe that Jesus is alive, that we have a relationship with Him, and that the church is His body. Paul has given us the great promises that we have been adopted into the family of God, that Christ is truly the one who saves us, and that the Holy Spirit has been given to keep us in His grace.

To be "in" Jesus means that our living Lord is with us. He shares our trials and heartaches (Hebrews 2:18). We grow in Christ as we appreciate this presence. As C. Austin Miles (1868–1946) wrote, "He walks with me, and He talks with me, and He tells me I am His own." We are never alone (Hebrews 13:5). We grow in Christ as we practice His presence, resting in the promises of His love and care.

B. Prayer

Our Father, we praise You for our undeserved status as Your adopted sons and daughters. May we ever rest securely in Your promises for our eternity. In Jesus' name, amen.

C. Thought to Remember
Remain in Christ.

VISUALS FOR THESE LESSONS

The visual pictured in each lesson (example: page 125) is a small reproduction of a large, full-color poster included in the *Adult Resources* packet for the Winter Quarter. That packet also contains the very useful *Presentation Helps* on a CD for teacher use. Order No. 020029212 from your supplier.

INVOLVEMENT LEARNING

Some of the activities below are also found in the helpful student book, Adult Bible Class.
Don't forget to download the free reproducible page from www.standardlesson.com to enhance your lesson!

Into the Lesson

Have this completion statement on display as learners arrive: *Adoption is an act of _____.* Ask your class to complete it, jotting responses on the board. Receive several responses before you stop to discuss. Expect such responses as grace, love, choice, unselfishness, compassion. Leave the list on display as the class proceeds. Return to the list as you conclude class, noting which terms apply to God's adopting us in Christ.

Option: Invite an adoptive parent to give a three- to five-minute description of the adoptive process that he or she was involved in. Ask your guest to give special attention to the motivations for entering the process. Do this before the completion exercise above.

Into the Word

Give each learner a handout titled *He Has.* Put the following as the headers for three columns, one each: "What the Father Has Done" / "What the Son Has Done" / "What the Spirit Has Done." Direct learners to look at Ephesians 1:3-14 and write as many "He has" statements as possible in each column.

Call for responses after an appropriate amount of time. Possible responses for the Father column include "He has 'blessed us with all spiritual blessings'" (v. 3) and "He has 'chosen us in him'" (v. 4). Possible responses for the Son column include "He has redeemed us 'through His blood'" (v. 7) and "He has 'accepted' us" (v. 6). Possible responses for the Spirit column include "He has become a seal of our relationship to the Father" (v. 13) and "He has guaranteed our inheritance by being an 'earnest'" (v. 14). Some learners may offer responses that you do not clearly see in the text; in those cases, ask the responder to clarify.

Next, give each learner a handout titled *Ranking Our Blessings.* The handout will include this list of words, in this order: *adopted, chosen, for-*

given, included, informed, loved, marked, redeemed, saved, united. (*Option:* You can include this exercise on the same handout as the *He Has* exercise above, but do so only if you think it will not distract your learners as they work on *He Has.*) Give this direction: "Rank-order these spiritual blessings from 1 to 10, with 1 signifying 'most wonderful,' 2 signifying 'second most wonderful,' etc. This will be difficult, but try to make the hard decisions anyway."

After a few minutes, ask two or three volunteers to read their lists in ranked order. Then ask, "How does one decide which of God's blessings is the best? How did you decide?" Let several respond. Also ask, "What are some fallacies in making such a list?" Learners should note that some of the terms are virtually synonymous (example: *redeemed* and *saved*), and thus cannot be separated into different rankings. Learners should also note that some terms presuppose other terms (example: we are *united* because we have been *redeemed*).

Wrap up by saying, "Paul, by the Spirit, writes in straightforward language so there's no question about what we have in Christ. As a result, we will have the joy of salvation and be fully thankful!" Time permitting, you can have learners complete the "Happy Birthday in Christ" activity on the reproducible page, which you can download.

Into Life

Distribute copies of the "Praise . . . Praise" activity from the reproducible page. Have learners complete it and take it home for use in personal devotions in the week ahead, as indicated.

Option: Give each learner a strip of paper that is printed with the statement *Act Like a Child of God Today!* Suggest that learners post it in a place where they will see it each morning for a time. This will remind them not only of their blessed relationship as an adopted child of the king, but also of their obligations to represent "the family name."

Blessed in Christ

ONE IN
JESUS CHRIST

DEVOTIONAL READING: Ephesians 3:14-21
BACKGROUND SCRIPTURE: Ephesians 2, 3

EPHESIANS 2:11-22

11 Wherefore remember, that ye being in time past Gentiles in the flesh, who are called Uncircumcision by that which is called the Circumcision in the flesh made by hands;

12 That at that time ye were without Christ, being aliens from the commonwealth of Israel, and strangers from the covenants of promise, having no hope, and without God in the world:

13 But now in Christ Jesus ye who sometimes were far off are made nigh by the blood of Christ.

14 For he is our peace, who hath made both one, and hath broken down the middle wall of partition between us;

15 Having abolished in his flesh the enmity, even the law of commandments contained in ordinances; for to make in himself of twain one new man, so making peace;

16 And that he might reconcile both unto God in one body by the cross, having slain the enmity thereby:

17 And came and preached peace to you which were afar off, and to them that were nigh.

18 For through him we both have access by one Spirit unto the Father.

19 Now therefore ye are no more strangers and foreigners, but fellowcitizens with the saints, and of the household of God;

20 And are built upon the foundation of the apostles and prophets, Jesus Christ himself being the chief corner stone;

21 In whom all the building fitly framed together groweth unto an holy temple in the Lord:

22 In whom ye also are builded together for an habitation of God through the Spirit.

KEY VERSE

In whom all the building fitly framed together groweth unto an holy temple in the Lord.

—Ephesians 2:21

JESUS IS LORD

Unit 1: Victory in Jesus

LESSONS 1-5

LESSON AIMS

After participating in this lesson, each student will be able to:

1. Explain the spiritual dimension of the separation that existed between Jew and Gentile before Christ came.

2. Compare and contrast the separation between Jew and Gentile in Paul's day with the separation that exists between Christians and non-Christians.

3. Suggest an evangelistic campaign that focuses more on uniting people with Christ than on music, programs, or social benefits.

LESSON OUTLINE

Introduction
    A. The Divided Church
    B. Lesson Background
 I. Humanity Divided (EPHESIANS 2:11, 12)
    A. By Ritual (v. 11)
    B. By Boundary (v. 12)
II. Humanity United (EPHESIANS 2:13-22)
    A. By Christ's Peace (vv. 13-15)
      Bringing Down a Wall
    B. By God's Spirit (vv. 16-18)
      Cross Power
    C. As God's Family (v. 19)
    D. To Be God's Temple (vv. 20-22)
Conclusion
    A. The United Church
    B. Prayer
    C. Thought to Remember

Introduction

A. The Divided Church

A central agenda for the Christian faith is to unite all of humanity into a single entity, the church of Jesus Christ. Jesus himself prayed for the day when "all may be one" (John 17:21). Jesus was well aware of the barriers to this goal. Sin separates people from God; it also separates people from each other.

We still fall short of Jesus' desire for a united humanity, even within the church itself. By some estimates, there are over 30,000 distinct denominations of the church today. The divided state of Christianity has been and still is a heartfelt concern for many Christians. Most distressing is to see divisive tensions within local churches themselves. Conflict occurs over things like worship styles, leadership loyalties, and minor doctrines. Rather than submit to Christ and find unity in Him, some folks seem determined to create and perpetuate divisions. Those who have been through a church fight or split know that a divisive spirit can drain all the joy of the faith from the soul.

In Paul's day, there was tension (if not outright division) within the church between those who came from a Jewish background and those who did not (Gentiles). While this specific problem is rarely encountered today, the human reasons fueling it are still with us, as are Paul's instructions for overcoming this spirit of division.

B. Lesson Background

In about AD 51, a dozen or so years before writing his letter to the Ephesians, Paul participated in a meeting we sometimes call "the Jerusalem Council." This is described in Acts 15 and Galatians 2. The Jerusalem Council was convened to resolve a pressing question for the church of that day: *Is it necessary for Gentile men to be circumcised in order for them to be considered Christian believers?* Simply put, the question was whether a person had to become a Jew first before becoming a Christian. Was the gateway to the church only to be found in the synagogue?

The epic decision of the Jerusalem Council was that circumcision was not to be required of Gentiles. However, this decision was not accepted by all. Even a dozen years later there were some who were teaching that Gentiles needed to be circumcised and otherwise "toe the line" regarding the Law of Moses. Thus Paul found the need to revisit this issue.

I. Humanity Divided
(EPHESIANS 2:11, 12)
A. By Ritual (v. 11)

11. Wherefore remember, that ye being in time past Gentiles in the flesh, who are called Uncircumcision by that which is called the Circumcision in the flesh made by hands.

We may struggle to understand the significance of the circumcision issue for the church of Paul's day. Circumcision was an important sign of the covenant for the Jewish people. The roots of circumcision date back to the patriarch Abraham, making the practice more ancient than the Law of Moses (Genesis 17:10-14).

Circumcision was also a source of pride for the Jews, for they considered the uncircumcised to be unclean and inferior (see 1 Samuel 17:26). From the Jewish perspective, there were only two kinds of people-groups in the world: the circumcised and the uncircumcised. The circumcised mainly are Jews, although converts to Judaism can be included (Exodus 12:48). The Jews had even come to use the word *uncircumcision* as a term of derision to describe the person whose heart stubbornly opposed God's will (see Jeremiah 9:26; Acts 7:51). Before Jesus came, it was unthinkable for a Jew to consider an uncircumcised man as part of the people of God.

We have our own issues that divide us today, and circumcision is not one of them. Even so, Paul's instructions for overcoming this divisive issue of his day can be of great value for us in the twenty-first century.

B. By Boundary (v. 12)

12. That at that time ye were without Christ, being aliens from the commonwealth of Israel, and strangers from the covenants of promise, having no hope, and without God in the world.

To understand Paul's argument here, we should examine the four ways in which he describes Gentiles in contrast with the Jewish people. First, the fact that Gentiles are not part of *the commonwealth of Israel* means they were excluded historically from being part of the chosen people of God; thus Gentiles have no part in *the covenants of promise* (compare Romans 9:4). The Old Testament tells of several covenants God made with His people (see Exodus 2:24; 24:8; Psalm 89:3; etc.). All of these were terms of a special relationship offered by God.

The promises of each of these covenants were founded essentially on the same idea: that God would bless the world through His chosen people (example: Genesis 12:3). As Paul knows, this blessing is realized in Jesus Christ, the descendant of Abraham and David (Matthew 1:17). Jesus is the Savior of all people, not just the Jews.

Seeing Jesus as the fulfillment of the ancient promise helps us understand Paul's third and fourth descriptions of the Gentiles: *having no hope* and being *without God* (compare 1 Thessalonians 4:13). There is no true hope in any of the pagan religions since none of them worship the only true God, the God of Israel. Without Christ, the Gentiles are cut off from the blessings that God had directed toward and through the Jewish people.

> **What Do You Think?**
> In what ways does your church bring the hope of Christ to people around the world? How can it do more in this regard?
> *Talking Points for Your Discussion*
> - Budget priorities
> - Short-term mission opportunities
> - Long-term mission support
> - Church vision and strategic planning
> - Other

II. Humanity United
(EPHESIANS 2:13-22)
A. By Christ's Peace (vv. 13-15)

13. But now in Christ Jesus ye who sometimes were far off are made nigh by the blood of Christ.

The fourfold description of Gentiles in verse 12 is now expanded: they *were far off*. The image is that of people in a distant country. That distance is now negated, for the Gentiles *are made nigh by the blood of Christ*, which refers to the atoning death of Jesus for sin (compare Galatians 3:28). The explanation that follows is one of the most beautiful and meaningful descriptions of Christ's sacrifice to be found in the Bible.

14, 15a. For he is our peace, who hath made both one, and hath broken down the middle wall of partition between us; having abolished in his flesh the enmity, even the law of commandments contained in ordinances;

When Paul says that Christ *is our peace,* he has in mind the Jewish concept of *shalom,* a Hebrew word often translated "peace." In the Old Testament, *shalom* is more than suspension of hostilities. Leviticus 26:6-9 uses this word to describe a state of physical and spiritual well-being for an individual who is at peace with God and neighbor.

Other aspects of the Jewish concept of peace/ *shalom* are found in Leviticus 3. There the word *shalom* is translated "peace offering" in verses 1, 3, 6, and 9. The Old Testament also uses *shalom* as a verb to describe the idea of giving something to make satisfaction for an injustice or wrong. For example, if a valuable animal dies through the negligence of a neighbor, the negligent person is required to "make it good" (*shalom* in Leviticus 24:18) and "restore it" (*shalom* in 24:21); this is a type of righteous recompense.

This Old Testament pattern is a background for Paul's description of Christ's death as the adequate atonement for sin. This is the mighty truth behind the simple assertion *he is our peace.* The marvelous thing is that Christ's death serves not just the Jewish people, but Gentiles too. All stand in need of a Savior (Romans 3:22, 23). The problem of sin and its solution through the blood of Jesus transcends any arguments about circumcision or other things that might divide Jew from Gentile.

Paul portrays this in memorable language as the breaking down of a wall *(partition).* He may draw this image from a wall in the Jerusalem temple that is the boundary for Gentiles, marking the inner courts that are forbidden to them.

Such divisive barriers are now *broken down.* As a result, there is no more assumption of enmity, for all are equally loved in Christ and should be loving toward one another (compare John 13:34).

In this light, the law of the Jews (including circumcision requirements) has become moot as a divisive factor (compare Colossians 2:14). This does not mean there is no value in the law (Galatians 3:24), nor that Christianity is a lawless faith, an ethical free-for-all (Jude 4). It means, rather, that the specific requirements of the law that result in distinguishing Jew from Gentile are now powerless. Christianity is not a religion of rule-keeping, but a way of faith (Ephesians 2:8, 9).

15b. For to make in himself of twain one new man, so making peace.

The result of this is a new humanity, a people of God undivided by anything specific to being a Jew or a Gentile (Galatians 3:28). We are in relationship with one another because of the inclusive nature of our relationship with Christ. Paul sums this up as the result of *making peace,* returning to his idea of complete *shalom* as found in Christ for all people. This unity in Christ should overcome the divisive things within and between today's churches. If our focus is on our oneness in Christ, other things will fade into the background.

> *What Do You Think?*
> In what ways does our church promote oneness and unity in Christ? How can it do more in this regard?
> *Talking Points for Your Discussion*
> - Through the Web site
> - In small groups
> - In midsize groups
> - In new-member classes
> - In corporate worship
> - Other

❧ *BRINGING DOWN A WALL* ❧

In 1961, the Communist authorities of East Germany installed a wire fence to divide the city of Berlin. After years of construction, this barrier grew into a reinforced concrete wall that was 12 feet high with dozens of watchtowers. Anti-vehicle trenches, guard dogs, etc., provided extra deterrence to anyone who tried to cross. Nevertheless, some 5,000 people tried to do so over the years, with upwards of 200 dying in the attempt. When the Berlin Wall fell in 1989, the world celebrated as separated people were reunited.

One of the consequences of sin is division between people. It is true that God told the Israelites to separate themselves from idolatrous nations, but the ultimate purpose of that particular separation was to prepare a people to usher in the Messiah for everyone. Even given their set-apart status, the Israelites were commanded not to oppress the foreigners among them, and the same law was to apply to both (Exodus 12:48, 49; 23:9).

Even so, a wall still existed. By the first century AD, the Jews had made the wall even higher by adding tradition (Matthew 23:1-32; Mark 7:1-13). Jesus tore down this wall. Today, God continues to lead His church to fulfill His goal of a kingdom of every kindred, tongue, and nation (Revelation 7:9). May we not rebuild a wall that Jesus tore down! —A. W.

B. By God's Spirit (vv. 16-18)

16. And that he might reconcile both unto God in one body by the cross, having slain the enmity thereby.

To reconcile means to repair a broken relationship. For Paul, reconciliation has a dual aspect. First, we are reconciled to God *by the cross,* another reference to the saving effect of Christ's atoning death for sin (see Colossians 1:20, 22; 2 Corinthians 5:18). The relationship between God and humans, broken by sin, is restored through Christ.

HOW TO SAY IT

Gentiles	*Jen*-tiles.
Judaism	*Joo*-duh-izz-um or *Joo*-day-izz-um.
levitical	leh-*vit*-ih-kul.
patriarch	*pay*-tree-ark.
Persia	*Per*-zhuh.
shalom *(Hebrew)*	shah-*lome*.
synagogue	*sin*-uh-gog.

Second, this renewed relationship with God makes reconciliation between people possible, for we are shaped into *one body* in Christ. This body is the church (1 Corinthians 12:27), both on the local congregational level and the worldwide universal level. This is a place where there is no place for enmity, whether it be in the God-human relationship or in human-human relationships.

> **What Do You Think?**
> Is there such a thing as "healthy distinctives" among churches? If so, how do we keep these from becoming unhealthy divisions of the one body?
>
> *Talking Points for Your Discussion*
> - Differences in doctrine vs. differences in practice
> - Differences based on cultural expectations
> - John 17:11
> - 1 Corinthians 1:13; 11:19

⁂ CROSS POWER ⁂

In the old horror movies, all you needed to defend yourself from a vampire was a big ol' cross. Whip that thing out, and the enemy would hiss and hide his face in fear. He might even get a nasty cross-shaped burn if you touched him with it. Have you noticed crosses don't seem to work so well in the movies these days? Now if a heroine holds up a cross, her attacker may laugh diabolically and slap it aside as a worthless trinket.

To think that a physical object can provide magical protection is misguided in any case, of course. However, movie producers aren't exactly improving on popular theology. They seem to be tapping into a larger cultural skepticism about the power of Christ's death on the cross. Even within some Christian circles the cross is de-emphasized. In some churches it's hard to detect that the crucifixion and resurrection are central Christian doctrines.

Vampires aren't real, of course, but evil is. At the cross, Jesus didn't just make evil cringe—He defeated it. "The Son of God was manifested, that he might destroy the works of the devil" (1 John 3:8). That happened by the power of the cross. The cross will never lose that power. —A. W.

17. And came and preached peace to you which were afar off, and to them that were nigh.

While the Jews (them that were nigh) may have been closer to God than the Gentiles (you which were afar off) because of covenant relationship, neither was reconciled with their Creator. The gospel remains a necessary and welcome message for all people, Jew and Gentile (Isaiah 57:19).

> **What Do You Think?**
> How can our church communicate the good news more effectively?
> *Talking Points for Your Discussion*
> - Mission statement: important or unimportant?
> - "Truth is relative" obstacle of postmodernism
> - Technological enhancements vs. distractions
> - Training

18. For through him we both have access by one Spirit unto the Father.

A unifying factor in the church is the gift of the Holy Spirit. There is one Holy Spirit (Ephesians 4:4), and the presence of God's Spirit in the church and in the heart of each believer is a great source of unity (see 4:3). Just as Paul sees no difference between the Holy Spirit in the life of a Jew and the Holy Spirit in the life of a Gentile, so we today should understand that each and every Christian has the same gift of the Holy Spirit (Acts 2:38, 39; 10:44-47). He is the timeless, eternal Spirit of God who was present at creation (Genesis 1:2), is present in the life of Paul as he ministers (see Romans 5:5; 1 Corinthians 2:12), and is still active in the church today.

C. As God's Family (v. 19)

19. Now therefore ye are no more strangers and foreigners, but fellowcitizens with the saints, and of the household of God.

Paul now describes unity using terms of national citizenship and family homes. The word *ye* refers particularly to the Gentiles since Paul notes that they *are no more strangers,* referring to people from other nations. For example, to a Roman citizen living in Rome, a visitor from Persia is a stranger. This Persian has no rights as a citizen and is considered an outsider, even if he lives in Rome.

Paul also tells the Gentiles they are *no more . . . foreigners.* The Greek word here is translated "strangers" in Acts 7:29 and 1 Peter 2:11, so it may be a mistake to see too much of a difference between *strangers* and *foreigners.* The doubled usage stresses the "outsider" status of Gentiles in the Jewish mind of Paul's day.

Paul counters the negative image with two positive ones. Gentile believers are now *fellowcitizens with the saints.* Rather than being foreigners, these Gentiles now have full citizenship among the people of God. Furthermore, the Gentiles are now part *of the household of God.* They are not living "outside the house," but have full access and privileges as part of the people of God. All stand as equal citizens and family members within the church (compare Ephesians 3:8, 9).

D. To Be God's Temple (vv. 20-22)

20. And are built upon the foundation of the apostles and prophets, Jesus Christ himself being the chief corner stone.

Paul now describes this new people of God in terms of architecture: the church is a carefully crafted building, constructed on the foundation of God-ordained teachers. These teachers are both *apostles* (referring to teachers such as Paul and Peter; compare Revelation 21:14) and *prophets* (compare 1 Corinthians 12:28; 14:1; also see reference to Old Testament prophets in 1 Peter 1:10). Today we have the great blessing of finding their teachings in the pages of our Bibles. The Bible must be the authority for how the church understands itself.

Paul also includes a powerful reference to Jesus as *the chief corner stone* of the church. The early church understood the "head stone of the corner" reference of Psalm 118:22 as a prophecy of the Messiah, an understanding that Jesus himself taught (Matthew 21:42). In addition to seeing Jesus as the foundational stone upon which the church rests, we must also acknowledge the psalmist's portrayal of this stone as a miraculous work of God (Psalm 118:23).

21, 22. In whom all the building fitly framed together groweth unto an holy temple in the Lord: in whom ye also are builded together for an habitation of God through the Spirit.

One in Jesus Christ

As Paul writes, less than a decade remains before the magnificent temple in Jerusalem is destroyed in AD 70. The temple was intended to be a meeting place between God and people as mediated by the levitical priesthood. This building is central to the faith of the ancient Israelites and to the identity of their nation. As noted above, Gentiles are restricted to an outer court of the temple, with the inner courts being off-limits to them. Nothing demonstrates the separation between Jew and Gentile more than this building.

> *What Do You Think?*
> What would indicate that we are building a figurative "court of Gentiles" within our church? How do we keep this from happening?
> *Talking Points for Your Discussion*
> - Expectations from local tradition
> - Vested interests
> - Fear of change
> - Defensive mind-set

By contrast, the new people of God in Christ —the church—is the new temple of God. He dwells among His people through the presence of the Holy Spirit (see 1 Corinthians 3:16; compare 2 Corinthians 6:16). This echoes the teaching of Jesus that a time was coming when a physical temple in Jerusalem or elsewhere would no longer be necessary (John 4:21-23). The new temple of God is a spiritual edifice made up of Christians from all nations. They are the ones reconciled to God.

Conclusion

A. The United Church

Ephesians is the great book of Christian unity. In today's lesson text, Paul did more than argue against the necessity of circumcision. He went on to lay out the marvelous unity that Christians have in Christ and to explain why this unity is essential to the mission and purpose of the church.

The divided church of today is an unfortunate and scandalous reality. How may we overcome this? One way is to realize that God has given the church more unity than we sometimes realize. We have unity in a common Savior, Jesus Christ. We

Visual for Lesson 2. *Have this visual on display as you discuss verse 19. Ask, "What can our church do to bring us closer to one another in Christ?"*

have unity in a common gift, the Holy Spirit. We have unity in a common state, being reconciled to God. In God's eyes, all Christians are united into a spiritual temple for His dwelling place among men and women. This is not an edifice of our own plan. It is God's work.

There is a saying of uncertain origin but repeated by John Wesley (1703–1791) that speaks to Paul's concerns: *In essentials, unity; in nonessentials, liberty; in all things, love.* Paul shows us the essentials of the faith: our common salvation through faith in Christ. Paul also points to the nonessential of circumcision (compare Romans 2:25-29). And in all of his discussion, Paul exhibits the loving grace of Jesus Christ. If we could lay down our swords of controversy and adopt the spirit of Paul, our divided churches would have more hope of unity.

B. Prayer

Father God, You have been the Lord of the church for centuries. May we find unity through our shared relationship with You, for You have loved us and given Your Son as an offering in order to reconcile us to You. May we act with this spirit of reconciliation in all of our relationships, and especially within Your church. We pray these things in the name of Jesus, amen.

C. Thought to Remember

May our churches be places of peace and unity where the Spirit of God dwells.

INVOLVEMENT LEARNING

Some of the activities below are also found in the helpful student book, Adult Bible Class.
Don't forget to download the free reproducible page from www.standardlesson.com to enhance your lesson!

Into the Lesson

Bring in a large picture frame with a piece of blank poster board filling the image opening. Have a prominent label attached to the lower edge, bearing the title "A Sad Picture." Hold the frame up to your class, read the label, and ask, "What do you see in this image?" Encourage creative, imaginative responses. If need be, give this example: "I see a lonely child on a school playground." After several responses, say, "One verse in today's text is a sad picture indeed."

Into the Word

Have Ephesians 2:11-22 read aloud. Then ask, "Which verse epitomizes the idea of a sad picture?" When someone suggests verse 12, ask, "What are the sad components of that verse's picture?" As learners call them out, note them on the blank poster board inside the frame: (1) without Christ, (2) alienated from the commonwealth of Israel, (3) strangers from the covenants of promise, (4) having no hope, and (5) without God in the world.

Remark: "Now that is a sad picture indeed! But let's look at the remainder of the text and discover Paul's positive 'ye were' (past tense) and 'ye are' (present tense) conclusions." Have learners do so (can be a small-group activity). Verses 11-13, 17, 19, 22 will be most obvious, but the positive ideas are implied in the other verses as well. Comment, "God repainted the sad picture with the blood of His Son!"

Next, hold up two flash cards with the words *US* and *THEM,* one each. Ask, "Thinking very broadly, what differences divide people into groups?" Expect answers along the lines of gender, nationality, age, education level, political viewpoints, etc. Ask, "With regard to today's text, what was the key separation that existed before Christ?" (Expected answer: the Jewish-Gentile divide.)

Ask, "How does the text describe the elimination of this separation?" The answers span several verses: verse 14, Christ made peace between Jew and Gentile; verse 16, Christ negated enmity; verse 17, Christ enabled the gospel of God's peace to be preached to all; verse 18, Christ's work allows both Jew and Gentile to have access to the Father; verse 19, Christ made citizenship in God's household available to all; verses 21, 22, Christ established a new kind of temple for all people.

Ask, "In what sense does belief in Jesus and acceptance of His lordship break down the barrier between any of the *us* and *them* groups named earlier?" Allow free discussion.

Next, reveal a large sign that reads *Outsiders, Please Sit Outside!* Ask, "What does this idea have to do with today's study?" There should be two kinds of responses. The "historical context" answer relates to the fact that Gentiles were once not a part of God's people. The "right now" answer relates to problems churches may have in treating people as outsiders when they should not be treated that way.

Into Life

Distribute copies of the "Divided No Longer" activity from the reproducible page, which you can download. Have learners complete it in study pairs. Then push deeper as you ask, "What are some creative ways that our church can present to our community that Christ is the one who eliminates dividing walls?" Have someone record the responses. Then say, "I will pass along these ideas to our church leaders as possibilities to consider for extending our congregation's evangelistic efforts." Be sure to follow through. Also, encourage learners to choose from the list something that is possible on an individual basis.

Distribute copies of the "I Was . . . But No Longer Am" activity from the reproducible page. This exercise will be a time of personal reflection. Ask for volunteers to reveal their responses, but don't put anyone on the spot.

PART OF ONE BODY IN CHRIST

DEVOTIONAL READING: Romans 12:3-8
BACKGROUND SCRIPTURE: Ephesians 4:1-16

EPHESIANS 4:1-16

1 I therefore, the prisoner of the Lord, beseech you that ye walk worthy of the vocation wherewith ye are called,

2 With all lowliness and meekness, with longsuffering, forbearing one another in love;

3 Endeavouring to keep the unity of the Spirit in the bond of peace.

4 There is one body, and one Spirit, even as ye are called in one hope of your calling;

5 One Lord, one faith, one baptism,

6 One God and Father of all, who is above all, and through all, and in you all.

7 But unto every one of us is given grace according to the measure of the gift of Christ.

8 Wherefore he saith, When he ascended up on high, he led captivity captive, and gave gifts unto men.

9 (Now that he ascended, what is it but that he also descended first into the lower parts of the earth?

10 He that descended is the same also that ascended up far above all heavens, that he might fill all things.)

11 And he gave some, apostles; and some, prophets; and some, evangelists; and some, pastors and teachers;

12 For the perfecting of the saints, for the work of the ministry, for the edifying of the body of Christ:

13 Till we all come in the unity of the faith, and of the knowledge of the Son of God, unto a perfect man, unto the measure of the stature of the fulness of Christ:

14 That we henceforth be no more children, tossed to and fro, and carried about with every wind of doctrine, by the sleight of men, and cunning craftiness, whereby they lie in wait to deceive;

15 But speaking the truth in love, may grow up into him in all things, which is the head, even Christ:

16 From whom the whole body fitly joined together and compacted by that which every joint supplieth, according to the effectual working in the measure of every part, maketh increase of the body unto the edifying of itself in love.

KEY VERSES

There is one body, and one Spirit, even as ye are called in one hope of your calling; one Lord, one faith, one baptism. —**Ephesians 4:4, 5**

JESUS IS LORD

Unit 1: Victory in Jesus
LESSONS 1–5

LESSON AIMS

After participating in this lesson, each student will be able to:

1. Identify the source, expression, and result of unity in the body of Christ.

2. Compare and contrast the unity of the body of Christ with the sense of fellowship expressed in nonreligious groups.

3. Identify one's own role in the body of believers and make a commitment to fulfill that role in a manner that helps the body grow.

LESSON OUTLINE

Introduction
A. Selfish Gifts

Gift-giving is tricky because we have to watch our motives carefully as we give. Sometimes we give gifts because we gain satisfaction and pleasure from helping. Sometimes we give in order to fulfill a duty or responsibility we feel to support an organization or ministry. Sometimes we give in order to be acknowledged as a donor. While satisfaction, duty, and recognition may be effective motivations for giving, each is tinged to a degree with a "something in return" selfishness. Professional fund-raisers are aware of such motives and use them in fund appeals. Is it possible, though, to give without *any* hint of self-interest?

While it may be rare for us to give in a way that is completely selfless, *selflessness* describes the giving nature of God. He gives gifts to us without expectation of reward, for what sort of reward could we offer the king of the universe (Psalm 50:9, 10)? God does not give to coerce us into doing His will. He gives freely, for this is His nature. We are not God, but we can strive to be godly in the matter of giving. In today's lesson, we learn much about God as the perfect giver of gifts (see James 1:17).

B. Lesson Background

The background for Lesson 1 applies here, so that information need not be repeated. However, the additional picture of *unity* addressed in this week's lesson lends itself to some scrutiny. A specific Greek word for *unity* appears only twice in the New Testament—at Ephesians 4:3, 13, both verses of which are part of this week's lesson. This does not mean, of course, that Ephesians 4 is the only place in the New Testament that addresses the concept of *unity*. Other texts use various other words to project the idea of *unity* or *oneness* (examples: Acts 1:14; John 17:11, 21, 22).

We wonder why Paul would choose to address the topic of *unity* by using a word he uses nowhere else. (He uses different Greek words to discuss *unity* in Romans 15:5, 6; 1 Corinthians 1:10; Philippians 4:2; and Colossians 3:14.) On the one hand, we acknowledge that the difference may be no more than stylistic. On the other hand, per-

haps Paul uses a relatively rare word to stress to the Ephesian readers their need to pay close attention to the concept of *unity*.

Ephesus was one of the largest cities of the ancient world. It was home to the magnificent pagan temple of Diana (or Artemis; see Acts 19). To establish a church in the shadow of such an imposing structure had to be intimidating! Without unity, there was no way for the Ephesian church to survive in this environment.

I. Called to Unity
(EPHESIANS 4:1-6)
A. Hard Work (vv. 1-3)

1a. I therefore, the prisoner of the Lord,

Paul's reference to being a prisoner is more than a figurative way of referring to his deep sense of obligation to serve the Lord. Paul is a literal prisoner, under house arrest in Rome awaiting his requested hearing before the emperor (Acts 28:16; Ephesians 3:1). Paul understands his state as part of the cost he bears for his service to the Lord as a minister of the gospel (compare Revelation 1:9).

1b. . . . beseech you that ye walk worthy of the vocation wherewith ye are called.

To *walk worthy* is to live life in an acceptable, proper manner (compare Colossians 1:10). The Greek word translated *worthy* is the term from which we get our English word *axiom,* meaning a universal, fundamental correctness.

Paul defines this further by including a standard whereby one may measure the worthiness of one's living: *the vocation wherewith ye are called.* The sense of *vocation* is bigger than our employment choices. It is to be invited or summoned to something—in this case to a new life in Christ. The reader is being called to check his or her lifestyle to see if it is worthy of the high calling of

HOW TO SAY IT

Artemis	*Ar*-teh-miss.
Ephesus	*Ef*-uh-sus.
Eurydice	You-*rih*-dih-see.
Orpheus	*Or*-fyus or *Or*-fee-us.
Pentecost	*Pent*-ih-kost.

being a follower of Christ (Philippians 3:14). It is to be a life of holiness (1 Peter 1:15, 16).

❧ *THE PRESIDENT AND THE RABBIT* ❧

While fishing on a pond in 1979, President Jimmy Carter noticed a swamp rabbit, hissing and gnashing its teeth, swimming toward his boat. Not sure what was wrong with the critter, the president used his paddle to shoo it away. Unfortunately, the incident was caught on camera and reported in the press. As a result, the president was repeatedly (and unfairly) asked in public forums to explain what he had against poor, defenseless rabbits! To many, the president's action didn't seem to be, well, "presidential."

The world sometimes holds Christians to unreasonable standards as well. Unbelievers will distort minor incidents to create "evidence" that our faith is invalid, that we are all hypocrites. God doesn't do that. He works with us while we are still making progress rather than waiting for us to be perfect before putting us into service for Him.

Our lives should be a witness to unbelievers (1 Timothy 3:7; 1 Peter 2:12). Even so, to "walk worthy" of our calling does not mean that we serve God with timidity because we fear the world may misinterpret what we do. God is our judge, not the world. We live and serve in such a way that God, who sees the heart, will approve.   —A. W.

2, 3. With all lowliness and meekness, with longsuffering, forbearing one another in love; endeavouring to keep the unity of the Spirit in the bond of peace.

Paul explains the nature of this high calling in three categories. *Lowliness and meekness* characterize the submissive life, the life of a person who seeks to serve. The churches of the first century have their share of abrasive, self-serving persons, sometimes in leadership (compare 3 John 9, 10). Sadly, there are Christians today who seem to relish conflict and desire to dominate. Such behavior works against unity.

Second, we are to be *longsuffering,* meaning that we practice *forbearing one another.* There is nothing more central to the character of a self-centered person than impatience with others. To live in a

God-centered manner is to live as though having the patience of God. No church is made up of perfect people. There are many quirks and behaviors that can become divisive irritants if we let them.

Third, we live our lives so that we can contribute to the *unity of the Spirit* as characterized by *the bond of peace.* The church unity that Paul portrays is not the result of dynamic human leadership, grudging toleration of others, or mindless conformity. It is a work of God, a peaceful work of the Holy Spirit among God's people (see Acts 9:31).

What Do You Think?

What are some situations, if any, when one or more of Paul's three categories should not be practiced in the church? Why, or why not?

Talking Points for Your Discussion
- 1 Corinthians 4:21; 5:13
- 2 Corinthians 11:4
- 3 John 9, 10
- Jude 3

B. Grand Scope (vv. 4-6)

4. There is one body, and one Spirit, even as ye are called in one hope of your calling.

Paul now expounds on unity by giving us "the seven great *ones*" of the Christian faith in verses 4-6. The phrase *one body* reflects a favorite way for Paul to describe the church (see Ephesians 2:16). The fact that the human body is made up of many parts working together is a useful illustration that helps us understand that *unity* in the church does not mean *uniformity* (Romans 12:4, 5; 1 Corinthians 12:12-27). This way of understanding the church also lets Paul present the role of Christ as "head of the church" (Ephesians 5:23).

Continuing divisions in the church are our work, not God's. If we take Paul seriously, we come to realize there is more church unity than we may recognize at first glance. The second and third of Paul's "seven ones" show this.

The *one Spirit,* who indwells the church, is indivisible. Human folly cannot change that fact. Christians are also united by *one hope.* Elsewhere, Paul speaks of Christian hope in two related ways: it can be the hope we have for eternal life (Titus

1:2; 3:7), but also the confidence we have that Christ will come again (Titus 2:13). Either way, the Christian hope is a positive and encouraging view of the future.

5. One Lord, one faith, one baptism.

One Lord is the object of our one hope: the Lord Jesus. The recognition of Jesus as Lord is included in the earliest strands of Christian history (see Acts 2:36; 10:36; Romans 1:3; 1 Corinthians 8:5, 6). Jesus is the source of the church's hope and the focus of the church's *one faith.* Paul's call for unity draws the readers back to this simple fact. We have one faith because we have one Lord.

This unified faith is expressed in *one baptism.* The details of the practice of baptism have a long history in the church, with variations beginning to show by the end of the first century. But we should not forget that Christian baptism is always an act of faith in the one Lord, Jesus Christ (Matthew 28:19; contrast 1 Corinthians 1:13). This ageless and beautiful practice of the church began on the Day of Pentecost (Acts 2:41).

6. One God and Father of all, who is above all, and through all, and in you all.

Paul's final, climactic *one* is indeed a grand unifier: our realization that there is *one God.* The fourfold use of *all* keeps the focus on the unified church as she relates to the one God. The fact that He is *Father of all* is reflected also in 2 Corinthians 6:18; for the Father to be *above all* means that He is separate from and superior to the church (compare Romans 14:10-12); *through all* indicates God's working through the men and women of the church to accomplish His purposes (see Ephesians 3:10, 11); *in you all* points to God's living in the hearts of the believers who make up the church (see Ephesians 3:16).

What Do You Think?

Which of Paul's seven *ones* do you struggle with most? Why?

Talking Points for Your Discussion
- In terms of doctrinal understanding
- In terms of practical application in general
- In terms of practical application as focused on church unity

---

Part of One Body in Christ

II. Called to Service
(EPHESIANS 4:7-16)

A. Giving to Equip the Church (vv. 7-12)

7. But unto every one of us is given grace according to the measure of the gift of Christ.

Having laid out the grand vision of the basis for the unity of the church, Paul now moves to practical ways by which this may be achieved. Grace, at its heart, is the expression of a free gift. God's gifts to the church are universal in scope *(unto every one of us),* but the gifts are not identical. They are given according to the judgment of Christ, the Lord of the church. He knows both what we should be given and what the church needs (see 1 Corinthians 12:4-6).

8. Wherefore he saith, When he ascended up on high, he led captivity captive, and gave gifts unto men.

Paul draws on Psalm 68:18, written by David, to show that God's giving nature is not a new thing for Him. Paul has modified this verse from "received gifts for men" to *gave gifts unto men.* We can be sure that Paul does not make such an adjustment out of confusion. Paul, guided by the Holy Spirit, knows what he is doing. In the change of David's king as gift-receiver to Paul's king as gift-giver, Paul grabs the attention of any Jewish reader familiar with Psalm 68. In so doing, Paul turns the attention to his point that God is a giving God.

Paul's procedure does not give us warrant to change the language of Old Testament verses to suit our purposes, for we are not inspired authors of Scripture. But it does show us the priority of the New Testament and the supporting role of the Old Testament when it comes to doctrine.

9, 10. (Now that he ascended, what is it but that he also descended first into the lower parts of the earth? He that descended is the same also that ascended up far above all heavens, that he might fill all things.)

A murky belief in the early church proposed that Jesus descended into Hell during the time between His death and resurrection. This idea even became enshrined in some of the early creeds. It is based on an incorrect reading of this and other passages (see Romans 10:7; 1 Peter 3:19). This proposal has

Visual for
Lesson 3

Point to this visual as you work through the seven ones *discussion question associated with verse 6.*

more to do with the Greek myths of Orpheus and Eurydice than the teachings of the Bible.

Paul is describing, rather, Christ's descent from Heaven to earth (the incarnation; see John 1:14; Philippians 2:6, 7) and His subsequent ascension to God's right hand (Romans 8:34). This reenacts the triumphal procession portrayed in Psalm 68, including the giving of gifts from the largesse of the triumphant king (see 2 Corinthians 2:14).

11. And he gave some, apostles; and some, prophets; and some, evangelists; and some, pastors and teachers.

Some students think that Paul's focus here is on individual spiritual gifts. A better idea is that Paul is teaching that Christ gives *apostles, prophets, evangelists,* and *pastors and teachers* to the church. To be sure, these specialized servants are first given the capacity (spiritual giftedness) to minister in extraordinary ways. But Paul's emphasis throughout this section is on the God-given and God-protected unity of the church, not the spiritual fulfillment of individual believers.

Apostles are those commissioned by Jesus himself and given unique authority in matters of teaching. *Prophets* are those in the first-century church who speak the powerful Word of God as given to them by the Lord and as needed by the church. Both are necessary functions to guide the church in faith and practice before the New Testament is finished. While some churches still recognize one or both of these roles today, no one should be seen to have authority to supersede or add to the Bible (Revelation 22:18, 19).

Evangelists preach the gospel. They are considered to be close associates of the apostles as they preach in coordination with the apostolic ministry (see Acts 21:8; 2 Timothy 4:5). Today, evangelists are those who share the gospel with the unsaved.

Focused on a local congregation, *pastors* are the shepherds of the church, those who look after the spiritual needs of the flock. This is equated with the office of elder in 1 Peter 5:1, 2. An overlapping office is that of *teacher* (see 1 Timothy 3:2), one who explains the facts and implications of the gospel. Some students think that the overlap should cause us to think of a singular *pastor-teacher*.

12. For the perfecting of the saints, for the work of the ministry, for the edifying of the body of Christ.

The categories of church leaders named in verse 11 have a single, unified purpose: preparing the members of the church *(the saints)* with the necessary education, competencies, and attitudes to be confident in their own ministries. All Christians are called to be ministers. Each is to contribute to the work of the church.

The result should be *the edifying of the body of Christ,* meaning that believers are to serve in ways that make the church stronger and more effective. This equipping ministry should produce new generations of church leaders who will equip others in turn (2 Timothy 3:17).

What Do You Think?

Who has been most responsible for helping equip you to serve Christ? How will you help equip others to serve?

Talking Points for Your Discussion
- Through teaching
- Through encouraging
- Through example
- Through invitations to use talents and spiritual gifts

B. Loving to Grow the Body (vv. 13-16)

13. Till we all come in the unity of the faith, and of the knowledge of the Son of God, unto

a perfect man, unto the measure of the stature of the fulness of Christ.

Paul realizes that a perfect church will not be found in this world. Yet he still expects churches and their members to strive toward certain ideals of perfection. First, there is to be unity in matters *of the faith.* Sadly, faith issues often divide churches. Second, there is to be a commonly held knowledge concerning the Son of God. The most foundational doctrinal statement in this regard is that Jesus is "the Christ, the Son of the living God" (Matthew 16:16).

As we attend to these two, we grow up spiritually *(unto a perfect man).* The measuring rod in this regard is always Christ himself. Christ is the church's head. The body of Christ is to become worthy and pleasing to its Lord.

14. That we henceforth be no more children, tossed to and fro, and carried about with every wind of doctrine, by the sleight of men, and cunning craftiness, whereby they lie in wait to deceive.

Division may originate in the teachings of deceivers, those who teach self-serving doctrine contrary to the spirit and teachings of the apostles and of Christ. In the unified church envisaged by Paul, the members will have grown to the place that they are not confused about the essentials of the faith and will resist challenges. Christians find spiritual strength in the unity of a congregation that clearly teaches the primary, ancient doctrines of the church.

What Do You Think?

How is unity in the church similar to and different from the camaraderie of, say, a bowling team or a civic organization?

Talking Points for Your Discussion
- 2 Chronicles 30:12
- Psalm 133:1
- Romans 12:4-8; 15:5

15, 16. But speaking the truth in love, may grow up into him in all things, which is the head, even Christ: from whom the whole body fitly joined together and compacted by that which every joint supplieth, according to the

effectual working in the measure of every part, maketh increase of the body unto the edifying of itself in love.

In ending this section, Paul reviews his points. His vision of the unified church looks up to Christ, the head and pattern for all Christians. The unified church works harmoniously together, not wasting energy on fighting. The result is a healthy body that functions effectively.

> **What Do You Think?**
> Does the dispute between Paul and Barnabas in Acts 15:36-40 give us a precedent for allowing disunity in certain contexts? Why, or why not?
> *Talking Points for Your Discussion*
> ▪ Galatians 2:11-13
> ▪ 2 Timothy 4:11 as a follow-up to Acts 15: 36-40
> ▪ The "lesser of two evils" concept
> ▪ The "to get along you have to go along" concept

All is conditioned on love. To speak *the truth in love* can be quite a challenge since it's easy for loving confrontations to degenerate into bitter disputes. If the one doing the confronting is not careful, the *love* aspect can evaporate as the desire to "be right" takes over. Edification in love may lead us to confront those who are wayward (see Jude 20-23), but love may cause us to hold our tongues and lead by example at times.

❧ CHRISTIAN MULTITASKING ❧

A buzzword of our overcommitted society is *multitasking,* which refers to trying to do more than one thing at a time. There are plenty of funny YouTube® videos of people getting into difficulty as they multitask. The serious side of this problem presents itself when drivers crash their cars because they're distracted by cell phone usage, etc.

Multitasking presents dangers, even in the Christian arena (see Luke 10:38-42). Yet there is one area where Paul says we *must* multitask: speaking the truth in love. Plenty of people are more than willing to tell us the truth, no matter how hurtful or unwelcome. Others express what they intend as unconditional love no matter what sin the other person commits. Rare may be the friend who speaks truth from loving motives and in loving ways.

On two occasions I have been on the receiving end of loving correction from a minister at our church because of misunderstandings with others. Both times he spoke with me privately, allowed me to tell my side of the story, affirmed my worth and his friendship, then suggested a different way to look at these situations and a better way to handle them. While no one likes to be corrected, his gentle but forthright manner not only helped me restore relationships, but also gave me a model for confronting others lovingly when they need to hear uncomfortable truth.   —A. W.

Conclusion
A. Giving Ourselves

Christina Rossetti was a Christian poet of the nineteenth century. Life experiences of loneliness and disappointment often gave a melancholy aspect to her poetry. We see this in her poem "In the Bleak Midwinter," which has become a Christmas song. Here Rossetti sees life as hard and cold. We too may experience life this way. Even so, Rossetti shows us the hope that was the saving grace of her life: God's gift of a Savior. At the end of the poem, she speaks to the deep needs of our lives:

> *What can I give Him, poor as I am?*
> *If I were a shepherd, I would bring a lamb;*
> *If I were a wise man, I would do my part;*
> *Yet what I can I give Him—Give my heart.*

God has given us His Son so that we might be saved. God has given the church the necessary gifts to bring it unity and peace. God has blessed us with His precious Holy Spirit. Even in—or especially in—the winters of life, may we submit to Him in humility and gentleness, giving Him our hearts in the unity of the Spirit.

B. Prayer

O God, may You work through us to make Your church one so that the world may see this unity and be drawn to Your Son. In His name, amen.

C. Thought to Remember

Serve Christ by serving others in ministry.

INVOLVEMENT LEARNING

Some of the activities below are also found in the helpful student book, Adult Bible Class.
Don't forget to download the free reproducible page from www.standardlesson.com to enhance your lesson!

Into the Lesson

Create cutouts of the numeral 1 that are about 6" in height; give one to each learner as he or she arrives. Comment as you begin class, "Today's study is all about the number 1. As we study, jot down words or ideas that relate to the concept of *oneness*. We will look at your lists later."

Into the Word

Download the reproducible page in advance and make copies of the "The Put-Together Church" tangram puzzle, one for each learner. Cut these puzzles apart as indicated, and put the resulting sets of puzzle pieces into envelopes, one set each. Give each learner an envelope.

Say, "These are pieces of a church. Let's see if we can get the 10 pieces unified so we have a 'put-together' church." Ask learners to work individually as they scan today's text of Ephesians 4:1-16 to uncover 10 truths that should characterize an effective, mature, unified body of believers. Add: "Although it won't always be possible, try to make the truth match the piece in some way. Use your numeral 1 to remind yourself of *oneness* ideas as you work."

After an appropriate amount of time, call for conclusions. Possible responses include "the church must be built on a solid foundation: the fact that Jesus is the Christ and Lord" [written on the base rectangle] and "the door is always open wide, for whosoever will may come" [written on the door]. *Alternative 1:* Do not cut the pieces apart; simply give each learner a copy of the uncut diagram to write on. *Alternative 2:* Do not distribute copies; instead draw the diagram on the board to complete as a whole-class exercise. If you choose this alternative, expect the answers to overflow to more than 10.

Answers should include the seven *ones* of verses 4-7. Expect some variety in the remaining three answers. Discuss.

Say, "I'm going to read the text again. As I do, jot a note on your numeral 1 that speaks most powerfully to you personally." Read the text slowly and distinctly. At the conclusion, ask, "Who will tell us what you picked and why?" If there is no response after 15 seconds, you can give one of your own as a sample. For example, you might say, "I wrote *one hope* from verse 4 because I anticipate Heaven beyond the grave" or "I wrote *mature in the fullness of Christ* from verse 16 because that is my earthly commitment and my heavenly anticipation."

Into Life

Option 1: Hand each learner a sheet featuring the simple outline of a traditional tombstone (easy to find on the Internet). On the tombstone's rectangular base have the inscription *A Worthy Life*. Ask each learner to write his or her name at the top of the stone. Direct the class, "Write some key words from today's text for your tombstone, words that you wish will characterize your earthly life. You may write as many or as few words as you wish." (Remind learners to give attention to their numeral 1s as well.)

Option 2: Return to the "The Put-Together Church" activity. Ask, "What is your piece of the puzzle for the unified church? What's missing if you fail to fall into place in our church?" Display a commercial jigsaw-puzzle box that says *Interlocking Pieces* on the front so learners can visualize a key truth: pieces must be connected firmly into a beautiful whole. Ask, "What can you do to make yourself more of an interlocking piece?" Allow responses, but do not put anyone on the spot. Revealing an answer for yourself may make others more comfortable to do so.

Distribute copies of the "No Longer Children" activity from the reproducible page. This exercise calls for answers that are very personal, so it may be best as a take-home activity.

ALIVE IN THE *John 3*
LIGHT OF CHRIST

DEVOTIONAL READING: Psalm 97

BACKGROUND SCRIPTURE: John 1:1-14; Ephesians 4:17–5:14

JOHN 1:1-5, 14

1 In the beginning was the Word, and the Word was with God, and the Word was God.

2 The same was in the beginning with God.

3 All things were made by him; and without him was not any thing made that was made.

4 In him was life; and the life was the light of men.

5 And the light shineth in darkness; and the darkness comprehended it not.

· ·

14 And the Word was made flesh, and dwelt among us, (and we beheld his glory, the glory as of the only begotten of the Father,) full of grace and truth.

EPHESIANS 5:1, 2, 6-14

1 Be ye therefore followers of God, as dear children;

2 And walk in love, as Christ also hath loved us, and hath given himself for us an offering and a sacrifice to God for a sweetsmelling savour.

· ·

6 Let no man deceive you with vain words: for because of these things cometh the wrath of God upon the children of disobedience.

7 Be not ye therefore partakers with them.

8 For ye were sometimes darkness, but now are ye light in the Lord: walk as children of light:

9 (For the fruit of the Spirit is in all goodness and righteousness and truth;)

10 Proving what is acceptable unto the Lord.

11 And have no fellowship with the unfruitful works of darkness, but rather reprove them.

12 For it is a shame even to speak of those things which are done of them in secret.

13 But all things that are reproved are made manifest by the light: for whatsoever doth make manifest is light.

14 Wherefore he saith, Awake thou that sleepest, and arise from the dead, and Christ shall give thee light.

KEY VERSE

And the Word was made flesh, and dwelt among us, (and we beheld his glory, the glory as of the only begotten of the Father,) full of grace and truth. —**John 1:14**

JESUS IS LORD

Unit 1: Victory in Jesus
LESSONS 1–5

LESSON AIMS

After participating in this lesson, each student will be able to:

1. Make a list of the benefits of light according to today's lesson texts.

2. Explain why God's light on our lives should dispel fear rather than cause us to fear.

3. Identify one personal dark secret and bring that secret into God's light in prayer.

LESSON OUTLINE

Introduction

A. Grotesque Creatures of Darkness

Advances in technology allow researchers to penetrate the deepest parts of the oceans with cameras. This previously unseen world (where there is no light) was thought by some to be devoid of living creatures, but it has been revealed as having an astounding variety of creatures. The pictures are unsettling though, for the creatures are grotesque and fearsome. They have been given names such as coffinfish, fangtooth, vampire squid, and viperfish. They are creatures of literal, physical darkness.

Occasionally, we hear of people who thrive (in an earthly sense) in the figurative darkness of secrecy. Take, for example, the discovery in 2010 that the officials of a small city near Los Angeles were receiving exorbitant salary and benefit packages. The city manager's compensation was nearly double that of the President of the United States. The police chief of this small, working-class burg was receiving about 50 percent more than the police chief for the city of Los Angeles. This happened because the numbers were negotiated in secret and not made public until investigators revealed them. Public outrage was predictable (and justified). The darkness of secrecy had protected these city officials from the wrath of their constituents, at least for a time.

God is omniscient (all-knowing). Nothing is hidden from Him. We cannot keep secrets from God. We cannot fool Him. God has all the facts, all the time, for all men and women. There is no darkness in God (1 John 1:5), for He knows our every thought and action.

While some may find this terrifying, it should not be. Christians should take comfort in the belief that their God is light, utter light that completely dispels darkness and leaves no shadows. We, as the people of God, can and should live in God's light with joy and confidence. This is the focus of our lesson today.

B. Lesson Background

The Lesson Background to Lessons 1 and 3 mentioned briefly the presence of the Temple of Diana (Artemis) in the city of Ephesus. We should

           Alive in the Light of Christ

now say a bit more about this edifice since it played a key role in the spiritual darkness of that city.

The people of Ephesus were proud of this temple, one of the seven wonders of the ancient world. The Greeks worshipped Artemis as the goddess of wild animals and hunting; her counterpart in Roman mythology was Diana, so the famous Ephesian temple was called by both names.

This temple was one of the largest buildings of its time. Its rectangular footprint was about the size of an American football field, including the end zones. The temple was constructed entirely of marble (except for the roof) and featured more than 100 massive 60-foot columns. We estimate that this temple was 600 years old when Paul first visited Ephesus.

That temple was a place of pilgrimage, a type of tourist attraction. Religious sightseeing meant that the Ephesians' love for Diana/Artemis was motivated by both religious and economic considerations. Any threat to this temple would have been seen as an attack on the city's heritage, prestige, and economy. Paul's preaching in Ephesus brought many people to the Lord and caused them to change their religious practices. The threat posed by Paul's message alarmed some Ephesians who depended on the temple for their livelihoods (Acts 19:27). This led to mob violence, which resulted in Paul's departure from the city (20:1).

Paul was under house arrest in Rome when he wrote his letter to the Ephesians about five years later. It is likely that some of his Ephesian readers were former worshippers at the temple of Diana/Artemis. Undoubtedly, some were still struggling to make a clean break with their pagan past. Some may have been living a double life: respectable church member in public, goddess worshipper in private.

Paul was aware of the strong pull of a convert's former life, how tempting it was to participate in

HOW TO SAY IT

Artemis	*Ar*-teh-miss.
Bethlehem	*Beth*-lih-hem.
Ephesus	*Ef*-uh-sus.
omniscient	ahm-*nish*-unt.

things that are displeasing to God and shameful for Christians. This forms the backdrop of the message of Paul we will look at as a part of this week's lesson. But first we will consider a section from the Gospel of John.

I. Life-giving Light
(JOHN 1:1-5, 14)
A. At the Beginning (vv. 1, 2)

1, 2. In the beginning was the Word, and the Word was with God, and the Word was God. The same was in the beginning with God.

We are used to seeing Christmas lessons feature the birth of Jesus in Bethlehem. But that's not how John begins his treatment of Jesus' origin. Bible students will recognize John's language as borrowed from the opening lines of Genesis. John wants us to make this connection. He does this to help us understand the prehistory of Jesus, His existence before He was born in Bethlehem. The pre-Bethlehem Jesus is *the Word* (compare Revelation 19:13). This harkens back to the Genesis description of God's creative word, how God created the world by speaking it into existence (Genesis 1:3, 6, 9).

The phrase *the Word was with God* indicates a distinction between *the Word* and *God;* at the same time, the phrase *the Word was God* indicates unity. Christian belief in the deity of Jesus as the Son of God does not mean that Christians believe in two gods. There is only one God, and the pre-existent Christ is an essential part of God in ways we cannot fully understand (1 Corinthians 8:6).

B. In Creation (v. 3)

3. All things were made by him; and without him was not any thing made that was made.

If we have any doubts about John's intention to use the creation account to introduce Jesus, such doubts are now put to rest. John does not follow the detailed, day-by-day format of Genesis, but simply gives a summary statement: *all things were made by him.* This is a grand affirmation of the deity of the Word, for there is nothing more god-like than to be the Creator of everything (Colossians 1:16, 17; Hebrews 1:2).

C. In Contrast (vv. 4, 5)

4. In him was life; and the life was the light of men.

God's first act in creation was to command "Let there be light," light described as separated from darkness (Genesis 1:3, 4). Reading the creation account carefully, we notice that this light is something different from sunlight or moonlight, for sun and moon are not created until day four (1:16).

John sees *light* as much more than a physical phenomenon of electromagnetic radiation. Light is tied to life, and the source for both is the creating Word of God. All living creatures on earth depend on the light of the sun, either directly or indirectly. Even the denizens of the deep oceans where there is no light depend on food sources that drop to their levels from waters that do receive light.

But John is dealing with spiritual truths, not physical science. Everyone needs the light that comes from God in order to have life. This light is personified in Jesus, who later announces "I am the light of the world" (John 8:12).

What Do You Think?

Of the things God has revealed about himself through the Word (Jesus), which changes people the most in your experience?

Talking Points for Your Discussion
- Something Jesus said
- Something Jesus did
- Something in Jesus' nature

---

5. And the light shineth in darkness; and the darkness comprehended it not.

Light and darkness are not equal, opposing forces like the two poles of a magnet. If you enter a completely darkened room and light a small birthday candle, there will be light in that room. There is no equivalent for darkness. You cannot enter a brightly lit room and activate a darkness candle to dim the light. Light always trumps darkness.

John uses this physical truth to illustrate his spiritual message. The Greek word translated *comprehended* has a double meaning, with the second meaning being "to take down" or "to overcome." The forces of darkness can neither understand nor defeat the light of Jesus. The light of the Word will always shine, even in the darkest, most depraved human conditions.

D. Among Us (v. 14)

14. And the Word was made flesh, and dwelt among us, (and we beheld his glory, the glory as of the only begotten of the Father,) full of grace and truth.

If we were reading John 1 as a story, we would be surprised at the plot turn here. For the light of God to vanquish the darkness of sin, we might expect to read of some cataclysmic cleansing that burns sin out of existence. Instead, John tells us that the Word takes human form, becoming flesh.

We cannot fully understand how the Creator can be encapsulated in the form of a creature. But that is the message of Christmas! When God comes in the flesh (an event we call *the incarnation*), that does not mean that the power of God's light is minimized. John's word picture *we beheld his glory* evokes an image of blinding light (compare Matthew 17:1, 2; Luke 9:32). John is an eyewitness (1 John 1:1). Today we can behold God's glory through the eyes of faith. God is revealed through Jesus, His Son (John 14:9). Jesus reveals God's glory in His words and deeds (John 2:11).

The power of the enlightening message of Jesus is in the splendor of the truth it reveals. This message of God's love and salvation for all men and women is one of grace (John 3:17).

What Do You Think?

How does the fact that we do not serve a distant, impersonal God affect your life?

Talking Points for Your Discussion
- In the way you pray
- In the example you set
- In your speech patterns

II. Light-walking Life
(EPHESIANS 5:1, 2, 6-14)

A. Moving Toward God (vv. 1, 2)

1. Be ye therefore followers of God, as dear children.

Paul's *therefore* refers to his discussion in the previous verses of appropriate Christian behaviors.

These include speaking truth, controlling anger, foregoing thievery, sharing with the poor, using edifying speech, and forgiving others (Ephesians 4:25-32). As God's *dear children,* our lives should show the impact of this relationship.

2. And walk in love, as Christ also hath loved us, and hath given himself for us an offering and a sacrifice to God for a sweetsmelling savour.

Jesus' atoning sacrifice for human sins is the premier act of love that motivates sacrificial love in our own lives (see John 15:13). As we follow God, we will make loving sacrifices for others (compare Romans 14:15). Paul accentuates the sacrificial nature of Christ's death by borrowing language from Leviticus, which describes the burning of animal sacrifices as "a sweet savour" (see Leviticus 4:31). These were sin offerings, given as acts of atonement.

What Do You Think?

In what specific way do you need to grow in obedience to the command to "walk in love"? How will you do this?

Talking Points for Your Discussion

- Moving from word to deed (James 2:16)
- In keeping pure motives (Matthew 6:1-4)
- In embracing the area of ministry for which you are gifted (Acts 6:2-4)
- Regarding practices common at Christmas that could be continued year round

---

B. Moving Away from Darkness (vv. 6-8a)

6, 7. Let no man deceive you with vain words: for because of these things cometh the wrath of God upon the children of disobedience. Be not ye therefore partakers with them.

The Gospels picture Jesus as a "friend of publicans and sinners" (Luke 7:34), one who was willing to have fellowship with nonbelievers. How then can Paul advise us to *be not ye therefore partakers with them?*

We should note that in context Paul is speaking of false teachers *(them)* within the church. The *vain words* are the deviant teachings of those who advocate things that contradict Paul's teachings (see Colossians 2:4, 8). False teaching in Ephe-

Visual for Lesson 4. *Use this visual to start a discussion as you ask, "How does the imperative of Ephesians 5:8b follow from the fact of John 1:4?"*

sus might include some mix of Judaism with the Christian gospel. The result of such a mixture can be a doctrine that sees correct behavior as a way of earning salvation (contrast Ephesians 2:8, 9). Paul does not want to minimize the value of godly behaviors, but these actions flow from the life of the believer rather than being the requirement for God's favor.

Christians are to have a passion for souls, a strong desire to save the lost by sharing the gospel. This may entail having redemptive friendships with unbelievers. But we are not to allow those who push false doctrines to be our teachers in the church. We must not confuse our love for the lost with an affinity for false teaching.

8a. For ye were sometimes darkness.

Paul's language is strong and uncompromising. He does not say "Ye were once walking in darkness." Rather, he says *ye were sometimes darkness.* The word *sometimes* here does not mean "occasionally," but "then," "in the past," or "at one time." Paul speaks in absolute terms because the heart without Christ is not partially enlightened. It is dark, deep in sin, and without hope of salvation (compare John 3:19).

C. Living Right (vv. 8b-10)

8b. But now are ye light in the Lord: walk as children of light.

Paul matches the severity of his statement in verse 8a with the equally powerful assertion *now are ye light.* This is not a light of our own inner goodness, but *light in the Lord.* To be in the Lord's light means we see sin for what it is: a deadly lifestyle that keeps us from fellowship with God. Faith in Christ means we will live our lives in concert with the holiness of God, in whom we have put our trust (see Romans 13:12).

> ### What Do You Think?
> Who is a positive example of the phrase *walk as children of light*? How is darkness driven back by the influence of this believer?
> *Talking Points for Your Discussion*
> - Examples in the Bible
> - Examples from nonbiblical history
> - Examples from your life

❧ *BE A LIVING HISTORY* ❧

For the past several years, I have enjoyed being a Civil War reenactor. Sometimes our unit goes to an actual battlefield to depict what happened there. Other times we just put on a made-up battle somewhere to demonstrate to spectators what a battle would have looked like. For other occasions we do what we call a "living history": we make camp, set up tents, and just talk to visitors about what army life was like for the typical Civil War soldier.

At any of these of events, we have a campfire for cooking and sometimes for warmth. What the spectators don't see is what we do when we gather around the fire later that night: we enjoy the fire's warmth and the camaraderie that takes place as we enjoy casual conversation. I have noticed during such times that the campfire casts shadows around our circle, but the shadows occur only when something is blocking the fire's light.

Part of what it means to "walk as children of light" is that we do not cast shadows. Christians do not block the light of Jesus—quite the opposite! Christ gives us light—His light—and we walk in ways to defeat darkness. When we do so, we are a "living history" of Christ himself.   —J. B. N.

9, 10. (For the fruit of the Spirit is in all goodness and righteousness and truth;) proving what is acceptable unto the Lord.

There is a slight variation in the manuscripts at this point, with earlier manuscripts having "fruit of the light" instead of *fruit of the Spirit.* Paul's longer treatment of fruit of the Spirit is found in Galatians 5:22-26. It is possible that the Christians of Ephesus are familiar with Paul's letter to the Galatians, written a decade or so earlier.

But even if the Ephesians haven't heard Galatians read, the teaching of Paul during his lengthy stay in Ephesus would have included this material. So his words here serve as a reminder to them of what *is acceptable unto the Lord.* If we are walking in the light, living the life acceptable to God, there is nothing in the areas of *goodness and righteousness and truth* that is excluded.

D. Creating Visibility (vv. 11-14)

11. And have no fellowship with the unfruitful works of darkness, but rather reprove them.

In speaking of *the unfruitful works of darkness,* Paul has in mind behaviors that are opposed to Christian faith. Earlier he listed whoremongering, uncleanness, covetousness, and idolatry as examples (Ephesians 5:5; compare Galatians 5:19-21). The church must not ignore such activities among her members. The church is called to *reprove them.* Paul has more to say about having *no fellowship* in Romans 16:17; 1 Corinthians 5:11; and 2 Thessalonians 3:6. While the church is to be a refuge for sinners, it should not be a harbor for sin.

12, 13. For it is a shame even to speak of those things which are done of them in secret. But all things that are reproved are made manifest by the light: for whatsoever doth make manifest is light.

A central aspect of Paul's distinction between the deeds of darkness and the fruit of the Spirit is now explained: the matter of secrecy and shamefulness. Many sinful activities would be abandoned quickly if they were made public. Shame is still a powerful motivator for many people (although it seems to be less and less so today). Paul's logic goes like this: if you are doing things you would be ashamed to have made public, quit doing them.

14. Wherefore he saith, Awake thou that sleepest, and arise from the dead, and Christ shall give thee light.

While Paul knows that a full appreciation of God's complete awareness of our hidden actions may be a terrifying prospect, it has an encouraging aspect too. The pure light that godliness shines on our sin has not only the power to expose its evil, but also the power to transform us.

Paul does not intend the church to be a place of embarrassment and fear where sin is constantly outed. He intends the church to be a place where brothers and sisters work together to change sinful lives into lives of victory over sin. Christ is the light of the world to reveal the Father and draw us to Him. If we keep our focus on God and our paths directed toward Him, the issues of sin begin to fade away as our lives become more and more conformed to His will and the example of Christ.

The phrase *wherefore he saith* indicates that Paul is quoting something or someone. We don't know exactly what or who the source is, but some students see a general reference to Isaiah 60:1.

> **What Do You Think?**
> When was a time that a disclosure of one of your "secrets" resulted in you being freed from a burden? How were you transformed?
> *Talking Points for Your Discussion*
> - A secret you confessed voluntarily
> - A secret of yours revealed intentionally by someone else
> - A secret of yours revealed accidentally

❧ *RESURRECTION LIGHT* ❧

Photography did not exist in the first century to capture the detail of resurrection scenes. This allows artists to use considerable imagination when depicting the resurrections of Jesus, Lazarus, etc. Even so, there is an interesting constant in their paintings: the presence of streams of light.

Sometimes these rays of light come from the tomb itself, emanating from the background. Sometimes the rays of light originate from the figure who is emerging from the tomb, particularly if that figure is Jesus. Light and resurrection seem to be a common combination.

This combination fits with Paul's reference to sleepers awakening, rising from the dead, and receiving light. Perhaps it was my semirural upbringing, but when I was a youngster, people often referred to "that great getting-up morning." Most of us are greeted by light when we get up in the morning; on that great Resurrection Day, there will be light indeed! Even so, the reference here is more immediate: the risen Christ is shedding light *now* on those formerly dead in sin but now alive in Christ (Romans 6:1-14). What difference will that fact make in your life this week?   —J. B. N.

Conclusion
A. The Light Has Dawned

One of the most stirring prophecies of the Old Testament is found in Isaiah: "The people that walked in darkness have seen a great light: they that dwell in the land of the shadow of death, upon them hath the light shined" (Isaiah 9:2; see Matthew 4:16). During the Christmas season, we often celebrate by lighting candles. This has great symbolic power for us. Before the coming of the Christ, humanity lived in the darkness of sin with no hope. Even the nation of Israel, the chosen people of God, were inadequate in keeping their law and unwilling to share their blessings with Gentiles.

But light has come. Christ is the light of the world. He was present when the world was created, bringing physical light into the universe. He is present now as the living Word of God, breathing life into souls dead in sin. His light penetrates all darkness, exposes all secrets, and frees us from the bondage of hidden sin. Shine, Jesus, may You shine!

B. Prayer

Father, may we never be afraid of Your light. May we come out of darkness, and walk in Your brightly lighted road of righteousness. May we never cease to honor Christ with our lives, for He is our eternal light. We pray these things in Jesus' name, amen.

C. Thought to Remember

Take comfort in knowing
that nothing is hidden from God.

INVOLVEMENT LEARNING

Some of the activities below are also found in the helpful student book, Adult Bible Class.
Don't forget to download the free reproducible page from www.standardlesson.com to enhance your lesson!

Into the Lesson

Alternative 1: Have on display some images of sea creatures that live in the total darkness of the deepest ocean depths, as referred to in the lesson's Introduction. These are easy to find on the Internet. If you use PowerPoint®, you can create a slide show of these creatures; set your slide transition to automatic for these opening slides as learners gather. This will pique curiosity about the lesson.

Alternative 2: Ask, "When you were a child, what was it about the dark that caused you the most fear?" Let several respond. Ask also, "What is rational, if anything, about being afraid of what we cannot see?"

After either alternative, say, "Today's lesson evaluates the nature of spiritual darkness and why we need have no fear of anything that lurks there."

Into the Word

Distribute facedown copies of the "Important Truths" quiz from the reproducible page, which you can download. Give these instructions: "Don't turn these over yet! First, we're going to have a reading of today's texts of John 1:1-5, 14 and Ephesians 5:1, 2, 6-14. After I read these passages, close your Bibles, flip the quiz over, and mark each statement as either *J* (from John) or *E* (from Ephesians). You don't have to remember chapter and verse, just the correct book." Conduct the activity and discuss results.

Divide your class into two groups by sending around a paper bag containing an equal number of 2" squares of a dark colored paper and 2" squares of a light colored paper, with the total number of squares equaling the number of learners you have. Direct learners to draw out one square each without looking into the bag. Then say jokingly, "Now we separate the children of darkness [hold up a dark square] from the children of light [hold up a light square]!"

Assemble the two groups. (If your class is large, divide the two groups into four.) Give these directions: "I want you to develop an acrostic for the words *DARKNESS* (for the dark-squares group) and *HIS LIGHT* (for the light-squares group), based on today's study texts. You can use your key letters in any way—to begin words or phrases, to end words or phrases, or simply to fall in the middle of a word or phrase." (*Option:* Give each group a poster board with its word[s] in large caps arranged vertically down the center.) After learners complete and display their acrostics, ask for explanations of the relationship to ideas in the text.

Note the title of today's study ("Alive in the Light of Christ") and ask the class, "How would you state the opposite of today's lesson title?" (An obvious answer is "Dead in the Darkness of the Devil.") Then ask, "How does this 'opposite title' characterize nonbelievers?" Encourage free discussion.

Into Life

Distribute copies of the "The Lights of Christmas" activity from the reproducible page. Have learners complete this either in study pairs or small groups. After an appropriate amount of time, invite any who wish to share their responses with the class to do so. This can be a very meaningful time of reflection on the Christmas season.

As learners depart, give each one a lightly colored (white or yellow) sticky note (one brand name for these is Post-It®). Say, "I would like for everyone to have a 'light square' because we are all children walking in His light!" Suggest that they write the title of today's lesson, "Alive in the Light of Christ," on the note and affix it where they will see it at least once daily in the week ahead. You can also suggest that learners add additional thoughts to the note during each devotional time in the week ahead that reflects the "light nature" of the Christmas season.

Alive in the Light of Christ

CHRIST'S LOVE FOR THE CHURCH

DEVOTIONAL READING: John 3:16-21
BACKGROUND SCRIPTURE: Ephesians 5:15–6:9

EPHESIANS 5:18-33

18 And be not drunk with wine, wherein is excess; but be filled with the Spirit;

19 Speaking to yourselves in psalms and hymns and spiritual songs, singing and making melody in your heart to the Lord;

20 Giving thanks always for all things unto God and the Father in the name of our Lord Jesus Christ;

21 Submitting yourselves one to another in the fear of God.

22 Wives, submit yourselves unto your own husbands, as unto the Lord.

23 For the husband is the head of the wife, even as Christ is the head of the church: and he is the saviour of the body.

24 Therefore as the church is subject unto Christ, so let the wives be to their own husbands in every thing.

25 Husbands, love your wives, even as Christ also loved the church, and gave himself for it;

26 That he might sanctify and cleanse it with the washing of water by the word,

27 That he might present it to himself a glorious church, not having spot, or wrinkle, or any such thing; but that it should be holy and without blemish.

28 So ought men to love their wives as their own bodies. He that loveth his wife loveth himself.

29 For no man ever yet hated his own flesh; but nourisheth and cherisheth it, even as the Lord the church:

30 For we are members of his body, of his flesh, and of his bones.

31 For this cause shall a man leave his father and mother, and shall be joined unto his wife, and they two shall be one flesh.

32 This is a great mystery: but I speak concerning Christ and the church.

33 Nevertheless let every one of you in particular so love his wife even as himself; and the wife see that she reverence her husband.

EPHESIANS 6:1-4

1 Children, obey your parents in the Lord: for this is right.

2 Honour thy father and mother; which is the first commandment with promise;

3 That it may be well with thee, and thou mayest live long on the earth.

4 And, ye fathers, provoke not your children to wrath: but bring them up in the nurture and admonition of the Lord.

KEY VERSE

Submitting yourselves one to another in the fear of God. —Ephesians 5:21

JESUS IS LORD

Unit 1: Victory in Jesus

LESSONS 1–5

LESSON AIMS

After participating in this lesson, each student will be able to:

1. List three biblical principles for successful Christian family life.

2. Explain how being "filled with the Spirit" affects or relates to family relationships.

3. Commit himself or herself to fulfilling his or her role in the family in a Spirit-filled manner.

LESSON OUTLINE

Introduction

A. The Postmodern Family

The *nuclear family* (meaning mother and father living with their natural or adopted children) now represents fewer than 30 percent of American households. Sociologists refer to the *postmodern family* as they observe a bewildering array of family compositions. Economic stresses seem to have brought a return of the *extended family,* where children, parents, and grandparents live together; these are also known as *multiple-generation households.* There has been a rise in single-person households, "families" of one. We see more childless-by-choice households. Long-term relationships often do not include marriage. Many families consist of a single parent living with a child or children. *Blended families*—households having children from different parents—seem common. Whew!

All of this should cause Christians to look anew to the Bible as a guide for family and household structure. This is not so easy or simple, though. The Old Testament tells of families with multiple wives, something unacceptable today. The New Testament notes the existence of households with slaves, an unthinkable pattern now. But all is not lost! While family patterns may change, the Bible does indeed portray certain family relationships as having a God-ordained basis. Paul addresses this topic in the last two chapters of Ephesians.

B. Lesson Background

In Ephesians 5:21–6:9 and Colossians 3:18–4:1, Paul includes what has been called *a house table;* this is a list of obligations and duties to guide households (compare 1 Peter 2:18–3:7). Paul was not a husband (1 Corinthians 7:7; 9:5) and apparently a father only in a spiritual sense (1 Timothy 1:2). Yet his teaching as an apostle under the inspiration of the Holy Spirit is authoritative.

We also should remember that Paul came from a Jewish background, where the family was generally more stable and valued than in the pagan society of his day. In the Greco-Roman world, for example, some saw the prohibition of adultery as applying only to married women, with men allowed to have sexual relations with slaves or

Christ's Love for the Church

mistresses without social disapproval. We should understand, then, that Paul is particularly concerned to present a godly view of marriage and family that was familiar to his Jewish readers, but new for his Gentile readers.

I. Family of God
(EPHESIANS 5:18-21)
A. Spiritual Fulfillment (v. 18)

18. And be not drunk with wine, wherein is excess; but be filled with the Spirit.

Paul begins this section by contrasting a lifestyle of drunkenness (common among some Gentiles of his day) with the spiritually rich life of the Christian. To be *filled with the Spirit* is to be under the control of the Holy Spirit. To live a life of drunkenness, by contrast, means to be under the control of intoxicating beverages.

There is no absolute prohibition of alcohol consumption in the Bible. Even so, there is a consistent warning against drunkenness, seen as a destroyer of lives and families (see Proverbs 20:1; 23:20, 21, 29-35). Because there is an indistinct line between moderate alcohol consumption and excessive drinking, many Christians choose to abstain from alcoholic beverages altogether. Paul is not commanding abstinence, but his advice is to seek comfort in the fellowship of the Holy Spirit rather than in strong drink (compare Romans 8:5).

❧ OVERFLOWING WITH WHAT? ❧

It's interesting how drunkenness is displayed in movies and on TV. Often the person who is drunk stumbles around bumping into things, making weird faces, using slurred speech, and appearing happy and carefree. The scene is intended to be humorous and lighthearted. The reality as I have seen it is much different.

HOW TO SAY IT

Gentiles	*Jen*-tiles.
Judaism	*Joo*-duh-izz-um
	or *Joo*-day-izz-um.
messianic	mess-ee-*an*-ick.

I used to ride the bus to work. On two occasions, people who were drunk got aboard. One had lost control of himself and had wet his pants. It was not funny. Another had done worse, and the odor permeated the bus. That was not amusing for anyone. When I was a youngster, a man in my neighborhood—a man I knew and respected—sometimes got drunk. His slurred speech and stumbling ways were not funny. Coming from a person I knew and had respected, it was just sad.

How infinitely better to be filled with the Spirit! When I was in graduate school, a young woman who lived in our apartment building was the most Christlike person I had ever met. Her life radiated peace, tranquility, and calm. She was gentle in speech and kind in disposition. She manifested a beautiful soul. What a joy it was to see that the Spirit overflowed every aspect of her life and personality! Do people say this about you? —J. B. N.

B. Spiritual Worship (vv. 19, 20)

19a. Speaking to yourselves in psalms and hymns and spiritual songs.

Using musical analogies, Paul indicates five interrelated ways in which our spiritual filling is enjoyed. Three of these (here) are in fellowship since the word *yourselves* is plural; the other two (v. 19b, below) are on a personal level.

The *psalms* are associated with the worship tradition of Israel. By Paul's day, the psalms of Israel had been gathered into a collection spanning hundreds of years. The Old Testament psalms are seen by the first-century church as having a rich messianic tradition (see Acts 13:33), thereby making them particularly suitable for Christian worship.

Hymns are Christian compositions that give musical expression to doctrine. We may have two such hymns embedded in the letters of Paul (Philippians 2:6-11; Colossians 1:15-20). These hymns are shared among congregations, thus providing a common aspect to worship on a regional basis.

The word translated *songs* is a term from which we get our English word *ode,* referring to poetic words set to music. Such compositions can be secular, so Paul qualifies his intent as *spiritual songs,* meaning compositions directed toward worship and expression of the Christian relationship with

God. Such music is to be a natural way of realizing the filling of the Holy Spirit, which permeates the Christian's life.

19b. Singing and making melody in your heart to the Lord.

Paul now moves to instructions on the private level, indicated by *in your heart*. Times of corporate worship should be followed by ongoing personal worship. Our spiritual filling is not just for Sunday, but continues after the congregation disperses. The power of music in worship can be seen in those times during the week when the lyrics and/or melody of a piece of Christian music wells up in our souls, giving us a sense of worship.

> **What Do You Think?**
> In what ways have you seen music be a positive influence on Christians? How can we keep music from being a stumbling block?
>
> *Talking Points for Your Discussion*
> - Music styles in the church
> - The influence of secular music on believers
> - Using secular music within the church
> - Application of 1 Corinthians 8 to music issues
> - Other

20. Giving thanks always for all things unto God and the Father in the name of our Lord Jesus Christ.

Paul now shifts to the language of prayer: *giving thanks*. As spiritually minded believers, we should never lose sight of our dependence on God. Central to our thanksgiving is to remember what God has done for us through His Son, Jesus Christ. We should not make a hard distinction between the prayers of the church and the music of worship. A worship song addressed to God is a prayer.

> **What Do You Think?**
> Under what circumstances do you find it particularly important to express thanks to God?
>
> *Talking Points for Your Discussion*
> - During times of grief
> - During a family crisis
> - During a specific time of year
> - Other

C. Spiritual Submission (v. 21)

21. Submitting yourselves one to another in the fear of God.

This verse is a bridge between Paul's discussion of the spiritual life in the context of worship and his counsel on how to put the spiritual life into practice on the family level. The common factor is submission, a voluntary yielding of control. Recognition of God's power and submission to His authority are at the core when we worship.

The word translated *submitting* has a military background, carrying the sense of "complying with orders." This call should not be seen as an opportunity for church leaders to take an authoritarian position in demanding submission since *the fear of God* doesn't allow that. Rather, Paul is calling for mutual submission in the body of Christ, a spirit of loving others more than oneself.

> **What Do You Think?**
> Under what circumstances do you find it most difficult to follow the imperative of verse 21? Why is that?
>
> *Talking Points for Your Discussion*
> - Submitting to Christians who have no spiritual authority over us
> - Past experience with authority being abused
> - Cultural trends regarding authority/submission
> - Other

II. Family in Christ
(Ephesians 5:22–6:4)

A. Wives, Husbands, and Christ (vv. 22-24)

22. Wives, submit yourselves unto your own husbands, as unto the Lord.

Paul now calls for wives to have a spirit of humbleness and submission to the authority of their husbands (also Colossians 3:18). However, Paul is not giving husbands permission to act as tyrants over their wives. This becomes clear as Paul proceeds with his instructions.

23. For the husband is the head of the wife, even as Christ is the head of the church: and he is the saviour of the body.

In both the Jewish and the Gentile households of Paul's day, the father/husband is seen as having great authority within the home. Paul does not challenge this. But, using the analogy of Christ, he reminds us that this authority does not come without responsibility. Christ, who is both the head and Savior of the church, gave His life to save us. As the church's Redeemer, Christ has authority in the church as its ultimate leader (compare 1 Corinthians 11:3; Ephesians 1:22, 23).

24. Therefore as the church is subject unto Christ, so let the wives be to their own husbands in every thing.

We keep in mind that Paul is speaking of the family as an extension of the church, the Christian family. His use of *every thing* is thus not a blanket command for wives to obey their husbands in absolutely anything they ask. For example, Paul would not approve of a husband's asking his wife to participate in a criminal activity. Yet in general Paul sees the husband as the leader of the Christian home, and wives should respect that fact.

What Do You Think?

What are some ways a husband can make it easier for his wife to follow his lead?

Talking Points for Your Discussion
- Decision-making style
- Listening skills
- Personal priorities
- Other

B. Husbands, Wives, and Christ (vv. 25-33)

25. Husbands, love your wives, even as Christ also loved the church, and gave himself for it.

Now Paul focuses more explicitly on the expectations of the husband: he should *love* his wife. The kind of love in view is the godly, unselfish love that Christ has demonstrated. Rather than see his wife as a target for exploitation, the husband is to honor her with his own self-giving love and protection (Colossians 3:19; 1 Peter 3:7).

If the wife submits and the husband takes advantage of her submission, the marriage will be a failure. If the husband gives his all for the wife and the wife takes advantage of his self-sacrifice, the marriage will likewise fail. Although unmarried himself, Paul sees the ideal Christian marriage as a remarkable relationship of mutuality: the wife accepting the husband's leadership, and the husband putting his wife's needs before his own.

26, 27. That he might sanctify and cleanse it with the washing of water by the word, that he might present it to himself a glorious church, not having spot, or wrinkle, or any such thing; but that it should be holy and without blemish.

Paul's picture is reminiscent of wedding language where a bride is presented to her husband (see 2 Corinthians 11:2). This powerful image is based on the expected virginal status of a new wife, unspoiled by sexual contact while unmarried. In Paul's day, a never-married woman who is not a virgin is not a suitable bride within Judaism (Deuteronomy 22:13-29). Christ, though, does not allow the imperfection of His bride (the church) to stop their marriage. Christ himself purifies the church (Colossians 1:22) so that she becomes suitable to be wed to the Lamb of glory (Revelation 19:7, 8).

The *washing of water by the word* is baptism, seen as a symbolic enactment of the scrubbing of the sinful soul (Acts 22:16; Titus 3:5; compare Psalm 51:2). Baptism is an act of faith. So too the Christian marriage should be based on trust, with each party having the spiritual and physical welfare of the other as paramount.

✷ IRONING OUT THE WRINKLES ✷

Some of us are looking for "the perfect church." If we ever find one, we shouldn't join it because then it would no longer be perfect! My wife and I have lived in several states and have been members of various churches through the years. In every instance, the local congregation looked very inviting at first. But over time the luster would fade as we became aware of various issues and the personality characteristics of certain leaders. They were still good people, and we enjoyed the fellowship, but we knew it was not a perfect church.

Augustine once said, "The church that is without spot or blemish must ever pray, 'Forgive us our sins.'" Because the church is the bride of Christ, she is pure and clean. Because the church is made up of people, she must ask for forgiveness. When that happens, the result is a church worthy of being the pure bride of God's only Son.   —J. B. N.

SUBMIT TO
ONE ANOTHER

Visual for
Lesson 5

*Point to this visual as you introduce the discussion
question associated with verse 21 (page 156).*

**28. So ought men to love their wives as their
own bodies. He that loveth his wife loveth
himself.**

Paul puts the golden ethic of "love . . . thy
neighbour as thyself" (Luke 10:27) at the center
of the husband's obligations. Marriages that are
pleasing to God are based on selflessness. There is
no conflict between loving one's wife and loving
oneself. However, there is more to the expectation
of a husband loving his wife than his personal gain
from doing so, as Paul discusses next.

**29, 30. For no man ever yet hated his own
flesh; but nourisheth and cherisheth it, even as
the Lord the church: for we are members of his
body, of his flesh, and of his bones.**

The natural inclination of a man (or anyone, for
that matter) is to take care of his own body. We
may be guilty of destructive behaviors that damage
our health, but we all at least *want* to have healthy
bodies. Paul broadens his observation to include
the care that Christ has for *his body,* which is the
body of believers—the church (see Romans 12:5).

**31. For this cause shall a man leave his father
and mother, and shall be joined unto his wife,
and they two shall be one flesh.**

Paul's quotation of Genesis 2:24 presents a
biblical understanding of the basis for marriage
(see also Matthew 19:5). Children grow older,
break bonds with their parents, and establish
new families through their own marriages. The
newly forged bond between husband and wife is

intended by God to be strong, both spiritually and
physically, to the point that they are considered
one flesh (contrast 1 Corinthians 6:16).

Paul's point, then, is that the husband who
treats his wife in ways that strengthen their marriage is fulfilling God's intention to have men and
women in lifelong relationships as the foundation
for families and the building block for society.
This is true for the church as well, for strong marriages help build strong churches.

We should recognize, however, that Paul is not
saying these things to diminish those who are
unmarried, for elsewhere he commends the single life (1 Corinthians 7:8). He is speaking here
in pointed, specific terms to husbands and giving
them a Christlike, biblical example for the manner in which they are to honor their wives.

**32. This is a great mystery: but I speak con-
cerning Christ and the church.**

Paul's use of the term *mystery* usually implies
a truth from God that must be revealed through
an inspired messenger such as Paul himself (see
1 Corinthians 15:51). In this case, Paul is saying
that a deep, thoughtful understanding of God's
created pattern for marriage helps us understand
the relationship between Christ and His church,
a relationship of willing sacrifice. The great love of
Christ for His church is a guide for understanding
God's intentions for marriage, particularly concerning the role of the husband.

**33. Nevertheless let every one of you in par-
ticular so love his wife even as himself; and the
wife see that she reverence her husband.**

Paul's summary may seem obvious to those
who have grown up with Christian expectations
for marriage: the husband acts with great love
for his wife, and the wife responds with willing
respect. We should remember, however, that this
concept is countercultural for Paul's Gentile readers. In their households, the husbands often act
in self-serving ways, and wives harbor resentment
as a result. The "escape valve" of divorce is not a
ready remedy in Paul's day (especially for women),
and many families are very unhappy places. The
tendency today is either to divorce when things
get tough or to try to avoid the problems of marriage by engaging in unmarried cohabitation.

It does not have to be this way! The solution is to honor God's pattern for marriage by these foundational principles: a husband must love his wife and show it in his actions, and a wife must respond by honoring and supporting her husband as her own demonstration of love.

C. Children, Parents, and the Lord (6:1-4)

1. Children, obey your parents in the Lord: for this is right.

The patterns of godly, submissive Christian behavior also apply in the relationships between children and parents. Thus Paul reminds children that God's pattern for families includes respectful obedience (see Leviticus 19:3; Proverbs 6:20). *In the Lord* is the framework of submission to the lordship of Christ (see also Colossians 3:20).

2, 3. Honour thy father and mother; which is the first commandment with promise; that it may be well with thee, and thou mayest live long on the earth.

Paul invokes the Old Testament to help us understand the basis for children's obedience. The Ten Commandments express God's expectations for the behavior of His people, and this short list includes an injunction for children to honor their parents. This concept of *honoring* naturally includes obedience, for to disobey is to dishonor.

Paul points out that this commandment comes with a promise: the one who gives obedient honor to parents will be rewarded by God with a long and good life (Deuteronomy 5:16). Paul does not intend us to understand this in a simplistic, infallible cause-and-effect way, as in "if we honor our parents, then we are guaranteed to have a great life." Life is too complex and sin is too powerful for this to happen always. But Paul is confident that the Christian's life, family, and church will be stronger if submissive obedience by children is the rule (compare 1 Timothy 3:4, 5).

4. And, ye fathers, provoke not your children to wrath: but bring them up in the nurture and admonition of the Lord.

Selfish bullying or other mistreatment directed toward the children will result in bitterness in return. How can children be expected to honor a cruelly selfish father? The father should remember that rearing children is a God-given responsibility. The father is accountable to the Lord even within the walls of the family home.

> **What Do You Think?**
> How does a parent know when he or she is in danger of crossing the line from appropriate discipline to selfish bullying?
> *Talking Points for Your Discussion*
> - The age of the child
> - The issue of strong-willed children
> - The method of discipline
> - Other

Conclusion

A. Family Roles and Responsibilities

It may seem like a set of impossible expectations: a husband/father who acts with unfailing love for his wife and children; a wife/mother who supports her husband's decisions; and children who honor their parents with obedience. Many forces in society work against this ideal. Children are encouraged to be rebellious. Wives are belittled for not asserting their own interests. Husbands are tempted by examples of unfaithfulness that are presented in an appealing light. Is there any place for the pattern of the family as Paul sees it?

Throughout today's text, Paul keeps returning to Christ's love for the church. This is the key to understanding relationships. There is no greater love than what Jesus Christ showed in laying down His innocent life for our salvation. We are always to be guided by that profound example. Families may have complicated tensions resulting from generational history and sinful behavior. But this does not absolve us from seeking to live with Christ's love as our guiding principle.

B. Prayer

God, our great Father, make us more like Your Son. Help us overcome the pull of selfishness. May we love each other in our church and in our families as Christ has loved us. In His name, amen.

C. Thought to Remember

Let Christ's love show in your relationships.

INVOLVEMENT LEARNING

Some of the activities below are also found in the helpful student book, Adult Bible Class.
Don't forget to download the free reproducible page from www.standardlesson.com to enhance your lesson!

Into the Lesson

Use 12 large cards to prepare 4 sets of 3 cards in advance. On the first set, put the letters *L* and *O* on one card each, leaving the third card of the set blank. Do the same for the letters *O* and *B* for the second set, the letters *V* and *E* for the third set, and the letters *E* and *Y* for the fourth set. Tape the cards of each set together to form 4 triangles that will display the letters to your learners as the cards are stood on edge and rotated.

On a high stand easily seen, arrange the triangles so that your learners will see the letters *L-O-V-E* and *O-B-E-Y* in the correct order when those faces are showing. However, begin with the four blank faces showing. Say, "Two faces on each of these four triangles carry key concepts from today's text. When you think you know what the words are on the two faces, speak out." Rotate the triangles to reveal letters and blank spaces randomly for all to see clearly. When a learner eventually says that the words are *love* and *obey*, say, "Let's dig into today's text of Ephesians 5:18–6:4 to see why these words are important."

Into the Word

Say, "As we read today's text, be thinking how those two key concepts of *love* and *obey* are important to Paul's line of thought." Read Ephesians 5:18–6:4 aloud or have learners take turns reading the verses.

Call for an open discussion of *love* and *obey* as they relate to each other in the text. Push for comprehension beyond the superficial. For example, expect an observation that is something like "Obedience reflects a submissive attitude and spirit that is made easier when the relationship involves love." If this kind of "deeper" observation is not forthcoming, offer it yourself in the form of a question, such as, "How does a relationship characterized by love make easier the submissive attitude and spirit of obedience?" You also can reverse the question

this way: "How is it easier to express love in the presence of a spirit of submissiveness?"

Option: You may need to take some time to explore the concept of *submission* more fully since this can be an emotionally negative "trigger word" in today's culture. Try to avoid an overly defensive approach, which would involve a lengthy discussion on what this word "doesn't mean." Instead, adopt an affirmative approach by saying, "Let's take a glance at Philippians 2:5-11, which we will explore in Lesson 7." Read that passage aloud. Note Christ's submissiveness in obediently accepting death because He loved the Father, He knew that the Father loved Him, and He loved the church that was to come.

Direct the discussion back to today's lesson text by asking "How do *love* and *submission* relate to Paul's injunctions in Ephesians 5:18-21?" *Option:* At this point, you can use the "Drunken or Filled?" exercise from the reproducible page, which you can download.

Distribute handouts with the following "sub" words: *subhead, subject, sublet, submarine, subordinate, subsidiary, substitute, subway.* Say, "Scan through this list. What do these words imply about a relationship or relative position to something else?" If no one else does so, point out that the "under relationship" of each is one of function, not one of inferiority. Ask the class to look again at Ephesians 5:22–6:4 and identify the submissive relationships evident in verses that do not imply inferiority.

Into Life

Give each learner a copy of the "The Family (Re)defined" exercise from the reproducible page, which you can download. Depending on the nature and size of your class, this can be discussed in study pairs, small groups, or as a whole class. Ask, "What can you do this week personally to help our culture see God's ideal for the family?"

PROCLAIMING CHRIST

DEVOTIONAL READING: Psalm 119:169-176
BACKGROUND SCRIPTURE: Philippians 1

PHILIPPIANS 1:12-26

12 But I would ye should understand, brethren, that the things which happened unto me have fallen out rather unto the furtherance of the gospel;

13 So that my bonds in Christ are manifest in all the palace, and in all other places;

14 And many of the brethren in the Lord, waxing confident by my bonds, are much more bold to speak the word without fear.

15 Some indeed preach Christ even of envy and strife; and some also of good will:

16 The one preach Christ of contention, not sincerely, supposing to add affliction to my bonds:

17 But the other of love, knowing that I am set for the defence of the gospel.

18 What then? notwithstanding, every way, whether in pretence, or in truth, Christ is preached; and I therein do rejoice, yea, and will rejoice.

19 For I know that this shall turn to my salvation through your prayer, and the supply of the Spirit of Jesus Christ,

20 According to my earnest expectation and my hope, that in nothing I shall be ashamed, but that with all boldness, as always, so now also Christ shall be magnified in my body, whether it be by life, or by death.

21 For to me to live is Christ, and to die is gain.

22 But if I live in the flesh, this is the fruit of my labour: yet what I shall choose I wot not.

23 For I am in a strait betwixt two, having a desire to depart, and to be with Christ; which is far better:

24 Nevertheless to abide in the flesh is more needful for you.

25 And having this confidence, I know that I shall abide and continue with you all for your furtherance and joy of faith;

26 That your rejoicing may be more abundant in Jesus Christ for me by my coming to you again.

KEY VERSE

Every way, whether in pretence, or in truth, Christ is preached; and I therein do rejoice, yea, and will rejoice. —Philippians 1:18

JESUS IS LORD

Unit 2: Exalting Christ

LESSONS 6–9

LESSON AIMS

After participating in this lesson, each student will be able to:

1. Tell how Paul rose above his circumstances in order to rejoice in what God was doing.

2. Compare and contrast Paul's outlook with that of a contemporary figure who faces adversity.

3. Identify a source of opposition or adversity in his or her life and look for ways to rejoice in the midst of it.

LESSON OUTLINE

Introduction

A. Mixed Motives

Every so often, churches are shaken by the news that a leader has become tainted in some way. Whether the scandal centers on a national televangelist or a local youth minister, these situations raise serious questions. Can God really do His work through sinners? If a person who oversees an important ministry falls under a cloud of suspicion, is the ministry rendered invalid? Do wrong motives negate the positive effects of someone's work?

Our text today discusses this problem in the first-century church. Paul himself was tainted in the eyes of some by his imprisonment. Paul's enemies viewed the circumstances surrounding his Roman imprisonment as an opportunity to promote their own agenda. Both situations bear close scrutiny for how they speak to the church today.

B. Lesson Background

Philippians is one of Paul's four Prison Epistles, the others being Ephesians, Colossians, and Philemon. They are so called because Paul specifically refers to himself as a prisoner in these letters. These references situate the writing of Philippians late in Paul's career, when he was living in Rome under house arrest while awaiting a hearing before Caesar (see Acts 28:16, 30, 31) in about AD 63. Obviously, Paul was unable to visit the churches during this time, so he communicated with them through letters and a network of messengers. Two such messengers, Timothy and Epaphroditus, are mentioned in Philippians 1:1; 2:19-30.

Unlike many of Paul's letters, Philippians is characterized by a consistently warm and positive tone. This suggests that Paul was pleased with the progress that the church at Philippi had made. Paul had established that church on his second missionary journey, in about AD 53 (Acts 16:11-40). Thus the believers there had had about a decade to grow spiritually by the time Paul wrote his letter to them. The letter carries the tone of an extended thank-you note for the Philippians' spiritual and financial support of Paul (Philippians 1:5, 19; 2:25; 4:10-19).

While Paul was clearly thankful to and for the Philippians, other aspects of their situation were unsettling. During Paul's absence, itinerant teachers seem to have begun to circulate among the churches without his authorization. Such teachers could have a good message but wrong motives (Philippians 1:15-18, today's text). Others simply could have a bad message (3:2; see Lesson 8). It is against such a backdrop that today's lesson opens.

I. Gospel's Spread
(PHILIPPIANS 1:12-18a)

A. In Spite of Restrictions (vv. 12-14)

12. But I would ye should understand, brethren, that the things which happened unto me have fallen out rather unto the furtherance of the gospel.

This section opens with an autobiographical note that sets the tone for what follows. Paul's visit to Jerusalem in about AD 58 (Acts 21:1-26) marked the end of his third missionary journey. When Paul visited the temple in Jerusalem, he was seized by a mob and falsely accused of defiling the sacred precincts (21:27-30). Intervention by Roman soldiers saved Paul from death at the hands of the mob (21:31-36).

To appease the Jews and hoping for a bribe, the Roman governor Felix held Paul in custody for two years (Acts 24:24-27). In about AD 60, the new governor, Festus, took charge of Paul and his case (25:1-6). Paul's appeal to Caesar resulted in his ending up in Rome. There he spent two more years in custody, under house arrest (28:16, 30).

HOW TO SAY IT

Caesar	*See*-zer.
Diocletian	Dye-uh-*klee*-shun.
Donatus	*Don*-uh-tuss.
Epaphroditus	Ee-*paf*-ro-**dye**-tus.
Felix	*Fee*-licks.
Festus	*Fes*-tus.
Judaizers	*Joo*-duh-*ize*-ers.
Philemon	Fih-*lee*-mun or Fye-*lee*-mun.
Philippi	Fih-*lip*-pie or *Fil*-ih-pie.
traditores *(Latin)*	trad-ih-*tor*-ez.

All this is probably what Paul refers to in writing of *the things which happened unto me.* As a result of these unjust detentions, Paul has been unable to visit his churches for several years by the time the letter to the Philippians is written. In view of all this, the verse before us reflects a remarkable spirit of optimism. Looking at the positive, Paul focuses not on the chances he has missed but on the things he has been able to accomplish. His difficult situation has closed many doors but opened others, perhaps unexpectedly (next verse).

❧ GOOD FROM BAD ❧

Sometimes misfortune results in opportunities that would not have presented themselves had the misfortune not occurred. Such was the case at the Battle of Midway during World War II.

U.S. forces had located the Japanese fleet with its four aircraft carriers. Launching strike aircraft, the U.S. plan was to have low-altitude torpedo bombers and high-altitude dive bombers make a coordinated attack. But things went wrong, and the planes got separated. The slow torpedo bombers got to the enemy fleet first. Enemy fighters pounced and shot down every plane. But in so doing they abandoned their position high above the fleet. When the American dive bombers appeared, there was no fighter opposition at high altitude.

The result was devastating attacks on the Japanese carriers, with all four eventually sunk. What happened to the torpedo bombers was a misfortune of war, but it allowed the other U.S. planes to score a resounding victory that changed the course of the war in the Pacific Theater of Operations.

Paul's imprisonment seemed to be a great misfortune for the cause of the gospel. Christianity's chief spokesman was in jail! But Paul found opportunities to preach the gospel within this context. Perhaps the greatest opportunity and result is seen in the letters he wrote, which endure to this day. Do we allow troubling circumstances to paralyze us, or do we look for opportunities?   —J. B. N.

13. So that my bonds in Christ are manifest in all the palace, and in all other places.

Paul mentions his bonds (chains) or incarceration in the Prison Epistles also in Ephesians 3:1;

4:1; Colossians 4:3, 18; and Philemon 1, 9, 23. A notable result of Paul's imprisonment is stated here: many of the imperial guard, whom he otherwise would not have met, have heard his message. Some "of Caesar's household" have become believers (Philippians 4:22).

This verse reflects the situation described in Acts 28:16, which notes that Paul lives under house arrest under the watch of a solider. While some might view this as an unwelcome intrusion, Paul considers the guards to be a captive audience. The circumstances of Paul's arrest (see Acts 21) led many Romans to think Paul guilty of defiling the Jewish temple and/or inciting a riot in Jerusalem. Now, however, they can perceive the truth by his character, the events of Acts 27:1–28:10, etc.

What Do You Think?
How have you seen God use difficult circumstances for His glory?
Talking Points for Your Discussion
- In crisis resolution
- In divorce recovery
- In grief support
- During persecution
- Other

14. And many of the brethren in the Lord, waxing confident by my bonds, are much more bold to speak the word without fear.

Paul's outlook reflects a theme of Greco-Roman thought: suffering is worthwhile when it inspires others to action. Since Paul is a prominent Christian leader, his imprisonment can strike fear in the hearts of fellow believers, leading them to hide their faith (compare John 19:38). But his hardships actually have the opposite effect; Paul's willingness to preach an unsoftened message in the face of suffering inspire *many of the brethren in the Lord* to step out boldly. Their testimony is an aspect of Paul's affirmation in verse 12: if he had not been imprisoned, perhaps these people would not have found the courage they now demonstrate.

In the final analysis, then, imprisonment does not silence Paul's message, but amplifies it. He himself continues to spread the good news, and others add their voices to the chorus of witnesses.

What Do You Think?
How do you move past (or through) fear when it comes to doing God's work?
Talking Points for Your Discussion
- Drawing support from others (Ezra 10:4)
- Keeping priorities straight (Matthew 10:28)
- When acting alone (Mark 15:43)
- Looking to the ultimate source of strength (Hebrews 13:6)

B. In Light of Differing Motives (vv. 15-18a)

15. Some indeed preach Christ even of envy and strife; and some also of good will.

The "waxing confident" of verse 14 indicates enthusiasm. But this enthusiasm leads in turn to the fact that not everyone who is emboldened to proclaim Christ does so with good motives. The terms *envy, strife,* and *good will* probably refer to the attitudes people hold toward Paul rather than toward God (this will become clearer in vv. 16, 17). Some preach to support Paul's work, while others are rivals to his mission. This fact undoubtedly adds stress to Paul's already difficult situation, but he refuses to be discouraged. Paul proceeds to examine the various motives.

16. The one preach Christ of contention, not sincerely, supposing to add affliction to my bonds.

Those who have issues with Paul's leadership view his imprisonment as a chance to advance their own agendas. Some may merely want to be in charge (compare 3 John 9). Others may disagree with Paul's doctrinal viewpoints. The latter opponents probably are *Judaizers*—Jewish Christians who insist that Gentiles must be taught to obey the Law of Moses before they can join the church (compare Philippians 3:1-6). Paul consistently opposes the teaching of the Judaizers (Acts 15:1-21; Galatians 3:1-14; 2:14; 5:1-12).

For now, however, Paul cannot visit his churches to counteract either kind of adversary; he is confined to house arrest while his opponents are free to roam. Paul therefore must address the problem by writing letters. In so doing, Paul challenges the motives of his opponents: while they claim to be

Proclaiming Christ

concerned with the spread of the gospel, they are also clearly taking advantage of Paul's situation.

17. But the other of love, knowing that I am set for the defence of the gospel.

Positively, some have risen to the occasion to ensure that Paul's mission continues during his imprisonment. They further the cause of Christ by proclaiming the gospel from a motive of love. These individuals include Timothy (Philippians 2:19-24) and Epaphroditus (2:25-30). Inspired by Paul's example, they continue the work despite the risks. Paul's claim in verse 12 is thus verified further: the gospel advances through his suffering.

18a. What then? notwithstanding, every way, whether in pretence, or in truth, Christ is preached.

After stating both the positive and negative sides of the issue, Paul concludes that the situation calls for rejoicing. Despite wrong motives, Paul's enemies are at least proclaiming the gospel of Christ! This mature outlook affirms that even those who do things for wrong reasons can have a positive impact on the world. The effects of the message are more important than the motives of the messenger. This causes Paul to rejoice (next verse).

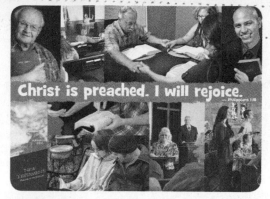

Visual for Lesson 6. *Point to this visual as you ask, "What are some ways we can express rejoicing one to another at the fact that Christ is preached?"*

> *What Do You Think?*
> How should we address a problem of wrong motives within a church's ministry teams?
> *Talking Points for Your Discussion*
> - Preventing wrong motives from developing
> - Addressing wrong motives after they have already developed
> - 1 Chronicles 28:9
> - 1 Corinthians 4:5

II. Paul's Outlook
(PHILIPPIANS 1:18b-26)

A. Joy and Expectation (vv. 18b-20)

18b. And I therein do rejoice, yea, and will rejoice.

The theme of rejoicing is prominent throughout Philippians. Several times Paul mentions the joy that he experiences, particularly when he hears good reports about the Philippians' progress in the faith (Philippians 1:4, 25; 2:2, 17, 18; 4:1, 10). He often urges his readers to rejoice as well (2:28, 29; 3:1; 4:4).

The backdrop of this letter suggests that Paul does not use the word *joy* in the emotional sense of "happiness" since he cannot be said to be happy either about his circumstances or what his adversaries are doing. Joy is, rather, a product of confident faith. It is an outlook on life that comes from the knowledge that God is in control and is making everything work toward His purposes. This kind of joy is like the "peace of God, which passeth all understanding" (Philippians 4:7).

19. For I know that this shall turn to my salvation through your prayer, and the supply of the Spirit of Jesus Christ.

Paul has a positive outlook not only because the spread of the gospel continues (v. 18a, above), but also because he remains confident that God is working out a plan that will lead to his release from prison. (The word *salvation* as used in this context refers to this anticipated release.) Christ will honor the Philippians' prayers and restore Paul to them soon. Paul definitely believes in the power of intercessory prayer (also 2 Corinthians 1:11).

20. According to my earnest expectation and my hope, that in nothing I shall be ashamed, but that with all boldness, as always, so now also Christ shall be magnified in my body, whether it be by life, or by death.

This verse puts a twist on what Paul has just said. Verse 19 implies that Paul expects to be vindicated and released from prison; now he specifies that the freedom he seeks is in Christ, regardless of the outcome of his anticipated trial. Paul desires to be faithful to his calling no matter the outcome of the imprisonment. Whether he lives or dies, he wants to honor Christ. If freed, Paul will continue preaching the message; if condemned, he will die with a clear conscience, unashamed.

This attitude explains Paul's ability to experience "joy" in his situation. He focuses on the bigger picture. This allows him to put his sufferings in proper perspective.

B. Life and Death (vv. 21-24)

21. For to me to live is Christ, and to die is gain.

This verse, perhaps better than any other, summarizes Paul's outlook on life (compare Galatians 2:20). If he is released, he will give all his energy to his ministry. If he is executed, God will reward him in Heaven. Obviously, the latter outcome would mean less work and quicker blessing for Paul, facts that lead him to view death as gain. Paul will return to this theme in chapter 3 (Lesson 8).

What Do You Think?

What might cause a person to hesitate to affirm, with Paul, that "to die is gain"? Why?

Talking Points for Your Discussion

- The nature of life in the age to come
- The difficulty of letting go of this life
- Other

❧ To Live Is Christ ❧

Martin Luther was the key figure at the beginning of the sixteenth-century Protestant Reformation. After a fruitful life of more than 62 years, Luther died peacefully in the town in which he was born. But his life was hardly free from stress and danger.

Once wracked by insecurity that God could not accept him, Luther finally achieved peace in the knowledge that we are saved by grace, not by our works. As a result of this realization, he ended up challenging many teachings of the Roman Catholicism of the day. This brought the wrath of the Holy Roman Emperor as well as the threat of other princes. At one point, Luther agreed to appear before the entire German government at a tribunal, even though his friends warned him it was a trap that would end in his arrest and execution. When the tribunal demanded that he renounce his beliefs, he refused, stating, "Here I stand. I can do no other. God help me. Amen."

I can do no other. That was Luther's equivalent to Paul's "to live is Christ." For Luther, to live was simply to follow the teachings of Scripture. He would follow Christ, or he would die. There was no middle ground, no compromise. Would that we had the same devotion today!   —J. B. N.

22, 23. But if I live in the flesh, this is the fruit of my labour: yet what I shall choose I wot not. For I am in a strait betwixt two, having a desire to depart, and to be with Christ; which is far better.

These two verses unpack verse 21. On the one hand, Paul is confident that he will continue to be productive as long as he lives. This confidence is based on the principle stated in verse 12: no matter what happens, God will somehow bring something good from the situation.

On the other hand, Paul is under no illusion that life will get better, even if he is released from custody. Things would be much more pleasant for him if he were simply in Heaven. There he could live eternally in the presence of Christ rather than in the presence of Roman soldiers (compare 2 Corinthians 5:8).

By the phrase *what I shall choose,* Paul is speaking hypothetically, as if he has a choice in the matter. But Paul knows that the choice is God's, not his. As Paul ponders the two possible outcomes, he is resolved to accept whatever God deems best. God knows which outcome is best for His purposes. For Paul to commit suicide in order *to be with Christ* would be to take the choice out of God's hands. Paul will not do this. God is in control, not Paul. Even so, Paul thinks he knows what God's choice will be (next verse).

24. Nevertheless to abide in the flesh is more needful for you.

Paul has eternity ahead of him in Heaven, but the Philippians need him now. Regardless of Paul's own preference, the fact is that God still has work for him. God's calling comes first. For now, God needs Paul to continue working, even though this means that Paul's suffering will continue.

C. Presence and Joy (vv. 25, 26)

25. And having this confidence, I know that I shall abide and continue with you all for your furtherance and joy of faith.

Confidence in God's wisdom provides Paul the rationale for his suffering. While Paul prefers freedom to imprisonment and while he is weary of his struggles with his enemies, Paul knows that his suffering will help the Philippians in their faith journey. His pain will lead to their joy. Paul's pain is beneficial to us some 2,000 years later: if he had not been imprisoned, then he may not have written the letter to the Philippians, which is an enduring treasure for the church.

What Do You Think?

How do you know you are being effective in your own ministry of "furtherance"?

Talking Points for Your Discussion

- Measuring spiritual growth (2 Peter 1:5-8)
- Handling unwarranted criticism (Romans 3:8; 2 Corinthians 10:10)
- Evaluating results (Acts 6:7)
- Other

---

26. That your rejoicing may be more abundant in Jesus Christ for me by my coming to you again.

Paul ends this section on a positive note, anticipating that God will not only preserve his life, but also will secure his freedom so he may visit the Philippians. Thus Paul provides additional encouragement to them.

Conclusion

A. One Reason for Joy

In AD 303, the early church faced the most severe persecution ever by the Roman Empire. Under a series of edicts from the Roman emperor Diocletian, Christians were forbidden from meeting and were required to offer sacrifices to pagan gods. Those who refused were tortured or killed.

Faced with these pressures, many Christians paid homage to the pagan gods and surrendered their churches and Scriptures for destruction. When the waves of persecution subsided, these individuals came to be called *traditores,* Latin for "surrenderers" or "ones who had handed over." They had surrendered church property, and sometimes the names of other Christians, to the Roman authorities.

A significant controversy arose within the church concerning the status of these individuals, especially because many *traditores* were clergy. If a preacher had given in to the pressure—at least outwardly if not inwardly—did that fact render his message invalid? Would the Lord honor a baptism or communion service that was conducted by someone who had yielded to the demands of pagan Rome?

A major segment of the church, led by Donatus of Carthage, argued that God could not honor the worship led by those whose faith was not pure. Many Christians, however, concluded that God could overlook the shortcomings and mixed motives of the *traditores,* and that the imperfections of a messenger do not corrupt the effects of the message.

Today's lesson suggests that Paul would have agreed with the second viewpoint. Paul could have argued that the results of his opponents' efforts were tainted by corrupt motives. In the end, however, Paul chose to focus on the fact that Christ was preached. May Paul's joy in this regard be ours as well!

B. Prayer

Father, sometimes we don't understand what motivates people to do what they do, and often our own motives aren't as pristine as they should be. Purify our hearts, help us not to become discouraged, and keep us focused on the ultimate goal. In Jesus' name, amen.

C. Thought to Remember

May the gospel shine through no matter what!

INVOLVEMENT LEARNING

Some of the activities below are also found in the helpful student book, Adult Bible Class.
Don't forget to download the free reproducible page from www.standardlesson.com to enhance your lesson!

Into the Lesson

Prepare a handout titled *Choruses*. Make three columns with the headings "Hymn Verse," "Chorus," and "Teaching or Testimony," one each. Print the following partial hymn verses under the first heading. 1. "I was sinking deep in sin." 2. "When peace, like a river, attendeth my way." 3. "I hear the Savior say, 'Thy strength indeed is small.'" 4. "Alas! and did my Savior bleed?"

Inform the class that many older hymns express praise in their choruses. Ask learners to write in the second column the beginning words of each hymn's chorus that corresponds to the first line of the hymn. They should also jot notes in the third column about what is taught by the testimony of the chorus. *(Answers for column two are 1. "Love lifted me!" 2. "It is well with my soul." 3. "Jesus paid it all." 4. "At the cross.")*

After completing the exercise, say, "Many hymns actually are testimonies by the hymn writers. Every Christian has a faith story to share. It may not be dramatic, yet it could be encouraging to someone who will hear it. Let's look at one person's dramatic testimony in today's text."

Into the Word

Deliver a fast moving mini-lecture based on the Lesson Background. Have the following words covered on a poster. Uncover each when appropriate in your mini-lecture: *Prison Epistle / House arrest / Messengers / Tone of letter / Itinerant teachers / Privilege of witnessing.*

The following activity may be done in three teams or as an entire class. If you choose to use teams, give each team a poster board and a marker. *Team 1* will focus on Philippians 1:12-14; *Team 2* will focus on 1:15-18; *Team 3* will focus on 1:19-26. Each team is to identify "impact" words or phrases; this means that learners will look for words or phrases that address results, changes, or values.

After an appropriate amount of time, ask teams to share their results. If learners are having difficulty identifying "impact" words, you may suggest the following examples: "my bonds in Christ are manifest in all the palace" (v. 13, for Team 1); "notwithstanding, every way, . . . Christ is preached" (v. 18, for Team 2); "to live is Christ, and to die is gain" (v. 21, for Team 3).

Distribute copies of the "What, How, and You" activity from the reproducible page, which you can download. This is best completed in small groups or study pairs. Since this exercise includes application, it can serve as a transition to the Into Life segment.

Into Life

Pose these two discussion questions: 1. Thinking of Paul's observations on motives in Philippians 1:15-17, what should be done, if anything, about this problem today? 2. Thinking of Paul's rejoicing in the fact that "Christ is preached" by those with impure motives (v. 18), what good have you seen come as a result of preaching done by someone who was later tainted by scandal?

Say, "Even while in chains, Paul affirmed that he was able to influence people around him. He added another affirmation that 'to live is Christ, and to die is gain' (v. 21). Use the following lines from hymns to identify bits of your own faith story; jot notes about your experience with Jesus."

1. "O happy day that fixed my choice on Thee, my Savior and my God!" (Philip Doddridge)
2. "All the way my Savior leads me; what have I to ask beside?" (Fanny Crosby)
3. "Moment by moment I'm kept in His love." (Daniel Whittle)
4. "Jesus is all the world to me." (Will Thompson)

Alternative: Use the "Forming a Testimony" activity from the reproducible page as a substitute for the above exercise.

IMITATING
CHRIST

DEVOTIONAL READING: James 3:13-18
BACKGROUND SCRIPTURE: Philippians 2

PHILIPPIANS 2:1-13

1 If there be therefore any consolation in Christ, if any comfort of love, if any fellowship of the Spirit, if any bowels and mercies,

2 Fulfil ye my joy, that ye be likeminded, having the same love, being of one accord, of one mind.

3 Let nothing be done through strife or vainglory; but in lowliness of mind let each esteem other better than themselves.

4 Look not every man on his own things, but every man also on the things of others.

5 Let this mind be in you, which was also in Christ Jesus:

6 Who, being in the form of God, thought it not robbery to be equal with God:

7 But made himself of no reputation, and took upon him the form of a servant, and was made in the likeness of men:

8 And being found in fashion as a man, he humbled himself, and became obedient unto death, even the death of the cross.

9 Wherefore God also hath highly exalted him, and given him a name which is above every name:

10 That at the name of Jesus every knee should bow, of things in heaven, and things in earth, and things under the earth;

11 And that every tongue should confess that Jesus Christ is Lord, to the glory of God the Father.

12 Wherefore, my beloved, as ye have always obeyed, not as in my presence only, but now much more in my absence, work out your own salvation with fear and trembling.

13 For it is God which worketh in you both to will and to do of his good pleasure.

KEY VERSE

Let this mind be in you, which was also in Christ Jesus. —**Philippians 2:5**

JESUS IS LORD

Unit 2: Exalting Christ

LESSONS 6–9

LESSON AIMS

After participating in this lesson, each student will be able to:

1. List ways that Christ serves as an example of humble service.

2. Contrast the attitude of humility that Jesus displayed with the attitude(s) that seem to be prized by modern culture.

3. Identify one area where his or her attitude needs to be closer to that of Christ and make a plan to change.

LESSON OUTLINE

Introduction

A. The Round Table

The legendary King Arthur is perhaps most famous for his round table. Challenging the hierarchical structure of medieval society, King Arthur is said to have built a table that had no "head," thus symbolizing that all the knights who gathered there had an equal voice.

If the legend is true, it means that Arthur believed that his round table would foster a spirit of camaraderie and mutual support—no one would feel the need to jockey for position. But it's possible to do so regardless of the shape of a table.

On one occasion, Jesus noticed how the guests at a dinner scrambled to secure seats of honor at the table. Reflecting on this human tendency, Jesus advised them to try a different course: rather than seeking the highest available seat, choose the lowest. It would be shameful if the host were to ask you to move down, but an honor to be asked to move up to a higher position. Further, and more significantly, God himself would bestow greater honor on a humble person (Luke 14:11).

Jesus not only taught humility, He also modeled it. Christ's willingness to come to suffer and die offers an incomparable illustration of self-sacrificing love. Only love would lead Christ to do what He did. This same motive should inspire us to love one another.

B. Lesson Background

Bible scholars are widely agreed that Philippians 2:6-11, part of today's text, is a quotation from an early Christian hymn. This would have been a song or chant used in worship and/or fellowship settings.

In addition to the poetic rhythm of the original Greek text, the content of this passage closely resembles other texts that also seem to cite ancient hymns; some possibilities are John 1:1-18; Luke 1:46-55; Colossians 1:15-20; and 1 Peter 3:18-22. These focus on the nature and work of Christ by highlighting His divinity and preexistence, role in creation, incarnation, painful death, resurrection, and exaltation (although not all these passages contain all these elements).

The hymn in Philippians 2 includes most of these elements, as we shall see. Just as listeners today recognize the words to familiar hymns or worship songs in sermons, Paul's readers would have recognized immediately the source of Paul's thoughts. They would have seen the relevance of Christ's example to their own situation of conflict.

I. Paul's Desire
(PHILIPPIANS 2:1-4)
A. If, Then (vv. 1, 2)

1. If there be therefore any consolation in Christ, if any comfort of love, if any fellowship of the Spirit, if any bowels and mercies.

Our text opens with a series of four *ifs* that expect a certain *then*. These "if-statements" summarize spiritual and emotional benefits that the Philippians—and indeed all Christians—enjoy (or should enjoy). The Philippian readers experience *consolation* to remain faithful through union with Christ. They know a sense of *comfort* in the face of difficulty that comes from experiencing His love. Their *fellowship of the Spirit* creates a unity unknown among pagan religions. The use of the word *bowels* may seem curious to us, but this is an older way of referring to "gentleness" or "softheartedness." All these things are the result of Paul's work among the Philippians. But how should they respond? What is the *then*?

2. Fulfil ye my joy, that ye be likeminded, having the same love, being of one accord, of one mind.

The desired outcomes of the four if-statements of verse 1 are here: Paul wants the Philippians to be unified in purpose, desire, affection, etc. The book of Philippians is widely known as Paul's "epistle of joy," as he frequently discusses his own joy and urges the reader to rejoice as well (see Phi-

lippians 1:4, 18, 25; 2:17, 18, 28, 29; 3:1; 4:4). Several times in the letter, as here, Paul uses the theme of joy to appeal to the Philippians' sense of loyalty to him. They will increase his joy by being *of one mind* (2:14-18; 4:2).

B. Not This, But That (v. 3)

3. Let nothing be done through strife or vainglory; but in lowliness of mind let each esteem other better than themselves.

Paul spends much of chapter 1 reflecting on his opponents who use his imprisonment as an opportunity to enhance their own influence. While Paul is pleased to know that others are preaching the gospel, it concerns him that these individuals are driven by less than pure motives (Philippians 1:15-18, last week's lesson). The proper attitude is described in the verse before us.

The Greek word translated *strife* is translated *contention* in Philippians 1:16 (last week's lesson), where it is set in contrast with *sincerely*. This speaks to wrong motives. *Vainglory* is a compound word that combines two terms that are in the Christ hymn in verses 5-11, as we shall see. The word *vain* carries the idea of "empty"; thus vainglory is "empty glory." This is what worldly people end up with as they amass power and praise for themselves. Their efforts are glorious only in the shallow sense of the word *glamour*. Ultimately, it is devoid of spiritual value.

Both strife and vainglory are part of the one-upmanship attitude that the Philippians are to avoid (compare Luke 22:24-26; 2 Corinthians 12:20; James 3:14-16). The model is to be Christ, as we shall see below.

C. Not Only, But Also (v. 4)

4. Look not every man on his own things, but every man also on the things of others.

The word *also* is critical here. Paul does not suggest that his readers should have no concern whatsoever for their own physical, emotional, and spiritual needs. Paul instructs, rather, that personal needs should not be all-consuming. We should not get "tunnel vision" regarding our *own things*. Instead, individuals should think of themselves as members of a larger group, assuming that what

HOW TO SAY IT

Colossians	Kuh-*losh*-unz.
Corinthians	Ko-*rin*-thee-unz (*th* as in *thin*).
Ephesians	Ee-*fee*-zhunz.
medieval	muh-*dee*-vul.
Philippians	Fih-*lip*-ee-unz.

is best for the group will ultimately be best for each one.

Our actions should contribute to the good of the whole, consistent with the spirit of unity that Paul desires for the church (v. 2, above). This is not to say, of course, that various boundaries are unnecessary or that we should simply do whatever people demand of us (Matthew 25:9); in many cases, what others desire may not be the best thing for either them or us to have. It *is* to say that Christians should fight against the natural impulse to put our own perceived needs before the needs of others, and especially that we should never seek to fulfill our desires at the expense of others (compare 1 Corinthians 10:24, 33).

> **What Do You Think?**
> How have you seen others reflect the lifestyle Paul encourages in verses 3, 4? How has this served as an example to you?
> *Talking Points for Your Discussion*
> - In parents caring for their children
> - In adult children caring for their aging parents
> - In a spouse addressing the needs of the other
> - In someone practicing benevolence
> - Other

II. Christ's Example
(PHILIPPIANS 2:5-11)
A. His Humility (vv. 5-8)

5. Let this mind be in you, which was also in Christ Jesus.

Paul now moves from exhortation to illustration: Christians should demonstrate the same attitude that Jesus did. This principle would seem obvious were it not for the fact that so many people in the church do not follow it!

Ideally, a Christian lives by the teaching and example of Jesus, not only in one's personal devotional life, but also (and especially) in the way that one interacts with others. The verse before us provides the rationale for the popular question, "What would Jesus do?" Before speaking or acting, particularly when the unity and mission of the church are at stake, we should pause to consider how Christ's example speaks to the situation.

> **What Do You Think?**
> In what situations have you noticed that your mind reflects or doesn't reflect that of Jesus? Why the difference?
> *Talking Points for Your Discussion*
> - In times of grief or sorrow
> - In times of financial distress
> - In times of family conflicts
> - In times when things are going well
> - Other

6. Who, being in the form of God, thought it not robbery to be equal with God.

The Lesson Background notes how ancient Christian hymns describe Christ's ministry path. Paul's citation in this regard begins with Christ's eternal position in Heaven, before His birth as the baby Jesus (compare John 1:1, 2; 17:5). *Being in the form of God* refers to Christ's status before He came to earth since verse 7 (next) will show us how Christ's form changed as He came to earth. The term *form* includes the idea of "invisibility" since the next use of *form* in verse 7 is a contrast with that of a visible human (compare Colossians 1:15).

The acknowledgement of the full deity of the Christ takes us into an area we cannot understand fully: the relationship among the persons of the Godhead. God has revealed himself to us in three persons—Father, Son, and Holy Spirit—and all share equal and complete divinity. Even so, Christianity does not teach that there are three gods, only one. But Paul's purpose is not to explain the mystery of the Trinity, so for us to try to push his explanation any further takes us into the area of speculation. Paul's purpose, rather, is to describe the great sacrifice that Christ made in becoming a human being. A key to understanding this sacrifice is to first establish what Christ's status was before He came as the baby Jesus in Bethlehem.

Christ made His sacrifice willingly, not holding on to His high position in glory. Christ had every right to hang on to this equality with God. To do so would not have been wrong since it was something that Christ rightfully possessed all along.

Imitating Christ

7. But made himself of no reputation, and took upon him the form of a servant, and was made in the likeness of men.

This verse has been the subject of much debate. The Greek translated *made himself of no reputation* carries the idea of "to empty" as part of the description of Christ's transition to human form. What, exactly, did Christ empty himself of in being *made in the likeness of men*? He obviously did not "empty" himself to the point of having absolutely *no reputation* whatsoever with regard to His divine nature; Christ never stopped being divine. Rather, the idea seems to be that He gave up certain privileges attached to His divinity.

While remaining equal with God in nature, Christ chose to become a human being with a low social position—a peasant laborer living on the outskirts of the Roman Empire (compare 2 Corinthians 8:9). Having previously borne the invisible form of God, Christ chose to take on the visible, physical *form of a servant* by becoming human. Paul stresses this stark contrast by repeating the word *form* from verse 6 (compare John 1:14).

We find it difficult to understand how Jesus could be both human and divine at the same time—but He was! Paul himself seems amazed that Christ became a human willingly, purely for the sake of others, and with no benefit to himself (compare Romans 8:3; Hebrews 2:14-18).

𝄞 *Sleeping by the* Parasha 𝄞

Victor Herman (died 1985) spent many years as a prisoner in Russia's gulags. His autobiography, *Coming Out of the Ice,* tells the story. For a time he was kept with 15 other prisoners in a cell 5½ by 10 feet. Herman says he was nearly insane after only 24 hours in the cell, surviving only because of a fellow prisoner known as "the Elder." That man was recognized as the leader, a man who looked out for the other prisoners. The Elder slept closest to the *Parasha*—the latrine—where the stench was the worst. He was also closest to the door, where he was the first to be beaten by the sadistic guards.

At the once-daily feeding time, the Elder counted the 16 bowls of soup, seeing that every man was fed, not letting anyone eat until all were

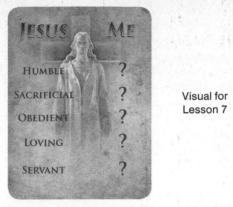

Visual for Lesson 7

Point to this visual as you ask, "In which area do you most need help in having the mind of Christ?"

served. At night, the men filled every bit of space on the cold stone floor. One could not turn without disturbing others, so twice a night the Elder called out for the men to turn.

Herman said that that cell would remain a model of Christian service to him for a long time. The cell reminded him that every situation in life, no matter how plain or grim, pointed to the need for a servant leader. But the cell told him also that the person who sits closest to the *Parasha*, the person most exposed to the blows of the system, could claim authority to lead and serve. That's something of what it meant for Jesus to "empty himself" for our sakes.   —C. R. B.

8. And being found in fashion as a man, he humbled himself, and became obedient unto death, even the death of the cross.

The fact that Christ *humbled himself, and became obedient unto death* was not a sign of weakness, but an expression of willpower since He could have stopped the process at any point (Matthew 26:53). Christ's decision to become a servant did not, at any moment, demonstrate a lack of strength—quite the opposite! His death was, among other things, an expression of obedience (Hebrews 5:8). The reference to the cross magnifies the point: Jesus not only died—something that God had never before experienced—He allowed himself to be killed in the most painful and humiliating way imaginable at the time.

> **What Do You Think?**
>
> What needs to happen in your life for you to walk the path of Christian humility?
>
> *Talking Points for Your Discussion*
>
> - Proverbs 16:19
> - Luke 22:26
> - John 13:5
> - 1 Peter 5:5
> - Other

B. His Exaltation (vv. 9-11)

9. Wherefore God also hath highly exalted him, and given him a name which is above every name.

The hymn now moves from Jesus' life on earth past Christ's resurrection to His return to Heaven. The opening word is significant. We don't use *wherefore* in modern English, but it has the sense of "by which" or "on which account." It was on account of Christ's humbling, obedience, and death that God exalted Him.

By implication, God also will exalt the Philippians if they put the needs of others before their own (vv. 3, 4, above). It is important to stress that Paul is not promising material honors to the Philippians, nor necessarily even something that will happen in this life. We may or may not end up with material blessings or positions of earthly prestige by humbling ourselves. Jesus was not honored that way, nor was Paul. But we, like Paul, certainly will receive spiritual blessings in the form of joy and peace in the face of trials. Imitating Christ always yields blessings (Mark 10:28-30).

The cross—the ultimate symbol of weakness and humiliation in the Roman world—became the means by which Christ achieved the most exalted position imaginable. The name *Jesus,* as glorious as it is, is not His only designation. He is also "King of kings, and Lord of Lords" (Revelation 19:16). Jesus is exalted over everything in God's domain, and everyone eventually will be forced to admit that this is true (next verse).

10, 11. That at the name of Jesus every knee should bow, of things in heaven, and things in earth, and things under the earth; and that every tongue should confess that Jesus Christ is Lord, to the glory of God the Father.

These verses describe the necessary human response to Christ given His status described in verse 9. The fact that the response includes *every knee* and *every tongue* leaves no one out (Isaiah 45:23). Absolutely everyone *should bow* and *should confess that Jesus Christ is Lord.*

The word *should* as used twice here conveys the idea of results that are expected. Everyone should acknowledge Jesus as Lord in the here and now, but God has given us free will to not do so. We are free to rebel against Him, and many foolishly choose that path.

But a time is coming when the *should* becomes *shall,* when the *expected* becomes *mandatory.* This is clear in Paul's use of Isaiah 45:23 in Romans 14:11: "every knee shall bow . . . and every tongue shall confess." The surrounding verses make clear that Paul is talking about Judgment Day in that context. Some will refuse to repent right up to the end (Revelation 9:20, 21; 16:9, 11), but they will be forced to bow and confess nonetheless.

III. Readers' Status
(PHILIPPIANS 2:12, 13)
A. Our Work (v. 12)

12. Wherefore, my beloved, as ye have always obeyed, not as in my presence only, but now much more in my absence, work out your own salvation with fear and trembling.

With the hymn completed, Paul moves to discuss implications. Paul is grateful that the Philippians *have always obeyed* him as their spiritual mentor. To obey Paul is to obey Christ since Paul is an apostle commissioned directly by Him. Obedience is closely connected with the goal of unity that Paul so fervently desires (see Philippians 1:27).

To *work out your own salvation* does not mean that we must do good works in order to be saved, a doctrine Paul opposes (see Ephesians 2:1-10). Now that we have been saved by grace, our obedience in putting others before ourselves, etc., is our "outworking" of that fact. The verse that follows adds clarity.

❧ WILLING TO DO GOOD ❧

Parents are pleased to see their children obeying them. Such obedience may initially come about because of a fear of punishment. Ideally, however, parental discipline is intended to provide a framework of godly principles that nurture a child along the bumpy path that leads to adulthood. Parents hope that by the time the child becomes an adult, he or she will have learned to *want* to do good.

A similar thing should happen with us as children of God. As we mature spiritually, we should find ourselves obeying God out of gratitude for His love and care rather than because we fear what He might do to us if we fail to obey. Maturity in Christ sometimes means deciding to do what's right even when part of us says, "I don't want to."

Someone has said, "Life is like a cafeteria line: the menu may be limited or not to our liking, but still we must make a choice." Paul encouraged the Philippians to be obedient to God in his absence just as they were when he was present. Mature faith produces good works with or without someone else watching over our shoulder. —C. R. B.

B. God's Work (v. 13)

13. For it is God which worketh in you both to will and to do of his good pleasure.

Realistically, the command to imitate Christ by putting others first, etc., seems overwhelming. Paul closes on a positive note by assuring the Philippians that they are not alone in this task, for *it is God which worketh in you.* This verse parallels Philippians 1:6, where Paul expresses confidence that God will complete "a good work" he had begun in the Philippians by helping them mature in their faith. God will work in them to help them both to desire *(will)* and act in a Christlike way. And so He will do with us too.

Conclusion
A. "Love Does Not Measure"

Mother Teresa (1910–1997) was the founder of the Missionaries of Charity in Calcutta, India, and winner of the 1979 Nobel Peace Prize for her selfless work for the poor. Her doctrinal beliefs are open to question on several points, but none can doubt her spirit of self-sacrifice. That spirit is reflected in some of her quotes:

> *I wouldn't touch a leper for a thousand [British] pounds; yet I willingly cure him for the love of God.*
> *I am a little pencil in the hand of a writing God who is sending a love letter to the world.*
> *Intense love does not measure, it just gives.*

Christ did not love on the basis of a measure of convenience or inconvenience for himself. Rather, He acted in terms of our need. To imitate Him, we must actively love others without regard for our own selfish desires. We must do this not only in the big decisions of life but also in everyday moments.

B. Prayer

Lord, we struggle to put others before ourselves. It's very hard to resist selfish urges. Help us understand what it means to love one another the way Christ loved us. In His name, amen.

C. Thought to Remember

The measureless love of Christ
is the model for all we do.

INVOLVEMENT LEARNING

Some of the activities below are also found in the helpful student book, Adult Bible Class.
Don't forget to download the free reproducible page from www.standardlesson.com to enhance your lesson!

Into the Lesson

Have this question on display as learners arrive: *When was the last time you saw someone humble himself or herself in Christian service?* Be prepared to voice your own response to this question, particularly if anyone is hesitant to go first. As situations are noted, ask learners to sum up their reactions in one or two words. Jot those responses on the board for later in the lesson.

Ask learners to offer definitions or synonyms of the word *humble;* list these on the board under that word. Come prepared with entries from a dictionary and a thesaurus to compare and contrast with learner responses. Then ask, "Is it always humiliating to be humble? Why, or why not?"

Make the transition to Bible study by saying, "Humility is a quality that the King of kings models for us in His life. Today's study even includes a segment of an early Christian hymn or chant that honors Jesus' humble service."

Into the Word

Create four study teams. Give each team a piece of poster board, a marker, and a copy of the following instructions appropriate to the team.

Team Hymns: Compare and contrast the Philippian hymn (Philippians 2:6-11) with the hymn of Colossians 1:15-20. Jot notes about common themes. Also note any themes unique to each.

Team Models: List instances from the life of Christ that demonstrate humble service. Do not include His teachings about service, only His actual models of humility.

Team Focus: Reflecting on Philippians 2:7, describe how Jesus could be both human and divine. Give examples from His life that illustrate His humanity and His divinity.

Team Culture: Read Philippians 2:1-13. Then list ways that our culture values attitudes contrary to Christ's model of humility. Feel free also to cite cultural encouragements to humble service.

Team Focus should also be given a photocopy of the lesson commentary on verse 7. Teams may be as small as two people, but no larger than four. If your class is larger, create additional teams and give duplicate assignments. *Option:* Add a fifth team, called *Team Humility.* Give members of that team copies of the "Characteristics of Humility" exercise from the reproducible page, which you can download, to complete per its instructions.

After an appropriate amount of time, call for conclusions. Encourage discussion.

Into Life

Pose the following discussion questions to your class: 1. What would you add to *Team Culture's* list of cultural values that are contrary to Jesus' model? 2. What great, godly things may happen as a result of living a life of humility? (Jot responses on the board under the word *Benefits.*) 3. What should we do and not do if someone tries to take advantage of our stance of humble service?

Next, say, "Now is the time to get personal and let Jesus' example touch our lives. I'm going to give you an opportunity to express your gratitude and your commitment by writing a prayer. You will work in the same teams as before, and you may write your prayer on the back of your poster board. Your prayer should include thanksgiving, recognition of Jesus' model of humility, and a commitment that reflects the heart of each of your team members. You may want to use the following starter words for each thought." Display the following model:

Dear Lord,
Thank You . . . / Your model . . . / We have learned . . . / Therefore, each of us on this team . . .

Alternative: Instead of having learners work as teams on the prayer exercise above, distribute copies of the "My Hymn" activity from the reproducible page for learners to work on individually. Invite learners to share their results.

Imitating Christ

KNOWING JESUS CHRIST

DEVOTIONAL READING: Matthew 13:44-46
BACKGROUND SCRIPTURE: Philippians 3:1-11

PHILIPPIANS 3:1-11

1 Finally, my brethren, rejoice in the Lord. To write the same things to you, to me indeed is not grievous, but for you it is safe.

2 Beware of dogs, beware of evil workers, beware of the concision.

3 For we are the circumcision, which worship God in the spirit, and rejoice in Christ Jesus, and have no confidence in the flesh.

4 Though I might also have confidence in the flesh. If any other man thinketh that he hath whereof he might trust in the flesh, I more:

5 Circumcised the eighth day, of the stock of Israel, of the tribe of Benjamin, an Hebrew of the Hebrews; as touching the law, a Pharisee;

6 Concerning zeal, persecuting the church; touching the righteousness which is in the law, blameless.

7 But what things were gain to me, those I counted loss for Christ.

8 Yea doubtless, and I count all things but loss for the excellency of the knowledge of Christ Jesus my Lord: for whom I have suffered the loss of all things, and do count them but dung, that I may win Christ,

9 And be found in him, not having mine own righteousness, which is of the law, but that which is through the faith of Christ, the righteousness which is of God by faith:

10 That I may know him, and the power of his resurrection, and the fellowship of his sufferings, being made conformable unto his death;

11 If by any means I might attain unto the resurrection of the dead.

KEY VERSE

What things were gain to me, those I counted loss for Christ. —**Philippians 3:7**

JESUS IS LORD

Unit 2: Exalting Christ
LESSONS 6–9

LESSON AIMS

After participating in this lesson, each student will be able to:

1. Tell what things Paul counted as loss in order to know Christ.

2. Suggest items in contemporary culture that a believer might count as loss in a manner similar to Paul's reckoning.

3. Identify one specific thing he or she should count as loss for Christ and give that to God in prayer.

LESSON OUTLINE

Introduction

A. Doctrine—Good or Bad?

What is your reaction when you hear the word *doctrine*? In a broad, general sense, that word simply means "something that is taught." Many Christians, however, think in terms of the specific teachings of a particular denomination or faith group when hearing that word. The word *doctrine* begins to take on decidedly negative overtones when connected with the idea of *indoctrinate* since this suggests something like "brainwashing." In this sense, those who want to have nothing to do with the church may explain their wariness in terms of a fear of "being indoctrinated."

But what about the doctrines taught by secular society? Our daughters are inundated (indoctrinated?) with images of what "the perfect body" is and what it takes to be accepted. Culture encourages us to chase after career accolades, striving to squeeze one more dollar into our bank accounts. We must get one more client or one more sale or have our names on the letterhead because society deems those to be worthy accomplishments. Various "reality" shows such as *Survivor* and *The Apprentice* teach viewers subtle and not-so-subtle lessons on how to beat the competition.

The supposed choice of being either "indoctrinated" by the church or living "doctrine free" in modern, secular society is a false choice. Culture has just as much doctrine—if not more—than the church. The real choice is whose doctrine will we choose to live by. The clash of doctrines and values between Christ and the world is vital to recognize.

B. Lesson Background

In his Pastoral Epistles (that is, 1 and 2 Timothy; Titus), Paul instructs leaders of the churches to protect sound, biblical doctrine. He sets that goal as one of their primary responsibilities. Sometimes we refer to false teachings and false doctrines as *heresies* (see 2 Peter 2:1). Heresies have taken various forms through the centuries. The primary heresy in Paul's day seems to have been the error of *Judaizing*. We discussed Judaizing in the commentary on Philippians 1:16 in Lesson 6, but perhaps a bit more can be said.

The Judaizers of Paul's day worked actively to undermine the message of salvation by faith. They taught that Gentile men had to be circumcised and otherwise adhere to the Law of Moses to be "true" followers of Christ. This implied that Christ's work on the cross was not sufficient for salvation.

There is debate among scholars as to whether the Philippian church had been infected with Judaizing. Paul's language in today's passage may lead us to believe this was the case, but the evidence is not conclusive. Perhaps Paul's language in Philippians 3 is preemptive in warning his readers should the teaching of the Judaizers ever come along. In other words, "forewarned is forearmed."

In any case, today's passage reveals some of Paul's deepest doctrinal convictions. These are gently blended with a discussion of the practical needs of the church at Philippi. When we study the churches of this formative era, we conclude that the spiritual maturity of most believers had not progressed very far (1 Corinthians 3:2; Galatians 3:1-5; Hebrews 5:12; etc.). We get the sense that there were few spiritually mature people for newer Christians to turn to for discernment.

The false teachers were crafty, and their message seemed compelling, so it was easy for new believers to be swayed. With this fact in mind, Paul decided that the issues of pedigree and accomplishments were important to address.

I. Actions to Take
(PHILIPPIANS 3:1-3)
A. Rejoice (v. 1)

1. Finally, my brethren, rejoice in the Lord. To write the same things to you, to me indeed is not grievous, but for you it is safe.

This is not the first time Paul has encouraged the Philippians to rejoice, nor will it be the last (see Philippians 2:18; 4:4). Given what follows below, Paul is reminding this community of believers to be joyful in the Lord no matter what doctrinal controversies and false teachers are presenting or will present themselves.

The statement *to write the same things to you* implies that Paul has addressed this issue with

the Philippians previously. Whether he did so in another letter we do not have or in person is not certain. What *is* certain is that Paul views this repetition as a safeguard. Those who *rejoice in the Lord* tend to be more unified. Negativity, on the other hand, opens the door of divisiveness.

What Do You Think?
How can we encourage fellow Christians to rejoice in the Lord when suffering trials? How do we avoid being flippant in doing so?
Talking Points for Your Discussion
- Habakkuk 3:17, 18
- Acts 5:41
- 2 Corinthians 4:17
- Hebrews 10:34
- 1 Peter 4:12, 13

B. Beware (v. 2)

2. Beware of dogs, beware of evil workers, beware of the concision.

This verse reminds the Philippian church of the dangers of the false teachers. As stated earlier, there is some debate among scholars whether the Philippian church is actually under the influence of false teachers (such as Judaizers) or if Paul is merely concerned about the possibility the church may fall victim (compare Galatians 3:1).

False teachers have a way of endearing themselves to the people they mislead, so Paul reminds the church of their true character and intentions in his use of the words *dogs* and *evil*. The word *concision* refers to circumcision in the negative sense of "mutilation" (compare Galatians 5:12).

HOW TO SAY IT

concision	kun-*sih*-zhun.
heresies	*hair*-uh-seez.
Judaizing	*Joo*-duh-*ize*-ing.
Moses	*Mo*-zes or *Mo*-zez.
Pharisee	*Fair*-ih-see.
Philippi	Fih-*lip*-pie or *Fil*-ih-pie.
Ponce de León	*Pohn*-say *day* Lay-**own.**
Sanhedrin	*San*-huh-drun or San-*heed*-run.

C. Identify (v. 3)

3. For we are the circumcision, which worship God in the spirit, and rejoice in Christ Jesus, and have no confidence in the flesh.

By using the word *we,* Paul is informing the Philippians that he and they collectively are the true believers *(the circumcision),* while those of "the concision" (v. 2, above) are not. The reason this is so is that Paul and the Philippians are the ones who (1) *worship God in the spirit,* (2) *rejoice in Christ Jesus,* and (3) *have no confidence in the flesh.* This implies that Paul's opponents don't do these things. The qualifier *in the spirit* overthrows any idea that proper worship is tied to external forms and specific places (John 4:23, 24).

Flesh is an important term in this regard, and Paul uses it frequently. His Jewish opponents hold their traditions and genealogical ties to be indicators of their status as the people of God. But elsewhere Paul notes that a person "is a Jew, which is one inwardly; and circumcision is that of the heart, in the spirit, and not in the letter" (Romans 2:29).

Confidence in the flesh is still a problem today. Think of the achievements that give people an elevated status in the eyes of the world and fuel their sense of self-importance (compare Matthew 6:1, 2). Within Christianity itself the problem of false confidence may be seen in things thought to be "necessary supplements" to the work of Christ on the cross. Christ has done everything necessary.

Paul draws a doctrinal boundary here: there is indeed such a thing as false doctrine. Some folks do not wish to grapple with the distinction between true and false doctrine, but we must.

What Do You Think?

What events tend to shake people out of their "confidence in the flesh"? How can we be witnesses for Christ during such times?

Talking Points for Your Discussion

- Meltdown in financial markets
- Loss of job
- Health crisis
- Family breakup
- Natural disasters
- Other

❧ *Vanities* ❧

Plastic surgery, in its foundational sense of "reconstructive surgery," has a long history. Such surgery was being done in India as early as 800 BC. First-century Roman surgeons performed minor facial repairs. In modern times, plastic surgery is used to repair birth defects, disfigurement from war or accidents, etc.

However, the late twentieth century saw a vast increase in the use of such surgery for reasons of personal vanity. In some cases, this kind of surgery seems to be done as part of the search for perpetual youth. The trend spawned at least two TV shows. Perhaps you snickered when you first heard the tale of Ponce de León's search in 1513 for the Fountain of Youth in Florida. Are modern attempts to remain perpetually youthful through vanity surgery any less laughable?

Paul's warning regarding *confidence in the flesh* was not directed to the problem of vanity surgery, of course. But the application is similar: to put confidence in the flesh in either the sense Paul is addressing or in a modern pursuit of maintaining an illusion of youth is to place trust in the wrong thing. Anything "of the flesh" in which we place trust—whether it be religious heritage, personal accomplishments, or youthful good looks—distracts us from Christ. Make sure this doesn't happen to you!   —C. R. B.

II. Example to Evaluate
(PHILIPPIANS 3:4-6)
A. Paul's Pedigree (vv. 4, 5)

4. Though I might also have confidence in the flesh. If any other man thinketh that he hath whereof he might trust in the flesh, I more.

If Paul were to dismiss the credentials of his opponents while lacking those same credentials himself, then he might be accused of having a "sour grapes" attitude. But it's another thing entirely for a critic to minimize the importance of certain credentials that the critic himself possesses.

If anyone has the pedigree according to Jewish law and tradition—*confidence in the flesh*—to be in right relationship with God, it is Paul! The Philippians are about to be reminded why.

5. Circumcised the eighth day, of the stock of Israel, of the tribe of Benjamin, an Hebrew of the Hebrews; as touching the law, a Pharisee.

Paul now describes his own Jewish heritage. The requirement for male Israelite infants to be *circumcised [on] the eighth day* is found in Leviticus 12:3 (compare Luke 1:59; 2:21). Paul was not exempted from this requirement.

Paul's ancestry is purely Jewish, as he also makes clear in Acts 22:3 and 2 Corinthians 11:22. The *tribe of Benjamin* is mentioned numerous times in the Old Testament. Paul announced his status as a Pharisee publicly on the occasions noted in Acts 23:6 and 26:5; the Pharisees are notable for their strict adherence to the Law of Moses.

B. Paul's "Accomplishments" (v. 6)

6. Concerning zeal, persecuting the church; touching the righteousness which is in the law, blameless.

This verse reflects Galatians 1:14, where Paul says he "profited in the Jews' religion above many my equals in mine own nation, being more exceedingly zealous of the traditions of my fathers." All of us have parts of our personal histories that we are ashamed of, and Paul's zeal in persecuting the church fits this category. Acts 8:3 and 9:1, 2 describe his actions in this regard. Paul doesn't try to hide his past (see Acts 22:4; 26:9-11).

As far as any perception regarding Paul's righteousness under the Law of Moses, no one can find fault with him. If there is anyone who holds the pedigree, qualifications, and works to earn a right relationship with God, it is Paul!

What Do You Think?

In what ways do you still tend to "rest on your laurels" of personal achievement? What is the danger in this?

Talking Points for Your Discussion
- Educational credentials
- Size of bank account
- Involvement at church
- Other

III. Attitude to Have
(PHILIPPIANS 3:7-11)

A. Regarding Rubbish (vv. 7, 8)

7. But what things were gain to me, those I counted loss for Christ.

The distinction between Paul and his opponents (who are described in v. 2, above) becomes sharper. What they still cling to as *gain* Paul has come to realize as *loss* (compare Matthew 13:44-46; Mark 10:28, 29; Luke 14:33). Paul thought for many years that his accomplishments and privileges as a Jew would allow him to be found blameless before God on Judgment Day. When Jesus intervened in Paul's life on the road to Damascus (when he was still known as Saul), he began the journey toward realizing that the accomplishments, pedigrees, and privileges of the flesh hold no sway with God. "For all have sinned, and come short of the glory of God" (Romans 3:23).

Society teaches that self-worth is based on our accomplishments in this world. Various status symbols help us "keep score" in this regard: the houses we own, the organizations we belong to, the size of our retirement accounts, etc. But such achievements hold no more weight with God than Paul's own heritage did. "All our righteousnesses are as filthy rags" (Isaiah 64:6). Christians are to find their self-worth in the fact that God sees us as worth saving and that He has taken the action necessary to bring that salvation about. The grace of God through the work of Christ is what we need for eternal life.

❧ *WHICH SCORECARD?* ❧

On January 1, 2011, the first baby boomers reached 65 years of age. The boomers (those born between 1946 and 1964) are the generation that became famous for self-absorption and a sense of entitlement. Boomers are those for whom TV first became a babysitter; as a result, youthful viewers ended up demanding from their parents all the toys, foods, and clothing that TV said would make them "special"—just like everybody else in their age group.

It would be easy enough to condemn the boomers for all the resulting focus on self. But boomers didn't get there without help! Parents and grandparents happily (and perhaps unknowingly) facilitated boomer self-centeredness and desire to "self-actualize." The result has been a stress on worldly accomplishment, with the pursuit of possessions and perks as the way to keep score.

The problem of judging a person's worth by personal accomplishments is as old as the human race, of course. But the baby boomer generation seems to have raised this value system to a new level. However, Paul says that none of this world's accomplishments—whether religious, secular, or material—is an indicator of our worth in the eyes of God. There are two kinds of bank accounts: earthly and heavenly (Matthew 6:19, 20; Luke 12:15-21; 2 Corinthians 6:10; 1 Timothy 6:6-10, 17-19). On which is your primary focus?

—C. R. B.

8. Yea doubtless, and I count all things but loss for the excellency of the knowledge of Christ Jesus my Lord: for whom I have suffered the loss of all things, and do count them but dung, that I may win Christ.

Paul's affirmation of his *loss for the excellency of the knowledge of Christ Jesus* exhibits his understanding of what is truly valuable. We should try to grasp the scope of what it has meant for Paul to *have suffered the loss of all things.* Paul (as Saul) seems to have been a rising star in Judaism at one time (Acts 22:3-5; Galatians 1:14), perhaps already having a seat on the Sanhedrin (Acts 26:10).

He gave up that career track for the cause of Christ. He lost his freedom on various occasions, sometimes for extended periods of time (one of which is in progress as he writes this letter). He lost the physical security and relative safety of a "normal" home life (2 Corinthians 6:3-10; 11:23-27). But Paul considers what he has gained in Christ to be worth all those losses and more.

Since Paul's ongoing desire is to know Christ Jesus in his life, *all things* in Paul's life must therefore fall in line with that desire. Just as our own accomplishments in this world are not necessarily evil in and of themselves, neither were the elements of Paul's Jewish upbringing. What was faulty was the way he put them to use (Acts 8:3;

9:1, 2). God gifts us in various ways, but how will we use our gifts and abilities? Counting all things as loss for Christ doesn't necessarily mean giving up what we're good at doing. It does mean, however, placing ourselves at God's disposal as we use those gifts and abilities.

What Do You Think?
In what ways have you seen people willingly suffer loss for the sake of Christ? How have things turned out for them?
Talking Points for Your Discussion
- Leaving a high-paying job for the mission field
- Downsizing one's lifestyle so more may be given to kingdom work
- Being ostracized by family members for becoming a Christian
- Other

B. Regarding Righteousness (v. 9)

9. And be found in him, not having mine own righteousness, which is of the law, but that which is through the faith of Christ, righteousness which is of God by faith.

Only God can provide what is necessary for salvation. Paul understands, as we must, that we cannot stand before God and expect to be declared righteous because of our works of the flesh or our adherence to the Law of Moses. Paul has much more to say about this in his extended discussion in Romans 3:9-31.

C. Regarding Resurrection (vv. 10, 11)

10, 11. That I may know him, and the power of his resurrection, and the fellowship of his sufferings, being made conformable unto his death; if by any means I might attain unto the resurrection of the dead.

The journey to *know [Christ], and the power of his resurrection* is ongoing. It continues throughout our lives. Much can be said about the power of Christ's resurrection, the event that proved Him to be the Son of God (Romans 1:4). It is Christ's resurrection that guarantees our own resurrection (1 Corinthians 15:1-34). We are *made conformable unto his death* initially in baptism (Romans 6:3,

4), but that conforming is also a daily process (see 2 Corinthians 4:10, 11).

The more we mature spiritually, the greater our awareness of our sins and the frequency with which we commit them. The more we study Scripture, the more questions we tend to have about our maturity. The more we strive to live the Christian life, the more we recognize how far we have to go in the struggle to become more like Christ. Spiritual maturity is reflected in the understanding of how much we fall short of God's glory, how far we have to go in our journey, and how incredible God's grace truly is.

Conclusion

A. What's Really Important

Paul's message to the Philippian church holds great relevance for us today. Satan will continue to attack the church and its message in creative ways. Today's lesson helps us develop a sense of discernment of the danger and presence of false teachings. When we have that discernment, we are able to draw boundaries to separate what is right from what is wrong.

One way that false doctrine creeps into the church is when believers fall victim to the old *appeal to authority* fallacy. The logical error here is to assume that a certain statement is true merely because the person who makes the statement seems to be an authority on the subject. Paul was aware of this danger, and he addressed it in today's text. The Philippians were not to accept a teaching just because those who were doing the teaching seemed to have credentials "of the flesh." If the validity of a teaching is determined on the basis of who has more credentials of the flesh, then Paul had more than any of his opponents! His Jewish genealogy was without flaw. His Jewish education was beyond question. His zeal as a Pharisee was unmatched. If anyone was going to accept truth under the *appeal to authority* logic, then they should listen to Paul!

But Paul was quick to make clear that "what things were gain to me, those I counted loss for Christ" (Philippians 3:7). The fact that Paul was willing to abandon the perks that his pedigree and accomplishments could gain him within Judaism lends credence to his message even 2,000 years later. What will (or must) we count as loss for Christ so that we can serve Him best?

B. Prayer

Father, use this passage from Your Word and the lesson from today to keep our perspective of life an eternal one. May we view our earthly accomplishments as Paul viewed his. Help us, Father, to discern biblical truth from error. We also pray that we would share Paul's passion and desire to come to know Christ and the power of His resurrection above all other things. In Jesus' name, amen.

C. Thought to Remember
Nothing compares with the value of knowing Christ.

Prestige

Status   Power

Wealth

What things were gain to me, those I counted loss for Christ

Visual for Lesson 8

Point to this visual as you introduce the discussion question associated with verse 8.

INVOLVEMENT LEARNING

Some of the activities below are also found in the helpful student book, Adult Bible Class.
Don't forget to download the free reproducible page from www.standardlesson.com to enhance your lesson!

Into the Lesson

Place in chairs copies of the "Paul's Blanks" exercise from the reproducible page, which you can download. Learners can begin working on this as they arrive.

Distribute paper and pencils as you say, "As I say a word, jot down the first thing that comes to your mind. There are four words in the game." Say the words *atheism, purgatory, hedonism,* and *reincarnation,* pausing for a few seconds between each for learners to write thoughts.

Allow class members to share a few responses after you finish reading all four. Then ask, "What do these four words have in common?" Answer: *All are false teachings.* (Atheism denies the existence of God; the doctrine of purgatory proposes there is a place of temporary punishment before admittance into Heaven; hedonism promotes pleasure as the only intrinsic good; reincarnation involves multiple deaths and rebirths.)

Say, "Today's study warns us about false teaching in the first-century church. Even more significantly, our text is a wonderful tribute to those who wish to know and follow Jesus."

Into the Word

Distribute copies of the following True/False quiz. Assure your learners that you will not collect the quizzes for grading; they will score their results themselves.

1. Paul resents having to write the same thing again to the Philippians because they didn't do it right the first time. 2. Paul uses the words *dogs* and *evil* in referring to false teachers. 3. According to Paul, he and the Philippian Christians are "the circumcision." 4. If anyone would have had good reason to put confidence in the flesh, it would have been Paul. 5. Paul's tribal ancestry was that of Judah. 6. One part of Paul's Jewish pedigree was that he was or had been a Sadducee, not a Pharisee. 7. There are a few things Paul regrets having

to give up in order to follow Jesus. 8. Paul teaches that true righteousness does not come by keeping the law, but through faith in Christ. 9. As a person gets to know Jesus better, suffering should be less and less a part of his or her Christian life. 10. Paul wants to become like Jesus in His death so that he can attain to the resurrection of the dead.

Option 1: Read Philippians 3:1-11 aloud, then have learners close their Bibles to take the quiz. Go over the answers as a class. *Option 2:* Have learners take the quiz as a closed-Bible pretest before you read Philippians 3:1-11. Then read the text and discuss answers. *(Answers: 1. false, verse 1; 2. true, verse 2; 3. true, verse 3; 4. true, verses 4, 5; 5. false, verse 5; 6. false, verse 5; 7. false, verses 7, 8; 8. true, verse 9; 9. false, verse 10; 10. true, verses 10, 11.)*

Into Life

Ask the class to help you plan a worship service honoring Paul's testimony and commitment. The theme for the service will be "Knowing Jesus and Sharing in the Suffering." Ask someone to write the ideas for the worship service on the board.

First Step: Say, "Assume we will have someone step on stage to welcome people and introduce the theme. What brief statement should this person use?" *Second Step:* Ask learners to select three or four appropriate songs. *Third Step:* Brainstorm ideas for a humorous skit that illustrates the theme. *Fourth Step:* Discuss creative ways to have the Scripture text read. *Fifth Step:* Select one major point for the sermon. *Sixth Step:* Decide what challenge or invitation to lay before the congregation when concluding the sermon.

Following the exercise, have ready the following phrases on three index cards, one each: "the fellowship of sharing in Christ's sufferings," "the wonder of knowing Jesus as Lord," and "the righteousness that comes from God." Give three learners one card each; ask each to word a brief closing prayer that uses the phrase on his or her card.

STANDING FIRM
IN CHRIST

[handwritten: Eph]
[handwritten: Bone of His Bone — Flesh of His Flesh]

DEVOTIONAL READING: Matthew 25:14-29
BACKGROUND SCRIPTURE: Philippians 3:12–4:1

PHILIPPIANS 3:12-21

12 Not as though I had already attained, either were already perfect: but I follow after, if that I may apprehend that for which also I am apprehended of Christ Jesus.

13 Brethren, I count not myself to have apprehended: but this one thing I do, forgetting those things which are behind, and reaching forth unto those things which are before,

14 I press toward the mark for the prize of the high calling of God in Christ Jesus.

15 Let us therefore, as many as be perfect, be thus minded: and if in any thing ye be otherwise minded, God shall reveal even this unto you.

16 Nevertheless, whereto we have already attained, let us walk by the same rule, let us mind the same thing.

17 Brethren, be followers together of me, and mark them which walk so as ye have us for an ensample.

18 (For many walk, of whom I have told you often, and now tell you even weeping, that they are the enemies of the cross of Christ:

19 Whose end is destruction, whose God is their belly, and whose glory is in their shame, who mind earthly things.)

20 For our conversation is in heaven; from whence also we look for the Saviour, the Lord Jesus Christ:

21 Who shall change our vile body, that it may be fashioned like unto his glorious body, according to the working whereby he is able even to subdue all things unto himself.

PHILIPPIANS 4:1

1 Therefore, my brethren dearly beloved and longed for, my joy and crown, so stand fast in the Lord, my dearly beloved.

KEY VERSE

Nevertheless, whereto we have already attained, let us walk by the same rule, let us mind the same thing.
—**Philippians 3:16**

Photo: Jupiterimages / Photos.com / Thinkstock

Jesus Is Lord

Unit 2: Exalting Christ

Lessons 6–9

Lesson Aims

After participating in this lesson, each student will be able to:

1. Recall what Paul tells the Philippians about how they should stand firm in the Lord.

2. List some characteristics of modern enemies of the cross.

3. Propose a process by which a Christian can overcome things that hinder growth in Christian maturity.

Lesson Outline

Introduction

A. No Walk in the Park

Living a life worthy of our calling in Christ is not a walk in the park. We dare not promote the idea that coming to Christ means that one's problems will be solved magically, life will be much better instantly, and all will be well going forward.

In fact, the opposite often happens: new problems and challenges crop up as Satan works feverishly to thwart God's work (Matthew 13:37-39). The Christian life is a continuous journey, many times with two steps forward and one step back. What keeps us going? The goal!

B. Lesson Background

In last week's lesson, we examined the interplay between Paul's exhortation to rejoice and his warning regarding false teachers. Paul reminded his readers that if right standing before God were based on personal pedigree and accomplishments, then he (Paul) would be at the head of the line.

Indeed, Paul's personal background is vital to the power of his argument. Paul, as Saul in his younger days (Acts 7:58), had been sent from Tarsus to Jerusalem to study under the famous rabbi Gamaliel (22:3). That man was a leading teacher of the day among the Pharisees (5:34). By today's standards, Pharisees were highly educated laypersons. To study successfully under a great teacher such as Gamaliel was the equivalent of doing doctoral work at a famous university. We surmise that Paul was one of the most educated people in all of Judaism, even in the entire Roman world (see Acts 26:24).

Yet Paul declared that he considered all he had accomplished to be loss for the sake of Christ (Philippians 3:7). Paul was no fool. He gave up certain things so the way could be clear to gain something better. That "something" to be gained demands special attention.

I. Pressing On

(Philippians 3:12-16)

A. Reality and Orientation (vv. 12-14)

12, 13a. Not as though I had already attained, either were already perfect: but I follow after, if

that I may apprehend that for which also I am apprehended of Christ Jesus. Brethren, I count not myself to have apprehended.

That which Paul wishes to attain is stated in the two verses just before this one (Philippians 3:10, 11, last week's lesson): "That I may know him, and the power of his resurrection, and the fellowship of his sufferings, being made conformable unto his death; if by any means I might attain unto the resurrection of the dead."

Paul seems to think that his current status in regard to those two verses deserves more explanation, so verse 12 is his clarification. His readers should understand that he does not see himself as having already attained everything set forth in verses 10, 11. Rather, Paul continues to keep those goals in front of him.

Paul makes his point with a play on words by the repeated use of *apprehended*. This word has the sense of "make something one's possession." In saying that he is *apprehended of Christ Jesus,* Paul therefore is affirming that he is Christ's own, Christ's possession. That is a fact, a done deal. But part of this process is Paul's apprehension, or capture of, himself. He knows that his own efforts in that regard are not complete. His job is not done, and his life is not perfect. He still has some race yet to run.

Sanctification is a lifelong process; it is something we should aspire to and work toward each

day. Paul wants the Philippian church to see him as one of their own—broken and sinful, but forgiven and striving to live the Christian life.

> **What Do You Think?**
> What most impedes your own growth in Christ? How will you address this obstacle?
> *Talking Points for Your Discussion*
> - Inadequate knowledge of God's Word (Hosea 4:6)
> - Addictions (Ephesians 5:18)
> - Pursuit of worldly approval (John 12:42, 43)
> - Other

13b, 14. But this one thing I do, forgetting those things which are behind, and reaching forth unto those things which are before, I press toward the mark for the prize of the high calling of God in Christ Jesus.

Both Paul and the Philippians must forget what is behind and strive toward what lies ahead. On the one hand, we may be tempted to rest on the work we have done for God and simply say, "I am where I need to be, and this is good enough." On the other hand, some folks shackle themselves with the guilt of their life before Christ.

There is no forward movement in either case. Both play right into Satan's desires. If he can convince us that the kingdom work we have accomplished is good enough, he will do so. If he can stop our progress by reminding us of our past shortcomings, he will do that too.

We can't let Satan win! We defeat him by *forgetting those things which are behind, and reaching forth unto those things which are before.* For us to forget does not mean we can erase our memories as if erasing a computer's hard drive. Rather, it means we no longer dwell on the past. The best way to do that is to keep our attention on what is to come. We must move forward. Our *high calling* is to be conformed every day into the likeness of Christ and to do the work God has called us to perform.

God has been working His plan of redemption throughout history. He works through us to accomplish His purpose. We must be willing to serve and be used with the understanding that our lives will be transformed in the process. Our

HOW TO SAY IT

chameleon	kuh-*meel*-yuhn.
Colossians	Kuh-*losh*-unz.
Corinth	*Kor*-inth.
Corinthians	Ko-*rin*-thee-unz (*th* as in *thin*).
Ephesians	Ee-*fee*-zhunz.
Gamaliel	Guh-*may*-lih-ul or Guh-*may*-lee-al.
Pharisees	*Fair*-ih-seez.
Philippi	Fih-*lip*-pie or *Fil*-ih-pie.
Philippians	Fih-*lip*-ee-unz.
rabbi	*rab*-eye.
Tarsus	*Tar*-sus.
Thessalonians	*Thess*-uh-*lo*-nee-unz (*th* as in *thin*).

hearts will become broken with the sin that so permeates the world and the needs of people who are lost. We will sacrifice time and relationships, even suffer opposition, as we do God's work.

Regardless, to know Christ, the power of His resurrection, and the fellowship of His sufferings is the goal (the mark) we pursue until the day God calls us home. Like training for a marathon, this requires preparation (1 Corinthians 9:24-27).

B. Maturity and Clarity (vv. 15, 16)

15. Let us therefore, as many as be perfect, be thus minded: and if in any thing ye be otherwise minded, God shall reveal even this unto you.

No sooner does Paul state that he has not attained perfection (v. 12) than he says *Let us, therefore, as many as be perfect, be thus minded.* Is Paul really moving from admitting imperfection to including himself among the perfect?

No, Paul is not inconsistent. The Greek word being translated *perfect* is something of a chameleon in that it "changes color" depending on the context in which it is placed. In this context, the idea is along the lines of "developed" as it is in other uses by Paul (1 Corinthians 2:6; 14:20; Ephesians 4:13; Colossians 1:28; 4:12). Thus Paul is referring not to those who have attained Christian perfection (which is not possible on this side of Heaven), but to believers who are spiritually mature.

Spiritual development has many facets. Here the idea is the ability to shift one's focus away from what we have accomplished (or failed to accomplish); instead, we focus on the work and path ahead. This path may end up being long and difficult, but it is here we must focus nonetheless. Those who are *otherwise minded* have not yet reached a level of spiritual maturity where they are able to do this.

What is to be done with such people? Paul dealt with this problem previously in a rather stern manner concerning the church at Corinth (1 Corinthians 3:1-4). Here, by contrast, Paul seems quite gentle with the Philippians, merely saying that God will reveal the truth to them as well. Paul tailors his message to his audiences and their unique situations.

16. Nevertheless, whereto we have already attained, let us walk by the same rule, let us mind the same thing.

This is a very difficult sentence in the Greek text. The main thing that is apparent, however, is the stress on church harmony. With maturity comes unity and agreement. What the Philippians *have already attained* seems to refer to a certain level of knowledge as revealed by God. By contrast, those of verse 15 who lack spiritual maturity will have their problem solved when they receive (or are able to digest) additional revelation from God. The New Testament obviously is not finished as Paul writes.

But church harmony and unity cannot wait until more revelation by God comes along to answer every question and address every disagreement. The church at Philippi is expected to be a unified church even though the believers there have yet to receive all of God's revelation in the form of the completed New Testament. How much more should twenty-first–century churches be unified now that we have that completion!

Some students think that what the Philippians *have already attained* also addresses their accomplishments to this point. Deviations from the truth can undermine the work that has been accomplished, resulting in the church's laboring in vain. But what about "forgetting those things which are behind" (v. 13)? Remembering vs. not-remembering the past is a fine line to walk. When *remembering* the past becomes *dwelling* on our past work, we end up immobilized—we don't move for-

Standing Firm in Christ

ward. But recalling accomplishments for God—spiritual victories—can be part of the touchstone that helps us *walk by the same rule*.

What Do You Think?
How will you use your church's spiritual victories as a launching pad for the future without trying to recreate the past?
Talking Points for Your Discussion
- In terms of upreach (worship)
- In terms of outreach (evangelism, benevolence, conscience of the community)
- In terms of inreach (growth in Christ)

❧ *Looking Both Ways* ❧

The Roman god Janus was depicted as having two heads or faces—one looking backward, the other looking forward. He was thought to be, among other things, the god of endings and beginnings; Janus looked to the past with one face as he looked to the future with the other. His name is the basis for calling the first month of the year *January*, the month of transition from the old year to the new.

The modern practice of making New Year's resolutions draws on this idea of looking to the past while looking to the future. We look to the past to reflect on our failures or incomplete successes, then we use these reflections to help us decide how we might do better in the coming year. We may resolve to be more punctual, more honest, or more gracious. We may resolve to be more diligent in carrying through on tasks we start but don't finish. Possible resolutions are legion.

Looking in both directions is how we are able to compare where we are now with where we need to be. Gauging where our spiritual growth is now can indicate where we need to be tomorrow. The level of spiritual maturity we now have should not result in a satisfied complacency. Rather, our current level of maturity should be the foundation upon which we build further maturity in Christ. Looking back is a valuable exercise if it provokes us to accept the challenges that lie ahead. Otherwise, looking back becomes mere nostalgia at best and deadening self-satisfaction at worst.   —C. R. B.

II. Following an Example
(Philippians 3:17–4:1)
A. Identify (v. 17)
17a. Brethren, be followers together of me.

Whether doctrinal error actually is infecting the church at Philippi or Paul merely fears it may do so, he has the cure—*be followers together of me*. He already has compared his credibility with those who teach error (Philippians 3:2-6, last week's lesson). The closer the Philippians examine Paul's life, the clearer it will be that it is he they should follow (compare 1 Corinthians 4:16; 11:1). But his example is not the only one available (next verse).

17b. And mark them which walk so as ye have us for an ensample.

Doctrinal issues can be very complicated, and sometimes the most practical way to resist those who teach error is to emulate someone whose life *(walk)* defines a strong Christian life. Watch how such a person lives and expresses faith in God. The Philippians can follow those who believe and live as Paul does. The Greek behind the older English word *ensample* would come across literally as "type." We may also think of the related words "model" and "exemplification." The idea is that of "a standard to be followed" (compare 1 Thessalonians 1:7; 1 Peter 5:3).

What Do You Think?
In what ways can you be an example for others without coming across as "holier than thou"?
Talking Points for Your Discussion
- In the use of time, talent, and resources
- In conduct toward others
- In entertainment choices
- Matthew 5:14-16 as contrasted with 6:1-6, 16-18

❧ *Don't Be a Counterfeit!* ❧

The story is told about a certain family that attended church regularly. One Sunday, the minister preached about family life. After the service, little Johnny began sobbing. He cried all the way home. His father asked him several times what was wrong. At last, Johnny blurted out, "The minister said every child ought to be raised in a Christian home, but I want to stay with you and Mom!"

Addressing also the point of counterfeit Christians, Samuel M. Shoemaker, who helped originate the concept of Alcoholic Anonymous, said, "When I find people who have all their lives been coming to church, and have never mastered a quick tongue, a disagreeable spirit, the touchiness which resents the slightest interference with one's own desires, and which makes one hard to get along with, I do not say that Christianity has failed. I say that we Christians have simply not surrendered our whole hearts to the Lord Jesus Christ."

There will always be those whose Christianity is counterfeit. We must make sure we aren't following them. We must make sure also that we are not *being* one of them! The genuine follower of Christ will not only choose godly models to emulate, but will be such a model as well.   —C. R. B.

B. Avoid (vv. 18, 19)

18, 19. (For many walk, of whom I have told you often, and now tell you even weeping, that they are the enemies of the cross of Christ: whose end is destruction, whose God is their belly, and whose glory is in their shame, who mind earthly things.)

Paul turns up the intensity of his warning. *The enemies of the cross of Christ* can include both Jew and Gentile (1 Corinthians 1:22, 23). The enemies are identified by four characteristics.

First, their *end is destruction*. This characteristic is not immediately observable since it points to end results. Even so, it is a warning: this is a finish line you don't want to cross. Second, their *God is their belly*. This means the enemies are not controlled by the Holy Spirit, but by the appetites of the flesh. If our life goal is gratification of carnal desires, we sink deeper and deeper into depravity (see Romans 7:18; 16:18).

Third, their *glory is in their shame* in that the enemies celebrate that which should embarrass them. How true this rings today in our celebrity culture, where people become (in)famous for strident immorality! To *mind earthly things* is not a criticism of dealing with issues of everyday life. Rather, it is the idea of losing any sense of spirituality as one

lives selfishly and materialistically. The enemies are oblivious to the danger of the destructive life they choose and celebrate (Romans 8:5, 6).

C. Await (v. 20)

20. For our conversation is in heaven; from whence also we look for the Saviour, the Lord Jesus Christ.

The Greek word translated *conversation* appears only here in the New Testament. It is a word from the political sphere and has the sense of "citizenship." Since Philippi is a Roman colony (Acts 16:12), the idea of citizenship resonates deeply with the people there. Paul no doubt tries to draw on civic pride by reminding the believers that they are citizens of Heaven.

Our heavenly citizenship is one of the most important truths of the Christian worldview. This world is not our final home. Christ will take us home, and we will be with Him forever (1 Thessalonians 4:17). We take joy in believing that our home in glory will remove us from the tears of this life (see Revelation 21:4). Citizenship in Heaven means that the fallen earthly realm we live in is not the final word regarding our status.

D. Stand (3:21; 4:1)

21. Who shall change our vile body, that it may be fashioned like unto his glorious body, according to the working whereby he is able even to subdue all things unto himself.

Paul offers two promises his readers can embrace until Christ returns. First, Christ will make our current bodies *like unto his glorious body.* What a remarkable promise for our future existence in Heaven! Our new bodies will be spiritual bodies (1 Corinthians 15:44), fit for the spiritual universe; they will be imperishable and immortal (15:53). The limitations of our fragile, earthly bodies will be set aside. Reminding ourselves of this daily helps keep our focus off of "earthly things" (Philippian 3:19).

A second, related promise is that Christ will *subdue all things unto himself.* All enemies will be vanquished, including the enemy of death (1 Corinthians 15:25, 26). Christ will be the complete master of all things (Philippians 2:10, 11).

4:1. Therefore, my brethren dearly beloved and longed for, my joy and crown, so stand fast in the Lord, my dearly beloved.

The apostle takes great satisfaction in the Philippians' continued faithfulness and good works. He is able to pray about them with joy (see Philippians 1:3-6), believing they will endure to the end. They are his crown in the sense that we might say righteous children are jewels on the crown of faithful parents (compare Proverbs 17:6). This is not the crown of power or dominion, but of reward for a job well done. It is the award crown given to the victor in athletic contests, the laurel of honor (see also 1 Thessalonians 2:19, 20).

Everything Paul has said should give his readers reason to *stand fast in the Lord.* However, he knows the only way that will happen is for the people to maintain unity. To stand fast is a unifying act because the Philippians all have the same Lord. The result of this is to give them security in their fellowship, the "safety in numbers" effect. Paul is not telling them to "go along with the crowd," but to stand together with others who follow Christ.

Conclusion

A. A Worthwhile Goal

The Christian life as lived in a fallen world is not easy on the best of days. We are placed in a position where we need to take a stand for Christ against the wisdom of the world and the norms of the culture we live in. Just as the Philippian church

Visual for Lessons 9 & 10. *As you discuss Philippians 4:1, point to this visual and ask, "What challenges you most in your stand for the Lord?"*

discovered, "enemies of the cross of Christ" are alive and active in our world. The lure of earthly things is simply a few keystrokes away on a computer connected to the Internet. Access is easy, and accountability is nearly a foreign concept.

Our ability to communicate in various forms of media and in speeds that have never been seen before is a double-edged sword for our Christian maturity. On the one hand, it allows us to get nearly instant help from many fellow believers scattered all over the world. On the other hand, such access exposes us to false doctrine and immorality with unprecedented speed and scope; this deepens the challenge we face in staying firm in the faith.

The continuing challenge is to take Paul's words to heart and remember that we are called to be conformed to the likeness of Christ. In doing so, we must follow the examples set forth by Christ, Paul, and the mature believers around us. Sanctification is a goal we keep in front of us, relentlessly pursuing it each day of our lives.

B. Prayer

Father, use today's lesson to remind us that Christian maturity is a worthy goal to pursue with all our hearts, souls, and minds. Help us to be examples of maturity. In Christ's name, amen.

C. Thought to Remember

Focus on heavenly things.

INVOLVEMENT LEARNING

Some of the activities below are also found in the helpful student book, Adult Bible Class.
Don't forget to download the free reproducible page from www.standardlesson.com to enhance your lesson!

Into the Lesson

List several athletic events or sports on the board (possibilities: cross-country running, archery, hurdles, boxing, and basketball). Ask, "Which of these best illustrates your Christian life or spiritual quest to this point? Why?" Encourage discussion. *Options:* You can divide the class into small groups to talk this question over (allow three minutes), or you can do it as a whole-class exercise if your class is smaller.

Alternative: Instead of the above, distribute copies of the "Valuable Goals" activity from the reproducible page, which you can download. Have learners complete the first column according to the instructions. The second column will be your first activity for the Into the Word segment.

Into the Word

Say, "Today's Scripture includes a testimony by Paul, an encouragement to follow his example, and reflections regarding those who do not follow his pattern. We can break that down into three categories of *I, We,* and *They.*"

Distribute 8½" x 11" handouts in landscape format (that is, with the shorter side of the paper as the vertical) with the title *Learning from Paul's Example.* The handout will have three columns: the first column headed "I," the second headed "We," and the third headed "They." Say, "Take a few minutes to scan Philippians 3:12–4:1 and write Paul's 'I' statements on the handout."

Learners should discover that the "I" statements are clustered primarily in verses 12-14, although verse 18 has one as well. After their discoveries, ask these discussion questions: 1. What do you learn about Paul in this testimony? 2. What does Paul mean in verse 12 when he says, "I am apprehended of Christ Jesus"? 3. What example can you give to illustrate Paul's encouragement to forget those things that are behind (v. 13)? Why is it important for us to do so?

Next, ask learners to scan the text and write the "we" statements on the handout. There are only two, in verses 16 and 20, but perceptive learners will also include the "us" statements of verses 15-17. When complete, pose these questions: 1. What major theme touches your heart in these statements? Why? 2. What risks are there in looking to others for a good example (v. 17)? 3. What is Paul trying to do when he reminds us of our heavenly home in verse 20?

Finally, ask learners to scan the text and write the "they" statements on the handout. There is only one, in verse 18, but perceptive learners will also include the "their" statement of verse 19. When complete, pose these questions: 1. What is different about the ones whom Paul contrasts with followers of Jesus? 2. What is Paul saying when he describes these people with the word picture "whose God is their belly"?

Option: Instead of using the above as a whole-class exercise, you can assign the I, We, and They tasks to three small groups, one each. If you choose this option, include the appropriate instructions on the handouts instead of verbalizing them. If your class is larger, you can form more than three groups and give duplicate assignments.

Into Life

Choose one or more of the following activities to help class members apply this lesson.

Option 1: Observing Others. Remind the class that Paul encourages us to look to others for models in Christian growth. Ask, "Who are some people you would name as models in that regard?"

Option 2: Growing Up. Ask learners to describe viewpoints they have changed or no longer hold because of their growth in Christ.

Option 3: Personal Commitment. Have learners complete the "My Personal Commitment" affirmation on the reproducible page. If time is short, distribute copies to learners as they depart.

FOCUSED SOLELY ON CHRIST

DEVOTIONAL READING: Ephesians 1:17-23
BACKGROUND SCRIPTURE: Colossians 1

COLOSSIANS 1:12-23

12 Giving thanks unto the Father, which hath made us meet to be partakers of the inheritance of the saints in light:

13 Who hath delivered us from the power of darkness, and hath translated us into the kingdom of his dear Son:

14 In whom we have redemption through his blood, even the forgiveness of sins:

15 Who is the image of the invisible God, the firstborn of every creature:

16 For by him were all things created, that are in heaven, and that are in earth, visible and invisible, whether they be thrones, or dominions, or principalities, or powers: all things were created by him, and for him:

17 And he is before all things, and by him all things consist.

18 And he is the head of the body, the church: who is the beginning, the firstborn from the dead; that in all things he might have the preeminence.

19 For it pleased the Father that in him should all fulness dwell;

20 And, having made peace through the blood of his cross, by him to reconcile all things

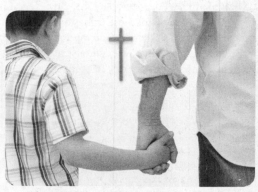

unto himself; by him, I say, whether they be things in earth, or things in heaven.

21 And you, that were sometime alienated and enemies in your mind by wicked works, yet now hath he reconciled

22 In the body of his flesh through death, to present you holy and unblameable and unreproveable in his sight:

23 If ye continue in the faith grounded and settled, and be not moved away from the hope of the gospel, which ye have heard, and which was preached to every creature which is under heaven; whereof I Paul am made a minister.

KEY VERSE

For it pleased the Father that in him should all fulness dwell. —**Colossians 1:19**

Photo: Stockbyte / Thinkstock

JESUS IS LORD

Unit 3: Imitating Jesus

LESSONS 10–13

LESSON AIMS

After participating in this lesson, each student will be able to:

1. Summarize Christ's relationship to the church.

2. Explain the supremacy of Christ by exposing the inadequacies of those things or people that are exalted as rivals in contemporary society.

3. Plan an event that will demonstrate or recognize the supremacy of Christ for the community.

LESSON OUTLINE

Introduction

A. Accept No Substitutes!

Are you a loyal customer of a particular product brand? Many people are. We have learned that our favorite brand delivers a level of quality or value that we cannot match in another product. When we have tried others, we have been disappointed. So we are loyal to our favorite brand.

Businesses know how we become loyal to a brand, so they try to play on that fact in their advertising. Extolling a product's virtues, they tell us to avoid inferior competitors. Common catch-phrases are "Accept no substitutes!" and "Beware of imitations!" Such sloganeering can be so much hot air, so much "puffing." But certainly some things are superior to others. If we want the very best, we will accept no substitutes.

Such is the message of Paul's letter to the Colossian church. Having come to faith in Jesus Christ, the Colossian Christians were later attracted to other, competing religious views (Colossians 2:20, 21; etc.). So Paul addressed them with a straightforward message: Jesus Christ is superior to all others, so it would be foolish to put faith in anything besides Him. Accept no substitutes!

B. Lesson Background

As noted in Lesson 6 (page 162), Colossians is one of four New Testament letters that the apostle Paul wrote during his imprisonment in Rome, about AD 63. The letter was written to the church in Colosse, a city in Asia Minor (modern Turkey). The city was about 100 miles from the western coast of that land mass. Paul himself did not visit the city on his missionary journeys (Colossians 1:9; 2:1). The gospel was carried there by Paul's associates (1:7).

Paul apparently learned that the faith of the Colossian Christians was being challenged by other belief systems. We can infer from the contents of the Colossian letter that something or some things that brought together various pagan ideas and Jewish practices were attracting believers (Colossians 2:4, 8, 20, 21, etc.). Paul's approach to this problem was unequivocal, as we shall see across our next four lessons.

I. Christ the Redeemer

(COLOSSIANS 1:12-14)

A. Thanks to the Father (v. 12)

12. Giving thanks unto the Father, which hath made us meet to be partakers of the inheritance of the saints in light.

As our text begins, Paul is continuing to share the content of his prayers, which are focused on thanksgiving for God's saving work in Christ. That in turn leads Paul to deliver a glorious, poetic description of the Christ who saves. Paul emphasizes that his prayers for God's blessing (Colossians 1:9-11) lead to prayers of thanksgiving.

The basis for that thanksgiving is God's plan to make us His own. To be *partakers of the inheritance of the saints* reminds us of Israel's receiving of the promised land. But the inheritance of the Christian is far greater than mere land, as we shall see.

The inheritance is shared by *the saints* (compare Ephesians 1:18), which literally is "the holy ones." This may make us think of people of exceptionally righteous behavior. But the basis for being a "holy one" is not one's own righteousness, but belonging to God's set-apart people. The Israelites were set apart because God delivered them from slavery in Egypt "to be a special people unto himself" (Deuteronomy 7:6); Christians are set apart to a much greater degree because God has delivered us from the slavery of sin.

In that regard, *made us meet* means "caused us to be sufficient." How this happens, Paul will proceed to describe. But the result is that God has put us in a new place. Christians are *in light,* an apt image for God's blessing and the new life that flows from it. As God first spoke light into existence (Genesis 1:3), now He has acted to give light to His people.

❧ *INHERITANCE ATTITUDE* ❧

On August 11, 1882, *The New York Times* relayed this interview from the *Religious Herald* of Richmond, Virginia:

> The widow of a Baptist deacon who died four years ago said to us a few days ago as we sat in her parlor: "The great mistake of my husband's life was leaving $200,000 to his children. My oldest son had not been in possession of his portion six months before he had acquired intemperate habits, and today, wrecked in health and morals, he hasn't a dollar left of the thousands his father left him. My daughter married an immoral man, who has spent her portion, and now her life is sad and dreary. It would have been a thousand times better had my husband devoted his means more largely to education and Christianity."

The fact that the $200,000 bequest equals more than $5,000,000 in today's money makes the widow's sad lament sharper still! Once again we are reminded how a sudden influx of money may be a curse rather than a blessing (Luke 15:11-16). It doesn't seem to matter whether the windfall comes by inheritance, lawsuit settlement, or lottery winnings.

But we know that it's not the money itself that's the problem. The problem, rather, is that of *an attitude of getting*—the recipient of the money may think of nothing but what he or she can get with it. By contrast, our inheritance from Christ promotes *an attitude of giving*—when we realize what Christ has done, we should want to give it to as many others as possible in turn. Is that your mindset as one of "the saints in light"? —C. R. B.

B. Kingdom of the Son (vv. 13, 14)

13. Who hath delivered us from the power of darkness, and hath translated us into the kingdom of his dear Son.

The light in which the Christian lives is very different from the old life, which is rightly called *darkness.* The God who delivered ancient Israel from slavery to freedom has *delivered us from the power of darkness,* rescued from sin slavery. Now we are in a situation greater than being in the promised land, and we are ruled by a king greater than David. This is the kingdom of God's beloved Son.

No concept is more familiar to us from the New Testament than Jesus as God's Son. The term is rich with significance. Sometimes it emphasizes Jesus' oneness with God the Father in authority and power. Sometimes it emphasizes Jesus' willing submission to God the Father. Sometimes it emphasizes what it does here: that Jesus rules over the kingdom of God as God has appointed and enthroned Him.

14. In whom we have redemption through his blood, even the forgiveness of sins.

Redemption is a powerful word in the New Testament, suggesting the liberation of slaves. In Paul's Jewish background, this word especially refers to God's freeing of the Israelites from Egyptian slavery (Psalm 106:10; etc.). But there is now a greater redemption in Christ, bringing freedom from the penalty for sin. Through *his blood* we are forgiven the punishment that we ought to receive.

II. Christ the Sovereign

(COLOSSIANS 1:15-17)

A. Firstborn (v. 15)

15. Who is the image of the invisible God, the firstborn of every creature.

To grasp the significance of our redemption, we need to realize not just what we are redeemed from and redeemed to, but who did the redeeming. Our Redeemer is no less than the world's eternal Ruler. That idea is suggested first in His description as *the image of the invisible God* (compare 2 Corinthians 4:4; Hebrews 1:3).

To this description Paul adds the term *firstborn*. We should recognize that the term as Paul uses it does not emphasize the idea of "birth" but of "priority," of being first. The firstborn son in an ancient Israelite family had first place over siblings (Deuteronomy 21:15-17). Christ is first both in time and in position. As the eternal God, He exists without beginning, and so exists before all things. And as the eternal God, He has authority over all things. Thus, Christ is supreme over everything created.

B. Creator (v. 16)

16. For by him were all things created, that are in heaven, and that are in earth, visible and invisible, whether they be thrones, or dominions, or principalities, or powers: all things were created by him, and for him.

Christ is sovereign over creation because He created all things. Everything owes its existence to Christ and ultimately exists for His glory. He created all, and so He rules over all (John 1:3).

Paul uses a series of expressions to stress that nothing is excluded from Christ's sovereignty. Genesis 1:1 uses the expression "the heaven and the earth" to refer to all creation, and so here Paul refers to things *that are in heaven, and that are in earth* to signify all creation. That includes both the physical world—things visible—and the world of the spirit—things invisible.

Expressions such as *thrones, or dominions, or principalities, or powers* are used in Paul's time to describe various groupings of spirits, whether angelic or demonic (Ephesians 1:21; 3:10; 6:12). Some in the Colossian church perhaps are tempted to try to gain spiritual power by following some teaching that purports to explain them. Paul's point is that whatever power such beings have, it is nothing compared with the power of Christ.

The issue of power is not confined to the invisible world of the spirit. Demonic spiritual forces are the inspiration behind the visibly evil actions among people in the world (compare John 13:27). But because Christ is supreme over all, His power is sufficient to enable His people to overcome evil (compare Romans 12:21).

C. Sustainer (v. 17)

17. And he is before all things, and by him all things consist.

Paul piles on terms to stress Christ's supreme rule. As the eternal, creator God, He exists prior to all creation (John 1:1; 8:58). But He did not merely create the world; He also sustains its existence. The word *consist* indicates "ongoing existence." Things do not exist on their own, Paul says. They owe their continuing existence to Jesus.

III. Christ the Head
(COLOSSIANS 1:18-23)
A. Supremacy (v. 18)

18a. And he is the head of the body, the church.

Jesus has a distinct relationship with His people. As their Creator, their Redeemer, and the perfect exemplar of who they are to be, Christ is unified with His people and rules over them. So He is to them as the head is to the body (compare Ephesians 1:22, 23; 4:15; 5:23).

His body is the church, and we should think about the use of the word *church* in Paul's time in order to understand it here. The word translated *church* is used among first-century Jews to refer to the assembly of God's people. Because Christ fulfills God's redemptive plan, makes the invisible God visible, and creates and rules as only God can do, Christ's people indeed are God's assembled people. There can be no higher status for a sinful human than to be welcomed into this assembly.

18b. Who is the beginning, the firstborn from the dead.

Christ *is the beginning* in multiple ways: existing before all creation, calling creation into existence, fulfilling the divine purpose for humanity. This sums up much of what Paul has stressed in the entire passage. For Christ's people, nothing is more vital than the fact that He is the beginning of their new life. As a Pharisee, Paul believed that God would one day raise His people from the dead so that He could bestow on them all His promised blessings (Acts 23:6-8). As an apostle, Paul now believes that God is fulfilling that promise in Jesus in a way that people did not expect.

God raised Jesus first, and Jesus imparts to His people the resurrection life.

We experience that resurrection life as Christ empowers us to overcome sin and live faithfully (Romans 6:1-14). And we look forward confidently to the coming day when Christ will raise the dead to be together with Him forever (1 Thessalonians 4:13-18). Thus Christ is *firstborn from the dead*, both the first one raised—never to die again—and the ruler over all whom He will raise.

> *What Do You Think?*
> What ideas have you heard that contradict what
>   Paul says about Jesus? How do you counter
>   these?
> *Talking Points for Your Discussion*
> - Regarding Jesus' preexistence
> - Regarding Jesus' authority
> - Regarding Jesus' resurrection
> - Other

❧ *BIRTH ORDER?* ❧

Does birth order in a family make any difference? Many Web sites are dedicated to the subject. The pop psychology on those sites may promote the idea that firstborn children are natural leaders because they have younger siblings as their followers. Middle children are "people pleasers" who must negotiate their way between the desires of younger and older siblings. Youngest children are the popular "clowns" who remain in some way "the baby" all their lives. The "only" child is spoiled since he or she need not share parental attention.

Research does not give strong support to these proposals. There are just too many exceptions, and all of us know many people who simply do not fit the stereotypes. Human stereotypes certainly do not fit Jesus, who is firstborn in a unique sense: that of firstborn from the dead.

Conclusions about birth-order characteristics also have no place in discussions about our rebirth in Christ. The characteristics most appropriate to all who have been reborn in Christ are gratitude and humility, regardless of how early or late in life we accepted that rebirth. See 1 Corinthians 15:8-11.   —C. R. B.

18c. That in all things he might have the preeminence.

Paul closes the verse by again stressing Christ's preeminent status. It is absurd to expect some greater benefit outside of Christ or some improvement on what Christ gives. None can be greater than He; none can give more than He does.

> **What Do You Think?**
> What can you do to help others see Jesus' supremacy affirmed in your church?
> *Talking Points for Your Discussion*
> - In worship
> - In leadership
> - In Bible-study curriculum
> - In ministry priorities
> - Other

B. Reconciliation (vv. 19-22)

19. For it pleased the Father that in him should all fulness dwell.

We naturally struggle to understand the concept of God that Paul presents in this passage. The Father and the Son are not rival deities, like the many fictitious pagan gods. The true God is one God, but existing as Father, Son, and Spirit. They share perfect love and unity of purpose. So God the Father's will is fulfilled in what God the Son has done, especially as the Son reveals the Father and accomplishes His plan to save and rule.

God is pleased that in Christ we find God's fullness, the "utter whole" of God's being. This may be what some in the Colossian church think they can find outside Christianity. Perhaps they believe that they can approach God's presence by looking elsewhere. But in Christ we find everything that God is (John 14:9). To look elsewhere is not to seek more of God but to turn away from God.

20. And, having made peace through the blood of his cross, by him to reconcile all things unto himself; by him, I say, whether they be things in earth, or things in heaven.

Human rebellion marred God's creation, making the world a painful place for our existence (Genesis 3:14-19; Romans 8:20-23). The divine Christ fulfills God's eternal purpose by restoring the entire creation to harmony and submission to His authority (Ephesians 1:10).

Amazingly, Christ accomplishes this universal reconciliation by suffering death *through the blood of his cross* (compare Ephesians 1:7). Death is the ultimate curse pronounced on human rebellion against God, but the Son of God takes our curse on himself! It was no ordinary death that Christ died, but death by crucifixion. This is the means by which a pagan empire demonstrates its ruthless, seemingly absolute power. But Christ defeated the power of death by willingly becoming its victim. No other being, no other power could so fully change our existence than has He.

21. And you, that were sometime alienated and enemies in your mind by wicked works, yet now hath he reconciled.

Christ's work is to reconcile all of creation, but the focus and center of that work is people. We are the ones who caused the alienation to begin with; it was our rebellion against God that brought the curse on us and on creation. As rebels we were God's enemies, driven away from fellowship with Him (see Genesis 3:23, 24). We were caught in a vicious cycle: our minds giving rise to rebellious acts *(wicked works)*, and our actions feeding our rebellious minds (Ephesians 4:17-19).

But Christ's work changes us: it first restores our relationship to God, then it transforms our minds and actions from rebellion to submission.

22. In the body of his flesh through death, to present you holy and unblameable and unreproveable in his sight.

The description of our reconciliation continues. Again Paul emphasizes that Christ has done this remarkable thing by means of His remarkable death. This wasn't some kind of figurative or spiritual death; it was an actual death *in the body of his flesh*. This was the same body that revealed the fullness of God (Colossians 1:19; 2:9).

HOW TO SAY IT

Colosse	Ko-*lahss*-ee.
Egyptian	Ee-*jip*-shun.
Pharisee	*Fair*-ih-see.
sloganeering	*slow*-guh-**nir**-ing.

It was Christ's death that allowed what was unholy to be made holy (*unblameable and unreproveable;* compare Ephesians 5:27). We had rejected God and wanted nothing to do with Him, making us anything but His set-apart people. But now through Christ we are reconciled to God; we belong to God again as His set-apart ones.

C. Proclamation (v. 23)

23. If ye continue in the faith grounded and settled, and be not moved away from the hope of the gospel, which ye have heard, and which was preached to every creature which is under heaven; whereof I Paul am made a minister.

Still, there is a condition attached to our reconciliation: what we receive in Christ, we must agree to receive. And we must cling to it (Hebrew 3:14). Our trust in Christ needs to be like a building on a firm foundation, solid and immovable. With everything that is available in Christ, what reason can we possibly have for abandoning our trust in Him? He has given us a confident expectation of the future, a real hope, when otherwise we would have nothing but fearful dread.

> **What Do You Think?**
> How do the example of Jesus and the strength of the Holy Spirit help you "continue in the faith"?
> *Talking Points for Your Discussion*
> ▪ For continuing in thought
> ▪ For continuing in action

That hope came to us through the gospel of Jesus Christ. Though once God revealed himself to a single nation, Israel, now He makes himself known to everyone, without borders, through this good news. Paul can speak of the gospel being *preached to every creature* even though it has gone only to a portion of the world in his lifetime. In God's plan, the gospel is moving forward without limitations.

God's plan is to redeem all the nations (Genesis 22:18), and this plan is fulfilled in Christ. So the preaching of Paul and others advances the progress of fulfilling that promise, the beginning of God's reconciliation, universally available, that can make people from every nation His people forever.

Visual for Lessons 9 & 10. *Point to this visual as you introduce the discussion question associated with verse 23.*

Of that good news Paul is *a minister.* That term may make us think of a preacher, which Paul is of course. But the word translated *minister* simply signifies "servant." Compared with Christ, Paul has no position of exaltation. Paul is but a lowly servant, yet he is entrusted as a steward of the message that reconciles the world to God.

And so are we. Confident that the divine Christ has made us His people, we are also called to be the agents of His reconciliation in the world.

Conclusion
A. What More Could We Want?

As we reflect on the description of Christ in today's passage, we realize how clear the apostle's message is. If Christ is preeminent, where else shall we turn to find what we need? If He has done all that Paul describes, what more could we want than for our lives to reflect our reconciliation to God, used to carry the message of Christ's reconciling power to everyone?

B. Prayer

Father, we fall before You in awe. Your Son, the author of life, died and rose to give us life. The lives He has given back to us we pledge to His service and glory. In Jesus' name we pray, amen.

C. Thought to Remember
Look only to Christ.

INVOLVEMENT LEARNING

Some of the activities below are also found in the helpful student book, Adult Bible Class.
Don't forget to download the free reproducible page from www.standardlesson.com to enhance your lesson!

Into the Lesson

Say, "I'm going to give you an eye test as we begin class today. Tell me what you see." Display a large blurry (out of focus) image of the letter *R*. After a few seconds for responses, do the same thing for the letters *S* and *H*. Next, do the same thing for the sharply focused letters *R, S,* and *H* in sequence. (These may be on the reverse sides of poster board used for the blurry letters, on Power-Point® slides, etc.).

Immediately give each learner an index card that has one of the letters *R* or *S* or *H* printed on it. (Prepare cards in advance so that the number of cards are equally distributed among the three letters.) Have learners gather in three groups according to the letters. Say, "Today's text of Colossians 1:12-23 divides easily into three parts: verses 12-14 for *R*, verses 15-17 for *S*, and verses 18-23 for *H*. A key role of Christ is sharply revealed in each segment. See if your group can figure out what word best characterizes Christ using the letter you received." This marks the transition to Into the Word.

Into the Word

Allow a few minutes for completing the task above, then call for conclusions. The anticipated responses are *Redeemer, Sovereign,* and *Head,* per the commentary's lesson outline. (Your learners may make a good case for different answers.)

Continuing in the "letters theme," prepare in advance an equal number of two handouts, one of which is headed *We Were/Are . . .* and the other *He Is . . .* Have all the letters of the alphabet printed vertically down the side of both handouts. Give each learner one of the two handouts so that the two versions are distributed equally.

Say, "Look at today's text and see how many words you can identify that correctly complete the heading on your sheet. You may use words from the text or concepts represented by the truths there." You can give these examples to get your

learners started: for the *We Were/Are . . .* group: A = alienated, verse 21; for the *He Is . . .* group: A = authority, verse 18a.

Allow six to eight minutes on this task, then ask for volunteers to read their lists. If someone includes a characterization that does not relate quickly to the text, ask for an explanation. Expect a range of responses; no doubt your learners will offer interesting and perceptive choices. Before leaving this task, ask, "Does anyone have any words we have not heard yet?"

Option: As a quick posttest, have learners complete the "The Results Are In" quiz on the reproducible page, which you can download. This option will go faster if you make it closed Bible. Assure your learners that you will not collect the quizzes. Go over the answers as they score the quizzes themselves.

Into Life

Have learners brainstorm the possibility of a community-wide project that will affirm the supremacy of Christ. One possible idea is to rent a prominent billboard to display a message (and advertise your congregation) that reads "Good, better, best . . . Christ is above the rest!" or something similar. If your community has a transit system, your learners may think of "rolling ads" with a message something like "Leaders come and leaders go, but one Leader is forever: Christ the Lord!" Your class may also suggest possible messages for your church's outdoor sign, if you have one.

Suggest your group draw their suggestions from today's text; one possibility along this line is "Jesus is the one God loves. What about you?" Pass along ideas to your church's leadership.

Move to personal application by having learners complete the "Are You Focused?" activity from the reproducible page. Connect this activity back to the blurry and sharply focused letters of the opening activity.

Focused Solely on Christ

RAISED WITH CHRIST

DEVOTIONAL READING: Romans 8:31-39
BACKGROUND SCRIPTURE: Colossians 2

COLOSSIANS 2:6-15

6 As ye have therefore received Christ Jesus the Lord, so walk ye in him:

7 Rooted and built up in him, and stablished in the faith, as ye have been taught, abounding therein with thanksgiving.

8 Beware lest any man spoil you through philosophy and vain deceit, after the tradition of men, after the rudiments of the world, and not after Christ.

9 For in him dwelleth all the fulness of the Godhead bodily.

10 And ye are complete in him, which is the head of all principality and power:

11 In whom also ye are circumcised with the circumcision made without hands, in putting off the body of the sins of the flesh by the circumcision of Christ:

12 Buried with him in baptism, wherein also ye are risen with him through the faith of the operation of God, who hath raised him from the dead.

13 And you, being dead in your sins and the uncircumcision of your flesh, hath he quickened together with him, having forgiven you all trespasses;

14 Blotting out the handwriting of ordinances that was against us, which was contrary to us, and took it out of the way, nailing it to his cross;

15 And having spoiled principalities and powers, he made a shew of them openly, triumphing over them in it.

KEY VERSE

Ye are complete in him, which is the head of all principality and power. —**Colossians 2:10**

JESUS IS LORD

Unit 3: Imitating Jesus

LESSON AIMS

After participating in this lesson, each student will be able to:

1. State some benefits that are available only in Christ.

2. Compare and contrast Christian baptism with Jewish circumcision.

3. Role-play a debate between a secular philosopher and a Christian.

LESSON OUTLINE

Introduction

A. Rejecting the "Yard Sale" Life

People find amazing items at yard sales. Among the piles of used clothes and dated bric-a-brac, savvy shoppers find bargains on rare collectibles, valuable antiques, and useful everyday items.

Most yard sales have a few items that have been barely used, if at all. Many of those nearly new items were probably bought in a spasm of self-improvement. A person thinks, "I need to start exercising," so he buys exercise equipment. Or a person says, "I need to eat healthier food," so she buys a juicer or vegetable steamer. Years later, that item sits unused in the closet or the basement.

Facing up to reality, the owner puts it up for sale at a fraction of its original cost. The hoped for self-improvement never happened. And by Saturday afternoon, the item is in the custody of another optimistic self-improver, perhaps to end up in yet another yard sale in a few more years.

Look closely at many lives and you will see more than neglected treadmills. You will also see unused ideas, beliefs, commitments—ways of life that people hoped would improve their lot but which end up ignored and set aside. No one wants a basement full of neglected stuff, once bought at high cost only to be sold for loose change at a yard sale. Likewise, no one should want a spiritual life that is characterized by an endless string of short-term, lukewarm enthusiasms. No one should miss the genuine, priceless treasure that commitment to Christ brings. Paul definitely didn't want this fate to befall the Colossian believers.

B. Lesson Background

The church of Colosse found itself surrounded by competing belief systems (sound familiar?). There were the old pagan religions—famous stories about the heroic gods and goddesses of Greece. There were newfangled "mystery" religions—small, cultlike groups that promised spiritual enlightenment for those willing to undergo a long and costly process of initiation. There were sophisticated philosophical systems—ways of life built around speculation on the nature of existence combined with commonsense observations. There was magic—

practices that were thought to manipulate spiritual beings into doing one's bidding. And there was Judaism—a firm commitment to but one God who revealed himself to a single nation and gave them an elaborate legal code to follow.

When the gospel came to Colosse, many saw in Jesus Christ what they had sought but not found in those other ideologies and faiths. Setting aside their old commitments at great cost, they committed to Christ. But old ways can reassert their appeal with time. Paul wanted to remind the Colossian believers of what was at stake in their flirtation with these old ways.

I. Stay Firm in Christ
(COLOSSIANS 2:6-8)
A. What to Do (vv. 6, 7)

6. As ye have therefore received Christ Jesus the Lord, so walk ye in him.

The supremacy of Christ demands that believers commit themselves to His supremacy. That is largely Paul's point in the entire Colossian letter, and this verse stresses it directly. So we should look carefully at how Paul makes the point.

Paul writes of receiving Christ, which for many Christians today sounds like a common description of conversion: to receive Jesus into one's heart. However, Paul's terms are more specific than that. The verb translated *received* normally refers to receiving a message, teaching, or tradition that is passed along. So here it refers to hearing and believing the gospel message (1 Thessalonians 2:13; etc.). Paul is reminding Christian believers who are flirting with (or may be tempted to flirt with) other beliefs of the message that first brought them to faith in *Christ Jesus the Lord*.

The one in whom they believe is God's exalted king, who delivers His people and rules over them. He is Jesus, the lowly man of Nazareth, who surrendered His life on the cross and was raised victorious. This makes Him Lord, the supreme sovereign over all.

Christ's identity makes a clear demand. To believe that Christ Jesus is Lord provokes constant thanksgiving, demands submissive obedience, and inspires unending loyalty. So to *walk . . . in him* means to live according to those demands. There is no place for other allegiances or to other lords if Christ Jesus is Lord.

❧ WALKING IN JESUS ❧

The expression "walk a mile in my shoes" is a challenge for others to identify with the situation of the speaker. Jesus did indeed walk a mile (and more) in our shoes when He came to the earth. As a result, He "was in all points tempted like as we are" (Hebrews 4:15).

Now it's our turn to identify with Jesus by walking in Him. But many refuse to do so. Some see His shoes as too big, and they stumble trying to walk in them because they don't draw on His strength for the journey. Others see His shoes as too small and confining, and they kick them off because of a desire to be free. But those who step into His shoes to walk by faith find strength and purpose for life.

Walking in the shoes of Jesus—walking along the path of His choosing—is what we must do full time. We don't stop doing so when no one is watching. We don't stop doing so when we are on vacation. Why would we even want to? Only Jesus provides us the path to eternal life.   —A. E. A.

7. Rooted and built up in him, and stablished in the faith, as ye have been taught, abounding therein with thanksgiving.

To emphasize how strong and sure the implication of verse 6 is, Paul piles up terms that indicate firmness and stability. *Rooted* brings to mind the immovability of a tree having roots deep in the soil. *Built up* suggests the solid, permanent foundation of a building (compare Ephesians 2:20). *Stablished* translates a word that indicates stability of all kinds, including a firmly settled legal arrangement. *Abounding* projects an image of a cup or jug filled beyond its capacity. Those images combine to suggest exceptional strength of

HOW TO SAY IT

Colosse	Ko-*lahss*-ee.
Colossians	Kuh-*losh*-unz.
Judaism	*Joo*-duh-izz-um or *Joo*-day-izz-um.

commitment and joyous gratitude to the supreme Christ. Such is the response that He deserves for who He is and what He has done.

B. What Not to Do (v. 8)

8. Beware lest any man spoil you through philosophy and vain deceit, after the tradition of men, after the rudiments of the world, and not after Christ.

Because Christ is supreme, He can have no rivals. Anything that seems to rival Him is inferior to Him, a pretender to His supreme position.

But rivals do present themselves, and Paul briefly characterizes them. *Philosophy* today often refers to academic argumentation about thought and logic. In Paul's time, it refers more broadly to the wisdom of various thinkers who seek to find the way to a good life. The ancient philosophers did indeed make some true observations, but the reality of the unseen God lay beyond their powers of observation. Philosophy is limited by the finiteness of the human observer. Paul knew what it was like to bump up against philosophers (see Acts 17:16-34).

Paired with philosophy is *vain deceit*. Here Paul refers not to honest inquiry, but to the sinful human tendency to mislead others for one's own advantage. *Vain* indicates emptiness or pointlessness (compare Ephesians 5:6; Colossians 2:4). Compared with knowing Christ, all human efforts at finding a right way to live are empty failures, and many are deliberately deceiving.

The tradition of men refers to teachings passed on by word of mouth. The problem here is not tradition in and of itself; after all, Christians follow the passed-along tradition of the gospel message. The problem Paul addresses, rather, is that of traditions that are purely human in origin, unlike the gospel of the divine Christ. All human teaching pales in comparison with the message of the supreme Lord, Jesus Christ (Matthew 15:9).

The phrase *rudiments of the world* is a difficult one, but it probably refers to belief in local spirits or deities thought to have authority over an area. Paul's point is not to argue their existence or nonexistence. Certainly, he would affirm with the rest of the Bible that the unseen world of the spirit has many spirit beings, some angelic and some

demonic. But none of these has an authority that even begins to compare with that of Christ.

All these challengers for the allegiance of the Colossian Christians suffer from the same deficiency: they are not Christ.

What Do You Think?
  What worldly traditions, principles, etc., present the greatest threats to a Christian's spiritual health? Why, and how do we resist?
Talking Points for Your Discussion
- Worldly views of sin
- Worldly views of human origins
- Worldly views of Jesus' person and work
- Other

II. Reasons for Firm Faith
(COLOSSIANS 2:9-15)

A. Christ Is Supreme (vv. 9, 10)

9. For in him dwelleth all the fulness of the Godhead bodily.

To make clear Christ's utter supremacy, Paul draws on a concept that he used earlier, in Colossians 1:19 (last week's lesson): Christ is the fullness, the entirety of God's being. To know Him is to know God fully. Here Paul adds a concept to specify further Christ's utter supremacy as God: Christ is *the fulness of the Godhead*. This indicates unmistakably that Paul speaks of Christ not just as a powerful spirit being, but as God himself. Christ is the one true God, the God of Israel.

Further still, the true God dwelt in Christ *bodily*. This indicates that God himself entered the world as a human with a physical body in the man Jesus. The wonder of the triune God (one God existing as Father, Son, and Spirit) and the wonder of the incarnation (God becoming human) are briefly and powerfully expressed here.

10. And ye are complete in him, which is the head of all principality and power.

Because Christ is the fullness of God, those who belong to Christ are complete or full because they belong to Him. Nothing else can surpass or add to what believers receive from the supreme Christ.

Because He is the fullness of the one true God, Christ is sovereign over any and every other spiritual being (*all principality and power;* also Ephesians 1:21, 22). Whatever power they possess, Christ is greater. Likewise, whatever they might empower among the people of this world, Christ is greater and imparts a greater power to His people.

So Christ's people have every reason to look nowhere but to Him. He, the fullness of God, gives us full, complete relationship with God. As the greatest power, He is supreme over every spiritual and worldly power. His supremacy gives us every reason to stand firm in our faith in Him.

> **What Do You Think?**
>
> How do you "go on unto perfection" (Hebrews 6:1) while realizing that you are already "complete in him" (here)?
>
> *Talking Points for Your Discussion*
> - Ephesians 4:13, 14 (Lesson 3)
> - Philippians 3:12-15 (Lesson 9)
> - Colossians 4:12 (Lesson 13)

B. Christ Transforms (vv. 11, 12)

11. In whom also ye are circumcised with the circumcision made without hands, in putting off the body of the sins of the flesh by the circumcision of Christ.

From His supreme position, Christ grants His people a victorious transformation that surpasses that of any other source. What Christ does fulfills God's promises made in the Old Testament to Israel, bringing the reality to which Israel's laws and practices pointed. God had commanded Abraham to circumcise all the males in His camp as a sign that they belonged to God through a covenant (Genesis 17:10, 11). Thereafter, circumcision was the definitive sign of membership in Israel, God's chosen people. Without that sign, a man could not be regarded as belonging to God's people.

But God's promise was always to bless not just Israel but all nations (Genesis 22:18; Isaiah 42:6). In Christ, Paul says, God fulfills that promise. Christ brings about a greater circumcision. This one is not done by human hands, but by Christ's divine power.

This new kind of circumcision is not the removal of a piece of flesh, as is "ordinary" circumcision.

Visual for Lesson 11. *Use this visual to start a discussion contrasting the "good" and "bad" captivities of Colossians 2:8 and 2 Corinthians 10:5, respectively.*

Rather, it is the removal of sin, pictured as if it were a piece of flesh. Christ removes the guilt of sin, granting us forgiveness, and He removes the power of sin as His power enables us to overcome the rebellious thoughts and actions that otherwise dominate our lives. That is a circumcision of the heart (Romans 2:29).

Thus Israel's practice of circumcision was intended by God to point toward something that later would truly mark God's people as belonging to Him. That "something" is the sin-overcoming transformation that Christ offers.

12. Buried with him in baptism, wherein also ye are risen with him through the faith of the operation of God, who hath raised him from the dead.

This verse continues the theme of the previous one, adding another image of Christ's transformation: baptism. At Jesus' command, His followers administer it "in the name of the Father, and of the Son, and of the Holy Ghost" on those who come to faith in Jesus (Matthew 28:19, 20; compare Acts 2:38). Religious washing ceremonies are common in ancient Judaism. But these are self-administered: a person dips himself or herself in water. Christian baptism differs in that it is administered by another. This represents a cleansing that one cannot do to oneself, but that God provides (compare Titus 3:5).

To this image of cleansing, the New Testament adds others. Notable images here are burial and resurrection (also Romans 6:4). Because the baptized person is taken under the water and then brought out of it, the action resembles Christ's resurrection from the dead. So now in baptism, the believer is united with Christ's death and resurrection, as God applies the power and benefits of the cross to believers. Baptism signals death to the old life of rebellion against God and resurrection to the new life of submission to Christ.

Of course, merely dipping someone in water cannot accomplish this. The baptismal water has no magical properties. Baptism is God's act, given to those who approach Him *through the faith of the operation* (work) of God. But baptism also is the biblical means by which we address ourselves to God, seeking cleansing from sin and new life from Him. In baptism the believer says, "God, please by the power of Christ make me clean from sin, make me dead to sin, give me new life in Christ."

> **What Do You Think?**
> Which part of Paul's description of baptism helps you most in staying rooted in Christ? Why?
> *Talking Points for Your Discussion*
> - Contrast with circumcision of the old covenant
> - Image of burial
> - Image of resurrection

❧ MARK OF THE BEST ❧

She has her mother's eyes. He has his father's smile. He acts like his big brother. She likes to dress like her sister. Each of these statements indicates a mark of identification of one person with another. Various symbols or marks of identification are all around us. Think of matching wedding bands, police uniforms, and gang tattoos.

The mark of identification in ancient Israel was circumcision. In the Christian era, baptism is one mark of identification of a repentant follower of Jesus Christ. But submitting to baptism as a mere outward ritual is without value. The goal of those who are identified with Christ is to become more and more like Him.

Some Christians spend a lot of time trying to interpret the meaning of "the mark of the beast" of Revelation 16:2; 19:20. They want to make

sure they are not identified in that manner. While some concern about this mark is called for, a better use of time and effort is to try to live up to the meaning of bearing "the mark of the best." We do so when our lives serve as examples of what living in Jesus Christ is all about. —A. E. A.

C. Christ Nullifies (vv. 13-15)

13. And you, being dead in your sins and the uncircumcision of your flesh, hath he quickened together with him, having forgiven you all trespasses.

Paul now combines images from the preceding section to emphasize the complete forgiveness that Christ gives His people (also Ephesians 2:1, 5). The Bible consistently associates death with sin, from God's first warning to Adam (Genesis 2:17) through Revelation's warning about the "second death" (Revelation 21:8). That death is more than the tragedy of physical death; it is the ongoing guilt, alienation, and disharmony that we experience because of disobedience to God. That is the experience of being *dead in your sins.*

> **What Do You Think?**
> How has your life changed in moving from "dead in your sins" to "dead indeed unto sin" (Romans 6:11)?
> *Talking Points for Your Discussion*
> - Things that used to get your attention but no longer do
> - Things that now get your attention that didn't before

Uncircumcision indicated separation from God's people, being God's enemy. That is another appropriate image of the old life. To that lost, helpless situation, God brings the answer in Christ. He grants new life in resurrection from the death of sin; He performs the removal of sin in spiritual circumcision. He forgives utterly. In every way that we have violated His will, He absolves.

Nowhere else is such forgiveness possible. Even the temple, given to Israel by God himself, cannot give full and final forgiveness since sacrifices there have to be offered over and over (Hebrews 10:1-4). Only Christ provides absolute release from sin's condemnation. *Quickened* is an older word that means "made alive," and that's what Christ does.

14. Blotting out the handwriting of ordinances that was against us, which was contrary to us, and took it out of the way, nailing it to his cross.

This verse has terms that are difficult to sort out, but the basic sense is clear. *The handwriting of ordinances* is probably one of two things: either the Old Testament Law of Moses or a figurative list of the sinner's violations of the law. The latter would indicate a sort of IOU that we cannot pay back. Probably the simpler choice is the first one.

For Israel, that law brought condemnation: the people knew it, but did not keep it. For Gentiles, the law excluded them from the people of God. Truly, it was against all of humanity in rebellion against God. Sin makes us God's enemies, and so God's law becomes our enemy because "sin is the transgression of the law" (1 John 3:4).

That condemning law is taken away by Christ's death. As Pilate literally nailed the proclamation "King of the Jews" on Jesus' cross (John 19:19), so God figuratively nailed the law to the cross as Christ took our punishment on himself as our willing representative. Jesus took the punishment that the law pronounces on sin, namely death, so that the law's blessing, life, can be ours.

If the Colossian Christians are contemplating a return to Judaism without Jesus, Paul certainly warns against that move. The Law of Moses does not save; it condemns. But in so doing, it points to our need of a Savior. Christ fulfills what the law anticipates (Galatians 4:23-25).

15. And having spoiled principalities and powers, he made a shew of them openly, triumphing over them in it.

Paul now pictures the end of our condemnation in terms of a great military victory. The *principalities and powers* are, as in verse 10, spirit beings —here demonic beings in particular. These now appear as defeated enemies. They are pictured as *spoiled,* as if their weapons and armor have been stripped by a victorious general. Then as defeated enemies they are led in a victory procession, paraded through the city. All this is to the glory of the victor and the shame of the vanquished.

We need not speculate about some specific disarming ceremony and victory procession in the spirit world to understand this statement. The point is that by His death and resurrection, Christ has defeated every power that opposes Him. Ironically enough, the Romans—pagans who are indifferent to the true God—crucified Him as a demonstration of their own power. But as things turned out, Jesus defeated all who rival Him as Lord.

So there is none to condemn Christ's people. And there is none with power greater than His.

What Do You Think?
How do you make sure that "principalities and powers" remain defeated in your life?
Talking Points for Your Discussion
- Jeremiah 1:17-19
- Romans 8:31-39
- Acts 2:42
- 1 John 5:5
- Other

Conclusion

A. Our Priceless Treasure

A popular television program shows people bringing antique family heirlooms for appraisal by experts. Much of the show's appeal comes from the surprise that people display when they learn the great value of what was for them just a sentimental memento. In today's text, Paul served as an expert appraising the priceless value of Christ's work. But we should not be surprised to hear his appraisal. We recognized Christ's supreme worth when we came to faith in Him, and each day teaches us how valuable are our "lives of no condemnation." There can be no surrendering this great treasure.

B. Prayer

O Lord, Your gifts to us are beyond value and beyond measure. In gratitude we pledge our lives to You again. By Your grace may we always grow in our commitment to You. We pray because of Christ's victory and in His name, amen.

C. Thought to Remember

Know what to keep and what to reject.

INVOLVEMENT LEARNING

Some of the activities below are also found in the helpful student book, Adult Bible Class.
Don't forget to download the free reproducible page from www.standardlesson.com to enhance your lesson!

Into the Lesson

Have on display a sign that says *Yard Sale* as learners arrive. Also have on display some sketches on the board of things for sale that are marked prominently "In Original Packaging!" or "Hardly Used!" Include primarily items intended for physical and spiritual self-improvement. Make sure to include sketches related to baptism, such as the typical white baptismal robe, to connect with Colossians 2:12, part of today's text.

With these images as a backdrop, summarize or paraphrase to the class the lesson writer's Introduction on "Rejecting the 'Yard Sale' Life." Add your own personal experiences with living that kind of life. You can invite learners to share their own experiences in this regard, but don't let this segment drag out too long.

Into the Word

Establish three small groups that you will call *The Rooted Group, The Strengthened Group,* and *The Thankful Group.* Groups should consist of no more than four learners each. (Larger classes can form more than three groups and give duplicate assignments.) Provide these directions to each group: "Look at Colossians 2:6-15 and complete the following sentence with ideas based on the text: 'I need to be _____ because _____.' Put the key term of your group in the first blank, which will be either *rooted, strengthened,* or *thankful.*"

If your learners need a stimulus to jump-start their thinking, you can offer the following: "I need to be rooted because there are those who will try to pluck me up"; "I need to be strengthened because there are those who will try to deceive me with empty words"; and "I need to be thankful because God has forgiven all my sins."

Challenge groups to think of at least three ways to complete the affirmation. Groups are allowed to count the examples you gave, provided they can identify a verse or verses as basis.

After about eight minutes, ask groups to report results. As each affirmation is read, ask, "On what verse or verses are you basing that truth?"

Distribute copies of the "Sounds Familiar" exercise from the reproducible page, which you can download. This will help your learners tie this week's lesson to last week's lesson.

Into Life

Distribute copies of the "At the Foot of the Cross" activity from the reproducible page. Say, "Some would like to 'spoil you through philosophy and vain deceit' today (Colossians 2:8). Let's see what some of those folks have to say." Recruit three class members to present the impassioned "sales pitches" below. Provide each with an appropriate sign to wear.

The Materialist: "I want you! I want you to want because our economy depends on your buying and buying. As they say, 'The one with the most toys wins!' Remember, 'What you see is what you get, for what you see is all there is.' You don't want to believe in things you can't see and touch, do you?"

The Politically Correct: "I want you! I want you to stop judging people and ideas to be 'wrong,' for the Bible clearly says 'Judge not' in Matthew 7:1. Your own faith says that everyone is equal—no religious, national, or lifestyle differences. We all believe in the same God, don't we?"

The Humanist: "I want you! I want you to stand tall, as an intelligent human being, fully capable of directing your own life. With all our marvelous advances in science and technology, what need do we have of a Supreme Being? Just to explain what we can't explain? Get busy! Work out the explanations. You are capable, you know."

Follow each presentation with a discussion. (Larger classes can use small groups for this.) Kick off each discussion in turn by asking, "What did you just hear that should be left at the cross? Why? How will you guard yourself against these?"

Raised with Christ

CLOTHED WITH CHRIST

DEVOTIONAL READING: Psalm 107:1-9

BACKGROUND SCRIPTURE: Colossians 3

COLOSSIANS 3:5-17

Rom 89

5 Mortify therefore your members which are upon the earth; fornication, uncleanness, inordinate affection, evil concupiscence, and covetousness, which is idolatry:

6 For which things' sake the wrath of God cometh on the children of disobedience:

7 In the which ye also walked some time, when ye lived in them.

8 But now ye also put off all these; anger, wrath, malice, blasphemy, filthy communication out of your mouth.

9 Lie not one to another, seeing that ye have put off the old man with his deeds;

10 And have put on the new man, which is renewed in knowledge after the image of him that created him:

11 Where there is neither Greek nor Jew, circumcision nor uncircumcision, Barbarian, Scythian, bond nor free: but Christ is all, and in all.

12 Put on therefore, as the elect of God, holy and beloved, bowels of mercies, kindness, humbleness of mind, meekness, longsuffering;

13 Forbearing one another, and forgiving one another, if any man have a quarrel against any: even as Christ forgave you, so also do ye.

14 And above all these things put on charity, *love* which is the bond of perfectness.

15 And let the peace of God rule in your hearts, to the which also ye are called in one body; and be ye thankful.

16 Let the word of Christ dwell in you richly in all wisdom; teaching and admonishing one another in psalms and hymns and spiritual songs, singing with grace in your hearts to the Lord.

17 And whatsoever ye do in word or deed, do all in the name of the Lord Jesus, giving thanks to God and the Father by him.

KEY VERSE

Above all these things put on charity, which is the bond of perfectness. —**Colossians 3:14**

JESUS IS LORD

Unit 3: Imitating Jesus
LESSONS 10–13

LESSON AIMS

After participating in this lesson, each student will be able to:

1. List some attitudes and behaviors that ought and ought not to characterize the Christian.

2. Explain what it means to "put to death" the sinful behaviors and attitudes of the flesh.

3. Write a prayer of gratitude for new life in Christ.

LESSON OUTLINE

Introduction
A. Clothes Tell the Story

Clothing announces who a person is, doesn't it? Doctors at the hospital wear white lab coats. Mechanics at the garage may wear blue shirts with their names embroidered in a patch on the chest. Servers at restaurants often wear uniforms that are distinctive to their restaurant chain. What kind of clothing announces that we are followers of Jesus? Our text today tells us.

B. Lesson Background

Christians in Colosse faced a choice: whether to continue in their new faith in Christ or to follow some other belief system. Pagan religions surrounded them, as did the philosophical teachings of the day. Judaism was also influential. Whether confronted by a single alternative or several, the Colossian Christians were faced with the temptation to give up faith in Jesus for something else (see the Lesson Background to last week's lesson).

In the first half of his letter to the Colossians (lessons for the previous two weeks), Paul points out Jesus' complete superiority. No other belief system can rival His good news. In the second half of the letter, Paul turns to the implications of faith in Christ. If God really did enter the world in the person of Jesus, then our world has been turned upside down and inside out. It demands a different kind of life from us.

Today's text comes near the beginning of this discussion of putting faith in Christ into practice. Paul has just told the readers to settle their thinking on Christ, who reigns from Heaven and who will one day return to receive His people in glory. That way of thinking leads (or should lead) to distinct behavior, which Paul describes in our text.

I. What to Put Off
(COLOSSIANS 3:5-11)
A. The Selfish Life (vv. 5-7)

5. Mortify therefore your members which are upon the earth; fornication, uncleanness, inordinate affection, evil concupiscence, and covetousness, which is idolatry.

This verse's many terms can make sense if we begin with the phrase *upon the earth*. This phrase focuses on the difference between thinking and living according to earthly powers and pressures in contrast with the reign of Christ in Heaven. In a survival-of-the-fittest world, people get for themselves what they can. But Christ lived differently. He refused to serve himself, instead giving His life for undeserving sinners. If we acknowledge His reign, we will reject the selfish life.

Paul begins to characterize that old life with a list of vices. All the terms in this verse name manifestations of selfishness. Most are specifically about seeking selfish gratification of sexual desire. We can look at each term individually to understand what they mean, remembering that Paul uses the combination of terms to paint a larger portrait.

The term *fornication* is used in the Bible to refer to any sexual activity outside of marriage (and marriage is understood in the Bible to be permanent, monogamous, and heterosexual). Human sexuality is an important aspect of God's creation that is "very good" (Genesis 1:31). But God's intention is that sexuality is to be exercised only within marriage. This places sex in a context of mutual commitment of selfless love.

Sex outside of marriage omits that selfless covenant. The sexually immoral person selfishly takes what rightly belongs to another person's spouse (or potential future spouse). Immoral sex is not a violation of an arbitrary rule; it is an act of selfishness that rejects the reign of the self-sacrificial Christ.

The other terms in the list continue this theme. *Uncleanness* is another term for sexual sin, emphasizing its degrading, shameful aspects. *Inordinate affection* in modern dialect is "strong desire," referring to desire for something to which one has no right. That is followed by *evil concupiscence*, or evil lust—a term reemphasizing desire for what is forbidden (see also Ephesians 4:19; 5:3, 5).

HOW TO SAY IT

Barbarian	Bar-*bare*-ee-un.
concupiscence	kon-*cue*-puh-sense.
Scythian	*Sith*-ee-un.

The next term, *covetousness,* should be familiar since it is part of the Ten Commandments (Exodus 20:17). While this may refer to a selfish desire for sexual gratification, the term is commonly used for the desire to have an abundance of anything —money, possessions, or pleasure. Following the other terms, it may widen the focus on sexual sin to include all kinds of selfish desires.

Paul equates this self-gratifying greed with *idolatry*. The connection is clear: if our selfish desires control us, we no longer live under the reign of the selfless Christ. We have displaced the true God for a false god of our own making: our own self-centered pleasure-seeking.

We can't reach any kind of halfway accommodation regarding these things—these *members*. Rather, we must *mortify* them; that is, we must put them to death (Romans 8:13). Just as Christ nailed the law and its condemnation of our sin to the cross (Colossians 2:14, last week's lesson), so we must let Him nail our selfish desires to the cross as well (Romans 6:5-14).

> *What Do You Think?*
> How do you protect yourself from rationalizing as you wrestle with Paul's list?
> *Talking Points for Your Discussion*
> ▪ The "between consenting adults" argument
> ▪ The "privacy of my own home" argument
> ▪ Other

6. For which things' sake the wrath of God cometh on the children of disobedience.

The selfish mind-set is utterly contrary to the nature of God, whom we know through Jesus. So God cannot let such things slip by. If He is at all true to himself, if He is at all just, He must bring justice to wrongdoers. God's solemn determination to punish evil is what the Bible calls His *wrath*. Those whose lives are characterized by rebellion against Him deserve His punishment (Ephesians 5:6). He would not be the God of justice without wrath against sin.

But God does not leave us without hope! God provides through Christ the way for His mercy by taking on himself the just punishment for our sin. His wrath remains, however, for those who refuse that gift, a refusal they declare with their stubbornly selfish existence.

7. In the which ye also walked some time, when ye lived in them.

Lest as the forgiven we become arrogant, Paul reminds us that we ourselves know the lifestyle of sin. All of us have belonged to the world's selfish way of life. All of us have participated in the patterns of life that provoke God's wrath.

Having lived the world's life and being surrounded by the world's ways even now, we find it hard to overcome the old life. The things that bring God's wrath have been part of our lives before. They can come back if we forget the Christ who rules over us, the wrath of God, and the cost of our redemption.

B. The Hostile Life (vv. 8-11)

8. But now ye also put off all these; anger, wrath, malice, blasphemy, filthy communication out of your mouth.

Again, Paul provides a list that characterizes the old life. This one focuses on our attitude and actions toward others. The Christ who rules over us is the Christ who did not retaliate when His enemies arrested, tortured, and killed Him. Our God is the God who offers mercy and forgiveness to sinners who repeatedly rebel against Him. So for those who submit to His rule, there can be no place for hostility toward other people, whether in thought, word, or action.

The terms in the list center on that point. *Anger* and *wrath* indicate hostility, seeking to harm another. These have no place in the life of a forgiven person who trusts God to bring whatever punishment needs to be brought on evildoers. *Malice* refers to a desire that others suffer injury, again an attitude opposite that of Christ.

Blasphemy is disrespectful speech about God and things associated with God. It is no accident that blasphemy appears in a list of sins against our fellow humans, for if we are willing to treat with contempt those who bear God's image, we show no respect for God himself. *Filthy communication* is shameful speech of all kinds; it can include vulgar talk, insults, gossip—any of the ways we use words to hurt others (see also Ephesians 4:25-31; 5:4).

9. Lie not one to another, seeing that ye have put off the old man with his deeds.

Falsehood is obviously inconsistent with submission to Christ. God is truth, so His people must live in truth. We use lies to gain our own selfish ends or to harm others, which is the very core of the old life (Ephesians 4:25).

Paul tells us again that we put off *the old man* when we became Christians (Ephesians 4:22). Calling on Christ in baptism, we asked Him to cleanse us from the old, putting to death our lives of rebellion and raising us to lives of submission to Him (Colossians 2:12, 13, last week's lesson). What are we saying to Him, and what are we saying about ourselves, if we continue to live as if we had never asked Christ to make us new?

❧ SENDING THINGS TO THE LANDFILL ❧

One day my wife began looking with great disfavor at my favorite jeans. She thought it was time for me to get rid of them. I realized they had holes, were frayed at the cuff, and otherwise generally worn out. But they were so comfortable that I was willing to turn a blind eye to their state of decay.

However, the day came when the decision to get rid of them had to be made. But then a thought popped into my mind: *Maybe someone else could get some good use out of them!* So I decided the yard sale was the place to put them. That would be the way to fool myself into believing that something that provided me with such comfort still had value. In reality, those jeans were good for nothing but the landfill. They needed to be discarded and forgotten.

We can struggle in a similar way with our bad habits and sins. They are so comfortable and familiar! They are such a part of our lives that we see them as part of who we are. What habits and practices in your life need to go straight to the landfill? —A. E. A.

10. And have put on the new man, which is renewed in knowledge after the image of him that created him.

Living as a Christian means more than just avoiding sin. It means acquiring a new, different perspective and lifestyle. That is *the new man,* a life modeled after Christ himself, who shows us what it means to live out our purpose.

This verse's point is built on the idea that God created us in His image (Genesis 1:26, 27). We are created to reflect who God is. But by choosing sin, we distort God's image, living in contempt of Him. But Christ lived in full submission to God, displaying God's righteousness and mercy. So the life that Christ lived is to be the new life that we live. That life is the expression of humanity as God originally intended, a genuine fulfillment of our Creator's blessed purpose for us.

> **What Do You Think?**
> How does the practice of putting off "the old man" (v. 9) interact with the practice of putting on "the new man" in your life?
> *Talking Points for Your Discussion*
> - 1 Samuel 7:3, 4
> - Proverbs 4:24-27
> - Luke 11:24-26
> - 2 Timothy 4:10a

11. Where there is neither Greek nor Jew, circumcision nor uncircumcision, Barbarian, Scythian, bond nor free: but Christ is all, and in all.

Sinful humans like nothing better than to find and exploit differences between themselves and others. People tend to focus on divisions such as nationality, socioeconomic class, etc. This results in giving ourselves permission to look down on others. The Bible's perspective is that such divisions are the consequence of our rebellion against God (Genesis 11:1-8; Psalm 2:1-3). In fact, we are all part of the same family, all descended from our first parents,

Visual for Lesson 12. *Have this visual on display as you pose the discussion questions associated with verses 10 and/or 12.*

all equally guilty of sin, and all equally in need of God's forgiveness (Romans 10:12).

So for those who know God's forgiveness in Christ, the old divisions can no longer divide. Belonging to Christ, we are one (1 Corinthians 12:13; Galatians 3:26-28). Our identity in Him matters far more than the identities that we used to use as excuses for ignoring or taking advantage of others.

So Paul lists some of the divisive identifiers of his day. Greeks are the culturally dominant people of the time, the people of privilege. Jews understand that they have received the promises of God and so can claim their own privilege. *Barbarian* refers in Paul's time simply to people who do not speak Greek; they are not utterly uncivilized, but certainly are uncultured. Scythians are a step further down the social ladder. These are people of Asia, distant from Greek culture, thought to be primitive and wild.

Bond refers to slaves; *free* refers to those not enslaved. Slavery is tragically common in Paul's world. Slaves are degraded as property, divided from those having the freedom to direct their own lives.

Christ obliterates these distinctions. God calls His people to lay aside the prejudices by which they have dehumanized others. He calls them to embrace all who belong to Christ as a new family. Christ did not die for one group or another; He died for everyone.

II. What to Put On
(COLOSSIANS 3:12-16)
A. The Grace-filled Life (vv. 12-14)

12. Put on therefore, as the elect of God, holy and beloved, bowels of mercies, kindness, humbleness of mind, meekness, longsuffering.

Completing the command to "put off" in verse 8, we now have the command to *put on* the attitudes and behaviors that befit the new life. Christians are called to do this as *the elect of God,* His chosen people (1 Peter 2:9). Israel was God's chosen people in the Old Testament (Exodus 19:3-6), but now Christ has fulfilled what Israel's law anticipated: believers in Christ are God's chosen. They belong to God and so are holy, or set apart. They are the objects of His love and grace and so are beloved. Their lives therefore need to reflect their identity as God's people, made His by His love.

The characteristics named in this verse all express that identity. The phrase *bowels of mercies* indicates a strong feeling of compassion for others. We are probably more accustomed to calling this a response of the heart, but we sometimes say that we feel something "in the gut." *Kindness* likewise indicates a positive, generous, gracious response to others' needs.

Humbleness of mind and *meekness* both stress adopting a position of lowliness, seeking to serve others instead of asserting one's own rights or privileges. *Longsuffering* indicates the willingness to wait as long as it takes for others to make the right response, just as God waited for us to respond to Him (Ephesians 4:32). Such "clothing" as this surely identifies a person as belonging to Christ.

> **What Do You Think?**
> How can a church develop in her members the things in Paul's "put on" list?
> *Talking Points for Your Discussion*
> - Through one-on-one methods
> - Through small-group methods
> - Through midsize-group methods

13. Forbearing one another, and forgiving one another, if any man have a quarrel against any: even as Christ forgave you, so also do ye.

The attitudes of the previous verse are to yield certain actions. *Forbearing* suggests "putting up with." The person who belongs to Christ will recognize that others' faults are small for us to put up with when compared with what Christ puts up with in His people! Forbearing leads to forgiving, as we do not simply keep our grievances quiet, but actually let them go.

We are called to respond with forbearance and forgiveness when we have a complaint against another; the term translated *quarrel* indicates any bone to pick, big or small. Paul's words do not give us a basis to withhold our forbearance and forgiveness when we believe our grievance is justified. Christ's forgiving us stands in the center of this discussion. It compels us to forgive (see Matthew 18:23-35). If we refuse to forgive, we treat Christ's forgiveness with contempt.

14. And above all these things put on charity, which is the bond of perfectness.

The entirety of the Christian's new clothing can be described with a single word: *charity* (in modern English, *love;* Romans 13:8, 10). Love is what motivates God's forbearance and forgiveness toward us, so it is also what motivates the same in us toward others. Charity/love *is the bond of perfectness,* a band that ties all the virtues together.

B. The Harmonious Life (vv. 15, 16)

15. And let the peace of God rule in your hearts, to the which also ye are called in one body; and be ye thankful.

If all Christ's people live as Paul describes, there will be no conflict among them, only harmony and acceptance. These are the two sides of God's peace: the absence of hostility and the presence of genuine fellowship. This peace begins inwardly, with attitudes remade in the image of Christ. So it rules *in your hearts.* It changes how we act, so it is observed in the way that the *one body* functions.

Making us one in Him is what Christ came to do. Sin divides us; His forgiveness unites us. We cannot tolerate division if we are true to our identity as Christ's people. The expression *let the peace of God rule* does not express something that happens passively. It can also be translated *the peace of God must rule.* This is not an option, but an imperative.

Thankfulness rounds out this section. Because our new lives are God's work, continual thanksgiving is a hallmark of the new life.

16. Let the word of Christ dwell in you richly in all wisdom; teaching and admonishing one another in psalms and hymns and spiritual songs, singing with grace in your hearts to the Lord.

We often read this verse as a mandate to worship together in song. It is certainly that, but it is more as well. Christ's Word needs to shape our attitudes and actions. It needs to do so *richly* as a mighty reality that transforms every aspect of our lives. It puts us in relationship with other believers, compelling us to strengthen them and be strengthened by them. See the commentary on Ephesians 5:19 in Lesson 5 (page 155) regarding the distinctions among *psalms and hymns and spiritual songs*.

III. Whom to Focus On
(COLOSSIANS 3:17)

17. And whatsoever ye do in word or deed, do all in the name of the Lord Jesus, giving thanks to God and the Father by him.

This verse sums up what the entire text emphasizes. If Christ reigns over all, if we are raised to new life in Him, then everything we do must be submitted to His authority—*in the name of the Lord Jesus*. That means adopting the attitudes that Christ demonstrated and then demonstrating them in our lives (1 Corinthians 10:31). That's the way we thank God for His magnificent gift. Thanksgiving in mere words is hollow and insincere. Thanksgiving in both word and action that reflect our Lord's character and will is true thanksgiving, worthy of the God we know as *the Father* (Ephesians 5:20).

What Do You Think?
How does living out "whatsoever ye do" manifest itself in different parts of your life?
Talking Points for Your Discussion
- During leisure time
- While serving in the church
- In the workplace
- Other

❧ *IN HIS NAME* ❧

In January 2011, a major donor to the University of Connecticut athletic program demanded the return of a $3 million donation. He also demanded that his family name be removed from the football complex at the university. He stated that he felt that he had received a "slap in the face" when the athletic director chose a new football head coach without hearing his voice on the subject. The donor did not want his family name associated with a search process he saw as flawed.

We can argue the propriety of the man's request. We may disagree with his attitude. We may wonder about the motive behind his donation. But we cannot fault him for wanting to protect his name by not allowing it to be associated with something that troubled him.

Christians bear the name of Christ. He paid a great price for our salvation. As such, He has claim over our lives and our decisions. When we fail to take off the old life of sin and put on the new spiritual clothing of righteousness, we dishonor and disrespect His name. May our association with the name *Jesus* bring honor to Him as He watches the way we live this week!   —A. E. A.

Conclusion
A. Our Sunday Best

Have you ever had a discussion about the right clothes to wear to church? Standards change, and people have different opinions about "Sunday best." But certainly today's passage tells us that there is a kind of clothing that really matters—the life-clothing we put on when we join Christ's people. The Christian's real "Sunday best" is simple: to become like Christ, inside and out. He gives us the clothing. It is up to us to continue to wear it, and not just on Sundays.

B. Prayer

Lord, teach us daily to make our thoughts, words, and deeds reflections of the love You so richly bestowed on us. In Jesus' name, amen.

C. Thought to Remember

"Love . . . as I have loved you" (John 13:34).

INVOLVEMENT LEARNING

Some of the activities below are also found in the helpful student book, Adult Bible Class.
Don't forget to download the free reproducible page from www.standardlesson.com to enhance your lesson!

Into the Lesson

Ask learners to watch carefully as you hold above your head a sign that says *THINGS*. With your other hand, lift a picture of a heart and then a picture of a brain; attach each in turn at the top of the *THINGS* sign. Ask, "What do you think I am representing?" If no one responds correctly, say (as you expect some groans at your corniness), "Look at verses 1 and 2 of Colossians 3, just previous to today's text. Those verses affirm our need to set our hearts and minds on things above. That is a prerequisite to clothing ourselves with Christ, as today's text teaches."

Alternative: Bring to class some kind of uniform on a hanger. Ask, "How do clothes reveal the person?" (See the lesson Introduction for thoughts on this.)

Into the Word

Have on display a small rectangular box that you (or an artistic class member) have decorated to look like a coffin. Read the first four words of Colossians 3:3, "for ye are dead." That will serve as a preface to 3:5, the first verse of today's text, which challenges us to "mortify" (put to death) earthly things. Say, "In the verses that follow, Paul speaks by the Spirit of the attitudes and behaviors that should die to the Christian when he or she is buried with Christ in baptism (Colossians 2:12; see last week's study)."

Using 8½" x 11" sheets of paper, cut from each sheet three strips so that you end up with strips that are approximately 2¾" x 11". Draw across the narrow width of each strip horizontal lines that are 1" apart. This will provide space for 11 entries on each strip. Give each learner a strip with these directions: "Read Colossians 3:5-11 and write in each segment an element that deserves to die in the life of a Christian."

Discuss results. Expect some differences in response given that some elements overlap one another in meaning; also, some learners may see prejudice implied in verse 11, although that word is not used there. *Option:* At this point, have learners complete the "Put Off Changed" activity from the reproducible page, which you can download.

Move to the positive, "put on" portion by saying, "Certain life clothing will reveal our role in Christ." Hand each learner a sheet of paper showing simple outlines of at least 10 common articles of clothing (slacks, pair of socks, shirt/blouse, etc.). Give these directions: "Look at Colossians 3:12-14 and identify elements as items of clothing that the Christian needs to 'put on.'"

As you discuss results, ask, "Are the imperatives of verses 15-17 referring to things to 'put on' or are they the expected *results* of the 'putting on' of verses 12-14?" *Option:* At this point, have learners complete the "Put On Changed" activity from the reproducible page.

Into Life

Give each learner an index card. Say, "Paul begins his letter to the Colossians with a word of thanks as he writes in Colossians 1:3, 'We give thanks to God and the Father of our Lord Jesus Christ, praying always for you.' Paul goes on to challenge his readers to be 'giving thanks unto the Father' in 1:12. Paul reemphasizes that call in 3:17, part of today's text, where we read 'whatsoever ye do in word or deed, do all in the name of the Lord Jesus, giving thanks to God and the Father by him.' What grand truths are you learning in these Colossian studies that merit a word of thanksgiving on your part? Make a list on your card and carry it with you for a time."

Option: Suggest that learners take home their "die" strips from Into the Word so they can clip off a segment daily for 11 days, putting them into a box representing a coffin. Also suggest that learners post their "clothing lists" somewhere they will see it as they get dressed daily in the week ahead.

Clothed with Christ

DISCIPLINED
FOR LIFE

DEVOTIONAL READING: 1 Corinthians 9:19-27
BACKGROUND SCRIPTURE: Colossians 4

COLOSSIANS 4:2-17

2 Continue in prayer, and watch in the same with thanksgiving;

3 Withal praying also for us, that God would open unto us a door of utterance, to speak the mystery of Christ, for which I am also in bonds:

4 That I may make it manifest, as I ought to speak.

5 Walk in wisdom toward them that are without, redeeming the time.

6 Let your speech be always with grace, seasoned with salt, that ye may know how ye ought to answer every man.

7 All my state shall Tychicus declare unto you, who is a beloved brother, and a faithful minister and fellowservant in the Lord:

8 Whom I have sent unto you for the same purpose, that he might know your estate, and comfort your hearts;

9 With Onesimus, a faithful and beloved brother, who is one of you. They shall make known unto you all things which are done here.

10 Aristarchus my fellowprisoner saluteth you, and Marcus, sister's son to Barnabas, (touching whom ye received commandments: if he come unto you, receive him;)

11 And Jesus, which is called Justus, who are of the circumcision. These only are my fellow-workers unto the kingdom of God, which have been a comfort unto me.

12 Epaphras, who is one of you, a servant of Christ, saluteth you, always labouring fervently for you in prayers, that ye may stand perfect and complete in all the will of God.

13 For I bear him record, that he hath a great zeal for you, and them that are in Laodicea, and them in Hierapolis.

14 Luke, the beloved physician, and Demas, greet you.

15 Salute the brethren which are in Laodicea, and Nymphas, and the church which is in his house.

16 And when this epistle is read among you, cause that it be read also in the church of the Laodiceans; and that ye likewise read the epistle from Laodicea.

17 And say to Archippus, Take heed to the ministry which thou hast received in the Lord, that thou fulfil it.

KEY VERSE

Say to Archippus, Take heed to the ministry which thou hast received in the Lord, that thou fulfil it.

—**Colossians 4:17**

JESUS IS LORD

Unit 3: Imitating Jesus
LESSONS 10–13

LESSON AIMS

After participating in this lesson, each student will be able to:

1. Identify the behaviors that cultivate growth in Christlikeness as they appear in the text.

2. Tell why prayer is stressed so much in the closing section of Paul's letter to the Colossians.

3. Commit to spending more time in prayer each day in the week ahead.

LESSON OUTLINE

Introduction

A. The Key to Success?

Why are some people highly successful and others not? There are many reasons, but one is *practice*. Highly successful people—from the Beatles to Bill Gates—have spent an exceptional amount of time and effort mastering what they do. Some research indicates that highly successful people commonly spend 10,000 hours practicing their craft. That is a huge figure! At an hour a day, one needs more than 27 years to amass 10,000 hours.

We can exaggerate the comparison, but the same principle can apply to our growth as Christians. Deliberately devoting time and effort to actions related to our faith in Christ is vital to our growth in Christ.

B. Lesson Background

In Paul's time, letters conventionally ended with a series of short, incidental instructions and a series of greetings from friends. Paul's letters normally end this way as well. But Paul also typically uses the closing section of his letters to reinforce themes that he stresses in the letter's main body.

That is the case in Colossians. Paul's closing, which is our text today, is at first glance a typical list of short instructions and greetings. But Paul also reinforces his message throughout this section, providing a guide to a genuinely growing spiritual life. To grow, the Colossians cannot add anything to faith in Jesus, but they can diligently pursue habits that will strengthen and deepen their faith.

Colossians is one of Paul's prison letters, written while he was in custody awaiting trial in Rome in about AD 63 (Acts 28:16-31). Remembering that setting helps us grasp the earnestness of his instructions: he writes as one who has lost his freedom because he is faithful to Christ.

I. Disciplines to Practice
(COLOSSIANS 4:2-6)
A. Persistent Prayer (vv. 2-4)

2. Continue in prayer, and watch in the same with thanksgiving.

The section begins with several statements urging the Colossians to pray. To *continue in prayer* means to devote faithful attention to it (also Ephesians 6:18; Philippians 4:6; 1 Thessalonians 5:17). Prayer is a natural habit for those who believe that the risen Christ reigns victorious in Heaven. In prayer we ask our powerful, gracious Lord to exercise His authority to sustain us as His people.

That instruction is accompanied with a reminder to watch. The term *watch* is used in Paul's day for a sentry or guard who is on alert for an enemy. Doubtless Paul's point is related. The enemy is indeed present, seeking to take advantage of God's people in a moment of weakness. Watchfulness in prayer means constantly relying on God's power to enable us to overcome the devil's opportunistic temptations (Matthew 6:13).

Such prayer is done *with thanksgiving*. Our enemy's activity should not make us forget what God has already given us. When we pray with thanksgiving, we make requests with confidence, remembering how richly God has blessed us in the past.

3. Withal praying also for us, that God would open unto us a door of utterance, to speak the mystery of Christ, for which I am also in bonds.

A disciplined prayer life is not just about oneself. So Paul urges the Colossians to pray for him and his associates in ministry as well (Ephesians 6:19; 2 Thessalonians 3:1). Because he is a prisoner, Paul might be expected to ask for prayers for his release. But he does not do this. Instead, he asks that a figurative door be opened for him to speak about Jesus (also 1 Corinthians 16:9).

The Christian message Paul desires to share he refers to as *mystery*. Paul uses this word to emphasize that the plan by which God would save the rebellious world had been hidden in the past, but now is revealed in Christ. It is a revealed mystery, something we could not have known on our own.

It is also a great challenge to our conventional way of thinking, a message we will not grasp if we judge it by the ordinary human way of judging things. The gospel tells us that the crucified Christ is victorious, that the prisoner Paul can have an open door. As we address God with our burdens and concerns, in response He reminds us of the great truths of the gospel. This teaches us to view our lives from His perspective instead of ours.

❧ THE CHALLENGE OF PRAYER ❧

One day our Sunday school class accepted Paul's challenge to "pray without ceasing" (1 Thessalonians 5:17). In so doing, we realized we couldn't limit our practice of prayer to times of sitting alone with eyes closed. Rather, we would need to develop an awareness of God's presence no matter what we were doing.

The next Sunday, one man reported back on his progress for the week. He said he would walk into his office and look at the dozen or more items that demanded his immediate attention. But before diving in, he would stop and acknowledge God and ask for His help. After a few minutes of focused prayer, he started his tasks, learning that several pressing problems had worked themselves out while he prayed. He had come to realize that maintaining one's focus continually on God was difficult, but everything else became easier as a result.

To think of prayer as just "one more item" on our already lengthy to-do lists is a terrible error.

HOW TO SAY IT

Archippus	Ar-*kip*-us.
Aristarchus	Air-iss-*tar*-cuss.
Epaphras	*Ep*-uh-frass.
Hierapolis	Hi-er-*ap*-o-lis.
Laodicea	Lay-*odd*-uh-*see*-uh.
Nymphas	*Nim*-fuss.
Onesimus	O-*ness*-ih-muss.
Philemon	Fih-*lee*-mun or Fye-*lee*-mun.
Tychicus	*Tick*-ih-cuss.

Prayer is communing with God, who created us to walk with Him continually. When we live prayerfully, we stay connected with the one who has the wisdom and power to run the universe. When we add an attitude of watchfulness, we anticipate that God is indeed moving on our behalf. As a result, we bless the God who is blessing us.   —V. E.

4. That I may make it manifest, as I ought to speak.

Paul's unrelenting focus is on proclaiming the gospel (Ephesians 6:20). He understands that this is the purpose of his imprisonment, and he uses his imprisonment to preach to all who will listen (Acts 28:30, 31). In Philippians, another prison letter, Paul states that his imprisonment has led to the evangelizing of many (Philippians 1:12-14). This is the bigger picture.

B. Divine Wisdom (v. 5)

5. Walk in wisdom toward them that are without, redeeming the time.

A life of prayer expresses dependence on God. So does a life that seeks God's wisdom daily. The wisdom of which Paul speaks is God's wisdom, expressed in Jesus and appearing to be foolish by the world's standards (1 Corinthians 1:18-25). Our wisdom is turned upside down by God's wisdom: His wisdom glorifies lowliness and brings victory through Christ's self-sacrificial death. That is the wisdom in which the Christian must walk, a figure of speech for habitual thoughts and actions.

Such wisdom is especially required when dealing with people who do not know Jesus, those *that are without*. Over time they can see the difference in our lives, and that difference will provoke many to want to know what creates it (1 Thessalonians 4:11, 12). By this means, our time in a corrupt world becomes something that accomplishes God's saving purpose. So we are *redeeming the time*: staying away from meaningless sin to join God in demonstrating His saving wisdom.

C. Redemptive Speech (v. 6)

6. Let your speech be always with grace, seasoned with salt, that ye may know how ye ought to answer every man.

Perhaps our most powerful ability is speech. Speech that is characterized by God's grace—His favor and love for the undeserving—is like carefully seasoned food. Such speech, regardless of its subject, testifies to the gospel (1 Peter 3:15). We may not know the most convincing responses to the questions and objections that unbelievers bring. But we can be confident that sincere speech that reflects God's grace can provoke skeptics to consider the gospel in a new light.

II. Mentors to Follow
(Colossians 4:7-15)
A. Tychicus (vv. 7, 8)

7, 8. All my state shall Tychicus declare unto you, who is a beloved brother, and a faithful minister and fellowservant in the Lord: Whom I have sent unto you for the same purpose, that he might know your estate, and comfort your hearts.

Paul's greetings to the Colossians name close associates who travel with him in his missionary work. Their descriptions make them in-the-flesh examples of the Christlike life. These people are not passing acquaintances of Paul's churches, but are well-known, well-loved members of God's family. In Paul's circle there are both apprentices learning the work of a missionary and those more mature, who multiply their influence by guiding others toward Christian maturity. Paul's method is doubtless deliberate: he recognizes that spiritual growth happens when young Christians are in a living relationship with mature Christians.

Of Tychicus we know relatively little. He is from Asia (the western region of modern Turkey; Acts 20:4), and he remains an associate of Paul to the end of Paul's life, sent on various ministry

Disciplined for Life

tasks (2 Timothy 4:12; Titus 3:12). We can infer that he is the one who carries the letter to Colosse for Paul, and that likewise he delivers Paul's letter to the Ephesians (Ephesians 6:21, 22).

Tychicus's description shows us that he does much more than deliver letters. He is a *beloved brother,* one who belongs to God's family and so to all the readers. He is also a *faithful minister,* a servant who discharges his duties with devoted consistency. As such, Tychicus should be welcomed, trusted, and imitated. He will update the Colossians personally about Paul's situation.

> **What Do You Think?**
> What are appropriate occasions and methods for publicly commending someone's service for the Lord? What cautions should be taken in doing so?
> *Talking Points for Your Discussion*
> ▪ Thank-you notes in the church newsletter
> ▪ Recognition banquets
> ▪ Eulogies at funerals
> ▪ Other

❧ MUTUAL SUPPORT ❧

The members of the administration and faculty of a certain Christian college routinely caution their students that only a small percentage of individuals who start out in vocational ministry will remain so throughout their lives. One professor adds insight to this unfavorable fact: he believes that it is not a random smattering of folks who stay in ministry for the long haul, but those who stand with others in mutual support. Those who hold each other up go the distance and finish well.

The theme of cooperative effort is woven throughout Scripture (Exodus 17:10-13; Proverbs 11:14; Ecclesiastes 4:12; etc.). Today's text demonstrates such effort being lived out in the first-century church.

We must acknowledge that God has planted gifts, talents, and abilities in each of His image-bearers. As we do, we are able to work together in ways that honor, respect, and encourage our fellow servants in Christ. This is the way to accomplish what God desires of us and for us. —V. E.

B. Onesimus (v. 9)

9. With Onesimus, a faithful and beloved brother, who is one of you. They shall make known unto you all things which are done here.

The story of Onesimus is told in Paul's letter to Philemon. There we see that the status of Onesimus is that of slave in the household of Philemon. Onesimus flees his slavery and goes to Rome, where he meets with Paul. As a result of that meeting, Onesimus agrees to return to Philemon. Paul urges Philemon to receive Onesimus as a Christian brother and, by implication, to free Onesimus (Philemon 10-16).

The description here of Onesimus as *a faithful and beloved brother, who is one of you* leads us to conclude that Philemon is a member of the Colossian church. This description is a deliberate stress on Onesimus's identity. For Philemon and the Colossian Christians, the challenge will be to live up to their faith principles by embracing, forgiving, and emancipating Onesimus.

C. Aristarchus and Marcus (v. 10)

10. Aristarchus my fellowprisoner saluteth you, and Marcus, sister's son to Barnabas, (touching whom ye received commandments: if he come unto you, receive him;).

Aristarchus is also one of Paul's missionary assistants (see Acts 19:29; 20:4; 27:2; Philemon 24). Paul description of him as *my fellowprisoner* suggests that he shares Paul's imprisonment in Rome (Acts 28:16, 30). Willing to surrender his freedom for the sake of the gospel, Aristarchus is the kind of Christian the Colossians should emulate.

Marcus is known also as John Mark in Acts 12:25; 15:37 (compare 13:13). Paul and Barnabas had disagreed about whether to take him on their second missionary journey after he left the team to return home during the first journey. That disagreement had been so sharp that Paul and Barnabas parted company (Acts 15:38, 39).

With that rift now settled, Paul commends them both. John Mark is now a welcome associate in Paul's ministry (2 Timothy 4:11; Philemon 24). Again, we have a story of God's grace at work, healing divisions and restoring relationships.

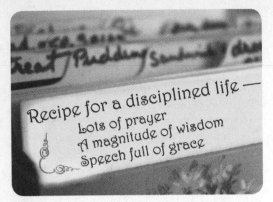

Visual for Lesson 13. *Point to this recipe as you ask, "What other ingredients can we add to develop a disciplined life?"*

D. Justus (v. 11)

11. And Jesus, which is called Justus, who are of the circumcision. These only are my fellowworkers unto the kingdom of God, which have been a comfort unto me.

Of Jesus Justus we know nothing except that he belongs to those *who are of the circumcision.* Thus he is a Jewish Christian who joins Paul in his preaching to both Jews and Gentiles. Since the Colossian Christians may be tempted to take up some alternative faith, they need examples of Jewish Christians who are committed to Jesus as the fulfillment of God's promises to Israel.

E. Epaphras (vv. 12, 13)

12. Epaphras, who is one of you, a servant of Christ, saluteth you, always labouring fervently for you in prayers, that ye may stand perfect and complete in all the will of God.

The phrase *who is one of you* means that Epaphras is part of the Colossian church (see the same description of Onesimus in v. 9, above). He is the one who brought the gospel to Colosse (Colossians 1:7). He is described as *a servant*—literally "a slave"—*of Christ.* That is a favorite term of Paul's to describe a Christian, emphasizing the relationship of submission and obedience that a Christian has with the supreme Christ.

As such a servant/slave, Epaphras labors or struggles in prayer for the Colossians. This sug-

gests the vivid image of Jacob wrestling with God and refusing to let go until he received a blessing (Genesis 32:22-30). One who agonizes in prayer is expressing deep concern for those being prayed for and dependence on God to meet the need.

Epaphras's prayer for the Colossians is for their spiritual maturity *(perfect and complete).* If some seek greater spirituality through other religious or philosophical systems, Epaphras's prayer is that they will find what they seek in the only place from which true spirituality comes: Jesus Christ. This maturity is focused on *the will of God,* not the desires of the individual. It is in God's will that we discover what we have always truly desired.

13. For I bear him record, that he hath a great zeal for you, and them that are in Laodicea, and them in Hierapolis.

Epaphras's prayers demonstrate the maturing faith of devotion to Christian brothers and sisters. His zeal embraces not just his hometown, but also the neighboring cities of Laodicea to the west and Hierapolis to the northwest. Epaphras provides a superb model for the Colossians to follow.

F. Luke and Demas (v. 14)

14. Luke, the beloved physician, and Demas, greet you.

Here we meet two more of Paul's associates, each mentioned only briefly. Luke is a medical doctor, held in such esteem that he can be called *beloved* without further comment. Luke is best known to us as the author of the Gospel of Luke and the Acts of the Apostles. He clearly plays a vital role in Paul's company.

Demas is mentioned positively here and in Philemon 24. But we learn in 2 Timothy 4:10 that he later forsakes his faith. Demas the positive example tragically ends up being a cautionary one.

G. Laodiceans and Nymphas (v. 15)

15. Salute the brethren which are in Laodicea, and Nymphas, and the church which is in his house.

Beyond Paul's associates, there are others who can serve the Colossian Christians as mentors in the pursuit of spiritual maturity. Nearby Laodicea also has believers. Prominent among them is a certain Nymphas, who provides the church with its meeting space. Christians commonly meet in homes in Paul's time, as few other spaces are available. In such settings, believers are in close relationship, sharing trials and learning together.

III. Responsibility to Discharge
(COLOSSIANS 4:16, 17)

A. Regarding Laodicea (v. 16)

16. And when this epistle is read among you, cause that it be read also in the church of the Laodiceans; and that ye likewise read the epistle from Laodicea.

The definitive aid to the Colossians' spiritual growth is the counsel of Scripture. Paul writes letters to churches as a substitute for his own presence, a "virtual" form of mentoring. But his letters are more than his own wise advice. Paul consciously writes from a position of authority, under God's inspiration, declaring to the church the meaning and implications of the good news of Jesus.

The churches recognize and affirm that authority, keeping his letters to read long beyond the situations that prompt them. They are copied for believers in other places to read. This process is the first step toward the collection of authoritative Christian documents we call the New Testament.

Here we see that Paul himself encourages this process. Laodicea also has received one of Paul's letters—perhaps the letter to the Ephesians, which may be sent to many churches, or perhaps a letter no longer in existence. The Christians in various locations can learn much from these letters, even though only one may be written directly to them. Paul's instructions are authoritative guides to what true growth in the Christian faith consists of.

> **What Do You Think?**
> What are some things churches in your area can and should do to cooperate in various ways?
> *Talking Points for Your Discussion*
> ▪ Cooperation with churches that are similar to your church
> ▪ Cooperation with churches that are not similar to your church

B. Regarding Archippus (v. 17)

17. And say to Archippus, Take heed to the ministry which thou hast received in the Lord, that thou fulfil it.

Archippus is Paul's "fellowsoldier" in Philemon 2. This man is to give closer attention to the responsibility he has as a Christian. We cannot be sure what that responsibility is since *ministry* here simply means "service." This may or may not imply leadership of the congregation. Whatever it is, Archippus and others in the church are aware that his responsibility is clear and important, something that belongs to him *in the Lord*.

While Archippus is singled out here, he is not alone. Everyone who belongs to Christ has a ministry, a call to service. There will be no spiritual growth without active service in response to what Christ has done for us.

> **What Do You Think?**
> How can you encourage someone today to fulfill a ministry in the Lord?
> *Talking Points for Your Discussion*
> ▪ A ministry begun but now abandoned
> ▪ A ministry that has turned out to be different from originally expected
> ▪ A ministry that seems impossible to maintain
> ▪ Other

Conclusion

A. Pursuing Maturity

Growing as a Christian is natural, but it is not accidental. We must pursue it deliberately. There is nothing mysterious about how it happens, but there is something very wonderful about what we receive when we devote ourselves to it. May we do so!

B. Prayer

Father, direct our minds and hearts to Your word. Make us a community that challenges each other to growth. Give us strength to be devoted to You in all things. We pray in Jesus' name, amen.

C. Thought to Remember

Serve to grow; grow to serve.

INVOLVEMENT LEARNING

Some of the activities below are also found in the helpful student book, Adult Bible Class.
Don't forget to download the free reproducible page from www.standardlesson.com to enhance your lesson!

Into the Lesson

Have on display this question as class begins: *If you were writing a letter to encourage other Christians, who are some friends in Christ that you might use as positive examples to challenge the addressees?* As names are given, ask for explanations of why the named person is a good role model for other Christians. Say, "Writing such a note is not a far-fetched idea. Paul did just that. Let's see how and why."

Distribute copies of the "Your Friends . . . and Paul's" activity from the reproducible page, which you can download. Ask learners to write in the space provided the names of Christian friends they have thought of during the discussion so far. Say, "As we work through today's text, draw connecting lines between your friends' names and the names of Paul's associates where you see similarities."

Alternative: Give each learner a copy of the "fill-in" letter below. Provide these directions: "Write three thoughts of encouragement, admonition, counsel, etc., to a hypothetical friend in Christ."

Dear Friend in Christ,

I was thinking of you today as I read the words of Scripture. A few thoughts came to my mind that I thought you would like to hear and consider. These ideas have encouraged me, and they may do so for you as well.

1. _____
2. _____
3. _____

In the words of the apostle John, "I wish . . . that thou mayest prosper and be in health, even as thy soul prospereth" (3 John 2).

Yours in Christ,

_____

Ask for volunteers to read their letters. After hearing several, say, "Now let's do a comparison between your letters and part of the letter Paul wrote to his fellow laborers in the Colossian church."

Into the Word

Read Colossians 4:2-17 aloud. Ask, "As you look at today's text, what five or six words of advice or counsel to the Colossian Christians do you see?" Let learners respond freely.

Verses 2-6 offer obvious truths, but encourage your learners to look also at the other verses as well. For example, one might gather from verse 10 the counsel to extend hospitality to a fellow worker in Christ. Verse 12 adds the significant challenge of wrestling in prayer for fellow Christians that they will stand firm in the will of God. Further, verse 17 includes the important admonition to finish what one has started in Christ. Your learners undoubtedly will see and relate other important truths the Christian needs to ponder daily—truths worth passing along.

List all ideas on the board. Wrap up by saying, "Wow! These are good words of advice for growing Christians. Perhaps you can use some of them in the week ahead."

Into Life

Distribute copies of the "Time Redemption" activity from the reproducible page. Allow two minutes for learners to fill out the "Week Past" column. Say, "The week just completed is just that —gone and done. But the week ahead is still an open book! Put this list in your Bible for reflection during your daily devotions. See if you can get all opportunities to be marked as a *T* (taken) before we gather again next week."

Option: Return to the "Your Friends . . . and Paul's" activity. Note that Paul names 11 associates in today's text. Ask learners if they listed at least that many of their own. Encourage everyone to expand their list to include at least that many and pray for them by name in the week ahead.

Drawing on Colossians 4:17, offer the encouragement "Take heed to the ministry!" to learners individually, by name, as they depart.

UNDYING

HOPE

Special Features

Lessons

Unit 1: The Kingdom of God

Unit 2: Resurrection Hope

Unit 3: A Call to Holy Living

QUARTERLY QUIZ

Use these questions as a pretest or as a review. The answers are on page iv of This Quarter in the Word.

Lesson 1

1. Daniel had a _____ that included visions from God. *Daniel 7:1, 2*

2. Daniel saw "the Ancient of days" wearing a purple robe, the sign of royalty. T/F. *Daniel 7:9*

Lesson 2

1. In his confession, Daniel affirmed that God keeps His "covenant and _____." *Daniel 9:4*

2. The curse God sent on Israel was according to what? (Law of Moses, Psalms, Job?) *Daniel 9:11*

Lesson 3

1. While beside the Ulai River, Daniel was visited by an angel named _____. *Daniel 8:16*

2. In Daniel's vision, the king of Grecia (Greece) is represented by a goat. T/F. *Daniel 8:21*

Lesson 4

1. Luke's account of the last supper features two cups. T/F. *Luke 22:17-20*

2. At the last supper, there was dissension among the disciples regarding who was the traitor and who was the _____. *Luke 22:23, 24*

Lesson 5

1. Jesus noted what emotion in the disciples on the Emmaus road? (joy, fear, sadness?) *Luke 24:17*

2. The disciples in Emmaus never realized that they had been talking to Jesus. T/F. *Luke 24:31-33*

Lesson 6

1. The resurrected Jesus invited the disciples to inspect both His hands and feet. T/F. *Luke 24:39*

2. After the resurrection, Jesus ate a piece of what? (fish, bread, fruit?) *Luke 24:42, 43*

Lesson 7

1. People were amazed to hear the disciples speak in other tongues because the people knew that those speaking were from _____. *Acts 2:6, 7*

2. People from Cyprus are noted as having been present on the Day of Pentecost. T/F. *Acts 2:9-11*

Lesson 8

1. The Lord's return will be accompanied by the _____ of the archangel. *1 Thessalonians 4:16*

2. The return of Jesus is compared with that of a _____ in the night. *1 Thessalonians 5:2*

Lesson 9

1. Paul said that the Thessalonians had much to fear about the future. T/F. *2 Thessalonians 2:2*

2. Christ's return will be preceded by a "woman of sin." T/F. *2 Thessalonians 2:3*

Lesson 10

1. Peter notes that the prophets were inspired by the Spirit of Christ. T/F. *1 Peter 1:10, 11*

2. Peter tells his readers to gird up the loins of their what? (spirit, mind, soul?) *1 Peter 1:13*

Lesson 11

1. We are to be diligent in making our calling and _____ sure. *2 Peter 1:10*

2. The Old Testament prophets gave their best personal opinions about the Messiah who was to come. T/F. *2 Peter 1:20, 21*

Lesson 12

1. Since "the end of all things is at hand," we are to do what two things? (fast and tithe, preach and teach, be sober and watch?) *1 Peter 4:7*

2. Charity (love) covers a multitude of _____. *1 Peter 4:8*

Lesson 13

1. For the Lord, a day is like what? (a waterfall, a thousand years, a walled city?) *2 Peter 3:8*

2. When Christ comes again, the old heavens and earth will be destroyed by _____. *2 Peter 3:10-12*

QUARTER AT A GLANCE

by Mark S. Krause

DORIS DAY had a huge hit in the 1950s with the song, "Que Sera, Sera (Whatever Will Be, Will Be)." More than 50 years later, this song expresses a common viewpoint of the future: whatever is going to happen, is going to happen. We have no control over the future, nor do we have any clues as to what it might be like.

The Bible does not share this view, for it is a book of hope. The Bible's outlook of hope is that of faith based on evidence. We believe God, who raised Jesus from the dead. This faith gives us the assured hope of salvation. Our future may have hardships ahead, but we are sustained by this glorious hope: one day we will be with the Lord forever (1 Thessalonians 4:17, Lesson 8).

Unit 1: The Kingdom of God

This quarter's lessons look at some of the key passages of Scripture that contribute to the Bible's message of hope. From the Old Testament we will have three lessons from Daniel, a man of God who was given glorious visions of the future. Although both frightening and mysterious, these visions have a theme of hope running through them. It is a hope for a future day when God will vindicate and reward His people. Daniel's hope is not based on human goodness or accomplishment, but on the mighty works and faithfulness of the Lord God.

Unit 2: Resurrection Hope

Hundreds of years after Daniel's time, Jesus came to Jerusalem to celebrate the Passover for the final time (Lesson 4). A tumultuous week ended with His crucifixion on Friday and burial in a borrowed tomb. Hope seemed to have died as well.

Yet that was not the end, for on the first day of the week Jesus began to appear to His disciples after He had risen from the dead (Lessons 5 and 6). The resurrected Lord gave hope to the community of disciples, a hope that continued after Jesus ascended into Heaven.

Jesus' departure left the core group of disciples in Jerusalem, waiting for what was to come next. On the Day of Pentecost, they experienced the powerful arrival of the Holy Spirit (Lesson 7), one of the most dramatic events recorded in the Bible! The gospel message of hope was launched into the world on that day.

The first-century church taught not only that Jesus was risen, but also that He would come again. Many expected that that would happen within a few days, months, or perhaps years. When that expectation went unmet, the apostle Paul wrote two letters of reassurance to his friends

> One day we will be with the Lord forever.

in Thessalonica (Lessons 8 and 9). His reassurance included warnings that some of the events preceding Jesus' return would be distressing. But when Christ comes again, those who have placed faith in Him will forget all pain and hardship as evil is finally and completely overthrown by Jesus.

Unit 3: A Call to Holy Living

We will investigate the two letters written by the apostle Peter to wrap up this quarter's study of hope. Peter wrote nearly 40 years after Christ ascended into Heaven, and some scoffed at the idea that Jesus would return. Peter's assurance is that though the return of Jesus may seem to be delayed, He will surely come. The church has held this assured hope for nearly two millennia.

Today's Hope

Hope is essential to our well-being. We need to believe that currently painful circumstances will be better in the future. In Jesus they will be! The Christian's salvation is sure. We of all people have cause for hope.

GET THE SETTING

by Ronald L. Nickelson

HOPE IS OUR FOCUS for the quarter. Perhaps a good working definition of *hope* is that it is the ability to envision and expect a better future.

We see this human ability throughout the pages of the Bible. Indeed, if you count the expressions of hope (and lack of hope) in the Bible, you will find dozens and dozens of occurrences. But what did hope (and lack of hope) mean to God's people?

One way to enrich our understanding of biblical hope is to examine it against the backdrop of how the pagan world of antiquity understood this concept. We can look at the ancient pagan's concept of *hope* in terms of two broad categories: what people hoped for in this life, and what people hoped for in the next life. We will consider these two categories in reverse order.

Hope Regarding Life After Death

One would think that we should approach our two categories in chronological order: first, investigate how ancient pagans expressed hope for their lives in this world, then take a look at what they hoped for in the hereafter. But there is a very good reason to do it the other way around.

Ancient pagans often expressed a very bleak view of what human existence would be like after death. Because they had such a despairing view of the afterlife, they ended up with a very "this worldly" focus regarding hope. In other words, we are considering the pagan outlook on hope for the afterlife first because their dismal outlook in this regard forced them to look to this life as the primary place for any hope.

An influential figure in creating a bleak outlook on the afterlife was the Greek poet Homer (that's a sculpture of him on the right). He may have lived

in the eighth century BC, about the time of biblical prophets such as Amos. In his famous work the *Odyssey,* Homer imagines Odysseus, king of Ithaca, taking a trip to the underworld, the abode of the dead. Odysseus finds this place (hades) to be one of misery.

In this underworld, Odysseus meets Achilles, a dead hero of the Trojan War. Achilles famously laments that he would rather be a slave to the lowest person among the living than to be king of all the dead of hades. Existence in this kind of afterlife was not something to be anticipated!

This wasn't the only pagan viewpoint, of course. Some philosophers proposed the possibility of a blissful afterlife, reincarnation, the rebirth of the earth after its destruction, etc. But these seem to have been minority viewpoints. One concept never considered in a positive light was that of *resurrection.* Acts 17:32 notes the scoffing of pagan philosophers when Paul mentioned this idea.

Hope in This Life

Since ancient pagans saw little to hope for in the hereafter, they tended to focus on what could be gained in this world. Greek mythology had a goddess of hope in this regard, named *Elpis.* The Roman equivalent was the goddess *Spes,* and the Romans built temples in her honor. The mythology behind Elpis/Spes is rather complicated. But the bottom line seems to be that human imagination created a goddess who could provide whatever humans hoped for.

These hopes included many things we value today, such as personal, family, and cultural stability. The most "enduring" thing a pagan could hope for was a good name, a good reputation that would outlive oneself. Perhaps Paul was reflecting on the emptiness of this viewpoint when he wrote, "If in this life only we have hope in Christ, we are of all men most miserable" (1 Corinthians 15:19). How great is the Christian's hope!

THIS QUARTER IN THE WORD

Answers to the Quarterly Quiz on page 226

Lesson 1—1. dream. 2. false. **Lesson 2**—1. mercy. 2. Law of Moses. **Lesson 3**—1. Gabriel. 2. true. **Lesson 4**—1. true. 2. greatest. **Lesson 5**—1. sadness. 2. false. **Lesson 6**—1. true. 2. fish. **Lesson 7**—1. Galilee. 2. false. **Lesson 8**—1. voice. 2. thief. **Lesson 9**—1. false. 2. false. **Lesson 10**—1. true. 2. mind. **Lesson 11**—1. election. 2. false. **Lesson 12**—1. be sober and watch. 2. sins. **Lesson 13**—1. a thousand years. 2. fire or heat.

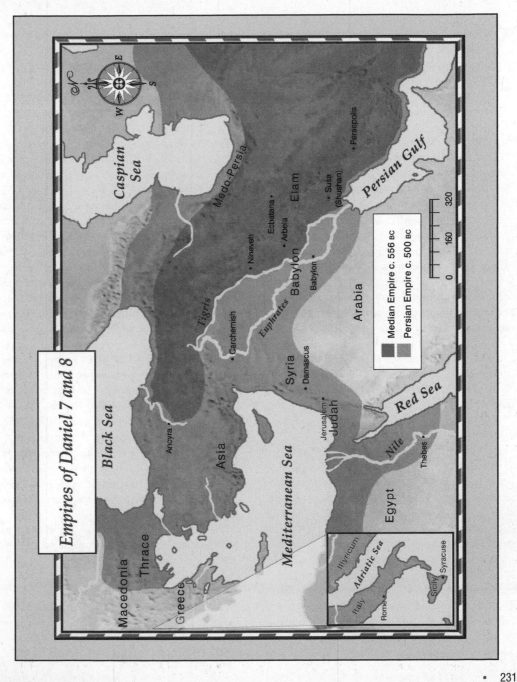

Empires of Daniel 7 and 8

Caspian Sea

Black Sea

Medo-Persia

Persian Gulf

• Persepolis

Elam

• Susa (Shushan)

Ecbatana •

• Arbela

Babylon

• Ninaveh

Babylon

Tigris

Euphrates

Arabia

• Carchemish

Syria

Damascus •

Red Sea

Asia

Ancyra •

Jerusalem •

Judah

Nile

Mediterranean Sea

Egypt

• Thebes

Macedonia

Thrace

Greece

Median Empire c. 556 BC

Persian Empire c. 500 BC

0   160   320

Illyricum

Adriatic Sea

Italy

Rome •

Sicily

Syracuse •

YOUR SEVEN DAYS

Teacher Tips by Brent L. Amato

YOU MUST TEACH on Sunday morning, but you've waited until Saturday night to begin preparing your lesson. Now time is short, and you're stuck on something. "I had seven days," you say to yourself. "Why did I put off preparing?" Does this sound like you?

An Issue of Stewardship

Teaching, like other activities of life, is an opportunity to glorify God (1 Corinthians 10:31). We are to be good stewards of how we use the gift of teaching, as we are to be good stewards of all our spiritual gifts (1 Peter 4:10). Each of us will give an account to the master teacher for each lesson that we teach (2 Corinthians 5:10). When that time comes, I want to hear those words, "Well done, thou good and faithful servant: thou hast been faithful" (Matthew 25:21). I am sobered that teachers are held to a higher standard (see James 3:1).

All this makes me ponder what I will do with the time between lessons. When do I start preparing for the next Bible lesson that I am to teach? What does good stewardship say about my seven days?

An Issue of Diligence

As Luke demonstrated diligence in preparing his Gospel (Luke 1:3, 4), we are to exercise diligence in preparing our lessons. Will we make the most of every preparation opportunity (Ephesians 5:15, 16)? Will our preparation time include diligent prayer (1 Thessalonians 5:17)? Will our preparation include intensive study of and meditation on God's Word (Psalm 1:2; 119:15; 2 Timothy 2:15)? Will we use our preparation time in an organized and orderly manner (1 Corinthians 14:40)? Will we prepare so that our learners will end up with a clear understanding of the truths of the lesson (Nehemiah 8:8)? Will we prepare in such a diligent way that we will not speak hastily during the lesson (Proverbs 29:20)? What will we do with our seven days?

An Issue of Quality

We live in a culture of instant gratification and quick fixes. The quicker we get one thing done, the quicker we can move on to something else. Witness the popularity of microwave ovens and fast-food restaurants. This mind-set can leak over into our approach to lesson preparation if we're not careful.

Think about the difference. Would you rather eat a prepackaged frozen dinner that has been zapped quickly in a microwave oven or a dish that has simmered all day in a slow cooker? Would you rather drink "instant" coffee or coffee that has been brewed slowly? Will your learners prefer "instant" spiritual food that was whipped up on Saturday night or spiritual food that has been prepared over the course of seven days?

An Issue of Percolation

Starting your preparation on Sunday afternoon for the following Sunday morning's lesson results in a process I call "percolating the lesson." Starting preparation on Sunday afternoon will result in an awareness of things going on around you. Over seven days you will be watching and listening for God to drop insights, large and small. Lessons are refined and improved over time. New ideas occur; material is focused, changed, even discarded; creativity blossoms!

We all know that a Saturday night or a Sunday morning sometimes "blows up" in a teacher's face because of the unexpected stuff of life. Starting to prepare sooner rather than later is a wonderful hedge against such challenges.

When I come home from church each Sunday, I have three options: (1) take a nap, (2) watch sports on TV, or (3) spend a few minutes on next week's lesson. Seven days. How will I spend them?

DANIEL'S VISION OF CHANGE

DEVOTIONAL READING: Daniel 6:25-28
BACKGROUND SCRIPTURE: Daniel 7

DANIEL 7:1-3, 9-14

1 In the first year of Belshazzar king of Babylon Daniel had a dream and visions of his head upon his bed: then he wrote the dream, and told the sum of the matters.

2 Daniel spake and said, I saw in my vision by night, and, behold, the four winds of the heaven strove upon the great sea.

3 And four great beasts came up from the sea, diverse one from another.

· ·

9 I beheld till the thrones were cast down, and the Ancient of days did sit, whose garment was white as snow, and the hair of his head like the pure wool: his throne was like the fiery flame, and his wheels as burning fire.

10 A fiery stream issued and came forth from before him: thousand thousands ministered unto him, and ten thousand times ten thousand stood before him: the judgment was set, and the books were opened.

11 I beheld then because of the voice of the great words which the horn spake: I beheld even till the beast was slain, and his body destroyed, and given to the burning flame.

12 As concerning the rest of the beasts, they had their dominion taken away: yet their lives were prolonged for a season and time.

13 I saw in the night visions, and, behold, one like the Son of man came with the clouds of heaven, and came to the Ancient of days, and they brought him near before him.

14 And there was given him dominion, and glory, and a kingdom, that all people, nations, and languages, should serve him: his dominion is an everlasting dominion, which shall not pass away, and his kingdom that which shall not be destroyed.

KEY VERSE

There was given him dominion, and glory, and a kingdom, that all people, nations, and languages, should serve him: his dominion is an everlasting dominion, which shall not pass away, and his kingdom that which shall not be destroyed. —**Daniel 7:14**

UNDYING HOPE

Unit 1: The Kingdom of God

LESSON AIMS

After participating in this lesson, each student will be able to:

1. Recall the elements of Daniel's dream.

2. Explain why Daniel's dream was important for his day and is important for ours.

3. List reasons why Daniel's dream is a source of comfort to him or her.

LESSON OUTLINE

Introduction

A. That's Just the Way It Is

While millions of people struggle to feed their families, professional athletes receive millions to move a ball and score points in a televised game. While innovative thinkers with life-improving ideas cannot gain a public hearing, the masses tune in daily to hours of mindless entertainment media. While innocent people fear for their safety and livelihood, the wicked profit from the vulnerable and strut arrogantly without a care.

This is nothing new. The earliest humans observed the wicked thriving and the righteous barely surviving. Some will say, "Get over it—that's life." It is enough to make one cynical, to make us give up on the idea of a better world.

We can get stuck in mental ruts, and when we do, we need to be jarred out of this world's "reality" and into God's reality. We need Jesus to remind us again that the poor in spirit have the kingdom, the meek inherit the earth, the merciful receive mercy, the pure see God, and the peacemakers are considered His children (Matthew 5:3-9).

Long before Jesus issued that mountaintop reality check, the prophet Daniel opened the eyes of Jews in the sixth century BC so they could see what God was and would be doing. What Daniel saw was the ultimate triumph that God's followers today still long to see. It therefore has power to spare us the cynicism that can so easily ensnare.

B. Lesson Background

Daniel was one of the prominent Jews from Jerusalem who were taken to Babylon by King Nebuchadnezzar (Daniel 1:1-7). There were several deportations (compare Jeremiah 52:28). The fact that Daniel was taken in one of the early ones indicates that he was considered to be among the cream of the crop of the Israelite people.

During the exile, Daniel and other Jews struggled to understand what God was doing in the world. Why were the wicked Babylonians thriving while God's people, who were not nearly as wicked, suffered? Had God given up on the Jewish people? Did they have a future worth waiting for and praying for?

Some Jews conspired to take matters into their own hands (compare Jeremiah 41). They believed that the best way to push forward was to rebel against the Babylonians. They did not believe the prophesies of Habakkuk, Jeremiah, and others that God had decided to allow the Babylonians to triumph over the Israelites for their unfaithfulness. They did not comprehend that God would indeed punish the Babylonians for their own wickedness.

Other Jews gave up altogether. They stopped following Israel's God and turned to false gods. They assumed that if their God was the one true God, then they should always triumph over their enemies. To them, Babylon's victory over Israel was a victory of Babylon's gods over Israel's God (compare Jeremiah 44:18). Why worship a losing deity? So they transferred allegiance.

During times of such confusion, the Israelites needed a word from God to set the record straight. One such word came from Daniel.

I. Vision Begins
(DANIEL 7:1-3)
A. Dream Recorded (v. 1)

1. In the first year of Belshazzar king of Babylon Daniel had a dream and visions of his head upon his bed: then he wrote the dream, and told the sum of the matters.

It is important to note which Babylonian king is reigning when Daniel has this dream. Two Babylonian kings are named in the book of Daniel: Nebuchadnezzar and Belshazzar. (Darius, a third king, is "the Median" by nationality in 5:31). Nebuchadnezzar reigned first, from about 605 to 562 BC. He was the one who destroyed Jerusalem

HOW TO SAY IT

Babylon	*Bab*-uh-lun.
Babylonians	Bab-ih-*low*-nee-unz.
Belshazzar	Bel-*shazz*-er.
Habakkuk	Huh-*back*-kuk.
Medo-Persia	*Mee*-doe *Per*-zhuh.
Messiah	Meh-*sigh*-uh.
Nebuchadnezzar	*Neb*-yuh-kud-**nez**-er.
Zechariah	*Zek*-uh-**rye**-uh.

and took many Jews into exile. The Babylonians seemed to realize that this was God's doing, but the Israelites did not (see Jeremiah 40:1-3).

Nebuchadnezzar is presented in Daniel as a king who has his own selfish agenda, but also as a king who is capable of respecting the true God (Daniel 4:34, 35). Belshazzar, who begins reigning about 553 BC, is presented less favorably. He is depicted as an arrogant king who mocks God by toying with the sacred Jerusalem temple vessels (5:2-4). God's response to such irreverence is not to humble Belshazzar as He did Nebuchadnezzar, but to bring him to deadly justice (5:18-30).

This is important because some world rulers whom God's people face after Daniel's day will be like Nebuchadnezzar, and others will be like Belshazzar. It is thus fitting that Daniel has his vision during the reign of Belshazzar, a vision about a future arrogant king whom God will bring to deadly justice.

❧ *"I SAW JESUS IN THE KITCHEN"* ❧

"Excuse me, I couldn't help noticing your shirt. Are you a priest?" I turned from browsing a jewelry display to see an older lady who had walked up. Surprised, I looked down and realized she had seen the Bible college logo on my T-shirt. She continued, "I need some advice. I saw Jesus in the kitchen last night. Do you think it means I'm going to die?" I confess my first thoughts were that she was mentally unbalanced or maybe had had a little too much to drink. But what if she really did see Jesus?

In Daniel's day, many people claimed to have direct communication with God. Some did, and some didn't. Telling them apart wasn't always easy. The Bible warns that false prophets are recognized by their untrue predictions (Deuteronomy 18:21, 22), promoting other gods (Deuteronomy 13:1-4), and/or bearing bad spiritual fruit (Matthew 7:15-20). Clearly, two of these tests require a "wait and see" approach.

Was the jewelry store lady a false prophetess? I don't know. But sorting that out in this brief encounter was not as important as pointing her toward Christ. "I think if Jesus appeared to you He would tell you He loves you and wants to be your Lord," I said. "I'd be glad to talk with you about that if you're interested." She looked at me strangely, politely declined, and went off to search for another minister. I think she thought *I* was the one who was crazy. —A. W.

B. Seas Stirred (v. 2)

2. Daniel spake and said, I saw in my vision by night, and, behold, the four winds of the heaven strove upon the great sea.

The sea is a place of fear and dread in the ancient world. It is also a symbol of chaos. Ancient people think that the sea is controlled by destructive gods and ruled by fierce beasts. They think this way because the earliest sailors who set out to navigate the open waters often do not come back. So people assume that such sailors have fallen victim to the sea's wrath. People learn that it is much safer to stick close to the shore when sailing.

So when *the four winds of the heaven* struggle *upon the great sea* in Daniel's vision, the reader should expect that chaos is brewing (compare Revelation 7:1). Normally, the wind blows from one direction only. The fact that it here blows from all directions may mean that a fearsome whirlpool is forming.

What Do You Think?
How does the blustery imagery of Daniel's dream resonate with your own experience of a turbulent time?
Talking Points for Your Discussion
- A time of spiritual turmoil
- A time of family turmoil
- A time of governmental turmoil
- John 16:33

C. Beasts Emerge (v. 3)

3. And four great beasts came up from the sea, diverse one from another.

Out of this chaotic sea emerge *four great beasts,* which represent four kings or kingdoms of the earth according to verse 17 (not in today's text). These beasts are described in greater detail in verses 4-8 (also not in today's text). Some students identify these four beasts with the empires of Babylon, Medo-Persia, Greece, and Rome. Not

all agree on this identification, however (see further discussion with verse 11, below).

What Do You Think?
Would it be useful to use images of animals, etc., to describe the governmental or spiritual powers that affect us today? Why, or why not?
Talking Points for Your Discussion
- Issue of respect (1 Peter 2:17)
- Cultural and cross-cultural contexts
- "A picture is worth a thousand words"

II. Ancient of Days Enthroned
(DANIEL 7:9, 10)
A. Thrones Set (v. 9)

9. I beheld till the thrones were cast down, and the Ancient of days did sit, whose garment was white as snow, and the hair of his head like the pure wool: his throne was like the fiery flame, and his wheels as burning fire.

The judgment scene is set. Thrones are installed and the judge has taken his seat. *The Ancient of days* is God, the one who always was and always will be (Revelation 4:8, 9). Other divine throne-scenes in Scripture include 1 Kings 22:19-22; Isaiah 6:1-9; Matthew 19:28; and Revelation 4.

That the everlasting God is judge is crucial to this vision. As one who sees everything, God alone can give a completely accurate account of what is really going on in world history. From the perspective of many Jewish exiles, God has lost to the Babylonian gods, and God's people have no future.

But God is not controlled by what "appears to be." He is not carried along by the momentum of the day. His *hair . . . like the pure wool* testifies to His ancient perspective, the same head of hair and perspective that the exalted Christ is depicted with in Revelation 1:12-16. The garment that is *white as snow* testifies to His purity. He is not a crooked judge, but is the source of true justice (compare Mark 9:3).

Another key component in this verse is fire. Both the throne and its wheels are aflame. Yet like the burning bush that Moses saw (Exodus 3:2), the fire does not consume the throne or its occupant. Fire is an image of judgment in Scripture. Positively, fire can purify a precious metal like gold; in burning up the impurities, fire brings out true qualities (Zechariah 13:9; 1 Peter 1:7; Revelation 3:18). Fire consumes what does not last, incinerating what is worthless (compare 1 Corinthians 3:12-15). Fire is an instrument of eternal punishment (Deuteronomy 32:22; Matthew 5:22; 2 Peter 3:7).

B. Books Opened (v. 10)

10. A fiery stream issued and came forth from before him: thousand thousands ministered unto him, and ten thousand times ten thousand stood before him: the judgment was set, and the books were opened.

The fire that streams from God's presence likely indicates that He is about to judge. The thousands who surround Him are heavenly beings, or angels. Their vast number testifies to God's majesty as it does in Revelation 5:11. Daniel 5:1 tells us that Belshazzar has 1,000 nobles who feast in his presence. This impressive number is dwarfed by the multitude that waits on Israel's God. That these servants are present at this judgment scene also indicates that God has plenty of witnesses both to corroborate His judgment and to carry it out. What He decrees will certainly come to pass.

The books that are opened pertain to judgment. This passage does not specify whether they contain a list of misdeeds according to which the beasts will be judged or whether they indicate the names of those whom God spares judgment and therefore saves. Elsewhere in Scripture, the "book of life" appears to be an indication of who is saved (Psalm 69:28; Daniel 12:1; Revelation 3:5; 13:8; 17:8; 20:15; 21:27; 22:19). Revelation 20:12 is the strongest parallel to this passage. It is also a judgment scene in which multiple books are opened, including the book of life; persons are judged according to their works as listed in those books.

❧ *WHAT IS A BOOK?* ❧

I read my first electronic book (or "e-book") just a few weeks ago. It's hard to wrap my mind around the concept that scrolling through a long document on a little computer counts as reading a book. Where are the pages? Where is the new (or old) book smell? How do I underline the good

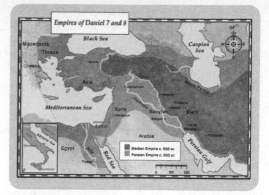

Visual for Lessons 1 & 3. *Keep this map posted as you study the lessons of Unit 1 to give your learners a geographical perspective.*

parts and find them again? But if we're feeling old, there are definite improvements: you can make the print larger with the push of a button, and if you still can't see it, then another button makes it read itself aloud!

When Daniel saw books opened in Heaven, he probably didn't see leather-bound tomes or computer monitors. Instead, he probably saw the scrolls or clay tablets familiar to his culture. Regardless of the format, the essence of a book is that of a permanent record.

Of course, God doesn't need the reminder of printed or digital pages as we might; His memory is perfect. But Daniel's vision serves as a warning to us that actions are recorded and that we will be called to account for them. Rather than trying to write the book of our life on our own, wouldn't it make sense to ask the author of life to help us write it?
                                                                    —A. W.

III. Beasts Defeated
(DANIEL 7:11, 12)
A. One Slain (v. 11)

11. I beheld then because of the voice of the great words which the horn spake: I beheld even till the beast was slain, and his body destroyed, and given to the burning flame.

The horn that is speaking belongs to the fourth, most terrifying beast (Daniel 7:7, 8). We learn more about this beast in verses 19-26. As mentioned above, some students identify this beast and its horns with the Roman Empire, although interpretations vary.

Our primary purpose, however, is not to identify this beast with a particular king or kingdom, but to focus on the kind of force this beast represents. Here we see audacity to speak and act against the one true God and His people. The impact of arrogant beasts (worldly rulers and their kingdoms) on the lives of God's people is felt during all ages. These beasts defy God Almighty and trample His people. King Belshazzar is neither the first nor the last to do this. Such beasts take many forms throughout history. If we are to resist their devouring ways, we must adopt God's view, which we get in the verses that follow.

What is most striking about the verse before us is what little effort God expends to strike this beast down. This beast is frighteningly powerful in the experience of those who suffer at its hands. Yet without fuss or fight, God simply slays the beast and burns its remains. When it comes to Israel's God, this beast is way out of its league. There cannot be a struggle, only instant defeat. God's people thus have no reason to fear even the most powerful humans. If God is for us, no one can stand against us (Romans 8:31).

What Do You Think?
When a situation turns out much differently from what most expect, how do we evaluate the presence or absence of God at work?
Talking Points for Your Discussion
- Political elections
- Healings
- Deliverance from danger
- Other

B. Others Deposed (v. 12)
12. As concerning the rest of the beasts, they had their dominion taken away: yet their lives were prolonged for a season and time.

By way of contrast, the other beasts receive considerably less judgment. Though it is true that they eventually lose control of their kingdoms, God allows them to retain control for a while.

This teaches us something about how God relates to the rulers and kingdoms of this world. All human institutions are fallen, and none is perfect. Their power is on loan from God (Romans 13:1). Some misuse that power so badly that God intervenes to bring them down. Other kings and kingdoms use their power in ways that God is willing to tolerate for a time. All human kingdoms ultimately will be replaced by God's kingdom. But some human kingdoms are better than others, and God relates to them in different ways.

What Do You Think?
Under what circumstances, if any, should a church "get involved in politics" to influence the course of a secular authority?
Talking Points for Your Discussion
- Regarding a biblical issue
- Regarding a non-biblical issue

IV. Son of Man Appears
(DANIEL 7:13, 14)
A. Arrival (v. 13)
13. I saw in the night visions, and, behold, one like the Son of man came with the clouds of heaven, and came to the Ancient of days, and they brought him near before him.

Daniel's vision does not end only with bad news for those who rebel against God. It goes on to announce good news for those who are faithful.

This good news happens when *one like the Son of man* arrives. This designation has been interpreted in various ways. On the most basic level, the role that this being plays in the vision should be noticed. Previously, Daniel saw four beasts that looked "like" certain animals. Now he sees a being that looks *like the Son of man,* that is, like a human. In contrast with the beasts, this figure is humanlike. This is good news for God's people, who do not fare well under the rule of the beasts.

In Daniel 8:17, the phrase "son of man" is used to contrast a human with an angel. From an angel's perspective, "son of man" is another way of saying "descendant of Adam." But it makes no sense in this vision for God to exalt a mere human the way He is going to exalt this particular *one like*

Daniel's Vision of Change

the Son of man. For the same reason, it makes no sense that this being would be an angel, such as Michael (Daniel 10:13, 21; 12:1). The ancient Jews never expect an angel to be given the kingdom (see Daniel 7:14, below).

Two positions remain. One asserts that the *Son of man* figure represents the people of Israel. This idea is drawn from Daniel 7:18, where God's people receive the kingdom. This makes sense in light of the biblical story, since God promises His people through the prophets that Israel is to be exalted above all nations. However, the New Testament is also very clear that Jesus identifies himself as this Son of man. In various places, He is the "Son of man" who is over "the kingdom" and whom people see "coming in the clouds" (Matthew 13:41-43; 16:28; 19:28; 24:30; 26:64).

We do not need to choose between these two options. Jesus is the one to whom God has given the kingdom, and God's people are the ones with whom Jesus shares His kingdom. For Jesus to receive the kingdom is thus for God's people to receive the kingdom as well. Since the ancient Jews expect a Messiah who will someday come and reign forever on David's throne, it is natural for them to identify this Son of man with that Messiah. We know that Messiah to be Jesus.

B. Exaltation (v. 14)

14. And there was given him dominion, and glory, and a kingdom, that all people, nations, and languages, should serve him: his dominion is an everlasting dominion, which shall not pass away, and his kingdom that which shall not be destroyed.

The fate of the Son of man is entirely different from that of the arrogant beast. The arrogant beast has dominion over many nations; the Son of man reigns over all nations and all people everywhere. The arrogant beast has power for a brief time; the Son of man rules forever. The arrogant beast is destroyed swiftly; the Son of man's kingdom *shall not be destroyed.*

The subjects of the Son of man therefore have nothing to fear. As long as they remain loyal to Him, they will share in a kingdom that *is an everlasting dominion.*

What Do You Think?

How does knowing that "God's people win in the end" affect the way you live right now? What changes do you need to make?

Talking Points for Your Discussion
- In lifestyle choices
- In speech patterns
- In relationships
- 2 Corinthians 4:16-18

Conclusion

A. Ah, But Don't You Believe Them

Note in today's Scriptures how world kingdoms end and how God's kingdom comes: God does it all. God's people do, however, have an important responsibility: to be God's heralds and witnesses (Matthew 28:19, 20). Our job is to tell the whole world that our king reigns, that His kingdom will never end, and that He has invited all people to become His subjects.

We must tell the world that while things appear bleak now, appearances can be deceiving. If anyone tells you, "That's just the way it is, some things will never change," don't believe them!

B. Prayer

We thank You, Lord, for giving us eyes to see. Though Daniel could only look forward to the coming kingdom, we can look back at its magnificent beginnings in Jesus. Yet we wait as Daniel waited, in anxious anticipation for the fullness of Your kingdom. Come, Lord Jesus; hasten that day. In Jesus' name, amen.

C. Thought to Remember

God's eternal kingdom surpasses all the fleeting kingdoms of this world.

VISUALS FOR THESE LESSONS

The visual pictured in each lesson (example: page 237) is a small reproduction of a large, full-color poster included in the *Adult Resources* packet for the Spring Quarter. That packet also contains the very useful *Presentation Helps* on a CD for teacher use. Order No. 020039213 from your supplier.

INVOLVEMENT LEARNING

Some of the activities below are also found in the helpful student book, Adult Bible Class.
Don't forget to download the free reproducible page from www.standardlesson.com to enhance your lesson!

Into the Lesson

Sketch on the board the image of a person sleeping in bed; have two large "dream balloons" above his or her head. Ask, "What are some elements of a 'bad dream'?" Jot answers inside one of the dream balloons. *(Possible responses: presence of monsters, the dreamer is threatened by a powerful force or bad weather, etc.)*

Also ask, "What are some elements of a 'good dream'?" Jot ideas inside the other dream balloon. *(Possible responses: the dreamer is among friendly companions, an arriving hero "saves the day," the ending is happy and satisfying.)* After the discussion runs its course, say, "Today we're going to look at a dream recorded in the Bible. As we do, we may see some of these elements in that dream."

Alternative: Place in chairs copies of one or both of the activities from the reproducible page, which you can download. Learners can begin working on this as they arrive. *Option:* Divide learners into study groups of three to five people; have half of the groups work on one activity while the others work on the other activity. Discuss results, but do not let this segment drag out too long.

Into the Word

Distribute copies of the following True/False quiz, which you have titled "Daniel's Dream." Ask learners to pair off to work together.

Give these instructions: "Read Daniel 7:1-3, 9-14 and indicate if the following statements are true or false." 1. Daniel had a dream when Belshazzar was king of Persia. 2. Daniel's dream opened with a gentle breeze blowing over a calm ocean. 3. The four great beasts were different from one another. 4. Daniel saw the Ancient of Days standing in His glory. 5. The throne was "fiery" in some sense. 6. A stream of water flowed from the throne. 7. Books were opened. 8. A horn was speaking. 9. The body of a slain beast was thrown into the churning sea. 10. All four beasts were slain at the same time. 11. The "Ancient of days" came to the "Son of man." 12. The resulting kingdom is never destroyed. *(Answers: 1-F, v. 1; 2-F, v. 2; 3-T, v. 3; 4-F, v. 9; 5-T, v. 9; 6-F, v. 10; 7-T, v. 10; 8-T, v. 11; 9-F, v. 11; 10-F, v. 12; 11-F, v. 13; 12-T, v. 14.)*

There are various ways you can use this quiz. One option is first to read the text aloud, then have learners take the quiz with Bibles closed; results will indicate where further review is needed as your lesson progresses.

To give the key verse of Daniel 7:14 special attention, prepare handouts with the heading "Daniel 7:14, Key Verse Analysis." Space the following phrases randomly around the page:

And there was given him / dominion, and glory, / and a kingdom, / that all people, / nations, and languages, / should serve him: / his dominion is / an everlasting dominion / which shall not pass away, / and his kingdom / that which shall / not be destroyed.

Have these instructions at the top of the page: "Daniel 7:14 is a marvelous statement of what the "Son of man" of verse 13 is given. Draw lines to connect these phrases in the correct order without using your Bible." After learners finish, have the class read the key verse in unison with you several times.

Into Life

Say, "Daniel's dream is one that should comfort a child of God." Give each learner a sentence strip that reads, "Daniel says, 'Good night! Sleep tight!'" Once each learner has a strip, ask, "What is there about Daniel's dream that can enable you to have a 'good, sleep-tight' night?"

As the discussion winds down, suggest that each learner take his or her strip home and put it where it will be seen just before going to sleep each night in the week ahead. This will serve as a reminder of today's lesson.

Daniel's Vision of Change

DANIEL'S
PRAYER

DEVOTIONAL READING: James 5:13-18
BACKGROUND SCRIPTURE: Daniel 9

DANIEL 9:4-14, 17

4 And I prayed unto the LORD my God, and made my confession, and said, O Lord, the great and dreadful God, keeping the covenant and mercy to them that love him, and to them that keep his commandments;

5 We have sinned, and have committed iniquity, and have done wickedly, and have rebelled, even by departing from thy precepts and from thy judgments:

6 Neither have we hearkened unto thy servants the prophets, which spake in thy name to our kings, our princes, and our fathers, and to all the people of the land.

7 O Lord, righteousness belongeth unto thee, but unto us confusion of faces, as at this day; to the men of Judah, and to the inhabitants of Jerusalem, and unto all Israel, that are near, and that are far off, through all the countries whither thou hast driven them, because of their trespass that they have trespassed against thee.

8 O Lord, to us belongeth confusion of face, to our kings, to our princes, and to our fathers, because we have sinned against thee.

9 To the Lord our God belong mercies and forgivenesses, though we have rebelled against him; Beast=nations Roman Crack ? read

10 Neither have we obeyed the voice of the LORD our God, to walk in his laws, which he set before us by his servants the prophets.

11 Yea, all Israel have transgressed thy law, even by departing, that they might not obey thy voice; therefore the curse is poured upon us, and the oath that is written in the law of Moses the servant of God, because we have sinned against him.

12 And he hath confirmed his words, which he spake against us, and against our judges that judged us, by bringing upon us a great evil: for under the whole heaven hath not been done as hath been done upon Jerusalem.

13 As it is written in the law of Moses, all this evil is come upon us: yet made we not our prayer before the LORD our God, that we might turn from our iniquities, and understand thy truth.

14 Therefore hath the LORD watched upon the evil, and brought it upon us: for the LORD our God is righteous in all his works which he doeth: for we obeyed not his voice.

· ·

17 Now therefore, O our God, hear the prayer of thy servant, and his supplications, and cause thy face to shine upon thy sanctuary that is desolate, for the Lord's sake.

KEY VERSE

To the Lord our God belong mercies and forgivenesses, though we have rebelled against him. —**Daniel 9:9**

UNDYING HOPE

Unit 1: The Kingdom of God

LESSONS 1–3

LESSON AIMS

After participating in this lesson, each student will be able to:

1. Summarize Daniel's prayer of confession.

2. Tell why confessing sin is important for groups (nations, etc.) as well as for individuals.

3. Write a prayer of confession for his or her own nation, community, or church.

LESSON OUTLINE

Introduction
  A. Confession and Apology
  B. Lesson Background
 I. Confession (DANIEL 9:4-6)
  A. God Approached (v. 4)
  B. Precepts Rejected (v. 5)
  C. Messengers Ignored (v. 6)
    When the Innocent Confess
 II. Realization (DANIEL 9:7-14)
  A. Sharp Contrasts (vv. 7-11a)
  B. Sobering Results (vv. 11b-14)
    The Surprising Course of History
 III. Appeal (DANIEL 9:17)
  A. To Hear (v. 17a)
  B. To See (v. 17b)
Conclusion
  A. Daniel's Example
  B. Prayer
  C. Thought to Remember

Introduction

A. Confession and Apology

The terms *confession* and *apology* are an interesting pair. They are used most often in their negative senses, although each also has a positive sense. Negatively, to apologize is to say that one is sorry; positively, to offer an apology is to offer a defense of one's position (as in the word *apologetics*). In both instances, the focus is image management. We do not want people to think that our true identity is represented by a particular wrongdoing, and so we say we are sorry. We do not want them to think that a position we hold is flimsy, and so we offer an apology (or an apologetic) to convince them that it is intellectually respectable.

Confession in its negative sense is more intense than saying we are sorry; it means admitting that what we did was wrong. In so doing, we are affirming the existence of a moral order that is larger than ourselves and submitting our plea to the mercy of the one we have wronged. Confession in its positive sense is to affirm what we believe or the way things should be. To confess "Jesus is Lord" is to confess in a positive sense. We confess Christ because we are so convinced of His lordship and its implications for all creation that we cannot help but share this good news with everyone.

There is a time and place for both confession and apology. The sixth century BC of Daniel's day was a time for confession by the Jews.

B. Lesson Background

Daniel's prayer in today's text is best understood when viewed through a wide-angle lens. The national identity of the Israelites had its roots in God's promise to Abraham (who, ironically, was originally from Babylon) that he would become a great nation and that through him all nations would be blessed (Genesis 12:1-3).

An important element of this promise was God's deliverance of Abraham's descendants from slavery in Egypt (about 1440 BC), bringing them into the promised land. The people's well-being depended on their keeping God's law. Should the Israelites fail in that, God vowed to deliver them into their enemies' hands (Deuteronomy 28:15-68).

Daniel's Prayer

By Daniel's time many centuries later, that is exactly what had happened. The Israelites had forsaken God's ways, and God had kept His Word to judge them. Judgment was not, however, God's last word. He also foretold that should the Israelites return to Him wholeheartedly, then He would restore their fortunes (Deuteronomy 30:1-10). This is the most important background to Daniel's prayer in today's text.

Daniel offered his prayer in "the first year of Darius . . . which was made king over the realm of the Chaldeans" (Daniel 9:1). We date this to about 522 BC. Thus Daniel's prayer in today's text took place some 64 years after the destruction of the temple in Jerusalem. The rebuilding of the temple was started in 538 BC as the first wave of the Jews returned from exile (Ezra 1:1–4:5), but subsequently halted (4:24). The work on the temple resumed in 529 BC and was completed in 515 BC (5:1–6:15). Thus Daniel offered his prayer during a time of transition for his people. (Note: the Chaldeans are the same as the Babylonians.)

I. Confession
(DANIEL 9:4-6)

A. God Approached (v. 4)

4. And I prayed unto the LORD my God, and made my confession, and said, O Lord, the great and dreadful God, keeping the covenant and mercy to them that love him, and to them that keep his commandments.

HOW TO SAY IT

apologetics	uh-*pah*-luh-*jeh*-tiks.
Assyria	Uh-*sear*-ee-uh.
Babylonian	Bab-ih-*low*-nee-un.
Chaldeans	Kal-*dee*-unz.
Constantine	*Kahns*-tun-*teen*.
Cyrus	*Sigh*-russ.
Darius	Duh-*rye*-us.
Lamentations	Lam-en-*tay*-shunz.
medieval	muh-*dee*-vul.
Nebuchadnezzar	*Neb*-yuh-kud-*nez*-er.
Theodosius	*Thee*-uh-*doe*-shus.
Wicca	*Wih*-kuh.

Daniel begins his prayer of confession by recognizing the great difference between God and His people. God is the one who is great. He is the one *keeping the covenant* while His people self-evidently do not. God's mercy is itself self-evident given the decree of Cyrus that already has been issued in the Jews' favor (Ezra 1). All the events to this point establish that God honors His Word and that His people forsake His commands. This difference is crucial for Daniel's request that we will see in verse 17, below. Since God is so different from His people, He may extend them mercy one more time.

Solomon used similar language of God in the dedication of the Jerusalem temple centuries earlier (1 Kings 8:23; 2 Chronicles 6:14). This is significant because Solomon's prayer anticipated the Israelites' eventual exile; in that light, his prayer beseeched God to remember them when they would cry out to Him. This is precisely what Daniel is doing. Several decades after Daniel's prayer, Nehemiah will describe God in nearly identical language. Nehemiah too will call on God to remember His people and restore them as they rebuild their city's walls (Nehemiah 1:5).

> *What Do You Think?*
> How is knowing God's character important for the way you pray? What adjustments do you need to make in this regard?
> *Talking Points for Your Discussion*
> - Exodus 33:13; 34:6, 7
> - Nehemiah 9:19-23
> - 2 Thessalonians 1:6
> - Hebrews 4:15; 6:10; 12:29
> - 1 John 1:5; 4:16

B. Precepts Rejected (v. 5)

5. We have sinned, and have committed iniquity, and have done wickedly, and have rebelled, even by departing from thy precepts and from thy judgments.

God wants His people to admit that they are responsible for their own demise. He wants them to recognize that disaster follows from sin. He wants them to become the type of people who do not repeat the same sinful mistakes, but grow in their knowledge of God and His requirements.

Daniel uses several expressions of confession in this light. The last expression in his list is perhaps the most noteworthy: the Israelites' sin has been the deliberate rejection of God's specific requirements (*thy precepts* and *thy judgments*). By naming the source of the problem, Daniel implies the path to recovery: the requirements of God that the people have left behind must be embraced anew.

What Do You Think?

When is confession of specific sins better than a general "I have fallen short" confession? When is a general confession more appropriate?

Talking Points for Your Discussion

- Leviticus 5:5
- Matthew 3:6
- Acts 19:18
- James 5:16
- 1 John 1:9

C. Messengers Ignored (v. 6)

6. Neither have we hearkened unto thy servants the prophets, which spake in thy name to our kings, our princes, and our fathers, and to all the people of the land.

God did not simply give His law to Moses, retreat to Heaven, wait for His people to violate it, and then judge them when they did. Out of compassion, He sent prophets time and again as they strayed. He did all He could to bring things under control. He sent these servants not just to those in charge, but to all the people. God had given the Israelites plenty of chances to rethink their unfaithfulness and get their lives in conformity with His will before things fell apart completely.

❧ WHEN THE INNOCENT CONFESS ❧

I have a friend who practices Wicca, a modern form of witchcraft. "Jill" turned to witchcraft in part because of abusive experiences in churches. Over the years, she has accumulated a whole litany of grievances against Christians, from the strangers who have criticized her for wearing a pentacle, to the church leaders of medieval and colonial eras who tortured accused witches in the name of God.

After several conversations regarding this, I wrote a sincere apology to Jill for the suffering she and similar people have experienced by misguided Christians. Although we both knew that I had never personally hurt her in these ways, taking this step let her know I empathized with her. This advanced both our friendship and her receptivity to the gospel.

Daniel confessed the sins of past generations of his people although he was personally innocent of those sins. His confession showed that he identified with God's outrage over Israel's behavior and wished that he could do something to change the situation. This placed him—and can place us—on God's side, ready to be used by Him to influence others.

—A. W.

II. Realization
(DANIEL 9:7-14)

A. Sharp Contrasts (vv. 7-11a)

7, 8. O Lord, righteousness belongeth unto thee, but unto us confusion of faces, as at this day; to the men of Judah, and to the inhabitants of Jerusalem, and unto all Israel, that are near, and that are far off, through all the countries whither thou hast driven them, because of their trespass that they have trespassed against thee. O Lord, to us belongeth confusion of face, to our kings, to our princes, and to our fathers, because we have sinned against thee.

Daniel continues to contrast God with His people. God is the one who is entirely in the right. He has done nothing wrong in judging His people as He has. He has made the terms of His covenant clear. He has established the consequences of rebellion. He has sent prophets to clarify the meaning of His covenant. He had warned that judgment was coming, giving plenty of opportunities to repent. Every step of the way, God has kept His word.

All this has left the Israelites entirely without excuse. The result is scandal or, as the *King James Version* translates it literally, *confusion of face*. The people are entirely responsible, and Daniel lets no one off the hook. Daniel faults not only the residents of Jerusalem and Judah, but all Israelites everywhere. Both those who stayed put in the land and those who have been scattered share the blame because all sinned against the Lord's commands. Powerful leaders are to blame (Jeremiah 44:17), as well as the average head of household (44:19).

9. To the LORD our God belong mercies and forgivenesses, though we have rebelled against him.

Daniel also knows that divine righteousness is not the only factor. God has also revealed himself to be a God of *mercies and forgiveness.* The Israelites have rebelled against God many times: by worshipping a golden calf (Exodus 32), by fearing the inhabitants of the promised land (Numbers 13), etc. Yet time and again, God worked through the sinful choices of His people, offering a way forward to His ultimate purposes for them. Daniel knows this about God.

What Do You Think?

How can you express gratitude for God's mercy today in ways other than prayer?

Talking Points for Your Discussion

- In interactions with fellow Christians
- In interactions with non-Christians
- In financial priorities
- In entertainment choices
- Other

10, 11a. Neither have we obeyed the voice of the LORD our God, to walk in his laws, which he set before us by his servants the prophets. Yea, all Israel have transgressed thy law, even by departing, that they might not obey thy voice.

After declaring God's mercy in verse 9, one might expect Daniel to conclude his prayer. He does not do so, however, because he is not after cheap forgiveness. Instead he continues to rehearse Israel's guilt.

It is worth remembering at this point why God sent prophets to urge His people *to walk in his laws:* God relentlessly pursues His people, not because they are special in and of themselves, but because He has called them to an important mission. They must walk in God's ways so the nations will see those ways and be drawn to God (Deuteronomy 4:5-8).

God is faithful when His people are faithless because God loves the whole world. His plan for saving this world involves forming a people to be His witnesses. The Israelites are not called to save the world; only God can do that. Yet even imperfect people can be used as witnesses to God. Why would the nations believe the witness of God's people if those people merely live like everyone else? They have to *be* different if they are going to *make* a difference. God knows that the credibility of His witnesses is crucial to the world's acceptance of their witness.

B. Sobering Results (vv. 11b-14)

11b. Therefore the curse is poured upon us, and the oath that is written in the law of Moses the servant of God, because we have sinned against him.

The curse of God that results should not be a surprise since a series of curses is presented in detail in Deuteronomy 28:15-68. All of the consequences listed there have come to pass. At the hands of Assyria, Babylon, and the smaller nations around Israel, God had brought judgment on His people in various ways through the centuries.

12. And he hath confirmed his words, which he spake against us, and against our judges that judged us, by bringing upon us a great evil: for under the whole heaven hath not been done as hath been done upon Jerusalem.

Daniel affirms his conviction that God is the one who has brought disaster on Israel. This conviction is itself an act of faith because not all Jews believe that God is the one who leveled Jerusalem and scattered His people. Some interpret these events as a sign of God's defeat. They think pagan gods have prevailed (see Jeremiah 44:17, 18). But Daniel has eyes to see God's hand at work.

This does not mean, however, that believers today are justified in attributing to God all the personal disasters that befall them. The Bible does not teach that all disaster comes from God. Even so, the Bible does affirm that God is capable of using all of our experiences to accomplish some good for us (Romans 8:28).

"God, hear the prayer of thy servant."

Visual for Lesson 2. *As you discuss verse 17, point to this visual and ask, "What are some barriers that would cause God not to hear our prayers, if any?"*

fer abject poverty (example: Sub-Saharan Africa). God's purpose in working with the nations is so that people should reach out to Him and find Him (Acts 17:26, 27). Our part is to point people to Him and wait patiently as the surprising course of history unfolds.

—A. W.

❧ THE SURPRISING COURSE OF HISTORY ❧

Rome built one of the greatest empires in history. The result was a uniting of the Mediterranean world with roads and aqueducts, an advanced legal system, and prosperous trade. At the same time, the Romans promoted idol worship, sexual immorality, slavery, and the torture of Christians. The demise of the Roman Empire clearly seems to have been a judgment of God (compare Revelation 17, 18).

There's a problem, though: Rome's final collapse did not come until *after* the empire had become Christianized! Constantine issued an edict of tolerance in AD 312, and Theodosius proclaimed Christianity the state religion in 380. These two emperors and others who followed worked vigorously to build churches, abolish immoral practices, promote doctrinal unity, and spread the faith to other lands. Yet within a few generations, barbarians had overrun their empire.

What's the explanation? Maybe they were false converts, just using Christianity for political ends. Maybe they were sincere, but it was simply too late. Or perhaps God knew that the migration of European tribes into Roman territory was the best way for new people groups to hear the gospel.

We cannot always pinpoint the reasons why nations rise and decline. Some of the least Christian nations in the world today are also among the most prosperous (examples: Saudi Arabia, Japan), while some predominantly Christian societies suf-

13, 14. As it is written in the law of Moses, all this evil is come upon us: yet made we not our prayer before the LORD our God, that we might turn from our iniquities, and understand thy truth. Therefore hath the Lord watched upon the evil, and brought it upon us: for the LORD our God is righteous in all his works which he doeth: for we obeyed not his voice.

Although Daniel continues to confess God's righteousness in bringing disaster on the Israelites, he further recognizes that there was a time when Israel could have averted it. Not only could the people have averted God's judgment by not sinning to begin with, they also could have averted it by reversing course once they had started sinning.

Notice in these verses that the Israelites need to do more than apologize for letting God down. When God's people sin, they need to turn from their sinful ways. Only in turning from sin do God's people show that they understand God's truth. God's truth is not simply an abstract set of intellectual principles to affirm or deny. Understanding God's truth means embracing the life to which God calls His people. This is made clearest in Jesus' claim to be the way, the truth, and the life (John 14:6). Confessing Jesus requires reordering our lives according to God's will. Anything short of this is a sham (see John 14:15).

What Do You Think?
What prayer burden is on your heart today? How have your prayer burdens changed as you have grown in spiritual maturity?
Talking Points for Your Discussion
- Prayers for yourself
- Prayers for fellow Christians
- Prayers for non-Christians
- Prayers for the church
- Other

Daniel's Prayer

III. Appeal
(DANIEL 9:17)
A. To Hear (v. 17a)

17a. Now therefore, O our God, hear the prayer of thy servant, and his supplications.

Daniel 9:15, 16 (not in today's text) continues the contrast between the nature of God and the sin of the people. With verse 17 Daniel begins his appeal. The final verse of our study is not the final verse of Daniel's prayer, since it does not end until verse 19. Verse 17 nonetheless captures the substance of verses 17-19. Daniel wants God to act, but Daniel realizes that God must first be willing to hear prayers (compare Lamentations 3:44).

What Do You Think?

In the four-step prayer formula *Adoration, Confession, Thanksgiving, Supplication* (ACTS), where do you need to make the most improvement? How will you do so?

Talking Points for Your Discussion
- Elements of the Lord's prayer (Matthew 6:9-13)
- Prayer environment (Matthew 14:23)
- The issue of doubt (James 1:6)
- The issue of motives (James 4:3)
- Other

B. To Shine (v. 17b)

17b. And cause thy face to shine upon thy sanctuary that is desolate, for the Lord's sake.

As Daniel brings his petition to a close, he bases his appeal on the Lord's own sake, not on the sake of the people. Israel's disaster means that God's name—which is attached to His people, His city of Jerusalem, His sanctuary (temple)—has been profaned among the nations (compare Ezekiel 36:21-23), His reputation tarnished.

Of course, God is not insecure about what the nations think of Him. They have misconstrued who He is for a long time. He is concerned, however, with how the nations understand His unique relationship with His people. This is because His strategy for drawing all humans to himself involves the witness of His people. Although it is important that God discipline His people when their trans-

gressions compromise His mission, to wipe them out altogether would also compromise that mission. God does not mind being known as the God who disciplines those whom He loves, but He also wants to be known as the God of mercy. Indeed, that's how Daniel himself knows God (Daniel 9:9, 18). The mercy that God shows His people is the same mercy He intends to show the nations.

For this reason, Daniel appeals to God's larger purposes. Daniel is committed to those larger purposes. The partially rebuilt temple (see the Lesson Background) is still a disgrace. Daniel calls on God to remember His plan because Daniel wants to renew Israel's commitment to that plan.

Conclusion
A. Daniel's Example

Daniel's prayer is a model in teaching us what it means to confess sins with integrity. We do not simply apologize to God. We must reorient our lives around God's mission. We must be honest about our past and deliberate about our future.

Daniel's prayer is also a wonderful example of corporate solidarity. In a world where leaders may not even own up to personal failings, it is remarkable to see someone who identifies with the sins of his people, both in his own generation and in generations past. Daniel makes no distinction between his behavior and that of Israel as a whole. Yet we know Daniel was a moral exemplar among his people. He took bold steps to honor God when his own life was on the line (Daniel 1 and 6).

But Daniel's life did not revolve around himself. If his people were not right with God, then God's mission was at stake. When God's mission is in jeopardy, God's people have to join together, confess together, and turn to God together.

B. Prayer

Lord, we continually fall short. We confess that we have a lot of growing up (and owning up) to do. Help us keep the bigger picture of Your mission in view. In Jesus' name, amen.

C. Thought to Remember

Confess sin and return to God.

INVOLVEMENT LEARNING

Some of the activities below are also found in the helpful student book, Adult Bible Class.
Don't forget to download the free reproducible page from www.standardlesson.com to enhance your lesson!

Into the Lesson

Write the names *Daniel, Nehemiah,* and *Solomon* on the board. Then ask three volunteers to stand up front and read 1 Kings 8:23; Daniel 9:4; Nehemiah 1:5, one passage each. The readers are not to reveal to the class the passages where the readings are found. Ask, "Who addressed God in each of these prayers?" as you point to the three names. Have the verses read again, if necessary.

After the three names are matched correctly, write on the board *1 Kings 8:22-53* (next to the name Solomon), *Daniel 9:4-19* (next to Daniel); and *Nehemiah 1:3-11* (next to Nehemiah). Then ask, "What is a common element across these three prayers?" Allow learners to check their Bibles for possibilities. More than one answer is possible, but in particular make sure your class sees *confession of sin* as the common element. If you think this segment will take too long (because the three passages are lengthy), you can simply point out this common element yourself in 1 Kings 8:47; Daniel 9:5, 6; and Nehemiah 1:6, 7. Say, "Let's take an in-depth look at Daniel's prayer."

Alternative: Place in chairs copies of the "Addressing God" activity from the reproducible page, which you can download. Learners can begin working on this as they arrive.

Into the Word

Say, "Prayer realizes who God is and who we are in relationship to and comparison with Him. When we understand His power and love and see our own weaknesses, asking for His help is the appropriate thing to do."

Read aloud today's text, Daniel 4:4-14, 17. Then say, "In his prayer Daniel seems to be answering the unstated question, 'Who is God?' What are some of the answers he comes up with?" Divide learners into groups of four to six to develop a list of answers. Suggest that learners look at verses 1-3 as well as the lesson text.

Ask groups to share their suggestions with the class as a whole. Expect suggestions to include (1) God is merciful (v. 4), (2) God expects obedience (v. 4), (3) God is righteous (v. 7), (4) God is forgiving and gracious (v. 9), (5) God punishes sin and disobedience (vv. 11, 12, 14), (6) God can answer prayers (v. 17). Other suggestions are possible.

Then ask, "What is the appropriate response we should have to God as we have seen Him described thus far?" Some expected responses are that we come to Him (1) as sinners, those who have done wrong (v. 5), (2) as rebellious people (vv. 5, 9), (3) as those who have rejected His commands and laws (v. 5), (4) as people who have refused to listen to those He sends with His Word (v. 6), (5) confused and ashamed (vv. 7, 8), (6) as unfaithful (v. 7), (7) with grateful awareness of His mercies and forgiveness (v. 9), (8) with sins that need to be forgiven (v. 11), (9) in anticipation that our prayers will be heard (v. 17). Your learners may, of course, see other possibilities.

As you work through the text from Daniel's viewpoint and how that viewpoint speaks to our own prayer lives, be sure to address the concept of confessing the sins of past generations. Naturally, the one doing the praying is innocent in such cases. You may find the illustration "When the Innocent Confess" on page 244 helpful in this regard.

Option: If time allows, supplement this section of the lesson with the "An Attitude of Prayer" activity on the reproducible page, which you can download.

Into Life

Say, "It's time to stop talking about praying and pray." Allow time for brief prayer responses as you suggest categories for prayer from today's text. You can encourage silent praying or ask volunteers to pray aloud. Use "we statements" from today's text as prayer stimuli, adjusting them as necessary for today's context.

GABRIEL INTERPRETS DANIEL'S VISION

DEVOTIONAL READING: Psalm 91:1-12
BACKGROUND SCRIPTURE: Daniel 8

DANIEL 8:1, 15-26

1 In the third year of the reign of king Belshazzar a vision appeared unto me, even unto me Daniel, after that which appeared unto me at the first. *Bel Sha er*

. . . .

15 And it came to pass, when I, even I Daniel, had seen the vision, and sought for the meaning, then, behold, there stood before me as the appearance of a man. *U LA I*

16 And I heard a man's voice between the banks of Ulai, which called, and said, Gabriel, make this man to understand the vision.

17 So he came near where I stood: and when he came, I was afraid, and fell upon my face: but he said unto me, Understand, O son of man: for at the time of the end shall be the vision.

18 Now as he was speaking with me, I was in a deep sleep on my face toward the ground: but he touched me, and set me upright.

19 And he said, Behold, I will make thee know what shall be in the last end of the indignation: for at the time appointed the end shall be.

20 The ram which thou sawest having two horns are the kings of Media and Persia.

21 And the rough goat is the king of Grecia: *Roman*
and the great horn that is between his eyes is the first king.

22 Now that being broken, whereas four stood up for it, four kingdoms shall stand up out of the nation, but not in his power.

23 And in the latter time of their kingdom, when the transgressors are come to the full, a king of fierce countenance, and understanding dark sentences, shall stand up.

24 And his power shall be mighty, but not by his own power: and he shall destroy wonderfully, and shall prosper, and practise, and shall destroy the mighty and the holy people.

25 And through his policy also he shall cause craft to prosper in his hand; and he shall magnify himself in his heart, and by peace shall destroy many: he shall also stand up against the Prince of princes; but he shall be broken without hand.

26 And the vision of the evening and the morning which was told is true: wherefore shut thou up the vision; for it shall be for many days.

KEY VERSE

The vision of the evening and the morning which was told is true. —**Daniel 8:26a**

UNDYING HOPE

Unit 1: The Kingdom of God

LESSONS 1–3

LESSON AIMS

After participating in this lesson, each student will be able to:

1. Identify the ram, the goat, and the king of fierce countenance of Daniel's vision.

2. Trace the fulfillment of Daniel's vision.

3. Write a prayer that praises God for His sovereignty over human events.

LESSON OUTLINE

Introduction

A. Left Behind?

Every once in a while a book series comes along that captures the imagination of millions of readers. What the Harry Potter series did for young people in the general public, the Left Behind series did for a broad range of Christian readers back around the turn of the millennium. That series is a imaginative account of the end of the world revolving around apocalyptic portions of Revelation. The events of Revelation are interpreted as if they were meant to give a literal play-by-play account of end-times tribulation.

This kind of interpretation draws a crowd partly because it plays off of the difficulty that readers have with apocalyptic texts such as the book of Revelation. The symbolic language of such texts is perplexing, and an interpreter who "connects the dots" in a way that seems fairly plausible can gain a wide hearing.

Daniel 8, today's lesson, is an apocalyptic text that can cause similar consternation since it involves key historical events represented symbolically by animals. This chapter is different from other apocalyptic texts, however, in that it also includes an angelic interpretation. We are not left guessing what the animals represent; we are told. Readers are led to understand better both the meaning of the animals in this chapter and the nature of *apocalypse* as a type of literature. This gives us clues for the proper reading of apocalyptic texts for which interpretations are not so obvious.

B. Lesson Background

Daniel 8 contains a vision of two animals and an interpretation of what they represent. The interpretation points to a future time long after the death of Daniel. Rather than focus on the Babylonian empire against which Daniel and the Jews of his time struggle, the vision focuses on the times of the Persians and Greeks that followed. A brief introduction to the Jewish encounter with these nations is therefore in order.

The Babylonians destroyed Jerusalem in 586 BC, carrying many Judeans into exile. Yet Babylon's dominance as a world power did not last much longer after that. With little struggle, Cyrus of Persia conquered Babylon by 539 BC.

Cyrus had come to power initially under the authority of the more powerful Median Empire. The Medes controlled a vast amount of territory north and east of the Babylonian Empire. Within roughly a decade, however, Cyrus conquered the Medes, assumed their territory, and declared himself king of Persia (modern Iran). His empire is thus referred to as either the Persian Empire or the Medo-Persian Empire.

The Persians ruled over the Judeans in a much more benevolent manner than the Babylonians had. The Persians sponsored the Jews' return to Jerusalem of 538 BC, allowing the Jewish people to rule themselves by their own laws. There were, of course, strings attached. Should the Jews rebel or withhold tribute, the Persians would beat them into submission.

This arrangement lasted until the 330s BC. At that time, Alexander the Great of Greece subdued the Persians and took control of Palestine. Alexander died in 323 BC, and his kingdom was divided among his generals. These Greek rulers continued Persia's more benevolent foreign policy for the most part. This lasted until about the middle of the second century BC, when the tide changed for the worse for God's people (see the non-biblical book of 1 Maccabees). Daniel's vision in today's lesson provides an important glimpse into some terrifying periods and God's decisive response.

HOW TO SAY IT

Antiochus Epiphanes	An-*tie*-oh-kus Ih-*piff*-a-neez.
apocalypse	uh-*pock*-uh-lips.
apocalyptic	uh-*pock*-uh-**lip**-tik.
Belshazzar	Bel-*shazz*-er.
Lysimachus	Lie-*sih*-meh-kus.
Maccabees	*Mack*-uh-bees.
Macedon	*Mah*-suh-dun.
Medes	Meeds.
Ptolemy	*Tahl*-uh-me.
Seleucus	Suh-*loo*-kuss.
Ulai	*You*-lye or *You*-luh-eye.

I. Meeting the Interpreter
(DANIEL 8:1, 15-19)
A. Second Vision Is Received (v. 1)

1. In the third year of the reign of king Belshazzar a vision appeared unto me, even unto me Daniel, after that which appeared unto me at the first.

The third year of the reign of king Belshazzar of Babylon computes to 550 BC, about 36 years after the fall of Jerusalem. As noted in Lesson 1, Belshazzar was a wicked ruler who made sport of the sacred vessels that were confiscated from the Jerusalem temple (Daniel 5). It is thus fitting that this particular vision, which concerns a future arrogant king who also makes sport of the Jewish faith (see Daniel 8:23-25, below), takes place during the reign of Belshazzar.

The substance of Daniel's vision is presented in Daniel 8:3-14, although that section is not included in today's text. As we focus on the interpretation of the vision, we will be referring to verses 3-14 as necessary to help us understand the interpretation. The vision of four beasts in Daniel 7 (last week's lesson) is likely the one described here as *that which appeared unto me at the first.*

B. Gabriel Is Commissioned (vv. 15, 16)

15. And it came to pass, when I, even I Daniel, had seen the vision, and sought for the meaning, then, behold, there stood before me as the appearance of a man.

Daniel tries to understand what he has seen thus far; the vision is not yet ended. Explanation begins to come with *the appearance of a man.* This figure should not be confused with the one who looks "like the Son of man" in Daniel 7:13. The word used here for *man* in the original language is different. It is a technical term meaning "mighty one" (example: Isaiah 42:13), and it is nearly identical to the name of the vision's interpreter (next verse).

16. And I heard a man's voice between the banks of Ulai, which called, and said, Gabriel, make this man to understand the vision.

Daniel is still near the Ulai River, the place where he saw himself at the beginning of his vision (Daniel 8:2). In this part of the vision, Daniel hears an unidentified voice calling to the one who looks like a man in verse 15. This man is named Gabriel, which means "mighty one of God" in the original language. Gabriel is appointed to help Daniel *understand the vision.* Gabriel will make another appearance about 28 years later, in Daniel 9:21 (compare Luke 1:19, 26).

C. Daniel Is Resuscitated (vv. 17, 18)

17. So he came near where I stood: and when he came, I was afraid, and fell upon my face: but he said unto me, Understand, O son of man: for at the time of the end shall be the vision.

Daniel is terrified as Gabriel approaches. Reverence and fear are common reactions throughout the Scriptures when humans encounter angelic beings (examples: Numbers 22:31; Joshua 5:14; Luke 1:12; Acts 10:3, 4; Revelation 19:10).

Daniel must understand that the vision concerns not the time of his own day in the mid–sixth century BC, but *the time at the end.* The phrase *the end* can be interpreted in more than one way, depending on context.

Sometimes *the end* means "the end of history as we know it," which comes about when Jesus returns. In other instances, *the end* refers to the end of a specific time period in history (example: Ezekiel 7:1-7). In still other cases, it seems to be both, as if the events of the somewhat near future are only the beginning of a long string of events that find their fulfillment in the final judgment and reign of Christ. We will dig into this further as the interpretation of the vision unfolds.

What Do You Think?

What circumstances, if any, should cause us to react in reverence as Daniel did? Why?

Talking Points for Your Discussion

- Deuteronomy 9:18, 25
- 1 Chronicles 29:20
- Ecclesiastes 3:7b
- Habakkuk 2:20
- Revelation 5:8, 14; 7:11; 19:4

---

18. Now as he was speaking with me, I was in a deep sleep on my face toward the ground: but he touched me, and set me upright.

The appearance of Gabriel has so startled Daniel that he has fainted or is otherwise knocked out cold! But Daniel needs to be prepared to hear the message, so Gabriel revives him and sets him on his feet. Though God's messengers are frightening to behold, humans can nonetheless handle being in their presence. Angels are to be respected as God's messengers, but they are not to be worshipped (see Revelation 19:9, 10 and 22:8, 9).

D. Interpretation Is Introduced (v. 19)

19. And he said, Behold, I will make thee know what shall be in the last end of the indignation: for at the time appointed the end shall be.

When Gabriel first speaks to Daniel in verse 17, he tells him that the vision pertains to "the end." Gabriel's decision to repeat that here may indicate that Daniel did not hear him the first time, having lost consciousness.

Regardless, Gabriel adds at this point that the end being discussed is *appointed,* presumably by God. This means that as disturbing as the events may be, God remains in control. He knows what is going to happen, and He will somehow bring events in line with His plans. This does not mean that God will cause the events to happen or is pleased by them. His power is demonstrated in the fact that He takes disordered human decisions and orders them for His own saving purposes.

❧ SOME THINGS CAN'T BE RUSHED ❧

For every expectant mother who patiently contemplates the new life growing inside her, there are a dozen others who are ready for their baby to be born now! Folk advice abounds on how to hurry labor. My wife's aunt had her husband drive over bouncy country roads in an attempt to initiate labor, to no effect. A wise grandmother gave probably the best advice: "That baby will come when she wants to come."

We easily imagine Daniel's mixed emotions at the troubling visions and interpretations. Yes, his people would be delivered, but their salvation would involve further suffering first. Like receiving news of a needed surgery, this message must have brought a mixture of dread and anticipation. Gabriel's words brought reassurance that everything was going according to plan; Daniel had only to wait.

Finishing school, paying off debt, recuperating from illness—such things can make us feel like something is holding us back from achieving our goals. Modern technology allows us to speed many things up, but some things simply can't be rushed. Strained relationships can take a long time to heal. Non-Christian friends aren't always receptive to our witness. God will work all our experiences together for good (Romans 8:28), but we dare not try to rush His timing. —A. W.

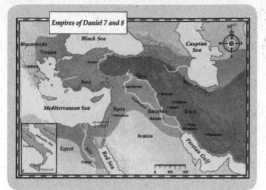

Visual for Lessons 1 & 3. *Help your learners keep a geographical perspective by referring to this map frequently as you study the three lessons of Unit 1.*

> **What Do You Think?**
> When was a time you resisted (or failed to resist) the temptation to try to rush God's timing? How did things turn out?
> *Talking Points for Your Discussion*
> - In making a vocational choice
> - In starting a church building program
> - In making a personal commitment
> - Numbers 14:40-45
> - Other

II. Receiving the Interpretation
(DANIEL 8:20-26)
A. Ram Is Identified (v. 20)

20. The ram which thou sawest having two horns are the kings of Media and Persia.

The first thing Daniel saw in his vision, back in verse 3, was a ram standing beside the Ulai River. One of its two horns is "higher" than the other. The ram moves relentlessly in triumph "westward, and northward, and southward" (v. 4). These details align perfectly with Gabriel's statement that the ram represents *Media and Persia*. The facts of history affirm that the Medo-Persian kingdom expands in these three directions.

The ram is depicted fittingly in Daniel 8:3 as a single animal with two horns of unequal length since Media and Persia are two kingdoms that collapse into one, with the Cyrus of Persia becoming prominent (see the Lesson Background). The disproportionate horn length may be parallel to the image of the bear in the previous vision that was raised up on one side (Daniel 7:5).

B. Goat Is Identified (vv. 21, 22)

21. And the rough goat is the king of Grecia: and the great horn that is between his eyes is the first king.

The animal of Daniel 8:5-7 is a one-horned goat that charges from the west, tramples the ram, and shatters the ram's two horns. Gabriel now identifies this animal as *the king of Grecia* (Greece). The record of history informs us that *the great horn . . . the first king* is Alexander the Great, who will be born about 194 years after this vision. After coming to power, Alexander moves quickly from west to east to take control of the Medo-Persian Empire.

22. Now that being broken, whereas four stood up for it, four kingdoms shall stand up out of the nation, but not in his power.

According to Daniel 8:8, the great horn is broken as it becomes strong, being replaced with four horns pointing "toward the four winds of heaven." Gabriel clarifies here that these horns are four kingdoms that lack Alexander's power.

This is exactly what ends up happening historically. Alexander dies at age 33 in 323 BC, and His kingdom eventually is divided among four of his generals: Cassander rules over Macedon and Greece (west); Lysimachus rules Thrace and Asia Minor (north); Seleucus rules Syria and Babylon (east); and Ptolemy rules Egypt (south). Since each of these kingdoms receives only a portion of Alexander's empire, none of them matches *his power*.

C. Wicked King Is Judged (vv. 23-25)

23, 24. And in the latter time of their kingdom, when the transgressors are come to the full, a king of fierce countenance, and understanding dark sentences, shall stand up. And his power shall be mighty, but not by his own power: and he shall destroy wonderfully, and shall prosper, and practise, and shall destroy the mighty and the holy people.

These verses focus on the "little horn" of Daniel 8:9-12. It wreaks havoc in the south and east and "toward the pleasant land" (v. 9). It wages war against "the host of heaven," "the prince of the host," and even "the place of his sanctuary" (vv. 10, 11). No one seems able to stop this rampaging king.

Gabriel clarifies here that this king comes later than the others and that he stands out in ferocity and darkness. In particular, this king seeks to destroy *the holy people*. This is Gabriel's way of identifying "the pleasant land" of verse 9. That land is Judah. The Greek king most known for attacking God's people in their homeland is Antiochus IV, also known as Antiochus Epiphanes. He rules from 175 to 164 BC.

It is not clear what it means that this king's prosperity is not *by his own power*. The book of Daniel makes no reference to satanic influence. If the reference is to God, the point is that Antiochus can have power over God's people only as God allows it. Any power Antiochus is to have will be on loan from God. This does not mean that God is the cause of this king's wicked deeds. But it *does* mean that God can easily take that man's power away.

What Do You Think?
What are some ways that Christians should respond and not respond to an oppressive government?
Talking Points for Your Discussion
- Matthew 5:39
- Mark 12:17
- Luke 2:1-4
- Acts 4:19; 5:29; 16:35-37; 22:25
- Romans 13:1-7
- Ephesians 6:12
- 1 Peter 2:17

25. And through his policy also he shall cause craft to prosper in his hand; and he shall magnify himself in his heart, and by peace shall destroy many: he shall also stand up against the Prince of princes; but he shall be broken without hand.

Wickedness thrives during the reign of Antiochus. Jews with money and a willingness to abandon faith can rise to prominence within his corrupt regime. Jews who resist his policies are persecuted from 170 to 164 BC. Antiochus ends up being so arrogant that he rises up against God himself by defiling the Jerusalem temple in 167 BC. Jews are killed for reading Scriptures, honoring the Sabbath, abstaining from unclean food, etc. (This is described in the nonbiblical 1 Maccabees 1:54-61.)

This period proves to be one of the most distressing eras in Jewish history. Yet God is still in control. The verse before us ends with a clear and simple statement that Antiochus *shall be broken*, although not by human agency *(without hand)*. God is the one who brings him to justice. When God decides that the time is right, He will destroy Antiochus as easily as he does the ferocious beast in Daniel 7:11. This remarkable prophecy is given over 380 years before it comes to pass!

What Do You Think?
How do we know when we should "let God handle it" and not try to "assist" Him?
Talking Points for Your Discussion
- Deuteronomy 32:35 (Hebrews 10:30)
- Isaiah 6:8-10 (Acts 28:26)
- Ezekiel 22:30
- Zechariah 4:6b
- Matthew 28:19, 20

D. Vision Is Sealed (v. 26)

26a. And the vision of the evening and the morning which was told is true.

The last thing Daniel heard before Gabriel began revealing his interpretation in Daniel 8:17 was an angelic voice stating that the sanctuary is to be restored "unto two thousand and three hundred days" (v. 14). Gabriel now stresses that this will indeed happen. God will not allow His holy place to be violated indefinitely.

This prophecy is fulfilled in 164 BC, three years after the temple's defilement; that's when the temple is rededicated. Three years adds up to roughly 1,150 days or a combination of 2,300 evenings and mornings (see 1 Maccabees 4:36-58).

26b. Wherefore shut thou up the vision; for it shall be for many days.

What is fascinating about this passage is what Daniel is *not* called to do: he is not charged to do anything to keep these terrible events from happening. Instead, he is told to seal up the vision and wait for it to unfold.

The purpose of this advance notice is not to keep certain things from happening, but to help the reader develop a "God's-eye view" of these events when they do happen. Those faithful to God must trust that God is in control; in the midst of persecution, God's people are to bear witness to their trust in that fact.

❧ GOOD SECRETS ❧

We are keeping a secret from our daughter. In a few months, my wife is taking her on her first overseas trip to visit friends on the mission field. At just 9 years old, she will be deeply affected by this experience, perhaps even becoming inspired to be a missionary herself one day.

But there is no way we are going to tell her about the trip now! If we did, she would be distracted from her schoolwork, have tension with her younger siblings, and perhaps even dread the thought of the trip rather than look forward to it. Even though what we plan is a good thing, her not knowing is, in our judgment, better for her right now than knowing.

God told Daniel about some future events, but not all the precise details regarding Israel's future rescue. Likewise, God does not lay out detailed road maps of everything that He has in store for us. Think about it: if as a child you had been given to know everything that would happen to you by now, would you have been able to understand it or bear it? May we praise the all-wise God who tells us just what we need to know when we need to know it! See 1 Corinthians 2:9.   —A. W.

Conclusion

A. Apocalypse Now!

If Daniel 8 is an indication of how biblical apocalypses function, then there are a few lessons that we learn about how to read them. We learn about the nature of symbolic language. We learn that God does not give us glimpses into the future so we can use that knowledge to take control of how things turn out. We learn that sometimes God gives us only enough knowledge of the future to embolden us to remain radically faithful in the present.

Yet not all apocalyptic texts are the same. Daniel 8 is different in many ways from Daniel 7 and Daniel 10–12. The book of Daniel as a whole is different from the book of Revelation, which in Greek is called *Apocalypse*. Yet these differences are not so great that a proper reading of Daniel cannot prepare us for a proper reading of Revelation. Though some of the events foretold in Revelation pertain to the end of time when Jesus brings His kingdom in its fullness, much of that book also pertains to events of the first-century church. In all this, one thing remains clear: God is in control. May we approach God's Word with that fact in mind. Our side wins.

B. Prayer

Lord God, we confess that You are Lord over world history. Deliver us from the temptation to try seizing control. Give us eyes to see the bigger picture and to embrace a future that ultimately is in Your benevolent arms. In Jesus' name, amen.

C. Thought to Remember

God is faithful and able to deliver His people.

INVOLVEMENT LEARNING

Some of the activities below are also found in the helpful student book, Adult Bible Class.
Don't forget to download the free reproducible page from www.standardlesson.com to enhance your lesson!

Into the Lesson

Early in the week, ask one of your learners to prepare a mini-lecture of the Lesson Background. Display or project a map of the world powers being described during the presentation. If you don't have such a map, create and distribute handouts of one (easy to find on the Internet).

Option: Before class, place in chairs copies of the "Visions and Interpretations" activity from the reproducible page, which you can download. Learners can begin working on this as they arrive (before the mini-lecture above). After discussing results, say, "God does not always provide interpretations of symbolic language, but we sure do appreciate it when He does! Today's study takes us to one such instance. But first we need some background." Then introduce the mini-lecture above.

Into the Word

Have learners take turns reading aloud the verses of today's printed text, Daniel 8:1, 15-26. *Alternative:* Learners can read the entirety of Daniel 8, but this will be a lengthy reading.

Option 1: Distribute copies of the "Proofreading Prophecy" activity from the reproducible page, which you can download. Say, "This will be a closed-Bible quiz. You get one point for circling each wrong item, and one point for writing the correct answer to replace the wrong item; thus there are 26 points possible. As soon as you are finished, open your Bible and score the quiz yourself." (*Alternative:* You can have learners work as open-Bible study pairs.) Identify the two or three most missed errors for special attention.

Option 2: Write the following answers on the board in a scattered manner: *Alexander the Great, Antiochus Epiphanes, Belshazzar, Daniel, Gabriel.* Then distribute the following short notes to volunteers to be read aloud in a "Who Am I?" activity. Point to the names on the board as you say, "These individuals are part of today's text. See if

you can match names with descriptions." Distribute eight slips of paper to eight learners, one each. The slips will have the following statements, one per slip. Direct readers to read the clue statements but not the answer.

1. I was a conquering king. Daniel's vision pictured me as a mighty, shaggy goat from the west. *(Alexander the Great; see Daniel 8:21)* 2. I spoke on behalf of God to Daniel, and I also spoke for God to two people in Luke 1. *(Gabriel; see Daniel 8:15, 16; Luke 1:19, 26)* 3. I was a wicked king who inherited a small portion of Alexander's empire. I desecrated the Jews' holy place. *(Antiochus Epiphanes; see the lesson notes on Daniel 8:23-25)* 4. As king, I saw "the handwriting on the wall." This happened as I was desecrating the holy vessels of the Jerusalem temple. *(Belshazzar; see Daniel 5:1-5; 8:1)* 5. Through Gabriel I received the meaning of my vision as a hope for my people Israel. *(Daniel)*

Into Life

Say, "God's sovereignty is an important concept in today's study." Discuss dictionary definitions of the words *sovereign* and *sovereignty* with your class. Then give each learner a copy of this acrostic:

   S —supreme, Savior
   O—overcomer, omnipotent, omniscient
   V—victorious, vision-giving
   E—eternal, excellent, enabler
   R—righteous, ruler, revealer
   E—everlasting, elevated (on a throne)
   I —invincible, invisible, indivisible (yet triune)
   G—gracious, governing
   N—not limited, not defeated

Say, "In your devotional times this week, see how many of these concepts you can introduce into your prayers as you praise God for His sovereignty over history." Use some of the above concepts in closing your class with prayer. Distribute copies of the "Standing Against the Prince of Princes" from the reproducible page as a take-home activity.

THE LORD'S SUPPER

DEVOTIONAL READING: 1 Corinthians 10:14-22

BACKGROUND SCRIPTURE: Luke 22:1-38

LUKE 22:14-30

14 And when the hour was come, he sat down, and the twelve apostles with him.

15 And he said unto them, With desire I have desired to eat this passover with you before I suffer:

16 For I say unto you, I will not any more eat thereof, until it be fulfilled in the kingdom of God.

17 And he took the cup, and gave thanks, and said, Take this, and divide it among yourselves:

18 For I say unto you, I will not drink of the fruit of the vine, until the kingdom of God shall come.

19 And he took bread, and gave thanks, and brake it, and gave unto them, saying, This is my body which is given for you: this do in remembrance of me.

20 Likewise also the cup after supper, saying, This cup is the new testament in my blood, which is shed for you.

21 But, behold, the hand of him that betrayeth me is with me on the table.

22 And truly the Son of man goeth, as it was determined: but woe unto that man by whom he is betrayed!

23 And they began to enquire among themselves, which of them it was that should do this thing.

24 And there was also a strife among them, which of them should be accounted the greatest.

25 And he said unto them, The kings of the Gentiles exercise lordship over them; and they that exercise authority upon them are called benefactors.

26 But ye shall not be so: but he that is greatest among you, let him be as the younger; and he that is chief, as he that doth serve.

27 For whether is greater, he that sitteth at meat, or he that serveth? is not he that sitteth at meat? but I am among you as he that serveth.

28 Ye are they which have continued with me in my temptations.

29 And I appoint unto you a kingdom, as my Father hath appointed unto me;

30 That ye may eat and drink at my table in my kingdom, and sit on thrones judging the twelve tribes of Israel.

KEY VERSE

He that is greatest among you, let him be as the younger; and he that is chief, as he that doth serve.

—**Luke 22:26b**

UNDYING HOPE

Unit 2: Resurrection Hope
LESSONS 4–9

LESSON AIMS

After participating in this lesson, each student will be able to:

1. Retell the events of the instituting of the Lord's Supper.

2. Note the irony of the disciples' dispute about who was the greatest as juxtaposed against Jesus' words about His impending sacrifice.

3. Confess that he or she sometimes focuses on self even in the midst of worship events that focus on Christ.

LESSON OUTLINE

Introduction

A. Last Supper, Lord's Supper

Christians have shared in the Lord's Supper millions of times in the last 2,000 years. These celebrations trace their origin to a single meal shared by Jesus and His disciples in an upstairs room in Jerusalem. That was a bittersweet time for Jesus: He had looked forward to this fellowship meal, yet He knew that He would be betrayed that night by one of His friends. He knew that that betrayal would set in motion a series of events leading to His crucifixion.

At that historic meal, Jesus asked His disciples to remember Him whenever they reenacted the meal in the future. This week's lesson studies Luke's account of this meal so that we might better understand and remember what our Savior faced on that night.

B. Lesson Background

Each of the four Gospels has an account of the last supper, with varying details. For example, John records the meal, but makes no mention of the institution of the Lord's Supper by Jesus. Luke is unique is telling of more than one cup used by Jesus. These distinctives are not in conflict, and each adds to the rich picture of the last supper.

Luke 22:7, which precedes today's lesson text, describes the occasion of the last supper as "the day of unleavened bread, when the passover [lamb] must be killed." This would have been Friday, before the Sabbath/Saturday of that week. We must remember, however, that most Jews reckoned a new day as beginning at sundown, so their Friday would have begun at sundown on Thursday by our system. Sundown would have been at about 6 PM, so this Passover celebration by Jesus and His disciples probably took place within the time frame of 7–10 PM on Thursday night by modern reckoning.

I. Somber Celebration
(LUKE 22:14-20)
A. Last Passover (vv. 14-16)

14. And when the hour was come, he sat down, and the twelve apostles with him.

Mention of *the hour* indicates the time for the meal after all the preparations are finished. These preparations likely include the provision of a low table with pillowed couches around it. If such a configuration is correct, then *sat down* means that the participants are reclining on their sides (compare Matthew 26:20).

15. And he said unto them, With desire I have desired to eat this passover with you before I suffer.

Jesus' opening comments introduce both a uniqueness and a sense of finality to this meal. He reveals (again) that He anticipates a disturbing thing that is coming: His suffering. This is the word sometimes translated as "passion" (see Acts 1:3); it refers to the humiliation and pain that Jesus endures in His trials, flogging, and being nailed to a wooden cross to die.

The writers of the Gospels present Jesus as being aware of this inevitable passion-time. These writers also depict the disciples as being generally oblivious in this regard. It is doubtful that any of those 12 imagine that the lifeless body of Jesus will be lying in a tomb less than 24 hours after this meal concludes.

16. For I say unto you, I will not any more eat thereof, until it be fulfilled in the kingdom of God.

At the same time, Jesus introduces a note of hopeful anticipation. He reveals that He will eat again, but only under very different circumstances. His future eating will be in connection with the fulfillment of *the kingdom of God*. This will be feasting on the other side of death, celebration in a new reality. We are reminded of Jesus' picture of a future messianic banquet (see Luke 14:15-24; 22:29, 30), a table where people from all nations will be welcome (13:29).

B. Last Cup (vv. 17, 18)

17. And he took the cup, and gave thanks, and said, Take this, and divide it among yourselves.

Luke mentions two instances in which Jesus and the disciples share a cup at this meal: here and in verse 20 (below). Since this is a Passover feast (called *seder* by modern Jews), there are several traditional parts to the meal. We do not

know exactly how Jesus and His disciples organize these traditions, but celebration of a modern seder involves drinking from four cups during the meal. Some identify the cup in this verse with the seder's third cup, called "the cup of blessing."

The Greek word behind *gave thanks* is the origin of the word *Eucharist*. This designation is used in some Christian traditions for the Lord's Supper.

18. For I say unto you, I will not drink of the fruit of the vine, until the kingdom of God shall come.

As in verse 16, Jesus emphasizes the finality of this occasion. There will be no more festive meals for Him *until the kingdom of God shall come.*

There is debate over what constitutes the establishment *(shall come)* of God's kingdom. Luke 24:41-43 records that Jesus does indeed eat with His disciples after His resurrection. But there is no indication that that meal involves *the fruit of the vine,* and it certainly is not a Passover celebration. We should understand that the language of the verse before us indicates a transition: Jesus and His followers are moving from one era into another. In the new era, Jesus' disciples (Christians) will share the cup with Jesus each time they reenact this last supper as the Lord's Supper.

What Do You Think?

How can we keep the Lord's Supper from becoming a source of division rather than unity?

Talking Points for Your Discussion

- Differences in doctrinal interpretation
- Undue focus on accessories
- Entrenched traditions
- Other

There is also debate over what is meant by *fruit of the vine.* If taken literally, this refers to grapes. But you do not drink grapes, so we can assume that Jesus is referring to the juice of grapes. The debate concerns whether or not this juice is fermented— whether it is wine or fresh grape juice.

Many scholars conclude that it is unlikely that first-century Jews would use fresh grape juice at a Passover meal, so they think that it is wine. Others stress the point that the gospel texts say *fruit of the vine* specifically (Matthew 26:29; Mark 14:25), not *wine* as in, for example, Acts 2:13. At any rate, the importance in using this beverage is not its alcohol content, but its color. It is a deep red with a hint of blue—a purplish-red color we call *crimson*. This is very close to the color of blood, making this cup filled with the fruit of the vine a meaningful symbol for use in the Lord's Supper (see Luke 22:20, below).

C. Last Loaf (v. 19)

19. And he took bread, and gave thanks, and brake it, and gave unto them, saying, This is my body which is given for you: this do in remembrance of me.

Passover traditions dictate that bread used at this feast be baked without leaven (yeast). This is in accordance with the first Passover meal, celebrated on the eve of the Israelites' departure from Egypt. On that occasion, the people needed to bake their bread quickly, not having time for dough to rise. Thus it was unleavened (Exodus 12, especially v. 39).

After giving thanks again (see also Luke 24:30), Jesus makes two enduring comments. The first one is the statement *this is my body*. Some Christian traditions take this to mean that the bread used in Communion services today is somehow transformed into the physical body of Christ. However, this is not what Jesus intends for us to understand. The rich symbolism of the bread lies in breaking the loaf (as Christ's body is damaged on the cross), in giving the loaf (as Christ gives His life willingly as a sacrifice for our sins), and in the sharing of the loaf among all participants (as Christians share a common faith in Christ).

The other enduring comment is the command *this do in remembrance of me*. This indicates two things. First, there is a coming time when the disciples of Jesus will celebrate this meal without His being physically present—after all, you don't have to "remember" someone who is right there with you physically. Jesus is to be remembered for all He did and said, and most of all for the salvation His death provides (see Hebrews 10:10).

Second, Jesus' command indicates that the disciples are to reenact His symbolic actions in the future. As they do, the last supper becomes the

Lord's Supper in the church (compare 1 Corinthians 11:20-26).

> **What Do You Think?**
> Besides *this do in remembrance of me*, what would be some good inscriptions for Communion tables?
> *Talking Points for Your Discussion*
> - Matthew 26:26, 27
> - Mark 14:24
> - Luke 22:17
> - Acts 2:42
> - 1 Corinthians 11:26
> - Other

D. New Covenant (v. 20)

20. Likewise also the cup after supper, saying, This cup is the new testament in my blood, which is shed for you.

The word *likewise* indicates that this particular cup is also blessed with a thanksgiving and shared among the disciples. As already mentioned, a traditional Passover meal can involve several cups, each symbolizing something different. With this final cup of the evening, Jesus ties the contents of the cup to His death. He does so by comparing the cup with His blood, which is soon to be shed in His upcoming torture and crucifixion.

The fact that this cup signifies *the new testament* indicates a new agreement between God and humanity. This is the new covenant promised in Jeremiah 31:31-34, a covenant of forgiveness (compare Exodus 24:8). The old regime of law is passing, and a new era of grace is beginning. Whenever we drink the cup in our celebrations of the Lord's Supper, we should remember what a great blessing it is to live under this covenant.

II. Sobering Prediction
(LUKE 22:21-30)
A. Hand of Betrayal (vv. 21, 22)

21, 22. But, behold, the hand of him that betrayeth me is with me on the table. And truly the Son of man goeth, as it was determined: but woe unto that man by whom he is betrayed!

The reality of dark deeds yet to come again creeps into the meal. We easily imagine that Jesus' tone of voice changes dramatically as He reveals that there is a traitor within the group. While there have been warnings about this before (see John 6:70, 71), this is the most blatant declaration thus far. Jesus demonstrates His divine knowledge of the plot against Him (compare Luke 22:1-6).

Jesus also reveals that His own future *was determined,* meaning that it has been part of God's plan for human salvation all along. Judas Iscariot's act of betrayal accomplishes God's purpose, but Judas's decision to turn traitor is his own choice, foreseen by God (Acts 1:16-20); Judas will be held responsible for his treachery (1:25).

Judas's actions remain one of the great mysteries of human history. How could one who was on such close terms with the Savior of the world betray his friend and teacher? We do not understand this fully, but Luke records that Judas is motivated by the presence of Satan in his heart (Luke 22:3) and the lure of money (22:5).

> *What Do You Think?*
> What are some ways people betray Jesus today? How do you protect yourself from doing so?
> *Talking Points for Your Discussion*
> - In thought life
> - In the workplace
> - In entertainment choices
> - "Don't assume you are the good soil [of Luke 8:15]" (Francis Chan, *Crazy Love*).
> - Other

❧ *FAMOUS (OR INFAMOUS) TRAITORS* ❧

Benedict Arnold had a distinguished career during America's Revolutionary War. Some of his military actions on land and water were simply brilliant. But Arnold was not nearly as good at "playing politics," and he was passed over for promotion as a result. In anger, he negotiated with the British and planned to turn over to them the American fort at West Point.

The unsuccessful plot resulted in Arnold's name becoming virtually synonymous with the word *traitor;* it is a label that overshadows all of Arnold's military successes. When someone is referred to as "a Benedict Arnold," we instinctively know that the reference is not to that man's military brilliance!

The same is true of Judas Iscariot. As an apostle, he took part in the magnificent physical and spiritual victories described in Luke 9:1-6. But to call someone "a Judas" today is not to affirm that person's devotion to the work of the Lord—quite the opposite! The church has had her traitors and defectors throughout the centuries. We do well to remember that "No man, having put his hand to the plough, and looking back, is fit for the kingdom of God" (Luke 9:62). —C. R. B.

B. Head of Boasting (vv. 23, 24)

23, 24. And they began to enquire among themselves, which of them it was that should do this thing. And there was also a strife among them, which of them should be accounted the greatest.

In the chaotic discussion that follows, we can imagine each disciple trying to outdo his companions by pledging higher and higher levels of loyalty to Jesus. At some point, this discussion seems to degenerate, making a transition from claims of having the greatest love for the Master to claims of being the greatest (compare Luke 9:46).

This discussion seems nearly insane from our perspective. Yet Jesus uses this confusion to give one of His last teaching lessons before the crucifixion.

> *What Do You Think?*
> Is there any place for a competitive spirit within the church? Why, or why not?
> *Talking Points for Your Discussion*
> - 1 Corinthians 11:19
> - Philippians 2:3
> - Hebrews 10:24
> - Other?

❧ *"GETTING IT"—OR NOT!* ❧

"You just don't get it!" is a common expression of frustration when people are disagreeing about something. It is a way of characterizing someone as uncaring or clueless. A wife may use this expression when her husband fails to perceive the level of importance she places on his attendance at a dinner with her family. In turn, he may use this expression when she doesn't grasp the importance of his playing golf for the second time in a week as part of the process of sealing a business deal.

We can imagine Jesus thinking *You just don't get it* during the last supper. He was trying to prepare His disciples for what He would be facing later that evening and the following morning. There He was about to confront the greatest crisis of His life, and His disciples were arguing over who would be greatest! They "didn't get it."

"Not getting it" can result from *tunnel vision,* an extreme narrowness of viewpoint. Jesus had to confront tunnel vision throughout His earthly ministry. May we heed both the problem and Jesus' responses to it.   —C. R. B.

C. Heart of Service (vv. 25-27)

25. And he said unto them, The kings of the Gentiles exercise lordship over them; and they that exercise authority upon them are called benefactors.

Rather than condemning the disciples for vying for position, Jesus uses an example that grabs their attention: that of earthly rulers. This includes the Romans, the hated occupiers of the Jewish homeland. Jesus' point is that the kings and other rulers exercise their power over people in a self-serving manner while thinking of themselves as benefactors in the process. Jesus' implication is that these Gentile rulers primarily benefit themselves. This underlying truth is well-known to Jesus' disciples.

26. But ye shall not be so: but he that is greatest among you, let him be as the younger; and he that is chief, as he that doth serve.

HOW TO SAY IT

Eucharist	*You*-kuh-rust.
Gethsemane	Geth-*sem*-uh-nee (G as in *get*).
Judas Iscariot	*Joo*-dus Iss-*care*-ee-ut.
messianic	mess-ee-*an*-ick.
seder	*say*-der.

Having established the pattern of self-serving rulers, Jesus gives two other examples of social priority to make his point. Younger men of the first century are considered social inferiors to their elders. Slaves or servants are always in a lesser position than their masters. Jesus turns this leadership model inside out by proclaiming the greatest one is not the person ordering others around, but the one who serves others.

27. For whether is greater, he that sitteth at meat, or he that serveth? is not he that sitteth at meat? but I am among you as he that serveth.

Jesus goes on to use the example of a banquet, asking if the one who is being served *(he that sitteth at meat)* is greater than the one who serves. This is the image of the rich man who presides over a lavish feast versus the servant who brings the food and clears the dishes. The immediate assumption of the rich man being the greater is thrown out when Jesus places himself in the role of the servant. Greatness in God's kingdom is found in serving others rather than self.

> *What Do You Think?*
> When was a time you were surprised to be blessed as you served someone else?
> *Talking Points for Your Discussion*
> - In a benevolence setting
> - In a teaching setting
> - In a counseling setting
> - Other

D. Honor of Faithfulness (vv. 28-30)

28. Ye are they which have continued with me in my temptations.

Jesus turns from His corrective rebuke to commend His disciples for staying true to Him during His temptations. By this Jesus refers to the times when He and His disciples were in physical danger from Jesus' opponents (compare John 11:8, 16). He may also be referring to the satanic attacks that were present throughout His ministry.

Sadly, however, the disciples will fall asleep during Jesus' great trial of agony in the Garden of Gethsemane (Luke 22:39-46). This disappointing performance by the disciples will be minor compared with what follows, however. When a mob led by one of the disciples comes to arrest Jesus, the disciples will abandon Jesus in the darkness and confusion.

29, 30. And I appoint unto you a kingdom, as my Father hath appointed unto me; that ye may eat and drink at my table in my kingdom, and sit on thrones judging the twelve tribes of Israel.

Finally, Jesus points the disciples to a wondrous future time when there will be another great fellowship meal. This will be in Jesus' kingdom. It is a marvelous image: a lavish table of food and drink, with the disciples reunited with Jesus. They will no longer be reclining on cushions since the table will be crowded with thrones for Jesus and the disciples. The disciples will have judging authority over the people of God, represented as *the twelve tribes of Israel.* But Jesus is the master king at this table, for it is His table. He is the King of kings, as appointed by God.

Conclusion

A. Remembering

Collective memory is important. It has been said that the one who controls the memories of a community controls its future. Some cultures value elderly people because they are the ones whose memory stretches back the furthest. As important as the issue of remembering is, however, another important issue is that of forgetting.

Sometimes we wish we had more control over our forgetting, for there are things we would like to forget but cannot. But certain things should be—must be—remembered. A memory that is neglected and unused will fade over the years. Memory works best when it is "jogged." How do we jog our memories about the most important things in life, things that must not be lost? Families may do this by taking out photo albums of past events, remembering loved ones who are gone but not forgotten. The church has a superb way of remembering the essential truths of the Christian faith in its celebration of the Lord's Supper.

Although there may be many variations in its practice, the Lord's Supper should always serve to

Visual for Lesson 4. *As you study verse 19, point to this visual and ask, "How can we better prepare ourselves for observing the Lord's Supper?"*

help us remember. The broken bread we use helps us remember the body of Christ, broken in the death on that lonely cross outside of Jerusalem. The cup should help us remember that our salvation was made possible through the blood of Christ, given freely as an acceptable sacrifice for our sins.

A paradox of the Lord's Supper is that while it symbolizes bloody brokenness, it is also a great unifying factor for the church. We remember Christ's body broken for us, but we should also look for the unbroken body, the church, which is the body of Christ on earth. We should share around the Lord's table in fellowship, not isolation. This is why it is called *Communion,* for we have communing fellowship with other Christians and with the Lord.

The next time you participate in your church's celebration of the Lord's Supper, take time to remember these things: blood as a price for your forgiveness, a body broken out of our Savior's love for us, and a body (the church) united in allegiance to its Lord.

B. Prayer

Father, as we remember Your Son in the loaf and cup, may You lead our hearts in joyful obedience toward Your throne of glory. We pray in the name of the one who died for us, amen.

C. Thought to Remember

Sharing in the Lord's Supper sustains our spirits.

INVOLVEMENT LEARNING

Some of the activities below are also found in the helpful student book, Adult Bible Class.
Don't forget to download the free reproducible page from www.standardlesson.com to enhance your lesson!

Into the Lesson

As learners arrive, give each a piece of red yarn that is 10" in length. Say, "Tie this in a loose bow on a finger. Keep it on until later in the class."

As class begins, summarize Joshua 2:1-13, then read Joshua 2:14-21. Comment: "That scarlet red cord became a mark that would tell the destroyers of Jericho, 'Pass over this house.' It was therefore similar to the blood marks the children of Israel had put over their doors in Egypt to escape God's avenging angel (Exodus 11, 12). Today we will use this red cord *[point to the one on your own finger]* to remind us of a Passover of greater significance: the one that directly preceded the crucifixion of Jesus, where His shed blood became the 'red stripe' that saves us from God's wrath."

Into the Word

Read today's text, Luke 22:14-30, aloud. Say, "Prepositions can be very significant. Let's see how." Prepare in advance four very large flash cards with the following prepositions, one each: *AMONG, BEFORE, UNTIL,* and *WITH.* As you show each word, ask, "What is the significance of this word as you see it in today's text?" This will encourage a close examination of the text; encourage free discussion. If your class is larger, you may wish to do this in small groups.

You should point out the following key concepts if learners do not do so. For *BEFORE,* Jesus notes this supper precedes His suffering (v. 15). For *UNTIL,* Jesus states what He will not do until fulfillment or coming of the kingdom of God (vv. 16-18). For *AMONG,* three matters may be noted: the cup and bread were shared among the group (vv. 17, 19), questions of betrayal and greatness occurred among the disciples (vv. 23, 24), and Jesus' response dealt with what it meant for Him to be among them (vv. 26, 27). For *WITH,* note that Judas's hand—the hand of the betrayer—was with that of Jesus on the table (v. 21).

As you move to discuss verses 24-27, distribute the "Who's the Greatest?" activity from the reproducible page, which you can download. This will highlight Jesus' utter superiority. You can do this as a whole-class response activity or have learners work in study pairs. Follow by asking two learners to read aloud Matthew 18:1-4 and Matthew 19:13, 14, one each. Then ask, "How could the 12 disciples dare argue about such an issue, especially considering the gravity of the occasion?" Discuss.

Option: Distribute copies of a facsimile "report card" with three subjects noted: (1) knowledge of the truth, (2) personal self-evaluation, and (3) spiritual progress. For each have the letter-grade *F* already assigned. Say, "The three *Fs* stand for 'Forgetting First Facts.' That was the disciples' mistake; it is often our mistake as well: we forget the basic facts of Jesus' sovereignty, we think more highly of ourselves than we should, and we end up looking like spiritual babies!" Discuss.

Into Life

Distribute copies of the "Eager" activity from the reproducible page, which you can download. This will get learners thinking about their level of enthusiasm for the things of the Spirit, including participation in the Lord's Supper. This can be a take-home activity if time is short.

Draw class attention back to the red yarn. Say, "Find a prominent place to hang this at home or work for the week ahead. Let it remind you daily that you are blessed indeed by the blood of Jesus."

Option: Prepare in advance "coins" made from lightweight cardboard. One side of the coins will carry the statement *I AM THE GREATEST!* The other side will say *JESUS IS THE GREATEST!* Give each learner a coin as you say, "This coin represents the choice to be made daily, but it's not a matter to be decided by a casual 'coin flip.' It is a matter of the will. Which side of the coin will you put up each day?"

THE LORD
LIVES

DEVOTIONAL READING: Luke 24:22-26
BACKGROUND SCRIPTURE: Luke 24:1-35

LUKE 24:13-21, 28-35

13 And, behold, two of them went that same day to a village called Emmaus, which was from Jerusalem about threescore furlongs.

14 And they talked together of all these things which had happened.

15 And it came to pass, that, while they communed together and reasoned, Jesus himself drew near, and went with them.

16 But their eyes were holden that they should not know him.

17 And he said unto them, What manner of communications are these that ye have one to another, as ye walk, and are sad?

18 And the one of them, whose name was Cleopas, answering said unto him, Art thou only a stranger in Jerusalem, and hast not known the things which are come to pass there in these days?

19 And he said unto them, What things? And they said unto him, Concerning Jesus of Nazareth, which was a prophet mighty in deed and word before God and all the people:

20 And how the chief priests and our rulers delivered him to be condemned to death, and have crucified him.

21 But we trusted that it had been he which should have redeemed Israel: and beside all this, to day is the third day since these things were done.

. . . .

28 And they drew nigh unto the village, whither they went: and he made as though he would have gone further.

29 But they constrained him, saying, Abide with us: for it is toward evening, and the day is far spent. And he went in to tarry with them.

30 And it came to pass, as he sat at meat with them, he took bread, and blessed it, and brake, and gave to them.

31 And their eyes were opened, and they knew him; and he vanished out of their sight.

32 And they said one to another, Did not our heart burn within us, while he talked with us by the way, and while he opened to us the scriptures?

33 And they rose up the same hour, and returned to Jerusalem, and found the eleven gathered together, and them that were with them,

34 Saying, The Lord is risen indeed, and hath appeared to Simon.

35 And they told what things were done in the way, and how he was known of them in breaking of bread.

KEY VERSE

And their eyes were opened, and they knew him; and he vanished out of their sight. —**Luke 24:31**

UNDYING HOPE

Unit 2: Resurrection Hope

LESSONS 4–9

LESSON AIMS

After participating in this lesson, each student will be able to:

1. Retell the encounter between Jesus and the two disciples on the road to Emmaus.

2. Explain how the two disciples changed from seeing Jesus as having failed their hopes to be Redeemer of Israel to energizing their hope that He is Savior of the world.

3. Sing a hymn or chorus that celebrates the risen Lord.

LESSON OUTLINE

Introduction

A. After the Funeral

In some traditions, a wake is held in the home of the deceased after a funeral. The body of the deceased is present in this ceremony, and food and drink are served to those who have come to pay their respects. In some churches, a meal is held in the church fellowship hall. But no matter what the tradition, everyone eventually goes home after a funeral. We cannot stay at the church, the funeral parlor, or the cemetery very long. We go home.

Jesus died less than 24 hours after He celebrated a Passover meal with His disciples. His body was buried late on a Friday afternoon, a rushed interment to beat the arrival of the Sabbath that began at sundown (John 19:31). The stunned disciples stayed together (John 20:19), but they shared sadness and shock more than food or drink. There had been no proper funeral for their friend and teacher.

The next day, Sunday, some of Jesus' disciples apparently did what we do after a funeral: they started for home. Two set out for Emmaus, a village outside Jerusalem. The unexpected turn that this trip took is the subject of this week's lesson.

B. Lesson Background

The Gospels highlight the role of the 12 apostles, but there were other followers of Jesus as well. We see this in the plurality of candidates available to replace Judas (Acts 1:23). The other, non-apostolic disciples included both men and women (see Luke 8:1-3). About 120 of them were gathered together in Jerusalem sometime between Jesus' resurrection and the Day of Pentecost (see Acts 1:15).

Our story today concerns two such disciples. The name of one is given as *Cleopas*. We have no other confirmable information about this man. But one intriguing suggestion is that he is the same as the *Cleophas* of John 19:25, mentioned as being the husband of one of the women named *Mary* who stood by the cross as Jesus died. That leads to the further theory that the other, unnamed disciple in today's lesson could be that Mary. If these two are husband and wife walking back to their home village of Emmaus in Luke 24:13, that would throw a certain light on today's story regarding the hospitality they offered to Jesus. But if (1) Mary the wife of Cleophas is the same as "Mary the mother of James," who had witnessed the empty tomb (Luke 24:10), and (2) Luke 24:22-24 establishes that the two disciples in today's text had not witnessed the empty tomb, then (3) the unnamed disciple of today's study would not be Mary the wife of Cleophas.

Jerusalem was the largest city in the region, perhaps 30,000–50,000 in population. It was surrounded by many small villages of a few hundred people each. The residents of these villages tended vineyards, fields, orchards, flocks, and herds. The temple city of Jerusalem was fed economically by these villagers, who traveled to Jerusalem several times a year for festivals and to pay an annual temple tax. Emmaus was one such village. Today we are uncertain of its actual site, since the village was likely destroyed in the Roman military campaign that swept through Palestine in AD 66–70.

I. Sad Walk
(LUKE 24:13, 14)

A. Departing from Jerusalem (v. 13)

13. And, behold, two of them went that same day to a village called Emmaus, which was from Jerusalem about threescore furlongs.

Our story begins with two people leaving Jerusalem for nearby Emmaus. The phrase *of them* refers back to "the eleven and . . . all the rest" of

HOW TO SAY IT

Cleopas	*Clee*-uh-pass.
Cleophas	*Klee*-o-fus.
Emmaus	Em-*may*-us.
Gorbachev	*Gore*-bah-*choff*.
Magdalene	*Mag*-duh-leen
	or Mag-duh-*lee*-nee.
Mikhail	Mih-kha-*ill*.
Nazareth	*Naz*-uh-reth.
Pentecost	*Pent*-ih-kost.
Sadducee	*Sad*-you-see.
Sanhedrin	*San*-huh-drun
	or San-*heed*-run.
Sergeyevich	Ser-*ghe*-yeh-vich.

Luke 24:9; thus these two are followers of Jesus. Their walk of *threescore furlongs* (about seven miles) will take them two or three hours. Luke does not say why the pair is going to Emmaus, but the likely reason is that they are returning home.

The phrase *that same day* refers us back to Luke 24:1, which discusses events on "the first day of the week" (compare Luke 24:21, 22). This is Sunday. Earlier that day, Mary Magdalene had led a group of women to Jesus' tomb in order to give His body a more fitting burial (Luke 23:55–24:10). They had found the tomb open and empty, being told by two angels that Jesus was risen from the dead.

This was reported to the apostles and others (Luke 24:9), but the report was met with general disbelief. Peter, however, went to check. He too found an empty tomb (24:11, 12).

B. Discussion on the Road (v. 14)

14. And they talked together of all these things which had happened.

The two disciples are talking freely, unconstrained by the atmosphere of fear in Jerusalem (compare John 20:19). They have much to talk about, given recent events! These include the triumphal entry of Jesus into Jerusalem, the controversial cleansing of the temple, Jesus' arrest and trials, the crucifixion and quick death of Jesus, His burial, and (especially) the reports of the empty tomb and angelic announcements of Jesus' resurrection. There certainly is a lot to talk about!

II. Stranger Joins
(LUKE 24:15-21)

A. Concealed Identity (vv. 15, 16)

15. And it came to pass, that, while they communed together and reasoned, Jesus himself drew near, and went with them.

Luke pictures the two disciples engaged in heavy discussion. We are not told where Jesus comes from, and the two disciples seem too engrossed in conversation to notice. By the time they are aware of His presence, He is walking alongside them. It is not unusual in Jesus' day for unacquainted travelers to walk together and talk. This would be something like talking with a fellow passenger during a plane flight today without expecting to see that person again.

16. But their eyes were holden that they should not know him.

This is an early spring day, so there is likely a chill in the air. The travelers perhaps are "bundled up" a bit, with facial features not easily seen. The failure of the two disciples to recognize Jesus is attributable to more than a scarf across the bottom half of His face, however. The fact that *their eyes were holden* indicates a divine prevention of recognizing Jesus until the proper time (compare Mark 16:12).

❧ GRIEF-FILLED WALKS AND TALKS ❧

Assassinations form a dark thread in the tapestry of American history. Many of us are old enough to remember the assassinations of President John F. Kennedy in 1963, of Dr. Martin Luther King, Jr. in 1968, etc. We retain vivid mental images of such tragic days. Those were days of shock, disbelief, and grief. Many attempted to cope by talking through their anguish with others.

Jesus' walk with two disciples on the road to Emmaus was both similar to and different from those events. The sadness at the violent, unjust death of a leader was a similarity. Also similar was the shared anguish as the disciples talked through their grief. But one thing was very different: unbeknownst to those grieving disciples, their leader was alive and talking with them!

Grief is part of the human condition. But when we lift our grief to God in prayer, we do so in the name of our living leader, our living Lord! Because He lives, He is the one who ultimately dries all tears (Revelation 21:4).   —C. R. B.

B. Questioned Conversation (v. 17)

17. And he said unto them, What manner of communications are these that ye have one to another, as ye walk, and are sad?

Whether by tone of voice or facial expression, Jesus notices the sadness of the two disciples. Perhaps their talking is punctuated by sobs of grief. We can also surmise that Jesus sees the deep sadness in their hearts (see John 2:25).

The question Jesus asks does not mean that He is trying to get information that He lacks. He already knows why they are sad. The question, rather, is intended to be a conversation starter.

> *What Do You Think?*
> If Jesus visited you this week, what would He most likely find you discussing?
> *Talking Points for Your Discussion*
> ▪ Over lunch at work
> ▪ With family in the evenings
> ▪ While socializing with friends
> ▪ With fellow Christians after Sunday worship
> ▪ Other

C. Incredulous Response (v. 18)

18. And the one of them, whose name was Cleopas, answering said unto him, Art thou only a stranger in Jerusalem, and hast not known the things which are come to pass there in these days?

With the city walls of Jerusalem perhaps still in sight, the two disciples know that this stranger has also come from Jerusalem. It is therefore difficult for them to understand how He can be unaware of the stunning events of the past week. On the identity of Cleopas, see the Lesson Background.

D. Recounted Events (vv. 19-21)

19. And he said unto them, What things? And they said unto him, Concerning Jesus of Nazareth, which was a prophet mighty in deed and word before God and all the people.

Jesus is not mocking these two. Rather, He is drawing them into a conversation. Their reply to His question *What things?* gives us a four-point perspective regarding what at least some followers of Jesus believe about Him.

First, Jesus' background is known: He is from Nazareth, a village in Galilee (compare Luke 4:16). Jesus' opponents also are aware of this (Luke 4:34; John 19:19). Second, Jesus is understood to be a prophet (compare Matthew 21:11). This means that the people see Jesus as having been appointed by God to speak for God.

Third, Jesus has been *mighty in deed and word* (compare Acts 7:22). Jesus' reputation among the people has been built on both His miracles (Luke

7:21) and His powerful preaching (4:22). Fourth, Jesus' ministry has been done in the presence of *God and all the people*. These were not secret things, but have been accomplished in public, widely known (compare Acts 26:26).

> **What Do You Think?**
> How is the way you explain Jesus similar to and
>   different from the way Cleopas explained Him?
> *Talking Points for Your Discussion*
> - Matthew 10:32, 33
> - Acts 17:22-31
> - 1 Corinthians 9:19-23
> - 1 Peter 3:15

20. And how the chief priests and our rulers delivered him to be condemned to death, and have crucified him.

The chief priests are the temple elites from the Sadducee party. The *rulers* are the members of the Jewish high council, the Sanhedrin. How Jesus ended up on a Roman cross is not a mystery to the people. They realize that the Jewish masters of Jerusalem had collaborated with the Romans to secure Jesus' death. This is the big news that the stranger seems to have missed—the death of a prophet through the hands of their own religious leaders. We can detect in this response a note of dismay and awareness of injustice.

21. But we trusted that it had been he which should have redeemed Israel: and beside all this, to day is the third day since these things were done.

The first half of this verse reveals the biggest reason for the disciples' sadness. Above all, Jesus' death seems to have signaled an end to their hope of Jesus being the one chosen by God to lead their nation out of bondage (compare Luke 1:68; 2:38).

In all of this, Luke wants us to understand that although these two disciples hold a very high estimate of Jesus that is correct in many ways, they have missed the central aspect of what He has been doing. He did not come to redeem Israel politically, but to save people from the bondage of sin.

If seen in a political or nationalistic sense, the death of Jesus is a tragic end to such hopes. If seen according to the plan of God, though, Jesus' death is part of a strategy to bring salvation. It is necessary that Jesus' death be followed by His resurrection to show God's vindication (see Acts 2:31-36). The fact that *to day is the third day since these things were done* ties this conversation to Luke 24:1, 46.

> **What Do You Think?**
> When was a time for you that dashed hopes eventually resulted in something unexpected and ultimately better?
> *Talking Points for Your Discussion*
> - Regarding a health issue
> - Regarding a family issue
> - Regarding a church issue
> - Regarding a relationship issue
> - Other

III. Savior Reveals
(LUKE 24:28-35)
A. Hospitality Extended (vv. 28, 29)

28, 29. And they drew nigh unto the village, whither they went: and he made as though he would have gone further. But they constrained him, saying, Abide with us: for it is toward evening, and the day is far spent. And he went in to tarry with them.

When the trio arrives at Emmaus, the two disciples have reached their destination. It is late afternoon, but Jesus (whose identity is still hidden) seems as if He is continuing on. Although unaware of the identity of this stranger, the two disciples extend Him hospitality. *Abide with us* is an invitation for a meal and a bed for the night.

We wonder what motivates the two to extend such hospitality (compare Judges 19:15-21). One clue may be found in the preceding verses of Luke 24:25-27 (not in today's text). There Luke tells us that this mysterious stranger has given the pair an in-depth lesson on the prophecies of Scripture concerning the Messiah. They want to hear more from this man, for the wheels are turning in their heads.

B. Bread Broken (vv. 30, 31)

30. And it came to pass, as he sat at meat with them, he took bread, and blessed it, and brake, and gave to them.

HOW WERE YOUR EYES OPENED?

Visual for
Lesson 5

Point to this visual as you introduce the discussion question associated with verse 32.

Some think that what happens here is reminiscent of the last supper (see Luke 22:19). At least two things work against this idea: Jesus' statement in Luke 22:16 (see last week's study) and the lack of any cup mentioned (compare 22:17, 20). Further, the blessing and breaking of bread was not a new thing at the last supper (see Matthew 14:19). Since the eyes of these two disciples are opened to recognize Jesus only after the blessing and breaking of bread (v. 31, next), they likely see something personally familiar in Jesus' actions.

31. And their eyes were opened, and they knew him; and he vanished out of their sight.

What happens now is completely unexpected. Whatever has been keeping the two disciples from recognizing Jesus is removed, and they now realize the risen Lord has been sitting right there with them! No sooner does this glorious realization dawn on these two than Jesus is gone. He does not merely duck into the shadows—He vanishes. Jesus' postresurrection appearances and disappearances have an aura of "suddenness" about them (compare Matthew 28:9; John 20:19, 26; 21:4).

❧ BLINDNESS AND CHANGE ❧

K'hron Green was 15 years old when he lost his sight in May 2008 as a result of a car accident. He was sent to a rehabilitation facility in the Detroit area, where he was angry and defiant at first. But over the next three years, he became a mentor to others who had sustained traumatic brain injuries

as he had. Green's physical eyes were effectively closed, but the eyes of his heart were opened. His speech therapist describes the change in his outlook on life as "just shy of a miracle."

Jesus' disciples suffered great trauma in seeing their leader killed. But that trauma wasn't what kept the disciples on the road to Emmaus from recognizing Jesus. Their "blindness" was from God, and it was He who lifted it.

The disciples' temporary blindness in this regard was accompanied by a spiritual blindness of mistaken expectations of what the Messiah was to accomplish. Jesus had to contend with this kind of blindness right up until His ascension (see Acts 1:6). But the one who opened the eyes of the physically blind (Luke 7:21, 22) still works to correct spiritual blindness. As He does so in our lives, may we be mentors to those who still need to "see" Jesus.   —C. R. B.

C. Hearts Burned (v. 32)

32. And they said one to another, Did not our heart burn within us, while he talked with us by the way, and while he opened to us the scriptures?

Not only do the two disciples understand that Jesus is risen, they also are better able to interpret their experiences on the road with Jesus. They now realize why they had experienced a sensation described as a burning in the heart. At the time, they probably could explain that sensation only in terms of the marvelous Scripture lesson they were receiving from the stranger. But now they realize the supernatural cause: the presence of the risen Lord. They have been getting information from the best possible source!

> *What Do You Think?*
> What was an occasion when you had "a goose bump moment" regarding a sudden realization about Jesus?
> *Talking Points for Your Discussion*
> ▪ During a time of personal Bible study
> ▪ During a sermon
> ▪ When sharing the gospel with another
> ▪ Other

D. Risen Lord Proclaimed (vv. 33-35)

33. And they rose up the same hour, and returned to Jerusalem, and found the eleven gathered together, and them that were with them.

These two disciples cannot wait until morning to share their experience. So they scurry back to Jerusalem, perhaps even arriving after dark. Their return must be surprising to the apostles who are gathered with other disciples, but not as surprising as the news the two from Emmaus are given even before they share their own experience.

What Do You Think?

When was a time you were convicted to do something "the same hour" of your conviction? How did things turn out?

Talking Points for Your Discussion
- Administering or receiving baptism (Acts 16:33)
- Performing an act of benevolence
- Confronting wrongdoing
- Other

---

34. Saying, The Lord is risen indeed, and hath appeared to Simon.

The Greek sentence structure indicates that this is the report of those still in Jerusalem. Earlier that day, Simon Peter himself had encountered the risen Lord (see 1 Corinthians 15:5). Placed alongside Luke 24:36-39 (next week's lesson), what we see here is a mixture of belief and unbelief among the members of this core group. Any remaining doubts will be dispelled soon enough. The report we see here has been repeated every Easter, every Resurrection Sunday since: *The Lord is risen indeed!*

35. And they told what things were done in the way, and how he was known of them in breaking of bread.

Now the two disciples from Emmaus tell their own story. The fact that they relate the story from *what things were done in the way* to *how he was known of them in the breaking of bread* means that they do not leave anything out.

We should not expect to have a visual experience of the risen Christ today, nor is it necessary. We rest in His promise that "where two or three are gathered together in my name, there am I in the midst of them" (Matthew 18:20). As Simon Peter affirms many years later, "whom having not seen, ye love; in whom, though now ye see him not, yet believing, ye rejoice with joy unspeakable" (1 Peter 1:8). Hallelujah, He is risen indeed!

Conclusion
A. He Is Risen Indeed!

During the twentieth century, the Soviet Union was officially an atheist state where persecutions of Christians and the church were common. The final days of the Soviet Union witnessed a beginning of *glasnost* (meaning "openness") in that society, and some interesting things happened.

One of these took place during one of the last great May Day parades in Moscow. After the parade's seemingly endless procession of troops and military equipment, a small, ragtag group entered Red Square. The group consisted of shabbily dressed priests and other Christians—those who had felt the government's persecution firsthand. The leader carried a large cross, which he raised high as they approached the reviewing stand.

On the reviewing balcony was Mikhail Sergeyevich Gorbachev, the ruler of that Communist empire. The small group stopped in front of and below this powerful man and his entourage, the masters of millions of people. The huge crowd watched with interest, and a hush came over the people when the Christians stopped. The leader, holding the cross, raised his voice as he said, "Mikhail Sergeyevich, Christ is risen!"

In a world soaked with unbelief, this message never changes. Christ is risen from the dead. The world can never be the same because the Son of God has conquered death. May our hearts burn with the reality of the risen Lord!

B. Prayer

Father, Your Son is risen indeed! Help us to open eyes to see that fact. We pray this through the power of Jesus' precious name, amen.

C. Thought to Remember

Encounter the risen Christ again today.

INVOLVEMENT LEARNING

Some of the activities below are also found in the helpful student book, Adult Bible Class.
Don't forget to download the free reproducible page from www.standardlesson.com to enhance your lesson!

Into the Lesson

Before learners arrive, draw on the board a large time line with the following reference points: *Palm Sunday, Monday, Tuesday, Wednesday, Thursday, Friday, Saturday, Resurrection Sunday.* Give each learner a few index cards and a hymnal or other song book of Christian music. Say, "Find compositions with lyrics that depict one or more events of Jesus' final week. Write lines from your discoveries on the index cards, one entry per card."

As a group, discuss how the cards should be arranged on the time line; affix cards in the proper location as conclusions are reached. (You may wish to consult a final-week chronology in a Bible dictionary in advance.) Emphasize that while the story of the crucifixion and resurrection is familiar to many, it should never lose its significance in our lives.

Alternative: Place in chairs copies of the "Jesus' Final Week" activity from the reproducible page, which you can download, for learners to work on as they arrive. Your discussion of the results will serve as the transition to Into the Word.

Into the Word

Bring construction paper for five pairs or groups of three to have two sheets each. (Smaller classes can delete the assignment for Group 3.) Furnish each pair/group a handout with the following identical instructions: "Read your assigned verses and identify the emotions expressed or implied in the passage. Then draw faces that express those emotions, one emotion per face. Answer the questions posed." Below these common instructions, each handout will include one of the following sets of individualized instructions.

Group 1: Luke 24:13-17. What were the "all these things" (v. 14) that these disciples were discussing? What emotion or emotions do you think they were experiencing? Why? What happened that interrupted their intense conversation?

Group 2: Luke 24:18-21. What emotion or emotions do you think the disciples experienced as the result of Jesus' question in verse 17? Why? Does verse 21 indicate an additional emotion? If so, what was it?

Group 3: Luke 24:22-27. Although these verses are not part of the lesson text, they reveal that the two disciples had heard a report of the resurrection. What emotion did they seem to experience as they recalled that report? How do you think their emotions changed, if at all, as Jesus chided them and began to explain the Scriptures?

Group 4: Luke 24:28-31. What emotion did the two disciples reveal as they urged Jesus to stay with them? What did Jesus do that drew the disciples' reaction? What emotion do you think they experienced because of the way Jesus left them?

Group 5: Luke 24:32-35. What emotion did the disciples experience as Jesus talked with them about the Scriptures? What role do you think this emotion played in their decision to return to Jerusalem right away? What emotion might they have been feeling as they shared the story of their encounter with Jesus?

Give each group time to show the faces they have drawn and give brief explanations. Stress the point that there was a major transformation in their emotions once they realized Jesus was alive.

Into Life

Ask learners to share times when they were disappointed or in despair over unmet expectations, only to have their expectations exceeded by something else. What role did Christian faith (or lack of faith) play in all this?

Option 1: End the class with a time of praise and a prayer of thanks for the "exceeded expectations" we have in Christ. *Option 2:* End the class by having one of your musically gifted learners lead in singing some stanzas of a familiar hymn or song about the resurrection.

The Lord Lives

THE LORD
APPEARS

DEVOTIONAL READING: 1 Corinthians 15:1-8
BACKGROUND SCRIPTURE: Luke 24:36-53

LUKE 24:36-53

36 And as they thus spake, Jesus himself stood in the midst of them, and saith unto them, Peace be unto you.

37 But they were terrified and affrighted, and supposed that they had seen a spirit.

38 And he said unto them, Why are ye troubled? and why do thoughts arise in your hearts?

39 Behold my hands and my feet, that it is I myself: handle me, and see; for a spirit hath not flesh and bones, as ye see me have.

40 And when he had thus spoken, he shewed them his hands and his feet.

41 And while they yet believed not for joy, and wondered, he said unto them, Have ye here any meat?

42 And they gave him a piece of a broiled fish, and of an honeycomb.

43 And he took it, and did eat before them.

44 And he said unto them, These are the words which I spake unto you, while I was yet with you, that all things must be fulfilled, which were written in the law of Moses, and in the prophets, and in the psalms, concerning me.

45 Then opened he their understanding, that they might understand the scriptures,

46 And said unto them, Thus it is written, and thus it behooved Christ to suffer, and to rise from the dead the third day:

47 And that repentance and remission of sins should be preached in his name among all nations, beginning at Jerusalem.

48 And ye are witnesses of these things.

49 And, behold, I send the promise of my Father upon you: but tarry ye in the city of Jerusalem, until ye be endued with power from on high.

50 And he led them out as far as to Bethany, and he lifted up his hands, and blessed them.

51 And it came to pass, while he blessed them,  he was parted from them, and carried up into heaven.

52 And they worshipped him, and returned to Jerusalem with great joy:

53 And were continually in the temple, praising and blessing God. Amen.

KEY VERSE

He said unto them, These are the words which I spake unto you, while I was yet with you, that all things must be fulfilled, which were written in the law of Moses, and in the prophets, and in the psalms, concerning me. —Luke 24:44

UNDYING HOPE

Unit 2: Resurrection Hope

LESSON AIMS

After participating in this lesson, each student will be able to:

1. List the points of evidence for believing in Jesus' resurrection.

2. Relate the importance of this evidence to the call to be witnesses for Christ.

3. Make a list of opportunities that he or she will have to be a witness for Christ in the next few weeks.

LESSON OUTLINE

Introduction
  A. Where Does God Live?
  B. Lesson Background
I. Seeing Jesus (LUKE 24:36-43)
  A. Startling Appearance (vv. 36, 37)
  B. Challenged Belief (vv. 38-40)
  C. Unmistakable Demonstration (vv. 41-43)
    Seeing Ghosts?
II. Understanding Scripture (LUKE 24:44-49)
  A. Imperative (v. 44)
  B. Explanation (vv. 45, 46)
  C. Commission (vv. 47, 48)
  D. Promise (v. 49)
III. Worshipping Jesus (LUKE 24:50-53)
  A. Dramatic Departure (vv. 50, 51)
    Lies, and Where Hope Lies
  B. Joyous Reaction (vv. 52, 53)
Conclusion
  A. Where Did Jesus Go?
  B. Prayer
  C. Thought to Remember

Introduction

A. Where Does God Live?

Many parents have been challenged by a small child who asks innocently, "Where does God live?" Our answer may reflect a struggle to answer on the child's level. We might say, "God lives in our hearts," only to be met with a quizzical, "How?" We might say, "God lives in Heaven," only to be asked, "Where is Heaven?" We might say, "God lives in the church," only to have the child wonder which church in town that might be.

Where does God live? The problem with this question is that the one asking it may assume that God has a physical need to live somewhere, and our answers may reflect this. How we answer may be true in one sense but inaccurate in another sense at the same time.

Our desire to understand "where God lives" is addressed in today's lesson, which concerns the ascension of Jesus Christ. That was a dramatic moment unlike anything ever witnessed (with the possible exception of 2 Kings 2:11). Jesus did not rise from the dead to resume His earthly life and eventually die again. He rose to be with His disciples for a short time and then return to the Father.

B. Lesson Background

The ancients believed in an "up-down" universe. "Below" was the underworld that housed the dead; "above" was Heaven, the realm of celestial beings. When Jesus returned to the Father, He *ascended*—that is, He went up into the sky. Everyone who witnessed this would have understood that to be the proper way to reach Heaven (compare 2 Corinthians 12:2).

Even so, we know that there is no physical "place" in the sky (or anywhere else) where God lives because we understand the abode of God in a spiritual, nonspatial way, as Paul did (see Acts 17:24). Thus when reading of Jesus' ascension, we should not be sidetracked by trying to account for all of the physical characteristics of His departure.

What is important is to grasp the significance of Jesus' ascension and to remember His final words just before that event. In so doing, we share the faith of those who heard those words as confirmation that Jesus had been dead, had come back to life, and then underwent an amazing transition.

In last week's lesson, we saw Jesus joining in mysterious fashion two disciples on the way to Emmaus (Luke 24:15). He later disappeared from their sight after they recognized Him (24:31). These disciples returned to report their encounter to the larger group in Jerusalem (24:33). In today's lesson, Jesus appears to the disciples in a startling way.

I. Seeing Jesus
(LUKE 24:36-43)

A. Startling Appearance (vv. 36, 37)

36, 37. And as they thus spake, Jesus himself stood in the midst of them, and saith unto them, Peace be unto you. But they were terrified and affrighted, and supposed that they had seen a spirit.

We are given the impression that this appearance of Jesus is sudden, and no further explanation of that fact is offered here. As we try to understand this, we can note a couple of things.

First, there is no sense that Jesus opens a door and walks into the room (compare John 20:19, with the detail given of a locked door). This is not depicted as Jesus walking through walls, but as the reality that walls and locked doors cannot keep the risen Lord from appearing in the room.

Second, we can see that Jesus' appearance is completely unexpected and startling. These disciples know for certain that Jesus had died, and to see Him standing among them causes shock and fear. They recognize Jesus immediately—that's the very reason for their terror! His identity is not hidden as it was in Luke 24:16 (last week's lesson).

Just two verses prior, the gathered disciples had affirmed that "the Lord is risen indeed" (last week's lesson). Thus we see a mixture of belief and unbelief when that statement is placed alongside the fact that the disciples now interpret His appearance to be that of a spirit (compare Matthew 14:26). The lingering unbelief of those gathered is about to be thoroughly dispelled.

Jesus' greeting *Peace be unto you* is not just a way of saying "Hello," but is intended to calm the

fears of the disciples (compare John 20:19-21). He wants to bring peace to their hearts.

B. Challenged Belief (vv. 38-40)

38. And he said unto them, Why are ye troubled? and why do thoughts arise in your hearts?

Jesus does not ask His questions because He needs information that He lacks. He already knows why they are troubled. The questions are for the benefit of the disciples—they need to examine their own doubts, their own hearts. Their doubting hearts make them unwilling to trust what their eyes see. It is a critical moment, the line between belief and disbelief. Jesus fully intends to give the disciples cause to believe that He is risen from the dead so they will put their faith in Him, the risen Lord.

39, 40. Behold my hands and my feet, that it is I myself: handle me, and see; for a spirit hath not flesh and bones, as ye see me have. And when he had thus spoken, he shewed them his hands and his feet.

Jesus does not expect the disciples to trust their eyes alone, so He invites them to touch Him (compare John 20:25-27; 1 John 1:1). By examining His hands and feet, they can see the wounds from the nails used to fasten Him to the cross.

While the crucifixion narratives in the Gospels themselves do not describe Jesus specifically as being nailed to a wooden cross, the use of nails and the resulting puncture wounds are clearly in

Visual for Lesson 6. *Point to this visual as you ask, "What are times in your life when the promised presence of Christ of Matthew 28:20 seems most real?"*

mind here (compare John 20:25; Acts 2:23). The Romans sometimes tie their victims to crosses using ropes, but nails are also a common method to affix hands and feet. Jesus shows His hands and feet because they bear marks of recent nail wounds. This indicates that the apparent Jesus in the room is neither an imposter nor a spirit.

For Jesus to say that He has *flesh and bones* is not intended to give us great insights into the nature of His resurrected body. Rather, Jesus' simple intent is to demonstrate that He is physically present. It is in this light that the disciples are invited to view His body and touch it.

What Do You Think?

How should you react when someone claims to have seen Jesus either physically or as a disembodied spirit?

Talking Points for Your Discussion

- Luke 17:23, 24
- John 20:29
- Acts 9:27; 10:41; 23:11
- 1 Corinthians 9:1
- Revelation 1:7
- Other

C. Unmistakable Demonstration (vv. 41-43)

41. And while they yet believed not for joy, and wondered, he said unto them, Have ye here any meat?

Jesus, knowing that some still doubt, offers an even more substantive demonstration of His physical presence: He asks for food so that He can eat it while they watch. *Meat* is used here in an older sense of our English word to mean "food in general" (as opposed to drink). Jesus has shown in His ministry a certain disregard for food (Matthew 4:1-4; Luke 12:22, 29; John 4:31-34). Thus it is highly unlikely that Jesus asks for food merely to satisfy a sense of hunger. Rather, His request is intended to dispel any lingering doubts about the reality of His physical existence as the disciples watch Him eat.

Before we are too critical of these disciples, we should put ourselves in their place. Imagine that you saw a person die right before your eyes. Then you attended an open-casket funeral, after which you witnessed the casket being lowered into the ground and the grave being filled with dirt. Then you gather with others somewhere for a memorial meal. Over the course of time, some people show up claiming that the deceased is alive again—you're confused. Suddenly, the person whose body was buried appears in the living room and begins to talk with you. You would be hard pressed to understand immediately what is happening! That is what is going on with these disciples.

42, 43. And they gave him a piece of a broiled fish, and of an honeycomb. And he took it, and did eat before them.

Jesus' request is honored quickly. His eating proves He is no ghost. He is the real man they have followed for over three years, now risen from the dead. If He were merely an apparition or figment of their imaginations, the tomb would not be empty (Luke 24:3).

❧ SEEING GHOSTS? ❧

People are fascinated with ghost stories. Witness the popularity as a tourist attraction of the 160-room Winchester Mystery House™ in San Jose, California. Some claim that visitors have experienced the presence of ghosts there hundreds of times. Many people visit in order to have just such an experience.

This house owes its quirks of construction to Sarah Winchester (1839–1922). She believed that her late husband, the inventor of the Winchester rifle, was cursed because of all the deaths caused by his invention. A spiritualist convinced her that she too was cursed and could escape only if she were involved in continuous construction on the house. She acted on that belief for decades.

Consulting the spirits of the dead was one of "the abominations" to ancient Israel (Deuteronomy 18:9-13). But Jesus did not stand in the midst of the disciples because they held a séance to "call Him up" (compare 1 Samuel 28). They weren't expecting Him at all! And Jesus appeared in bodily form, not as a spirit or apparition. Sarah Winchester may well have been delusional, but Jesus proved that the disciples were not. May we seek the living Jesus only.   —C. R. B.

II. Understanding Scripture
(LUKE 24:44-49)
A. Imperative (v. 44)

44. And he said unto them, These are the words which I spake unto you, while I was yet with you, that all things must be fulfilled, which were written in the law of Moses, and in the prophets, and in the psalms, concerning me.

When Jesus conversed with the two on the Emmaus road, "he expounded unto them in all the scriptures the things concerning himself" (Luke 24:27). Jesus' use of Scripture is now described a bit more fully, as He is said here to use *the psalms,* not mentioned in the Emmaus episode. His death had been horrific, but it was a fulfillment, not a thwarting, of God's plan.

Jesus' approach reflects the Jewish threefold division of their Scriptures (our Old Testament). *The law of Moses,* the first five books of the Bible, is also known today as the *Torah* (literally, "instruction"). *The prophets* are also known as the *Nevi'im* (which is merely the Hebrew word for "prophets"). *The psalms* are part of the third section, which is known as the *Ketuvim* (literally, "the writings").

Christian editions of the Old Testament have all the same books, but we arrange their order differently. Jesus' comments on this occasion and that of Luke 24:27 indicate the importance for Christians to study the Old Testament for a full understanding of the Messiah. The fact that the New Testament authors quote extensively from the Old Testament further establishes the importance of studying the Old Testament.

What Do You Think?
What improvements do you need to make in your study of the Old Testament?
Talking Points for Your Discussion
- In frequency of study
- In depth of study

Of all the events recorded in the Bible, this may be the one for which we would most like to have been present. Imagine having the comfort of knowing from firsthand experience that Jesus is risen from the dead! Combine that with an oppor-tunity to sit at the Master's feet and hear Him explain Scripture, how it applies to Him, and what is accomplished through His death, burial, and resurrection (compare John 20:9)—what earthly experience could top this?

B. Explanation (vv. 45, 46)

45, 46. Then opened he their understanding, that they might understand the scriptures, And said unto them, Thus it is written, and thus it behooved Christ to suffer, and to rise from the dead the third day.

There is no single passage in the Old Testament that includes all of what Jesus says here, so we should understand this to be a summary of several passages (see Isaiah 53:3-12; compare Acts 8:32-35). Jesus' understanding of the fulfillment of the three-day time frame regarding His death and resurrection draws on the experience of Jonah (see Matthew 12:40).

This is a crucial moment in history because the significance of Jesus' death will be lost if His disciples do not understood it themselves. Jesus' lingering for 40 days between His resurrection and ascension (Acts 1:3) serves both to prove that He is risen and to teach His disciples the meaning of His death and resurrection. The preaching of the church depends on these proofs and explanations.

Some students think this teaching occurs at a later time, immediately before Jesus' ascension (and within this viewpoint there is a debate regarding whether the transition begins here or at v. 44). In any case, we are reading some final instructions given by Jesus to His disciples before He leaves them to be with the Father.

HOW TO SAY IT

Bethany	*Beth*-uh-nee.
Emmaus	Em-*may*-us.
Jonah	*Jo*-nuh.
Ketuvim *(Hebrew)*	*Ket*-you-vim.
Messiah	Meh-*sigh*-uh.
Nevi'im *(Hebrew)*	*Neh*-vih-im.
Pentecost	*Pent*-ih-kost.
syncretism	*sin*-kreh-*tih*-zum.
Torah *(Hebrew)*	*Tor*-uh.

C. Commission (vv. 47, 48)

47, 48. And that repentance and remission of sins should be preached in his name among all nations, beginning at Jerusalem. And ye are witnesses of these things.

The coming of the Son of God into the human sphere is only one phase of God's plan. It was prophesied and therefore intended that Jesus should die and be resurrected, but this is not the end. The disciples are now witnesses who can testify about the resurrection. They are therefore commissioned by the risen Lord to begin the next phase: the preaching of repentance and the resulting *remission of sins* to *all nations* (compare Matthew 28:19, 20; 1 Timothy 3:16).

This is a key message that Luke wants his readers to hear. Faith must be shared, for the salvation of the world is at stake (compare Acts 1:8). Jesus saves the lost (Luke 19:10) as this message is spread.

These words are not simply for the disciples who are gathered to watch Jesus depart; these words are for us too. As we follow the biblical plan of salvation in accepting Jesus as our Lord, we become witnesses who are charged with spreading this good news.

What Do You Think?

How can your church better help people make a connection between the Easter story and their daily lives?

Talking Points for Your Discussion

- Special events
- Special studies or sermon series
- Through existing programs
- Other

D. Promise (v. 49)

49. And, behold, I send the promise of my Father upon you: but tarry ye in the city of Jerusalem, until ye be endued with power from on high.

Remember that the Gospel of Luke is the first volume of a two-volume set. The author intends us to read the next volume, Acts, where the promise of the verse before us is fulfilled (Acts 1:8; 2:1-4). The *power from on high* is the outpouring of God's

Holy Spirit on the disciples. (This will be the focus of next week's lesson.)

What Do You Think?

Which promises of God most influence choices you make daily and for the future? Why?

Talking Points for Your Discussion

- Fulfilled promises
- Promises yet-to-be fulfilled

III. Worshipping Jesus
(Luke 24:50-53)

A. Dramatic Departure (vv. 50, 51)

50. And he led them out as far as to Bethany, and he lifted up his hands, and blessed them.

This particular Bethany is undoubtedly the one on the southeast flank of the Mount of Olives. This village was something of a headquarters for Jesus during His final week (Matthew 21:17; Mark 11:11, 12; John 12:1). It is the home of Lazarus, Mary, and Martha (John 11:18, 19).

John 11:18 specifies that the distance between Jerusalem and Bethany is "about fifteen furlongs," which equates to less than two miles. Acts 1:12 tells us that the disciples will return "unto Jerusalem from the mount called Olivet, which is from Jerusalem a sabbath day's journey," which is less than one mile. Putting these two ideas together lets us conclude that the trip toward Bethany ends up somewhere on the Mount of Olives. It is here that Jesus blesses His followers while lifting His hands to Heaven in the posture of prayer.

51. And it came to pass, while he blessed them, he was parted from them, and carried up into heaven.

While still pronouncing a blessing, Jesus is physically removed from the group. The description of Jesus' being *carried up into heaven* is further noted as being "taken up; and a cloud received him out of their sight" in Acts 1:9.

There is no description of anyone on this occasion being privileged to witness Jesus being exalted to "the right hand of God" (Acts 2:33). Stephen will be privileged to see that result as he dies (Acts 7:55, 56; compare Romans 8:34; Colossians 3:1; and Hebrews 10:12). Even so, Luke leaves no doubt that the disciples experience Jesus' ascension as a return to His Father in Heaven.

❧ LIES, AND WHERE HOPE LIES ❧

San Diego police discovered evidence of a mass suicide on March 26, 1997. The victims were members of the "Heaven's Gate" cult, founded by Marshall Applewhite and Bonnie Nettles. The pair had claimed to be the two witnesses mentioned in Revelation 11:3. Their belief system was a combination of Christian ideas, New Age philosophy, evolutionary theory, and science fiction.

The result of such syncretism was a conclusion that the earth would soon be destroyed, and the only way to survive was to leave earth immediately. Thus did Applewhite induce 38 of his followers to commit mass suicide with him so their souls could board a spacecraft thought to be behind the Hale-Bopp comet.

The world is still looking for a way to transcend the bonds of this life. Jesus' ascension into Heaven left His followers filled with hope that they too would someday go to be with Him (compare John 14:1-4). We share that hope because we trust Jesus, not the lies of false prophets such as Applewhite (compare 1 John 4:1).   —C. R. B.

B. Joyous Reaction (vv. 52, 53)

52, 53. And they worshipped him, and returned to Jerusalem with great joy: and were continually in the temple, praising and blessing God. Amen.

The disciples' return to Jerusalem is also noted in Acts 1:12. Rather than express anything like disappointment at being abandoned, the mood of the disciples is that of joyous worship (compare John 14:28; 16:22).

The atmosphere of worship does not cease that day of return to Jerusalem since the disciples are *continually in the temple,* meaning every day. Daily gatherings at the temple are part of the practice of Jesus' followers after His ascension (Acts 2:46; 3:1; 5:20, 21). That massive edifice has many places available for congregating in its spacious courts.

Therefore we should not picture the disciples cowering uncertainly in hiding in the days between Jesus' ascension and the Day of Pente-

cost. This is not what Luke wants us to see. The reality of Jesus' resurrection and the implications of His return to the Father are now embraced fully by this group of disciples. They will wait, but it will be with joyous anticipation of what the future holds, for Jesus has promised to send a great gift of power to them.

> **What Do You Think?**
> What impact can and should Jesus' ascension have on your witness for Him?
> *Talking Points for Your Discussion*
> - Regarding relatives
> - Regarding former church members who have "fallen away"
> - Regarding coworkers
> - Regarding unsaved friends
> - Other

Conclusion
A. Where Did Jesus Go?

Where did Jesus go? He did not "go" anywhere in the sense of "not being here," for He is not far from us (see Acts 17:27; Hebrews 13:5). He did indeed go to the right hand of God, where He serves as our advocate and priest in Heaven (Hebrews 4:14–5:10; 8:1), but Jesus is also with us because this is what He promised (Matthew 28:20).

N. T. Wright has said, "Ascension doesn't mean absence . . . it means sovereignty." We serve a risen Lord, and we serve Him with joyous anticipation of His return. We serve our Savior by heeding His words and taking the message of forgiveness and grace to all the world. We serve the King of kings, the one who has an impact on our lives today, some 2,000 years after the Bethany event.

B. Prayer

Father, may we be obedient as we take Your Son's message to the world. May we be joyous in our service as we worship and praise You. May we be expectant in our waiting, for our deepest desire is to be with You forever. In Jesus' name, amen.

C. Thought to Remember

The risen Jesus is also the present Jesus.

Involvement Learning

Some of the activities below are also found in the helpful student book, Adult Bible Class.
Don't forget to download the free reproducible page from www.standardlesson.com to enhance your lesson!

Into the Lesson

Draw two columns on the board. Above one column write *Bible*; above the other write *People*. Ask learners to brainstorm what Scripture says about the "dwelling place" of God. Jot responses in the *Bible* column. Then ask learners what they've heard people say about "where God lives." Write these responses in the *People* column. Their observations can be from fellow believers, televangelists, children, ancient mythology, etc.

Compare the two lists. Discuss possible reasons for wrong ideas. Say, "Today's lesson focuses on one of the most crucial moments in history. Let's see how our understanding of the biblical text affects our witness for Christ."

Into the Word

Form learners into groups of no more than six, then distribute the following assignments. (Larger classes can form additional groups with duplicate assignments.) *Group 1:* List the actions of Jesus and the disciples' reactions in Luke 24:36-43. *Group 2:* Identify Jesus' explanations to the disciples in Luke 24:44-49. *Group 3:* List what the disciples saw and heard and how they responded to Jesus' instructions in Luke 24:50-53.

Ask groups to share their findings, which should include the following:

Group 1: Jesus stood in their midst (v. 36); disciples reacted with terror and fright (v. 37). Jesus asked the disciples why they reacted as they did (v. 38), showed them His hands and feet, offering to let them touch Him (vv. 39, 40); disciples reacted with joy and wonder (v. 41); Jesus asked for something to eat (v. 41); disciples gave Him some food (v. 42). Discuss the logical sequence of actions and reactions. Note that Jesus acted in ways to give the disciples time to adjust to His unexpected presence. Use the lesson commentary for verses 38-43 to help learners see the significance of accepting these unusual events.

Group 2: Jesus commenced His explanations once the disciples accepted the fact of His physical presence. What had happened was a fulfillment of Scripture, not a thwarted plan (v. 44); the intent of this plan was repentance and forgiveness of sins for everyone (vv. 45-47); the vehicle for moving the plan forward was the disciples, who would be empowered to do so (vv. 48, 49). Use the lesson commentary for verses 44-49 to establish how the resurrection was a key part of the plan for the redemption of the world.

Group 3: The disciples heard and saw Jesus blessing them (v. 50); they saw Jesus carried up into Heaven (v. 51); they worshipped Him (v. 52); they obeyed by returning to Jerusalem (v. 52); they exhibited great joy (v. 52); they went to the temple and praised God (v. 53). Discuss how the disciples not only accepted what Jesus told them, but enthusiastically embraced it.

Distribute copies of the "An Amazing Story" activity from the reproducible page, which you can download. Assign to the same three groups the three rows in the exercise, one row each. Say, "Think of additional objections that skeptics might raise." After several minutes, have someone from each group present the case for the skeptics, then have someone else give the biblical response.

Into Life

Say, "We have seen how Jesus presented evidence of His resurrection not just to the disciples but to generations to come. That evidence compelled the disciples to be witnesses of God's plan to the nations. How does that same evidence compel us to be witnesses of that plan as well?" Discuss. Then have learners record names of people with whom they need to share the gospel. Follow with prayer for your learners' witness to them.

Alternative: Instead of the above, distribute copies of the "My Witness" activity from the reproducible page. Complete and discuss.

The Lord Appears

THE LORD SENDS
THE SPIRIT

DEVOTIONAL READING: John 15:1-7
BACKGROUND SCRIPTURE: Acts 2:1-41

ACTS 2:1-16

1 And when the day of Pentecost was fully come, they were all with one accord in one place.

2 And suddenly there came a sound from heaven as of a rushing mighty wind, and it filled all the house where they were sitting.

3 And there appeared unto them cloven tongues like as of fire, and it sat upon each of them.

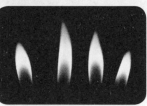

4 And they were all filled with the Holy Ghost, and began to speak with other tongues, as the Spirit gave them utterance.

5 And there were dwelling at Jerusalem Jews, devout men, out of every nation under heaven.

6 Now when this was noised abroad, the multitude came together, and were confounded, because that every man heard them speak in his own language.

7 And they were all amazed and marvelled, saying one to another, Behold, are not all these which speak Galilaeans?

8 And how hear we every man in our own tongue, wherein we were born?

9 Parthians, and Medes, and Elamites, and the dwellers in Mesopotamia, and in Judaea, and Cappadocia, in Pontus, and Asia,

10 Phrygia, and Pamphylia, in Egypt, and in the parts of Libya about Cyrene, and strangers of Rome, Jews and proselytes,

11 Cretes and Arabians, we do hear them speak in our tongues the wonderful works of God.

12 And they were all amazed, and were in doubt, saying one to another, What meaneth this?

13 Others mocking said, These men are full of new wine.

14 But Peter, standing up with the eleven, lifted up his voice, and said unto them, Ye men of Judaea, and all ye that dwell at Jerusalem, be this known unto you, and hearken to my words:

15 For these are not drunken, as ye suppose, seeing it is but the third hour of the day.

16 But this is that which was spoken by the prophet Joel.

KEY VERSE

They were all filled with the Holy Ghost, and began to speak with other tongues, as the Spirit gave them utterance. —**Acts 2:4**

UNDYING HOPE

Unit 2: Resurrection Hope

LESSONS 4–9

LESSON AIMS

After participating in this lesson, each student will be able to:

1. Describe what happened leading up to Peter's dramatic sermon on the Day of Pentecost.

2. Explain how the unusual events of that day helped convince the God-fearing Jews who were present that the message of the apostles came from God.

3. Suggest some ways to get people's attention today as an open door to evangelism.

LESSON OUTLINE

Introduction

A. The Ruined Vacation

Have you ever had a vacation ruined by an ugly incident? an accident or illness? a car breakdown? being victimized by a thief? bad news from home? I have friends who were happily vacationing in New York City on 9/11. Needless to say, their vacation was ruined.

Early first-century Jerusalem was full of visitors every spring. They were Jewish pilgrims from all over the Mediterranean world who came for the great Passover celebration and stayed until Pentecost, roughly two months later. This was like a religious vacation. In the year of today's lesson text (probably AD 30), the vacation of these visitors was disrupted. A visiting rabbi, named Jesus, was at first greeted by joyous crowds in a festive atmosphere. But things turned ugly. The visiting rabbi was in conflict with the Jewish authorities. The conflict escalated to the point that He was seized, given quick trials, and executed. It must have left a bad taste in everyone's mouth.

Coming seven weeks after Passover, the Feast of Pentecost was the end-event for most of these visitors. They would have begun to disperse the following week. That year, they might have left with this murderous memory weighing heavily on their hearts, a once-in-a-lifetime vacation ruined. But God, in His wisdom, did not let these pilgrims leave Jerusalem before experiencing an astounding event. The result was the birth of the church.

B. Lesson Background

The ancient Jewish calendar of special days had a great sense of history to it. One of the most important days on the calendar was Passover. That was a time to remember when God's angel of death "passed over" the Jewish households in Egypt that had been marked with the blood of a Passover lamb (Exodus 11 and 12). This feast day is connected with the exodus of the nation of Israel from Egypt, from their lives of slavery. Thus, Passover had the flavor of a day of national independence, something like America's Fourth of July. The single-day Passover celebration occurred in conjunction with the seven-day Feast of Unleavened Bread (Leviticus 23:5, 6). Thus these two came to be seen functionally as one celebration.

Pentecost, also called the Feast of Weeks, came seven weeks plus one day later (compare Exodus 34:22; Leviticus 23:15-21; Deuteronomy 16:9, 10). This length of time computes to 50 days, and *Pentecost* is a Greek word that simply means "fiftieth day." Today's lesson takes us to the first Day of Pentecost after Jesus' resurrection.

I. Disciples Energized
(ACTS 2:1-4)
A. Long-Awaited Day (v. 1)

1. And when the day of Pentecost was fully come, they were all with one accord in one place.

Since Pentecost is 50 days after the Passover Sabbath, that means it falls on the first day of the week, Sunday. Jesus had lingered on earth for 40 days following His resurrection (Acts 1:3), so there is a period of less than two weeks between Jesus' ascension and this Pentecost day.

The mention of *all . . . in one place* leads us to investigate who is included in this "all." The group of disciples in Jerusalem at this time includes 11 of the 12 original apostles (Acts 1:13), the mother and brothers of Jesus (1:14), plus others for a total of about 120 (1:15). While waiting, they have taken care of at least one piece of vital business: choosing a replacement for Judas Iscariot to reconstitute the apostles to be 12 in number (1:15-26).

The gathering this particular morning seems according to the pattern the group has been fol-

HOW TO SAY IT

Cappadocia	Kap-uh-*doe*-shuh.
Diaspora	Dee-*as*-puh-ruh.
Elamites	*Ee*-luh-mites.
Euphrates	You-*fray*-teez.
Galilaeans	Gal-uh-*lee*-unz.
Mesopotamia	*Mes*-uh-puh-*tay*-me-uh.
Pamphylia	Pam-*fill*-ee-uh.
Parthians	*Par*-thee-unz (*th* as in *thin*).
Phrygia	*Frij*-e-uh.
proselytes	*prahss*-uh-lights.
Tigris	*Tie*-griss.

lowing for several days. Acts 1:4-8 provides a promise that something profound is about to happen.

We don't know where the *one place* is. It could be the house of Mary, the mother of John Mark (see Acts 12:12). It may also be the place where the last supper had been celebrated, "a large upper room" (Luke 22:12; compare Acts 1:13). It may be in the temple courts outdoors. Wherever it is, it is large enough to accommodate 120 people.

> **What Do You Think?**
> How should the modern church celebrate the Day of Pentecost as the day of the church's birth, if at all?
> *Talking Points for Your Discussion*
> - Low-key observances
> - High-visibility observances

B. Attention-Grabbing Phenomena (vv. 2, 3)

2. And suddenly there came a sound from heaven as of a rushing mighty wind, and it filled all the house where they were sitting.

The first sign that this is a special day is auditory: a noise like *a rushing mighty wind*. We should notice that there is no mention of an actual wind blowing things about, but only the *sound* of a wind. This by itself is understood as a supernatural sign—a loud noise recognizable to be like the wind, but with no accompanying air movement.

3. And there appeared unto them cloven tongues like as of fire, and it sat upon each of them.

As the first phenomenon is wind-like sound without mention of moving air, the second phenomenon is a fire-like display without mention of heat. The description *cloven* seems to indicate a fire-like image that divides, with a tongue resting on each person. These are not fiery replicas of human tongues, but flame-like extensions of the fire.

C. Spirit-Given Speech (v. 4)

4. And they were all filled with the Holy Ghost, and began to speak with other tongues, as the Spirit gave them utterance.

The third phenomenon is the greatest of all. We might call it a combination of the fire/tongues and the wind/spirit (vv. 2, 3, above) as the gathered disciples begin to speak *with other tongues, as the Spirit* enables them. The tongues are known languages (see vv. 6, 8, below), but unlearned by the disciples.

Luke, the author, describes this as happening when the disciples are *all filled with the Holy Ghost* (compare Acts 4:31). To be *filled* in this sense is to be "controlled." This does not mean that the disciples have lost all personal control, becoming zombies of some kind. Rather, it means that the ability to speak in the unlearned languages is coming from a source outside themselves: the Holy Spirit (see also Acts 10:44-46). This is a miracle!

This is fulfillment of John the Baptist's promise "he shall baptize you with the Holy Ghost" (Matthew 3:11; Luke 3:16; compare Acts 1:5). The word *wind* is closely related to the word *spirit* (or *ghost*) in the Greek language, as both are understood to be invisible but real forces.

What Do You Think?
How has God worked in your church in unexpected but nonmiraculous ways? How does this strengthen your faith?
Talking Points for Your Discussion
- In the birth of your church
- During moments of crisis and change
- In extending its outreach
- Other

II. Visitors Confounded
(ACTS 2:5-13)

A. Many Languages (vv. 5-11)

5. And there were dwelling at Jerusalem Jews, devout men, out of every nation under heaven.

The author briefly changes focus. In so doing, he sets the scene for the next surprising developments by reminding us that Jerusalem is full of foreign Jews at this time. Most of these are in town temporarily, having come for the Passover-through-Pentecost season of temple observances. Many will be headed home shortly (see the Lesson Background).

Luke's comment that they are from *every nation under heaven* is a testimony to the presence of Jews from across the Roman Empire. Such Jews are referred to as *the Diaspora,* meaning the dispersed nation of Israel (see John 7:35; James 1:1; compare Acts 21:21). We will get more details regarding the makeup of this international group in verses 9, 10, below.

What Do You Think?
What experiences have helped you most to appreciate the "every nation" nature of God's kingdom? Why?
Talking Points for Your Discussion
- At your church
- While on mission trips
- At Christian conventions
- Other

6, 7. Now when this was noised abroad, the multitude came together, and were confounded, because that every man heard them speak in his own language. And they were all amazed and marvelled, saying one to another, Behold, are not all these which speak Galilaeans?

This Holy Spirit–inspired speaking in other tongues begins to draw a crowd. These visiting Jews probably are fluent in Greek. It is likely that they are fluent in Hebrew as well according to Acts 22:2 (which probably refers also to a Day of Pentecost, per Acts 20:16). They could expect to hear one of these two languages on the lips of Galileans, but certainly not their mother tongues!

The question *Behold, are not all these which speak Galilaeans?* is disparaging. Whether because of the speakers' dress or accent (compare Matthew 26:73), the foreign Jews know that the ones speaking are from the rural area to the north. Galilee is part of the ancient territory of Israel, but at this time is a separate Roman district ruled by Herod Antipas (see Luke 3:1). The Jews of Galilee are considered uneducated and unsophisticated (compare Acts 4:13). Thus there is real surprise to witness people from that area as masters of many languages.

8. And how hear we every man in our own tongue, wherein we were born?

Because of the wide range of cities from which these Jews come (vv. 9-11, below), it is possible that there are very few representatives of certain languages in the multitude. Yet each person hears his or her local language being spoken! This is something they do not expect to hear until they return home.

9a. Parthians, and Medes, and Elamites, and the dwellers in Mesopotamia.

Luke now lists some of the regions represented. He begins with regions east of Jerusalem that are generally outside Roman control. We know from the Old Testament that many Jews remained in the east long after the return of Jews to Judea in 538 BC when many were released from captivity (Ezra 1, etc.).

The primary rival to the Romans is the Parthian Empire to the east. It controls the territory that encompasses the Parthians, Medes, and Elamites. These ancient peoples are located in what is modern Iran.

The Greek word *Mesopotamia* means "between the rivers," referring to the area between the Tigris and Euphrates Rivers. This territory is often called *Babylon* in the Bible; it is part of modern-day Iraq. This area is also controlled by the Parthians in the first century AD.

9b, 10a. And in Judaea, and Cappadocia, in Pontus, and Asia, Phrygia, and Pamphylia.

Next comes a listing of the easternmost provinces of the Roman Empire. Judea is the region around Jerusalem, and naturally there are many Judeans in this crowd. Cappadocia, Pontus, Asia, Phrygia, and Pamphylia are all areas in modern Turkey. Several of these areas are visited by the apostle Paul during his missionary journeys.

10b. In Egypt, and in the parts of Libya about Cyrene.

The third grouping consists of areas located in what we consider to be the northern part of Africa. These make up the southern provinces of the Roman Empire. We remember that the man forced to carry Jesus' cross was from Cyrene (Luke 23:26; compare Acts 13:1).

10c. And strangers of Rome, Jews and proselytes.

The *strangers of Rome* are subdivided into two groups: Jews and proselytes. There is a large Jewish population in the city of Rome and in other cities of southern Italy at this time. These Roman/Italian Jews are active in seeking converts *(proselytes)* to Judaism. So what the author is saying here is that the Roman Jews in Jerusalem on this day are represented by traditional Jewish families as well as by Gentiles who have converted to the Jewish faith.

There are three requirements for a Gentile man converting to Judaism: circumcision, a ritual bath, and the offering of a sacrifice at the temple. Some of these proselytes may be in Jerusalem at this time to complete the third requirement.

11. Cretes and Arabians, we do hear them speak in our tongues the wonderful works of God.

We now come to the last two people groups named. Those of the first are from the island of Crete, which has a sizable Jewish population. Crete is a prosperous center of trade because of its strategic location in the Mediterranean Sea. Arabians are Jews from the desert regions to the south of Jerusalem, especially from the Sinai peninsula and the northwest parts of the Arabian peninsula.

This verse gives us insight into the content of the marvelous speaking that is coming from the disciples as inspired by the Holy Spirit. The proclamation of *the wonderful works of God* is the language of praise. This is adoration of the Lord for His mighty works of creation and for His providential care (see Psalm 71:19; compare Luke 1:49; Revelation 15:3).

❧ BABEL REVERSED ❧

Pioneer Bible Translators and Wycliffe are two organizations dedicated to providing the people groups of the world with the Bible in their native languages. By one estimate, there are more than 6,900 spoken languages in the world today, with more than 30 percent of these not having any part of the Bible yet translated.

This tells us two things. First, there is still a lot of work to do before each and every people-group can have the gospel in its own language. Second, God did a very thorough job when He confounded the language of the people at Babel in Genesis 11!

When we contrast God's actions at confounding languages in Genesis 11 with the Holy Spirit's empowering on the Day of Pentecost, we see God drawing the peoples of the world back together. He wasn't giving back to people a common spoken language, but rather the message of a one-and-only Savior.

The miracle of enabling the disciples to speak in various languages was part of the proof. Now, some 2,000 years later, God is still drawing people to His Son through the gospel by means of the common spiritual language of *love* (John 3:16). We might call this "Babel reversed." What part will you play in God's plan?   —C. R. B.

B. Mixed Reaction (vv. 12, 13)

12, 13. And they were all amazed, and were in doubt, saying one to another, What meaneth this? Others mocking said, These men are full of new wine.

When Luke tells us that a crowd is amazed or astonished, it generally means that the people are confused about something they have just witnessed because it does not square with their normal expectations (examples: Luke 2:47, 48; Acts 9:21). They have no reasonable explanation, so they begin to doubt. They suspect trickery. This is an attitude we see in the crowd on this Day of Pentecost in Jerusalem.

This spirit of doubt results in the conclusion by some that those who are speaking are drunk. To be drunk in public is scandalous behavior, so this accusation is strongly demeaning.

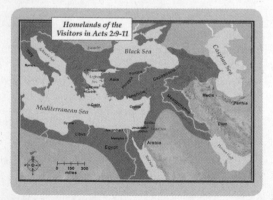

Visual for Lesson 7. *As you discuss verses 9-11, ask, "How can our church best respond to the increasing diversity of our country today?"*

What Do You Think?
What are some ways that people scoff at God's work today? How should you respond?
Talking Points for Your Discussion
- Acts 13:40, 41; 23:6-8
- 1 Corinthians 4:12, 13
- 2 Corinthians 5:11, 12
- Colossians 4:6
- 1 Peter 3:15
- 2 Peter 3:3, 4

III. Peter Emboldened
(Acts 2:14-16)

A. Explanation Offered (vv. 14, 15)

14a. But Peter, standing up with the eleven, lifted up his voice, and said unto them.

Peter comes forward as the spokesman for the group, as he did in the selection process of a new apostle (Acts 1:15). Peter is portrayed in the Gospels as a strong personality prone to making mistakes (compare also Galatians 2:11-13). But having been reinstated personally by Jesus (John 21:15-17), Peter's boldness now is better directed.

What Do You Think?
When did you do something for God that you never pictured yourself doing? How did things turn out?
Talking Points for Your Discussion
- Public witness
- Counseling situation
- Evangelistic opportunity
- Benevolence opportunity
- Other

14b, 15. Ye men of Judaea, and all ye that dwell at Jerusalem, be this known unto you, and hearken to my words: for these are not drunken, as ye suppose, seeing it is but the third hour of the day.

The disciples' speaking in foreign tongues probably ceases to allow Peter to have the undivided attention of the gathered people. Appealing to common sense, Peter begins by refuting the insulting charge that the disciples are drunk. It is only *the third hour of the day,* which is about 9:00 AM. While there might be the rare person here or there who begins drinking wine immediately on arising, this would not be the case with a group such as the one the crowd is witnessing. Furthermore, drunkenness cannot explain what the crowd is experiencing. Inebriation does not lead to extraordinary language skills—quite the opposite!

B. Prophecy Fulfilled (v. 16)

16. But this is that which was spoken by the prophet Joel.

Last week's lesson considered the final words of Jesus in teaching the disciples that His death and resurrection were part of the plan of God as prophesied in Scripture. Peter now extends this idea to include the Pentecost phenomena. Not only was what happened to Jesus foreseen centuries before by God's prophets, so also was this outpouring of God's Holy Spirit foreseen.

Fulfillment of prophecy is not complete with Jesus' ascension; fulfillment continues among the works of the apostles ~~in the first-century church~~. This sets the stage for ~~Peter's marvelous sermon,~~ based on the book of Joel and other Old Testament texts. The result of this sermon is the beginning of the church.

❧ *FLAWED VESSELS* ❧

Peter was a flawed vessel, presented in the Gospels as a man given to rashness. To human thinking, he seems an unlikely person to be chosen by God to preach the first gospel sermon, the sermon that established the church! But this was not the last time that God would work through a flawed individual to advance His plan. It has happened many times in the church's history.

One of the better known examples is that of John Newton (1725–1807). Newton spent his early life at sea, eventually becoming involved in the slave trade. But Newton underwent a spiritual conversion during a storm at sea in 1748. In time, he became an Anglican priest (1764), published his now-famous hymn "Amazing Grace" (1779), and wrote forcefully against the slave trade (1788).

Both Peter and John Newton continued to be flawed vessels long after they encountered Jesus, but God's grace worked to change those two. How is God working to change you? Where are you resisting God's changes? —C. R. B.

Conclusion
A. The Comforter Has Come

The account of that glorious Day of Pentecost has at least three abiding lessons for us. First, we recognize that the Holy Spirit has come to the church as part of the new covenant. The Old Testament certainly knows of God's Holy Spirit, but there is no sense there that the Spirit is a gift given to all the people of God. The coming of the Holy Spirit was foreseen by the Old Testament prophets and was promised by Jesus (John 14:15-26). The presence of the Holy Spirit is a primary difference between the people of God in the Old Testament and New Testament eras.

Second, we see that the Holy Spirit does not come passively, but with power. Many Christians today are uncomfortable talking about any sense ~~of supernatural power from the Holy Spirit. They~~ ~~are...~~ Christian should be speaking in tongues, etc. (see 1 Corinthians 12:30). But it does mean that every Christian has the blessed gift of God's presence.

Third, Peter's bold speech shows us that the Holy Spirit empowers the preaching of the gospel. The display of tongues on the Day of Pentecost showed the diverse Jewish crowd that God was active in their midst. It set the stage for Peter to preach the entire gospel message. There is still power in the message that exceeds that of the messenger. When we share the gospel faithfully, God's Spirit is active in the reception of the message. This is true whether preaching from a pulpit or sharing with a friend.

B. Prayer

O Lord, may the presence of Your indwelling Spirit empower our worship, our love for You, and our sharing of the gospel. In Jesus' name, amen.

C. Thought to Remember

The coming of the Holy Spirit
changes everything.

INVOLVEMENT LEARNING

Some of the activities below are also found in the helpful student book, Adult Bible Class.
Don't forget to download the free reproducible page from www.standardlesson.com to enhance your lesson!

Into the Lesson

Have learners share times when something they had planned went wrong (examples: a ruined vacation, a botched surprise party, or stolen Christmas presents). Discuss how they felt and what they did to try and rectify the problem. Using the information from the lesson introduction, move learners from their own experiences to how the visitors to Jerusalem must have felt about the crucifixion of Jesus during Passover. Say, "Sometimes God has to change our perspective in order to get our attention. In today's lesson we will again see how God used extraordinary means to accomplish His purpose."

Ask learners what they know about the meaning and significance of the Passover and Pentecost observances. If responses reveal deficiencies in knowledge, use the Lesson Background to fill in the gaps.

Into the Word

Have a volunteer read Acts 2:1-4. Ask, "What are the extraordinary events that these verses mention? Why are these events important?" Jot responses on the board, but do not evaluate the correctness of the suggestions at this point—just list them.

Next, have a volunteer read Acts 2:5-11. Ask, "What is noteworthy in these verses? What could be the reason or reasons for the stated facts of these verses?" Jot responses on the board. Again, do not evaluate the correctness of the suggestions at this point.

Next, read Acts 2:12 but make no comment. (You'll come back to this verse later.) Finally, have someone read Acts 2:13-16. As before, ask learners to brainstorm the significance of these verses while you jot their unevaluated responses on the board.

Return to the class's earlier musings regarding the rationale for events noted in verses 1-4 and the significance of the facts noted in verses 5-11. Use the lesson commentary for these two sections to

correct misconceptions and to answer questions the learners may have.

Use the results of this discussion to answer the question of verse 12: "What meaneth this?" Guide learners to the realization that God uses extraordinary means in Scripture to catch people's attention as He establishes that He is the source of what is happening. For today's lesson text, this helped the people recognize that the extraordinary things they were witnessing validated Peter's message of verses 14 and following as being from God and helped set aside the resistance of verse 13. Be sure to stress that what happened in today's text was nothing less than the birth of the church.

Option: Distribute copies of the "Not Your Typical Sunday Morning" activity from the reproducible page, which you can download. Have learners form study pairs to complete the activity. Encourage learners not to look at the suggested answers, but to see what they can recall from the study just completed. Allow sharing of conclusions, expecting some variety.

Into Life

Say, "As we think about the events surrounding the gospel sermon that accompanied the birth of the church, which parts can and should we expect to replicate in evangelistic sermons and messages today? Which parts should we not expect to replicate?" Expect responses that revolve around "attention getting" from miraculous and nonmiraculous angles.

Alternative: Distribute copies of the "Attention! Attention!—The Right Way" activity from the reproducible page. Form learners into small groups to complete this exercise. Have groups share their ideas with the class as a whole. Try to achieve consensus on the two best ideas, given the context of the community where your church is located. Tell the class that you will present those two ideas to your church's leadership, and do so.

The Lord Sends the Spirit

THE LORD WILL RETURN

DEVOTIONAL READING: Psalm 38:9-15
BACKGROUND SCRIPTURE: 1 Thessalonians 4:13–5:11

1 THESSALONIANS 4:13-18

13 But I would not have you to be ignorant, brethren, concerning them which are asleep, that ye sorrow not, even as others which have no hope.

14 For if we believe that Jesus died and rose again, even so them also which sleep in Jesus will God bring with him.

15 For this we say unto you by the word of the Lord, that we which are alive and remain unto the coming of the Lord shall not prevent them which are asleep.

16 For the Lord himself shall descend from heaven with a shout, with the voice of the archangel, and with the trump of God: and the dead in Christ shall rise first:

17 Then we which are alive and remain shall be caught up together with them in the clouds, to meet the Lord in the air: and so shall we ever be with the Lord.

18 Wherefore comfort one another with these words.

1 THESSALONIANS 5:1-11

1 But of the times and the seasons, brethren, ye have no need that I write unto you.

2 For yourselves know perfectly that the day of the Lord so cometh as a thief in the night.

3 For when they shall say, Peace and safety; then sudden destruction cometh upon them, as travail upon a woman with child; and they shall not escape.

4 But ye, brethren, are not in darkness, that that day should overtake you as a thief.

5 Ye are all the children of light, and the children of the day: we are not of the night, nor of darkness.

6 Therefore let us not sleep, as do others; but let us watch and be sober.

7 For they that sleep sleep in the night; and they that be drunken are drunken in the night.

8 But let us, who are of the day, be sober, putting on the breastplate of faith and love; and for an helmet, the hope of salvation.

9 For God hath not appointed us to wrath, but to obtain salvation by our Lord Jesus Christ,

10 Who died for us, that, whether we wake or sleep, we should live together with him.

11 Wherefore comfort yourselves together, and edify one another, even as also ye do.

KEY VERSE

God hath not appointed us to wrath, but to obtain salvation by our Lord Jesus Christ.
—1 Thessalonians 5:9

UNDYING HOPE

Unit 2: Resurrection Hope
LESSONS 4–9

LESSON AIMS

After participating in this lesson, each student will be able to:

1. Tell what will happen to believers—both those who have died and those who remain alive—when Christ returns.

2. Contrast the lifestyles of the children of the day with the children of darkness.

3. Write a prayer of encouragement based on the hope of resurrection.

LESSON OUTLINE

Introduction

A. Famous Returns

Julius Caesar returned to Rome in 49 BC as a victorious general, having extended the territory of the Romans to the North Sea. During World War II, General Douglas MacArthur returned triumphantly to the Philippines with a strong military force, having been forced to flee to Australia two years earlier. After his arrival he uttered the famous words, "I have returned." In 1979, Ruhollah Khomeini returned to Iran from his exile in Paris to lead a revolution. He became the Supreme Leader of the Islamic Republic of Iran.

Caesar, MacArthur, and Khomeini were heroes to some and villains to others. Such is the nature of history, for the triumphant return of a powerful leader can disrupt the power structures already in place. Caesar's return resulted in civil war, with Caesar eventually emerging as the master of the empire. MacArthur's return was the beginning of the end for Japanese occupation of the Philippines. Khomeini's return caused a revolt against the remnants of the previous regime, with opposition brutally suppressed.

The Bible tells us about the return of a leader who is perfectly just, unrivaled in power, and fully blessed by God. To be sure, there will be some who will rue the day of His return, for it will not be good news for "the powers that be" that have rejected Him. His return will not signal a new era in human history, but the end of history as we know it. This is the return in power and glory of the risen Lord, Jesus Christ, the Son of God.

B. Lesson Background

The return of Jesus is also called *the second coming* or *the Parousia*. It is referred to in 21 of the 27 New Testament books (absent only in Galatians, Ephesians, 1 Timothy, Philemon, 2 John, and 3 John). This teaching was an integral part of the preaching of Paul, and it was eagerly received by the churches he planted.

One such church was located in the city of Thessalonica. Paul was able to spend only about three weeks there (see Acts 17:1-10), and after his departure certain misunderstandings arose in the

Thessalonian church concerning Christ's return. The lessons for this week and next week will look at two letters Paul wrote to that church to correct wrong perceptions.

I. About Ignorance
(1 Thessalonians 4:13-18)
A. Status (vv. 13-15)

13. But I would not have you to be ignorant, brethren, concerning them which are asleep, that ye sorrow not, even as others which have no hope.

Paul's teaching among the Thessalonians perhaps has created great excitement and anticipation for the second coming of Jesus. As a result, these believers eagerly look for the Lord's return. However, a complication arises when some in their fellowship die. Working backward from Paul's response to the Thessalonians' unstated question, we easily can imagine that this situation has created a concern that these dead friends have missed out on Christ's return.

Paul always lives and preaches as if the Lord's return is imminent. He teaches his churches the great prayer of anticipation, "Maranatha!" which means, "Come, Lord!" (1 Corinthians 16:22; compare Revelation 22:20). The Thessalonians seem to be caught between this expectation and the present reality of death.

Paul's response is to chide his readers gently, warning that they are acting like nonbelievers, who *have no hope*. These are the ones who are without Christ (see Ephesians 2:12). The death of a beloved fellow Christian is certainly sad. But there should be no worry about the fate and status of that dead person.

We can note in passing that sleep is a common figure of speech in the Bible for death (examples: John 11:11-13; Acts 13:36). This does not require us to accept a theory of "soul sleep," the idea that human souls are in an unconscious state between death and resurrection. Although full details of what happens to people after death are not given in the Bible, there is no expectation of a period of unawareness between our deaths and our future existence beyond death (compare Luke 16:22-31).

14. For if we believe that Jesus died and rose again, even so them also which sleep in Jesus will God bring with him.

The Christian understanding of the resurrection of men and women is built on the fact of Jesus' resurrection (see Romans 6:5). Jesus is the "firstfruits" of our own resurrection from the dead (1 Corinthians 15:20). This means that Christ's victory over death is a new reality that paves the way for the general resurrection of those who die. Paul understands that it is nonsensical to preach the resurrection of Christ if we do not see this as a harbinger of our own resurrections (1 Corinthians 15:12-16).

15. For this we say unto you by the word of the Lord, that we which are alive and remain unto the coming of the Lord shall not prevent them which are asleep.

Paul's statement *by the word of the Lord* means that what Paul is about to say is as ironclad as it can be: those who die before Christ comes again will not miss out. But Paul also introduces a relative element by the use of the word *prevent*. Today, we use this word to mean "to keep something from happening," but when the *King James Version* was first published the word *prevent* meant "to go or arrive before." Thus Paul's meaning is something like "those who are still alive when the Lord comes back will not go ahead of the others who are already dead." Any mourning for deceased Christians therefore should not be based on fear and regret that their deaths will cause them to be left behind when Christ returns.

B. Sequence (vv. 16, 17)

16. For the Lord himself shall descend from heaven with a shout, with the voice of the archangel, and with the trump of God: and the dead in Christ shall rise first.

Paul briefly describes what will happen when Christ returns, a sequence of events. This is definitely a physical description, not some fuzzy, spiritualized scenario. Christ himself will be seen coming out of the sky. This will be a supernatural appearance, for Revelation 1:7 tells us that "every eye" will witness this event. It will not be blocked by the earth so that those in, say, England are able to see Christ while those in Australia are not.

The Lord's descent will be heralded by three loud, supernatural noises. The first is *a shout*. Paul's word is a military term, giving the sense of a shout of victory. The second noise will be *the voice of the archangel*, signaling that Christ will return with an angel army (see Matthew 24:30, 31; 2 Thessalonians 1:7). This will be accompanied by the blast of *the trump of God* (think "trumpet"). This signals the participation of God himself (1 Corinthians 15:52). We can assume these three mighty sounds will be heard universally, waking all who are asleep (dead) and startling those who are alive.

Christ will come to take His people home. Those who are dead (like those who are the subject of concern for the Thessalonians) will be resurrected, coming back to life with new bodies. The fact that their resurrection comes *first* means it comes before what we see in the next verse.

17. Then we which are alive and remain shall be caught up together with them in the clouds, to meet the Lord in the air: and so shall we ever be with the Lord.

Having addressed the status and future of deceased Christians, Paul now discusses the issue of believers who are alive when Christ returns. Paul pictures the triumphant Lord above the earth, as if riding on the clouds (see Psalm 68:4). We can assume that the bodies of these still-living believers will be changed into immortal, resurrection bodies at that time, although Paul does not include that detail here (see 1 Corinthians 15:52). Thus there will be a great gathering of all God's people, living and dead.

The ascent of living people into the sky is sometimes called *the rapture*. The word *rapture* comes from the Latin translation of this verse and is reflected in the older English verb *rapt,* which once meant "to be snatched" or "to be caught up quickly." Many Christians give attention to theories of "the end times" that involve this term. Some scholars use a certain interpretation of *the rapture* to propose a sequence of end-time events.

Difficulties arise, however, when the picture of being *caught up* in the verse before us is integrated with ideas from other texts. The book of Revelation mentions a great tribulation, the revealing of the beast, the establishment of a 1,000-year (millennial) reign of Christ, etc. The difficulties involved in putting all these together in a time line cause some students to propose a "secret rapture," but that is not Paul's language.

Since interpretation of figurative language is uncertain at many points, there is room for disagreement regarding theories of the end times. This should not cause us to shy away from the Bible's teachings concerning the end times (called

Visual for Lesson 8. *As you discuss verse 16, point to this visual and ask, "Would you like to have this inscribed on your tombstone? Why, or why not?"*

The Lord Will Return

eschatology). What Scripture says in this area can be of great comfort to us.

Paul does not say here where the gathered multitude goes, simply that they will *ever be with the Lord*. In other passages, this final dwelling place is seen as Heaven (example: Revelation 7:9). We should remember that Paul's purpose here is not to give all the details of Christ's second coming, but to assure the Thessalonians that those who have died will not be left out.

❧ MUCH ROOM, NO DIVORCE ❧

The so-called "wedding of the century" (the twentieth century, that is) took place on July 29, 1981, in London. A global audience of 750 million watched on TV as Lady Diana Frances Spencer was wed to Charles, Prince of Wales. Hundreds of thousands lined the streets to watch Diana's procession to the cathedral. It seemed that everyone wanted to be part of this "fairy-tale wedding"!

However, only 120 people were invited to the wedding dinner at Buckingham Palace after the ceremony. Sadder still, the fairy-tale wedding did not last. The marriage was in trouble within just a few years. Eventually, both Charles and Diana committed adultery. Formal separation was announced in 1992, followed by divorce in 1996 and Diana's tragic death in 1997.

Whether we are alive or not when Christ returns, none who are prepared for that event will have to worry about being left out of "the marriage supper of the Lamb" (Revelation 19:7-9). There will be room for everyone! There will be

HOW TO SAY IT

Corinth	*Kor*-inth.
eschatology	ess-kuh-*tah*-luh-gee.
Julius Caesar	*Joo*-lee-us *See*-zer.
Maranatha *(Aramaic)*	Mah-ruh-*nay*-thuh.
Parousia *(Greek)*	Par-*oo*-see-uh.
Ruhollah Khomeini	Rue-*hoe*-lah Ko-*may*-nee.
Silas	*Sigh*-luss.
Thessalonians	*Thess*-uh-**lo**-nee-unz (*th* as in *thin*).
Thessalonica	*Thess*-uh-lo-**nye**-kuh (*th* as in *thin*).

no possibility of adulterous affairs with false gods (contrast Jeremiah 3:6-9). The church need not worry about divorce from her bridegroom, Jesus. What a future we have!

—C. R. B.

C. Support (v. 18)

18. Wherefore comfort one another with these words.

This is Paul's main point. The Bible's teaching on the second coming of Christ can be confusing and disturbing for some. But it should not be so for believers, who trust Christ as Lord and look forward to His coming (compare Jude 21). We have not been abandoned by the risen Lord, for He will come to take us home (John 14:3).

> *What Do You Think?*
> How was your church a source of comfort to you when a loved one died?
> *Talking Points for Your Discussion*
> ▪ Acts of service
> ▪ Funeral or memorial service
> ▪ Personal words of comfort
> ▪ Other

II. About Times
(1 THESSALONIANS 5:1-5)
A. Thief in the Night (vv. 1-3)

1, 2. But of the times and the seasons, brethren, ye have no need that I write unto you. For yourselves know perfectly that the day of the Lord so cometh as a thief in the night.

Paul realizes that his readers desire to know more specifics regarding the timing of Christ's return. Don't we all! This is not information they receive, though, for this will happen in the Father's undisclosed timing (see Matthew 24:36; Acts 1:6, 7). If we pay attention to this fact, we will appreciate the folly of setting dates for Christ's return. Our job is not to decipher prophecies to determine a plausible date, but to be ready always for His return. If Christ lingers until after our deaths, we must die ready. If we are alive at His return, we must live ready (see Matthew 24:44).

The comparison of Christ's second coming with that of *a thief in the night* emphasizes sudden arrival at an unexpected time. This comparison was made by Jesus himself (Matthew 24:43; compare 2 Peter 3:10; Revelation 3:3; 16:15).

Jim was "actively dying," as members of the health-care profession sometimes refer to conditions such as his. He was afflicted with multiple life-threatening ailments—chronic heart and lung problems, as well as spreading cancer. Any one of these conditions could take his life quickly, but he clung tenaciously to life.

Jim's doctors, nurses, social workers, and the hospice chaplain had prepared his family for his imminent demise, but Jim held on. He died only after his son, who lived overseas, was able to come and say good-bye. Such a scene takes place with surprising frequency: a dying person "chooses" the time of his or her death.

Jim's "choosing" was that only in a very limited sense, however. He would have died eventually even if he had stubbornly "chosen" not to. A mark of emotional and spiritual maturity is being able to recognize where we have choices and where we do not. We cannot choose the time of Christ's return, nor can we choose whether we shall be alive or not at that moment. What we *can* choose is whether that event will be a time of joyful celebration or tragic despair.   —C. R. B.

3. For when they shall say, Peace and safety; then sudden destruction cometh upon them, as travail upon a woman with child; and they shall not escape.

Paul reminds us of the warnings of the prophets. Jeremiah warned people in his day not to believe the false prophets who proclaimed "Peace, peace; when there is no peace" (Jeremiah 6:14; 8:11; compare Ezekiel 13:10). Paul also invokes language from the warnings of Jesus that destruction will come on those who are not ready (Matthew 24:39; Luke 21:34-36), with an illustration of the suddenness of labor pains (see Mark 13:8).

B. People of the Day (vv. 4, 5)

4, 5. But ye, brethren, are not in darkness, that that day should overtake you as a thief. Ye are all the children of light, and the children of the day: we are not of the night, nor of darkness.

Paul reminds the Thessalonians that they have nothing to fear regarding the second coming of Christ. This should not lead to complacency, however, for Paul's readers are expected to be ready. As Paul notes in Romans 13:12, being ready involves casting off "the works of darkness" and putting on "the armour of light." *Children of light . . . day* behave differently from those *of the night . . . darkness* (compare Ephesians 5:8, 9).

This difference should be obvious. Christians have nothing to hide from God (1 John 1:5, 6; 2:28). Instead, we long deeply for Christ to come again so we might receive a "crown of righteousness" (2 Timothy 4:8). Paul has more to say about expected behavior in our next verse.

> *What Do You Think?*
> How does (or should) the anticipation of Jesus' return influence your response to troubling circumstances?
> *Talking Points for Your Discussion*
> ▪ Political turmoil
> ▪ Financial ups and downs
> ▪ Health problems
> ▪ Other

III. About Behavior
(1 THESSALONIANS 5:6-11)
A. What to Do (vv. 6-8)

6, 7. Therefore let us not sleep, as do others; but let us watch and be sober. For they that sleep sleep in the night; and they that be drunken are drunken in the night.

Unlike Paul's explanation concerning the resurrection of the dead believers, this is probably material that the Thessalonians have heard before, since it speaks to everyday behavior. It bears repeating. Those who are ready for the Lord's return will *watch and be sober* as opposed to the unready who will be asleep and drunk (compare Luke 12:45). It is a mistake to sift the teachings of Jesus for exact details concerning His second coming and end up missing His main point: we must be alert and "Watch!" (Mark 13:37).

8. But let us, who are of the day, be sober, putting on the breastplate of faith and love; and for an helmet, the hope of salvation.

Many are familiar with Paul's description of spiritual armor in Ephesians 6:11-17. Since 1 Thessalonians is written 11 or so years before Ephesians, we detect that this is a favorite teaching of the apostle. Here Paul mentions the two most important defensive pieces of armor for a Roman soldier (compare Isaiah 59:17).

The mighty breastplate protects the chest, abdomen, and their vital organs. A spiritual breastplate is composed of *faith and love,* two sustaining Christian virtues (see 1 Corinthians 13:13). The helmet protects the head from blows that can cause instant death. Spiritually, such protection is *the hope of salvation,* the central message of this entire section. Christ's promised return is a cause for hope. Hope is so central to the Christian faith that Paul refers to the gospel message as "the hope of Israel" (Acts 28:20; compare Romans 8:24).

What Do You Think?

How does Paul's description of spiritual armor help you shine as a child "of the day"?

Talking Points for Your Discussion

- Regarding faith
- Regarding love
- Regarding hope

B. Why to Do It (vv. 9, 10)

9, 10. For God hath not appointed us to wrath, but to obtain salvation by our Lord Jesus Christ, who died for us, that, whether we wake or sleep, we should live together with him.

Closely connected with the second coming of Christ is the concept of final judgment. This judgment will be the justice of God delivered to sinners, here expressed as God's wrath. Part of Paul's message is that Jesus will deliver us from this wrath when He comes in glory (1 Thessalonians 1:10). As sinners, we deserve the anger of God (Romans 1:18; 3:23); salvation from this deserved wrath is offered to us by Jesus, our Savior (5:9).

Paul's picture of a wrathful God is not a popular topic today. We prefer the picture of a for-

giving, loving God, the God of endless second chances and do-overs. Paul knows the loving side of God too (see Romans 5:8; compare Jeremiah 31:3). But Paul stresses that we must place our faith in Christ in order to escape God's wrath.

C. How to Interact (v. 11)

11. Wherefore comfort yourselves together, and edify one another, even as also ye do.

Paul ends this section by reminding the Thessalonians to use his words as mutual comfort. Paul (probably writing from Corinth) is not there to comfort them in person, and he does not need to be. They have the ability and the responsibility of building up one another. They can live as people of hope as they face the future.

Conclusion

A. Living Encouragements

The Christians in Thessalonica seem to have been a close-knit group. They depended on one another for support and encouragement. They had a close attachment to Paul and his coworkers (Silas, Timothy, and perhaps Luke). These men had brought a message of hope because salvation in Jesus Christ had come.

Sadly, the Thessalonians apparently had lost some in their fellowship to death after Paul's departure. This put hope to the test. Could the message of the gospel overcome the doubts of death? Paul's encouraging answer: those who die in Christ will not miss out on His blessed and glorious return.

In our age of overly privatized religion, we can miss an important part of Paul's message: the comfort we are to offer one another is based on our confidence in Christ's return. In this we become living encouragements.

B. Prayer

Father, may we never lose our hopeful anticipation of Your Son's return. May He find us ready. May He find us encouraging one another with His message of hope. In Jesus' name, amen.

C. Thought to Remember

Share comfort in the hope of Christ's return.

INVOLVEMENT LEARNING

Some of the activities below are also found in the helpful student book, Adult Bible Class.
Don't forget to download the free reproducible page from www.standardlesson.com to enhance your lesson!

Into the Lesson

Have the sentence fragment *In Heaven . . .* on the board as learners arrive. Give each an index card. Say, "Complete this sentence on your card." As learners finish, have them affix their cards to the board (provide masking tape). *Option:* Have playing a song that speaks about Heaven as learners complete their cards. (One possibility is "I Can Only Imagine" by MercyMe.)

Discuss some of your learners' ideas. Then say, "At His first coming, Christ sealed the promise of resurrection and Heaven for us; at His second coming, that promise becomes eternal reality. But the second coming also raises questions. Let's see how Paul addressed this issue for the Thessalonians."

Into the Word

Prepare three handouts with the following headings, one heading per handout: *Group 1: "Events of the Second Coming"*—1 Thessalonians 4:13-18; *Group 2: "Warnings/Comparisons"*—1 Thessalonians 5:1-3; and *Group 3: "Night vs. Day"*—1 Thessalonians 5:4-11.

Form learners into three groups, and give each a handout. Ask Group 1 to examine its passage and summarize the events associated with Jesus' second coming. Ask Group 2 to examine its passage to identify warnings and their respective comparisons. Ask Group 3 to examine its passage to identify contrasts between dark and light.

Preface Group 1's presentation by saying, "The Thessalonians seem to have been concerned that their deceased Christian friends would somehow miss out. How did Paul allay their fears?" *(Expected responses: Jesus will come out of the sky, there will be three loud noises, the dead will be resurrected, the living will be caught up to meet Jesus in the air, all who are in Christ will spend eternity with Him.)*

Preface Group 2's presentation by saying, "Paul didn't just write to answer the fears, but also to warn about those who weren't ready. What warn-ings did he give? To what did he compare those warnings?" *(Expected responses: No need to know times and dates / Jesus will come as thief in the night; sudden destruction and no escape / woman in labor.)*

Preface Group 3's presentation by saying, "Scripture offers several contrasts between those who will spend eternity with God and those who will not. Paul compared these two groups with light and darkness. What does he say in this regard?" *(Expected responses: **Night/Darkness**—surprised, asleep, unaware, drunk, suffers wrath; **Day/Light**—ready, sober, alert, clad with spiritual armor, encouraging one another.)*

Option: For extended study on the Night/Darkness and Day/Light contrast, distribute copies of the "Darkness and Light" activity from the reproducible page, which you can download. Have learners work in pairs. Allow time for discussion.

Close this segment by saying, "Paul's message is two-fold: some will spend eternity with God and some will not. Regarding the former, what should our response be?" *(encouragement)* "Regarding the latter, what should our response be?" *(evangelism)*

Into Life

Before class, make a list of names and addresses of your church's members who are elderly, shut-in, and/or terminally ill. Also bring Bible concordances as well as greeting cards that are appropriate for those on the list.

Say, "As a way to encourage some of our saints, I've brought some greeting cards we can send them. I'd like you to choose a name or two from the list and write a note of encouragement. Since Paul charged the Thessalonians to encourage one another with the promise of Jesus' return, include some verses that speak of Heaven." Learners can use the concordances to discover appropriate passages. Offer to mail the completed cards.

Alternative: Substitute the "Songs of Hope" activity from the reproducible page for the above.

The Lord Will Return

THE LORD WILL TRIUMPH

DEVOTIONAL READING: Titus 3:1-7
BACKGROUND SCRIPTURE: 2 Thessalonians 2

2 THESSALONIANS 2:1-4, 8-17

1 Now we beseech you, brethren, by the coming of our Lord Jesus Christ, and by our gathering together unto him,

2 That ye be not soon shaken in mind, or be troubled, neither by spirit, nor by word, nor by letter as from us, as that the day of Christ is at hand.

3 Let no man deceive you by any means: for that day shall not come, except there come a falling away first, and that man of sin be revealed, the son of perdition;

4 Who opposeth and exalteth himself above all that is called God, or that is worshipped; so that he as God sitteth in the temple of God, shewing himself that he is God.

. . . .

8 And then shall that Wicked be revealed, whom the Lord shall consume with the spirit of his mouth, and shall destroy with the brightness of his coming:

9 Even him, whose coming is after the working of Satan with all power and signs and lying wonders,

10 And with all deceivableness of unrighteousness in them that perish; because they received not the love of the truth, that they might be saved.

11 And for this cause God shall send them strong delusion, that they should believe a lie:

12 That they all might be damned who believed not the truth, but had pleasure in unrighteousness.

13 But we are bound to give thanks alway to God for you, brethren beloved of the Lord, because God hath from the beginning chosen you to salvation through sanctification of the Spirit and belief of the truth:

14 Whereunto he called you by our gospel, to the obtaining of the glory of our Lord Jesus Christ.

15 Therefore, brethren, stand fast, and hold the traditions which ye have been taught, whether by word, or our epistle.

16 Now our Lord Jesus Christ himself, and God, even our Father, which hath loved us, and hath given us everlasting consolation and good hope through grace,

17 Comfort your hearts, and stablish you in every good word and work.

KEY VERSES

Now our Lord Jesus Christ himself, and God, even our Father, which hath loved us, and hath given us everlasting consolation and good hope through grace, comfort your hearts, and stablish you in every good word and work. —2 Thessalonians 2:16, 17

Undying Hope

Unit 2: Resurrection Hope

LESSONS 4–9

LESSON AIMS

After participating in this lesson, each student will be able to:

1. Summarize Paul's argument that believers are to reject the deception of false teachers while remaining confident in the Lord's ultimate victory at His return.

2. Compare and contrast the deception in Paul's day with speculative teaching about "the end times" today.

3. Share with the class his or her best practices for avoiding evil deceptions.

LESSON OUTLINE

Introduction
  A. The Great Evil at the End
  B. Lesson Background
  I. Unshaken Believers (2 THESSALONIANS 2:1-4)
    A. Day of Christ (vv. 1, 2)
      Using Discernment
    B. Man of Sin (vv. 3, 4)
  II. Deceived Believers (2 THESSALONIANS 2:8-12)
    A. Revealing of the Wicked (vv. 8-10)
    B. Sending of a Delusion (vv. 11, 12)
  III. Chosen Believers (2 THESSALONIANS 2: 13-17)
    A. Glorious Christ (vv. 13, 14)
    B. Firm Traditions (v. 15)
      Traditions, Good and Bad
    C. Encouraging Prayer (vv. 16, 17)
Conclusion
  A. Restraint, Rebellion, Reward
  B. Prayer
  C. Thought to Remember

Introduction

A. The Great Evil at the End

Once upon a time. These words signal the beginning of a fairy tale, a fanciful story of castles and kingdoms, dragons and princesses. We read these stories with certain expectations. Some of our favorites are full of tension, as when it seems Snow White will not wake from the poisoned apple or the prince will fail to find Cinderella. We are not surprised to hear of the craftiness and power of evil witches and wolves, but we would feel betrayed if the story ended with the bad guys winning.

The Bible has no fairy tales, but it does have a grand narrative about the end of time. We revel in the finale of this story: the triumphant return of the Lord Jesus Christ, addressed in last week's lesson. This week we will look at some other issues related to the end of time.

B. Lesson Background

The technical word for the field of Bible study that deals with end-time prophecies is *eschatology.* Daniel in the Old Testament and Revelation in the New Testament are used often as primary sources for information in this area. A number of Old Testament passages speak of the "day of the Lord" (examples: Isaiah 13:9; Ezekiel 30:3; Zephaniah 1:14). Many of these predict the destruction of the Jerusalem temple by the Babylonians (which happened in 586 BC), but there is often a sense of additional fulfillment beyond that catastrophic event.

Jesus himself spoke of events associated with the end of time, particularly in the Olivet Discourse (also called the Apocalyptic Discourse) in Matthew 24, 25; Mark 13; and Luke 21. We can see in Jesus' words certain predictions of the destruction of the temple in AD 70, but there are elements within the teaching that speak of the end of time as well. Jesus speaks of a period of great suffering that is followed by His own triumphant appearance (see Mark 13:24-26).

This great period of suffering and persecution is often called *the tribulation;* some scholars identify this as a well-defined period in the future that necessarily precedes the coming of the Lord. Several places in the New Testament speak about one or more figures who are to personify evil and opposition to the kingdom of God (see Revelation 13:1, 11; 16:13; 1 John 2:18, 22; 2 John 7). Paul's second letter to the church in Thessalonica, today's study, also discusses a figure of evil.

The letter of 2 Thessalonians begins with Paul offering support to Christians for the "persecutions and tribulations" they had been enduring (2 Thessalonians 1:4). Details of this persecution are not given. We can guess, however, that it may have involved pressure from the envious Jews of Acts 17:5, 13. They might have been upset with fellow Jews who had accepted Jesus as Messiah. The distress could have taken the form of social pressure, economic pressure, even physical intimidation (Acts 17:6).

I. Unshaken Believers
(2 Thessalonians 2:1-4)

A. Day of Christ (vv. 1, 2)

1. **Now we beseech you, brethren, by the coming of our Lord Jesus Christ, and by our gathering together unto him.**

Paul narrows his focus to details concerning Christ's return that are causing uncertainty within the congregation. He begins by summing up his teaching from the previous letter, that the Lord's return will result in a *gathering together unto him* of believers (compare 1 Thessalonians 4:13-17, last week's lesson).

HOW TO SAY IT

apocalyptic	uh-*pah*-kuh-**lip**-tik.
apostasy	uh-*pahs*-tuh-see.
Babylonians	Bab-ih-*low*-nee-unz.
Caligula	Kuh-*lig*-you-luh.
eschatology	ess-kuh-*tah*-luh-gee.
hyperbole	high-*per*-buh-lee.
Judas Iscariot	*Joo*-dus Iss-*care*-ee-ut.
Olivet	*Ol*-ih-vet.
Thessalonians	*Thess*-uh-**lo**-nee-unz
	(*th* as in *thin*).
Zephaniah	Zef-uh-*nye*-uh.

2. **That ye be not soon shaken in mind, or be troubled, neither by spirit, nor by word, nor by letter as from us, as that the day of Christ is at hand.**

Paul plunges into his discussion with a primary, reassuring point: the Thessalonians have nothing to fear regarding the timing of *the day of Christ*. Any teaching that proposes that Christ's return has already happened is false teaching. Paul warns that false teaching may come, perhaps by a letter that purports to be from him.

We know that Paul had sent Timothy (and perhaps others) to the believers in Thessalonica so they would have the advantage of clarifications from one or more of Paul's trusted assistants (see 1 Thessalonians 3:2, 6). Although this is a new church with no veteran Christians, they nonetheless have resources to protect against false teaching.

> **What Do You Think?**
> Thinking of the failed end-time prophecies of years gone by, how will you react to end-time prophecies you may hear in the years ahead?
> *Talking Points for Your Discussion*
> - *Left Behind* movies and books
> - Harold Camping
> - Mayan calendar
> - Y2K
> - 1 John 4:1

❧ USING DISCERNMENT ❧

Who hasn't received one of those e-mails from Nigeria that promises millions of dollars for helping with a monetary transaction? The details of the e-mails vary, but the theme is consistent: someone needs confidential assistance in making a money transfer, and you can help by providing your bank account information. After the millions are transferred into your account, you will be allowed to keep a certain percentage for your trouble.

This deception works because it appeals to a certain aspect of human nature. But those foolish enough to give out bank account numbers quickly discover that it is their own funds that end up being transferred! The FBI's Web site warns of numerous variations of this scam.

Paul warned the Thessalonians not to believe letters fraudulently claiming to have come from him. The frauds could be persuasive by appealing to what the Thessalonians "wanted" to be true. Even so, the frauds could be identified by their contradiction of what Paul preached or the letters he himself had written. The warning to the Thessalonians still applies!　　　　—C. R. B.

B. Man of Sin (vv. 3, 4)

3a. Let no man deceive you by any means: for that day shall not come, except there come a falling away first.

Paul believes throughout his ministry that the return of the Lord is near. But Paul also knows there will be some signs preceding the Lord's return (compare Luke 21:31). He introduces one such sign in this half-verse: *a falling away* (literally, "apostasy").

Paul is not specific about those who will fall away after believing in Christ for a while. This kind of news is troubling in any case, for we want to think that all of our Christian brothers and sisters will remain faithful to the end. But this is not the picture given in the New Testament (see Matthew 13:20, 21; 1 Timothy 4:1; 2 Timothy 4:10). An ongoing heartbreak for Christians is the abandonment of the faith by fellow believers.

> **What Do You Think?**
> What are some safeguards a church might use to help people avoid being deceived by false teachers?
> *Talking Points for Your Discussion*
> - In its Christian education ministry
> - In its library or resource center
> - In its constitution and/or bylaws
> - In its small-group ministry
> - Other

3b, 4. And that man of sin be revealed, the son of perdition; who opposeth and exalteth himself above all that is called God, or that is worshipped; so that he as God sitteth in the temple of God, shewing himself that he is God.

Another great sign preceding the Lord's return will be the rise and revealing of a powerfully evil person, pictured as having a worldwide impact. He will set himself up as a false god, a rival to the Lord God himself. This is portrayed dramatically as the deceiver going so far as to occupy *the temple of God.*

About a decade prior to Paul's writing here, the mad Roman Emperor Caligula ordered a pagan statue to be erected in the Jerusalem temple. Naturally, this created a crisis in Judea. Some students think that Paul is evoking images of that notorious incident as a "type" or "foreshadowing" of something that will happen in the future: the use of idolatrous things to pollute the holy things reserved for God. Others take this imagery to be part of a prophetic drama that requires the temple to be rebuilt in Jerusalem sometime after its destruction in AD 70 (which destruction is less than 20 years in the future as Paul writes) and then be desecrated by the evil person whom Paul describes.

Paul gives this evil person two descriptive titles. First, he is *that man of sin,* which points to someone who violates God's laws with impunity and arrogance. Second, Paul calls him *the son of perdition,* meaning the one whose future destruction is sure (compare Revelation 17:11). He will doubtlessly present himself like Paul's description of Satan as an "angel of light" (2 Corinthians 11:14). He is not a man of victory or triumph, however, but one who will be defeated, judged, and condemned (see 2 Peter 3:7).

> **What Do You Think?**
> What are some consequences of failing to discern satanic activities? How do we guard against this error?
> *Talking Points for Your Discussion*
> - In family life
> - In politics
> - In the church
> - Other

We can note in passing that both the Greek and English wording for *the son of perdition* here exactly match the wording in John 17:12. But the reference there is to Judas Iscariot, who obviously is not the one Paul is talking about here. We can also note that the further description of this man as one who *exalteth himself above all that is called God* is similar to Daniel 11:36. But that passage refers to Antiochus IV, long dead by this point (see discussion in Lesson 3).

All this analysis can get very complicated! But before we get too wrapped up in this, we do well to keep Paul's intent in mind. Some Thessalonians are worried that "the day of Christ is at hand" (v. 2, above) or perhaps has already come and gone. Paul's correction is to say that that's not possible since a falling away and the revealing of a man of sin must happen first, and they haven't.

II. Deceived Believers
(2 THESSALONIANS 2:8-12)
A. Revealing of the Wicked (vv. 8-10)

8. And then shall that Wicked be revealed, whom the Lord shall consume with the spirit of his mouth, and shall destroy with the brightness of his coming.

Our lesson text skips over verses 5-7, but we should summarize what Paul says there: the person of evil being discussed is currently restrained. Yet there will come a time when this restraint is removed so that the final events may proceed in the plan of God. The removal of restraint on *that Wicked* person allows him to *be revealed,* to be out in the open. This will be followed by the Lord's coming, which will bring down the man of sin. The picture is one of instantaneous destruction.

The glorious coming of the Lord will overpower any and all opposition. The result is Jesus' unquestioned reign (see Matthew 25:31). If the power of evil is still at work in the world—and it is—then the Lord's coming has not yet happened.

9. Even him, whose coming is after the working of Satan with all power and signs and lying wonders.

Paul now explains that the source of this great wickedness is Satan. Does this mean that the "man of sin" is Satan himself? Or is Paul referring to two individuals—Satan and a man of sin who is in league with Satan? Scholars have argued for both positions. Either way, what we see here is a powerful pattern of deception (compare Matthew 24:24). The greatest of these lies is for this satanic

figure to set himself up as if he were God (2 Thessalonians 2:4, above).

10. And with all deceivableness of unrighteousness in them that perish; because they received not the love of the truth, that they might be saved.

The tragic side of all this is that many will believe the lie and reject the truth. God does not want any to perish (2 Peter 3:9). But when the Lord Jesus comes again, there will be no more opportunities for switching allegiances to join the winning side. Those who have rejected Jesus will not be saved when He returns.

B. Sending of a Delusion (vv. 11, 12)

11, 12. And for this cause God shall send them strong delusion, that they should believe a lie: that they all might be damned who believed not the truth, but had pleasure in unrighteousness.

On the surface, these two verses are very challenging, for Paul seems to be saying that the ultimate source of deception is God himself—that God causes some to *believe a lie* and thus *be damned.* Yet we know that Satan, not God, is the great deceiver, the father of lies (John 8:44; compare 2 Corinthians 4:4). We also know that God doesn't tempt anyone with evil (James 1:13). How can we resolve the seeming contradiction?

A good rule in Bible study is to note what the surrounding statements say. This keeps things in context. In this case, verses 10 and 12 both contrast *truth* with *unrighteousness.* It is impossible to love both truth and evil at the same time. Those who reject God's truth end up embracing the deceptive nature of the pleasures of lawless wickedness. This in turn opens these unbelievers

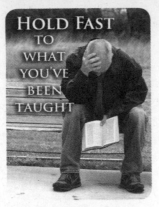

Visual for
Lesson 9

*As you study verse 15, point to this visual and ask,
"What challenges do you face in holding fast?"*

to God's judgment since they have chosen to be deceived. They have already made up their minds. So when Paul says *God shall send them strong delusion,* he may be using the same kind of "God gave them up/over" conclusion that he uses in Romans 1:24, 26, 28. What we are seeing, then, is a declaration of God's judgment.

A second possibility is to see *God shall send them strong delusion* as hyperbole. For example, Luke 14:26 speaks of the need to "hate" family members when becoming a follower of Christ. But we do not expect literal hatred toward one's family members by Christians. If the text before us is to be taken as hyperbole as well, it means that God is still in control despite the activities of Satan and those in league with him. Thus *send them strong delusion* is taken to mean "permits them to be deceived." We can compare Job 1:12, where the Lord is said to permit Satan's testing of Job, with Job 2:3, where the Lord is said to be the one who acted in the testing.

III. Chosen Believers
(2 Thessalonians 2:13-17)
A. Glorious Christ (vv. 13, 14)

13. But we are bound to give thanks alway to God for you, brethren beloved of the Lord, because God hath from the beginning chosen you to salvation through sanctification of the Spirit and belief of the truth.

Paul now leaves the gruesome picture of the unbelievers' future to give thankful comfort to the Thessalonian believers. Paul is confident that they are not among the deceived. Because of their response to the gospel, they are among the chosen.

Paul gives several reasons for their hope of salvation. First, the Thessalonians are *beloved of the Lord.* Everything begins with God's love for us (John 3:16). Second, they have been sanctified (made holy) by the Holy Spirit. Third, God knows that they have a confident *belief of the truth.* As they hold fast to the things Paul has taught, their salvation is not in question. Holding fast means they won't be deceived by a "man of sin" figure.

14. Whereunto he called you by our gospel, to the obtaining of the glory of our Lord Jesus Christ.

Fourth, the Thessalonians have the hope of salvation because of the gospel. This is the good news that Jesus died for their sins, rose from the dead, and will return to gather all of His people (whether dead or alive at the time) to be with Him forever. This is the picture of *the glory of our Lord Jesus Christ,* a glory that all believers will have the privilege to witness and to share (1 John 3:2).

B. Firm Traditions (v. 15)

15. Therefore, brethren, stand fast, and hold the traditions which ye have been taught, whether by word, or our epistle.

Paul sums up this section with simple advice: just keep doing what you know to be right. The Thessalonians have been taught well (2 Thessalonians 2:5), even though Paul's stay with them was brief. They do not need to look for new teachings that will lead them astray. They have memories of Paul's preaching, and they now have two letters filled with doctrinal treasures to guide them as they continue to be lovers of the truth.

❧ *Traditions, Good and Bad* ❧

All my fathers have been churchmen,
Nineteen hundred years or so,
And to every new suggestion
They have always answered, "No!"

Isn't that how many churches function? Several years ago, a certain church almost split over the

The Lord Will Triumph

decision to begin a second Sunday service, which featured contemporary music and worship style. Some members left, but the church survived.

Then an interesting thing happened: the older, "traditional" service became less traditional, using visual media, singing some contemporary songs, and generally enjoying a new vitality. On the other hand, the newer, "contemporary" service, became locked into the format it had used from its inception. One church member who enjoys popping the balloons of pretense sometimes chides the "contemporary" folks by calling their service *traditional* and the "traditional" service *transitional*. His point is that the latter found freedom to adapt, while the contemporary worship became mired in its own set of traditions!

Paul admonished his Thessalonian readers to stay rooted in "the traditions which ye have been taught." By this he meant the apostles' instructions, not entrenched practices of human tradition. How can we make sure we distinguish between the two?　　　　　—C. R. B.

C. Encouraging Prayer (vv. 16, 17)

16, 17. Now our Lord Jesus Christ himself, and God, even our Father, which hath loved us, and hath given us everlasting consolation and good hope through grace, comfort your hearts, and stablish you in every good word and work.

Paul ends this section with a prayer asking that God continue to safeguard the faith of the Thessalonians. There is unity between the Father and the Son (John 10:30), so there is a unified purpose in the strengthening and encouragement of these believers.

Worthy of note are the three "goods" Paul lifts up: *good hope, good word,* and *[good] work.* Paul has not taken up this much space in these two Thessalonian letters to address the second coming of the Lord simply to provide details for those fascinated by the intricacies of prophecy. Paul's purpose in teaching about Christ's return is to give his readers excellent expectations, a good hope concerning what the future holds. Having this hope should result is goodness in the believers' lives, whether in speech or deed. If our hope is in the Lord, our lives will bear His fruit.

What Do You Think?

How will your service for Christ this week be influenced by your expectation of His return?

Talking Points for Your Discussion
- In your witness at work or school
- In your faithfulness in worship and Bible study
- In your family relationships
- Other

Conclusion

A. Restraint, Rebellion, Reward

John Stott describes Paul's scenario in 2 Thessalonians 2 as "Restraint, Rebellion & Reward." For a time, the power of evil is restrained by God. At some point, this restraint is removed, with the result of rebellion among those who reject God's truth. This is followed by just and sure rewards from God. The wicked are punished, and those who have embraced the hope of the gospel are gathered to begin eternity with their risen Lord.

Throughout the history of the church, there have been those who have interpreted the events of their day as indicators of the Lord's soon return. This continues today. The modern interpreters may be as wrong as those of previous centuries, or they may be correct. Christ may return very soon, or He may delay for thousands of years. For believers, it does not matter. We have a blessed hope whether we live to see Christ return in power or are among the dead who are awakened by His call.

We should have no fear of "the man of sin," whoever he is, for we are among those who have washed our robes in the blood of the lamb. We will stand before God to worship and praise Him forever (Revelation 7:14-17).

B. Prayer

Lord God, may we continue to trust in You when evil gains power and when others reject the truth. May Paul's encouragement to the Thessalonians be ours as well. In Jesus' name, amen.

C. Thought to Remember

Celebrate Christ's past, present,
and future victory.

INVOLVEMENT LEARNING

Some of the activities below are also found in the helpful student book, Adult Bible Class.
Don't forget to download the free reproducible page from www.standardlesson.com to enhance your lesson!

Into the Lesson

Option 1: Form learners into small groups to share beliefs about how and when Jesus will return, listing ideas on a piece of poster board. Read the remarks as you affix each poster to the wall.

Option 2: For a whole-class brainstorming activity, say, "Sometimes people predict dates for the Lord's return. What are some of these predictions, and who made them?" Jot responses on the board or ask a "scribe" to do so.

Say, "There are many ideas about how and when Jesus will come again. We find questions surfacing in the pages of the Bible on how and when this will happen. Our lesson text will show us how Paul encourages the church in Thessalonica about this issue."

Into the Word

Give each learner a handout with the heading "Discovering the Day of Christ." Include these instructions: "Today's passage, 2 Thessalonians 2:1-4, 8-17, is packed with information about the *who, what,* and *when* associated with 'the day of Christ.' Search the verses listed below, looking for information about this day; note that information beside the verse number." Have the following verse numbers listed vertically down the left side of the handout: 2, 3, 4, 8, 9, 10-12, 13, 14, 15, 16, 17. (Note: This activity may be done in pairs, in small groups, or as a whole class activity. If you do it in pairs or small groups, you can create two or more handouts with fewer verses each so the pairs or groups have different ranges of text to examine.)

As you discuss conclusions as a class, possible discoveries include the following: verse 2, don't believe false teaching that the day of Christ has already come; verses 3, 4, the day will be preceded by apostasy and the appearance of a "man of sin"; verse 8, the wicked one will be revealed and destroyed; verse 9, the wicked one will perform lying wonders; verse 13, believers are loved

and sanctified; verse 14, believers will experience in some way the glory of Jesus; verse 15, believers must stand fast; verse 16, 17, God's love for believers gives comfort and hope.

Ask learners to turn their handouts over, draw a vertical line down the center, write "Wicked One" at the top of the left column and "Followers of Paul's Teachings" at the top of the right column. Say, "We now want to contrast the characteristics of the wicked one and of those who follow the gospel teaching of Paul. Take five minutes to scan the text and jot characteristics in the appropriate column." Review and discuss discoveries.

Tie the two activities together by asking, "How does satanic deceit make itself known in our culture today?

Option: Distribute copies of the "The End-Times News" activity from the reproducible page, which you can download. Ask learners to complete one of the three writing opportunities. Discuss results and compare with the lesson text.

Into Life

Say, "Truth and deceit are contrasted sharply in today's text. What are occasions in our daily routines where we may be challenged to ignore truths we've been taught about God and act in a manner contrary to that teaching?" Coax circumstances that reflect a variety of settings (as social events, work environments, parenting, private times when no one sees you, etc.).

As you jot ideas from a learner on the board, ask other class members, "What would you say to a Christian facing this situation that will encourage him or her to 'stand fast'?" After filling out the list, point to it as you ask, "Which of these is the highest-risk circumstance for you? You will not need to share your response here, but you need to identify it if you are going to 'stand fast.'" Form prayer teams to pray for each other's faithfulness when the deceiver attacks.

LIVING
HOPE

DEVOTIONAL READING: Lamentations 3:19-24
BACKGROUND SCRIPTURE: 1 Peter 1

1 PETER 1:3-16

3 Blessed be the God and Father of our Lord Jesus Christ, which according to his abundant mercy hath begotten us again unto a lively hope by the resurrection of Jesus Christ from the dead,

4 To an inheritance incorruptible, and undefiled, and that fadeth not away, reserved in heaven for you,

5 Who are kept by the power of God through faith unto salvation ready to be revealed in the last time.

6 Wherein ye greatly rejoice, though now for a season, if need be, ye are in heaviness through manifold temptations:

7 That the trial of your faith, being much more precious than of gold that perisheth, though it be tried with fire, might be found unto praise and honour and glory at the appearing of Jesus Christ:

8 Whom having not seen, ye love; in whom, though now ye see him not, yet believing, ye rejoice with joy unspeakable and full of glory:

9 Receiving the end of your faith, even the salvation of your souls.

10 Of which salvation the prophets have enquired and searched diligently, who prophesied of the grace that should come unto you:

11 Searching what, or what manner of time the Spirit of Christ which was in them did signify, when it testified beforehand the sufferings of Christ, and the glory that should follow.

12 Unto whom it was revealed, that not unto themselves, but unto us they did minister the things, which are now reported unto you by them that have preached the gospel unto you with the Holy Ghost sent down from heaven; which things the angels desire to look into.

13 Wherefore gird up the loins of your mind, be sober, and hope to the end for the grace that is to be brought unto you at the revelation of Jesus Christ;

14 As obedient children, not fashioning yourselves according to the former lusts in your ignorance:

15 But as he which hath called you is holy, so be ye holy in all manner of conversation;

16 Because it is written, Be ye holy; for I am holy.

KEY VERSE

Blessed be the God and Father of our Lord Jesus Christ, which according to his abundant mercy hath begotten us again unto a lively hope by the resurrection of Jesus Christ from the dead. —1 Peter 1:3

UNDYING HOPE

Unit 3: A Call to Holy Living
LESSONS 10–13

LESSON AIMS

After participating in this lesson, each student will be able to:

1. Tell what Peter says is the source, object, and expression of hope for the Christian.

2. Explain the relationship between personal holiness and salvation.

3. Identify one area of unholiness in his or her own life and make a plan for change.

LESSON OUTLINE

Introduction

A. Wishes vs. Hope

"I hope that the weather improves tomorrow." "I hope that the repairs on my car do not cost too much." "I hope that the home team has a good season this year." You probably have made statements like these at one time or another.

What do we mean when we say *hope* in these kinds of statements? We mean that there is one outcome that we prefer over another. We are expressing a wish. Such wishes may not be expressed with much confidence. They are what we *desire* to occur but not necessarily what we *expect*. It is easy to confuse the common usage of the word *hope* with the way that word is used in the New Testament. Today's study helps us avoid such confusion.

B. Lesson Background

Today's text comes from the first of the New Testament letters of the apostle Peter. As we learn from the letter's opening, Peter wrote to Christians in "Pontus, Galatia, Cappadocia, Asia and Bithynia" (1 Peter 1:1). These designations refer to an area that corresponds to modern Turkey. That region was controlled by Rome in Peter's day.

The Romans respected Judaism because of its antiquity. At first, the Romans viewed Christianity as merely an offshoot of Judaism, so the respect applied to Christians as well. But eventually the Romans came to see Christianity as a new religion in its own right. This created suspicion of Christians being "a class of men given to a new and mischievous superstition," as one ancient Roman historian put it in describing a Roman attitude during Nero's reign (AD 54–68).

Although the believers remained law-abiding citizens, they fell under suspicion of disorderly or criminal behavior, even insurrection against the government. Consequently, Christians in this region came under persecution. They faced insults, exclusion, loss of livelihood, arrest, and even violence. The churches of western Asia Minor were persecuted, suffering churches. The letter of 1 Peter, written about AD 64, addressed those Christians with a powerful reminder of the reality that lay beyond their suffering.

I. Hope Founded

(1 PETER 1:3-5)

A. Basis (vv. 3, 4)

3. Blessed be the God and Father of our Lord Jesus Christ, which according to his abundant mercy hath begotten us again unto a lively hope by the resurrection of Jesus Christ from the dead.

Letters in New Testament times usually start with a brief word of greeting and a statement of thanksgiving to a god. New Testament letters typically begin this way, with the thanks offered to the one true God. First Peter follows this common pattern, with the thanksgiving beginning here.

Note how many key ideas are contained in the beginning of this word of thanks. God is *Father,* a good and wise protector and provider for His people. He has the relationship of Father to Jesus, who himself is *Lord,* the divine ruler over all. Through Jesus we have received mercy, God's accepting us as friends and restraining our just punishment.

That mercy leads to our being *begotten* or born again. The expression "born again" in our time is widely taken to mean that one has had a dramatic conversion experience. Genuine conversion to faith in Jesus is often dramatic, but in its biblical usage that is not the emphasis of the expression. Instead, it stresses that through faith in Jesus one has a new family relationship. Under God's covenant with ancient Israel, one was "born" into His people. But in Christ anyone can be "reborn" into God's family. In fact, that is the only way one becomes part of God's family (John 3:3-8).

The result of this new family relationship is a new expectation of the future, a new hope. Like a family member with a sure inheritance, members of God's family can be confident of their future.

That hope can rightly be called *lively* (or "living") because it is founded on the triumph of life over death. Jesus' resurrection is the basis and guarantee for our future as believers in Him. Because God raised Jesus from the dead and because as believers we belong to Jesus, we have every reason for a confident hope that God will raise us up as well (1 Corinthians 15:20-23).

For all these reasons and more, Peter gives thanks to God. The term *blessed* when applied to God means to be worthy of praise and thanks.

What Do You Think?

Which Scripture passage(s) do you find most helpful in strengthening your "lively hope"? Why?

Talking Points for Your Discussion

- Acts 24:15
- Romans 15:13
- 2 Corinthians 3:10-12
- Hebrews 6:16-20
- Other

---

4. To an inheritance incorruptible, and undefiled, and that fadeth not away, reserved in heaven for you.

Now Peter focuses on the object of our confident hope. Reborn as members of God's family, we have a claim to "the family estate." But our inheritance with God is not the kind of thing that can fall apart or lose value as ordinary inheritances so often do. Rather, it is permanent: incapable of decay of any kind. That is because it is found in Heaven, in the presence of the eternal God (compare Matthew 6:20). It is, in fact, eternal life in God's presence, the very thing for which we were first made. That inheritance is now reserved for us, kept back for us to have on our arrival.

What Do You Think?

How does the inheritance we have in Christ contrast with worldly inheritances?

Talking Points for Your Discussion

- With regard to value
- With regard to how long they last
- With regard to how they may or may not be shared
- With regard to how they are obtained
- Other

❧ DECAY ❧

Virtually everything on earth will decay. Food will rot. Clothing will mildew. Paper will decompose. Asphalt will disintegrate. Concrete will weather and crumble. Bones of dinosaurs can be dug up, but the mere existence of such bones testifies to the fact that the life they were once part of is no more.

Incorruptibility is not a characteristic of life on this earth. It doesn't happen in physical things, and it probably never happens in moral standards either. We see such standards decline as descriptions are cleverly reworded. For example, *prostitutes* are now called *sex workers* in some areas. This is merely a way to "call evil good" (Isaiah 5:20); it is a way to claim to be without sin (contrast 1 John 1:8). Such is the decay of the world.

Yet Peter promises that ultimately we will receive something incorruptible: an eternal inheritance reserved for us in Heaven. As Paul said, "This corruptible must put on incorruption, and this mortal must put on immortality" (1 Corinthians 15:53). A time is coming when all the decaying things of this world will be behind us. What a joy that will be!　　　—J. B. N.

B. Protection (v. 5)

5. Who are kept by the power of God through faith unto salvation ready to be revealed in the last time.

As we anticipate receiving our inheritance, we can be confident not just that the inheritance is there but that we will indeed receive it. That confidence is not based on our own ability to "get through" to the end, however. It is founded on God's ability to see us through. God's power guards us through the hardships that we face as believers, allowing our faith to endure and even flourish when we might expect it to be quenched (compare 2 Corinthians 1:3-10; Revelation 3:10).

The outcome is the promised end-time salvation of God. To say that it will *be revealed in*

HOW TO SAY IT

Asia	*Ay*-zha.
Bithynia	Bih-*thin*-ee-uh.
Cappadocia	Kap-uh-*doe*-shuh.
Galatia	Guh-*lay*-shuh.
Nostradamus	*Nahss*-truh-**dah**-mus.
Pontus	*Pon*-tuss.

the last time is not a frightening prospect for the Christian. God's end time indeed means the climax of His righteous judgment, but that is to be experienced by God's enemies. For those who are His family, the end means salvation, the final deliverance from all the problems and persecutions we face. It means God's victory, a victory that He shares with the entire family.

II. Believers Refined
(1 PETER 1:6-9)
A. Trials, Value, Result (vv. 6, 7)

6. Wherein ye greatly rejoice, though now for a season, if need be, ye are in heaviness through manifold temptations.

Eternal life in God's family is certainly something to rejoice about. But Peter makes clear that our rejoicing goes on even when the present is difficult. The Greek word behind the translation *temptations* is also translated "trial" in 1 Peter 4:12. Trials or persecutions can tempt believers to abandon the faith so that the persecution may stop. But those reading Peter's letter can face persecution because God's promise of final victory is sure.

That promise changes the believer's perspective on suffering in the present. The sufferings may be many and of all kinds. But compared with eternity, they are slight. So from the perspective of faith, they last *for a season*, just a short time.

Those sufferings are no accident; they do not happen because God's power has failed. Rather, they play a role in His plan. God does not cause them, but in His wisdom He uses them.

7. That the trial of your faith, being much more precious than of gold that perisheth, though it be tried with fire, might be found unto praise and honour and glory at the appearing of Jesus Christ.

The reasons for God allowing His people to suffer are many. No single explanation is sufficient, and much remains a mystery to us. But here Peter reminds readers of one outcome of our suffering under God's plan: faith that has endured suffering has been strengthened and proved genuine, like gold that has been refined and purified in a super-hot fire. If fire can refine earthly gold, which passes away with this present age, then suffering can refine faith that endures forever and is immeasurably more valuable than gold (compare Isaiah 48:10; Zechariah 13:9; 1 Corinthians 3:13).

> **What Do You Think?**
> What difficulty has served as the most severe "trial of your faith" to this point? How have things turned out?
>
> *Talking Points for Your Discussion*
> - Challenges on the job to act in line with Christian ethics
> - Cultural acceptance of immoral lifestyles
> - Discrimination due to of faith conviction
> - Other

B. Joy, Love, Goal (vv. 8, 9)

8. Whom having not seen, ye love; in whom, though now ye see him not, yet believing, ye rejoice with joy unspeakable and full of glory.

In the end, Jesus will be revealed to all as Lord; for now, He is unseen. But those with faith affirm His lordship even though we, like everyone else, cannot see Him. Therein lies the essence of faith: a confident belief and commitment in the unseen reality of the true God (John 20:29; 2 Corinthians 5:7; Hebrews 11:1).

That unseen reality enables us to rejoice even when what we do see is profoundly difficult. The suffering of the faithful is very real. But so is the power of the Lord, and so is the promise of His final victory. As a result, our rejoicing can continue at all times. It is *joy unspeakable* because it is based on the Lord who is beyond comparison with anything else. It is *full of glory* because it acknowledges Christ's unseen glory and anticipates the time when His glory will be revealed to all.

9. Receiving the end of your faith, even the salvation of your souls.

Again Peter reminds suffering Christians that their confident expectation of the future transforms their present. *The end* refers to a goal or intended outcome (compare Romans 6:22). The goal that God has for us is that we should be rescued from evil and so share in His victory. Troubles are real, but are insignificant compared with eternity.

III. Plan Fulfilled
(1 PETER 1:10-12)

A. Prophets Had Searched (vv. 10, 11)

10. Of which salvation the prophets have enquired and searched diligently, who prophesied of the grace that should come unto you.

Peter has put the present in perspective by comparing it with the future. Now he compares the future with the past, reminding believers that they are the objects of God's favor at the very climax of His historic plan of salvation.

The Old Testament prophets were God's inspired messengers, delivering His authoritative message to successive generations of Israelites. Their message both interpreted the present and promised the future that God would bring to reality. The present, according to those prophets, is characterized by rebellion against God. But God will prevail and accomplish His purpose, which is to turn the rebels into friends. That can come about only by God's grace—the favor and blessing He gives to those who do not deserve it.

The prophets had announced that one day God would accomplish that saving goal. But they did not live to see its coming. As faithful people, they longed to experience the climax of God's plan, or at least to know more about it (Matthew 13:17; Luke 10:24). Now believers in Christ are in the very position that the ancient prophets longed for!

❧ *WHICH PROPHECIES?* ❧

Belief in prophets, oracles, and seers was common in the paganism of the first century AD. Various "signs" were taken to indicate a person's future greatness. The problem is that these were recorded *after* the individual did in fact become great. Outside the Judeo-Christian heritage, there is virtually no evidence of valid predictive prophecy of a person's greatness before the person was born.

More recently, Nostradamus wrote a book of prophecies in the sixteenth century. Modern followers have claimed that he predicted world events centuries in advance. But a more objective view is that such claims are based on (sometimes deliberate) mistranslations or strained explanations of his original words.

Visual for Lesson 10. *Point to this visual as you introduce the discussion question that is associated with verse 16.*

By contrast, the Old Testament offers prophecies of influential leaders far in advance of their appearance (examples: Isaiah 45:1, 13; Daniel 8:9-11, 20, 21). The most important of these prophecies were those of Jesus and His ministry. Which prophets and prophecies do you trust? —J. B. N.

11. Searching what, or what manner of time the Spirit of Christ which was in them did signify, when it testified beforehand the sufferings of Christ, and the glory that should follow.

Through prophets, God repeatedly promised that He would deliver His people. The prophets knew the certainty of that promise, but they did not know exactly how God would fulfill it.

Writing from the perspective that knows how God fulfilled His promises, Peter discusses just how amazing God's plan is. The prophets delivered God's promise to His suffering people, and the prophets were themselves at the very center of the suffering (Matthew 5:12; 23:30, 35). In fulfilling the promise given through the prophets, God entered the world in the person of Jesus. He willingly accepted suffering and death. By that means Jesus overcame the sin and death that oppressed them. The prophets had revealed glimpses of this plan (Isaiah 53:1-12; Zechariah 13:7; etc.), but only as it is fulfilled do we see it clearly.

It was well established among believers in Israel's God that God's Spirit inspired the prophets to deliver their message. But here Peter refers to God's Spirit as *the Spirit of Christ*. This emphasizes not just that Jesus is the divine Son of God, but also that the Spirit of the Christ who suffered is the one who inspired the prophets who suffered. That in turn reminds the readers, who are experiencing suffering of their own, that the same Spirit lives in them. He enables them to fulfill God's plan in the midst of their difficulty.

To that reminder the readers can add the hope of future deliverance. Christ suffered, but then rose in glory. Presently Christ's people suffer, but at His return they will share in His glory. Since God has faithfully fulfilled His promise to send Christ, and since God faithfully raised Christ from the dead, then God will be faithful to send Christ again to bring the fullness of salvation to His people.

B. Answer Is Revealed (v. 12)

12. Unto whom it was revealed, that not unto themselves, but unto us they did minister the things, which are now reported unto you by them that have preached the gospel unto you with the Holy Ghost sent down from heaven; which things the angels desire to look into.

Believers in Christ stand at the focus of everything that God has done in history. We are the beneficiaries of the promises God made through the prophets. What the Holy Spirit promised through the prophets we have now received. Even the angels through the ages have longed to have a glimpse of what Christians now have.

The first readers of this letter may think of themselves as anything but privileged. But their position from God's perspective is quite different. They already have the blessings of the ages. That reminder provides them with a firm basis for the confident expectation that God will indeed deliver them fully when Christ returns.

IV. Holiness Required
(1 PETER 1:13-16)
A. Results Expected (vv. 13-15)

13. Wherefore gird up the loins of your mind, be sober, and hope to the end for the grace that is to be brought unto you at the revelation of Jesus Christ.

Peter now brings the issue of hope to the action step. To move quickly in biblical times, a man needs to pull up the hem of his robe and tie it around his waist with his cloth belt. This is what it means to *gird up the loins*—it signifies being ready for action (compare Luke 12:35).

For believers under persecution, the need is to have the mind fully instilled with the reality of the gospel. That perspective demands a specific attitude. It begins with soberness, or seriousness of mind. That does not imply humorlessness. Rather, it means that we have a sound, wise, and realistic assessment of the world around us. The sober person does not waste life on meaningless things. The gospel allows us to focus on God's purposes.

> **What Do You Think?**
> What specifically can you do to "gird up the loins of your mind" this week?
> *Talking Points for Your Discussion*
> - Regarding your knowledge of God's Word
> - Regarding your prayer life
> - Regarding your entertainment choices
> - Other

14. As obedient children, not fashioning yourselves according to the former lusts in your ignorance.

Those who believe that their lives belong only to themselves imagine that they are free to do as they please. Those are the lusts of ignorance. But matters are different for those with a new birth into God's family. We want to please our Father. Saved in the past, with a hope for the future, our outlook in the present is entirely transformed.

15. But as he which hath called you is holy, so be ye holy in all manner of conversation.

To say that God is holy is to say that He is set apart and distinct—untouched by uncleanness. As members of His family, we are called to maintain the family resemblance. We live so that we are distinctly identified with God's character and purpose. The first-century readers are being persecuted because of their distinct lifestyle. Peter reminds them that they need to maintain that distinction despite its costs because of their vital identity as God's children. The word *conversation*

in the *King James Version* here refers to all kinds of interaction with people, not just speech.

B. Reason Established (v. 16)

16. Because it is written, Be ye holy; for I am holy.

This quotation is found repeatedly in Leviticus (11:44, 45; 19:2; 20:7). That book emphasized to the Israelites how they were to live distinctively as God's people among the pagan nations. Because through the gospel Christians have the fulfillment of Israel's promises and confident expectation for the future, our obligation is all the greater to live in a way that shows our identity as God's people.

> **What Do You Think?**
> What do you most need to lay aside in your pursuit of holiness? How will you do it?
> *Talking Points for Your Discussion*
> - A material possession
> - A secret sin
> - A habit
> - Other

Conclusion
A. Confident Expectation

A wag once said, "Christians are too heavenly minded to be any earthly good." That may be the most inaccurate assessment of Christianity ever given! Genuine hope, founded on the gospel, gives Christians the power to overcome all kinds of obstacles in the present as we live out God's plan and purpose in the world. A confident expectation of God's salvation does not make us passive and useless. It empowers us to live in a way that testifies to the Christ whose return we assuredly await.

B. Prayer

O God, You have done amazing things to make us part of Your family. Strengthen our hope for the future so that we can live as Your people in the present. In Jesus' name, amen.

C. Thought to Remember

"Those who have a 'why' to live can bear with almost any 'how.'"   —Victor Frankl

INVOLVEMENT LEARNING

Some of the activities below are also found in the helpful student book, Adult Bible Class.
Don't forget to download the free reproducible page from www.standardlesson.com to enhance your lesson!

Into the Lesson

Have the following on the board as learners arrive: *Name things we accept or believe as true, even though we cannot or have not personally seen them.* Jot responses on the board. Possible responses among many are gravity, DNA molecules, carbon dioxide, germs, etc.

Ask, "Why do we accept these things as real?" After discussion, make the transition to Bible study by saying, "Peter reminds believers that we accept Jesus and His resurrection as true even without seeing Him. He calls this acceptance 'hope.' Hope should be a key word for every Christian's life."

Alternative: Place in chairs copies of the "Discovering the Key" activity from the reproducible page, which you can download. Learners can begin working on this exercise as they arrive.

Into the Word

Divide the class into five study teams of two to five each. (Larger classes may form additional teams to study duplicate topics; smaller classes can form fewer teams and double up some assignments.) Give each team a copy of the appropriate segment of the lesson commentary, a poster board, a marker, and the following instructions:

Hope Team: Clarify the intent of the word *hope* for today's study. Read the lesson's Introduction and Lesson Background for ideas. Illustrate how the word *hope* is used in 1 Peter 1:3.

Resurrection Team: Focusing on 1 Peter 1:3-5, clarify how Peter looks to the resurrection of Christ to bring hope to believers. Explain why verse 3 may be called *the key verse* for today's text. Explain how believers are "kept by the power of God through faith unto salvation" (v. 5).

Trials Team: Focusing on 1 Peter 1:6-9, clarify and illustrate Peter's teaching that hope is often refined in trials. Give a contemporary example of his gold illustration in verse 7.

Salvation Team: Focusing on 1 Peter 1:10-12, summarize and clarify how the past gives hope for our salvation, our future deliverance.

Action Team: Focusing on 1 Peter 1:13-16, list, explain, and illustrate how hope transforms the lives of believers.

Allow time for groups to share their conclusions.

Into Life

Say, "The word *hope* is a very common word in the Christian vocabulary. The *Hope Team* reminded us that Christians do not use that word in the way that it is used in many contemporary settings. We can illustrate the Christian idea of *hope* with songs." Ask each team to select a song that reflects any of the principles of hope taught in today's text. (*Option:* Distribute hymnals and/or other Christian songbooks for learners to consult for their selections.) Teams will share why they chose particular songs and tell how those songs demonstrate hope as taught in today's study.

Say, "Music is one way to share and teach hope to a new generation of believers. Why do you think it is important for each generation to learn this concept?" After some discussion, ask, "What are some other ways we can teach a new generation about this kind of hope?"

Distribute handouts with this heading: *My Last Will and Testament of Spiritual Things.* Include the following below the heading:

I, _____, being spiritually minded, do wish to pass to my physical and/or spiritual children and grandchildren, this thought: _____

Ask learners to write a sentence stating what spiritual heritage they would like to pass along. The statement should include the word *hope*.

Option: Distribute copies of the "Sharing Our Hope" activity from the reproducible page. Use this as a case study to discuss how the lesson text could be used to comfort a suffering Christian.

SURE
HOPE

DEVOTIONAL READING: Psalm 130
BACKGROUND SCRIPTURE: 2 Peter 1

2 PETER 1:2-15, 20, 21

2 Grace and peace be multiplied unto you through the knowledge of God, and of Jesus our Lord,

3 According as his divine power hath given unto us all things that pertain unto life and godliness, through the knowledge of him that hath called us to glory and virtue:

4 Whereby are given unto us exceeding great and precious promises: that by these ye might be partakers of the divine nature, having escaped the corruption that is in the world through lust.

5 And beside this, giving all diligence, add to your faith virtue; and to virtue knowledge;

6 And to knowledge temperance; and to temperance patience; and to patience godliness;

7 And to godliness brotherly kindness; and to brotherly kindness charity.

8 For if these things be in you, and abound, they make you that ye shall neither be barren nor unfruitful in the knowledge of our Lord Jesus Christ.

9 But he that lacketh these things is blind, and cannot see afar off, and hath forgotten that he was purged from his old sins.

10 Wherefore the rather, brethren, give diligence to make your calling and election sure: for if ye do these things, ye shall never fall:

11 For so an entrance shall be ministered unto you abundantly into the everlasting kingdom of our Lord and Saviour Jesus Christ.

12 Wherefore I will not be negligent to put you always in remembrance of these things, though ye know them, and be established in the present truth.

13 Yea, I think it meet, as long as I am in this tabernacle, to stir you up by putting you in remembrance;

14 Knowing that shortly I must put off this my tabernacle, even as our Lord Jesus Christ hath shewed me.

15 Moreover I will endeavour that ye may be able after my decease to have these things always in remembrance.

. . . .

20 Knowing this first, that no prophecy of the scripture is of any private interpretation.

21 For the prophecy came not in old time by the will of man: but holy men of God spake as they were moved by the Holy Ghost.

KEY VERSE

According as his divine power hath given unto us all things that pertain unto life and godliness, through the knowledge of him that hath called us to glory and virtue. —**2 Peter 1:3**

UNDYING HOPE

Unit 3: A Call to Holy Living
LESSONS 10–13

LESSON AIMS

After participating in this lesson, each student will be able to:

1. List some of the gifts God has given us so that we have everything we need for a life of godliness.

2. Contrast Peter's concept of partaking of the divine nature with pagan concepts of "becoming gods."

3. Identify the quality of 2 Peter 1:5-7 where he or she is weakest and make a plan for change.

LESSON OUTLINE

Introduction

A. How Permanent Is "Permanent"?

As children we look forward to losing our temporary teeth and getting permanent ones. As adults we go to great effort to make those so-called permanent teeth last. We may go to the dentist for a temporary crown, to be replaced a week later with a permanent one. Then years later, that supposedly "permanent" work has to be repeated. Permanent did not turn out to mean "forever"!

It seldom does. A temporary worker has a job for a short period of time, but no job position is truly permanent. A temporary tattoo will wash right off, but even the permanent kind fades with time. Perhaps most difficult to make permanent is a change in one's life. Most humans know that they need a better kind of life. But finding a way to make the right change and make it permanent is difficult. Today's text is about making change that is permanent for this life and beyond.

B. Lesson Background

In many respects, 2 Peter is the sequel to 1 Peter (see the background to last week's lesson). The focus of 2 Peter is on that apostle's final instructions as he anticipates his pending death. We might say that this letter is Peter's "last will and testament." As such, it is a discourse on what he realizes the rising generation of Christians needs, the lessons he has learned through a lifetime of following Jesus in a sinful world.

The letter focuses on a few key topics, including the life that results from the genuine message of God (2 Peter 1), resistance to false and immoral teachers (2 Peter 2), and patience and expectancy regarding Christ's return (2 Peter 3). This week's text belongs to that first section. We think 2 Peter was written in AD 67 or 68.

I. Hope's Resources
(2 PETER 1:2-4)
A. Knowledge (vv. 2, 3)

2. Grace and peace be multiplied unto you through the knowledge of God, and of Jesus our Lord.

This letter begins with the kind of greeting that we find in most New Testament letters. Having identified himself and addressed the readers in verse 1, Peter now offers a salutation that is significant for what he is about to say. In the Greek language of the New Testament, the word for *grace* sounds much like another word commonly used as a greeting. Christians play on that similarity, turning their word of greeting into a reminder of God's undeserved favor. *Peace* is the standard greeting among Jewish people. It is used by Christians, both Jews and non-Jews, to affirm that God's long-anticipated peace is now delivered by Christ.

Peter here does not simply proclaim that these gifts are available, but prays that they may grow for the readers. Because the readers of this letter have true knowledge of God, not some myth or human creation, they are on a path that must yield an ever-increasing change in their lives.

3. According as his divine power hath given unto us all things that pertain unto life and godliness, through the knowledge of him that hath called us to glory and virtue.

The gifts in Christ provide the sure foundation for the life that God intends for us. Four key words, appearing in two pairs, express this. The first word in each pair describes a gift from God, and the second describes our response.

The first pair is *life and godliness.* The word *life* is a reminder that real life is available only as God's gift in Christ. *Godliness* refers to a style of life that properly honors God in obedience.

The second pair is *glory and virtue.* The preposition *to* in front of this pair is a little tricky because there is no preposition in the Greek text; it has to be supplied by the translator for smooth reading. Perhaps your copy of the *King James Version* has a footnote that offers *by* as a possible alternative. In either case, we look forward to the time when God's glorious nature will be revealed fully. We share His glory because He promises to share His victory with the people who belong to Him by His grace.

Virtue, the second half of this pair, may sound like an old-fashioned word to us. In its biblical context it refers to an excellent style of life, one that reflects the real purpose for which we exist.

What Do You Think?
In which areas that deal with living a life of godliness have you grown the most in the past year? Why?
Talking Points for Your Discussion
- With regard to your prayer life
- With regard to your worship
- With regard to your Christian service
- With regard to your Bible knowledge
- Other

B. Promises (v. 4)

4. Whereby are given unto us exceeding great and precious promises: that by these ye might be partakers of the divine nature, having escaped the corruption that is in the world through lust.

Again, Peter emphasizes the way that God has given gifts that motivate lasting and growing change. The *exceeding great and precious promises* are the ones now fulfilled in Christ, though also awaiting ultimate fulfillment at Christ's return.

The result is that we belong to God. To be *partakers of the divine nature* means not that we become part of God, as if we are somehow absorbed into His being. Rather, it means that we share identity with Him as members of His family. The blessing of union with Christ gives us resurrection life and power but also unites us with Him in suffering in a sinful world (1 Peter 4:13; 5:1).

By contrast, the people who belong to the world share an existence characterized by corruption, the decay that comes from death. Such a life is driven by out-of-control desires *(lust)*.

What Do You Think?
What helps you most to resist falling back into worldly corruption? How so?
Talking Points for Your Discussion
- An accountability partner
- Support of fellow believers
- Personal Bible study
- Prayer
- Other

II. Hope's Character
(2 Peter 1:5-9)
A. Virtue Ladder (vv. 5-7)

5a. And beside this, giving all diligence, add to your faith virtue.

Having reflected on how the gifts of the gospel provide the basis for lasting and growing change, Peter now details the nature of that change. He does this with a ladder of virtues, a step-by-step description of the characteristics that build on one another as a person grows in Christian hope. The steps of this ladder are of supreme importance. Therefore, this process demands that we give *all diligence* in displaying a consistent energy and enthusiasm befitting these most valuable pursuits.

The foundational virtue is *faith*. Faith, of course, is the response of belief and trust that we give God as He reaches out to us with the gospel.

The first step up from faith is *virtue*. We can refer to the entire ladder as listing virtues, but here the word is used more specifically to mean "excellent behavior" (see also v. 3, above). Faith is always to produce behavioral change. What kind of person truly believes something yet does nothing about it? Lasting change founded on Christ depends on these first two steps.

5b. And to virtue knowledge.

The antidote to false ideas is true *knowledge,* founded on what God has done and revealed in history, climaxing in Jesus. Just as initial faith must lead to behavioral change, it must also lead to a thirst to know more fully the good news that prompts our faith.

6a. And to knowledge temperance.

Older uses of the word *temperance* may lead us to think in terms of "sobriety" (avoidance of alcoholic beverages). But the idea is broader than that—along the lines of "self-restraint." Without God in the picture, a person has no clear reason to restrain desires and impulses as they arise. Through Christ we receive both the reason and the power to put our desires under control.

❧ *"Give Me a Drink!"* ❧

Some years ago, a friend of mine was telling me of his years as an Air Force chaplain. At one assignment he met a young man struggling with alcohol. The man's marriage was about to come apart, and he was in danger of being dishonorably discharged for unreliability.

Through discussion, Bible study, and a good deal of prayer, the young man accepted Christ as Lord and found the power to overcome his addiction. His marriage revived, and he became a respected individual.

Then one day he wandered into the club on base where alcoholic drinks were available. The bartender, aware of the young man's previous condition, urged him not to drink. The young man insisted. As the bartender continued to refuse, the young man raised his voice.

Finally, the bartender relented and asked him what he wanted to drink. "Seven-Up," the young man replied. With a smile, the bartender served him. The young man took his drink, turned to the crowd that was staring at him, raised his glass in a toast, drank it down, and walked out. The power of the gospel had helped him regain the virtue of self-restraint. It can do so for us as well.—J. B. N.

6b. And to temperance patience.

Patience especially signifies endurance in hardship. When we belong to Christ, we have a powerful impulse toward such endurance in the assurance of salvation already granted and the hope of salvation's fullness yet to be received. We can face the troubles of the present knowing that God is faithful.

6c. And to patience godliness.

Godliness has already been mentioned in verse 3. In Peter's time, most people believe in showing proper respect to the gods. But which god or gods are true? Knowing the true God is the foundation of genuine godliness, and the gospel teaches us to know Him as both righteous and merciful. So true godliness pursues righteousness and mercy in respectful imitation of God himself. To do otherwise is to deny the faith on which all the virtues are founded.

7a. And to godliness brotherly kindness.

As godliness looks up to God, brotherly kindness looks around to others. God's love compels us to love others. Such regard is expressed in tangible deeds (1 John 3:17). This is the characteristic that people should see among us as we live according to our identity as the people of God.

7b. And to brotherly kindness charity.

God loves the unlovable, the sinner. So the Christian's love does not stop at the church door. To brotherly kindness we are compelled to add the gracious, unconditional love—here called *charity*—that God has shown to us. These two steps of the virtue ladder should speak to the intensity and universality of God's love as practiced by His people.

We should note well the overall scope of the ladder of virtues. It begins with *faith,* the foundational characteristic. It ends with the exercise of *love,* the deep expression of God's relationship with us. The ladder is grounded throughout on *hope,* the confident expectation of God's saving actions yet to come. The three great keystones of the Christian life—faith, love, and hope—are very much on display here (compare 1 Corinthians 13:13).

B. Fruitful Relationship (v. 8)

8. For if these things be in you, and abound, they make you that ye shall neither be barren nor unfruitful in the knowledge of our Lord Jesus Christ.

Unfruitfulness is a grave danger! The Scriptures repeatedly use images of plants that do not bear fruit to remind God's people how serious is their response to God (examples: Isaiah 5:1-7; Luke 13:6-9; John 15:1-8). What Peter describes is the necessary, vital fruit of a relationship with Christ. These fruits need to *abound,* growing more abundant as time passes to reflect the magnitude of what God has done for us.

What Do You Think?

How do you recognize when unfruitfulness is starting to manifest itself in your life?

Talking Points for Your Discussion

- Matthew 13:22
- Luke 19:20-23
- John 15:2-6
- Ephesians 4:29-31; 5:3, 4
- 2 Timothy 4:10
- Other

"Make your calling and election sure."
—2 PETER 1:10

Visual for Lesson 11. *Point to this visual as you explore the connection between a good personal harvest and making one's calling sure.*

C. Spiritual Sight (v. 9)

9. But he that lacketh these things is blind, and cannot see afar off, and hath forgotten that he was purged from his old sins.

To claim faith and then not live as Peter has described reflects spiritual blindness, or at least something like nearsightedness—the inability to see beyond our own noses to the truth of what God has done and how we need to respond. If we remember that God has cleansed us from the rebellion that was our old life, then we will want nothing more than for the new life to take root and bear fruit in every way.

III. Hope's Persistence
(2 PETER 1:10-15)
A. In the Present (v. 10)

10. Wherefore the rather, brethren, give diligence to make your calling and election sure: for if ye do these things, ye shall never fall.

With a confident expectation of the future, we can persist in the present. Peter insists on this, reminding us that we do not want to lose out on what belongs to us by God's grace.

This calls for *diligence,* the same kind of characteristic named in verse 5. What is at stake is our *calling and election.* These two terms remind us of ancient Israel's identity as God's people, called His "chosen" or "elect" (Isaiah 42:1; 45:4; etc.). By His saving death and resurrection, Christ has made His followers the called and elect.

To keep that identity, Christ's followers need to maintain connection with Him. If we abandon the faith, we lose our standing as His people (compare Hebrews 2:1; 6:11; 10:35, 36). We should note carefully what Peter says here. He is not discussing the ongoing struggle with sin that every believer experiences. Rather, he warns that if we ignore the mandate to grow in virtue then we can lose the gift that we have received by faith. That is what it means to *fall*. A growing faith is a secure faith.

B. For Eternity (v. 11)

11. For so an entrance shall be ministered unto you abundantly into the everlasting kingdom of our Lord and Saviour Jesus Christ.

With our eyes clearly on the object of our hope, we have every reason to persist in the present. What God has for His called and chosen people is citizenship under His king, Jesus, who will rule without end in justice and peace. This is the gift He has prepared for us in the future, even as we are experiencing Christ's rule now through our growing faith. That future connects with our present, reminding us how important are the changes that God is working in our lives.

❧ EVERLASTING ❧

The related words *eternal, everlasting,* and *forever* are often used in a loose sense. I once saw a commercial for a cemetery that offered "eternal care" for grave sites. I doubt that the cemetery will last that long. When our family was younger and we were taking a long car trip, the children would often complain, "It's taking forever!" Not quite, but it seemed a very long time to them.

There is a very interesting usage of the word *forever* in Roman Catholic history. In the eighteenth century, the Jesuits had become a significant force within the church. Individual Jesuits were very active in the governments of several Catholic countries. Many folk in those countries came to fear the organized power of the Jesuits and demanded their elimination. The Jesuits were banished from country after country, and ultimately Pope Clement XIV banned the order "forever" in 1773. In the next century, however, the political situation changed drastically, and Pope Pius VII restored the Jesuit order in 1814. Apparently, *forever* meant 41 years!

In spite of the fact that earthly conditions can and do change, we can be assured that the *everlasting* kingdom of Jesus really is *forever*.   —J. B. N.

C. Until Death (vv. 12-15)

12. Wherefore I will not be negligent to put you always in remembrance of these things, though ye know them, and be established in the present truth.

Peter's life is about to reach its end (v. 14, below), but he is determined to use the time he has left to reinforce God's saving message. *These things* of which he writes are well-known among his readers, but they are so important that they bear repeating. Peter does not stress them because he questions his readers' standing with God, but because this is the most important message he can share.

13, 14. Yea, I think it meet, as long as I am in this tabernacle, to stir you up by putting you in remembrance; knowing that shortly I must put off this my tabernacle, even as our Lord Jesus Christ hath shewed me.

Peter uses the word *tabernacle,* or tent (Exodus 40:2), to indicate his physical body (compare 2 Corinthians 5:1). He chooses this image to stress the shortness of his life. As the end of life approaches, we expect people to do what matters most to them. Because time is short, it is precious and must be used for what is most valuable. Peter, at the end of his life, stresses that what matters most to him is encouraging believers by reminding them of what they have received.

We wonder how the Lord Jesus showed Peter that his death was near (compare John 21:18, 19). Though we cannot answer that question, we can observe Peter's confidence in knowing that Christ will deliver him into His presence.

HOW TO SAY IT

Corinthians	Ko-*rin*-thee-unz (*th* as in *thin*).
Isaiah	Eye-*zay*-uh.
tabernacle	*tah*-burr-*nah*-kul.

15. Moreover I will endeavour that ye may be able after my decease to have these things always in remembrance.

Peter wants to ensure that Christians will have access to this valuable message after he departs, so he writes it in a letter. The letter should not end up on a dusty shelf. Its message is not only to be preserved, but copied and circulated.

What Do You Think?

What words of spiritual encouragement would you like to pass on to others before you die? What's keeping you from doing this now?

Talking Points for Your Discussion

- To a child or grandchild (2 Timothy 1:5)
- To a child "in the faith" (1 Timothy 1:2)
- To a close friend in Christ
- To an unbeliever
- Other

IV. Hope's Foundation
(2 Peter 1:20, 21)
A. What Is True (v. 20)

20. Knowing this first, that no prophecy of the scripture is of any private interpretation.

In verses 16-19 (not in today's text), Peter reminds his readers that he is an eyewitness to the ministry of Jesus. Coupled with the assurance of such testimony is the message of Israel's Scriptures, what we call the Old Testament.

Because all the books of Scripture are the products of God's inspiration, they can all be referred to as *prophecy*. In this regard, *prophecy* means not just prediction of the future, but also the announcement of God's message. The sacred writings are not the product of human imagination. *Private interpretation* does not refer to an individual's own reading and explanation of the Scriptures, but to their being written in the first place. The Scriptures exist because God himself has provided them. The next verse makes this clearer.

B. Why It's True (v. 21)

21. For the prophecy came not in old time by the will of man: but holy men of God spake as they were moved by the Holy Ghost.

Peter reminds us that the witness of the Old Testament is the consequence of God's actions through His Holy Spirit. This is what Christians call *the doctrine of inspiration*: that the Holy Spirit worked through the writers of Scripture to produce the genuine Word of God (2 Timothy 3:16). It is true in all that it affirms, focused on the precise message that God wants delivered.

Our hope is founded on this divinely inspired message that points to the one of whom Peter was a witness: Jesus Christ. We have every reason to be confident in the truth of Jesus' message, in the certainty of what He has done to save us.

What Do You Think?

How should we respond to a fellow believer who expresses doubts about the inspiration and infallibility of Scripture?

Talking Points for Your Discussion

- In attitude
- In teaching
- In fellowship
- Deciding how he or she may or may not be used in the church's various ministries
- Other

Conclusion
A. The Power of the Gospel

The truth of the gospel is a powerful force. When we discover it, it inspires a confident expectation of the future that transforms our present lives. It inspires us to pursue the virtues that spring from the gospel and to grow in them consistently and constantly. No wonder Peter was compelled to share again that message in his last days on earth! The question is, what will we do with the message that he shared?

B. Prayer

Father, we are overwhelmed at what You have done! We look back and find reassurance. We look forward and have hope. Empower us to grow in our devotion to You. In Jesus' name, amen.

C. Thought to Remember

Make Peter's focus your own.

INVOLVEMENT LEARNING

Some of the activities below are also found in the helpful student book, Adult Bible Class.
Don't forget to download the free reproducible page from www.standardlesson.com to enhance your lesson!

Into the Lesson

Apply a temporary tattoo on your hand as the class watches. Say, "These things are temporary, they will wash off quickly. Permanent tattoos, however, are much more durable. What are some other illustrations of 'temporary' versus 'permanent'?" Jot answers on the board.

Ask, "Are the things we have listed as 'permanent' really permanent? Why, or why not?" The lesson Introduction will give ideas why nothing in this world is really permanent, including tattoos. Say, "Today's study is about making a life change that is permanent in an eternal sense."

Into the Word

Read the printed text aloud, and then distribute a handout featuring two activities. The first activity will have the heading *Gifts and Responses, 2 Peter 1:3, 4.* Under it have three short columns, headed "Gifts," "Our Response," and "Interpretation or Application." Under the first column, list the word *life.* Say, "Peter wishes to help believers be effective and fruitful. In that light, he assures us of the gifts God has given and our appropriate responses. One gift is already listed for you. List one more gift and two responses cited in verse 3. You don't need to address the third column yet." Call for discoveries. *(Answers under "Gifts": life, glory; under "Our Response": godliness, virtue.)* Discuss per the lesson commentary.

Call learners' attention to the third column as you pose these questions: 1. How and why is *godliness* an appropriate response to the gift of life in Christ? 2. How and why is *virtue* (an excellent lifestyle) an appropriate response now to the glory we will share in Christ?" Consult the lesson commentary to clarify responses. Conclude the activity by saying, "Verse 4 reminds us that God has given promises that motivate growing change. Peter builds on this as he sketches what might be called 'a ladder of virtues.'"

The second activity on the handout, headed *Ladder of Virtues, 2 Peter 1:5-9,* will include the image of a ladder with eight rungs. Say, "In verses 5-9, Peter uses what might be called *a ladder of virtues* to discuss the nature of growth that should be evident in our lives. These characteristics build on one another as we grow in Christian hope."

Ask learners to scan the verses and write the characteristics on the ladder in ascending order. The characteristics, in order, are: *faith, virtue, knowledge, temperance, patience, godliness, brotherly kindness,* and *charity.* Ask for definitions or examples of each rung or step of Peter's ladder of virtues. Be sure to discuss the different senses of the word *virtue* as that word is used to describe both the ladder as a whole and as a specific rung on the ladder.

Option 1: To reinforce this segment of the lesson, distribute copies of the "Discovering a Sure Hope" activity from the reproducible page, which you can download. Say, "Please close your Bibles and see if you can complete this from what you have learned so far." Have learners score their own results.

Option 2: For a contrast with the "Ladder of Virtues" activity above, distribute copies of the "Bad Ladder" activity from the reproducible page. Have learners complete it as indicated.

Into Life

Say, "A *collage* is a collection of pictures of related scenes. We will attempt to create a 'verbal collage' from the eight rungs of our 'ladder of virtue.'" Scatter around the board the eight words of the ladder of virtues. Ask the class for word pictures to represent the eight words on the board. The resulting verbal pictures should illustrate how to live out the characteristics. For example, the verbal picture "someone reading the Bible" could be placed next to *knowledge.* Discuss how to personalize these depictions.

ACTIVE
HOPE

DEVOTIONAL READING: Luke 16:10-13
BACKGROUND SCRIPTURE: 1 Peter 4

1 PETER 4:1-11

1 Forasmuch then as Christ hath suffered for us in the flesh, arm yourselves likewise with the same mind: for he that hath suffered in the flesh hath ceased from sin;

2 That he no longer should live the rest of his time in the flesh to the lusts of men, but to the will of God.

3 For the time past of our life may suffice us to have wrought the will of the Gentiles, when we walked in lasciviousness, lusts, excess of wine, revellings, banquetings, and abominable idolatries:

4 Wherein they think it strange that ye run not with them to the same excess of riot, speaking evil of you:

5 Who shall give account to him that is ready to judge the quick and the dead.

6 For for this cause was the gospel preached also to them that are dead, that they might be judged according to men in the flesh, but live according to God in the spirit.

7 But the end of all things is at hand: be ye therefore sober, and watch unto prayer.

8 And above all things have fervent charity among yourselves: for charity shall cover the multitude of sins.

9 Use hospitality one to another without grudging.

10 As every man hath received the gift, even so minister the same one to another, as good stewards of the manifold grace of God.

11 If any man speak, let him speak as the oracles of God; if any man minister, let him do it as of the ability which God giveth: that God in all things may be glorified through Jesus Christ, to whom be praise and dominion for ever and ever. Amen.

KEY VERSE

As every man hath received the gift, even so minister the same one to another, as good stewards of the manifold grace of God. —1 Peter 4:10

Photo: Jupiterimages / Comstock / Thinkstock

UNDYING HOPE

Unit 3: A Call to Holy Living
LESSONS 10–13

LESSON AIMS

After participating in this lesson, each student will be able to:

1. Describe key differences between the old, worldly life and new life in Christ.

2. Explain why and how Christ's physical suffering bears on the believer's behavior today.

3. Identify one gift God has given him or her and describe how he or she is using it—or will use it—as a steward of God's grace.

LESSON OUTLINE

Introduction

A. Wearing the Team Colors

Perhaps you have noticed that people like to wear clothing that bears the colors and logos of their favorite sports teams. People dress this way to make their loyalties clear.

How do followers of Jesus display their "team colors"? Some Christians wear distinctive clothing, and one can buy T-shirts and caps emblazoned with Christian slogans. But we recognize that something other than clothing is what declares a person to be a follower of Jesus.

That "something different" is a way of life. Our lifestyle reflects what Christ has already done, what Christ will do in the future, and who we are as a result. It has to do with how we think, how we speak, and how we act. Without exception, the new way of life is what the New Testament provides as the distinguishing mark of the Christian. That subject is the focus of today's text.

B. Lesson Background

Today's text takes us back to 1 Peter to address the situation faced by its original readers. They were subjects of the Roman Empire, living in places and a time when the Romans were increasingly hostile to Christianity. With some localized exceptions (such as in Acts 18:2), Roman hostility did not extend to Jews as such. Roman respect for Judaism is traced to decisions and actions of Emperor Julius Caesar, who died in 44 BC.

Roman suspicion of Christians grew as the Romans began to realize that Christianity was a new faith, not just a subset of Judaism. The result was increasing persecution of Christians (see the Lesson Background to Lesson 10). This is probably why Peter refers to Rome by the code word "Babylon" in 1 Peter 5:13.

Identity was important to these Christians. It was their identity that had created the trouble they were experiencing. Could they maintain that identity, expressing it consistently in the face of pressure to abandon it? Their challenge was to be true to their Lord. Their lives were to reflect what He had done and promised to do, not simply enduring the pressure that they faced.

I. Distinctive Life

(1 PETER 4:1-6)

A. Dead to Sin (vv. 1, 2)

1. Forasmuch then as Christ hath suffered for us in the flesh, arm yourselves likewise with the same mind: for he that hath suffered in the flesh hath ceased from sin.

Peter begins by reminding his readers how their life with Christ began. It is first of all Christ's death that makes them His. By dying on the cross, He took the penalty for the sins of the world. Rising from the dead, He overcame and defeated sin. His death and resurrection therefore mean, in a very real and important sense, that sin is over. Its rule is finished.

Christians are united with Jesus in His resurrection and its victory over sin (Romans 6:3-6). The resurrection life is, ideally, a life free from sin. That does not mean that sinful behaviors and temptations suddenly disappear. Sin and Satan remain active in this present age, though they are genuinely defeated. Those united with Christ in His death and resurrection have to fight deliberately against sin with the consciousness of a new life and the strength that Christ provides.

So Peter uses a military expression, *arm yourselves,* and focuses on our foundational issue of intent, *with the same mind.* We must believe and insist that we are dead to sin so that we can live the resurrection life to keep sin in its defeated state. Since we have eternal life, we ought to pursue sin's defeat now, not just wait for its full and final elimination in eternity.

What Do You Think?

What attitudes and practices of Jesus do you most need to develop as you "arm" yourself for the Christian life?

Talking Points for Your Discussion

- Jesus' method and practice of prayer (Luke 5:16)
- Jesus' choice of companions (Luke 7:34)
- Jesus' sense of priorities (John 4:31-34)
- Jesus' self-denial (John 6:38)
- Other

---

2. That he no longer should live the rest of his time in the flesh to the lusts of men, but to the will of God.

Our transformation in Christ is to produce the identifying signs of new life in Him. In the old life, there is nothing to drive a person except one's own desires (*the lusts of men* refers to all kinds of desires, not just sexual desires). In Christ our motivation is changed: doing God's will is now paramount.

The good news of Jesus shows us how miserable our lives were when we pursued our own desires. The good news shows us how much God has done for us, driving us to replace a focus on our own desires with a focus on God's will.

B. Different from Pagans (vv. 3-6)

3. For the time past of our life may suffice us to have wrought the will of the Gentiles, when we walked in lasciviousness, lusts, excess of wine, revellings, banquetings, and abominable idolatries.

The persecuted Christians who read this letter live in a world dominated by pagan religions. These offer little or no moral teaching, and some even encourage indulgence in sex and alcohol. The lives of pagans, or *Gentiles* in this verse, reflect the excesses of human desires without boundaries.

So Peter reminds his readers of the kinds of self-destructive behaviors still around them, behaviors they used to practice themselves. *Lasciviousness* is unrestricted sexual activity. *Lusts* also suggests strong sexual desire, underlining the excesses of the old life. *Excess of wine* is drunkenness, of course. *Revellings* and *banquetings* add additional underlines that refer to gatherings for overindulgence in food, intoxicating drink, and immoral activity.

The list reaches its high point (or low point!) with *abominable idolatries.* This is the worship of false gods, a practice that lies at the heart of all the others. It often accompanies the most obvious displays of self-indulgence. Idols may be broadly described as gods made to fulfill human desires, gods made in human image. It is little wonder, then, that idolatry is listed alongside the things described here—human desires gone out of control. In worshipping idols, people in effect worship their own desires (compare Philippians 3:19).

❧ *UNDO* ❧

When I replaced my old computer years ago, I discovered to my enjoyment that the new computer came equipped with a few games. I told myself that I could play a game or two while between projects because it was a bit of a break that kept my mind fresh. My favorite games became Free Cell and Spider Solitaire. I usually won at both, but occasionally I would work myself into a hole and lose. This happened in spite of the fact that both games had an "undo" feature that allowed me to reverse the last move. But reversing just the last move often wasn't enough; I still lost.

Then a couple of years ago I bought a laptop. The Free Cell and Spider Solitaire games that came with it also had an "undo" feature, but this one was different. It wasn't limited to just the last move; I could "undo" all the way back to the beginning if necessary. Since then I haven't lost a game!

I have often wondered, *Wouldn't life be more satisfying if it came with an "undo" feature?* Yet the sacrifice of Christ on the cross is exactly that! It undoes all the sin we have committed and gives us a clean slate with God. With this great "undo" available, why would we ever want to "redo" our sinful moves and go back to our old, eternally losing behavior?　　　　　　　—J. B. N.

4. Wherein they think it strange that ye run not with them to the same excess of riot, speaking evil of you.

The behaviors of verse 3 used to be the norm for the readers of Peter's letter. But now such behaviors are part of the past. This fact is a source of tension between Peter's audience and their pagan neighbors. The harsh words of pagans against the restrained Christian lifestyle undoubtedly hurts. That very fact demonstrates the enormous change that has come to the Christians' lives.

5. Who shall give account to him that is ready to judge the quick and the dead.

Though the pagans ridicule the Christians' new behavior, they have reason to consider the matter soberly. In the end, all people—both *the quick* (living) and *the dead*—will stand before the true, righteous God who judges all His creation (also Acts 10:42; 2 Timothy 4:1). The difference between

the pagans and the Christians will tell the story of judgment. One group rejects God and worships its own desires. The other turns to God for His mercy. The marks of identity are clear for each.

The idea of God's coming judgment is not pleasant to contemplate, but humans universally long for justice to prevail. If in the end there is no judgment from God, then there is no justice in the world. But if God does judge and I am guilty, what can I do? That realization drives us to accept God's offer of mercy.

> *What Do You Think?*
> What is your attitude when thinking of the judgment that unbelievers face? What changes do you need to make in this regard?
> *Talking Points for Your Discussion*
> - Satisfaction—they will get what they deserve
> - Thankfulness—"I was lost, but now I'm found"
> - Guilt—for ever sharing their lifestyle
> - Helplessness—just knowing their fate
> - Compassion—how can I reach them?
> - Other

6. For for this cause was the gospel preached also to them that are dead, that they might be judged according to men in the flesh, but live according to God in the spirit.

This verse is difficult to understand. However, with care for the setting of the letter, we probably can make good sense of Peter's meaning. The phrase *them that are dead* seems to refer to Christian victims of persecution. The gospel had been preached to them, and they believed it before dying. Therefore, even though humans have judged them harshly by worldly standards, with God those deceased believers enjoy life everlasting. They are the recipients of life everlasting through God's mercy that they had received while alive.

The outcome for the faithful stands in stark contrast with that of the pagans. In the final judgment, the latter will find themselves without hope, having rejected God's offer of mercy in the gospel. When we as Christians assess our own place in the world, we need to remember that the human view and God's view are very different. By the human view, the persecuted Christians were judged as wrongdoers. From God's perspective, it will be their persecutors who deserve judgment.

God's purpose in announcing the coming judgment is to enable sinful people to escape His wrath. The announcement of judgment is an act of God's mercy. How ironic it is, then, if people reject the warning because they find it harsh!

II. Expectant Life
(1 Peter 4:7-11)
A. Alert and Praying (v. 7)

7. But the end of all things is at hand: be ye therefore sober, and watch unto prayer.

The end or goal for which God has prepared the world *is at hand,* Peter reminds his readers (compare Romans 13:11, 12; 1 John 2:18). His previous discussion of God's judgment raises this topic to the forefront. But to our minds, the question we ask ourselves is how *the end of all things* could truly have been *at hand* in the first century since nearly 2,000 years now have passed and Christ still has not returned. To understand Peter's statement, we need to think carefully about what the New Testament teaches about the nearness of the end in comparison with the uncertainty of its timing.

Jesus affirmed both that His return was "near" (Matthew 24:33, 34) and that no one could know the time in advance (24:36). In light of both statements, we can understand that the nearness of His return is not calculated by a specific measure of time. Rather, the nearness of Jesus' return is a word of personal assurance to all His people: Jesus returns soon enough to rescue every one of His people from the sinful world and bring them together into the fullness of His kingdom.

With that assurance, coupled with the knowledge that the time is uncertain, we realize that we need to live expectantly and urgently. We anticipate Christ's return, and so we live with confidence while valuing every moment as an opportunity for serving Christ.

That is the message of this verse—that believers be *sober,* meaning "serious-minded." We are to be like sentries on the watch, always alert. But our alertness is directed to prayer, calling on God for assistance and relying on Him to guide and sustain us in these last days. Recognizing that our time on earth is short, we prayerfully grasp the urgency of the moment: to do God's will now.

> *What Do You Think?*
> How does (and should) the nearness of the end affect your daily service for Christ?
> *Talking Points for Your Discussion*
> ▪ Matthew 24:36-48
> ▪ 1 Corinthians 7:29-31
> ▪ 1 John 2:18, 24-28
> ▪ Revelation 1:3
> ▪ Other

B. Loving (v. 8)

8. And above all things have fervent charity among yourselves: for charity shall cover the multitude of sins.

Our identity with Christ is based on the self-sacrificial, unconditional love of God that sent His Son into the world. As a result, nothing is more important in the life of the Christian than expressing that same self-sacrificial, unconditional love (here translated as *charity*) for others. So Peter says that living love—love that is *fervent* or especially strong—is the supreme pursuit of the Christian who lives in hope of Christ's return.

The expression *charity shall cover the multitude of sins* is a quotation of Proverbs 10:12. It is also found in James 5:20, and through repetition it has passed into our language as a cliché. Because the phrase is so familiar, we need to pay careful attention to get its meaning. In Proverbs and so here, it can mean that because of love, we should willingly forgive and forget the sins of others. When we do, we effectively hide their sins with loving forgiveness. Or Peter could be reminding us that

HOW TO SAY IT

Caesar	*See*-zer.
Gentiles	*Jen*-tiles.
lasciviousness	luh-*sih*-vee-us-nuss.
Lucian	*Loo*-shun.
Samosata	Suh-*mah*-suh-tah.

God's love, the love that sent Christ, hides our sin as Christ removes it. Or He could be suggesting that by living in love, we will avoid sinning against others, hiding sin by eliminating it.

In all these cases, the supreme importance of love is stressed. The reminder is to respond to God's love with active, sincere love for others in all situations. For believers facing persecution, this is a special reminder not to retaliate against the persecutors. Instead, we respond to evil with good, showing love even to enemies (Luke 6:27, 35).

C. Hospitable (v. 9)

9. Use hospitality one to another without grudging.

One practical expression of love is to share one's home and food. The practice of hospitality is vital to the first-century church. It is a means of providing for people in material need, for furthering the work of traveling evangelists, and for nurturing the fellowship of the church (Romans 16:23; 3 John 8). Hospitality is particularly important in times of persecution, as Christians meet the needs of their suffering brothers and sisters by welcoming them into their homes.

Lucian of Samosata, who lived in the second century AD, wrote humorously about Christians overwhelming their imprisoned brothers and sisters with gifts of food and clothing while standing outside their cells singing hymns to God hour after hour. It is impressive when a humorist can

Visual for Lesson 12. *As you consider verses 10 and 11, point to this visual and ask, "What ministry opportunities will you seek out in the week ahead?"*

find nothing to ridicule about Christians except their great devotion to hospitality!

> **What Do You Think?**
> What are some specific ways that you can better extend hospitality?
> *Talking Points for Your Discussion*
> - Toward the needy (Matthew 25:35)
> - Toward enemies (Romans 12:20)
> - Toward strangers (Hebrews 13:2)
> - Toward fellow Christians (3 John 5-8)

But such practical expressions of love can be a costly chore. So Peter reminds believers to practice hospitality *without grudging*—without the kind of muttering grumbles that characterizes a person who is irritated or angry. Real love is generous, and real generosity is free of resentment. We are to remember that our hospitality is an expression of love in response to God's love for us.

❧ THE PRACTICE OF HOSPITALITY ❧

I have heard of, read about, and experienced numerous instances of people living in impoverished countries who provided extraordinary hospitality to visitors. Those providing the hospitality may have very little compared with American standards, but they have been known to offer abundant food and even housing to Western visitors nonetheless.

When national church conventions were held in the nineteenth century, the members living in the host cities usually opened up their homes and provided sleeping arrangements for out-of-town visitors. In such a setting, one individual was known to have 30 guests sleep in his house, and he fed even dozens more than that!

Perhaps the reason this custom does not prevail today is simply because more people are able to afford hotels and restaurants. But there seems to be more to it than that. Could it be that the more money we have, the more aloof we become? Many today would feel it demeaning or intrusive to depend on a host family for food and lodging. Times and customs change, but the requirement to be hospitable never goes away. How can we put Peter's challenge into practice today?   —J. B. N.

D. Serving (vv. 10, 11)

10. As every man hath received the gift, even so minister the same one to another, as good stewards of the manifold grace of God.

The community of faith is made up of all kinds of people. That diversity is part of God's plan, so that His people can be equipped to do all kinds of service. We are different by design and are differently empowered by God's Spirit (1 Corinthians 12:12-31). From this perspective, those differences are gifts, the consequence of God's grace for each of His people.

The point of such gifts is that they are to be used in loving, self-giving service for others. To *minister . . . one to another* is simply to serve, providing useful benefits for others that reflect the way that God has generously served and blessed us. This kind of behavior is an exercise of stewardship, meaning responsible management of the resources that God has given to His people. Primary among those resources is God's saving grace, which reminds us that our service is not based on others' deserving it, but on the favor that God has shown us even though we are undeserving.

It is no accident that Peter discusses this as he reminds the readers of the nearness of Christ's return. Jesus told parables about servants who were left with a stewardship to perform in their master's absence. He used the stories to illustrate the faithful service expected from those awaiting His return (Matthew 24:45-47). A church that is faithfully awaiting Christ's return is one in which each Christian exercises his or her distinct gifts to demonstrate God's love to others (Romans 12:6-8).

11. If any man speak, let him speak as the oracles of God; if any man minister, let him do it as of the ability which God giveth: that God in all things may be glorified through Jesus Christ, to whom be praise and dominion for ever and ever. Amen.

Peter now uses two specific examples to illustrate selfless service in the exercise of gifts. Some may be gifted by God to speak. Although they could speak all kinds of things, the grace of God compels them to speak God's Word for the benefit of others. Similarly, the one who is gifted to minister, or to serve practically, should do so to the full extent that God enables, not holding back for selfish reasons.

The readers should see the pattern in these examples and apply them to the exercise of their own distinct gifts. Whatever it is we can do, God's grace compels us to do it in God's service, for the benefit of others, and with the generous measure by which God has given to us.

The result of such service is God's glory. Christians demonstrate to the world who God really is when we serve with self-sacrificial energy and a focus on others. We reflect what God did for us through Jesus when we serve this way. Thus Peter fittingly ends this section with a prayer that Christ receive the praise and power that are rightfully His.

> **What Do You Think?**
> Which spiritual gifts do you think you have? How will you better put these into practice?
> *Talking Points for Your Discussion*
> - Romans 12:6-8
> - 1 Corinthians 12:7-10
> - Ephesians 4:11

Conclusion

A. Past, Present, and Future

It is often said that the Christian life is lived in three tenses: past, present, and future. In the past, God saved us through Jesus' death and resurrection. In the present, our sins are forgiven and our lives are being transformed. In the future, Christ will come for His people and establish His rule among them fully and forever. The past and the future shape our present, Peter reminds us. Together, they demonstrate who we are: God's people, bought with the blood of Jesus Christ.

B. Prayer

God Almighty, we reflect with amazement on what You have done for us. You have filled our greatest need. You transform us to fulfill Your highest purpose. We offer our lives to You in service that reflects Your glory. In Jesus' name, amen.

C. Thought to Remember

Live as if you belong to Christ—because you do.

INVOLVEMENT LEARNING

Some of the activities below are also found in the helpful student book, Adult Bible Class.
Don't forget to download the free reproducible page from www.standardlesson.com to enhance your lesson!

Into the Lesson

Mount several large poster boards on different walls of the classroom. Each poster should have the heading *My Favorite Team*. As learners enter, distribute marker pens and say, "Please go to a poster and write the name of your favorite team from any sport. Also sketch something that represents that team (logo, mascot, etc.)." Ask for explanations as appropriate.

Make the transition to Bible study by saying, "When someone dresses in clothing that bears the colors and logo of his or her favorite sports team, observers know the loyalties of that individual. Some Christians even wear clothing with Christian sayings and emblems to show their allegiance to Jesus. However, there is a better way to show our Christian identity."

Into the Word

Early in the week, ask a class member to play the part of Peter for an interview. Give him a copy of the lesson commentary and the questions below in advance. Ideally, your actor should wear a Bible-times costume; if that is not available, he can wear a very large name tag.

Summarize the Lesson Background, then introduce "Peter." Ask the following interview questions, pausing for responses: 1. "Peter, thank you for coming. We're glad you're here to help us know how to live consistently with our identity as Christians. Let me start by asking, did you really cut off the ear of the servant of the high priest?" *(See John 18:10. Peter's embarrassed response may describe the setting, his intent to cut off more than an ear, his subsequent denial of Jesus, etc.)* 2. "Peter, you really have grown in Christ since that day! So when you tell us in verse 1 to 'arm yourselves,' I'm sure you mean something other than a sword. Would you clarify what you mean?" 3. "How can we resist the temptation to fall back into our previous sins?" 4. "In verse 6 you mention that the gospel was preached to those who are dead. Can you clarify?" 5. "Since the end of all things is near, what tips can you give us for living expectantly?" Lead a round of applause for "Peter" as the interview concludes.

Ask learners to work in pairs or trios. Prepare slips of paper with the following topics and Scripture texts, one each. Give one slip to each team: (1) *mind-set,* 1 Peter 4:1, 2, 7; (2) *sex,* 1 Peter 4:2-4; (3) *God's judgment,* 1 Peter 4:5, 6; (4) *prayer,* 1 Peter 4:7; (5) *love,* 1 Peter 4:8, 9; (6) *serving others,* 1 Peter 4:10, 11. Have this printed on each strip: "What are people's attitudes and actions toward your subject while they are unbelievers? How should the attitudes and actions change after accepting Christ?" Ask teams to share conclusions with the class.

Switch to a "big picture" view as you say, "Peter tells us that the end of all things is near. How does remembering that fact help you do a better job of living in a way that glorifies God?"

Alternative: In place of either of the above activities, distribute copies of the "Living as a Disciple" activity from the reproducible page, which you can download. Have learners work in small groups then share discoveries with the class.

Into Life

Say, "First Peter 4:3 lists several things the early Christians needed to give up or otherwise resist as they grew in their new faith." Then pose the following discussion questions: 1. What have you had to change, give up, etc., to make room for spiritual activities or the cultivation of Christian virtues? 2. How has the trade-off been worth it? 3. What behavior or value do you think the Lord still wants you to change or strengthen? 4. How will you make this change? *Option:* Put these questions on a handout for study pairs to consider.

Alternative: Use instead the "Still Growing!" fill-in prayer activity from the reproducible page. This can also be a take-home exercise.

PATIENT HOPE

DEVOTIONAL READING: John 14:1-7
BACKGROUND SCRIPTURE: 2 Peter 3

2 PETER 3:3-15A, 18

3 Knowing this first, that there shall come in the last days scoffers, walking after their own lusts,

4 And saying, Where is the promise of his coming? for since the fathers fell asleep, all things continue as they were from the beginning of the creation.

5 For this they willingly are ignorant of, that by the word of God the heavens were of old, and the earth standing out of the water and in the water:

6 Whereby the world that then was, being overflowed with water, perished:

7 But the heavens and the earth, which are now, by the same word are kept in store, reserved unto fire against the day of judgment and perdition of ungodly men.

8 But, beloved, be not ignorant of this one thing, that one day is with the Lord as a thousand years, and a thousand years as one day.

9 The Lord is not slack concerning his promise, as some men count slackness; but is longsuffering to us-ward, not willing that any should perish, but that all should come to repentance.

10 But the day of the Lord will come as a thief in the night; in the which the heavens shall pass away with a great noise, and the elements shall melt with fervent heat, the earth also and the works that are therein shall be burned up.

11 Seeing then that all these things shall be dissolved, what manner of persons ought ye to be in all holy conversation and godliness,

12 Looking for and hasting unto the coming of the day of God, wherein the heavens being on fire shall be dissolved, and the elements shall melt with fervent heat?

13 Nevertheless we, according to his promise, look for new heavens and a new earth, wherein dwelleth righteousness.

14 Wherefore, beloved, seeing that ye look for such things, be diligent that ye may be found of him in peace, without spot, and blameless.

15a And account that the longsuffering of our Lord is salvation.

18 But grow in grace, and in the knowledge of our Lord and Saviour Jesus Christ. To him be glory both now and for ever. Amen.

KEY VERSE

The Lord is not slack concerning his promise, as some men count slackness; but is longsuffering to us-ward, not willing that any should perish, but that all should come to repentance. —2 Peter 3:9

UNDYING HOPE

Unit 3: A Call to Holy Living

LESSON AIMS

After participating in this lesson, each student will be able to:

1. Describe the argument of the scoffers and how Peter answers them.

2. Explain how the promise of Christ's return should inspire faithful patience in believers.

3. Write a letter to encourage a hypothetical young believer who is discouraged about the apparent hopelessness of winning the lost or about the apparent delay in Christ's return.

LESSON OUTLINE

Introduction

A. Distance and Perspective

Judging distance is a tricky business. It is often a matter of perspective. For example, mountain peaks may appear to be very close together if viewed from a distance. But if we fly over the mountains in an airplane, we may see that they are, in fact, widely separated.

The passing of time can also be a matter of perspective. When we are young, time seems to drag on forever. Just a few weeks in school feels like an eternity. But as more time passes, the more quickly it seems to pass. Adults commonly ask themselves "Where did the time go?" as they think back across decades.

So how does time appear from God's perspective? That question underlies today's study.

B. Lesson Background

Today's lesson brings us again to 2 Peter, the great apostle's letter of final instructions before his impending death (see the Lesson Background to Lesson 11). By the time of the letter's writing, a generation had passed since the resurrection of Jesus. The faith had spread widely. Churches had been established all over the eastern part of the Roman Empire, and the Christian movement had become controversial. Christianity was the object of curiosity, ridicule, and even persecution.

At the heart of the controversy was the declaration that Jesus, who had been crucified by the Romans, had not only risen from the dead but now reigned as king at God's right hand. He would one day return to establish His rule fully and finally. That belief challenged the way that many Jewish people understood how God would send the promised king, whom they expected to appear as a military and political ruler. It challenged the Roman Empire's claim to absolute authority, as a man crucified by the Romans as a criminal was declared to be king.

The idea that Jesus would return to establish His rule fully, ending this present age and ushering in a new Heaven and earth, disturbed the widely held notion that the world would continue forever. The promise of Christ's return was challenged on another front as well. Years had passed since Jesus' death and resurrection. Why had He not returned, as His followers said He would? His people appeared to be forgotten, abandoned, or—worst of all—mistaken and misled. What were the believers of the latter half of the first century AD to make of this difficult issue? Today's lesson confronts this problem head-on.

I. Scoffers' Perspective
(2 PETER 3:3, 4)
A. What They Do (v. 3)

3. Knowing this first, that there shall come in the last days scoffers, walking after their own lusts.

Peter's warning focuses on activity *in the last days* (compare Jude 18). While that may sound to us as if such a period of time still lies in the future, the context shows that Peter understands the problem he is describing to be present already. From the perspective of the New Testament, the last days began with the appearance of Jesus, especially with His death and resurrection (compare Hebrews 1:2). Jesus inaugurated the last days when He came as the fulfillment of God's end-time promises.

Because the last days represent the climax of God's saving activity, they also represent the climax of opposition to God's plan (compare 1 John 2:18). So in the last days the faithful can expect to experience intense opposition to their faith, as the forces of the enemy try to frustrate God's program.

That is Peter's implication here: the last-days battle is going on already. The opposition is led by people who are driven by their own selfish desires instead of devotion to God. They ridicule and mock sacred ideas, hoping to discredit them so that they can remain free to do as they wish.

HOW TO SAY IT

Habakkuk	Huh-*back*-kuk.
Noah	*No*-uh.
patriarchs	*pay*-tree-arks.
Thessalonians	*Thess*-uh-*lo*-nee-unz
	(*th* as in *thin*).

It seems that scoffers have always been with us. Almost every technological innovation has been met with skepticism at first. When John Ericsson first proposed the ironclad *Monitor* during America's Civil War, many said it would not even float, much less be a useful warship. When the Wright brothers built their first airplane, many said it would never get off the ground. The list is endless.

Scoffers find it hard to accept anything that is not within their own experience. When I was a youngster in the 1950s, we spent Saturday mornings watching space travel with Buck Rogers on TV. We knew it was all science fiction—with a big emphasis on the *fiction* part. Little did we know that we eventually would put a man on the moon. No reasonable person scoffs about this now.

But it's not always wrong to be a skeptic. Jesus teaches us to be skeptical of various claims concerning His return (Mark 13:32; Luke 17:22-24). William Miller predicted Jesus' return for 1843; Charles Taze Russell predicted it for 1914; Edgar Whisenant wrote a pamphlet, "88 Reasons Why the Rapture Could Be in 1988"; Harold Camping predicted it twice for 2011. Skepticism of these predictions turned out to be well founded! Even so, we are confident that Christ will come again because that is what He promised.   —J. B. N.

B. What They Say (v. 4)

4. And saying, Where is the promise of his coming? for since the fathers fell asleep, all things continue as they were from the beginning of the creation.

Here we clearly see that Peter is addressing a situation that is already present in his own time. A generation has passed since Jesus arose and the gospel went forth. Christians have proclaimed repeatedly Jesus' coming as being near. But 30-plus years seems a long time, enough for skeptics to call into question the church's belief in Jesus' return.

The sarcastic rhetoric of the skeptics is captured here. "Today is just like every other day since the beginning of time," they say. "The ancient patriarchs, long dead, would see nothing different today from then. There is no change so far, so we should expect no change in the future."

From the impatient perspective of selfish humanity, three decades seems to be more than enough time to show that the promise of Christ's return is empty. Yet in holding this perspective, the skeptics are ignoring certain evidence, as we see next.

What Do You Think?

How do you respond to unbelievers who laugh at the false predictions of Christ's return?

Talking Points for Your Discussion

- Person-to-person responses
- Responses in a group setting

II. History's Perspective
(2 Peter 3:5-7)

A. Destroyed by Water (vv. 5, 6)

5. For this they willingly are ignorant of, that by the word of God the heavens were of old, and the earth standing out of the water and in the water.

Peter will not allow the mockery of the scoffers to stand. When they affirm that "all things continue as they were from the beginning of the creation" (v. 4), they should realize that the very fact of creation is itself a witness to change.

The earth standing out of the water echoes the description of God's action in Genesis 1:6-10. This demonstration of God's power begins to make Peter's case. Since the world exists because God called it into existence, then God has the power to call it out of existence as well. Since the world began in this way, it is not at all reasonable to assume that it will go on forever. Its continued existence is subject to the will of its Creator.

What Do You Think?

What challenges you most in keeping a historical perspective? How do you overcome this?

Talking Points for Your Discussion

- "The tyranny of the urgent"
- "History is more or less bunk" (Henry Ford)
- A focus on "what works"
- Other

6. Whereby the world that then was, being overflowed with water, perished.

The account of the great flood in Genesis 6–8 is the illustration ready at hand that shows God's power to destroy what He created (compare 2 Peter 2:5). God can and will do with His creation what He chooses to do. This should give pause to anyone who mocks the idea of Christ's return. This is also an additional challenge to the skeptics' claim that "all things continue as they were from the beginning of the creation."

B. Destroyed by Fire (v. 7)

7. But the heavens and the earth, which are now, by the same word are kept in store, reserved unto fire against the day of judgment and perdition of ungodly men.

Having looked back in biblical history, Peter now looks toward what we might call "future history." God preserves the world presently for the judgment that He will bring in the future. That one will not be with flood waters, but with fire. That event will mean God's guilty verdict (*judgment*) and ruin (*perdition*) on all those who, like the scoffers of Peter's day, reject Him to follow their own selfish desires.

III. God's Perspective
(2 Peter 3:8, 9)

A. His Timetable (v. 8)

8. But, beloved, be not ignorant of this one thing, that one day is with the Lord as a thousand years, and a thousand years as one day.

The perspective now shifts from past and future history to the throne room of the eternal God. God's existence is not bound by time as is ours. Because He exists without beginning or ending, the passing of time is to God not the problem that it is for us. "Soon" on God's calendar is not a matter of days, but of great epochs.

The scoffers have failed to reckon with this reality. God's timetable may be very different from our own. What seems like forever to us is insignificant to the God who has existed forever (compare Psalm 90:4).

The failure to grasp this perspective betrays human self-centeredness. We tend to judge everything by our own experience. In a human lifetime,

30 years is a long time. From God's perspective, though, it is not. The same is true for 2,000 years or for any finite number of years we may imagine.

What Do You Think?
How has your perspective on time changed through the years? How has this affected the way you face various issues?
Talking Points for Your Discussion
- Regarding financial issues
- Regarding possessions
- Regarding priorities
- Regarding relationships
- Regarding health concerns
- Other

B. His Patience (v. 9)

9. The Lord is not slack concerning his promise, as some men count slackness; but is long-suffering to us-ward, not willing that any should perish, but that all should come to repentance.

Granted that the passing of time is different from God's perspective, the scoffer could still ask why God bothers to delay the return of Christ at all. Certainly, God may not find the time significant, but why bother at all to leave a period of time between Christ's resurrection and the establishment of His full reign? Why not begin the final judgment immediately, if indeed there is to be such a thing?

Peter's reply to such an objection is vital to our understanding of God's dealings with the world. It expresses the implication of God's essential nature. God is just; therefore, He must bring judgment on evil. But God is also merciful, wanting to forgive those who have committed evil. So in His mercy, God withholds judgment while He invites rebellious humans to accept His offer of forgiveness and be reconciled to Him. Without a delay between Christ's resurrection and His return, no such opportunity would exist.

So, says Peter, God has in no way been late or neglectful in fulfilling His promises. In fact, He is faithfully fulfilling His promise to save by allowing sinful humans time to hear His gracious offer in the gospel and come to Jesus in repen-

tance. This is an expression of God's patience as He pursues His profound desire to bring all people to repentance and reconciliation, if only they are willing (compare 1 Timothy 2:4).

From God's perspective, this is no delay at all (compare Habakkuk 2:3). He is working out His plan to bring as many people as possible into an eternal relationship with Him. From the beginning, God has advanced His plan by which His enemies can become His friends. The seeming postponement of Christ's return is another step in that plan, allowing more rebellious humans to accept His terms of mercy.

IV. Believers' Perspective
(2 PETER 3:10-15a, 18)

A. Future Event (vv. 10-13)

10a. But the day of the Lord will come as a thief in the night;

The perspective now shifts to what faithful believers know about Christ's return and how they will be affected. The Lord's return as *a thief in the night* echoes Jesus' own words in Matthew 24:42-44 and Luke 12:39, 40 (compare 1 Thessalonians 5:2, 4 [Lesson 8]; Revelation 16:15). For those who reject the gospel and do not expect Christ's return, His coming will be a disastrous surprise.

The outcome will be different for believers. We expect Christ's return, and we will welcome Him when He arrives. For the scoffer, He returns with judgment; for the believer, He returns with blessing.

10b. In the which the heavens shall pass away with a great noise, and the elements shall melt with fervent heat, the earth also and the works that are therein shall be burned up.

The description now shifts to the fate of the universe as a whole: it *shall melt with fervent heat.* The world that the scoffer takes to be eternally unchanging, the place where the scoffer puts confidence and hope, will be destroyed. This includes *the works that are therein*—the things people have made, which they count as sources of security and power. Every pretension of humanity will come to nothing when Christ returns. For those who do not know Him as Savior, His coming means the destruction of what they think will save them.

11. Seeing then that all these things shall be dissolved, what manner of persons ought ye to be in all holy conversation and godliness?

For the believer, the knowledge that Christ will one day destroy this present existence has transformative power. We realize that there is no basis for security in the things of this present age. Relying on power or status on the world's terms is foolish because the world has no staying power.

Instead, what matters is *holy conversation and godliness*. The word *conversation* means not just speech, but all kinds of proper interaction with others. A life of *godliness* speaks to proper devotion to the true, eternal God. Our confident hope for the future demands that we live with an eternal perspective every day.

12. Looking for and hasting unto the coming of the day of God, wherein the heavens being on fire shall be dissolved, and the elements shall melt with fervent heat?

Unlike the scoffer, the Christian lives in expectation of Christ's return. The expression *looking for* implies "watching expectantly." We can compare this with children who look out the window waiting for a parent to arrive home after work.

The phrase *hasting unto the coming of the day of God* is difficult. Taken literally, it could mean that we somehow are able to "speed up" the timetable of Christ's return. Taken figuratively, the phrase carries the idea of "waiting eagerly" for that return. Such waiting is not passive, but involves applying energy and enthusiasm to obeying the Lord in anticipation of His return. As we do, we sit lightly on the things of this present age, knowing that such things are marked for destruction.

13. Nevertheless we, according to his promise, look for new heavens and a new earth, wherein dwelleth righteousness.

The Christian's perspective is to be defined by Christ's promises. Thus importance is placed not on the world that is passing away, but on the one to come.

The description that Peter provides is important, and we ought to pay careful attention to the language. First, we must remember that the combination "heavens and earth" is based on Old Testament usage, as in Genesis 1:1. As such, "heavens and earth" refers to the entirety of God's creation.

This causes us to realize that what Peter describes is not the destruction only of the earth so that the heavens remain. Rather, what is in view is the replacement of this present realm with a new one, *new heavens and a new earth*.

The new heavens and earth will be characterized by righteousness. In this new sphere, God's will shall be done perfectly. This is the promise of the Old Testament prophets (Isaiah 65:17; 66:22), renewed here and in the closing chapters of the New Testament (Revelation 21:1).

B. Present Response (vv. 14, 15a, 18)

14. Wherefore, beloved, seeing that ye look for such things, be diligent that ye may be found of him in peace, without spot, and blameless.

If our destination is a righteous world, the way we live in the present should reflect that destination. Considering the scope of Christ's return, our duty in the present is clear. We are like servants whose master is away: we want to be found doing His work when He returns (Luke 12:35-40).

As servants of Christ, we therefore pursue what He taught, namely true purity that exists inside and out, being spotless and blameless even where only the Lord himself can see—in our minds and hearts. Likewise, we pursue peaceful, positive relationships with others, just as Christ commanded. Servants with this kind of life will be commended by their master at His return.

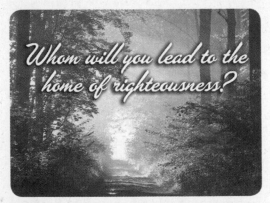

Whom will you lead to the home of righteousness?

Visual for Lesson 13. *Pose the question on this visual when your study reaches verse 13. Allow a time of sharing of responses.*

❦ TWO KINGDOMS ❦

An influential doctrine of Martin Luther (1483–1546) was his teaching of the two kingdoms. We live in a world governed by earthly authorities, authorities that God instituted (Romans 13:1, 2). At the same time, we live in a kingdom not of this world, a kingdom governed directly by God. The tricky part is to live responsibly in both at the same time so that we do not disregard one in favor of a total emphasis on the other.

Living in both kingdoms means we are to be heavenly minded (Colossians 3:1, 2) while also being salt and light in this world (Matthew 5:13-16). Peter was certainly aware of the fleeting nature of earthly existence. But this did not cause him to treat our earthly existence lightly; we see quite the opposite attitude as he encouraged his readers to live "in peace, without spot, and blameless."

The two kingdoms need not be in conflict, but a Christian certainly needs to know which one is the higher calling. We demonstrate that awareness in the way we live. —J. B. N.

15a. And account that the longsuffering of our Lord is salvation.

In the meantime, we may become impatient for the Lord's return. When life is difficult, we will long for Christ to return and put an end to the evil that we suffer. But if we understand the perspective that Peter shares, we will view the wait for Christ's return as God views it: an expression of God's patience. He waits for more people to return to Him. So we wait along with God himself, with our focus being what His focus is: bringing others to reconciliation with Him.

18. But grow in grace, and in the knowledge of our Lord and Saviour Jesus Christ. To him be glory both now and for ever. Amen.

After a brief discussion regarding how the apostle Paul also affirms these truths (vv. 15b-17, not in today's text), Peter turns to a closing word of encouragement. Knowing that Christ will indeed return compels that we continue in the gifts we have received from Him. We *grow in grace* as we respond consistently to God's unmerited gift of salvation. We *grow . . . in the knowledge* as we put into practice what we have learned through the gospel. By these means Christ is glorified.

Conclusion

A. Patient Endurance

How do we respond to the reality of Christ's expected return? We may be reluctant to desire His return when we feel comfortable; we may be anxious for His return when we are suffering. Whatever our circumstances, we need to recognize how important to our faith is the promise of His return to save and to judge. Remembering this promise will strengthen the patient endurance we need to stand firm and grow in our faith in a hostile world.

B. Prayer

Father, may Your Son return quickly! But if He tarries, we know it is so that more may be saved. Make us the agents of that reconciliation as You give us the strength to wait. In Jesus' name, amen.

C. Thought to Remember

"Behold, I come quickly; and my reward is with me" (Revelation 22:12).

INVOLVEMENT LEARNING

Some of the activities below are also found in the helpful student book, Adult Bible Class.
Don't forget to download the free reproducible page from www.standardlesson.com to enhance your lesson!

Into the Lesson

Form four teams of no more than five learners each. Give each team several Christian songbooks and/or hymnals. Say, "Select a song that speaks of the second coming of Christ. The reference may be in the song as a whole or in a specific line or verse." Ask teams to share their selections and reasons for choosing them. Say, "Christian music anticipates and celebrates Jesus' second coming. We must always remember that He will come again!"

Into the Word

Read the printed text, then assign the following four passages of Scripture to the same four groups above, one each: 2 Peter 3:3-7; 2 Peter 3:8, 9; 2 Peter 3:10-13; and 2 Peter 3:14, 15, 18. (*Option:* Depending on the nature of your class, you may wish to provide copies of the lesson commentary for the verses assigned.)

Ask each group to create an artistic depiction that represents or interprets its passage. They may choose a drawing, clay sculpture, new song lyric to an existing tune, or poetry. For example, a team may choose to write an additional verse to the children's song "Jesus Loves Me" to express truths of the passage. Make available sheets of poster board or paper, marker pens, colored pencils, modeling clay, and Christian songbooks or hymnals. Allow no more than 15 minutes for this creative activity.

After teams share results with the class, say, "Artistic representations of Scripture can be emotionally uplifting! But we also want to wrestle with the text mentally."

Distribute copies of the following questions to the same four teams, one set per team as numbered. Each team will have two questions to explore and answer for the class. *Team 1*—verses 3-7: What argument is given by the "scoffers"? How does Peter use creation and the flood to answer their argument? *Team 2*—verses 8, 9: How is God's perspective on time different from

ours? What important reason does Peter give for God's apparent delay in fulfilling His promise? *Team 3*—verses 10-13: What facts does Peter give about what "the day of the Lord" will be like? How should Christians act in light of these facts? *Team 4*—verses 14, 15, 18: As we await Christ's return, what can we do in the meantime? What comfort and encouragement does Peter give to Christians who are suffering?

Alternative: If you choose not to do the artistic depiction exercise above, you can follow the text examination exercise with the "What We Need to Have" activity from the reproducible page, which you can download. Distribute copies for the four teams to complete as a closed-Bible exercise.

Into Life

The next activity may be done as a whole class or in the teams that have been working together through the lesson thus far. Read the following situation, then distribute handouts with the same wording:

> One of your coworkers has been experiencing extreme hardship for two years. The problems began when she went through a difficult divorce, losing custody of her children to their father. Living on a very limited income from her secretarial work, she has been hammered by bills for car repairs and a mistake she made on her income tax return. This past week she discovered she will need surgery. You have become very concerned about the possibility that she will take her own life when you heard her say, "I just don't want to be here anymore. I have nothing to live for."
> You have invited her for lunch to talk and provide support. Using today's passage of Scripture as a foundation for your discussion, what can you say to her, without being flippant, to encourage perseverance?

Alternative: Instead of the above, distribute copies of the "Living in Hope" exercise from the reproducible page. After allowing a few minutes for personal reflection, ask volunteers to share thoughts.

GOD'S PEOPLE
WORSHIP

Special Features

Lessons

Unit 1: The Prophet and Praise

Unit 2: Worshipping in Jerusalem Again (Ezra)

Unit 3: Worshipping in Jerusalem Again (Nehemiah)

QUARTERLY QUIZ

Use these questions as a pretest or as a review. The answers are on page iv of This Quarter in the Word.

Lesson 1

1. Isaiah's vision of the Lord occurred in the year king _____ died. *Isaiah 6:1*

2. Isaiah thought he was doomed because he was a man of _____ lips. *Isaiah 6:5*

Lesson 2

1. Isaiah was joyful because God's _____ had been turned away. *Isaiah 12:1*

2. Isaiah pictured salvation as a well from which water is drawn. T/F. *Isaiah 12:3*

Lesson 3

1. God accused His people of honoring Him only with their feet. T/F. *Isaiah 29:13*

2. Through Isaiah, God promised that the wisdom of the wise would endure. T/F. *Isaiah 29:14*

Lesson 4

1. Isaiah foresaw a future of no premature death. T/F. *Isaiah 65:20*

2. Isaiah's vision of the future, peaceful kingdom of God included a wolf eating alongside a _____. *Isaiah 65:25*

Lesson 5

1. When the temple was rebuilt, who was one of the leaders? (Moses, Zerubbabel, Ahab?) *Ezra 3:2*

2. The Israelites who were the first to return from exile did not sacrifice on the altar until the temple was completely rebuilt. T/F. *Ezra 3:6*

Lesson 6

1. A Levite had to be at least ___ years old to help oversee rebuilding the temple. *Ezra 3:8*

2. Those supervising the rebuilding of the temple were all from the tribe of Judah. T/F. *Ezra 3:9*

Lesson 7

1. One prophet who served during the rebuilding of the temple was Haggai. T/F. *Ezra 6:14*

2. Who was king of Persia when the temple was completed? (Cyrus, Darius, Saul?) *Ezra 6:15*

3. The dedication of the rebuilt temple included the sacrifice of over 700 animals. T/F. *Ezra 6:17*

Lesson 8

1. What was Ezra's primary role? (cupbearer, governor of Judea, teacher of the law?) *Ezra 7:10*

2. Ezra did not ask the king for an armed escort for the journey to Jerusalem. T/F. *Ezra 8:22*

Lesson 9

1. Ezra and his group brought very little silver and gold to Jerusalem. T/F. *Ezra 8:26, 27*

2. On arrival in Jerusalem, Ezra's group rested for how many days? (zero, three, six?) *Ezra 8:32*

Lesson 10

1. Only male heads of households heard Ezra's reading of the law. T/F. *Nehemiah 8:3*

2. Those who heard the law read built _____ for a celebration. *Nehemiah 8:16*

Lesson 11

1. Before their confession, the Israelites separated themselves from _____. *Nehemiah 9:2*

2. God had used the prophets to warn Israel of their danger. T/F. *Nehemiah 9:30*

Lesson 12

1. Nehemiah used two large companies to give thanks. T/F. *Nehemiah 12:31*

2. The musical instruments used in the dedication of the walls traced back to which king? (David, Uzziah, Josiah?) *Nehemiah 12:36*

Lesson 13

1. Nehemiah was distressed when he saw the _____ day being profaned. *Nehemiah 13:15-18*

2. "Men of Tyre" were part of the problem that Nehemiah noted. T/F. *Nehemiah 13:16*

QUARTER AT A GLANCE

by Douglas Redford

AN OFTEN QUOTED maxim is, "You never know how much you miss something [or someone] until it [or that person] is gone." Such was the case with the people of God in the Old Testament who were accustomed to having the magnificent temple of Solomon in their midst.

Many had come to assume that the presence of the temple gave them a kind of "immunity" from any disaster. The people became spiritually apathetic. This in turn affected their worship, which became shallow at best and idolatrous at worst.

Dismantling Structures and People

Prophets such as Isaiah (whose book is the source of the four lessons in **Unit 1**) confronted the people with the hard truth that God was quite aware of their hollow ritualism (Isaiah 29:13). The people wouldn't listen, so the unthinkable happened: God brought about the destruction of that supposedly indestructible temple.

Sometimes we are guilty of the attitudes that characterized the ancient Israelites. We become complacent. Worship becomes a routine. We take the place we meet for granted, assuming it will always be there for us. But suppose the building where we meet to worship were destroyed by fire, a tornado, or some other disaster? Suddenly worship would take on an entirely different perspective. (Some who are reading this now have actually gone through such an experience.)

This—and worse—is what happened to God's people in 586 BC. Everyone could see the temple lying in ruins. A great many also found themselves trudging hundreds of miles into captivity, to Babylon. Psalm 137 in particular conveys the captives' deep sorrow.

Yet the Babylonian captivity was not a *period* for God's people, but a *comma;* the exile did not mark the end for them, but a pause. God had promised, through Isaiah and other prophets, that the captives would return and rebuild their lives in the promised land. This is the focus of the lessons of **Units 2 and 3** in this quarter's studies, drawn from the books of Ezra and Nehemiah.

Rebuilding Structures and People

One of the first orders of business for the initial wave of exiles returning from captivity was the restoration of worship. The people needed an altar for offering the required sacrifices, so they built one; they also determined to keep the Feast of Tabernacles. A bit later, they laid the foundation for a new temple.

But it was not just altars and buildings that needed to be rebuilt; the people themselves needed renewal. Ezra and Nehemiah, who traveled home-

> *Mistakes of the past can be repeated if one is not vigilant.*

ward in different groups after the first, took the initiative to see that the people of God were spiritually in tune with Him. Both men set about making sure that certain spiritual disciplines were not neglected. Both were passionate about instructing the people in the Word of the Lord. They encouraged giving attention to fasting, prayer, giving gifts, and observing sacred times as prescribed by the Lord. They did not want to see the people go through the heartache of another captivity!

Keeping Worship Fresh

Ezra and Nehemiah knew that mistakes of the past can be repeated if one is not vigilant. That is why it is also important to look ahead. The prophet Isaiah did just that in his description of worship that will take place in the coming new heavens and new earth (lesson 4).

May our desire to share someday in that incomparable worship experience keep our present worship fresh and focused.

GET THE SETTING

by Lloyd M. Pelfrey

ISRAEL'S TEMPLE was not distinctive in the ancient world. In 1936, archaeologists working in the area of Turkey that is closest to Israel observed remains of an ancient temple that had features similar to the one described in the Bible. Other ancient temples in that region have since been discovered that have the same general design.

Temple Design and Purpose

Two basic types of structures were used for temples: the "long-room" edifice and the "wide-room" building. Israel's temple was the long-room type, having two specific areas included in its length: the Holy Place and the Most Holy Place. It also had a portico that can be considered a third room. One crucial difference from pagan temples is that Israel's did not have a statue of God.

Ancient people had several reasons for building temples: to fulfill an innate desire to worship, to have a central place to gather, and/or to enable rulers to claim a type of divinity to help them control their subjects. These motivations were quite powerful, as seen in the fact that huge stones would be quarried, moved several miles, and stacked to form gigantic structures. The determination to do all this becomes even more amazing when we realize that temples were often built on hills!

Temples in Wrong Places

The Lord declared that only one place was acceptable for Israel to worship, a precept repeated frequently in Deuteronomy, beginning in 12:5. Israel did not obey this injunction faithfully. Major violations occurred when the nation divided after Solomon died (see 1 Kings 12:28-30). The result was idolatry.

The Babylonian exile essentially cured the Israelites' desire to be involved in idolatry. It is in this light that the people returned from exile to build a temple and renew proper worship in Jerusalem. However, another Jewish temple was in existence at the time; it was on Elephantine Island in Upper Egypt. It is easy to imagine that the Jews who returned to Palestine from exile wanted nothing to do with that rival temple, since there was only one proper place to have the Lord's house: in Jerusalem.

Papyri tell of a conflict that resulted in the Elephantine temple being vandalized in about 407 BC, so we know it continued to exist into the period of time between the Old and New Testaments. Appeals for help in rebuilding were sent to Johanan, a priest in Jerusalem who was a son of Eliashib; both are mentioned in Nehemiah 12:23. Receiving similar letters were the two sons of Sanballat, who were over Samaria. Sanballat is mentioned in Nehemiah 2:19.

Although the Babylonian exile settled for the Jews the "whom to worship" question, it apparently did not settle fully the "where to worship" question, even by Jesus' day. Another Jewish temple was located in the Nile Delta at Leontopolis; it was destroyed about AD 73.

Temples Today

We see the "where" issue presenting itself in John 4:20-24. In Jesus' response to the woman at the well, He declared that in His kingdom genuine worship would not be confined to one place. Today, each Christian functions as a temple in which the Holy Spirit dwells (1 Corinthians 6:19). This allows Christianity to be taken wherever we go—or perhaps we should say it *requires* Christianity to be taken wherever we go!

THIS QUARTER IN THE WORD

Answers to the Quarterly Quiz on page 338

Lesson 1—1. Uzziah. 2. unclean. **Lesson 2**—1. anger. 2. true. **Lesson 3**—1. false. 2. false. **Lesson 4**—1. true. 2. lamb. **Lesson 5**—1. Zerubbabel. 2. false. **Lesson 6**—1. 20. 2. false. **Lesson 7**—1. true. 2. Darius. 3. true. **Lesson 8**—1. teacher of the law. 2. true. **Lesson 9**—1. false. 2. three. **Lesson 10**—1. false. 2. booths. **Lesson 11**—1. strangers. 2. true. **Lesson 12**—1. true. 2. David. **Lesson 13**—1. Sabbath. 2. true.

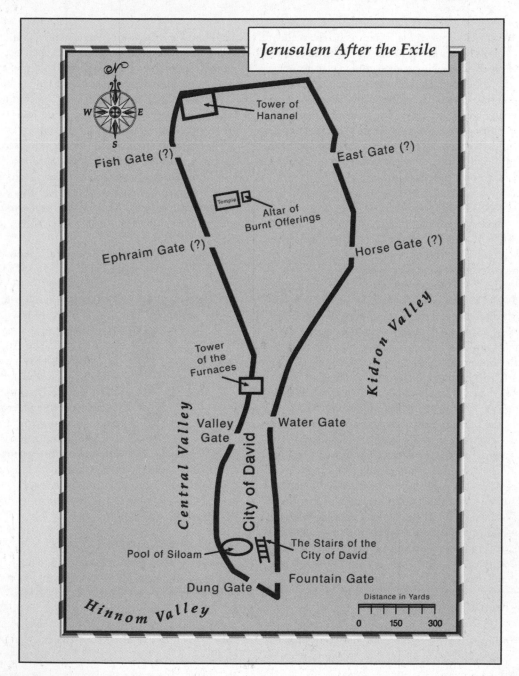

Jerusalem After the Exile

TOOLS OF THE TRADE

Teacher Tips by Brent L. Amato

JUST AS A master craftsman requires excellent tools for his or her profession, a skilled teacher of the Bible knows about and takes advantage of available resources to enhance the lesson. Imagine yourself starting to prepare your next lesson, with your Bible and *Standard Lesson Commentary* open. You sense Luke's diligence as he wrote his Gospel (Luke 1:3, 4), and you want to have that diligence as your own as you prepare. What "tools" might help?

Two Spiritual Tools

Resist the temptation to rely only on tools that can be bought in a store or accessed online. There is no substitute for the two spiritual resources that are already on hand for teachers!

The first is the power of the Holy Spirit, who dwells within us (1 Corinthians 6:19). A Spirit-filled teacher will teach a Spirit-filled lesson (Ephesians 3:16). Those blessed with the spiritual gift of teaching should be developing that gift through the power of the Holy Spirit (Romans 12:6, 7; 1 Corinthians 12:1, 28). Paul challenged Timothy to give himself wholly to his gift (1 Timothy 4:13-15), and that challenge is ours as well.

The second spiritual tool is prayer. Many times we teachers prepare to teach a biblical passage by studying its technicalities without first spending much time praying about and meditating on that passage. Through prayer we invite God to engage our minds and hearts in the truth of His Word (Psalm 119:18). If that doesn't happen, how can we communicate it properly to our students? It is through prayerful meditation that the Word becomes a way of life to be modeled to our students (Psalm 1:2, 3).

Three Man-Made Tools

You're teaching on the humility of Christ from Philippians 2:5-8. You reach into your teacher's toolbox and open a book that lists every place in the Bible where the word *humility* and its variants appear. You discover more than 70 such occurrences you can draw from to enrich your preparation. You've just used a *concordance*!

You're teaching on John 21:15-17 concerning a dialogue between Jesus and Peter after Jesus' resurrection. You've heard from sermons or other teachers that different words for *love* are used in the Greek that stands behind the English translation. You want to know if the difference is important or merely stylistic, so you reach into your teacher's toolbox, grab a book, and open it to the entry on *love* that explains the issue. You've just used a *Bible dictionary*!

You're teaching about the special friendship between Jonathan and David, and you read in  1 Samuel 23:15, 16 that "David was in the wilderness of Ziph in a wood. And Jonathan . . . went to David." You reach into your teacher's toolbox and open a book that has a map indicating the location of this wilderness area. Comparing that with Jonathan's starting point, you come away with a much deeper appreciation of Jonathan's journey and, consequently, insight into Jonathan's commitment to David. Your lesson is better illustrated because you've examined *a Bible atlas*!

Don't Let the Tools Get Dusty!

Every time you sit down to prepare to teach, the toolbox should be at your side! It should be ready to be opened and its contents used so that you too "mightest know the certainty of those things" (Luke 1:4). When you use your tools to that end, your students will end up knowing the things of God as well.

Photo: Dynamic Graphics / Liquidlibrary / Thinkstock

WORSHIP AND RESPOND

DEVOTIONAL READING: Joshua 24:14-24
BACKGROUND SCRIPTURE: Isaiah 6

ISAIAH 6:1-8

1 In the year that king Uzziah died I saw also the Lord sitting upon a throne, high and lifted up, and his train filled the temple.

2 Above it stood the seraphims: each one had six wings; with twain he covered his face, and with twain he covered his feet, and with twain he did fly.

3 And one cried unto another, and said, Holy, holy, holy, is the LORD of hosts: the whole earth is full of his glory.

4 And the posts of the door moved at the voice of him that cried, and the house was filled with smoke.

5 Then said I, Woe is me! for I am undone; because I am a man of unclean lips, and I dwell in the midst of a people of unclean lips: for mine eyes have seen the King, the LORD of hosts.

6 Then flew one of the seraphims unto me, having a live coal in his hand, which he had taken with the tongs from off the altar:

7 And he laid it upon my mouth, and said, Lo, this hath touched thy lips; and thine iniquity is taken away, and thy sin purged.

8 Also I heard the voice of the Lord, saying, Whom shall I send, and who will go for us? Then said I, Here am I; send me.

KEY VERSE

One cried unto another, and said, Holy, holy, holy, is the LORD of hosts: the whole earth is full of his glory.
—Isaiah 6:3

GOD'S PEOPLE WORSHIP

Unit 1: The Prophet and Praise
LESSONS 1–4

LESSON AIMS

After participating in this lesson, each student will be able to:

1. List the key details of Isaiah's call to become a prophet of the Lord.

2. Explain the connection between Isaiah's vision and his response to God's call, "Who will go?"

3. Make a commitment to be faithful in worship and faithful in service through the summer months.

LESSON OUTLINE

Introduction

A. Remember Who's in Control

I was in my office at the Christian university where I teach on the morning of 9/11. That was a Tuesday morning, when the school was to hold its regularly scheduled chapel service later at 10:00 AM. One of my colleagues was to speak for chapel, and naturally he already had a sermon prepared. But as news of the tragic events of that day became known across campus, he decided to change the content of his message. He ended up reading a series of Scriptures appropriate for the occasion and offered brief comments on each one.

One of the Scriptures he read that morning was the first verse of today's printed text, from Isaiah 6:1: "In the year that king Uzziah died I saw also the Lord . . . high and lifted up." His point was that when tragedy occurs—even a tragedy that touches an entire nation—the Lord *is* still in control.

B. Lesson Background

The prophet Isaiah lived in turbulent times. In fact, prophets usually served in such times; that is why they were called to their ministry. God raised them up to provide a divine perspective on the events unfolding before His people—events that sometimes appeared to be spiraling out of control.

Isaiah's ministry occurred during the period of Old Testament history known as the divided monarchy. His prophetic call came, as today's text states, "In the year that king Uzziah died" (Isaiah 6:1); that was 740 BC, about 191 years after the nation of Israel had divided into the northern kingdom of Israel and the southern kingdom of Judah. The northern kingdom was in decline in 740 BC, both politically and spiritually. Concurrently, the Assyrians to the northeast had gained in strength and vigor, thanks to the efforts of Tiglath-pileser III, who ruled 745–727 BC. A few years after his reign ended, the northern kingdom of Israel fell to the Assyrians, in 722 BC (2 Kings 17:5, 6).

Isaiah's ministry was concentrated in the southern kingdom of Judah. All the kings mentioned in the opening verse of his book are kings of Judah (Isaiah 1:1). Approximately 20 years after Israel fell, the Assyrians targeted Judah just as they had targeted Israel. But Judah was spared from destruction during the reign of godly King Hezekiah, who received counsel from Isaiah (37:21-38).

Thus the prophet Isaiah served during a time of both divine judgment (upon the northern kingdom of Israel) and divine deliverance (granted to the southern kingdom of Judah). It was during times that seemed as uncertain and foreboding as those that occurred on 9/11 that Isaiah was called to remind the people that God was in control. Isaiah himself was allowed to experience that truth in a unique, unforgettable way. His experience is the subject of today's printed text.

We may wonder why Isaiah's call is not recorded until chapter 6 of his book. In the cases of the prophets Jeremiah and Ezekiel, the calls appear toward the beginning of the records, where one would expect them to be (Jeremiah 1:4-19; Ezekiel 1:1–3:27). Perhaps Isaiah's call actually did precede his messages of Isaiah 1–5, but the account of the call is placed in Isaiah 6 to make a crucial point: the first five chapters explain *why* a prophet like Isaiah was so desperately needed by God's people. Isaiah 5 in particular is a compelling description of the extent of corruption within a people originally called by God to be "a kingdom of priests, and an holy nation" (Exodus 19:6). Isaiah uses the imagery of a vineyard and a garden to describe both the Lord's care for Israel and Judah and His disappointment that they had not produced the desired crop (Isaiah 5:1-7).

There follows a series of woes (six to be exact) that depict the depths of depravity to which God's people had plunged. Isaiah 5:20 is an especially powerful indictment of how the people of God had misplaced their priorities; they were guilty of calling "evil good, and good evil."

It is noteworthy that the "woe" that Isaiah cries in our printed text (Isaiah 6:5) is the seventh in this series. Perhaps his "woe" is designed to complete the set (the number seven is often a symbol of completeness or perfection in the Bible). The prophet's own sense of woe compelled him to address the woes that have placed God's people in a position of being ripe for His judgment.

I. Splendor Displayed
(ISAIAH 6:1-4)
A. Seeing the Lord (vv. 1, 2)

1. In the year that king Uzziah died I saw also the Lord sitting upon a throne, high and lifted up, and his train filled the temple.

Uzziah reigned from about 792 to 740 BC. His 52-year reign is one of the longest recorded in Scripture (2 Chronicles 26:3). Uzziah was one of Judah's better kings from a spiritual standpoint. "He did that which was right in the sight of the Lord, according to all that his father Amaziah did. And he sought God in the days of Zechariah, who had understanding in the visions of God: and as long as he sought the Lord, God made him to prosper" (26:4, 5).

However, Uzziah did not finish as well as he could have. "But when he was strong, his heart was lifted up to his destruction: for he transgressed against the Lord his God, and went into the temple of the Lord to burn incense upon the altar of incense" (2 Chronicles 26:16). Entering the temple was restricted to the priests; and when some of the priests confronted Uzziah with his action, he became enraged with them. In the midst of his ranting, the king was stricken with leprosy and was quickly ushered from the temple. He lived in isolation until his death (26:17-21). Uzziah is also known as *Azariah* in 2 Kings 14:21 and 15:1.

The vision that Isaiah sees in the year of Uzziah's death is marvelous indeed: *the Lord sitting upon a throne, high and lifted up, and his train filled the temple.* We wonder which temple this is—is it

HOW TO SAY IT

Amaziah	Am-uh-*zye*-uh.
Assyrians	Uh-*sear*-e-unz.
Azariah	Az-uh-*rye*-uh.
cherubims	*chair*-uh-bims.
Hezekiah	Hez-ih-*kye*-uh.
Kathmandu	Kat-man-*due*.
seraphims	*sair*-uh-fims.
theophany	thee-*ah*-fuh-nee (*th* as in *thin*).
Tiglath-pileser	*Tig*-lath-pih-*lee*-zer.
Uzziah	Uh-*zye*-uh.
Zechariah	*Zek*-uh-*rye*-uh.

Jerusalem's temple, built by Solomon, or is it the heavenly temple, which Isaiah is seeing by means of a vision? Given what happened to King Uzziah when he ventured into a sacred space, some suggest that Isaiah likely does not physically enter the Jerusalem temple. The grandeur and splendor of all that Isaiah sees, including the presence of the seraphims (v. 2, next), suggests that this is the heavenly temple. Isaiah is seeing in a vision something perhaps similar to the surroundings that the apostle John is privileged to see in Revelation 4:1-11.

The fact that Isaiah sees the Lord should not be seen as contradictory to John 1:18: "No man hath seen God at any time." Other individuals in Scripture are described as seeing God in a limited way that allows them to continue to live (Exodus 24:9-11; 33:18-23; 34:5-7; Judges 13:22, 23). The technical term for such an appearance of God to humans is *theophany*.

The fact that the Lord is *sitting upon a throne* may suggest that He is in a position of judgment (Proverbs 20:8; Matthew 25:31-33; Revelation 20:11, 12)—a judgment deserved by the nation of Judah, as Isaiah 1–5 shows. One detail in the scene before Isaiah especially catches the prophet's eye: *his train*. The Hebrew word translated "train" refers to the hem of a garment. The hem is often used as a mark of identity for people of stature, such as kings or priests (see the description of the high priest's "hem" in Exodus 28:33-35).

Visual for Lesson 1. *Use this visual to introduce the discussion question that is associated with Isaiah 6:3 (top of page 349).*

The fact that this part of the Lord's robe fills the temple testifies to the majesty and splendor of the one who occupies the throne. The prophet does not include further details of the train, perhaps because his attention is drawn to something else.

❧ A FADED PALACE ❧

The royal palace complex in Kathmandu, Nepal, looks like an imposing center of power when viewed from a distance. With its fences, guards, and security checkpoints, you would think a king still ruled there, receiving foreign dignitaries from his golden throne.

Once inside the palace walls, however, visitors get a different impression. The decor has not been updated since the 1960s. The ceilings are discolored with water damage, the wallpaper is peeling, and the tiger skin rugs are dusty and worn. In the unkempt garden outside is a marker describing the massacre of the royal family in 2001 under mysterious circumstances. In the political upheaval that followed, Nepal became a republic and opened the palace to the public as a poignant memorial to a once glorious monarchy.

As an outsider, I could observe the effects of this political change with some detachment because I knew I would soon leave for the stability of my own country. Yet I know that no nation's stability is permanent (see Acts 17:26).

The rising and falling of earthly powers should motivate us to reach for the security that can be found only in the Lord. The next time we lift our eyes to our country's flag, let us lift our spiritual gaze further yet, to Heaven. We belong to another kingdom—a kingdom that will never fade.
—A. W.

2. Above it stood the seraphims: each one had six wings; with twain he covered his face, and with twain he covered his feet, and with twain he did fly.

Today's text is the only place in the Bible where *seraphims* are mentioned. They may be similar to the "cherubims" mentioned in Ezekiel 10; but they are not the same, since that prophet describes cherubims as having four wings each, not six (see 1:1-11 and 10:20-22). The word *seraph* comes from a Hebrew word meaning "to burn." Perhaps this is meant to describe the radiance that is part of their appearance.

The seraphims also appear to be similar to the "four beasts" mentioned in Revelation 4:6-8; they too have six wings each but have other characteristics that are not included in the description of the seraphims. The beasts declare God's holiness as do the seraphims (Isaiah 6:3, below).

Four of each seraph's six wings cover parts of their bodies. In the ancient Near East, covering the feet and covering (or, usually, bowing) the head are expressions of homage, used especially in the presence of kings. Isaiah himself will soon acknowledge that he is in the presence of a king (v. 5, below).

B. Hearing the Seraphims (vv. 3, 4)

3. And one cried unto another, and said, Holy, holy, holy, is the LORD of hosts: the whole earth is full of his glory.

Isaiah hears the seraphims proclaiming the holiness of the Lord to one another, using for special emphasis the familiar (to us) threefold refrain of *Holy, holy, holy* (compare Revelation 4:8). This experience seems to have an unforgettable impact on Isaiah, since he more than any other Old Testament writer uses the expression "Holy One of Israel" to describe God. (The phrase is used 26 times in Isaiah and only 6 times in the rest of the Old Testament.)

The quality of holiness implies separation or distinctiveness. This separation is primarily ethical or moral and only secondarily positional or geographical. This is why Isaiah becomes so distraught at being in the Lord's presence (v. 5, below); he knows how unholy, how sinful, he and his people are.

Although Isaiah is privileged to view the Lord in His heavenly surroundings, he is reminded by the seraphims' words that *the whole earth is full of his glory*. God's creation is a testament to His glory, a theme often echoed in the Psalms (examples: Psalms 8:1; 19:1; 24:1-3).

4. And the posts of the door moved at the voice of him that cried, and the house was filled with smoke.

Elsewhere Scripture tells how the voice of God produces dramatic results that cannot be ignored (Job 40:9; Psalm 29:3-9; Ezekiel 43:1, 2). Here the voice of His messengers has an impressive impact as well in that it moves *the posts of the door*. Why this portion of the heavenly temple is affected this way is unclear. Perhaps the entire temple moves, but the prophet senses this especially at the place where he is positioned—the doorway.

Smoke is sometimes associated with the presence of God (as on Mount Sinai, Exodus 19:18) and can be used in scenes depicting God's judgment (Psalm 18:8; Joel 2:30, 31; Revelation 9:1-3; 18:9, 10, 17, 18). At this point, three of Isaiah's senses—those of sight, hearing, and smell—are taking in this awe-inspiring drama. Touch will be included later as well (v. 7).

II. Sin Cleansed
(ISAIAH 6:5-7)
A. Isaiah's Remorse (v. 5)

5. Then said I, Woe is me! for I am undone; because I am a man of unclean lips, and I dwell in the midst of a people of unclean lips: for mine eyes have seen the King, the LORD of hosts.

Isaiah now feels compelled to speak, and his words express a sense of utter unworthiness to be witnessing the sights and sounds before him. The Lesson Background notes that Isaiah's *woe* may be considered the seventh in a series of seven that begins in Isaiah 5:8. This man acknowledges that he has no right whatsoever to be in the presence of the holy God (even in a vision), for he knows that he himself is the complete opposite of holiness. One wonders if what happened to Uzziah when he dared to enter the Lord's temple comes to Isaiah's mind at this point (again, 2 Chronicles 26:16-21).

Isaiah's mention of his lips being unclean contrasts sharply with the seraphims' acknowledgement of the Lord's holiness. Isaiah also notes that his *eyes have seen the King, the Lord of hosts*. If the Lord's eyes are too pure to "look on iniquity" (Habakkuk 1:13), then a human's eyes must be unfit to look upon deity. But Isaiah's condition is not unique to him; he knows he is *in the midst of a people of unclean lips*. He does not say this to excuse his own condition; he is simply confessing that the sin problem is nationwide (as Isaiah 1–5 shows).

> **What Do You Think?**
> How can we make sure *confession* receives the emphasis it should in our prayers?
> *Talking Points for Your Discussion*
> - Of personal sin, publicly and privately (Nehemiah 9:2a; Daniel 9:20a)
> - Of corporate sin, publicly and privately (Nehemiah 9:2b; Daniel 9:20b)

B. Seraphim's Remedy (vv. 6, 7)

6. Then flew one of the seraphims unto me, having a live coal in his hand, which he had taken with the tongs from off the altar.

At this point *one of the seraphims* goes into action: with *the tongs from off the altar* that is present in the heavenly temple, he takes *a live coal*. The exact purpose for this altar is unclear. In the tabernacle, coals of fire are taken from the altar of incense (the altar "before the Lord") on the Day of Atonement and brought within the Most Holy Place to atone for both the high priest's sins and the sins of Israel (Leviticus 16:11-17). An altar is part of the scenery that the apostle John witnesses during his visions of Heaven (Revelation 6:9; 8:3-5; 9:13).

7. And he laid it upon my mouth, and said, Lo, this hath touched thy lips; and thine iniquity is taken away, and thy sin purged.

Now comes a gesture specifically aimed at addressing Isaiah's problem of "unclean lips" (v. 5). Much as is the case with the coals used on the Day of Atonement, this coal is a symbol of purification from sin. Fire is used elsewhere in Scripture to symbolize refining or purifying of some kind (Zechariah 13:9; Malachi 3:2, 3; 1 Peter 1:7).

It is certainly noteworthy that the Lord's response to Isaiah's admission of his sinfulness is not immediate judgment, but mercy. This fact seems to fuel many of this prophet's appeals to God's people, such as we see in Isaiah 55:7.

> **What Do You Think?**
> What are some figurative "fires" that God uses to remove things from our lives so we can serve Him better? How have you seen this work?
> *Talking Points for Your Discussion*
> - Fires of financial difficulty
> - Fires of family turmoil
> - Fires of personal health problems
> - Other

III. Service Offered
(ISAIAH 6:8)

A. The Lord's Question (v. 8a)

8a. Also I heard the voice of the Lord, saying, Whom shall I send, and who will go for us?

Isaiah has heard the seraphims speak; now he hears the Lord himself pose two questions. The *us* in the second question may be a reference to the other persons of the Trinity (similar language is used in Genesis 1:26; 11:7), or it may simply designate the Lord and those seraphims who are part of Isaiah's intense experience. Such considerations are likely not going through Isaiah's mind at this point; all he hears is the call for someone to *go* on the Lord's behalf. Isaiah's response follows immediately.

We were sad when our friends decided to move to the west coast. But an exciting idea popped into my mind: I could help them drive cross-country to their new home! Free vacation, right? So I volunteered to help them with anything they needed in their move, "anything at all."

They took me up on the offer and got me to do what they needed most: put their furniture into local storage and sell their broken-down SUV. Not exactly what I had in mind! I completed the tasks, though, because I cared about my friends. And because they also cared about me, they didn't ask me to do anything too difficult or inappropriate.

To many, the two questions in Isaiah 6:8a are threatening, since they evoke the specter of overseas missions. Many Christians feel that they "should" want to go anywhere, but they desperately hope that God will use them in familiar surroundings. They may sing the old hymn "I'll Go Where You Want Me to Go" with a bit of unease. Ultimately, however, this verse is not about missions; it's about a trusting relationship. Isaiah volunteered to be sent without knowing what the assignment would be, but he knew who the sender was. That was enough for him. Is it enough for us?

—A. W.

B. Isaiah's Response (v. 8b)
8b. Then said I, Here am I; send me.

Unlike Adam and Eve, who heard the voice of the Lord and went into hiding (Genesis 3:8), Isaiah does not shrink at the Lord's voice. He is now a cleansed man; his formerly unclean lips are ready to declare whatever the Lord desires. He is prepared to go wherever the Lord may send him.

What Do You Think?
Why do some Christians hesitate when sensing a call from God for a task? How do we know if our hesitation is prudent or sinful?
Talking Points for Your Discussion
- Exodus 4:13
- Judges 6:15, 36-40
- Jeremiah 1:6
- Acts 4:19; 5:29; 9:13, 14; 10:9-23

Conclusion
A. From Service to Service

Those familiar with the *Star Trek* television series of the 1960s can probably recall parts of the introductory words to the program, which described the mission of the starship *Enterprise.* The concluding line of that introduction remains an oft-quoted piece of television history, if for no other reason than its infamous split infinitive: "To boldly go where no man has gone before!"

That line is very appropriate for describing the impact that worship is meant to have on the worshipper. Isaiah's experience of God's presence did not leave him content to remain there, satisfied to let the sinners around him perish. When he heard the Lord's questions asking for someone to go on His behalf, Isaiah replied without hesitation: "Here am I; send me." His was not the attitude of "Let others do it" (compare Exodus 4:13) or "I'm not ready yet" (compare Jeremiah 1:6). Worship challenged Isaiah to confront his world, not ignore it because he had found a refuge from it.

An old story tells of a man who entered a church building as the worshippers were leaving. He asked the minister, "Say, is the service over?"

"No," replied the minister, "it's just beginning." Real worship will move us to real service.

B. Prayer

Father, may our worship never become a means of shutting ourselves off from the world around us. May worship be a refuge for us, not so that we may stay safe within it, but so that we may help others find it. In Jesus' name, amen.

C. Thought to Remember
True worship compels us
to confront the world, not avoid it.

VISUALS FOR THESE LESSONS

The visual pictured in each lesson (example: page 348) is a small reproduction of a large, full-color poster included in the *Adult Resources* packet for the Summer Quarter. That packet also contains the very useful *Presentation Helps* on a CD for teacher use. Order No. 020049213 from your supplier.

INVOLVEMENT LEARNING

Some of the activities below are also found in the helpful student book, Adult Bible Class.
Don't forget to download the free reproducible page from www.standardlesson.com to enhance your lesson!

Into the Lesson

Ask each learner to jot quickly a list of "woes" that have occurred within the past decade that have caused him or her to mourn the moral direction of the country. Allow no more than three minutes. When time is up, have someone read Isaiah 5:8, then discuss how the "woe" described there matches a "woe" that one or more learners noted. Repeat this procedure for Isaiah 5:11; 5:18, 19; 5:20; 5:21; and 5:22, 23. (You may wish to discuss fewer than these six to keep this segment short.)

Say, "We struggle with 'woes' similar to those of Isaiah's day. Let's see God's response to those problems."

Into the Word

Ask learners to close their Bibles and listen carefully as a volunteer reads today's text, Isaiah 6:1-8. After the reading, distribute copies of the "Isaiah's Vision" exercise from the reproducible page, which you can download. Learners can work in pairs to put the events in the correct order. Then say, "That's a good introduction to today's study; now let's dig a bit deeper."

Divide the class into four groups and give each group one of the cards described below, which you have prepared in advance; smaller classes can form two groups to work on two assignments each. (*Alternative:* Display the words and associated references on the board and let learners choose individually which they would like to research.) The four cards will have these words and associated Scripture references, one set per card: *Temple* (1 Kings 6:11-13; Psalm 27:4; Revelation 4); *Throne* (Proverbs 20:8; Matthew 25:31-33; Revelation 20:11, 12); *Altar* (Genesis 8:20, 21; Leviticus 4:32-35); *Coals* (Leviticus 16:11-13).

Allow a few minutes of study as learners prepare themselves to discuss the significance of *Temple, Throne, Altar,* and *Coals* in terms of "association" as you work through the lesson text.

When groups have finished their research, read the lesson text aloud again, but read only verses 1-7, not verse 8. Pause after verses 1 and 6 to let groups suggest associations. Expected responses: verse 1—*throne:* place of judgment; verse 1—*temple:* heavenly realm, where God is present; verse 6—*coal:* atonement; verse 6—*altar:* where sacrifices are offered. Use the lesson commentary to expand on the groups' information as appropriate.

Say, "Let's look at our four words and identify possible Christian correlations." Discuss how Isaiah's vision in general and the four elements in particular counteract the modern "woes" that learners noted in the Into the Lesson segment. Responses may include (1) *throne* as Judgment Day; (2) *temple* in terms of our bodies, where the Holy Spirit resides; (3) *altar* as Calvary, the place of the ultimate sacrifice for sin; and (4) *coal* with regard to the atonement that comes through the blood of Christ.

When you finish this comparison, remind learners that the power and glory of God that Isaiah saw in his vision are available to us. Comment: "When it seems as though all hope is gone, we need to remember that God is on His throne and He is in control."

Into Life

Say, "Let's read the final verse in today's text and see how Isaiah's response to God's question can be our response as well." Have someone read Isaiah 6:8. Discuss other possible responses that were available to Isaiah besides, "Here am I; send me" (example: Exodus 4:10, 13).

Display the Thought to Remember; point to it as you discuss what causes Christians to hesitate to place themselves at God's disposal. Explore learners' willingness to commit themselves, individually or as a class, to a "summer of service" rather than a "summer of vacation." *Option:* Use the "Summer of Service" activity from the reproducible page to suggest ideas.

WORSHIP WITH THANKSGIVING

DEVOTIONAL READING: Psalm 92:1-8
BACKGROUND SCRIPTURE: Isaiah 12

ISAIAH 12

1 And in that day thou shalt say, O LORD, I will praise thee: though thou wast angry with me, thine anger is turned away, and thou comfortedst me.

2 Behold, God is my salvation; I will trust, and not be afraid: for the LORD JEHOVAH is my strength and my song; he also is become my salvation.

3 Therefore with joy shall ye draw water out of the wells of salvation.

4 And in that day shall ye say, Praise the LORD, call upon his name, declare his doings among the people, make mention that his name is exalted.

5 Sing unto the LORD; for he hath done excellent things: this is known in all the earth.

6 Cry out and shout, thou inhabitant of Zion: for great is the Holy One of Israel in the midst of thee.

KEY VERSE

Praise the LORD, call upon his name, declare his doings among the people, make mention that his name is exalted. —**Isaiah 12:4**

Photo: George Doyle & Ciaran Griffin / Stockbyte / Thinkstock

GOD'S PEOPLE WORSHIP

Unit 1: The Prophet and Praise
LESSONS 1–4

LESSON AIMS

After participating in this lesson, each student will be able to:

1. List the actions and attitudes of the worshipper in the text.

2. Explain how the themes of the text can be applied to praise from a Christian's perspective.

3. Write out a personal tribute or testimony of praise that includes the themes emphasized by Isaiah.

LESSON OUTLINE

Introduction

A. Many Reasons to Say "Thank You"

My wife's mother and father both celebrated their eightieth birthdays in 2010. When my wife prepared cards to send them, she included with each card 80 memories that she recalled about each. Needless to say, her parents were quite touched to read the lists and to consider all that my wife remembered about what each had done for her. Her father was especially amazed and surprised at all the seemingly insignificant actions that she recalled.

Gratitude to our heavenly Father should be one of the distinctives of the Christian life. Paul encourages his readers to be "giving thanks always for all things unto God and the Father in the name of our Lord Jesus Christ" (Ephesians 5:20). In addition to "always," some days may provide special opportunities to reflect on and remember our Father's goodness and faithfulness to us.

In today's passage, the prophet Isaiah speaks of a day when praise will be the common language of God's people—a message so strong and clear that the world will not be able to ignore it. Isaiah's words remind us that our praise is not meant to be hoarded, but to be proclaimed to the world.

B. Lesson Background

Today's text, Isaiah 12, reads like a psalm. With only six verses, Isaiah 12 is rather brief, as are many of the psalms. It concludes a series of messages by the prophet that have been characterized by both judgment and hope.

Last week's lesson text recorded Isaiah's eager response to the Lord's call for someone to go on His behalf (Isaiah 6:1-8). However, when we read Isaiah's "job description" that follows in 6:9-13, it seems that he was in for an extremely discouraging ministry! Essentially Isaiah was called by God to confirm His judgment upon His people (vv. 9, 10). When Isaiah inquired, "How long?" the response was, "Until the cities be wasted without inhabitant, and the houses without man, and the land be utterly desolate" (v. 11). A remnant, however, would be preserved, indicating that the "holy seed" would not be destroyed completely (v. 13).

Worship with Thanksgiving

If Isaiah entertained any reservations about having been so eager to answer the Lord's call, we are not told. The Scriptures indicate that he proceeded to carry out his commission, starting with an encounter with obstinate, rebellious King Ahaz of the southern kingdom of Judah. Faced with an invasion from the combined forces of the northern kingdom of Israel and Syria (Aram), Ahaz refused to heed Isaiah's plea to trust the Lord.

That king's lack of faith was just one illustration of why both northern and southern kingdoms were in such a low spiritual condition. Isaiah 9 and 10 include a series of indictments against the people, punctuated with this repeated refrain: "For all this his anger is not turned away, but his hand is stretched out still" (Isaiah 9:12, 17, 21; 10:4).

But these chapters are not limited to proclamations of gloom and doom. Within them we find some of the most stunning prophecies of Jesus in the Old Testament. Isaiah 7:14 prophesies His virgin birth. Isaiah 9:6 begins, "For unto us a child is born, unto us a son is given," and declares some of the magnificent titles that this child will wear.

Isaiah 11:1 predicts the coming of "a rod out of the stem of Jesse" and a "Branch" that "shall grow out of his roots." On this special individual will rest the Spirit of the Lord, empowering Him in all of the areas necessary for godly and competent leadership (11:1-5). The impact of this coming one is described in language that portrays natural enemies living at peace with one another (11:6-9). Verse 10 then labels the one to come as "an ensign of the people; to it shall the Gentiles seek." This verse is quoted in Romans 15:12 as fulfilled in Jesus.

HOW TO SAY IT

Ahaz	*Ay*-haz.
Aram	*Air*-um.
Babylon	*Bab*-uh-lun.
Elim	*Ee*-lim.
Gentiles	*Jen*-tiles.
Isaiah	Eye-*zay*-uh.
Syria	*Sear*-ee-uh.
Yahweh *(Hebrew)*	*Yah*-weh.
Zion	*Zi*-un.

The last six verses of Isaiah 11, just before today's lesson text, describe an event reminiscent of the exodus from Egypt. This wording might be understood to depict God's people returning from captivity in Babylon (which Isaiah later predicts to happen; see 39:5-7). But the scope of the return (involving even "the islands of the sea," 11:11) appears to point to something far more significant. The New Testament, particularly the previously mentioned quotation in Romans 15:12, leads one to consider Isaiah's language as pointing forward to the worldwide impact of Jesus' Great Commission. No wonder the prophet burst forth in the words of praise in today's text!

I. Personal Praise
(ISAIAH 12:1-3)
A. For God's Comfort (v. 1)

1. And in that day thou shalt say, O LORD, I will praise thee: though thou wast angry with me, thine anger is turned away, and thou comfortedst me.

The phrase *in that day* is most likely linked to the identical wording in Isaiah 11:10. There *that day* is connected with the coming root of Jesse, described as an ensign, or banner, that even the Gentiles will seek. The pronoun *thou* is second person, singular in the Hebrew text, indicating that the subject and initial focus in this praise is on the individual who offers praise for what the Lord has done. This focus on the individual is further seen in the pronouns *me, my,* and *I* in the verse before us and the next.

The praise is expressed because *though thou wast angry with me, thine anger is turned away.* This most certainly indicates a reversal of the situation described previously in Isaiah 9:12, 17, 21; 10:4, where God's anger is portrayed as "not turned away."

What has happened to turn away this anger? Certainly, those who end up returning from captivity in Babylon will find Isaiah's words appropriate to express the joy of that release when the time comes. However, references to Jesus in Isaiah 11 are important to consider (see the Lesson Background). In a later prophecy, Isaiah will portray the coming Servant of the Lord as one upon whom the Lord will lay "the iniquity of us all" (Isaiah 53:6). It is because of Jesus' sacrifice at the cross that God's anger is "turned away" from sinners. This is at the heart of what the New Testament calls *reconciliation* (see 2 Corinthians 5:17-21).

> **What Do You Think?**
> From what source do you most often experience God's comfort? Why is that?
> *Talking Points for Your Discussion*
> - Comfort through Scripture
> - Comfort through prayer
> - Comfort from fellow believers
> - Other

B. For God's Salvation (vv. 2, 3)

2. Behold, God is my salvation; I will trust, and not be afraid: for the LORD JEHOVAH is my strength and my song; he also is become my salvation.

God is my salvation is an appropriate declaration for Isaiah to make since the name *Isaiah* means "The Lord is salvation." The Lord does not merely provide salvation or strength or a song—He himself *is* all of these. Only by means of a personal relationship with such a God can these blessings be known. Paul makes similar claims of Jesus when he writes that "he is our peace" (Ephesians 2:14) and "for to me to live is Christ" (Philippians 1:21).

Isaiah has experienced the Lord's salvation in a very personal way through his earlier call to service (see last week's study). Isaiah recognized how separated he was from a holy God, but Isaiah received a divine purging that cleansed him and prepared him for service (Isaiah 6:6-8).

The title *Lord Jehovah* translates two Hebrew words that are very closely related. The word *Lord* is a translation of Hebrew *Yah*, which is a shortened version of *Yahweh;* that is how the divine name is often rendered. We see the shortened form appearing as the last three letters in the word *Hallelujah* (with *j* substituted for *y*), which is a literal exhortation to "praise the Lord." The word *Jehovah*, for its part, is the word *Yahweh* in its full form.

The declaration *I will trust, and not be afraid* provides a stark contrast with the attitude of King Ahaz as seen in Isaiah 7. That king was told by Isaiah not to fear the threats to him and his people (7:3, 4), but the weak king refused Isaiah's counsel (7:12). The alternative to fear is always to trust in the Lord and in His sovereign purposes.

> **What Do You Think?**
> What common fears can result in a lack of trust in God? What attitudes and actions can we take to demonstrate our trust in Him?
> *Talking Points for Your Discussion*
> - At the personal level
> - At the family level
> - At the congregational level
> - At the national level
> - Other

❧ SINGING IN THE DARK ❧

I was afraid of the dark as a child. I used to pull the sheets up around my head and surround myself with stuffed animals, even on the warmest nights. With my mind racing, I found comfort in singing Sunday school songs such as "Jesus Loves Me."

I thought I had left those days behind until I became a missionary in Ukraine. Our city experienced blackouts on many nights. Walking in pitch darkness through the city streets to my apartment, there was always the danger of being mugged or falling into an open manhole. Sometimes as I ascended the stairwell of my building, quietly murmuring voices or the light of a cigarette would be the only clues that people were lurking just a few feet away on the landing. Just as I did in childhood, I would let my mind dwell on songs of faith. Even in my 30s, "Jesus Loves Me" still brought courage and peace.

Christian music can bring peace to our souls as the words remind us of scriptural truths. Even so, the prophet Isaiah proclaimed that God himself was His song. God provides to full perfection all the teaching, comfort, and inspiration we might derive in partial form from music. Can you honestly say that God is *your* song? —A. W.

3. Therefore with joy shall ye draw water out of the wells of salvation.

The pronoun *ye* is plural. This serves to expand the enjoyment of the blessings of salvation to include others besides just the individual (which is the focus of the previous two verses).

The image of drawing *water out of the wells* is in keeping with the exodus language that is seen at the conclusion of Isaiah 11. After the Israelites left Egypt, they proceeded to the wilderness of Shur, where the only available water was too bitter to drink. When the people complained, the Lord enabled Moses to make the water drinkable (Exodus 15:22-25). Not long afterward the people reached another site, Elim, where there were 12 wells of water (v. 27). On a later occasion still, God again provided water by means of a well (Numbers 21:16-18).

Water becomes a symbol in Scripture for spiritual refreshment and renewal (Psalm 23:2; Isaiah 49:10; 58:11). Jesus describes himself to the Samaritan woman at the well as the source of living water (John 4:10-14). He describes the Holy Spirit in terms of "rivers of living water" that will flow from within anyone who believes in Jesus (John 7:37-39). Joy is just one of the blessings that a person experiences when he or she, like the woman at the well, embraces Jesus as "the Christ, the Saviour of the world" (John 4:42).

What Do You Think?

If you were designing a church logo that incorporates an image of water, what else would your logo include to convey the idea of "spiritual refreshment"?

Talking Points for Your Discussion
- Image of an inanimate object
- Image that includes a part of the human body
- Image that is countercultural
- Other

II. Public Praise
(ISAIAH 12:4-6)
A. Let the World Hear (vv. 4, 5)

4. And in that day shall ye say, Praise the LORD, call upon his name, declare his doings among the people, make mention that his name is exalted.

This verse begins as verse 1 does, only this time with the plural pronoun *ye* (as in v. 3). It pictures the community of the saved joining in a tribute of praise to the Lord. There is, however, another important ingredient in this call to praise: those who voice their praise are to *declare his doings among the people*. The blessing of salvation is not to be hoarded; salvation is a message for everyone, not just the people of Israel since the Hebrew word translated *people* is plural, literally "peoples." This too points to the impact of Jesus' life, death, and resurrection and to the worldwide declaration of those events. The apostle John was told, "Thou must prophesy again before many peoples, and nations, and tongues, and kings" (Revelation 10:11; compare 17:15).

Thus Isaiah's experience of a personal call (Isaiah 6:1-8, last week's lesson) is to be reproduced, in a sense, in the lives of all faithful servants of the Lord. Isaiah is eager to go forth in response to God's call for workers (6:8). But the message Isaiah is to bring, as found in 6:9-13, is primarily one of judgment and devastation. How much more should we be willing to *make mention that his name is exalted* as we take the gospel of Christ to the world!

5. Sing unto the LORD; for he hath done excellent things: this is known in all the earth.

The praise of God's people is to erupt in song because *he hath done excellent things*. This is another parallel to the events surrounding the exodus, for that act of deliverance was followed by a song of Moses and the Israelites, recorded in Exodus 15:1-18. That song includes the words, "The Lord is my strength and song, and he is become my salvation" (v. 2), which are very similar to the words of Isaiah 12:2, above. The exodus was also something to be acknowledged *in all the earth*. The Lord had declared to Pharaoh through Moses, "And in very deed for this cause have I raised thee up, for to show in thee my power; and that my name may be declared throughout all the earth" (Exodus 9:16).

Those who have experienced the Lord's salvation from spiritual bondage to sin have their own *excellent things* for which to give thanks. Isaiah can only prophesy of these blessings and view them from a distance; we are privileged to live in the era of fulfillment.

> **What Do You Think?**
> What should your own "life's song" say about the "excellent things" of God in your life?
> *Talking Points for Your Discussion*
> - Personal victories
> - Victories that blessed your family or community
> - Victories that blessed your church family

B. Let God Be Exalted (v. 6)

6. Cry out and shout, thou inhabitant of Zion: for great is the Holy One of Israel in the midst of thee.

We come to the final exhortation in this prophetic psalm. Earlier uses of the word *Zion* refer to the section of Jerusalem that provides the primary source of defense for the city (2 Samuel 5:6, 7). Eventually, *Zion* becomes a synonym for the city of Jerusalem (Psalm 74:2; 87:2; 137:3; Micah 4:2). Previously, Isaiah has had very little positive to say about Zion (see Isaiah 3:16–4:1). Now the shouts of praise and triumph reflect gratitude for all God accomplishes for His people, as climaxed by the dramatic events described in Isaiah 11.

The declaration *great is the Holy One of Israel in the midst of thee* is another echo from the call experience of Isaiah. We noted in lesson 1 that *the Holy One of Israel* is used as a title for God far more often in Isaiah than in any other book of the Old Testament. Its prominence likely reflects Isaiah's encounter with the holiness of God through the cry uttered by the seraphims (Isaiah 6:2, 3).

Previously, Isaiah had found himself overwhelmed by God's holiness as contrasted with his own sinfulness and that of his people (Isaiah 6:5). Thus the idea that God has come *in the midst of* His people is a blessing not thought possible at first by the prophet. Here, however, he exults in the thought that the holy God has come to provide salvation for His people. This is certainly a foreshadowing of the day when the Word will become flesh and dwell among us (John 1:14).

> **What Do You Think?**
> What are some ways that we can remind ourselves that God is indeed "in the midst" of us today? Why is it important to do so?
> *Talking Points for Your Discussion*
> - Scripture passages
> - Personal experience
> - Other

❧ MAKE SOME NOISE! ❧

When was the last time you were so happy you screamed your head off? All sorts of things can make us yell with joy: our team scores, a loved one returns from war, we receive a special gift, we ride a roller coaster, we find out a new baby is on the way, etc. Some of us are pretty reserved and express ourselves this freely only on rare occasions. But at some point each of us has been so happy about something that we literally screamed.

When was the last time you were so happy in church that you shouted? Some churches feature exuberant worship every Sunday. In other churches, a tentative "amen" from the back pew would surprise everyone, including the preacher. Yet even in these congregations, some of the most placid pew-sitters transform into maniacs in the bleachers of a high school basketball game.

So it's not a matter of cultural differences in general, it's a matter of church culture. This is not a criticism of churches that have subdued, reflective worship services; there is indeed great value in times of quiet worship when we can be undisturbed as we contemplate our relationship with God. But the salvation we have really is something to yell about! Isaiah reminds us it is perfectly appropriate to praise God with shouting—even, at times, in church.

—A. W.

Conclusion

A. Alone or with Someone

An older gentleman in the church in Indiana that I served some years ago liked to describe his fondness for pie (any kind, he was not picky) by saying, "The only times I'll eat pie is when I'm alone or with someone." Of course, what he meant was that he could eat a piece of pie anytime!

Among the thoughts drawn from today's study is that worship is to be both "alone or with someone." Some pronouns used by Isaiah in today's passage are singular, while others are plural. There is certainly a place for "closet praise," where one can give thanks in private (Matthew 6:6). When someone has gone through an especially dark, difficult "valley" and has emerged from it with God's help, then his or her praise may be far too personal to share in public. The tears that can erupt in the midst of such praise may be something best shared between only the worshipper and God.

On the other hand, public (corporate) worship also has a vital role in the Christian's life. Hebrews 10:25 is frequently quoted in this regard: "not forsaking the assembling of ourselves together." This bears repeating (and memorizing). Faithful and meaningful personal worship should drive us to seek worship with others. Meaningful corporate worship should result in a renewed commitment to maintaining our private fellowship with the Lord between Sundays.

The encouragement that comes from worship with others makes us realize that no one is ever alone in his or her walk with God. This gives the worshipper a renewed perspective for encountering a lost world. It is a world where many voices clamor to be heard—some worthwhile and others completely worthless. We have been placed in the midst of that noisy din to bear witness to the Holy One of Israel—to "declare his doings among the people" and make known the "excellent things" that He has done.

B. You Never Know Who's Listening

A couple of weeks before Christmas in 2010, my wife accompanied a group from our church to a local nursing home to do some Christmas caroling. The group planned to visit the section of the facility where the residents suffered from Alzheimer's disease since a lady from our church was there. My wife began the caroling by asking if anyone had a favorite carol he or she would like to sing. But the impact of Alzheimer's made it virtually impossible for any to respond verbally.

Visual for Lesson 2. *Have this poster displayed prominently as you pose the discussion question associated with Isaiah 12:5.*

So my wife began to sing a familiar carol, and those from the church joined in. Before long, something quite amazing happened: many of the residents began to mouth or sing the words of the song once they recognized the tune. Smiles appeared on some of the residents' faces. Facility employees were cheered as well. Praise and thanksgiving can have that kind of impact, sometimes in places where we may least expect it.

The verbalizing of one's faith pictured by Isaiah in today's text is hard to miss. Within verses 4-6 is a cluster of such words: *praise, call, declare, make mention, sing, cry out,* and *shout.* In a world where it is easy to become intimidated into silence about our faith, let us remember that there are many in our world who desperately need some good news, a witness from someone of God's love and grace. Each of us has a particular sphere of influence where we can offer a word of encouragement. We never know the impact our words may have.

C. Prayer

Father, whether we worship in the quietness of our homes or amidst the songs of a congregation, may we, like Isaiah, refuse to be silenced in our thanksgiving. You have done and will do excellent things! In Jesus' name, amen.

D. Thought to Remember

Praise is not just part of our worship, it is also our witness to the world.

INVOLVEMENT LEARNING

Some of the activities below are also found in the helpful student book, Adult Bible Class.
Don't forget to download the free reproducible page from www.standardlesson.com to enhance your lesson!

Into the Lesson

Begin class by asking learners to identify things for which they are thankful; jot responses on the board under the heading *Reason*. Then ask learners to share what they do to demonstrate their thankfulness; jot responses on the board under the heading *Action*. Finally, ask learners what attitudes other than thankfulness they experience for their blessing; jot responses on the board under the heading *Attitude*. When you finish, you should have three columns of responses on the board, but be sure to leave the bottom half of the board blank for the Into the Word segment.

Say, "Today we're going to look at a passage from Isaiah where we find the prophet moved to worship because of his thankfulness."

Into the Word

Draw across the board a horizontal line to separate learners' responses above from discoveries they will make from today's text. As you work your way through the verses of Isaiah 12, ask learners to identify the *action* Isaiah engaged in, the *reason* for the action, and his *attitude*. The entries on the resulting chart can resemble the listing below; the three descriptions following the verse enumerations are *action / reason / attitude,* respectively.

Verse 1: Praise / God comforts me; His anger turned away / Thanksgiving

Verse 2: Acknowledgment / God is strength, song, salvation / God has done it, not me

Verse 3: Able to draw water from wells of salvation / The Lord has enabled / Joy

Verse 4: Praise, call upon, declare, mention / Seeing all that God has done / Awe

Verse 5: Sing / The excellent things God has done / Thanksgiving

Verse 6: Cry out, shout / The Holy One is in the midst of His people / Humility

Use the lesson commentary to explain the significance of the actions in Israel's history as you complete the chart. Also note that verses 1, 2 deal with individual responses, while verses 3-6 depict corporate responses. Discuss the need for both individual and corporate worship and how they relate to each other (see the commentary).

Say, "The book of Isaiah is known for its messianic prophecies. While today's text is not a direct prophecy in that regard, it does foreshadow the gospel message of the New Testament in certain ways. Let's see if we can think of New Testament parallels for the reasons for Isaiah's actions and attitudes from today's text." Ask learners to look at actions and attitudes in your listing and suggest such parallels.

Possible responses: verse 1—Christ turned God's wrath from us, Romans 5:9-11; verse 2—Jesus is our source of salvation, Ephesians 1:13; verse 3—we are enabled to serve, Luke 1:74; verse 4—we spread the gospel message, Matthew 28:19, 20; verse 5—we testify to what God has done, 2 Timothy 1:8; verse 6—God dwells in our midst, 1 Corinthians 6:19; Ephesians 2:22. Consult the commentary for further guidance.

Into Life

Option 1. As a class, construct a prayer of adoration to God that includes these themes discussed in the lesson: 1. God's anger has been taken away. 2. God has provided salvation. 3. God continuously "waters" our souls. 4. I must tell others. 5. God's ways are excellent. 6. God sent His Son to dwell among us, and the Holy Spirit came after Jesus' ascension.

Option 2. Have learners complete the "From Worship to Witness" activity from the reproducible page, which you can download and copy.

Option 3. Have learners complete the "Worthy of Worship" activity from the reproducible page.

You can mix and match the three options above, depending on the nature of your class and the amount of time available.

WORSHIP WITH
MEANING

DEVOTIONAL READING: Luke 8:9-15
BACKGROUND SCRIPTURE: Isaiah 29

ISAIAH 29:9-16

9 Stay yourselves, and wonder; cry ye out, and cry: they are drunken, but not with wine; they stagger, but not with strong drink.

10 For the LORD hath poured out upon you the spirit of deep sleep, and hath closed your eyes: the prophets and your rulers, the seers hath he covered.

11 And the vision of all is become unto you as the words of a book that is sealed, which men deliver to one that is learned, saying, Read this, I pray thee: and he saith, I cannot; for it is sealed:

12 And the book is delivered to him that is not learned, saying, Read this, I pray thee: and he saith, I am not learned.

13 Wherefore the Lord said, Forasmuch as this people draw near me with their mouth, and with their lips do honour me, but have removed their heart far from me, and their fear toward me is taught by the precept of men:

14 Therefore, behold, I will proceed to do a marvellous work among this people, even a marvellous work and a wonder: for the wisdom of their wise men shall perish, and the understanding of their prudent men shall be hid.

15 Woe unto them that seek deep to hide their counsel from the LORD, and their works are in the dark, and they say, Who seeth us? and who knoweth us?

16 Surely your turning of things upside down shall be esteemed as the potter's clay: for shall the work say of him that made it, He made me not? or shall the thing framed say of him that framed it, He had no understanding?

KEY VERSE

The Lord said, . . . this people draw near me with their mouth, and with their lips do honour me, but have removed their heart far from me, and their fear toward me is taught by the precept of men. —Isaiah 29:13

GOD'S PEOPLE WORSHIP

Unit 1: The Prophet and Praise

LESSONS 1–4

LESSON AIMS

After participating in this lesson, each student will be able to:

1. Tell what Isaiah had to say about the shallow worship of God's people and God's response to that.

2. Explain how worship can deteriorate to the point where it becomes mere lip service to God.

3. Suggest ways to avoid the insincere worship described by Isaiah.

LESSON OUTLINE

Introduction

A. "If I Only Had a Heart"

The words in the above heading will be recognized by many as a theme sung by the Tin Man in the classic movie *The Wizard of Oz*. The Tin Man was hollow, he said, because he had not been given a heart when he was made. He was encouraged by Dorothy and the Scarecrow to travel to Oz to see whether the wizard would provide him one.

Our maker did not forget to put a literal heart within us when He created us. Neither did He forget to give us the capacity to "have a heart for" various things. But sometimes we fail to "put our hearts into" things we should, including worship. In today's lesson, we will see the prophet Isaiah describing what amounts to the "heartless worship" by God's people.

B. Lesson Background

In last week's study, we noted how Isaiah called on God's people to include the nations among the audience as they praised the Lord for His great works (Isaiah 12:4). The prophet then proceeded in chapters 13–23 to cite specific nations and cities (including Jerusalem) as the recipients of either judgment or blessing (in some cases, both) from the Lord.

Isaiah 24–27 continues the theme of global judgment. Yet interspersed within that message are several glimmers of hope. Isaiah 25:8 is a particularly noteworthy example, foreshadowing the destruction of death in language found in the description of Heaven in Revelation 7:17; 21:4.

Isaiah 29, from which today's printed text is drawn, begins with a "woe" directed toward Ariel. The word *Ariel* means "altar hearth." The fact that Ariel is also called "the city where David dwelt" in verse 1 indicates that this term designates Jerusalem. The picture of an altar hearth (a place where a fire burns) is quite fitting for Jerusalem as the home of the temple, where many sacrifices are offered. But it also portrays what awaits Jerusalem, for it is to come under siege and is to be set on fire as part of God's judgment against it (v. 3).

In time, however, the "multitude of all the nations that fight against Ariel" (Isaiah 29:7) will themselves be judged and humbled before the Lord (vv. 5-8). They will become "like small dust" and "as chaff that passeth away" (v. 5).

Following this promise of deliverance comes the indictment of the people's shallow worship in today's text. It seems that the people of God were their own worst enemies. The insincere worship of the people was just a symptom of a far greater problem that could be remedied only by a serious self-examination and a realignment of the people's thinking toward God's holy purposes.

I. People's Apathy
(ISAIAH 29:9-12)
A. Staggered Walk (v. 9)

9. Stay yourselves, and wonder; cry ye out, and cry: they are drunken, but not with wine; they stagger, but not with strong drink.

Isaiah begins with two commands for his readers. *Stay yourselves* means "to delay" or "to be indecisive." *Wonder* carries the idea of "being bewildered" or "being dumbfounded."

Together, these convey how indecisive the people have become about spiritual matters. One is reminded of the lack of response to Elijah's challenge to those gathered on Mount Carmel concerning whom they would follow: the Lord or Baal. "And the people answered him not a word" (1 Kings 18:21).

The phrase *cry ye out, and cry* renders a Hebrew word that can mean "to take delight in." Those described in the verse as *drunken* may be crying out in celebration during their times of drunkenness; while so doing, they are oblivious to their sad spiritual state. One sees a description of individuals who have put themselves in a position where they have lost their spiritual bearings and are stumbling about. As such, they are completely unaware of the doom that awaits them.

HOW TO SAY IT

Baal	*Bay*-ul.
Corinthians	Ko-*rin*-thee-unz (*th* as in *thin*).
Elijah	Ee-*lye*-juh.
Isaiah	Eye-*zay*-uh.

What Do You Think?
  What are some indicators of spiritual apathy?
    How do we fix this problem when we see it?
Talking Points for Your Discussion
- In corporate worship
- In private devotional time
- In unmet ministry needs
- Revelation 3:15-18
- Other

B. Spiritual Sleep (v. 10)

10. For the LORD hath poured out upon you the spirit of deep sleep, and hath closed your eyes: the prophets and your rulers, the seers hath he covered.

This verse attributes the people's lethargy to the Lord: it is He who *hath poured out upon you the spirit of deep sleep, and hath closed your eyes.* The word for *deep sleep* is the same as that used of the deep sleep brought upon Adam by the Lord in Genesis 2:21, prior to God's removing a rib from Adam to create Eve. The word also describes a deep sleep that came upon Abram (Genesis 15:12) and one that the Lord brought upon King Saul (1 Samuel 26:12).

The purpose of the sleep forms part of the Lord's judgment of His wayward people. The Lord's action here may be similar to that described in Romans 1:24, 26, 28, where He "gave them up" or "over" to the consequences of their evil actions.

That the Lord has closed the people's eyes also calls to mind His words to Isaiah following that prophet's response to the Lord's call: "Shut their eyes; lest they see with their eyes, and hear with their ears, and understand with their heart, and convert, and be healed" (Isaiah 6:10). Scripture uses the idea of *blindness* not only as that of a physical condition but also of a spiritual one (Matthew 23:16, 17; John 9:40, 41; 2 Peter 1:9).

Further acts of divine judgment are pictured in the remainder of the verse: *the prophets and your rulers, the seers hath he covered.* Thus the normal means by which God has revealed His truth to His people have been rendered useless. Those who would usually be considered the spiritual leaders of the people are unable to provide any degree of guidance. They are all pictured as having their heads "covered," thus making it impossible for them to truly "see" any message from the Lord.

The combination of human choice and divine judgment in verses 9 and 10 is summarized quite well in this thought from John N. Oswalt: "There can be no more frightening motivation to listen to God than this, the thought that if you refuse to hear today, one day you might no longer be able to hear." The sobering thoughts in the verse before us make themselves felt again in Romans 11:8.

> **What Do You Think?**
> What things today contribute most to spiritual blindness and deafness? How do we recognize and resist these influences?
> *Talking Points for Your Discussion*
> - Matthew 13:18-22
> - Colossians 2:8
> - 1 Timothy 1:18, 19; 6:9, 10, 20, 21
> - 2 Timothy 4:10a
> - Other

C. Sealed Vision (vv. 11, 12)

11. And the vision of all is become unto you as the words of a book that is sealed, which men deliver to one that is learned, saying, Read this, I pray thee: and he saith, I cannot; for it is sealed.

The vision now being discussed probably refers to the prophetic message uttered by Isaiah to this point. But even as Isaiah's prophetic vision is committed to writing, those who should be able to read the resulting book (scroll) cannot because *it is sealed*. The seal here may not be literal; it may be a figurative symbol, much as drunkenness (v. 9) and blindness (v. 10) are in this passage. It may represent the people's opinion that the prophet's message is too difficult or mysterious to try to understand.

The apostle John weeps when he learns of a book that apparently no one is able to open (Revelation 5:1-4). Here the situation is quite different. No one weeps because of the inability of anyone to open or read this book. Apparently, no one has any desire

even to try. Lack of education is not the problem, since the *one that is learned* knows how to read! This person seems to have no desire or passion to discover more about the message of the book. This individual is content to remain ignorant.

12. And the book is delivered to him that is not learned, saying, Read this, I pray thee: and he saith, I am not learned.

Another person is pictured as receiving the book. This time it is someone who *is not learned* and therefore cannot read. This is the reason why the book remains sealed to this individual. Once more, the issue appears to be one of desire or interest. If this person really wants to learn the contents of the book, he or she can consult someone who *can* read the contents. This is a matter of personal initiative. After the people return from exile, they will indeed take this initiative (see Nehemiah 8:1-3, lesson 10). But that is not the mind-set in Isaiah's day.

In the cases of both the learned and the unlearned cited by Isaiah, the problem can be traced to the lack of desire to learn more about Isaiah's message. Cannot this be compared with the lack of interest today among many Christians regarding the opening and reading of our book, the Bible?

Many may consider the Bible to be too challenging or too "ancient" to grasp, so the book remains "sealed" to them. Others have not been taught how to study the Bible or have not bothered to learn how to do so. Like *him that is not learned* in this verse, they do not know how to "read"—they end up "seeing" but not "perceiving" (Mark 4:12; Acts 28:26, 27; both quoting Isaiah 6:9, 10). Then the question must be raised, "Where are the leaders in the church who are willing to 'unseal' the book—to teach others how to read it?" Have they become just as apathetic as the people?

> **What Do You Think?**
> What excuses do Christians offer for never having read the Bible in its entirety?
> *Talking Points for Your Discussion*
> - Excuses offered by those who are "learned"
> - Excuses offered by those who are "not learned"

Periodic cleaning always turns up some surprises at our house: a half-eaten piece of toast behind the couch, a long-overdue library book, swim goggles mysteriously cloistered behind pots and pans, water damage in the hall closet (related to the swim goggles?), etc. This past spring we actually discovered unopened Christmas gifts in my oldest daughter's room. Shocking!

We began to draw all kinds of conclusions about the unopened gifts: Maybe she forgot about them. Maybe she didn't like them. Maybe she's just getting too much. When we asked her, it was none of that. It turned out that she just wanted to save them up, keep them nice, and use them a little at a time "to make Christmas last." Fair enough. On the downside, however, waiting too long to use the presents means that one day they will seem old and uninteresting before they have even been used.

Some people start with a positive attitude toward God and His Word, but put off fully committing themselves until some ideal future time: after college, after getting settled in a career, when the children are a little older, etc. But the years quickly slip away, and eventually Christ seems blasé even though He has never really been tried.

My daughter has another gift she has used every day since she was a toddler: "Lambie," a stuffed lamb that shows the evidence of having been clutched close to her heart for years. I hope that's the kind of gift the Lamb of God is to us.—A. W.

II. God's Awareness
(ISAIAH 29:13-16)
A. Disgusting Worship (v. 13)

13. Wherefore the Lord said, Forasmuch as this people draw near me with their mouth, and with their lips do honour me, but have removed their heart far from me, and their fear toward me is taught by the precept of men.

We now see a consequence of the failure to open the scroll and learn the message of Isaiah's prophecy: the people's worship has become empty and meaningless. *With their mouth, and with their lips* the people profess loyalty and devotion to God, but they *have removed their heart far*

from Him. They are merely "going through the motions." During his call experience, Isaiah had confessed his own and his people's unclean lips (Isaiah 6:5). Here the lips appear to speak what is right, but whatever they utter is nullified by a heart that has little passion or desire for a genuine relationship with God. Centuries later, Jesus applies these very words to the scribes and Pharisees in His day (Matthew 15:1-9).

> ### What Do You Think?
> Which Scripture best describes the status of your heart for worship today? Why?
> *Talking Points for Your Discussion*
> - Isaiah 29:13
> - John 4:23, 24
> - Romans 12:1
> - Hebrews 12:28, 29
> - Other

ﻬ *POTEMKIN VILLAGES* ﻬ

In 1787, Catherine the Great of Russia went on a tour of the newly conquered Crimean peninsula. According to legend, Grigory Potemkin, the commander of the military campaign, ordered that façades of villages be built along the barren riverbanks to impress the empress.

Some historians believe that this story is fictional, circulated by Potemkin's rivals to discredit him. Even so, the expression *Potemkin village* has endured as a description of an elaborate deception meant to hide an embarrassing truth. During the Cold War, for example, gullible foreigners taking tours of the Soviet Union would be allowed to see "showcase" factories that were nothing like the typically decrepit Soviet facilities.

Spiritually, the problem of Potemkin villages of Isaiah's time was just as real in Jesus' day (see Matthew 23:27) and is so today. A church may appear to be full of well-adjusted, spiritually mature people. When asked how we are, the answer is always "fine." We rarely confess our sins to one another as James 5:16 instructs. If anyone starts "getting real," the rest of us start getting really nervous. Is that because we realize that our own spiritual lives are false fronts for spiritual barrenness?

God has the power to bring vibrant life to our emptiness, and He isn't fooled by our façades. He waits, however, for us to realize our need and invite Him in. Why maintain such a transparent deception when help is so close? —A. W.

B. Divine Action (v. 14)

14. Therefore, behold, I will proceed to do a marvellous work among this people, even a marvellous work and a wonder: for the wisdom of their wise men shall perish, and the understanding of their prudent men shall be hid.

The Lord's response to irreverent, fraudulent worship is to shatter the people's apathy with *a marvellous work among this people, even a marvellous work and a wonder*. Literally the promise is, "I will treat this people wonderfully, wonderfully and with wonder." This is something wonderful beyond description!

What is this "wonderfully wonderful wonder"? The second half of this verse is cited by Paul in 1 Corinthians 1:19 just after he notes that "the preaching of the cross is to them that perish foolishness," but "the power of God" to the saved (v. 18). Paul goes on to comment on how God has "made foolish the wisdom of this world" and brought it down to nothing by means of the cross (vv. 19-25).

The cross of Christ should move us to humble worship—the kind that is sadly lacking in Isaiah's day. No "precept of men" (Isaiah 29:13), no matter what it may be, can produce the degree of worship that the wonder of the cross can. May we who have accepted the crucified (and risen) Christ as Savior never lose our sense of wonder at that which so-called "intellectual" people of the world so often ridicule.

C. Defiant Thinking (vv. 15, 16)

15. Woe unto them that seek deep to hide their counsel from the LORD, and their works are in the dark, and they say, Who seeth us? and who knoweth us?

Those who fancy themselves to be wise and intelligent are frequently those who *seek deep to hide their counsel from the Lord*. This means that they go to great depths to conceal their sinful plans from God. If only they would exert similar efforts to discover the truth that God has gone to "great depths" to reveal to (and not hide from) humanity!

The wayward seem to believe that God is subject to the same limitations that restrict humans. Supposedly, He cannot know or see what is planned or done *in the dark*. But as David rightly observes, "Yea, the darkness hideth not from thee; but the night shineth as the day: the darkness and the light are both alike to thee" (Psalm 139:12).

What Do You Think?

What are some instances of defiant thinking that you've encountered? How do you protect yourself in this regard?

Talking Points for Your Discussion

- In popular media and art
- In secular education
- In law
- In your own past beliefs
- Other

16. Surely your turning of things upside down shall be esteemed as the potter's clay: for shall the work say of him that made it, He made me not? or shall the thing framed say of him that framed it, He had no understanding?

The reason that the plotters and schemers of verse 15 think and act as they do is that they have a faulty view of God. They have turned the authority structure *upside down*. Such is the inevitable outcome when humans refuse to acknowledge that they are created in the image of God (Genesis 1:26). They think of themselves as the potter, as if they were in charge.

But *the potter's clay* has no right to command the potter, and it is utter foolishness for the clay to deny that the potter made him or her (see Romans 9:21). It is noteworthy that the Hebrew word translated *framed* in this verse is the word used to describe how "the Lord God *formed* man of the dust of the ground" in Genesis 2:7.

True worship can never come from a mind-set that considers human beings to be the potter. This displays the utmost contempt for the true potter, who is God alone.

Conclusion

A. "Wonder"-ing About Worship

Like many words, the word *wonderful* has become overused. People can have a "wonderful" time at an almost unlimited number of activities: a baseball game, a family reunion, a birthday party, or for that matter a church gathering. The feeling of *wonder,* by contrast, seems to be fading from the contemporary frame of reference, especially in the Western world. Advances in technology have become so impressive that seldom do people feel a sense of true wonder at anything anymore.

It is easy to forget what makes Christian worship distinct: the wonder of "the old rugged cross." The people in Isaiah's day no longer associated the idea of *wonder* with God. Their worship had become stale and routine. Any weekly worship was done "weakly." So Isaiah announced the Lord's response: "Behold, I will proceed to do a marvellous work among this people, even a marvellous work and a wonder" (Isaiah 29:14).

Paul says that this wonder has been provided by something that at first glance does not appear to be all that wonderful as the term is commonly used—the cross of Christ. One reason the cross must remain at the center of Christian worship is because of what it says about the wisdom of this world. That wisdom, as impressive as it may seem at times, receives a grade of *F* in matters of the spiritual realm (1 Corinthians 1:18-23). And nothing says that more clearly than "the offence of the cross" (Galatians 5:11). Only as we keep the wonder of the cross uppermost in our preparation for corporate worship can real worship occur.

B. A Word About the Word

Another factor affecting the people's worship in Isaiah's day was their attitude toward God's revealed truth. For the leaders of the people of God, the words of the prophet had become a sealed document. No one, whether educated or uneducated, had a real hunger to know what the scroll contained.

Not long after I became a Christian, someone gave me a copy of a *Halley's Bible Handbook,* a classic Bible-study tool. This handbook is still in print

Visual for Lesson 3. *Point to this visual as you ask, "Where do Christians seem to need the most help in making worship meaningful to God? Why?"*

today. Some of its contents are now a bit outdated, but one portion of that book has always stuck with me. In the back of the handbook is a challenge to Christians to make Bible reading a top priority. From page 816 of the 24th edition (1965):

> Every Christian ought to be a Bible reader. It is the one habit, which, if done in the right spirit, more than any other one habit, will make a Christian what he ought to be in every way. If any church could get its people as a whole to be devoted readers of God's Word, it would revolutionize the church. If the churches of any community, as a whole, could get their people, as a whole, to be regular readers of the Bible, it would not only revolutionize the churches, but it would purge and purify the community as nothing else could do.

What a tragedy that many Christians do not make a more determined effort to know God's Word better! Our worship will remain shallow if our Bibles remain "sealed" and unused.

C. Prayer

Father, may we keep our hearts close to You so that our worship may be in spirit and in truth. May we never lose our sense of wonder whenever we consider the cross of Christ. In His name, amen.

D. Thought to Remember

True worship is founded on who God has revealed himself to be.

INVOLVEMENT LEARNING

Some of the activities below are also found in the helpful student book, Adult Bible Class.
Don't forget to download the free reproducible page from www.standardlesson.com to enhance your lesson!

Into the Lesson

Place in chairs copies of the "Steps Away from Proper Worship" activity from the reproducible page, which you can download. Learners can begin working on this as they arrive.

Ask learners to spend a few moments thinking of things they do on a regular basis to which they give only halfhearted effort (possible responses: cleaning the house, mowing the lawn, etc.). Ask why this is so.

Then ask, "Do Christians ever give a half-hearted effort to their worship of God?" Discuss why this is so (possible responses: dissatisfaction with church, boredom with spiritual endeavors, weighed down by the problems of life, etc.). Say, "In today's lesson we will look at the problem of shallow worship and how God responded."

Into the Word

Form learners into study pairs. Ask each pair to read today's lesson text, Isaiah 29:9-16, and identify characteristics of Judah's worship and God's response to that worship. As they work, write the following headings on the board: *Judah's Worship / God's Response.* When the pairs have finished, read the text aloud to the class, two verses at a time. After each such reading, stop and let the pairs share what they gleaned from the verses.

For *Judah's Worship,* some possible answers are that the people are dazed or in a stupor (v. 9); God's words are like a sealed book that no one can read (v. 12); worship is simply an empty, "going through the motions" ritual (v. 13); people try to hide their deeds from God, thinking He doesn't see them (v. 15); people try to take God's place and don't acknowledge Him as their Creator (v. 16). For *God's Response,* some possible answers are that the Lord puts the people in a kind of trance (or allows it to happen) so they can't see their condition (v. 10); and God will perform a great wonder that startles Judah out of spiritual apathy (v. 14).

As you work through the text, use remarks from the lesson commentary to lead discussions about why Judah had become so apathetic. While doing so, brainstorm whether the same circumstances are possible or even are present in twenty-first century Christianity. To aid you in this discussion, you can make and distribute copies of the following *Agree/Disagree* statements:

1. Modern technology that is used to enhance the worship experience instead ends up promoting apathy in worship as people become spectators rather than participants.

2. The "busyness" of life robs people of time needed to read and study God's Word.

3. People are too focused on the rituals of their familiar worship traditions.

4. Today's culture makes it easy for people to "hide" in church and not share their changed lives with others.

5. People are more interested in filling their personal needs than in obeying God.

Discuss differences of opinion and explore possible solutions to these problems.

Into Life

Say, "From our lesson and discussion, let me propose three simple steps to avoid insincere or apathetic worship: (1) be learners of God's Word; (2) remember that God is God, and we are to be in awe of Him; and (3) keep the cross at the center of all we do." After you write these on the board, spend some time identifying specific strategies your learners can use personally to ensure that these steps are carried out.

Distribute copies of the "Making Worship Wonderful" activity from the reproducible page; ask learners to complete it, assuring them that this is for their eyes only—you will not collect them. *Option:* This can be a take-home exercise if time is short. End with prayers of commitment to be sincere worshippers.

Worship with Meaning

WORSHIP IN THE
NEW CREATION

DEVOTIONAL READING: Isaiah 42:1-9
BACKGROUND SCRIPTURE: Isaiah 65

ISAIAH 65:17-25

17 For, behold, I create new heavens and a new earth: and the former shall not be remembered, nor come into mind.

18 But be ye glad and rejoice for ever in that which I create: for, behold, I create Jerusalem a rejoicing, and her people a joy.

19 And I will rejoice in Jerusalem, and joy in my people: and the voice of weeping shall be no more heard in her, nor the voice of crying.

20 There shall be no more thence an infant of days, nor an old man that hath not filled his days: for the child shall die an hundred years old; but the sinner being an hundred years old shall be accursed.

21 And they shall build houses, and inhabit them; and they shall plant vineyards, and eat the fruit of them.

22 They shall not build, and another inhabit; they shall not plant, and another eat: for as the days of a tree are the days of my people, and mine elect shall long enjoy the work of their hands.

23 They shall not labour in vain, nor bring forth for trouble; for they are the seed of the blessed of the LORD, and their offspring with them.

24 And it shall come to pass, that before they call, I will answer; and while they are yet speaking, I will hear.

25 The wolf and the lamb shall feed together, and the lion shall eat straw like the bullock: and dust shall be the serpent's meat. They shall not hurt nor destroy in all my holy mountain, saith the LORD.

KEY VERSES

Behold, I create new heavens and a new earth: and the former shall not be remembered, nor come into mind. But be ye glad and rejoice for ever in that which I create. —**Isaiah 65:17, 18a**

GOD'S PEOPLE WORSHIP

Unit 1: The Prophet and Praise

LESSONS 1–4

LESSON AIMS

After participating in this lesson, each student will be able to:

1. List characteristics of the new heaven and the new earth.

2. Tell what made the qualities of the new heaven and new earth particularly appealing to the Lord's people in Isaiah's day.

3. Write a prayer that acknowledges that the future is in the Lord's hands.

LESSON OUTLINE

Introduction

A. Isaiah: A "Mini-Bible"

Many have called attention to how the book of Isaiah resembles a Bible in miniature. Part of this observation is due to the number of chapters in Isaiah and their division. The first 39 chapters make up the first major division of the book, and the final 27 chapters constitute the second. This corresponds nicely to the arrangement of our Bibles into the 39 books of the Old Testament and the 27 books of the New.

The topics covered in these two divisions are noteworthy as well. Isaiah's message begins with an appeal to the heavens and the earth (Isaiah 1:2), just as Genesis begins with the creation of the heaven and the earth (Genesis 1:1). Isaiah 40, which begins the second portion of Isaiah, includes within the opening verses a reference to "the voice of him that crieth in the wilderness, Prepare ye the way of the Lord" (Isaiah 40:3). This prophecy is fulfilled in the proclamation of John the Baptist, whose ministry preceded that of Jesus (Mark 1:1-3).

Within the chapters following Isaiah 40 come some of the most powerful and vivid prophecies about Jesus found in the entire Old Testament. They are often labeled "servant passages" or "servant songs" because they refer to a special servant of the Lord and His ministry on the Lord's behalf. Although there is some variation, these are generally recognized to be the texts of Isaiah 42:1-9; 49:1-6; 50:4-9; 52:13–53:12; 61:1-4.

The conclusion of the book of Isaiah brings us to today's lesson text, Isaiah 65:17-25. This text, with its prediction of "new heavens and a new earth" (a promise restated near the end of the book in 66:22) brings to mind the conclusion of the New Testament, where the apostle John records his vision of "a new heaven and a new earth" (Revelation 21:1).

While it may be considered a happy coincidence that the numbering, etc., of Isaiah works out in such a fascinating manner, there is nothing coincidental about the links between Isaiah's words and John's in Revelation. Isaiah was one of the "holy men of God" who were "moved by the

Worship in the New Creation

Holy Ghost" (2 Peter 1:21) to write those prophecies whose fulfillment support the uniqueness of the Scriptures as "given by inspiration of God" (2 Timothy 3:16).

B. Lesson Background

As noted above, Isaiah 40–66 includes some of the most significant prophecies of Jesus and the impact of His life and ministry. The section begins with a word of "comfort" to God's people and assures Jerusalem "that her warfare is accomplished, that her iniquity is pardoned" (Isaiah 40:1, 2). This appears to describe how the captivity of the people in Babylon, predicted in Isaiah 39, is coming to an end.

However, there was another captivity affecting God's people that was far more serious and oppressive: the captivity of *sin*. The bondage to sin—the failure of God's chosen people to serve and obey Him alone faithfully as their God—was the primary cause for the heartbreak of the exile experienced by both the northern kingdom of Israel (to Assyria in 722 BC) and the southern kingdom of Judah (to Babylon in 586 BC). This had to be addressed, and "the servant songs," cited above, do so. Today's text pictures the glorious future worship of those delivered from the chains of spiritual bondage by this servant.

I. God's Promise
(ISAIAH 65:17)
A. New Foretold (v. 17a)

17a. For, behold, I create new heavens and a new earth.

HOW TO SAY IT

Assyria	Uh-*sear*-ee-uh.
Babylon	*Bab*-uh-lun.
Ecclesiastes	Ik-*leez*-ee-*as*-teez.
Gentiles	*Jen*-tiles.
Herodotus	Heh-*rod*-uh-tus.
Isaiah	Eye-*zay*-uh.
Judah	*Joo*-duh.
messianic	mess-ee-*an*-ick.
Zephaniah	Zef-uh-*nye*-uh.

The verb translated *create* is the same verb used of God's creative activity in Genesis 1:1. Previously, Isaiah has been heralding the coming of "new things" from the Lord (Isaiah 42:9; 48:6). With the passage before us, Isaiah reaches the climax of God's new work—the climax described by John in Revelation 21:1.

What Do You Think?

What can you do today to prepare yourself for the new heavens and new earth?

Talking Points for Your Discussion
- Matthew 6:19-21
- Hebrews 11:13-16; 12:1-3
- Revelation 21:1-5; 22:12
- Other

B. Old Forgotten (v. 17b)

17b. And the former shall not be remembered, nor come into mind.

Along with the coming of the new, Isaiah notes the disappearance of the old. This too is in keeping with John's description of "a new heaven and a new earth," where "the former things are passed away" (Revelation 21:4). Followers of Jesus receive a foretaste of this experience in the present life since "if any man be in Christ, he is a new creature: old things are passed away; behold, all things are become new" (2 Corinthians 5:17).

What Do You Think?

What things do Christians seem to have the most trouble "forgetting" regarding their previous status as rebellious sinners? Why is that?

Talking Points for Your Discussion
- Criminal acts
- Unethical acts
- Immoral acts
- 1 Corinthians 15:9

The conclusion to Isaiah's book includes significantly more hope than his introduction. The first five chapters (prior to Isaiah's call in chapter 6) are characterized primarily by messages of judgment that indict God's people for their rebellion against Him. Now, because of the servant's fulfillment of His duties (see the Introduction and Lesson

Visual for Lesson 4. *Point to this visual as you quote Isaiah 65:17a. Then ask the discussion question associated with this half-verse (page 371).*

Background), the bad news has been eclipsed; hope takes center stage.

❧ GONE FOR GOOD! ❧

Posttraumatic stress disorder (PTSD) is a phrase familiar to most. The phrase came into being in the 1970s to describe the symptoms that were appearing in combat veterans of the war in Vietnam. In earlier wars, the malady was referred to as "shell shock" or "battle fatigue." One of the first recorded descriptions of this condition comes to us from the ancient Greek historian Herodotus. He described a physically uninjured soldier who went blind during the Battle of Marathon (490 BC; see the Lesson Background of lesson 8) after seeing a comrade-in-arms die.

Although combat may be the best-known cause of PTSD, any serious trauma may trigger the symptoms. Some people relive the trauma over and over in dreams or flashbacks. Others become hypervigilant, as if to avoid being caught by surprise.

In the new creation, there will be no flashbacks, no need for hypervigilance. That's because there will be no traumatic events to cause such things. And the traumas we suffer now will no longer be remembered. God will use His power to wipe from our memory every evil thing we have experienced, every word, act, or situation that has caused us pain or grief. What a blessed future awaits us!

—C. R. B.

II. God's Provision
(ISAIAH 65:18-25)
A. Joy (vv. 18, 19)

18, 19. But be ye glad and rejoice for ever in that which I create: for, behold, I create Jerusalem a rejoicing, and her people a joy. And I will rejoice in Jerusalem, and joy in my people: and the voice of weeping shall be no more heard in her, nor the voice of crying.

In the remaining verses in our printed text, Isaiah concentrates specifically on Jerusalem. This is the city that suffers such misery as a result of being punished "double for all her sins" (Isaiah 40:2). The Jerusalem that is part of the new heavens and new earth will be a place of immeasurable delight and joy. What a contrast with the sadness and despair of living in captivity in Babylon! Those sad days (or for that matter, *any* sad days) will become a distant memory (compare Isaiah 25:7, 8). John echoes this "no more tears" language in his description of the marvelous future that awaits the faithful servants of Jesus (Revelation 7:17; 21:4).

The sense of joy that this New Jerusalem creates is not only for its inhabitants, but also for God himself. The New Jerusalem will be the climax of God's great redemptive plan, when His bride is fully ready to meet Him, "adorned for her husband" (Revelation 21:2). The prophet Zephaniah uses the image of God singing to portray His personal pleasure with this Jerusalem (Zephaniah 3:17).

B. Life (v. 20)

20. There shall be no more thence an infant of days, nor an old man that hath not filled his days: for the child shall die an hundred years old; but the sinner being an hundred years old shall be accursed.

Isaiah proceeds to offer further descriptions of life in the New Jerusalem. The limitations of age that are part of earthly life will no longer exist. A lengthy life will be the norm. No premature deaths will occur. Even someone who lives to be a *hundred years old* will be considered a mere child. The term *sinner* literally means "someone who misses the mark." Here the idea seems to be that an individual who "misses the mark" in failing to attain the age of 100 years *shall be accursed*. This is quite a noteworthy statement, since 70 is considered the normal life expectancy (Psalm 90:10).

The contents of this verse raise the question of how this language can be applied to the New Jerusalem (or Heaven), where there is to be no dying whatsoever (Revelation 21:4). Death does take place in Isaiah's description, albeit following an extended life. The thought of someone being accursed seems to counter what John states of the heavenly city, that "there shall be no more curse" (Revelation 22:3).

Isaiah appears to be using figurative language to convey how wonderful life in the new heavens and earth will be. Pictures of what an ideal life would be like here on earth are employed to convey the wonders of life in the new heavens and earth. Instead of trying to think in specific terms, such as an actual age of 100 years, it is more valid to look for a principle that undergirds what Isaiah is describing.

In the verse before us, the key theme is a reversal of the curse of death. Isaiah's language portrays a place where death has been stripped of its power. This is in keeping with Isaiah's earlier promise that the Lord will "swallow up death in victory" and "wipe away tears from off all faces" (Isaiah 25:8). In the passage before us, death may not appear to be "swallowed up" since people are still pictured as dying; but the thrust of Isaiah's overall description is that it is.

C. Abundance (vv. 21-23)

21. And they shall build houses, and inhabit them; and they shall plant vineyards, and eat the fruit of them.

This verse also uses the description of an ideal life on this earth, especially from the standpoint of an Israelite under the old covenant, to portray the blessedness of life in the New Jerusalem. To be able to inhabit one's own house and to *plant vineyards, and eat the fruit of them* are just a part of the numerous blessings associated with life in the promised land (see Deuteronomy 8:7-14).

Is it possible that activity such as building houses and planting vineyards can actually occur in the new earth? To see this promise in more lit-

eral terms does not necessarily violate other portions of Scripture (which is the problem in seeing verse 20 in more literal terms). Perhaps building and planting in the new earth is to be part of the reversal of the curse that was pronounced on humanity following the sin in the Garden of Eden, that work would be a drudgery (Genesis 3:17-19). Later in today's text comes the promise of peace within the animal kingdom (v. 25); this too may signal the end of the "bondage of corruption" that causes the "whole creation" to groan in pain, waiting for the day of "redemption" (Romans 8:20-23).

For those who spend most or all of their earthly lives in poverty, in want, and/or in places where the fruits of their labors are wrongly seized by others, the promise of a place free from such oppression is refreshing indeed. All Christians wait in hope to see how the promises of Isaiah and other inspired writers will come to pass.

> **What Do You Think?**
> What are some ways to keep our focus on the heavenly abundance that awaits while in the midst of the struggles of this life?
> *Talking Points for Your Discussion*
> - Issues of attitude
> - Issues of behavior

22. They shall not build, and another inhabit; they shall not plant, and another eat: for as the days of a tree are the days of my people, and mine elect shall long enjoy the work of their hands.

The promise we see here reflects a reversal of one of the curses that the Israelites would experience if they disobeyed God: "Thou shalt build an house, and thou shalt not dwell therein: thou shalt plant a vineyard, and shalt not gather the grapes thereof" (Deuteronomy 28:30). Added to this reversal is another promise of longevity: *as the days of a tree are the days of my people.*

In the new heavens and new earth, long life (that is, eternal life) allows one to enjoy the product of his or her labors for an unending period of time. One of the frustrations of life in a fallen world is that a person may pour himself or herself into a project and then not live long enough to see it completed or to experience the genuine satisfaction of a job well done (compare Ecclesiastes 2:21).

23. They shall not labour in vain, nor bring forth for trouble; for they are the seed of the blessed of the LORD, and their offspring with them.

Another sad, tragic consequence of life in a sin-cursed world is that children—described here as those whom their mothers *bring forth*—are often afflicted. They have to undergo pain, heartache, and a host of burdens that children should not have to bear. Isaiah's promise should not be taken as an indication that childbearing will occur in the new heavens and the earth (see Matthew 22:30). Most likely it is another illustration of how conditions in a sin-cursed world will be reversed.

Whereas punishment of children for their father's sin is extended "unto the third and to the fourth generation" according to Exodus 34:7, no such punishment is in place in the new heavens and new earth. Family members who have been faithful to the Lord will be reunited for eternity, never to be separated.

> **What Do You Think?**
> Besides the end of death, what promised reversals of this sin-cursed world encourage you the most today? Why?
> *Talking Points for Your Discussion*
> - Issues of poverty
> - Issues of injustice
> - Issues concerning relationships
> - Other

D. Access (v. 24)

24. And it shall come to pass, that before they call, I will answer; and while they are yet speaking, I will hear.

This verse depicts the level of closeness that God's people will experience with Him in the New Jerusalem (see Revelation 22:4). Many times we wrestle with questions of God's purpose for the suffering that we, our family members, or our friends confront. We can sympathize with the anguished cry of David when he asks, "Why standest thou afar off, O Lord? why hidest thou thyself in times of trouble?" (Psalm 10:1). But in the New Jerusalem, the closeness between God and His people will be akin to what Adam and Eve must have experienced in the Garden of Eden prior to the destructive intrusion of sin.

❧ REAL "INSTANT MESSAGING" ❧

There was a time when communication over long distances was very slow. In the early nineteenth century, a letter sent from America's east coast could take months to reach the west coast. The famous Pony Express of 1860–1861, combined with the telegraph, reduced that time to "only" 10 days. October 24, 1861 saw the completion of the telegraph line linking the eastern and western coasts of America, allowing near-instantaneous communication across the continent.

Improvements in communication technology since that time have been profound. Today's e-mail circles the globe at the speed of light. Many of us grew up taking the telephone for granted. Today's youth feel deprived without a so-called "smartphone"; these devices offer Internet connectivity, GPS navigation, etc. With a smartphone, one need never be "disconnected"!

Yet all of this pales in comparison with Isaiah's description of how closely we shall be connected with God in the new creation: "Before they call, I will answer." And it's possible even now! Our prayers are in God's ears even as they are being offered. The communication lines are open on God's end—are they open on ours?   —C. R. B.

E. Peace (v. 25)

25. The wolf and the lamb shall feed together, and the lion shall eat straw like the bullock: and dust shall be the serpent's meat. They shall not hurt nor destroy in all my holy mountain, saith the LORD.

The language in this verse brings to mind an earlier, similar description in Isaiah 11. There Isaiah describes the "rod out of the stem of Jesse" and the "Branch" that "shall grow out of his roots" (v. 1), whom the Spirit of the Lord will empower (vv. 2, 3). Verse 10 of that chapter pictures this "root of Jesse" as an ensign, or banner, that even the Gentiles will seek. The messianic age is in view.

Worship in the New Creation

Some suggest that the verse before us is using the image of changed relationships between animals that are typically hostile to one another to describe the impact of the gospel message on human relationships. The love of Christ has on numerous occasions produced reconciliation among people whose mutual hatred seemed irreversible. However, the description in the verse before us may be a portrayal of life in the new earth (similar to what was suggested under Isaiah 65:21, above).

The promise that *dust shall be the serpent's meat* is noteworthy. The reference to the serpent may be that of Satan and his tempting of humans to sin, which brought about conditions that Isaiah promises are to be reversed. When God cursed the serpent, He told it, "Upon thy belly shalt thou go, and dust shalt thou eat all the days of thy life" (Genesis 3:14); that sentence is reaffirmed by Isaiah. The serpent will not harm anyone, not even a child (Isaiah 11:8), but will remain in a position of submission. Perhaps that serves to reinforce what the establishment of the new heavens and new earth will signify: that the God of peace keeps His promise to "bruise Satan under your feet" (Romans 16:20).

Regardless of the specific details, Isaiah's new heavens and new earth will be a marvel for the eyes of the redeemed to look upon and to experience. May we all live life each day faithfully awaiting the time when God will bring these wonderful promises to their fulfillment.

What Do You Think?

How do you react to this comparison: "In light of heaven, the worst suffering on earth . . . will be seen to be no more serious than one night in an inconvenient hotel" (Mother Teresa)?

Talking Points for Your Discussion

- Agreement, and why
- Disagreement, and why

Conclusion

A. Reverse the Curse

When the Boston Red Sox won the World Series over the St. Louis Cardinals in 2004, their triumph signaled the end of one of the longest dry spells in the history of sports. The Red Sox had not won a World Series since 1918, when a young pitcher by the name of Babe Ruth was one of their star players.

Following that season, the Red Sox traded Ruth to the New York Yankees, which (in the opinion of many) began the legendary "curse" that doomed the Red Sox to constant frustration. On several occasions after 1918, the Red Sox came close to winning a championship; but all their loyal fans could do was "wait till next year." Finally in 2004, the "curse" was lifted, and Red Sox fans everywhere rejoiced.

Reverse the Curse! may be considered the theme of the Bible following the sin of Adam and Eve in Genesis 3. At that point, the curse of sin shattered the harmony of God's "very good" creation (Genesis 1:31). The world became a place of pain and sorrow, not at all what God created it to be. From Genesis 3 on, we see God working to get back what is rightfully His. He was (and is) out to "reverse the curse."

This is exactly what He accomplishes through Jesus. "For this purpose the Son of God was manifested, that he might destroy the works of the devil" (1 John 3:8). That destruction began at the cross and empty tomb. It awaits the consummation —the "grand finale"—when Jesus returns. The curse will be lifted fully on that great day, completely reversed for eternity.

As one reads Revelation and sees Isaiah's precious promises coming to pass, the only appropriate response is humble and grateful worship. John's closing words in Revelation will do nicely: "Even so, come, Lord Jesus" (Revelation 22:20).

B. Prayer

Father, Creator of Heaven and earth, thank You for the promise of a new heavens and a new earth, "wherein dwelleth righteousness" (2 Peter 3:13). May our lives on this present, unrighteous earth reflect true worship so that we may worship You in Your perfect home for eternity. In Jesus' name, amen.

C. Thought to Remember

God's plan is to reclaim what is rightfully His.

INVOLVEMENT LEARNING

Some of the activities below are also found in the helpful student book, Adult Bible Class.
Don't forget to download the free reproducible page from www.standardlesson.com to enhance your lesson!

Into the Lesson

To help set the context for today's lesson, review the six woes from Isaiah 5:8-23 (that is, v. 8; v. 11; vv. 18, 19; v. 20; v. 21; and vv. 22, 23), which were discussed in the Into the Lesson segment of lesson 1's Involvement Learning.

Say, "Three weeks ago we looked at several 'woes' of Isaiah's day (and some of our own). In so doing, we saw that God had a very clear message He wanted to convey. Isaiah had a vision of God on His throne, in all of His majesty. We realized we have access to the same power and glory of God that Isaiah experienced in that vision. When it seems as though all hope is gone, we need to remember that God is on His throne and He is in control. In today's lesson, we see an even greater manifestation of that power and glory."

Into the Word

Before class, prepare five index cards printed with the following Scripture references, one each: (1) Leviticus 26:3-13; (2) Deuteronomy 28:15, 30-48; (3) Isaiah 1:7-9; (4) 2 Kings 17:24; 25:8-12; (5) Isaiah 3:1; 5:7. Divide the class into five groups; assign one index card to each group. (Smaller classes can form five study pairs or assign more than one card to fewer groups.)

Within their groups, have learners read their Scripture texts and summarize either God's promise/warning (cards 1 and 2) or the circumstances in which the Israelites found themselves (cards 3, 4, and 5). After a few minutes, have group 1 summarize its text *(expected response: God tells Israel the blessings that await them if they obey His commands).* Discuss what some of those promised blessings were and whether they came to fruition.

Next, have group 2 summarize its text *(expected response: God warns what will happen if His people do not obey His commands).* Following that, read Isaiah 65:17 and discuss the hope that the ancient Israelites could have seen in this verse.

Next, ask group 3 to summarize its texts *(expected response: God's warning came true for Judah—cities burned, fields stripped, people taken away).* Then read Isaiah 65:18, 19. Discuss the hope that the ancient Israelites may have seen in these verses.

Next, ask group 4 to summarize its texts *(expected response: more fulfillment of God's warnings —Assyria took Israel into bondage and put other people to live in the land; Babylon took Judah captive and left only the poorest people to work the land).* Follow by reading Isaiah 65:21, 22. Again, discuss the hope these verses held for the Israelites.

Finally, have group 5 summarize its texts *(expected response: God withdrew His favor from His people—stripping away supply, support, and protection—because of their rebellion).* Follow by reading Isaiah 65:23-25. Again, discuss the hope these verses held for the Israelites.

Return to group 1's text (Leviticus 26:3-13) and brainstorm its possible application to Christians today. Say, "God's Word is timeless, thus we can also find hope in the words from Isaiah when we face the curses of life—whether brought on by our own disobedience or as a result of living in a fallen world."

Into Life

Say, "The words from our text today bring to mind verses from the book of Revelation that are familiar to many. Let's see how they compare." *Option 1:* Distribute copies of the "A Choral Reading" activity from the reproducible page, which you can download. Conduct the choral reading as indicated. *Option 2:* Instead of the choral reading, read aloud Revelation 21:1-4, 23, 24; 22:3, 4, 20.

Under either option, discuss how the prophecies of Isaiah are fulfilled in the vision the apostle John saw and recorded in Revelation. Close with a prayer expressing confidence in the fact that God is in control and the battle has been won.

Worship in the New Creation

RESTORING JOYFUL WORSHIP

DEVOTIONAL READING: Matthew 23:29-39
BACKGROUND SCRIPTURE: Ezra 1:1–3:7

EZRA 3:1-7

1 And when the seventh month was come, and the children of Israel were in the cities, the people gathered themselves together as one man to Jerusalem.

2 Then stood up Jeshua the son of Jozadak, and his brethren the priests, and Zerubbabel the son of Shealtiel, and his brethren, and builded the altar of the God of Israel, to offer burnt offerings thereon, as it is written in the law of Moses the man of God.

3 And they set the altar upon his bases; for fear was upon them because of the people of those countries: and they offered burnt offerings thereon unto the LORD, even burnt offerings morning and evening.

4 They kept also the feast of tabernacles, as it is written, and offered the daily burnt offer-

ings by number, according to the custom, as the duty of every day required;

5 And afterward offered the continual burnt offering, both of the new moons, and of all the set feasts of the LORD that were consecrated, and of every one that willingly offered a freewill offering unto the LORD.

6 From the first day of the seventh month began they to offer burnt offerings unto the LORD. But the foundation of the temple of the LORD was not yet laid.

7 They gave money also unto the masons, and to the carpenters; and meat, and drink, and oil, unto them of Zidon, and to them of Tyre, to bring cedar trees from Lebanon to the sea of Joppa, according to the grant that they had of Cyrus king of Persia.

KEY VERSE

They kept also the feast of tabernacles, as it is written, and offered the daily burnt offerings by number, according to the custom, as the duty of every day required. —**Ezra 3:4**

GOD'S PEOPLE WORSHIP

Unit 2: Worshipping in Jerusalem Again (Ezra)

LESSONS 5–9

LESSON AIMS

After participating in this lesson, each student will be able to:

1. Describe the worship of the former exiles after they returned to Jerusalem.

2. Explain the significance of the altar and the Feast of Tabernacles to the former exiles.

3. Suggest a way to prevent worship practices from becoming routine or mere ritual.

LESSON OUTLINE

Introduction

A. A Journey with Purpose

The word *journey* has become a popular term to describe the events that take place in the pursuit of life, liberty, and happiness. Many of the journeys of life will have one or more purposes. The expenses of miles, meals, and motels are not undertaken simply to spend money. Pleasure, business, religious conventions, or spiritual retreats are often combined to bring satisfaction and fulfillment to an individual or several members of a family.

Marketers know that many people find the words *journey* and *purpose* to be enticing. No one wants to live a life devoid of purpose. An Internet search reveals that there are several books that have titles with those two words. The idea being promoted is that you can find purpose, happiness, or fulfillment in your journey if you buy the recommended books.

Some people, however, suffer from the self-inflicted problem of filling their time with too many activities as they try to have lives that are rewarding and fulfilling. They become stressed in their efforts to complete the goals they have set. As the old saying goes, they "confuse activity with accomplishment." The concept of *balance* is ignored. Such people need to assess what they are doing and then work to bring balance into their lives.

Today may not be January 1, but it is still a good time to make resolutions to evaluate one's priorities. The lesson for today is about thousands of people who took a journey together. Their journey had spiritual purposes, and their purposes were realized.

B. Lesson Background

The book of Isaiah provided the texts for the first four lessons this quarter, and that prophet's ministry came to an end in about 700 BC. The lesson for today is from the first part of the book of Ezra, and the events described took place about 165 years later. Isaiah provides several fascinating prophecies that find their fulfillments in the early chapters of the book of Ezra.

Restoring Joyful Worship

Assyria was the world superpower during Isaiah's day. But he prophesied that it would be Babylon that would take captives from Judah (Isaiah 39:6, 7). Babylon was just a city of the Assyrian Empire when Isaiah wrote, but that status was to change.

Nebuchadnezzar and his allies destroyed Nineveh, the capital of Assyria, in 612 BC. By defeating the Egyptians in 605 BC, Nebuchadnezzar established what was known as the neo-Babylonian Empire. The people of Judah were not compliant subjects, however, and Nebuchadnezzar destroyed Jerusalem in 586 BC (see 2 Kings 25). That was over a century after the time that Isaiah wrote.

At the time when Babylon was just a city, Isaiah had prophesied that captive Israelites would return from there, and it all came to pass. An amazing prophecy in Isaiah is that of the specific name of the person who was to capture Babylon: King Cyrus the Great (Isaiah 44:28; 45:1, 13). Isaiah also predicted that Cyrus would declare that the temple would be rebuilt.

The troops of Cyrus captured Babylon in October of 539 BC. Ezra 1:2 (which repeats the last verse of 2 Chronicles) notes Cyrus's authorization to rebuild the temple. His declaration is usually dated in the spring of 538 BC, at the annual New Year's festival in Babylon.

The Cyrus Cylinder, found in 1879, is an important archaeological discovery in this regard. This artifact does not mention Judah, but it has the actual decree of Cyrus that all captured idols were to take residence again in their respective dwellings. The Israelites could not take a statue of their God since there wasn't any, but they could take vessels to the temple that they planned to rebuild. Ezra 1 tells us that this is what they did, which fulfilled the prophecy in Jeremiah 27:21, 22, given about 597 BC.

Ezra 2:64, 65 reveals that there were 49,897 in the first wave of exiles who made the journey from Babylon to Jerusalem, a trip of 880 miles. The primary purpose of the journey was spiritual: to rebuild the temple in order to renew the worship and rituals that had been given through Moses. The year of the return is one of the mysteries of history. The dates suggested by scholars range from 538 to 533 BC; we will use the date of 538.

When Jerusalem was destroyed in 586 BC, there remained no nation of Judah, no capital city of Jerusalem, and no temple. Normally it would be impossible for a nation to come into existence again after an absence of 50 years. God was in this situation, however, and the impossible became a reality. As Jeremiah stated, nothing is too difficult for God (Jeremiah 32:17).

I. Rebuilding the Altar
(EZRA 3:1, 2)
A. Convening (v. 1)

1. And when the seventh month was come, and the children of Israel were in the cities, the people gathered themselves together as one man to Jerusalem.

Many scholars assume that the returning exiles reach Jerusalem in about the fifth month of the year, for this is the timetable that Ezra uses later (Ezra 7:8, 9). If so, it means that the people take two months to locate themselves in their ancestral lands and villages (see 2:70). Now, in *the seventh month,* it is essential for them to get serious about the purpose of their journey, so the people come *together as one man to Jerusalem.*

Most of the people are from the tribes of Judah and Benjamin, but people from other tribes are also present. It is therefore appropriate that the ancient name *Israel* is used to describe the people who assemble to fulfill their spiritual goals.

What Do You Think?
What special "gathering events" have made lasting impressions on your faith? Why?
Talking Points for Your Discussion
- Milestone celebrations
- Building dedications
- Other

The seventh month, called *Tishri* or *Ethanim* (1 Kings 8:2), is considered to be the most important month in the Hebrew year; it is equivalent to late September and early October. On the first day of the month, the people are to celebrate the Feast of Trumpets (Leviticus 23:23-25). The tenth of the month is the Day of Atonement, when special sacrifices are offered for the sins of the people (see Leviticus 16 for details). The Feast of Tabernacles (or Booths) begins on the fifteenth day and continues for seven days, with a special eighth day as a holy convocation. (Leviticus 23:33-43 gives more information; see also the Lesson Background of lesson 10.)

B. Constructing (v. 2)

2. Then stood up Jeshua the son of Jozadak, and his brethren the priests, and Zerubbabel the son of Shealtiel, and his brethren, and builded the altar of the God of Israel, to offer burnt offerings thereon, as it is written in the law of Moses the man of God.

The total number of priests in this return is 4,289 (Ezra 2:36-39), and the high priest is a certain Jeshua (or Joshua). It is the priests who take the lead in constructing *the altar of the God of Israel* for the purpose of sacrificing burnt offerings. This is according to that which *is written in the law of Moses the man of God* as recorded in, among other places, Leviticus 1.

Zerubbabel the son of Shealtiel is a grandson of King Jehoiachin, the next to last king of Judah (see Matthew 1:12, where Jehoiachin is listed by the alternate name *Jechonias;* see also Jeremiah 24:1; 27:20; 28:4; 29:2). We will have more to say about both Jeshua and Zerubbabel when we consider Ezra 3:8 in next week's lesson.

What Do You Think?
  What do you remember about a church leader (or group of leaders) being a steadying influence during a time of transition?
Talking Points for Your Discussion
  ▪ During a time of internal church conflict
  ▪ During a time of pressure from an outside source (culture, government, etc.)
  ▪ During a natural disaster
  ▪ Other

Sacrifices have not been offered in Jerusalem since 586 BC, when the Babylonians broke through the city defenses (see 2 Kings 25:3, 8). Now, some 50 years later, it is a momentous occasion when the God-ordained sacrifices resume.

The size of the new altar is not given. The dimensions of the original altar used for the tabernacle were width and length of 5 cubits each (a cubit is about 18 inches) and height of 3 cubits (Exodus 27:1). That altar was constructed about 1446 BC, while the Israelites were still at Sinai.

Solomon began to build the temple about 480 years later (1 Kings 6:1), and the altar of burnt offerings was huge: 20 cubits wide and long and 10 cubits high (2 Chronicles 4:1). The new altar after the Babylonian captivity does not need to have such dimensions. A smaller one will suffice.

II. Resuming the Offerings
(EZRA 3:3-6)

A. Daily Requirements (v. 3)

3. And they set the altar upon his bases; for fear was upon them because of the people of those countries: and they offered burnt offerings thereon unto the LORD, even burnt offerings morning and evening.

There is no question about where to build the altar: it will be on the same place as the previous altars on this site. David had an altar constructed here after purchasing the threshing floor (2 Samuel 24:18-24), and this is where Solomon, David's son, built the altar for the temple. The people are doing their best to follow the instructions given by Moses and to follow the examples of godly leaders of centuries past.

What Do You Think?
  What are some good ways to honor the godly examples of your church's leaders, past and present?
Talking Points for Your Discussion
  ▪ "Big" ways (banquets, etc.)
  ▪ "Small" ways (notes in the church bulletin, etc.)

The Law of Moses prescribes that the *burnt offerings morning and evening* are to include one lamb each, on a daily basis (Numbers 28:1-4); Sabbath days require additional sacrifices (28:9, 10). Such offerings represent commitment and dedication.

There are other inhabitants in the region who do not appreciate the fact that almost 50,000 peo-

Restoring Joyful Worship

ple have suddenly arrived in "their" land. They are probably a mixture of non-Israelites and a few Israelites who had been left behind by the Babylonians. The new arrivals have moved into the villages of ancestors, and now the city of Jerusalem is becoming their religious center. Animosity develops, and this creates fear for the Israelites. But God's people have struggled to make their journey, and they intend to finish what they have started.

B. Feast of Tabernacles (v. 4)

4. They kept also the feast of tabernacles, as it is written, and offered the daily burnt offerings by number, according to the custom, as the duty of every day required.

The feast of tabernacles goes by other names, and it's easy to get confused. The first mention of this festival in the Bible calls it the Feast of Ingathering (Exodus 23:16b). It takes place in the fall at the end of the harvest season.

This festival is sometimes referred to as the Feast of Booths. Leviticus 23:33-43 instructs the Israelites to use tree branches to construct "booths," and the people are to live in them during the feast, hence the name Feast of Booths. The purpose of living in these makeshift structures is to remind the people that their ancestors lived in tents during the 40 years of the wilderness wanderings.

This event, then, is something like a seven-day campout, with feasting every day. It is a day for everyone to rejoice—the widows, orphans, Levites, and strangers (Deuteronomy 16:13-15).

HOW TO SAY IT

Assyria	Uh-*sear*-ee-uh.
Cyrus	*Sigh*-russ.
Ethanim	*Eth*-uh-nim.
Jechonias	*Jek*-o-**nye**-us.
Jehoiachin	Jeh-*hoy*-uh-kin.
Jeshua	*Jesh*-you-uh.
Nebuchadnezzar	*Neb*-yuh-kud-**nez**-er.
Nineveh	*Nin*-uh-vuh.
Shealtiel	She-*al*-tee-el.
tabernacles	**tah**-burr-**nah**-kuls.
Tishri	*Tish*-ree.
Zerubbabel	Zeh-*rub*-uh-bul.

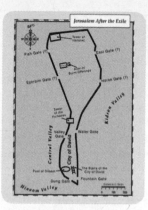

Visual for
Lessons 5 & 12

This map provides perspective, although the walls would not be rebuilt until Nehemiah's day.

The harvest is over, and it is a time to celebrate. (See further discussion in lesson 10.)

The emphasis here, however, is on the altar. Detailed instructions regarding the types of sacrificial offerings that are to be made throughout the feast are found in Numbers 29:12-39. The altar has been built, and the people are experiencing the joy that comes from being able to worship the Lord again in the promised land.

C. Other Requirements (v. 5)

5. And afterward offered the continual burnt offering, both of the new moons, and of all the set feasts of the Lord that were consecrated, and of every one that willingly offered a freewill offering unto the Lord.

This verse makes the very important point that sacrifices continue to be offered after the initial enthusiasm that is associated with the completion of the altar. The priests offer the morning and evening sacrifices, and they fulfill their obligations at the beginning of each month, as determined by a new moon.

In addition to the Feast of Tabernacles, the Israelites are conscientious about *all the set feasts of the Lord* (Deuteronomy 16:16; etc.). These include the one-day Passover observance (Exodus 12:6, 43-49) that is followed immediately by the seven-day Feast of Unleavened Bread (Leviticus 23:5, 6). These take place in the spring of the year; they commemorate the exodus from Egypt.

Another important observance is the one-day Feast of Harvest (Exodus 23:15, 16); its name is in line with the fact that the grain harvests are usually completed in Israel by early June. This festival is celebrated approximately seven weeks after Passover (Leviticus 23:15, 16). It is also called the Feast of Weeks (2 Chronicles 8:13; etc.), eventually coming to be known as Pentecost (compare Acts 2:1).

The last part of the verse indicates that freewill offerings are being made on a regular basis by people who are thrilled to be able to express their gratitude to God in this way. We know that the dedication of a new facility brings a surge in attendance. But without true commitment, enthusiasm will cool as other things assume a higher priority. That does not seem to be the case here!

What Do You Think?
What can you do to keep a sense of joy in your worship?
Talking Points for Your Discussion
▪ Before a worship service begins
▪ During a worship service

D. Significant Date (v. 6a)

6a. From the first day of the seventh month began they to offer burnt offerings unto the LORD.

This half-verse reviews the results of a successful and significant undertaking: the altar of burnt offerings is complete, ready to be used on the *first day of the seventh month,* when the Feast of Trumpets occurs (see discussion above). The people can now fulfill the obligations that God has prescribed for this special month.

E. Challenge Noted (v. 6b)

6b. But the foundation of the temple of the LORD was not yet laid.

The building of the altar is only phase one. A much bigger task is still ahead: the rebuilding of the temple. King Cyrus has authorized this task (see the Lesson Background).

The first step of a building project of this kind is to lay the foundation. That has not been done at this point since the construction of the altar had to come first.

The Ryugyong Hotel in Pyongyang, North Korea, was intended to impress the world with the supposed glories of that Communist state. Work on the 105-story edifice was begun in 1987, but construction came to a halt in 1992. It was still unfinished as of the time of this writing. A lack of funding and a shortage of electrical power, among other things, are said to be reasons for failure to complete it. Further, engineers say it is unsafe to continue construction.

The above reminds us of Jesus' observations about the importance of "counting the cost" in Luke 14:28-30. Those who led the various returns from exile did indeed count the cost. They knew what it would take to rebuild the altar, the foundation of the temple (see below), and the temple itself (lesson 6). They also knew the ability of God to provide.

Today, we "as lively stones, are built up a spiritual house, an holy priesthood" (1 Peter 2:5). God paid a big price to start this "building project"—the life of His Son. Have we counted the personal cost to be included (see Luke 14:25-33)? More importantly, have we counted the cost of *not* doing so?
—C. R. B.

III. Resources for the Temple
(EZRA 3:7)

A. Paying the Craftsmen (v. 7a)

7a. They gave money also unto the masons, and to the carpenters.

During King David's final days, he informed his son Solomon of the many preparations he (David) had made for the building of the temple. David had provided gold and silver in abundance, and he reminded Solomon that there were many skilled workmen available for the project (1 Chronicles 22:14, 15). As those men were paid for their services, and as workmen also were fairly compensated when the temple was repaired some 150 years after that (2 Kings 12:6-14), so also these workmen are paid. The masons serve as stonecutters, and the carpenters have the task of shaping the timber that will be coming from Lebanon (v. 7b, next).

Restoring Joyful Worship

Funding for this project is partly from those who stayed behind in Babylon. They have sent along much wealth with those Israelites who have made the journey to Jerusalem (Ezra 1:6). King Cyrus also has provided funding (6:3-5). The returnees establish a special treasury on arrival, and they too have contributed to it (2:68, 69).

B. Purchasing the Cedar (v. 7b)

7b. And meat, and drink, and oil, unto them of Zidon, and to them of Tyre, to bring cedar trees from Lebanon to the sea of Joppa, according to the grant that they had of Cyrus king of Persia.

Solomon completed the first temple over 400 years previously. He too had obtained *cedar trees from Lebanon,* so his efforts were similar to what we see here (2 Chronicles 2:8-10). The procedure of transporting the timber "in floats by sea" to Joppa is also repeated (2:16). A sea voyage from the port of Zidon (or Sidon) south to Tyre is about 25 miles; from Tyre to Joppa is an additional sea voyage of about 90 miles. The overland distance from Joppa to Jerusalem is about 38 miles.

The grant that they had of Cyrus king of Persia has two interpretations. The first is that this is a reminder that the entire project is authorized by him; this fact becomes very important in Ezra 5 and 6. The second view is that *the grant* refers to the funding provided by Cyrus for building of the temple (again, Ezra 6:3-5).

❧ GOD AND GIVERS ❧

Devout people through the centuries have showed their faith by building places of worship. These include grandiose cathedrals of the Middle Ages and following. In many cases, the resources were insufficient to complete the buildings within the lifetimes of those who started the construction. Some cathedrals took centuries to complete.

Some Christians argue that such structures are more examples of human pride than of devotion to God. Thus, the reasoning goes, the money might well have been better spent on ministry and works of mercy. In response, some recall Jesus' rebuke to those who condemned a woman for "wasting" expensive ointment by anointing Him (Mark 14:3-9). Thus they argue that these artistic structures gave glory to God and provided generations of craftsmen and artisans an outlet for their God-given talents.

God providentially provided the money, material, and manpower needed for the construction we see in this week's lesson and the next. In working for the Lord, what examples of similar providential help have you experienced? —C. R. B.

Conclusion

A. Things That Are First!

The first day of the week is Sunday, the Lord's Day. For the Christian, this is the primary day to assemble with other believers (Acts 20:7; 1 Corinthians 16:2; Hebrews 10:25). It is a matter of priorities.

Those who made the trip from Babylon to Judah set an excellent example in the matter of establishing priorities. On arrival, they did well in putting first things first: they continued their work in spite of the early opposition. Later opposition deterred them for a time, but they eventually completed the task. It was a matter of priorities.

B. Prayer

Almighty God, thank You for the example of the thousands of people in today's lesson who were willing to sacrifice personally to honor You. May that be my desire this day and every day! In Jesus' name, amen.

C. Thought to Remember

Seek first the kingdom of God.

INVOLVEMENT LEARNING

Some of the activities below are also found in the helpful student book, Adult Bible Class.
Don't forget to download the free reproducible page from www.standardlesson.com to enhance your lesson!

Into the Lesson

Option 1. Display the following series of letters as class members arrive: *APJUORUPRONSEEY.* Say, "There is a 'hidden title' for today's study in this series of letters. Can anyone see the title?" After a short time, assist learners by beginning to underline alternate letters starting with the first *P*. Someone will finally see "A Journey [with] Purpose." (See the title of the lesson's Introduction.)

Option 2. Place in chairs copies of the "Words of Worship and Joy" word-search activity from the reproducible page, which you can download. Learners can begin working on this as they arrive.

Once either the title is decoded (Option 1) or most have completed the word-search activity (Option 2), ask the following questions, pausing for responses between each: 1. From your past studies of the book of Ezra, what journeys were being taken? 2. Who took the first such journey? 3. What was the purpose of that journey? *Answers: (1) from captivity in Babylon back to the promised land; (2) about 50,000 Jewish exiles who chose to return; (3) to restore the altar and, ultimately, the temple in Jerusalem for worship as God intended.*

Into the Word

Have prepared in advance the following words as poster-size flash cards, with letters large enough to be read across your learning space: *PAYMENT / OBEDIENCE / SACRIFICE / INCOMPLETE / UNITY / WORKERS.*

Ask learners to read the lesson text, Ezra 3:1-7. Then divide your class into two groups. Label one *The Obvious Group;* label the other *The Not-So-Obvious Group.* Say, "I'm going to show you some flash cards. For each word, *The Obvious Group* will explain what is obvious about that word in the lesson text; then *The Not-So-Obvious Group* will suggest a connection that is not so obvious."

Begin displaying the cards, one by one. If the class needs an example, show the word *payment*

and say, "Obviously, verse 7 speaks of payment to workers and for materials; not so obviously, the burnt offerings of verse 3 could be considered figuratively as 'payments of gratitude' to God."

Here are possible responses for the other five words. For *obedience,* verse 2 says all was done exactly as Moses commanded, but obedience also presents itself as the people did what Cyrus had authorized per verse 7. For *sacrifice,* references to animal and other burnt offerings is obvious in verses 2-6, but we must not overlook the sacrifice made by those who returned 880 miles from exile, leaving behind friends and family members. For *incomplete,* verse 6 notes that the foundation for the temple remained missing, but not so obviously verse 3 indicates an incomplete faith when the worshippers feared the surrounding peoples. For *unity,* verse 1 indicates that the people from all towns assembled as one, but not so obviously they all participated in the offerings made. For *workers,* verse 7 notes the role of construction craftsmen, but perhaps not so obviously, the project called for hard work from the citizens of Lebanon.

Into Life

Display this fill-in title: "Restoring _____ Worship." Note that the lesson for today fills it in with the word *Joyful.* Ask, "What other words could be used here, especially words that relate to our own needs in worship?" Jot responses on the board (possibilities: *meaningful, sincere, personal, real*). Following each suggestion, immediately ask, "How do we do that?" This will help push the discussion beyond superficial responses. Be careful not to allow the discussion to become a gripe session about your church's current worship format.

Distribute copies of the "All on the Altar He/ We Lay" activity from the reproducible page. As learners complete this, they should begin to see the connection between the New Testament concepts of *sacrifice* and God-pleasing *worship.*

RESTORING THE TEMPLE

DEVOTIONAL READING: Psalm 66:1-12
BACKGROUND SCRIPTURE: Ezra 3:8-13

EZRA 3:8-13

8 Now in the second year of their coming unto the house of God at Jerusalem, in the second month, began Zerubbabel the son of Shealtiel, and Jeshua the son of Jozadak, and the remnant of their brethren the priests and the Levites, and all they that were come out of the captivity unto Jerusalem; and appointed the Levites, from twenty years old and upward, to set forward the work of the house of the LORD.

9 Then stood Jeshua with his sons and his brethren, Kadmiel and his sons, the sons of Judah, together, to set forward the workmen in the house of God: the sons of Henadad, with their sons and their brethren the Levites.

10 And when the builders laid the foundation of the temple of the LORD, they set the priests in their apparel with trumpets, and the Levites the sons of Asaph with cymbals, to praise the LORD, after the ordinance of David king of Israel.

11 And they sang together by course in praising and giving thanks unto the LORD; because he is good, for his mercy endureth for ever toward Israel. And all the people shouted with a great shout, when they praised the LORD, because the foundation of the house of the LORD was laid.

12 But many of the priests and Levites and chief of the fathers, who were ancient men, that had seen the first house, when the foundation of this house was laid before their eyes, wept with a loud voice; and many shouted aloud for joy:

13 So that the people could not discern the noise of the shout of joy from the noise of the weeping of the people: for the people shouted with a loud shout, and the noise was heard afar off.

KEY VERSE

All the people shouted with a great shout, when they praised the LORD, because the foundation of the house of the LORD was laid. —Ezra 3:11b

GOD'S PEOPLE WORSHIP

Unit 2: Worshipping in Jerusalem Again (Ezra)

LESSONS 5–9

LESSON AIMS

After participating in this lesson, each student will be able to:

1. Relate basic details regarding the laying of the foundation of the temple.

2. Summarize the role and importance of Zerubbabel.

3. Make a commitment to be influential in helping others worship the Lord sincerely and faithfully.

LESSON OUTLINE

Introduction
  A. His First Bridge
  B. Lesson Background
 I. Laying the Foundation (EZRA 3:8, 9)
  A. Appropriate Time (v. 8a)
  B. Able Leaders (vv. 8b, 9)
    Getting the Foundation Right
II. Celebrating the Completion (EZRA 3:10, 11)
  A. Preparing (v. 10)
  B. Praising and Giving Thanks (v. 11)
III. Contrasting the Responses (EZRA 3:12, 13)
  A. Mixed Emotions (v. 12)
    Tears of What?
  B. Far-reaching Sounds (v. 13)
Conclusion
  A. Whatever It Takes!
  B. Prayer
  C. Thought to Remember

Introduction

A. His First Bridge

He was a college student, and his summer job became a learning experience. He had been accepted as a worker for a highway department, and he was assigned to one of the bridge crews. One day, the men of the crew traveled to the site of the bridge that they were ready to build. With the old structure already removed, the men made their way down the banks to the stream bed. The work was ready to begin—way down there—and the goal was to build a bridge that would be about 15 feet above them—way up there!

The young man simply did as he was instructed. The bridge floor would be poured "up there" some day, but first there was much work to be done below the surface of the ground. It was essential to have a solid foundation that would provide support for the bridge. Such a foundation included two abutments anchored deep in the ground and "wings" that deflected water away from the abutments and back into the streambed.

When the bridge was finished, the student began to understand the reasons behind all the preliminary work. The necessity of the early work "down there" made sense; the stability of the new structure depended on the foundation—all the work in the ground that had to be completed before the superstructure could be built.

Today's text takes us back to certain events surrounding a foundation that was laid centuries before the bridge in this story.

B. Lesson Background

One word summarizes the reason why the nation of Judah had to experience captivity in Babylon. The word is *disobedience*! One word is also behind what led to their disobedience. That word is *idolatry,* for the people had had a fascination with it. The Israelites seemed determined to want a pluralistic religion that involved the one true God alongside other, fictitious gods.

In Moses' farewell addresses, he warned the nation of the negative consequences for disobedience: idolatry would cause them to be scattered among the nations. From those distant places

Restoring the Temple

they would decide to seek the Lord (Deuteronomy 4:25-30; 30:1-3), and this is what they did. While in Babylon, almost 900 miles from home, the captives finally realized that God meant what He said. The temple had been destroyed, and they knew the reason was their disobedience to God.

The prophets had said that there would be a return, and many people were ready to make the trip back. When they returned, they planned to build a new temple. It might not be as glorious as the one that Solomon had built, but they knew that acceptable worship for them could be complete only by having a temple that they would dedicate to God. It is generally true that it took the Babylonian captivity to cure the people of idolatry. There would be minor exceptions, but it was never again the problem it once was.

I. Laying the Foundation
(EZRA 3:8, 9)

A. Appropriate Time (v. 8a)

8a. Now in the second year of their coming unto the house of God at Jerusalem, in the second month.

Throughout the process of renewal of worship in Jerusalem, it is evident that there are parallels between the temple that was completed by Solomon and its replacement. The month for the construction to begin is the same for both the first and the second temples—*the second month* of the Hebrew calendar (1 Kings 6:1). That corresponds to late April and early May. The rainy season is ending, and it is an excellent time to begin work on the foundation.

The previous lesson described the construction of the new altar of burnt offerings. It was completed in order to be used on the first day of the seventh month (September/October). A period of seven months thus has passed since that time.

During the interval, the leaders make arrangements for securing building materials for the temple itself. Some items, such as the marble, are available in the surrounding areas. Any wood from previous constructions in Jerusalem was burned when the Babylonians destroyed Jerusalem in 586 BC (2 Kings 25:8, 9) or has otherwise

perished by exposure to the elements over several decades. Thus more wood has to be procured, so cedar is ordered from Tyre (Ezra 3:7, last week's lesson). Wood will be used in every fourth layer of the temple: three layers of stone and then one of wood (Ezra 6:4). For the time being, however, the emphasis is the foundation.

The fact that it is *the second year* since Ezra's group arrived from Babylon has significance. The people had arrived in the fifth month (July/August) of the previous year (Ezra 7:8), which had allowed time for sowing of grain. By the time of the second month of *the second year of their coming unto the house of God at Jerusalem,* the reaping has already started in the Jordan valley, where it is warmer. Such reaping begins there in the first month (March/April). Workers not involved in construction thus can take care of the task of supplying food for those who work on the foundation.

B. Able Leaders (vv. 8b, 9)

8b. Began Zerubbabel the son of Shealtiel, and Jeshua the son of Jozadak, and the remnant of their brethren the priests and the Levites, and all they that were come out of the captivity unto Jerusalem; and appointed the Levites, from twenty years old and upward, to set forward the work of the house of the LORD.

We offered introductory remarks on both Zerubbabel and Jeshua (also called Joshua) in last week's lesson in commentary on Ezra 3:2, so that information need not be repeated here. Probing a bit deeper now allows us to see additional interesting connections.

Zerubbabel the son of Shealtiel is a descendant of David, the king over Israel from 1010 to 970 BC. The easiest place to confirm Zerubbabel's place in the lineage of David (and Jesus) is Matthew 1:12, 13, where the spelling is a bit different. The prophet Nathan had told King David that one of David's descendants would build a house for the name of God (2 Samuel 7:12, 13); the "for ever" factor in that prophecy tends to show that the ultimate fulfillment is in Jesus. Solomon, a son of David, was the one who oversaw the building of the first temple; now another descendant of David is one of the leaders overseeing the construction of the second.

Jeshua the son of Jozadak is the high priest at this time (see Haggai 1:1). Thus it is fitting that he provides religious oversight to this project. His grandfather was Seraiah (1 Chronicles 6:14, 15); that man was the high priest when the forces of Nebuchadnezzar destroyed Jerusalem. Seraiah was taken to Riblah, about 65 miles north of Damascus, where he was executed (2 Kings 25:18-21). But family members made the journey to Babylon.

It was at Riblah that a prophecy of Ezekiel began to be fulfilled. He had prophesied that the prince of Judah would be taken to Babylon, but he would not see it (Ezekiel 12:13). That "prince" was Zedekiah, the last king of Judah. Zedekiah, a relative of Zerubbabel, had to watch the execution of his sons. Then he was blinded before being taken to Babylon (2 Kings 25:7).

Zerubbabel and Jeshua surely know these accounts about their ancestors. We surmise that this shared history serves as a bond as they work together in the construction of the new temple that Cyrus has authorized (Ezra 1:1-4).

Ezra 2:40-42 records that there are 341 Levites among the people who have returned from Babylon. From the wilderness wanderings under Moses (Numbers 4:46, 47) to the time of Jeshua (Joshua), the ages at which Levites begin to serve have varied from 30 to 25 to 20, depending on the situation at the time (see Numbers 4:46, 47; 8:24; 1 Chronicles 23:24-27). In this particular case, it is those Levites who are at least *twenty years old* who serve as supervisors *(set forward)* for the work on the temple.

> **What Do You Think?**
> Are there any offices or ministry tasks that a church should set "minimum age limits" for? Why, or why not?
> *Talking Points for Your Discussion*
> - Elder
> - Deacon
> - Teacher
> - Other

9. Then stood Jeshua with his sons and his brethren, Kadmiel and his sons, the sons of Judah, together, to set forward the workmen in the house of God: the sons of Henadad, with their sons and their brethren the Levites.

The names *Kadmiel* and *Judah* reflect the listing of Levites in Ezra 2:40, with a minor difference. The name *Judah* is used in the *King James Version* in the verse before us, but in Ezra 2:40 it is given as *Hodaviah*. The words are very similar in the original Hebrew, and the difference is not of any consequence; the references are the same. One of *the sons of Henadad* is named in Nehemiah 3:18, 24; 10:9.

The important thing is that this is a team effort that demands cooperation and coordination. It seems reasonable that men with experience in such matters are the ones who are prompted by God to leave Babylon so they can contribute their talents in building the temple in Jerusalem (Ezra 1:5; compare Exodus 35:30–36:1).

> **What Do You Think?**
> Under what circumstances, if any, should participants in various projects be honored by name?
> *Talking Points for Your Discussion*
> - Matthew 10:2, 3
> - John 3:30
> - 1 Corinthians 3:5-9
> - Philippians 2:25-30
> - 1 Timothy 5:17
> - Philemon 1, 2, 23, 24

❧ GETTING THE FOUNDATION RIGHT ❧

Visitors to Dawson City in Canada's Yukon Territory are often surprised by what they see: hundred-year-old houses that have sunk into the ground, tilted at odd angles. Visitors are also surprised to see that the modern homes in Dawson City are built *above* the ground, with space beneath that is open to the frigid elements. Shouldn't houses in this kind of climate be built right on the ground so that the bottom floors can be sealed off from the cold wind?

The problem here is that the "ground" is actually permafrost, which never melts. Never, that is, unless the heat from a building above it causes melting. This realization makes it clear why the old buildings have tilted and why the newer buildings have that space beneath them for frigid air to flow through.

Knowledge of circumstances and environment determines what the nature of the foundation must be. In the case of the rebuilt foundation of the temple, the issue was not just that of location, design, qualified craftsmen, and proper construction materials. It was also an issue of spiritual preparedness. This has important implications for the advancement of the gospel today. See 1 Corinthians 3:10-15. —C. R. B.

II. Celebrating the Completion
(EZRA 3:10, 11)

A. Preparing (v. 10)

10. And when the builders laid the foundation of the temple of the LORD, they set the priests in their apparel with trumpets, and the Levites the sons of Asaph with cymbals, to praise the LORD, after the ordinance of David king of Israel.

The biblical accounts often compress descriptions of events into just a few words. We see that here as the narrative moves immediately from the preparations for laying the foundation to the completed project. Nothing is said about the depth, dimensions, or other factors that are involved in having a solid, level foundation.

> **What Do You Think?**
> What experiences have you had (good or bad) that have helped you appreciate the importance of a good foundation?
> *Talking Points for Your Discussion*
> - Concerning buildings
> - Concerning financial issues
> - Concerning spiritual issues (Luke 6:46-49; 1 Corinthians 3:10-15; etc.)

The people of the Middle East like to celebrate, and noise plays a part. The completion of the foundation is cause for a noisy celebration! But we can be certain that God hears when His people praise Him sincerely, regardless of the decibel level that results.

The fact that it is the priests who sound trumpets matches what happened at the dedication of the first temple (see 2 Chronicles 5:12). At that time, 120 priests with trumpets stood on the east side of the altar. Priests often wear white robes, so it would be an impressive sight.

The reference to *the sons of Asaph with cymbals* also brings a certain nostalgia. When David celebrated the moving of the ark of the covenant to Jerusalem in about 1000 BC, it was Asaph who played the cymbals (1 Chronicles 16:5). He was still playing them when the first temple was dedicated in 959 BC (2 Chronicles 5:12), about 425 years before the event being described here. It is interesting that Asaph's descendants are maintaining this family talent! (Some think, however, that the designation *sons of Asaph* is a title for the musicians, not a reference to genealogy.)

B. Praising and Giving Thanks (v. 11)

11. And they sang together by course in praising and giving thanks unto the LORD; because he is good, for his mercy endureth for ever toward Israel. And all the people shouted with a great shout, when they praised the LORD, because the foundation of the house of the LORD was laid.

This is a great day for the Jews who have made the trip from Babylon! They can see their dreams being fulfilled one step at a time. The altar of burnt offerings was put into use the previous fall (last week's lesson), and now *the foundation of the house of the Lord* is finished.

The praise *he is good, for his mercy endureth for ever toward Israel* is very similar to what was voiced on two earlier occasions. One was when the ark of the covenant was brought into Jerusalem (1 Chronicles 16:34); the other was at the dedication of the first temple (2 Chronicles 5:13).

The fulfillment of a prophecy by Jeremiah should also be mentioned. That prophet was a prisoner in the days just before the Babylonians destroyed Jerusalem (Jeremiah 33:1). The Lord assured him that even though the city would become desolate, a time would come when praises again would be heard; words very similar to those in the verse before us are given in Jeremiah 33:11.

The type of singing that is being done is usually thought to be antiphonal—when one choir sings and another choir answers (compare Deuteronomy 11:29; Joshua 8:33). The word translated *sang* can take the meaning "to answer" in this regard. This is indicated by the phrase *by course*. Psalm 136 is often cited as demonstrating this type of singing, for the same refrain occurs in all 26 verses.

III. Contrasting the Responses
(EZRA 3:12, 13)
A. Mixed Emotions (v. 12)

12. But many of the priests and Levites and chief of the fathers, who were ancient men, that had seen the first house, when the foundation of this house was laid before their eyes, wept with a loud voice; and many shouted aloud for joy.

There are other loud expressions at this special celebration. The differing emotional responses to the same situation are shaped by previous experiences. The text indicates that the difference in the two reactions is that of age.

Jerusalem was destroyed in 586 BC, and it is now about 50 years later. This means that some of the older people present had seen the original temple before they were taken from Jerusalem. It is usually suggested that their weeping indicates that they are mentally comparing the foundation of the new temple with the previous one, and they

Visual for Lesson 6. *Point to this visual as you ask, "What elements are necessary for ensuring that a Christian's spiritual foundation is strong?"*

realize that the new temple will not have the same splendor as what they had seen in their youth; thus their tears are those of grief.

The text, however, does not explain why they are weeping, and another option must be considered. The older people do indeed have painful memories of the long siege that ended in 586 BC. They had endured an unpleasant trip to Babylon, but in old age have returned to Jerusalem with hopeful anticipation. They are seeing the temple and the city of David begin to rise again. Thus some propose that the tears may be those of joy and gratitude. However, the contrast we will see in verse 13 seems to imply that this weeping is due to something other than joy.

❧ TEARS OF WHAT? ❧

People shed tears for a variety of reasons, and different emotions may present themselves at the same event. At weddings, the bride may shed tears of joy for the new life she sees ahead, while her parents weep because they are "losing" a daughter. At a memorial service, children may weep in sadness because a beloved grandparent has been taken from them, while adults in attendance shed tears of relief because the lengthy suffering of the deceased is finally over and agony is swallowed up in the victory of Christ's resurrection.

But things get even more complicated when we realize that a person's shedding of tears may be due to the presence of two or more conflicting emotions within him or her at the same time! The tears of the bride's parents may be due both to the emotions of loss and of shared joy. A person attending a funeral may shed tears of grief that are comingled with tears of joy of Christ's triumph over death.

Even though "big boys don't cry" (as the saying goes), some aged men who saw the beginnings of the temple's reconstruction freely expressed their emotions with tears, whatever emotions might have been behind those tears. God is the one who has given us the ability to shed tears, and He respects our weeping. Even so, we recall Jesus' words, "Blessed are ye that weep now: for ye shall laugh" (Luke 6:21).   —C. R. B.

B. Far-reaching Sounds (v. 13)

13. So that the people could not discern the noise of the shout of joy from the noise of the weeping of the people: for the people shouted with a loud shout, and the noise was heard afar off.

Which sound is more pleasing to God—a joyful celebration or a loud wailing? The answer to this question, as to many questions, is in two words: *it depends.* The key factor is the heart of the person. The emotion being expressed must be sincere, and not just an imitation of what others are doing.

God is pleased with the broken, muffled sob of a contrite heart when sincere repentance occurs (Psalm 51:17). There may be a tear-stained face when some partake of the Lord's Supper. Meditation about the agony that Christ endured moves some to have eyes that are moist. "Blended worship" includes more than different types of music; it may include sounds of joy mixed with those of sorrow. There is "a time to weep, and a time to laugh" (Ecclesiastes 3:4).

HOW TO SAY IT

Asaph	*Ay*-saff.
Haggai	*Hag*-eye or *Hag*-ay-eye.
Henadad	*Hen*-uh-dad.
Hodaviah	*Hoe*-duh-***vie***-uh.
Jozadak	*Joz*-uh-dak.
Kadmiel	*Cad*-mih-el.
Levites	*Lee*-vites.
Nebuchadnezzar	*Neb*-yuh-kud-***nez***-er.
Seraiah	Se-*ray*-yuh or Se-*rye*-uh.
Shealtiel	She-*al*-tee-el.
Zerubbabel	Zeh-*rub*-uh-bul.

What Do You Think?
When have you observed mixed emotions within the same worship event? Why did that happen?
Talking Points for Your Discussion
- A special worship service that occurs yearly
- A weekly worship service
- A one-time observance
- Other

The blended sounds of weeping, shouting, and even louder shouting reverberate eastward to the Mount of Olives and to the south and north along the Kidron Valley. People of ancient times are not bombarded by the kinds of loud noises of today—power equipment, electronically amplified sound, etc. Loud sounds for them are trumpets, waterfalls, the excitement of large crowds, etc. This time the loudness is that of thousands of people rejoicing for the visible progress that has been made to have a temple again.

Even so, about 20 years will pass before the temple is actually completed. Opposition will result in a work stoppage (Ezra 4:1-5, 24) followed by spiritual lethargy. The temple will be built when God provides a new stimulus in the preaching of two prophets, Haggai and Zechariah (Ezra 5:1, 2).

Conclusion

A. Whatever It Takes!

The Israelites who made the journey from Babylon were willing to give up houses, friends, and family—whatever it took to restore genuine worship in Jerusalem. It would have been easier to remain in Babylon, as so many other Jewish exiles did. But those who returned felt compelled to do so. Are we as willing to leave our comfort zones for God's purposes?

B. Prayer

Heavenly Father, may the joys and sorrows in my life always be associated with dedication to You. In the name of the Christ, amen.

C. Thought to Remember

Go where God leads you—and rejoice as you do!

INVOLVEMENT LEARNING

Some of the activities below are also found in the helpful student book, Adult Bible Class.
Don't forget to download the free reproducible page from www.standardlesson.com to enhance your lesson!

Into the Lesson

To highlight the "building blocks" nature of today's text, hand each learner a child's alphabet block as he or she arrives. You will use these blocks in the Into the Word segment below in addition to their initial curiosity value. You might be able to borrow such blocks from someone who has young children or from a preschool classroom in your church (ask permission).

Alternatively, you may know someone who enjoys woodworking who would be happy to cut two-inch square blocks from available scrap; it's fine if the resulting blocks are somewhat crude, and you can add your own letters and numerals with markers. (If all else fails, you can create the blocks from construction paper.)

Ask if anyone has any memories of using alphabet blocks as a child. You also can invite a few stories about children and grandchildren using such blocks, but don't let this segment drag out. Say, "Today we look at how the returning exiles applied the ABCs of building to the tasks for which they had returned."

Into the Word

Read the lesson text, Ezra 3:8-13, aloud. Then begin calling out the following letters: *A, B, C, D, F, G, H, I, J, K, L, N, P, S, T.* (You will need to ensure that each letter occurs on at least one of the blocks you have distributed; if your class is smaller, you may need to give learners two or more blocks each.) As you call out a letter, ask, "Who has this one?" When a learner responds, ask, "How does your letter relate to today's text?" More than one response will be appropriate for some letters. For those, either ask for a second or third response, or call the letter again later. At each response, you will have an opportunity to ask discussion questions or offer commentary.

For example, if someone notes *Asaph* for the letter *A,* you could ask, "How do we relate Asaph's ministry in 1 Chronicles 16:5 and 2 Chronicles 5:12 to the occasion of our text?" (See the lesson commentary for help with this.) You will need to plan out your questions in advance for possible responses.

Here is a list of potential responses, although your learners may note others: *A*—Asaph (v. 10); *B*—builders (v. 10), brethren (vv. 8-10); *C*—cymbals (v. 10); *D*—discern (v. 13); *F*—foundation (vv. 10-12); *G*—God (vv. 8, 9), good (v. 11); *H*—Henadad (v. 9), house (vv. 8, 9, 11, 12); *I*—Israel (vv. 10, 11); *J*—Jeshua (vv. 8, 9), Jerusalem (v. 8), Jozadak (v. 8), joy (vv. 12, 13); *K*—king (v. 10), Kadmiel (v. 9); *L*—Levites (vv. 8-10, 12); *N*—noise (v. 13); *P*—priests (vv. 8, 10, 12), praise (vv. 10, 11); *S*—shout (vv. 11-13), second month/year (v. 8); *T*—temple (v. 10).

Option. At this point, have learners complete the "Building Blocks" activity from the reproducible page, which you can download. This exercise can serve as a bridge to the Into Life segment since it calls for application.

Into Life

Say, "Worship can become 'self-contained' in both positive and negative senses. It is a good thing that worship is intensely personal. But it is a bad thing when our worship has no impact on others around us. How can we worship in a manner that will influence others positively in their own worship?"

Jot responses on the board. Do not allow the discussion to become critical of how worship services are conducted at your church; keep the discussion focused on that of personal witness.

Option: Have learners complete the "Joy and Weeping, Spirit and Truth" exercise from the reproducible page. This can be a small-group exercise. Keep the proposals positive ("what we could do") so the discussion does not become a gripe session ("what we should stop doing").

DEDICATING THE TEMPLE

DEVOTIONAL READING: Ezra 5:1-5
BACKGROUND SCRIPTURE: Ezra 6

EZRA 6:13-22

13 Then Tatnai, governor on this side the river, Shetharboznai, and their companions, according to that which Darius the king had sent, so they did speedily.

14 And the elders of the Jews builded, and they prospered through the prophesying of Haggai the prophet and Zechariah the son of Iddo. And they builded, and finished it, according to the commandment of the God of Israel, and according to the commandment of Cyrus, and Darius, and Artaxerxes king of Persia.

15 And this house was finished on the third day of the month Adar, which was in the sixth year of the reign of Darius the king.

16 And the children of Israel, the priests, and the Levites, and the rest of the children of the captivity, kept the dedication of this house of God with joy.

17 And offered at the dedication of this house of God an hundred bullocks, two hundred rams, four hundred lambs; and for a sin offering for all Israel, twelve he goats, according to the number of the tribes of Israel.

18 And they set the priests in their divisions, and the Levites in their courses, for the service of God, which is at Jerusalem; as it is written in the book of Moses.

19 And the children of the captivity kept the passover upon the fourteenth day of the first month.

20 For the priests and the Levites were purified together, all of them were pure, and killed the passover for all the children of the captivity, and for their brethren the priests, and for themselves.

21 And the children of Israel, which were come again out of captivity, and all such as had separated themselves unto them from the filthiness of the heathen of the land, to seek the LORD God of Israel, did eat,

22 And kept the feast of unleavened bread seven days with joy: for the LORD had made them joyful, and turned the heart of the king of Assyria unto them, to strengthen their hands in the work of the house of God, the God of Israel.

KEY VERSE

The children of Israel, the priests, and the Levites, and the rest of the children of the captivity, kept the dedication of this house of God with joy. —**Ezra 6:16**

GOD'S PEOPLE
WORSHIP

Unit 2: Worshipping in Jerusalem Again (Ezra)

LESSON AIMS

After participating in this lesson, each student will be able to:

1. Describe the sequence of events in the completion and dedication of the second temple.

2. Compare and contrast the importance of the temple with the importance of church buildings today.

3. Dedicate himself or herself, as the temple of the Holy Spirit, to honoring God as sincerely as did the former exiles in Ezra 6 in dedicating the physical temple.

LESSON OUTLINE

Introduction
 A. The Importance of Places
 B. Lesson Background
 I. Decree Obeyed (Ezra 6:13-15)
 A. Diligence of the Officials (v. 13)
 B. Determination in Building (v. 14)
 C. Date of Completion (v. 15)
 II. Temple Dedicated (Ezra 6:16-18)
 A. Occasion for Joy (v. 16)
 B. Offering of Sacrifices (v. 17)
 Willing to Sacrifice
 C. Offices of Priests and Levites (v. 18)
 III. Passover Kept (Ezra 6:19-22)
 A. Celebration (v. 19)
 B. Purification (v. 20)
 C. Participation (v. 21)
 Purity Priority?
 D. Realization (v. 22)
Conclusion
 A. Real Joy
 B. Prayer
 C. Thought to Remember

Introduction

A. The Importance of Places

She was a stranger. She came to the door and introduced herself with an unusual request: she wanted to know if it would be all right if she came into the house just to see it again. She explained that she had lived there when she was a little girl and that her father had built the garage that was next to the house. The home owner's first impulse was to think she might have ulterior motives, but she seemed genuine. Permission was granted. She shared her memories of events in the house, and it was a rewarding experience both for her and the current occupants.

It has been said that you cannot go back to a place and expect it to be the same. That is true, but you can return and have your mind flood with memories. The place may have changed from a house to a parking lot, from a school to an office building, from a rural setting to a sprawling subdivision, from a church building where your wedding took place to a retail business. The place may not be the same, but the memories still return.

The lesson today continues the account of people who bravely made the journey to a very special place—Jerusalem. It was in Jerusalem where the temple had been built, and it was only there that they could obey many of the ordinances given by Moses. Jerusalem was indeed a very special place!

B. Lesson Background

We must know two things in order to interpret the book of Ezra correctly. The first is that the book has two major parts: chapters 1–6 and chapters 7–10. The first section describes the events associated with the first return from Babylon to Jerusalem. The book begins with the decree of Cyrus that permitted the return, and this decree was perhaps given in the spring of 538 BC.

Ezra 6 concludes the first section as it describes the completion of the temple 23 years later. The final four chapters of the book of Ezra provide information about a second return to Jerusalem that Ezra himself led in about 458 BC. Events associated with this second return are subjects of the next two lessons.

The second important factor for understanding the book of Ezra is to recognize that much of Ezra 4 is a parenthesis. Ezra 4:1-5 tells how opposition to the building efforts in Jerusalem became very intense. The result was that the rebuilding of the temple came to a halt. The parenthesis of Ezra 4:6-23 indicates the continuation of this hostility, primarily during the reigns of two future kings: Ahasuerus (also known as Xerxes, reigned 485–465 BC) and his son Artaxerxes (reigned 465–425 BC). Ahasuerus was the king who became the husband of Esther. Artaxerxes was the Persian king in the days of both Ezra and Nehemiah. After the parenthesis, the narrative returns to the time of Darius (reigned 522–486 BC).

Something special happened on August 29, 520 BC: the Lord sent a message of rebuke and challenge through Haggai the prophet (Haggai 1:1). "Is it time for you, O ye, to dwell in your ceiled houses, and this house lie waste?" (1:4). While making sure their own houses were comfortable, the people were ignoring the sad state of God's temple! The message produced positive and almost immediate results. Slightly over three weeks later, on September 21, the work on the temple began again (1:14, 15).

In February of 519 BC, another prophet provided additional encouragement with these words: "My house shall be built" (Zechariah 1:7, 16). Both Haggai and Zechariah are cited in Ezra 5:1, 2 as being the prophets who stimulated Jeshua

and Zerubbabel to resume their leadership roles in completing the house of God.

Political reactions also occurred, and the Jews heard from Tatnai, the regional governor (Ezra 5:3). He took a reasonable approach in that he did not compel the Jews to stop building while he waited for an answer to his question in a letter to King Darius: Was it true that King Cyrus had authorized the building of the temple as the Jews claimed (5:7-17)?

A copy of the decree of Cyrus was found (Ezra 6:1, 2), and the issue was settled: the Jews had the right to build the temple (6:3-5). In a sternly worded reply, King Darius said that not only could the Jews continue to build, but also that supplies and sacrifices for the God of Heaven were to be provided from the Persian treasury (6:6-10). Anyone who violated the royal decree was to suffer severe consequences (6:11). That leads us to the reactions to the decree.

I. Decree Obeyed
(EZRA 6:13-15)

A. Diligence of the Officials (v. 13)

13. Then Tatnai, governor on this side the river, Shetharboznai, and their companions, according to that which Darius the king had sent, so they did speedily.

A Babylonian document has been found that affirms that a certain Tattennu is a governor at the time in the region that is cited here. The document seems to indicate that he is an assistant to the satrap of a larger area, and this governor may have his headquarters in Damascus. Shetharboznai probably functions as his recorder or secretary. The river in view in the phrase *this side the river* is the Euphrates.

Disobedience to the king will bring a rapid end to any political career (if not to one's life), so the officials act immediately to comply. Although not stated, we can imagine the Jews briefly celebrating when this good news comes.

B. Determination in Building (v. 14)

14. And the elders of the Jews builded, and they prospered through the prophesying of

HOW TO SAY IT

Ahasuerus	Uh-haz-you-*ee*-rus.
Artaxerxes	Are-tuh-*zerk*-seez.
Cyrus	*Sigh*-russ.
Darius	Duh-*rye*-us.
Euphrates	You-*fray*-teez.
Haggai	*Hag*-eye or *Hag*-ay-eye.
Hezekiah	Hez-ih-*kye*-uh.
Jeshua	*Jesh*-you-uh.
Shetharboznai	She-thar-*boz*-nye.
Tatnai	*Tat*-nye or *Tat*-eh-nye.
Xerxes	*Zerk*-seez.
Zechariah	Zek-uh-*rye*-uh.
Zerubbabel	Zeh-*rub*-uh-bul.

Haggai the prophet and Zechariah the son of Iddo. And they builded, and finished it, according to the commandment of the God of Israel, and according to the commandment of Cyrus, and Darius, and Artaxerxes king of Persia.

The elders of the Jews have much to do as they oversee the reconstructions. Ezra 6:4 states that there are to be "three rows of great stones, and a row of new timber" in the design. The purpose of the wood in this regard is not clear. It may provide a means to attach interior paneling. Another possibility is that it provides "flex" so that mild earthquakes will have minimal effects.

The Lesson Background explains the roles of the prophets Haggai and Zechariah. In addition, the names of three Persian monarchs are cited. The first two are easy to explain: Cyrus is the one who gave the original mandate, and Darius, one of his successors, ordered the rebuilding to continue (again, see the Lesson Background).

The fact that *Artaxerxes* is included seems strange, for he will not become the king until about 56 years later. One suggestion is that Ezra has the "big picture" in mind. Just as he included Artaxerxes in chapter 4, where opposition is described, so Ezra looks ahead to the time of his (Ezra's) writing of this book, when Artaxerxes is reigning. Ezra's purpose under this theory is to commend Artaxerxes for giving permission for Ezra to lead his own return to Jerusalem (458 BC) with large gifts for a completed temple (see the next two lessons).

Ezra 6:16 is the key verse for this lesson, but one scholar has suggested that Ezra 6:14 is the key verse for the entire book. This verse shows that God is the primary source for the command to build, but also that pagan kings are used to fulfill God's purposes.

C. Date of Completion (v. 15)

15. And this house was finished on the third day of the month Adar, which was in the sixth year of the reign of Darius the king.

The construction of a building as large as the temple takes time. Older sources interpret the year of completion as being 516 BC, but *the third day*

of the month Adar, . . . in the sixth year of the reign of Darius is generally agreed now to be March 12, 515 BC. That is less than five years since construction resumed on September 21, 520 BC (Haggai 1:14, 15; see the Lesson Background). The completion date is determined to be a Sabbath, and the joyous celebration that follows is looked upon as very appropriate for a day of rest.

By comparison, the temple of Solomon took seven years to build (1 Kings 6:38). The details of the furnishings inside or outside *this house* (the second temple) are not given. This is in contrast with the detailed descriptions that are provided for the furnishings of the first temple in the days of Solomon (1 Kings 6, 7).

II. Temple Dedicated
(EZRA 6:16-18)
A. Occasion for Joy (v. 16)

16. And the children of Israel, the priests, and the Levites, and the rest of the children of the captivity, kept the dedication of this house of God with joy.

The *dedication of this house of God* is a joyous occasion for all the people of Israel! The ones who left Babylon to come back had first dedicated themselves to endure the travel and toil. Things have not gone just as they had wished, but the wait is worth it.

The celebration when the foundation was laid some two decades prior included the sounds of weeping (Ezra 3:12, 13, last week's lesson). Nothing is said about any such emotion this time, but there are probably some who have moments of quiet reflection about family members who have died in the years since the return, family members who did not live to see this milestone.

Dedicating the Temple

What Do You Think?

How can dedicating a physical building be of spiritual benefit today?

Talking Points for Your Discussion

- For adults
- For children
- For posterity
- For witness to unbelievers

B. Offering of Sacrifices (v. 17)

17. And offered at the dedication of this house of God an hundred bullocks, two hundred rams, four hundred lambs; and for a sin offering for all Israel, twelve he goats, according to the number of the tribes of Israel.

Most of the people who have returned from exile are from the tribes of Judah and Benjamin, but it's reasonable to assume that people from the other 10 tribes of Israel are also in the group. Thus the sacrifice of *a sin offering for all Israel, twelve he goats.*

Most of the animals sacrificed are peace offerings (Leviticus 3, 7:11-14). Most of the flesh of the animals is used for food in these situations in a feast or picnic atmosphere (7:15, 16). It takes much to feed all the people who have returned (almost 50,000), and that number probably has increased in the years that have passed.

It is customary to contrast the number of animals for this dedication with the number used when Solomon dedicated the first temple (1 Kings 8:63). The difference is easily explained: there were more people present at the earlier event (8:65), which took place in 959 BC.

❧ WILLING TO SACRIFICE ❧

A nation's war memorials honor those who have made the ultimate sacrifice in service to their country. But reactions to these memorials can differ depending on the nature of the conflict in which the sacrifices were made. World War II memorials, for example, may evoke thoughts that the lives sacrificed were "for a good cause." Frequently drawing an opposite reaction is the Vietnam Veterans Memorial in Washington, D.C.

Visitors who view the names of the nearly 60,000 honored dead inscribed there may think, "What a tragedy that our leaders sacrificed these lives in such a questionable endeavor!"

God's people sacrificed established homes and livelihoods to be able to return to Jerusalem after the exile. They sacrificed still more to dedicate the rebuilt temple, as the verse above reveals. Unlike the tragic waste of lives, homes, and livelihoods of 586 BC, the various sacrifices of 515 BC were for the best cause possible: renewal of proper worship of the one true God as He had prescribed.

Today, animal sacrifices are no longer necessary because God himself has provided the ultimate sacrifice in the life of His Son (Hebrews 9:11–10:18). Even so, Christians are called to make certain sacrifices (see Luke 18:28-30). The nature of our "good cause" is never in doubt, but what about our willingness to make sacrifices for it?   —C. R. B.

C. Offices of Priests and Levites (v. 18)

18. And they set the priests in their divisions, and the Levites in their courses, for the service of God, which is at Jerusalem; as it is written in the book of Moses.

We must remember that the ultimate goal is not to erect a building, but to serve God as He has directed. This requires many people for the multiple tasks involved. Moses was the one who first made distinctions between the duties of the

Visual for Lesson 7. *Point to this visual as you ask, "What connections do you see between Ezra 6:16 and 2 Corinthians 6:16, if any? Why?"*

priests and Levites (see Numbers 18). The priesthood at that time consisted of only Aaron and his sons. The number of priests grew, and 400 years later it was David who organized both groups into rotating divisions so that everyone had the privilege of serving God at the temple (1 Chronicles 23–26). We recall that all priests are Levites, but not all Levites are priests.

What Do You Think?

What benefits and challenges are there in using a "rotation system" for teachers in the church?

Talking Points for Your Discussion
- Consistent leadership vs. preventing burnout
- Experience vs. involving more people
- Recruiting "lifers" vs. recruiting for short-term service

III. Passover Kept
(Ezra 6:19-22)
A. Celebration (v. 19)

19. And the children of the captivity kept the passover upon the fourteenth day of the first month.

The date assigned to this event is April 21, 515 BC, so several weeks have passed since the dedication. Passover was first observed on the night that the Israelites left Egypt in about 1446 BC. The references to Passover in the Old Testament after that memorable night are associated with special events or covenant renewals. Of special significance in the New Testament is the fact that Jesus and the apostles observe Passover on the night before Jesus' crucifixion. Christ is referred to as "our passover" in 1 Corinthians 5:7.

What Do You Think?

What annual celebrations could your church hold to give the members a sense of connection with their ancestors in the faith?

Talking Points for Your Discussion
- "Our First Worship Service" remembrance day
- "Laying the Foundation" remembrance day
- "Mortgage Burning" remembrance day
- Other

B. Purification (v. 20)

20. For the priests and the Levites were purified together, all of them were pure, and killed the passover for all the children of the captivity, and for their brethren the priests, and for themselves.

Ritual purification ordinarily involves sexual abstinence, cleansing the body, and washing clothing (Exodus 19:10, 14, 15; Leviticus 16:28). Following revival, the observance of the Passover that Hezekiah initiated just before 700 BC had to be postponed to the second month because there were not enough priests who were ritually pure in the first month (2 Chronicles 30:1-3). Moses did not specify that Levites had to be the ones to kill the Passover animals. But at the time of the revival in Hezekiah's day, Levites were to kill the animals for anyone who was unclean (30:17).

What Do You Think?

What are some "purity issues" that we should address to help us prepare for worship? Where do Christians need the most help in this regard?

Talking Points for Your Discussion
- Matthew 5:8
- Titus 1:15, 16
- James 1:27
- 1 John 3:3
- Other

C. Participation (v. 21)

21. And the children of Israel, which were come again out of captivity, and all such as had separated themselves unto them from the filthiness of the heathen of the land, to seek the LORD God of Israel, did eat.

Two groups of people are mentioned as participating in this Passover: (1) those who had made the journey from Babylon to Jerusalem and (2) the people of the area who decide to separate themselves from the unclean pagan customs in which they have been involved. This second group includes the few Jews who had remained in the land, but until now have not been careful to disassociate themselves from the unholy customs of the people around them. The enthusiasm of the

Israelites in recent weeks may be responsible for this second group's desire to return to their roots.

❧ PURITY PRIORITY? ❧

An ample supply of pure water is a luxury in many parts of the world, even in some places in the U.S. Take, for example, the situation of Lake Mead, which serves as a reservoir to supply water for the city of Las Vegas. A combination of drought, evaporation, and increased water usage caused the lake's surface to drop by some 120 feet between the years 2000 and 2010. Some authorities speculate that Lake Mead could dry up by the year 2025, putting Las Vegas in crisis mode.

Various solutions are being implemented. One is called "toilet-to-tap." This involves using high-tech filtration techniques to make the dirty water from a city's sewer system pure enough for human consumption. However, the "yuk factor" of this process usually creates considerable resistance!

Purity was also an issue at the observance of Passover in today's text. But the kind of purity at issue in that instance is what we might call "set-apart-ness" purity as people "separated themselves unto them from the filthiness of the heathen of the land." Modern culture places a high value on purity in the water and food supplies, while moral and ethical purity is given little attention. What message do you see in this for modern Christians?

—C. R. B.

D. Realization (v. 22)

22. And kept the feast of unleavened bread seven days with joy: for the LORD had made them joyful, and turned the heart of the king of Assyria unto them, to strengthen their hands in the work of the house of God, the God of Israel.

The Passover is followed immediately by the seven-day *feast of unleavened bread* (Exodus 12:15-20; Leviticus 23:6). These two essentially are blended together into one observance, and the word *Passover* is used to refer to the entire period of this celebration.

One phrase in this verse may seem strange: *the king of Assyria*. It is now 515 BC, but the infamous Assyrian Empire had collapsed in 609 BC

after its capital city of Nineveh was destroyed in 612 BC. Why then does the author refer to *the king of Assyria* almost 100 years later?

The Assyrians were the first major group to begin the process of taking the people of God away from their land (2 Kings 17:1-23). Given that fact, one suggestion is that the phrase *king of Assyria* is used as a figure to represent others who had oppressed the Israelites in the same way.

It is also true that some kings, when proclaiming their greatness, like to include the names of other regions. To refer to a king of Persia also as king of Assyria therefore is a compliment to him. Even so, the participants realize that ultimate credit belongs to the Lord.

Conclusion
A. Real Joy

Joy is associated with the feasts that Israel kept. *Joy* is listed among the fruit of the Spirit in Galatians 5:22. Paul states in Philippians 4:4 that Christians are to rejoice, and then he repeats it: "Again I say, rejoice." Paul stresses this yet again in 1 Thessalonians 5:16, the shortest verse in the Greek New Testament: "Rejoice evermore!" (In the Greek, this is shorter than the two words "Jesus wept" of John 11:35.)

The dedication of a new building produces joy for the ones who had the vision for it, but there is a greater joy for people in Christ. As expressed in 1 Peter 1:8, we have not seen Jesus Christ, but we love Him and believe Him, and we rejoice "with joy unspeakable and full of glory." The people of Ezra's day built a building with stones; for our part, we "are built up a spiritual house, an holy priesthood, to offer up spiritual sacrifices, acceptable to God by Jesus Christ" (1 Peter 2:5). Rejoice!

B. Prayer

My Father in Heaven, today I am grateful for the people who went before me, who gave of themselves to build my life in Christ so that I can be a living stone for Him. In the name of Jesus, amen.

C. Thought to Remember

Continue to let God build your spiritual house.

INVOLVEMENT LEARNING

Some of the activities below are also found in the helpful student book, Adult Bible Class.
Don't forget to download the free reproducible page from www.standardlesson.com to enhance your lesson!

Into the Lesson

As learners arrive, hand each a self-adhesive name tag reading, "Hi, my name is . . ." or something comparable. Say, "Don't do anything with this right now. We'll use it later."

Recruit a class member to help you with this skit: as class begins, open a bag and pull out small boards, nails, and a hammer. Start nailing the pieces together. After a couple of hammer blows, your fellow actor will jump up and run toward you, saying, "Wait! You can't be building here. Who gave you the authority for this? I'm going straight to our leaders to see if you should be doing this." He or she huffs off angrily.

Look a bit stunned, pausing for dramatic effect. Then turn to the class and say, "This is what happened to the Jews of last week's success story: strong opposition arose to their building project."

Have a good oral reader ready to read the following verses that you have premarked in a Bible. These will serve as a bridge between last week's and this week's study: Ezra 4:1-5, 24; 5:1-6; 6:1-3, 6, 7, 12.

Into the Word

Give each learner a half sheet of paper that is divided into two columns; one column is headed *Good Guy(s)* and the other is headed *Bad Guy(s)*. Have the following 12 names/designations on large flash cards, one each: *Artaxerxes / Cyrus / Darius / Elders of the Jews / Exiles Who Had Returned / Heathen of the Land / Haggai / Levites / Priests / Shetharboznai / Tatnai / Zechariah*. Say, "When I show and say the name of a person or a group, please write the name into the appropriate column on your sheet." Read and show the cards; allow enough time between each for learners to reflect on the choice before you move to the next card.

After all 12 entries are read, go back through the cards, pausing on each one to ask, "How many of you put _____ in the 'good guy' category? in the 'bad guy' category?" What will make for an interesting discussion is the fact that the answer is not always clear cut. For example, one could say that Tatnai and Shetharboznai were "bad guys" for questioning the work on the temple (per Ezra 5:3, 4, 6-10), or they may be considered "good guys" for fully and immediately submitting to the king's orders regarding the Jews (Ezra 6:13).

For some of the entries, a general knowledge of Scripture may influence your learners' views. For example, the elders of the Jews, the Levites, and the priests are often presented in a negative light in the New Testament. Yet all three are presented positively in Ezra 6:14, 16, 18, 20. The returned exiles in general are depicted as "good guys" in Ezra 6:16, 19, 21, 22, although they seem to become "bad guys" when they draw criticism in the books of Haggai and Zechariah. The discussion of how to categorize these individuals and groups will give a thorough look at today's text.

Option. If you wish to highlight the theme of *joy* (Ezra 6:16, 22), at this point have learners complete the "Joyful" activity on the reproducible page, which you can download.

Into Life

Direct learners' attention to the name tag you handed out at the beginning of class. Say, "I have a name I want you to write on your tag. The name is T-E-M-P-L-E," spelling the word letter by letter. Continue: "The apostle Paul wants us to think of ourselves collectively as a temple." Have someone read 1 Corinthians 3:16, 17; discuss. Challenge learners to wear their name tags sometime in the week ahead to elicit opportunities to explain this concept to an inquiring friend or acquaintance.

Option. To enhance this segment of the lesson, distribute copies of the "Dedicated To, Separated From" activity on the reproducible page. Have learners complete it per the instructions.

FASTING AND PRAYING

DEVOTIONAL READING: 2 Chronicles 7:12-18
BACKGROUND SCRIPTURE: Ezra 7:1–8:23

EZRA 7:6-10

6 This Ezra went up from Babylon; and he was a ready scribe in the law of Moses, which the LORD God of Israel had given: and the king granted him all his request, according to the hand of the LORD his God upon him.

7 And there went up some of the children of Israel, and of the priests, and the Levites, and the singers, and the porters, and the Nethinims, unto Jerusalem, in the seventh year of Artaxerxes the king.

8 And he came to Jerusalem in the fifth month, which was in the seventh year of the king.

9 For upon the first day of the first month began he to go up from Babylon, and on the first day of the fifth month came he to Jerusalem, according to the good hand of his God upon him.

10 For Ezra had prepared his heart to seek the law of the LORD, and to do it, and to teach in Israel statutes and judgments.

EZRA 8:21-23

21 Then I proclaimed a fast there, at the river of Ahava, that we might afflict ourselves before our God, to seek of him a right way for us, and for our little ones, and for all our substance.

22 For I was ashamed to require of the king a band of soldiers and horsemen to help us against the enemy in the way: because we had spoken unto the king, saying, The hand of our God is upon all them for good that seek him; but his power and his wrath is against all them that forsake him.

23 So we fasted and besought our God for this: and he was intreated of us.

KEY VERSE

So we fasted and besought our God for this: and he was intreated of us. —**Ezra 8:23**

GOD'S PEOPLE WORSHIP

LESSON AIMS

After participating in this lesson, each student will be able to:

1. Summarize Ezra's qualifications, dedication, and preparations to lead thousands of people from Babylon to Jerusalem.

2. Explain how Ezra's preparation, including the decision not to request protection (Ezra 8:22), is sometimes the model for Christians to follow while Nehemiah's preparation, including the acceptance of protection (Nehemiah 2:9), can also be normative for Christians.

3. Plan and incorporate a time of fasting in an upcoming church or class activity.

LESSON OUTLINE

Introduction

A. Preparing for a Journey

Each person or family has different approaches to packing for a journey. Some people wait until the last minute, then pack quickly. Others begin packing days ahead of time, perhaps using a checklist to ensure that all important items are included. In some families, it is the mother or wife who packs for everyone. In other families, each person is expected to do his or her own packing.

The items packed for family trips change as the years go by and the family matures. The family that once needed to pack infant formula eventually becomes the family that has to make sure that denture cream and batteries for hearing aids are not forgotten. But one issue of preparation should never change, and it is easy to overlook: prayer for the journey! Many families or church groups have a custom of pausing to pray just before a trip begins. Such prayers are often said after everyone is inside a vehicle. Before the car or van is put in motion, a prayer is offered to God that expresses thanks and requests safety.

The lesson for today provides information about what is termed the second return from Babylon to Israel. This return was more than just one of physical relocation. It was also spiritual in nature. Prayer and fasting played a vital role in that regard before the group began to move toward its destination: Jerusalem.

B. Lesson Background

The previous lesson was about the completion of the new temple in Jerusalem, its dedication on March 12, 515 BC, observance of Passover on April 21, and celebration of the Feast of Unleavened Bread that immediately followed Passover. The first section of the book of Ezra comes to an end at this point (see the Lesson Background of last week's lesson).

Ezra 7 begins the second section of the book, and the date is 458 BC (see comments on Ezra 7:7b in this lesson). Thus there is a gap of 57 years, or about two generations, between the end of chapter 6 and the beginning of chapter 7. The Bible offers information in the account of Esther on some things that happened during that period of time. In January 478 BC, Esther became the queen for Ahasuerus (also known as Xerxes), king of the Persian Empire (Esther 2:16). Prior to that, however, three famous battles occurred that the Bible does not discuss. These battles, involving the Persians, are considered very important in the history of western civilization.

The first was the battle at Marathon, where the Athenians and their allies defeated the Persian army of Darius the Great in 490 BC. This is the same Darius who authorized the resumption of construction on the temple in Jerusalem (Ezra 6). This battle demonstrated to the Greeks that the Persians were not invincible, especially if the Greek city-states would unite instead of fighting each other.

The second was the battle at Thermopylae in 480 BC, where the Persians again confronted the Greeks. The six-month banquet of King Ahasuerus described in Esther 1 is often thought to be the planning of the military action against the Greeks that included this battle. The primary motivation for the Persian invasion may have been to avenge the defeat at Marathon suffered by Darius, father of Ahasuerus. During the ensuing campaign, 300 Spartans heroically defended the pass of Thermopylae for 7 days against a vastly superior Persian force. But through a betrayal, the Persians found the path around the pass and defeated the Spartans and their allies.

HOW TO SAY IT

Ahasuerus	Uh-haz-you-*ee*-rus.
Ahava	Uh-*hay*-vuh.
Assyrian	Uh-*sear*-e-un.
Babylon	*Bab*-uh-lun.
Darius	Duh-*rye*-us.
Euphrates	You-*fray*-teez.
Hosea	Ho-*zay*-uh.
Nethinims	*Neth*-ih-nims.
penitensya	pen-uh-*ten*-shah.
Salamis	*Sal*-uh-mis.
Susa	*Soo*-suh.
Thermopylae	Thur-*muh*-puh-lee.
Xerxes	*Zerk*-seez.

Third, and more significant, was the Greek victory at Salamis, which followed shortly after Thermopylae. This was a naval battle in which a heavily outnumbered Greek fleet decisively defeated the Persian fleet. Ahasuerus became discouraged after this reversal. Leaving one of his generals in charge to finish the campaign, he returned to Susa where an ancient historian says he found solace in his harem. The selection of Esther as his queen fits well into the historical reconstruction.

The events associated with the second wave of Jews returning from Babylon are in the final four chapters of the book of Ezra (today's lesson and next week's). The year being 458 BC means that the events described in today's text occur just 15 years after the final events of the book of Esther. The Persians are still in charge in Palestine, but their power is on the wane.

I. Mission Overview
(Ezra 7:6-10)

Ezra uses verses 1-5 of chapter 7 in his book to show that he has the priestly credentials to be the leader for the group that is preparing to go to Jerusalem. Giving the more prominent names, Ezra traces his ancestry all the way back to Aaron, the first high priest for the nation of Israel.

A. Ezra's Qualifications (v. 6a)

6a. This Ezra went up from Babylon; and he was a ready scribe in the law of Moses, which the Lord God of Israel had given.

Ezra further identifies himself as a *scribe*. The same Hebrew word is used to designate one of the officers or cabinet members for David in 2 Samuel 20:25. Therefore the word indicates a person who merits respect as one who is an intelligent, capable writer. In this case it is *the law of Moses* in which Ezra has expert knowledge. The reference to this law demonstrates that it (1) is already in existence, (2) is respected as coming from *the Lord God of Israel,* (3) is being studied, and (4) is being taught. We may assume that at least some of the captives finally understand why they are in Babylon: there has been a disdain for and disobedience of God and His Word.

B. Ezra's Request (v. 6b)

6b. And the king granted him all his request, according to the hand of the LORD his God upon him.

Ezra's credentials include receiving approval from Artaxerxes, king of Persia (Ezra 7:1), to lead this return of Jews from Babylon back to Palestine. (See the Lesson Background for more on Artaxerxes.) A key phrase is given as the reason the request of Ezra is granted: this was by *the hand of the Lord his God*. This and similar phrases are used several times across the books of Ezra and Nehemiah (see Ezra 7:9, 28; 8:18, 22, 31; Nehemiah 2:8, 18). God gets the credit!

The bold action on the part of Ezra leads some to think that he may have a position in the Persian government, perhaps as an official representative for the Jews. In any case, Ezra's plan has the full backing of the king. Pagan rulers do not want to offend any of "the gods." Perhaps Artaxerxes recalls the events in the days of Esther—how Haman and others who opposed the Jews had been annihilated. A good king would want to know about the nations in his domain, and Artaxerxes may have heard from Ezra about the miraculous events in the history of Israel. Some of those accounts show that the enemies of Israel can suffer severe consequences, such as the plagues on the Egyptians as recorded in Exodus.

C. Ezra's Traveling Companions (v. 7a)

7a. And there went up some of the children of Israel, and of the priests, and the Levites, and the singers, and the porters, and the Nethinims, unto Jerusalem.

Those who will take part in this trip are going to Jerusalem for a dual purpose: (1) to return to the land that God had promised to the patriarchs and (2) to serve God in the activities associated with the temple.

The reference to *the Levites* has an interesting background that is given in Ezra 8. As Ezra evaluates the composition of the group preparing to travel with him, he does not find any Levites. They are the ones most closely associated with assisting the priests (Ezra 8:15). Ezra therefore sends several trusted men to one community with the task of locating Levites who are willing to make the trip to Jerusalem. They search is successful: 38 Levites are found (8:18, 19) along with 220 others who also can assist (8:20). (See also the Lesson Background to lesson 12.)

The Hebrew behind the word *porters* is translated "doorkeepers" in 1 Chronicles 15:23, and that helps clarify its meaning. The word *Nethinims* refers to those who serve in the temple in various ways. The word seems to come from a root that means "give," and *Nethinims* may therefore refer to those who give themselves to such service.

D. Ezra's Trip (vv. 7b-9)

7b. In the seventh year of Artaxerxes the king.

The seventh year of Artaxerxes calculates as 458 BC. It has been almost 80 years since the first return (see Ezra 1, 2), and it has been 147 years since Daniel and his companions were taken to Babylon. Several generations undoubtedly have become comfortable in Babylon, so the people who want to return probably have a deep spiritual commitment that prompts them in their decision.

8. And he came to Jerusalem in the fifth month, which was in the seventh year of the king.

The word *he* refers to Ezra himself. The additional chronological note establishes the year and month of arrival, and verse 9 gives the day. These three pieces of data tell us that Ezra and his companions arrive in Jerusalem on August 4, 458 BC. The fact that the exact arrival date is given leads us to ask when the journey began. The answer to that comes next.

9a. For upon the first day of the first month began he to go up from Babylon, and on the first day of the fifth month came he to Jerusalem.

The fact that the journey begins on the *first day of the first month* means that the trip takes exactly four months. The Hebrews use a lunar calendar, and the new moon of the first month is determined to be April 8. The journey begins at the start of the dry season, and that is a good time of the year for travel.

A lunar month is 29.5 days, so the travel time from Babylon to Jerusalem is therefore 118 days. The group does not travel on a Sabbath day, so 18 or 19 days are spent resting along the way. Therefore the people take about 100 days to travel the 880 miles to Jerusalem. Thus we may conclude that the people average about 9 miles per day.

The next section indicates that there is a delay of at least three days at Ahava (Ezra 8:15, not in today's text), so the group does not travel on all non-Sabbath days. The group begins to move out from Ahava on the twelfth of the first month, or April 19 (Ezra 8:31, part of next week's lesson).

All in all, the group seems to travel at a rate of about 1 mile per hour. The standard rate of march for armies on foot is about 2 miles per hour, but Ezra's group includes animals that need to graze and be watered, children (Ezra 8:21), and lots of heavy cargo (8:24-30, next week's lesson). These factors result in a slower rate of travel.

9b. According to the good hand of his God upon him.

Ezra provides the proper evaluation for the successful trip: *the good hand of his God* is the reason that the journey goes so well. Ezra may have planned to the last detail, but he understands that God is the source of every blessing (compare James 1:17). At the end of the journey, each Israelite probably experiences a special surge of emotion as the city of Jerusalem comes into view.

E. Ezra's Dedication (v. 10)

10. For Ezra had prepared his heart to seek the law of the LORD, and to do it, and to teach in Israel statutes and judgments.

This is one of the best-known verses in the book of Ezra. It gives the threefold purpose that Ezra intends to continue governing his life when he reaches Jerusalem: to know *the law of the Lord*, to obey it, and to instruct others concerning it.

Before the northern nation of Israel had gone into Assyrian captivity, the Lord had said that His people were being destroyed for rejecting knowledge (Hosea 4:6). The southern nation of Judah did not learn from Israel's experience, so it went into captivity in Babylon. Now there is a new generation, and Ezra is determined to keep history from being repeated.

> *What Do You Think?*
> How would you go about preparing yourself for a new ministry task that you believed God wanted you to do?
> *Talking Points for Your Discussion*
> ▪ Questions you would ask other believers
> ▪ Answers you would seek from God's Word
> ▪ How you would pray
> ▪ Other

❧ KNOW, DO, TEACH ❧

Critics of the educational establishment sometimes recite the cynical aphorism, "Those who can't do, teach." Their skepticism may come from having known teachers who were ill-equipped to function adequately in the "real world" outside the classroom. A few couldn't function very well even *inside* the classroom!

On the other hand, the skeptic might simply believe that *learning* is less important than *doing*—or even that those two concepts are somehow contradictory. This attitude was revealed by a certain church elder one day. On hearing that the church's young minister had expressed the desire to get a master's degree in seminary, the elder said to him, "Preacher boy, don't go getting so much education that they ruin you as a preacher."

Ezra would have nothing to do with such an attitude. We are specifically told that he prepared his heart to know God's law. His knowledge of the Word of God came out of a decision to become a capable student of that law. Then, because of his love for God's Word, he devoted himself to practicing its principles daily. With this foundation,

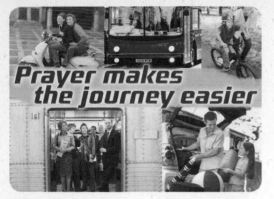

Prayer makes the journey easier

Visual for Lesson 8. *Use the variety of images on this visual to start a discussion on how prayer has made the journey easier for your learners.*

Ezra was equipped to be a faithful teacher of the law. He set a good example for all who would be leaders of God's people.   —C. R. B.

II. Mission Preparation
(EZRA 8:21-23)

Ezra 8:15, 21, and 31 indicate that a place by the Ahava waterway is a gathering point for the people who were going to Jerusalem. The exact location is not known, but it is assumed that it is near the Euphrates River, not too far north of the city of Babylon. Ezra 8 indicates that fewer than 1,800 male adults make the trip, so the total number in the group may be between 5,000 and 6,000 when we include women and children.

A. Gathering and Fasting (v. 21)

21. Then I proclaimed a fast there, at the river of Ahava, that we might afflict ourselves before our God, to seek of him a right way for us, and for our little ones, and for all our substance.

The Law of Moses mandates only one fast each year: during observance of the Day of Atonement. This is a fast in which the act of self-denial emphasizes the seriousness of sin (Leviticus 23:32). Otherwise, fasting is considered voluntary.

The Babylonian captivity causes the Jews to add four more days of fasting to the calendar. They are intended as reminders of major events associated with the fall of Jerusalem. Approximately 50 years

before Ezra's return, the Lord had said through the prophet Zechariah that the people should turn such days into days of feasting (Zechariah 8:19).

There is also the memorable three-day fast that was initiated by Esther before she presented herself to her king (Esther 4:16). Ezra would know about that fast, for he was alive at the time. Now he himself proclaims a special fast to ask God for safety before his group makes its spiritual pilgrimage to the city that God has chosen (1 Kings 11:13).

> **What Do You Think?**
> What emphasis should be put on fasting in the New Testament era? Why do you say that?
> *Talking Points for Your Discussion*
> - Matthew 6:16-18
> - Luke 5:33-35
> - Acts 13:2, 3; 14:23
> - Other

❧ SEEKING HIS GUIDANCE ❧

Penitensya is the rite of self-flagellation practiced by many Catholics in the Philippines during Lent. Wanting to take upon themselves the sufferings of Jesus, hundreds walk in procession bare-chested, whipping their backs until they ooze blood. The participants believe that *penitensya* will bring forgiveness of their sins. They also believe the practice will produce cures for illnesses and bring answers to prayers.

The ritual was practiced in Europe in the thirteenth and fourteenth centuries, but was later outlawed by the Catholic Church. The practice was begun anew in the Philippines during the Spanish rule there. Catholic bishops still condemn the practice, but to no avail. A reporter asked one Filipino why he was going to whip himself with bamboo sticks. His answer: to experience something of the pain and torture Jesus felt during His trial. He said, "This is our own way to atone for our sins and seek His guidance and protection."

Ezra urged his people to "afflict" themselves before God by fasting so that they might "seek of him a right way." The New Testament tells us that only Christ's sufferings can bring forgiveness of sin. But fasting such as we see in today's text can serve to humble us before God as we seek His guidance. Do we preach or practice the value of fasting as much as we should? —C. R. B.

B. King and God (v. 22)

22. For I was ashamed to require of the king a band of soldiers and horsemen to help us against the enemy in the way: because we had spoken unto the king, saying, The hand of our God is upon all them for good that seek him; but his power and his wrath is against all them that forsake him.

Ezra has expressed the fact that God provides special care to those who serve Him. Ezra confirms his belief by not asking King Artaxerxes for a military escort to provide protection on the journey. This is a powerful demonstration to the king.

Ezra's decision not to request a military escort is usually contrasted with the opposite approach when Nehemiah comes to Jerusalem 14 years later. In that case, Artaxerxes sends along a military guard, which Nehemiah does not refuse (Nehemiah 2:9). No explanations are given for the difference. Perhaps the king wants to protect his cupbearer, to demonstrate that Nehemiah's trip has royal sanction, and therefore negate opposition when Nehemiah begins rebuilding Jerusalem's walls. Nehemiah endures threats and ridicule, but actual military action against him never occurs.

> *What Do You Think?*
> Under what circumstances should Christians seek or accept the protection of earthly authorities, if any? Why?
> *Talking Points for Your Discussion*
> - 2 Kings 8:3
> - Nehemiah 2:1-9
> - Esther 8:1-14
> - Isaiah 30:1-3; 31:1
> - Acts 22:25-29; 25:11

The second part of Ezra's explanation is also important. The fact that God's *power and his wrath is against all them that forsake him* seems to be a subtle way of suggesting to King Artaxerxes that neither he nor anyone else should oppose this spiritual endeavor.

C. Prayer and Answer (v. 23)

23. So we fasted and besought our God for this: and he was intreated of us.

The fast becomes a reality, and the petitions for protection are genuinely expressed to God. As Ezra pens these words later, he can look back over the days and miles and know that God had indeed protected the group. They arrive safely, and Ezra is ready to begin his special ministry in Jerusalem of studying, obeying, and teaching the law of the Lord (Nehemiah 8:1-8; etc.).

> *What Do You Think?*
> What experiences have helped you to learn to depend on God? Explain.
> *Talking Points for Your Discussion*
> - Looking for a job
> - Making a major financial decision
> - Deciding where to attend church
> - Other

Conclusion

A. Preparing for Your Ministries

During the wilderness wanderings, Moses offered a special prayer each time the ark was moved and when it came to rest (Numbers 10:35, 36). Ezra's spiritual actions at the beginning of his journey were similar.

Many Christian leaders pray before beginning each task. Those who preach have the responsibility of ministering to hundreds or even thousands who have come for spiritual bread. The person who teaches lessons such as this one may begin the preparation with prayer. These facts lead us to a final thought regarding another direction for prayer: Did the Israelites pray for Ezra? Do your students pray for you, the teacher?

B. Prayer

O God, may this day be the day I resolve to know, do, and teach Your Word in my journey toward You. As I pray for my tasks, may I also seek the prayers of others. In Jesus' name, amen.

C. Thought to Remember

Remember to pray for God's enabling.

INVOLVEMENT LEARNING

Some of the activities below are also found in the helpful student book, Adult Bible Class.
Don't forget to download the free reproducible page from www.standardlesson.com to enhance your lesson!

Into the Lesson

Begin class by asking, "What are some jobs or career fields that people are expected to have credentials for?" Follow each response immediately with the question, "What credentials are needed for that job?" Jot all responses on the board.

Alternative. If you have the technology available, show a YouTube clip of the singing of "Lida Rose" from *The Music Man*. At the end, ask, "What was it those four men were appointed to get from Professor Harold Hill?" *(Answer: his "credentials.")*

After either of the above, briefly discuss the role of credentials in substantiating a person's training and experience for a task. Then say, "Our lesson for today begins by noting Ezra's credentials for leading the second wave of returnees to the promised land from Babylonian exile."

Into the Word

Read Ezra 7:6 aloud. (*Option:* also read verses 1-5, not in today's lesson text.) Ask, "What were Ezra's credentials for being a leader?" Expect responses that note (1) his proper lineage—he was no "pretender" (vv. 1-5, not in today's lesson text); (2) he was a well-informed teacher (v. 6a); (3) he was authorized by the reigning authority (vv. 1, 6); and (4) he had God's approval (v. 6).

Have Ezra 7:7-10 read aloud, and ask, "How do these verses confirm Ezra's credentials, and what further elements are added?" If learners do not do so, note Ezra's devotion to study and obedience, as well as his commitment to seeing the Word of God taught.

Have Ezra 8:21-23 read. Ask, "What additional insights are given concerning Ezra's qualifications for spiritual leadership?" Responses should note Ezra's realization of the need for fasting and praying (vv. 21, 23), as well as his confidence in God's presence and blessing of their decision (v. 22).

Option. To enhance the above discussions, distribute at the outset of this segment copies of the "Qualifications of a Spiritual Leader" activity from the reproducible page, which you can download. Learners can use this to note implications for Christian leadership as you work through the lesson text per above. After you finish considering Ezra 8:21-23, form study pairs or groups of three to discuss further the implications for Christian leadership. Let each study pair or group report conclusions to the class as a whole.

Into Life

Display a poster-size sign with the heading *Life in the FAST Lane*. Say, "This expression usually speaks of a certain lifestyle. Let me characterize it for you." Show each of these words (prepared as flash cards) one at a time: *Headlong, Frenzied, Self-Centered, Spontaneous, Impatient, Undisciplined*. Once all the words are introduced, say, "But notice that I put the word *FAST* on the poster in all capitals! From today's text, the concept of FAST doesn't mean what I have characterized by the words on the flash cards. Look again at the six words; what is an opposite for each? If you can figure that out, you will better characterize the biblical concept of 'the FAST Life.'"

"Opposite" responses may include *thoughtful* (for *headlong*), *organized* or *focused* (for *frenzied*), *altruistic* or *humble* (for *self-centered*), *planned* (for *spontaneous*), *patient* (for *impatient*), and *prudent* (for *undisciplined*). Note that the fast Ezra called for in Ezra 8:21 was a time for seeking the right way, God's way, to proceed. Ask, "What occasions in the life of our congregation could call for such a time of fasting?" Jot responses on the board. Consider using the responses to plan a time of fasting to precede a major event that is on your church's calendar.

Personalize today's lesson by having learners complete the "Three Steps to a Successful Life" activity on the reproducible page. This can be a take-home exercise if time is short.

Fasting and Praying

GIVING GIFTS FOR THE TEMPLE

DEVOTIONAL READING: Mark 12:38-44
BACKGROUND SCRIPTURE: Ezra 8:24-36

EZRA 8:24-35

24 Then I separated twelve of the chief of the priests, Sherebiah, Hashabiah, and ten of their brethren with them,

25 And weighed unto them the silver, and the gold, and the vessels, even the offering of the house of our God, which the king, and his counsellors, and his lords, and all Israel there present, had offered:

26 I even weighed unto their hand six hundred and fifty talents of silver, and silver vessels an hundred talents, and of gold an hundred talents;

27 Also twenty basons of gold, of a thousand drams; and two vessels of fine copper, precious as gold.

28 And I said unto them, Ye are holy unto the LORD; the vessels are holy also; and the silver and the gold are a freewill offering unto the LORD God of your fathers.

29 Watch ye, and keep them, until ye weigh them before the chief of the priests and the Levites, and chief of the fathers of Israel, at Jerusalem, in the chambers of the house of the LORD.

30 So took the priests and the Levites the weight of the silver, and the gold, and the ves-

sels, to bring them to Jerusalem unto the house of our God.

31 Then we departed from the river of Ahava on the twelfth day of the first month, to go unto Jerusalem: and the hand of our God was upon us, and he delivered us from the hand of the enemy, and of such as lay in wait by the way.

32 And we came to Jerusalem, and abode there three days.

33 Now on the fourth day was the silver and the gold and the vessels weighed in the house of our God by the hand of Meremoth the son of Uriah the priest; and with him was Eleazar the son of Phinehas; and with them was Jozabad the son of Jeshua, and Noadiah the son of Binnui, Levites;

34 By number and by weight of every one: and all the weight was written at that time.

35 Also the children of those that had been carried away, which were come out of the captivity, offered burnt offerings unto the God of Israel, twelve bullocks for all Israel, ninety and six rams, seventy and seven lambs, twelve he goats for a sin offering: all this was a burnt offering unto the LORD.

KEY VERSE

I said unto them, Ye are holy unto the LORD; the vessels are holy also; and the silver and the gold are a freewill offering unto the LORD God of your fathers. —**Ezra 8:28**

GOD'S PEOPLE WORSHIP

Unit 2: Worshipping in Jerusalem Again (Ezra)

LESSONS 5–9

LESSON AIMS

After participating in this lesson, each student will be able to:

1. Describe the procedures for financial accountability that Ezra and his companions used at the beginning and end of their journey to Jerusalem.

2. Give examples of how churches can take precautions to protect the persons who participate in various programs of the church, especially those who handle money.

3. Support and pray for missions that show evidence of careful stewardship in the handling of the gifts that are administered by them.

LESSON OUTLINE

Introduction

A. Tons to Transport

The *London Times* described it as "perhaps the biggest jigsaw puzzle in the history of architecture." The feat involved gathering, marking, and transporting 7,000 stones of a ruined church from England to Fulton, Missouri. The church building had been severely damaged in the bombing blitz on England during World War II.

Why rebuild the church in Missouri instead of London? Winston Churchill had delivered his famous "Iron Curtain" speech at Westminster College in Fulton, Missouri, on March 5, 1946. That speech is often cited to mark the beginning of the Cold War. Eventually, a decision was made to memorialize the famous speech at the place where it was delivered, thus the decision to transport the remains of the ruined church from London to Missouri. The immensity of the project was almost incomprehensible.

The first stones were delivered in time for the groundbreaking ceremony that took place on April 19, 1964. The remaining tons and tons of marked stones arrived soon thereafter, and reconstruction began. The dedication service was held on May 7, 1969. The outward appearance of the completed building very closely resembles pictures of the original. In 2009, the building was designated by Congress as the National Churchill Museum.

Today's study also relates a time when tons of material were transported a great distance to support a rebuilding effort. The occasion was the return from captivity that was led by Ezra in the spring and summer of 458 BC. The distance was 880 miles, from Babylon to Jerusalem.

B. Lesson Background

The biblical text for this lesson follows immediately after the previous study, so the historical background is the same. But perhaps a bit more can be said about Ezra's place in history. He was important in his own time, and he is often considered very important in shaping Judaism. His influence extended down to the Judaism of the first century AD and beyond.

Giving Gifts for the Temple

This high regard for Ezra has much to support it. First, he is termed a *scribe* (or teacher), and to have such a title was an honor. This meant that Ezra was an expert in the Law of Moses. It was said of Ezra that he was so worthy that the law could have been given through him "if Moses had not preceded him." Ancient rabbis wrote that if Ezra had lived at the same time as Aaron (Moses' brother, who became the first high priest), then Aaron would have been considered inferior to Ezra.

Ezra has also been called "a second Moses," and the two men can be compared and contrasted in various ways. Moses wrote down the law; Ezra went to Jerusalem to teach it. Both led groups on long trips to the promised land. Moses' group was protected by a special cloud; Ezra wrote that the hand of God provided protection. The Lord supplied manna and water in special ways for those in the exodus from Egypt; there is no record that this was done in Ezra's time. Moses performed miraculous signs before Pharaoh to persuade him to allow the Israelites to leave; Ezra had letters from the king of Persia that credentialed his mission. Moses' group received gifts from the Egyptians; Ezra's group had gifts from the king of Persia. The Israelites of Moses' day gave generously to build the tabernacle; those in Ezra's time gave generously for the house of the Lord. It took 40 years for the Israelites first to enter the promised land; it took Ezra's group 4 months. Moses appointed others to help him with administration; Ezra utilized priests and Levites to assist him for the trip.

HOW TO SAY IT

Ahasuerus	Uh-haz-you-*ee*-rus.
Apocrypha	Uh-*paw*-kruh-fuh.
Artaxerxes	Are-tuh-*zerk*-seez.
Binnui	*Bin*-you-eye.
Esdras	*Ez*-druss.
Hashabiah	Hash-uh-*bye*-uh.
Jozabad	*Jaws*-ah-bad.
Meremoth	*Mair*-ee-moth.
Noadiah	No-uh-**die**-uh.
Phinehas	*Fin*-ee-us.
Qumran	Koom-*rahn*.
Sherebiah	*Sher*-ee-**bye**-uh.

I. Consigning Offerings
(Ezra 8:24-27)

A. Selecting Trustworthy Men (v. 24)

24. Then I separated twelve of the chief of the priests, Sherebiah, Hashabiah, and ten of their brethren with them.

The verse just prior to this one tells of an important phase of preparation for the journey to Jerusalem: fasting and petitioning God for success of the mission (last week's lesson). The spiritual things are essential, but that is just one part of the preparation. Ezra now demonstrates that he is a careful administrator who knows how to plan his work and work his plan.

Ezra determines that the responsibility for transporting all the wealth listed in verses 25, 26 (next) should be divided among others. This is a security measure for him and for the valuables assigned to his care. Many churches have similar security procedures in place for the people who handle offerings. The purpose is to protect both the funds and those who have access to them.

Some students think that Ezra selects only a total of 12 men to assist him in this regard, and those *twelve of the chief of the priests* are, namely, *Sherebiah, Hashabiah, and ten of their brethren.* Other students think, however, that a total of 24 men is in view. Support for this proposal is seen in Ezra 8:18, 19, where Sherebiah and Hashabiah are mentioned as being leaders among the Levites (not the priests) who receive last-minute invitations to go to Jerusalem (compare Nehemiah 12:24).

Supporters of the first proposal counter that there is no contradiction with Ezra 8:18, 19 in seeing *Sherebiah, Hashabiah, and ten of their brethren* as being the 12 priests since all priests are Levites anyway. However, verse 30 clearly distinguishes between priests and Levites on this journey, which supports the idea that Ezra chooses a total of 24 men.

❧ *Acting in Faith and Wisdom* ❧

A few years ago, a certain church embarked on a building program. It needed to replace its old building with one that would better serve the growing congregation. The members gave generously to support the building program. One person was assigned the responsibility for the project, including the management of the building fund.

All went well as the work began. But soon rumors of trouble were being whispered. Contractors who had finished their part of the construction started complaining that they were not being paid. An investigation uncovered the distressing truth: the person in charge of the project had been using the money for his own purposes. As a result, there was insufficient money to pay the suppliers and builders.

Ezra demonstrated wisdom as an administrator. As he made plans to return to Jerusalem with a precious cargo to help complete the temple construction project, neither he nor any other one person was entrusted with the entire treasure. Ezra trusted God for safety during the journey. But Ezra also showed managerial expertise in the way he spread responsibility and accountability for the task. Those entrusted with overseeing the church's treasure today should be as wise!   —C. R. B.

B. Weighing Precious Metals (vv. 25-27)

25. And weighed unto them the silver, and the gold, and the vessels, even the offering of the house of our God, which the king, and his counsellors, and his lords, and all Israel there present, had offered.

The value of the donated silver and gold makes it imperative that there be a careful accounting.

Visual for Lesson 9. *Point to this visual to start a discussion on the idea of* consecration. *Use 1 Chronicles 29:2-5 (especially v. 5) to enrich the discussion.*

Coins are sometimes used at this time in history, but the precious metals in view here are in bulk form. Weighing is the best method to determine the amounts involved (see the next verse).

The special offerings are designated for *the house of our God,* with King Artaxerxes and others contributing toward this special project. The fact that *all Israel* participates shows that this mission is known by many.

What Do You Think?
Under what circumstances, if any, should the church solicit or accept financial aid from unbelievers? Why do you say this?

Talking Points for Your Discussion
- Genesis 14:21-24
- 2 Kings 5:15, 16
- Nehemiah 2:8
- 3 John 7
- Other

Last week's study revealed that Ezra did not ask to have a military escort protect his group (Ezra 8:22). Since many people know of the nature of the trip, the faith of Ezra in trusting God for protection is commendable. Ezra begins the journey with faith in God and in the men he has selected to guard the treasures.

26. I even weighed unto their hand six hundred and fifty talents of silver, and silver vessels an hundred talents, and of gold an hundred talents.

A talent is about 75 pounds. Thus the *six hundred and fifty talents of silver* weigh almost 24 tons, and the items made from silver weigh slightly less than 4 tons. The total weight of these metals indicates that wagons are used for transport (compare Numbers 7:2, 3).

The total weight of these precious metals represents enormous wealth. It is so great that some have suggested that a lesser weight (such as the mina, or 1.25 pounds) was in the original text. It must be remembered, however, that the Persian king, Artaxerxes, is exceedingly wealthy, and royal gifts such as the ones described are very possible. King Artaxerxes is aware of the great deliverance for the Jewish people in the time of Esther, for

Giving Gifts for the Temple

Esther's husband, Ahasuerus (or Xerxes), was his father. Artaxerxes does not wish to offend a God who has done so many mighty works in the past (Ezra 7:23).

Archaeologists have discovered evidence that several Jewish families in the Persian Empire were involved in banking. These people also can make sizable gifts. It is interesting that approximately 400 years after this event a king in Egypt paid Julius Caesar 6,000 talents of gold to have an official designation for Egypt as "Friend and Ally of the Roman People." The biblical amounts sound very reasonable!

27. Also twenty basons of gold, of a thousand drams; and two vessels of fine copper, precious as gold.

The weight *of a thousand drams* of the golden *basons* (bowls) is about 19 pounds—almost one pound each. The word *drams* translates the Hebrew word *darics*. The Persian king Darius the Great (reigned 522–486 BC, a grandfather to Artaxerxes) had introduced the *daric* as a golden coin of about 8.4 grams in weight. In value, it represents the wages for a soldier for one month.

The final two vessels in this listing are thought to be made of a special blend of metals that can be polished so that they almost resemble gold. They too are valuable.

II. Communicating Holiness
(EZRA 8:28-30)
A. Reminder Given (v. 28)

28. And I said unto them, Ye are holy unto the LORD; the vessels are holy also; and the silver and the gold are a freewill offering unto the LORD God of your fathers.

Ezra reminds those to be entrusted with the wealth that the Lord is the one who has set them apart in a special way: they belong to him (compare Numbers 3:11-13). Since the precious metals and vessels, also holy, have been given as a *freewill offering to the Lord,* it is a compliment to these men to be entrusted with gifts that are dedicated to God. Things given to God in any era are to be used, but not misused or abused through carelessness.

What Do You Think?
What does your church do to teach giving as an expression of worship? What more can it do?
Talking Points for Your Discussion
- To preteens
- To teenagers
- To adults

B. Responsibility Accepted (vv. 29, 30)

29. Watch ye, and keep them, until ye weigh them before the chief of the priests and the Levites, and chief of the fathers of Israel, at Jerusalem, in the chambers of the house of the LORD.

Ezra stresses the seriousness of guarding such a great treasure. These items are weighed at the beginning of the journey, and they will be weighed again on reaching Jerusalem (v. 33, below). At that time the gold and silver will be transferred to the care of *the chief of the priests and the Levites* and other leaders of the nation of Israel.

The first temple had three levels of chambers on three sides (1 Kings 6:5, 6). These rooms had multiple purposes. The verse before us shows that the second temple, which was dedicated 57 years before Ezra's arrival (see lesson 7), has similar compartments. Such rooms will be where the valuable gifts will be weighed.

30. So took the priests and the Levites the weight of the silver, and the gold, and the vessels, to bring them to Jerusalem unto the house of our God.

The priests and the Levites accept the seriousness of their charge of guarding the consecrated gifts for the temple of God in Jerusalem. They do not know whether they will encounter dangers along the way, but they are ready to demonstrate faithfulness to their task.

III. Completing the Mission
(EZRA 8:31-35)
A. Reviewing the Journey (v. 31)

31. Then we departed from the river of Ahava on the twelfth day of the first month, to go unto Jerusalem: and the hand of our God was upon

us, and he delivered us from the hand of the enemy, and of such as lay in wait by the way.

Ezra reflects on the magnitude of what he and his group experience. During the four-month journey *from the river of Ahava . . . unto Jerusalem* (see Ezra 7:8, 9, last week's lesson), they travel 880 miles while transporting tremendous wealth. Their journey takes them through areas where ambushes are often used to surprise and rob sojourners. As Ezra looks back in considering the distance, the days, and the dangers, there is only one conclusion: God had watched over them to protect them. Ezra seems to imply that such attacks did not occur, but the verse could also be interpreted to mean that such encounters did occur, but always failed.

> **What Do You Think?**
> When have you seen God's hand in safe deliverance through uncertain circumstances? How did you know it was not just "good luck"?
> *Talking Points for Your Discussion*
> ▪ Regarding a mission trip
> ▪ Regarding an untrue accusation
> ▪ Regarding a time of testing in a church
> ▪ Other

❧ AN EXAMPLE TO REMEMBER ❧

In an increasingly secularized culture, many Americans are ignorant of (or willfully overlook) the fact that their country's founders were, by and large, people of faith. For example, the U.S. Declaration of Independence acknowledges "the Laws of Nature and of Nature's God." The document appeals to "the Supreme Judge of the world" to validate the efforts of the colonies, avowing "firm reliance on the protection of Divine Providence." Speaking at the constitutional convention on June 28, 1787, the elderly Benjamin Franklin declared, "I have lived, Sir, a long time, and the longer I live, the more convincing proofs I see of this truth—that God governs the affairs of men."

How times have changed! Before embarking on a project big or small, how many political leaders —or anyone, for that matter—pause to reflect on the fact that God is in control? On completion of the project, how many stop to think about what God's part might have been in the undertaking?

Ezra was a leader who acknowledged God's care and protection. Pray that this lesson about faith and trust will be taught and retaught! —C. R. B.

B. Resting in Jerusalem (v. 32)

32. And we came to Jerusalem, and abode there three days.

It is very likely that a Sabbath is one of the *three days* involved here. An ancient calendar that was in use at a later time by the residents of the Qumran community near the Dead Sea indicates that Ezra's arrival in Jerusalem is on a Friday. Some of Ezra's group probably want to make certain that the accommodations to protect the wealth are ready, and it will take time to do the things that have to be done in that regard. A three-day rest in Jerusalem, including a Sabbath, is a real blessing after such a long trip.

> **What Do You Think?**
> How can Christians do a better job of watching out for one another in terms of ensuring adequate rest?
> *Talking Points for Your Discussion*
> ▪ Regarding the church's staff members
> ▪ Regarding the church's teachers
> ▪ Regarding the church's ministry teams
> ▪ Other

C. Delivering the Treasure (vv. 33, 34)

33. Now on the fourth day was the silver and the gold and the vessels weighed in the house of our God by the hand of Meremoth the son of Uriah the priest; and with him was Eleazar the son of Phinehas; and with them was Jozabad the son of Jeshua, and Noadiah the son of Binnui, Levites.

The gravity of the transfer that now takes place is seen in the fact that it occurs *in the house of our God*. Priests and Levites have had the task of safeguarding these valuables on their way to Jerusalem, and now their counterparts receive and weigh them. *Meremoth the son of Uriah the priest* will demonstrate 14 years later that he has other capabilities as well (see Nehemiah 3:4, 21).

Giving Gifts for the Temple

34. By number and by weight of every one: and all the weight was written at that time.

The implication is that everything tallies and matches the records that were made at the beginning of the four-month trip. The men who have the responsibility of delivering the dedicated gifts have fulfilled the trust that was placed in them.

> **What Do You Think?**
> What practices should a church have in place to provide transparency and accountability in the handling of assets?
> *Talking Points for Your Discussion*
> ▪ Regarding monetary assets
> ▪ Regarding property
> ▪ Regarding equipment
> ▪ Regarding intangible assets (use of the church name, etc.)

D. Demonstrating Dedication (v. 35)

35. Also the children of those that had been carried away, which were come out of the captivity, offered burnt offerings unto the God of Israel, twelve bullocks for all Israel, ninety and six rams, seventy and seven lambs, twelve he goats for a sin offering: all this was a burnt offering unto the LORD.

The material aspect of this trip now accomplished, Ezra and those who accompanied him turn their attention to something that is very important to every Israelite: being able to participate in offering sacrifices in the temple.

The Babylonians destroyed the first temple in August of 586 BC, and the date is August 4, 458 BC when Ezra's group completes its journey (see commentary on Ezra 7:8 in last week's lesson). They probably know that their ancestors established a day of fasting in the fifth month (late July and early August) in order to remember when the first temple was destroyed (see Zechariah 7:3). It is very likely that one motive that prompts people to make the trip with Ezra is that they will be able to worship in Jerusalem at the second temple. Now they can worship in the place God has chosen.

We can safely presume that those who *were come out of the captivity* undergo ritual washings and secure the help of priests and Levites for offering sacrifices. The enumeration of animals for these sacrifices is usually explained by saying that the numbers that are multiples of 12 represent the 12 tribes of Israel. The use of 77 lambs does not seem to have any symbolic significance. Some see it as a perfect number; others suggest that it is a figure of speech that simply means "many." A passage in the non-biblical collection known as the Apocrypha changes the number to 72, which creates an even multiple of 12 (1 Esdras 8:66), but there is no evidence to justify such a change.

Ordinarily, the priests receive a portion of each sin offering (compare Leviticus 6:26). This time, however, all the animals are treated as *burnt offerings* and are burned completely on the altar (except the skins, which go to the priests; see Leviticus 7:8). The burnt offering represents dedication or consecration to the Lord, and the people give a strong demonstration that their commitment does not end because one journey is complete.

Conclusion
A. Always Praying

A prayer of thankfulness is not mentioned after Ezra's arrival in Jerusalem. Even so, prayers would have accompanied the sacrifices of burnt offerings. Petitioning God is noted at the beginning of the trip (Ezra 8:23), and Ezra offers a lengthy prayer of confession in Ezra 9:6-15. Ezra is a man of prayer!

The familiar wording of the *King James Version* is a good reminder that God wants us to "pray without ceasing" (1 Thessalonians 5:17). In so doing, we will give "thanks always for all things unto God and the Father in the name of our Lord Jesus Christ" (Ephesians 5:20).

B. Prayer

Almighty God, You have gifted us to serve You in important ways. May our stewardship of those gifts, worth more than silver or gold, be part of our submission to You. In Jesus' name, amen.

C. Thought to Remember

Be a good steward of all your resources, especially the resource of prayer.

INVOLVEMENT LEARNING

Some of the activities below are also found in the helpful student book, Adult Bible Class.
Don't forget to download the free reproducible page from www.standardlesson.com to enhance your lesson!

Into the Lesson

As learners arrive, give each two to four toy coins of gold or silver. (These are readily and inexpensively available at "dollar" stores.) Say to each learner, "Guard these carefully." Keep a conspicuous tally on the board of the number distributed and to whom. When class begins, say, "I need to make an accounting of our coins." Turn to a learner and say, "[Name], how many do you have?" Do the same for all other learners.

As numbers are given, erase the tally stripes you used to record your gifts. (If you have any jokesters in class who are not honest in their responses, you will have to deal with them accordingly!) When you have a final accounting, say, "Our text today speaks of just such a bookkeeping strategy." Holding up your Bible, say, "Right now, let's do our own Bookkeeping—emphasizing *Book*."

Into the Word

Hand each learner a blank page from an accounting ledger (easy to find on the Internet). Instruct learners to add this heading: *A Bean Counter's Journal.* Say, "I want you to put the following numbers on your ledger down the left column (vertically): 1, 2, 2, 3, 3, 4, 4, 10, 12, 12, 12, 20, 77, 96, 100, 100, 650, 1,000." Read the numbers slowly to allow writing time, then read aloud today's text, Ezra 8:24-35. (*Option:* To save time, distribute the copies of ledger paper with the title and numbers already listed.)

Say, "Now I'm going to identify things from our text, and I want you to enter each beside an appropriate number. For example, if I say, 'number of rams offered in sacrifice,' you would write the word *rams* beside the number 96, per verse 35."

Work your way through the following (the answers and verse numbers are in italics—make sure not to verbalize those): number of types of precious metals mentioned *(3, v. 26, 27)*; the month Ezra's group left for Jerusalem *(1, v. 31)*; number of men to whom the gifts were counted out in the temple *(4, v. 33)*; the number of brothers of Sherebiah and Hashabiah who were responsible for part of the gift *(10, v. 24)*; talents of silver donated *(650, v. 26)*; number of male lambs in the burnt offering *(77, v. 35)*; number of days the travelers rested in Jerusalem before turning their gifts over at the temple *(3, v. 32)*; number of bulls included in the burnt offering *(12, v. 35)*; tally of the gold talents given *(100, v. 26)*; number of fine golden bowls in the gift *(20, v. 27)*; value of the golden bowls in the expressed unit of currency *(1,000, v. 27)*; tally of the weight of silver *(100, v. 26)*; number of articles of copper *(2, v. 27)*; the day of the month the Jews left for Jerusalem *(12, v. 31)*; the day Ezra's offering was turned over *(4, v. 33)*; number of times the gifts were weighed *(2, vv. 25, 33)*; number of male goats included in the sin offering *(12, v. 35)*.

Into Life

Choose one or more of the options below as you think appropriate for the nature of your class.

Option 1. Before class, research one or two of the financial reports of missions or parachurch organizations (Bible college, etc.) that your church supports. If possible, prepare copies for each learner in your group. Briefly discuss the adequacy (or inadequacy) of these accounts of stewardship (see also 2 Corinthians 8:19-21). Lead the class in prayers for these ministries and their wise and honest use of moneys provided to them.

Option 2. Distribute copies of the "Mind Your GAAP!" activity from the reproducible page, which you can download. Have learners complete in study pairs or small groups as indicated.

Option 3. Distribute copies of the "Set Apart to the Lord" activity from the reproducible page to be completed individually. Ask for volunteers to share their conclusions, but don't put anyone on the spot.

Giving Gifts for the Temple

FEAST OF TABERNACLES

DEVOTIONAL READING: Exodus 23:12-17
BACKGROUND SCRIPTURE: Nehemiah 7:73b–8:18; Leviticus 23:33-43

NEHEMIAH 8:2, 3, 13-18

2 And Ezra the priest brought the law before the congregation both of men and women, and all that could hear with understanding, upon the first day of the seventh month.

3 And he read therein before the street that was before the water gate from the morning until midday, before the men and the women, and those that could understand; and the ears of all the people were attentive unto the book of the law.

. . . .

13 And on the second day were gathered together the chief of the fathers of all the people, the priests, and the Levites, unto Ezra the scribe, even to understand the words of the law.

14 And they found written in the law which the LORD had commanded by Moses, that the children of Israel should dwell in booths in the feast of the seventh month:

15 And that they should publish and proclaim in all their cities, and in Jerusalem, saying, Go forth unto the mount, and fetch olive branches, and pine branches, and myr-tle branches, and palm branches, and branches of thick trees, to make booths, as it is written.

16 So the people went forth, and brought them, and made themselves booths, every one upon the roof of his house, and in their courts, and in the courts of the house of God, and in the street of the water gate, and in the street of the gate of Ephraim.

17 And all the congregation of them that were come again out of the captivity made booths, and sat under the booths: for since the days of Jeshua the son of Nun unto that day had not the children of Israel done so. And there was very great gladness.

18 Also day by day, from the first day unto the last day, he read in the book of the law of God. And they kept the feast seven days; and on the eighth day was a solemn assembly, according unto the manner.

KEY VERSE

All the congregation of them that were come again out of the captivity made booths, and sat under the booths: for since the days of Jeshua the son of Nun unto that day had not the children of Israel done so. And there was very great gladness. —**Nehemiah 8:17**

GOD'S PEOPLE WORSHIP

Unit 3: Worshipping in Jerusalem Again (Nehemiah)

LESSONS 10–13

LESSON AIMS

After participating in this lesson, each student will be able to:

1. List three important features of the Feast of Tabernacles.

2. Compare and contrast the Feast of Tabernacles with special celebrations in the life of his or her church.

3. Commit to some practice that involves a visual aid or unique action that will help him or her develop greater spiritual awareness.

LESSON OUTLINE

Introduction

A. Camping Experiences

I have always enjoyed camping, especially when I was in the Boy Scouts. In those days, I was part of a troop that went camping regularly in the woods of southern Georgia. Those woods were infested with poison ivy, snakes, and skunks. Danger lurked in the lakes and rivers, with water moccasins and tree stumps just below the surface. Perhaps the worst thing that ever happened to us was a thunderstorm that hit during one outing while we were asleep. We awoke to find ourselves lying in water and in danger of being hit by lightning that was striking all around. The troop leaders hustled us into the bus for safety.

Contrast that with my later experience of "camping" with my adult son and daughter and their families at a resort in Santa Claus, Indiana. In this environment, we slept in air-conditioned campers with soft beds. We cooked on two gas stoves, one inside and one outside. The children enjoyed the thrilling rides and the water park each day. We took warm showers in bathhouses that were just a brief walk away. I remember it as a joyful time with my extended family. But was it really "camping"?

The answer to that question depends on one's perspective. Those of us who had experienced camping as I did in the Boy Scouts had one viewpoint; those who had experienced camping only like the kind at this resort had another! The same can be said of the Israelites' experience in observing the Feast of Tabernacles, which reenacted a 40-year camping experience.

B. Lesson Background: Feast of Tabernacles

The Feast of Tabernacles was one of three annual festivals that the ancient Israelites were to celebrate before the Lord (Exodus 23:14-17; also Deuteronomy 16:16). This feast has different names, and it's easy to get confused. At first it was called the "Feast of Ingathering." Occurring in late September and early October, the name points to the final harvest of the season (Exodus 23:16b; 34:22b). Harvest was a cause for celebration, especially if the harvest was abundant.

The designation "Feast of Tabernacles" came later (Leviticus 23:34; Deuteronomy 16:13-16; 31:10; compare John 7:2). The "tabernacles" in view are also called "booths" (Leviticus 23:42, 43); we may think of these as huts or lean-tos. For seven days, the people were to dwell in these makeshift structures in a time of rejoicing (Leviticus 23:40; Deuteronomy 16:14, 15) as the Israelites remembered God's provisions during the wilderness wanderings of the exodus.

Living in tents was the normal lifestyle of the Israelites during the wilderness wanderings. Thus the Feast of Tabernacles recreated that lifestyle for succeeding generations that had not experienced it. But some of Nehemiah's audience in today's text had themselves experienced something like that lifestyle during their four-month trek from Babylon to Palestine—what some have called "a second exodus."

C. Lesson Background: Ezra and Nehemiah

The events of the books of Ezra and Nehemiah occur during what is called the Persian period. This period dates from the rise of Cyrus in 539 BC to the overthrow of the Persian Empire by Alexander the Great of Greece in the 330s BC. The Bible records three distinct returns from Babylonian exile during this period. We date the return of the first group—the one under Zerubbabel and Jeshua (or Joshua)—to 538 BC (see lessons 5, 6, and 7). The second return, under Ezra, is dated to 458 BC, some 80 years later (see lessons 8 and 9).

Our final four lessons of the quarter take us to the time of the third return, the one of 445 BC. Nehemiah led this return. The Bible does not mention anyone other than Nehemiah himself

HOW TO SAY IT

Artaxerxes	Are-tuh-*zerk*-seez.
Cyrus	*Sigh*-russ.
Ephraim	*Ee*-fray-im.
Gihon	*Gye*-hahn.
Jeshua	*Jesh*-you-uh.
Maccabees	*Mack*-uh-bees.
Nehemiah	*Nee*-huh-*my*-uh.
Zerubbabel	Zeh-*rub*-uh-bul.

in this group, but others undoubtedly came with him. (The list of returnees in Nehemiah 7 is that of the first group; compare Ezra 2).

Ezra and Nehemiah knew one another, and Ezra's personal actions are described in both Ezra 7–10 and Nehemiah 8 (or, as some think, in Nehemiah 8–10). Both were in Jerusalem to move the people in the right direction. This "push" included the proper celebration of the Feast of Tabernacles and covenant renewal. The events in Jerusalem of today's text occur during the reign of Artaxerxes I (see the Lesson Background to lesson 7).

I. Reading the Law
(NEHEMIAH 8:2, 3)

In Nehemiah 8:1, the people prevail on Ezra to read the book of the Law of Moses publicly. The Babylonian exile has "got the attention" of the people, and they are eager to hear God's Word.

A. Assembling to Hear (v. 2)

2. And Ezra the priest brought the law before the congregation both of men and women, and all that could hear with understanding, upon the first day of the seventh month.

The first day of the seventh month (in mid-September) is a holy and solemn day for Israel, marked by a blowing of trumpets. The month itself is an important one in Israel's year, for it not only includes the Feast of Trumpets (Leviticus 23:23-25), but also the Day of Atonement (23:26-32) and the Feast of Tabernacles (see the Lesson Background).

The gathering we see in the verse before us is for everyone! Those who are able to *hear with understanding* include children perhaps as young as age 12. The day on which the people assemble is a day of rest, a Sabbath according to Leviticus 23:24 and Numbers 29:1; this is a day sacred to God.

B. Hearing to Obey (v. 3)

3. And he read therein before the street that was before the water gate from the morning until midday, before the men and the women, and those that could understand; and the ears

of all the people were attentive unto the book of the law.

By this time, Nehemiah has finished repairing Jerusalem's walls and gates (Nehemiah 7:1). The place of gathering to hear the reading is near *the water gate,* which probably is located close to the Gihon Spring. This is south of the temple area, facing the Kidron Valley to Jerusalem's east. Most ancient cities have wide-open areas (which we call "plazas") adjacent to gates. Such areas can accommodate a standing crowd. *From the morning until midday* indicates a reading of several hours duration. But there is no hint that the people are restless and bored—quite the opposite!

What Do You Think?

When the Word of God is read, what are some appropriate ways to respond? What keeps us from always responding as we should?

Talking Points for Your Discussion

- Psalm 119:9
- Jeremiah 13:15; 15:16
- Acts 17:11
- 1 Thessalonians 2:13
- Other

Deuteronomy 31:10-13 requires that the law be read before the people—including children—every seven years at the Feast of Tabernacles. Whatever portion of the law is read by Ezra includes instructions as to how to celebrate this festival, as the next section of our text makes clear.

II. Heeding the Law
(NEHEMIAH 8:13-18)

The intervening verses that are not part of today's lesson provide some context. Ezra stands on an elevated platform so everyone can see and hear him during the reading. The platform is wide enough to accommodate 13 other men (Nehemiah 8:4). We know almost nothing about these men except that they are important to Ezra's task of making known the part of the law that is read. We presume they are leaders of some kind.

Nehemiah 8:5 tells us that the people stand when Ezra opens the scroll to read; this is a sign

of respect for the Law of Moses. Verse 7 lists the names of 13 Levites who assist in helping the people understand what is being read. This can include either translating from Hebrew to Aramaic or simply interpreting the text; perhaps they do both (v. 8). The people weep when they understand what is being read (v. 9), for they know they have not obeyed the law. It is a time of heavy emotion.

But Nehemiah, Ezra, and the Levites encourage the people to rejoice rather than mourn (Nehemiah 8:9, 10). The people are told to go home and enjoy the best of their food and drink, sharing with others who have nothing (vv. 11, 12). Joyous celebration fills out the rest of the first day of the month. Now we move to the second day.

A. Leaders Assembled (v. 13)

13. And on the second day were gathered together the chief of the fathers of all the people, the priests, and the Levites, unto Ezra the scribe, even to understand the words of the law.

The second day is a day for special study by Ezra for family leaders in addition to priests and Levites. Clearly, Ezra is placing the responsibility for knowing *the words of the law* on these groups! There is no excuse for not knowing God's Word and what it requires of God's people. One deficiency in particular that must be rectified presents itself in the next verse.

What Do You Think?

What methods, programs, etc., are best for equipping the leaders of families and leaders in the church to teach others? Why do you say that?

Talking Points for Your Discussion

- Electronic media
- Print media
- Special conferences
- Personal engagement
- Other

B. Law Examined (v. 14)

14. And they found written in the law which the LORD had commanded by Moses, that the children of Israel should dwell in booths in the feast of the seventh month.

Feast of Tabernacles

Ezra 3:4 notes that the Feast of Booths (also known as the Feast of Tabernacles; see the Lesson Background) was celebrated by the first group that returned from exile to Jerusalem. But apparently the requirement to observe this feast has been disregarded or marginalized in the 90 or so intervening years (compare Nehemiah 8:17, below).

There is no doubt that the text the verse before us is referring to is Leviticus 23:40-42 in reference to *booths*. This festival is connected with a vital part of Israel's salvation history: God's provisions during Israel's wilderness wanderings (see the Lesson Background). The law stipulates that this seven-day feast is to begin on the fifteenth day of the seventh month and end on the twenty-first day (Leviticus 23:34). Additionally, a "holy convocation" is to be observed on the eighth day to bring the celebration to a close (23:35).

> **What Do You Think?**
> In what ways has God's Word changed your life by reminding you of things you should do?
> *Talking Points for Your Discussion*
> - Concerning priorities (Matthew 6:33)
> - Concerning the need to seek wisdom (Proverbs 13:10)
> - Concerning use of the tongue (James 3:1-12)
> - Other

❧ *A LOST TREASURE* ❧

The phrase *lost treasure* conjures up images of ancient shipwrecks resting on the ocean floor with their precious cargo. In 2007, Odyssey Marine Exploration found such a treasure more than 3,000 feet below the surface of the Atlantic. Scattered over a wide area were 600,000 gold and silver coins valued at $500 million.

When this kind of treasure is found, it's easy to predict what will happen next: the legal wrangling over who really owns the treasure. Spain's government claims the treasure is theirs since the wreck is that of a nineteenth-century Spanish warship. Odyssey, the American treasure-hunting company, disputes that claim. The government of Peru has joined the litigation, claiming the coins to be "part of the patrimony of the Republic of Peru"

that was being transported from Peru to Spain in 1804. And so it goes.

God's law had become a "lost treasure" to the Israelites by Ezra's day. Its earlier "loss" (see 2 Kings 22:8-20) had carried dire consequences, and nobody wanted a repeat of those experiences. In Ezra's reading, the Jews rediscovered a precious treasure that belonged to them and them alone: the privilege of celebrating the Feast of Tabernacles to remind them how God provided for their ancestors during their wilderness wanderings.

The Bible is always at risk of becoming a "lost treasure." Sometimes its message ends up buried underneath human tradition (Mark 7:13). Sometimes its message is altered by desires to make its precepts "acceptable" to modern culture. What can we do to keep the treasure of God's Word from becoming lost all over again? —C. R. B.

C. Proclamation Made (v. 15)

15. And that they should publish and proclaim in all their cities, and in Jerusalem, saying, Go forth unto the mount, and fetch olive branches, and pine branches, and myrtle branches, and palm branches, and branches of thick trees, to make booths, as it is written.

Branches from specific trees are to be used, but the list of branches here differs from that of Leviticus 23:40. The listing in Leviticus seems to emphasize the importance of the tree branches as the people "rejoice before the Lord," perhaps waving the branches in procession. This kind of tradition is described in later texts. One of these is the non-biblical 2 Maccabees 10:6, 7, which describes the people keeping a certain "eight days with gladness, as in the feast of the tabernacles, remembering that not long afore they had held the feast of the tabernacles, when as they wandered in the mountains and dens like beasts. Therefore they bare branches, and fair boughs, and palms also, and sang psalms unto him that had given them good success."

On the other hand, today's text seems to emphasize the making of the huts themselves from these branches. Therefore, the list in Nehemiah is more robust in specifying olive, pine, myrtle, palm, and thick (or leafy) tree branches. Leviticus

23:40 does not mention as many, but includes "willows" that today's text does not.

This instruction is being read on the second day of the month, and the Feast of Tabernacles is to commence on the fifteenth day. Therefore, the people have two weeks to prepare. This is adequate time to *publish and proclaim in all their cities, and in Jerusalem.*

> **What Do You Think?**
> How can a church's ministry teams make sure to allow adequate time to prepare for the traditional observances on the church calendar?
> *Talking Points for Your Discussion*
> - Recruiting
> - Budgeting for and ordering of materials
> - Working around the schedules of likely participants
> - Other

D. Booths Built (v. 16)

16. So the people went forth, and brought them, and made themselves booths, every one upon the roof of his house, and in their courts, and in the courts of the house of God, and in the street of the water gate, and in the street of the gate of Ephraim.

The immediate obedience of the people is impressive! Five general locations are listed for placement of the booths. Those living in Jerusalem naturally have two options in this regard that visitors to Jerusalem do not have: the rooftops of personal houses and the courts (or courtyards) of those houses, where animals are kept.

Those who come from outside Jerusalem might find relatives who can share those two locations, but the visitors probably gravitate to the other three areas. Assuming that our conclusion about the location of *the water gate* is correct (v. 3, above), *the gate of Ephraim* is located about a third of a mile to the northwest of it, close to the temple mount (see 2 Kings 14:13; 2 Chronicles 25:23). Some think that the gate of Ephraim is the same as the gate of Benjamin (Jeremiah 37:13; Zechariah 14:10).

"Booths" constructed for modern-day celebrations of this feast have three sides enclosed, with the fourth side open. Branches are used for the roofs, and the structures are not rainproof. The idea is to experience some of the insecurity of the ancient Israelites in the wilderness; insecurity leads one to look to God for the provisions of life.

E. Joy Expressed (v. 17)

17. And all the congregation of them that were come again out of the captivity made booths, and sat under the booths: for since the days of Jeshua the son of Nun unto that day had not the children of Israel done so. And there was very great gladness.

The people know that they are obeying the very words of God: "At the end of every seven years, . . . in the feast of tabernacles, when all Israel is come to appear before the Lord thy God in the place which he shall choose, thou shalt read this law before all Israel in their hearing" (Deuteronomy 31:10, 11).

Both young and old have been privileged to hear the law as it was read, and we easily imagine all family members sharing the privilege of helping cut the branches, build the huts, and enjoy the produce of the fall harvest. The people are able to enjoy the tasty meat from the abundant sacrifices they make throughout the week (Numbers 29:12-38 notes the original stipulations for the animal sacrifices in this regard).

Jeshua the son of Nun has been dead for over 900 years at this point (Joshua 24:29). Comparing the reinstitution of a feast with earlier celebrations is not unusual in Scripture (see 2 Kings 23:22; 2 Chronicles 30:26; 35:18). Comparison with Jeshua (or Joshua) serves to emphasize the wilderness experience itself since that man had lived through it personally (Leviticus 23:43; Hosea 12:9).

> **What Do You Think?**
> What brings you the most joy and gladness as you live in the Lord? Why is that?
> *Talking Points for Your Discussion*
> - Worship (Psalm 100:2; 122:1)
> - Serving (Psalm 126:5, 6)
> - Victories (Psalm 21:1)
> - Difficulties (Matthew 5:11, 12; James 1:2)
> - Other

Feast of Tabernacles

F. Situation Summarized (v. 18)

18. Also day by day, from the first day unto the last day, he read in the book of the law of God. And they kept the feast seven days; and on the eighth day was a solemn assembly, according unto the manner.

It is difficult to know if this is a "year of release" (a seventh year) as prescribed in Deuteronomy 31:9-13, a year that the law is to be read. The reading from *the book of the law of God* could simply be part of a covenant renewal ceremony if this is not one of those seventh years. The description of the reading would be the same either way.

Leviticus 23:36 prescribes that the days of celebration are to end with "a solemn assembly," also called there "an holy convocation." On this day the people are required to reflect on the previous seven days and what their joy really signifies. Such reflection should accompany all our celebrations!

❧ CAN'T PUT IT DOWN . . . ! ❧

The Pulitzer Prize winning author James A. Michener (1907–1997) wrote many books of fiction and nonfiction. In the process, he became famous for what one reviewer calls his "told-from-the-beginning-of-time-saga" style of writing. His books tell stories of countries, places, eras, and events. He even wrote a novel about the writing and publishing of a novel!

Some of Michener's books are known for their length. Despite that, many readers find his books to be real page-turners—the reader keeps delaying other tasks in order to read "just one more page."

Have you ever had that kind of obsession regarding God's Word? The people of Ezra's day apparently did. During the Feast of Tabernacles, Ezra read from the law "day by day, from the first day unto the last day" as the people listened. But the peoples' fascination was not for a fictional story. No, the peoples' fascination was for *their* story. They had lived through the consequences of sin, consequences that had been written about beforehand. When was the last time in your Bible reading that you "just couldn't put it down" because you realized that it was *your* story?

—C. R. B.

Conclusion

A. Read, Obey, Celebrate

Many years ago, I had the privilege of baptizing a man known to be the town drunk. Since my father had been an alcoholic, I understood this man's problem. We helped him overcome his alcoholism and to surrender to the Lord.

The man was a good reader and had a deep baritone voice, so he read Scripture for worship services. This was a perfect fit because in those days we always read a large portion of Scripture that was relevant to the sermon. Many of us lament the fact that churches today do not have Scripture read in services as much as we used to.

Christians need to connect Scripture with celebrations of faith, especially with regard to Christmas and Easter. This can help us "experience" God's Word by reenacting what is meaningful to our faith. What improvements can your church make in this regard?

B. Prayer

Our Father, You have saved us from the exile of sin. You sacrificed Your Son that we might live eternally with Him. Help us to celebrate joyfully this great salvation in song, prayer, and Scripture reading. In Jesus' name, amen.

C. Thought to Remember

Celebrate in the Lord!

The Old Testament Jewish Calendar						
Hebrew Month	Religious Year	Civil Year	Modern Equivalent	Old Testament Observances	Day(s) of the Month	Old Testament References (partial)
Nisan (or Abib)	1	7	March—April	Passover	14	Exodus 12:6, 43-49; Leviticus 23:5; Numbers 28:16; Deuteronomy 16:1-2
				Feast of Unleavened Bread	15-21	Exodus 12:15-20; Leviticus 23:6; Numbers 28:17; Deuteronomy 16:3-4
Iyyar (or Ziv)	2	8	April—May			
Sivan	3	9	May—June	Pentecost (or Feast of Weeks, or Day of Firstfruits, or Feast of Harvest)	6	Exodus 34:22; Leviticus 23:15-21; Numbers 28:26-31; Deuteronomy 16:9-12, 16
Tammuz	4	10	June—July			
Ab	5	11	July—August			
Elul	6	12	August—September			
Tishri (or Ethanim)	7	1	September—October	Feast of Trumpets	1	Leviticus 23:23-25; Numbers 29:1-6
				Day of Atonement	10	Leviticus 23:26-32; Numbers 29:7-11
				Feast of Tabernacles (or Feast of Booths, or Feast of Ingathering)	15-21	Exodus 23:16b; 34:22b; Leviticus 23:33-36a, 39-43; Numbers 29:12-34; Deuteronomy 16:13-17; 31:10
				Assembly of the Eighth Day	22	Leviticus 23:36b; Numbers 29:35-38
Marchesvan (or Bul)	8	2	October—November			
Kislev	9	3	November—December			
Tebet	10	4	December—January			
Shebat	11	5	January—February			
Adar	12	6	February—March	Feast of Purim	14-15	Esther 9:18-28

Visual for Lesson 10. *Have this visual posted as you discuss the Feast of Tabernacles in relation to the Old Testament Jewish calendar as a whole.*

INVOLVEMENT LEARNING

Some of the activities below are also found in the helpful student book, Adult Bible Class.
Don't forget to download the free reproducible page from www.standardlesson.com to enhance your lesson!

Into the Lesson

Have the following on display as learners arrive:

Say, "Today's text describes an important practice, often ignored. Here it is, a letter at a time. When you think you know it, shout it out." The phrase to be discovered is *Read the Bible;* write letters slowly in this sequence: first the *A,* followed by the *Bs,* the *D,* the *Es,* the *H,* and the *I.* Someone will have the answer by this point.

Ask, "Is there enough of this practice in the church and in the Christian's life?" Allow brief responses, and then say, "Notice that in the verse just preceding today's text, Nehemiah 8:1, it is the people who called for the leadership to bring out God's Word for reading." Read that verse aloud.

Option. Before class begins, place in chairs copies of the "The Book" activity from the reproducible page, which you can download. Learners can begin working on this as they arrive.

Into the Word

Ask class members to stand as one of your good oral readers reads today's printed text. Before the reading, point out what the people did in Nehemiah 8:5. When the reading concludes, direct the group to be seated and ask, "How long did we stand, compared with Ezra's audience?" (Your reading probably was about two minutes, compared with the several hours reflected in verse 3.)

Ask learners to stand when they find the answers to questions you will ask. When you acknowledge someone who is standing, he or she will read aloud the appropriate part of the text that answers the question. Questions are given here in text order, but you may wish to scramble them. (Answers can be found in the verse references in italics; do not read those.)

1. What seems to be the qualification for taking part in the assembly? *(v. 2a)* 2. What was the exact date of the reading? *(v. 2b)* 3. How long did Ezra read on the first occasion? *(v. 3a)* 4. Where was the reading done? *(v. 3a)* 5. What attitude was reflected among those listening? *(end of v. 3 plus v. 13)* 6. On what day did the crowd hear of the neglected Feast of Tabernacles? *(v. 13a)* 7. From what portion of the Old Testament did the crowd hear about a feast involving booths? *(v. 14a)* 8. In which Hebrew month was the neglected feast to be celebrated? *(v. 14b)* 9. How were those not present to hear about the feast? *(v. 15a)* 10. What trees were to provide the branches for the peoples' booths? *(v. 15b)* 11. What five locations were used for the peoples' small booths? *(v. 16)* 12. What portion of the returned exiles participated in the Feast of Tabernacles? *(v. 17a)* 13. How long had it been since this feast was celebrated correctly? *(v. 17b)* 14. What atmosphere permeated the celebrators? *(end of v. 17)* 15. How many days did the reading and rejoicing continue? *(middle of v. 18)* 16. What happened on the eighth day? *(end of v. 18)*

The standing and being acknowledged can serve as a reinforcement of the idea of standing to honor God's Word.

Into Life

Give each learner two sheets of construction paper plus either a crayon, colored pencil, or marker suitable for drawing. Say, "Sketch some simple tree branches, such as palms. Don't worry about your art; just fill out the sheets quickly!" After three or four minutes, make this suggestion: "Tape these two sheets together along the long sides to form a tent. This week, stand this 'tent' over the Bible you use for study and devotion. Let it be a reminder of the importance of attending to the Word as did the returned exiles."

Option. Explore neglected practices in the modern church by having learners complete the "Eureka!" activity from the reproducible page.

COMMUNITY
OF CONFESSION

DEVOTIONAL READING: Luke 15:1-10
BACKGROUND SCRIPTURE: Nehemiah 9:1-37

NEHEMIAH 9:2, 6, 7, 9, 10, 30-36

2 And the seed of Israel separated themselves from all strangers, and stood and confessed their sins, and the iniquities of their fathers.

• •

6 Thou, even thou, art LORD alone; thou hast made heaven, the heaven of heavens, with all their host, the earth, and all things that are therein, the seas, and all that is therein, and thou preservest them all; and the host of heaven worshippeth thee.

7 Thou art the LORD the God, who didst choose Abram, and broughtest him forth out of Ur of the Chaldees, and gavest him the name of Abraham.

• •

9 And didst see the affliction of our fathers in Egypt, and heardest their cry by the Red sea;

10 And shewedst signs and wonders upon Pharaoh, and on all his servants, and on all the people of his land: for thou knewest that they dealt proudly against them. So didst thou get thee a name, as it is this day.

• •

30 Yet many years didst thou forbear them, and testifiedst against them by thy spirit in thy prophets: yet would they not give ear: therefore gavest thou them into the hand of the people of the lands.

31 Nevertheless for thy great mercies' sake thou didst not utterly consume them, nor forsake them; for thou art a gracious and merciful God.

32 Now therefore, our God, the great, the mighty, and the terrible God, who keepest covenant and mercy, let not all the trouble seem little before thee, that hath come upon us, on our kings, on our princes, and on our priests, and on our prophets, and on our fathers, and on all thy people, since the time of the kings of Assyria unto this day.

33 Howbeit thou art just in all that is brought upon us; for thou hast done right, but we have done wickedly:

34 Neither have our kings, our princes, our priests, nor our fathers, kept thy law, nor hearkened unto thy commandments and thy testimonies, wherewith thou didst testify against them.

35 For they have not served thee in their kingdom, and in thy great goodness that thou gavest them, and in the large and fat land which thou gavest before them, neither turned they from their wicked works.

36 Behold, we are servants this day, and for the land that thou gavest unto our fathers to eat the fruit thereof and the good thereof, behold, we are servants in it.

KEY VERSE

The seed of Israel separated themselves from all strangers, and stood and confessed their sins, and the iniquities of their fathers. —Nehemiah 9:2

GOD'S PEOPLE WORSHIP

Unit 3: Worshipping in Jerusalem Again (Nehemiah)

LESSONS 10–13

LESSON AIMS

After participating in this lesson, each student will be able to:

1. List the sins confessed by the former exiles and the acts of God that they acknowledged.

2. Tell why acknowledging God's faithful acts helps one put personal sin in perspective.

3. Plan a worship service in which songs of praise are followed by songs of confession and reading of Scripture.

LESSON OUTLINE

Introduction

A. The Burden of Unconfessed Sin

When I was about 14 years old, I did something that I knew my parents would not approve: I straddled the front fender of a car (when cars had conspicuously rounded fenders) while holding a rifle to shoot rabbits. I did this at night, when the rabbits would be paralyzed by the car's headlights. I must confess, even now, that I lied to my parents when confronted about it. Eventually, however, my conscience got the better of me, and I confessed.

My parents were more aggravated by my lie than by my poor judgment. Certainly, my actions had been dangerous to all the nonthinking teenagers connected with this incident, but perhaps the worst thing I did was to protect myself by lying.

When I did confess, I felt a huge burden lifted, and I was ready for any punishment. My parents grounded me for a year—yes, a whole year. They said it took that long for them to regain trust in me. After that experience I realized that the best way to live life before God is always to tell the truth, confess sins often, repent sincerely, and seek forgiveness before going forward.

The Word of God is filled with examples of sinful people confessing sins, repenting, and receiving forgiveness by a loving and gracious God. We will see one such example in today's lesson.

B. Lesson Background

Last week's lesson considered events that concluded with the weeklong observance of the Feast of Tabernacles in the seventh month of the Jewish calendar. Today's text takes us to "the twenty and fourth day" of that same month (Nehemiah 9:1); thus our Lesson Background is the same as that of last week's lesson.

Since the actions of today's lesson text follow so closely from those of last week's, we can see both as parts of a covenant renewal ceremony. This included historical reviews of the covenant relationship that highlighted the people's failures. There are many parallels to be drawn with the covenant renewal treaty of Moses in Deuteronomy 1–4. In addition to that example, the act of confession of sin by selectively rehearsing the history

Community of Confession

of God's people is found in Ezra 9; Psalms 78, 106; Daniel 9; and Acts 7, among others.

I. Confessing Sin
(NEHEMIAH 9:2)

Nehemiah 9:1 tells us that the event of today's lesson occurs on a particular day when the people gather to fast, put on sackcloth, and sprinkle "earth upon them." These are ancient practices of grief and contrition. We see fasting in this regard in 2 Samuel 1:12; Joel 2:12; etc. Donning sackcloth is connected with mourning in Genesis 37:34; 2 Samuel 3:31; etc. The sprinkling of dirt or ashes in such a context is seen in Jeremiah 6:26. Seeing all three together, then, is a powerful indicator of the serious nature of the occasion (compare Esther 4:3; Daniel 9:3; Jonah 3:5, 6).

A. Preparation (v. 2a)

2a. And the seed of Israel separated themselves from all strangers.

An important preparatory step for what is about to happen is the Israelites' decision to separate themselves from those not of Israelite descent *(strangers)*. The text does not tell us the extent of this separation. It can be as weighty as divorcing foreign wives (compare Ezra 9:1, 2; 10:3, 17) or as simple as physical distancing from the non-Israelites who are living in the land (2 Kings 17:24, 34; Ezra 4:1-3). In any case, only the *seed of Israel* can renew or reaffirm Israel's covenant with God!

HOW TO SAY IT

Assyrians	Uh-*sear*-e-unz.
Augustine	*Aw*-gus-teen or Aw-*gus*-tin.
Babylonians	Bab-ih-*low*-nee-unz.
Chaldees	*Kal*-deez.
Hagar	*Hay*-gar.
Isaac	*Eye*-zuk.
Ishmael	*Ish*-may-el.
Keturah	Keh-*too*-ruh.
Nehemiah	*Nee*-huh-*my*-uh.
patriarch	*pay*-tree-ark.
Ur	Er.
Yahweh (*Hebrew*)	*Yah*-weh.

B. Participation (v. 2b)

2b. And stood and confessed their sins, and the iniquities of their fathers.

Just as the people had stood to hear the law read a few days earlier (Nehemiah 8:5), so now they stand to confess their sins. Not only do the people confess their personal sins, they also identify themselves with the sins of their ancestors as Daniel does in Daniel 9. All Israelites share in *the iniquities of their fathers*. This outlook can be defined as "corporate" rather than "individualistic."

> **What Do You Think?**
> Should churches implement a time in the worship service for public confession of sins? Why, or why not?
> *Talking Points for Your Discussion*
> - 1 Samuel 7:5, 6
> - Acts 19:17-20
> - Other

❦ SEEING THE CONNECTION ❦

Augustine (AD 354–430) is one of the four "doctors" of the early church. He is certainly one of the most significant writers and leaders of that period in church history. I had a professor who once stated that 85 percent of everything that modern Christians believe comes through an Augustinian framework. Augustine, of course, got most of his content from the apostle Paul's writings. Even so, Augustine thoughts are stamped on much Christian doctrine today.

Augustine wrote many books, but probably the most popular and well-known is his *Confessions*. The book is set up as a prayer to God, and in this format Augustine confesses the errors of his life (he was about 45 when he wrote it; he would live another 30 years). He admits that he and his boyhood chums stole fruit from a neighbor's tree. He admits his error in following a deviant religion for almost 10 years. He confesses his struggles with sexual purity through his young adult years.

All in all, Augustine's book is an open and candid avowal of his sins. Later he would become the greatest theologian in early Christianity. Do we see the connection?

—J. B. N.

II. Acknowledging God
(NEHEMIAH 9:6, 7)

Nehemiah 9:3 (not in today's text) tells us that the people spend "one fourth part of the day" listening to the law being read and another fourth part confessing sins and worshipping. This is not silent meditation, since the people are led by several named Levites who set the example with loud voices (vv. 4, 5). The people are serious!

A. Creator of the Universe (v. 6)

6a. Thou, even thou, art LORD alone; thou hast made heaven, the heaven of heavens, with all their host.

The Hebrew creed is found in Deuteronomy 6:4: "Hear, O Israel: the Lord our God is one Lord." This short phrase has many implications, the most important being that Israel acknowledges Yahweh to be the only God. The power to create belongs only to Him. The Hebrew behind *with all their host* matches exactly that in Genesis 2:1 and Psalm 33:6, both translated "and all the host of them." This refers to the stars. Pagans often worship these as gods, but Israel is to know the stars simply as part of God's good creation (Deuteronomy 4:19; contrast 2 Kings 21:3).

> *What Do You Think?*
> What improvements can churches make in worshipping God intentionally as Creator?
> *Talking Points for Your Discussion*
> - Job 9:8, 9
> - Psalm 95:6; 121:1, 2; 134
> - Jeremiah 10:11-16
> - Revelation 14:7

6b. The earth, and all things that are therein, the seas, and all that is therein, and thou preservest them all;

The prayer continues to reflect the creation account of Genesis 1. The last phrase here reminds us that God not only creates, He also cares for and protects His good creation (see Genesis 2:5-15).

6c. And the host of heaven worshippeth thee.

The Hebrew behind the word *host* here and in verse 6a is the same. However, the phrasing here suggests that *host* is now being used differently: as angelic beings who constantly praise and worship God as Creator. To acknowledge God is to recognize Him first as Creator (as in Psalm 136:5-9).

B. Maker of Covenants (v. 7)

7. Thou art the LORD the God, who didst choose Abram, and broughtest him forth out of Ur of the Chaldees, and gavest him the name of Abraham.

Genesis 12:1-3 is a key text in the Bible. There we see God calling Abram to leave his country, people, and father's family to go to a promised land. The call is first pronounced in *Ur of the Chaldees* (see Genesis 15:7; compare Acts 7:4). Promises are made: (1) Abram will become a great nation; (2) God will bless him; and (3) Abram's name will become great. Abram's name is changed to *Abraham* in the midst of God's assigning circumcision as a sign of the covenant (Genesis 17:3-14). Leaving behind the designation "exalted father" (the meaning of *Abram*), this man becomes "father of a multitude" (the meaning of *Abraham*).

> *What Do You Think?*
> What changes should be apparent in our lives as our designation changes from *Lost* to *Saved*?
> *Talking Points for Your Discussion*
> - Changed attitudes
> - Changed behavior
> - Changed speech

Abraham did indeed become father of a multitude when we consider the descendants of Ishmael (Hagar's son; Genesis 25:12-18), Isaac (Sarah's son; 25:19-23), and Keturah (25:1-4). The covenant promise goes only through Isaac, however, and then through his son Jacob, the immediate patriarch of the 12 tribes. This is the "seed of Israel" of Nehemiah 9:2 (above), now reduced to a remnant.

III. Recalling Redemption
(NEHEMIAH 9:9, 10)

Nehemiah 9:8 summarizes the faithfulness of both God and Abraham. Our next verse then jumps more than 400 years ahead in time.

Community of Confession

A. Divine Presence (v. 9)

9. And didst see the affliction of our fathers in Egypt, and heardest their cry by the Red sea.

While enslaved in Egypt, the Israelites "cried, and their cry came up unto God by reason of the bondage" (Exodus 2:23). Israel's God "heard their groaning," "remembered his covenant with Abraham, with Isaac, and with Jacob," and "looked upon the children of Israel" (Exodus 2:24, 25).

The exodus events that followed become for subsequent generations of Israelites the symbol of God's great deliverance (see Psalms 78, 105, 106, 135, 136). The sequence of saving events occurred from the land of Goshen in Egypt to the Red Sea and beyond (see Exodus 7–14). God was with His people!

B. Divine Power (v. 10)

10. And shewedst signs and wonders upon Pharaoh, and on all his servants, and on all the people of his land: for thou knewest that they dealt proudly against them. So didst thou get thee a name, as it is this day.

The phrase *signs and wonders* surely refers to the plagues on Egypt (Exodus 7:14–11:10), but it also can include the earlier miracle of the snake (7:8-13) and the later miracle of crossing the Red Sea on dry ground (14:16-31). The song of Moses and Miriam that resulted (15:1-18, 21) confirms that God had indeed made a name for himself forever through these events.

The fame of God's power and name spread far ahead of the Israelites as they trekked toward the promised land (Joshua 2:8-11). The name of God is forever linked to the exodus events.

What Do You Think?

How important are *signs and wonders* to you? How has your understanding in this regard changed as you have grown spiritually?

Talking Points for Your Discussion

- Matthew 16:1-4; 24:3-31
- John 6:30-33; 10:40-42
- 1 Corinthians 1:22-24; 14:22
- 2 Thessalonians 2:9
- Other

IV. Admitting Truth
(NEHEMIAH 9:30-36)

Nehemiah 9:11-29, the intervening verses not in today's text, recount God's miraculous provisions for the Israelites during their journey toward the promised land. Also recounted are instances of Israelite disobedience and God's responses through the period of the judges and beyond.

A. Warning and Judgment (v. 30)

30. Yet many years didst thou forbear them, and testifiedst against them by thy spirit in thy prophets: yet would they not give ear: therefore gavest thou them into the hand of the people of the lands.

God's forbearance of Israelite disobedience has been remarkable. God's divine patience is best illustrated by His sending of many prophets to warn the people before judgment would come upon them. The stories of these servants of God are scattered throughout the period of the kings, from the unified kingdom under Saul, David, and Solomon (1050–931 BC) to that of the divided kingdoms of Israel and Judah.

Yet the people did not listen. As a result, the northern kingdom of Israel was destroyed by the Assyrians in 722 BC (2 Kings 17), and the southern kingdom of Judah was destroyed by the Babylonians in 586 BC. Only by God's patience did the kingdoms of Israel and Judah last as long as they did!

B. Grace and Mercies (v. 31)

31. Nevertheless for thy great mercies' sake thou didst not utterly consume them, nor forsake them; for thou art a gracious and merciful God.

God has great mercies (plural in Hebrew), so that God's people still survive even if only as a remnant (Isaiah 10:20-23). The fact that a remnant is allowed to return from exile reveals God's graciousness. The temple has been rebuilt (515 BC), the walls repaired (445 BC), and God's people are allowed to seek covenant renewal—a renewed commitment to God's law. No wonder God is described as *a gracious and merciful God*!

C. Then and Now (v. 32)

32. Now therefore, our God, the great, the mighty, and the terrible God, who keepest covenant and mercy, let not all the trouble seem little before thee, that hath come upon us, on our kings, on our princes, and on our priests, and on our prophets, and on our fathers, and on all thy people, since the time of the kings of Assyria unto this day.

Here begins the formal request for forgiveness while the sins of the people and their ancestors are confessed. God is once again addressed in majestic language. The word *terrible* has the sense of "inspiring terror"; God is to be feared. The fact that God *keepest covenant and mercy* refers to God's promise to Abraham, which God keeps intact by His own covenant loyalty. In spite of the unfaithfulness of the Israelites throughout their history as a people, God has always been faithful to His side of the covenant. (See the similar beginning of the prayer in Nehemiah 1:5.)

The hardships that came upon the Israelites during the time of the divided kingdoms of Israel and Judah (931–586 BC) continue to haunt the remnant that has returned from Babylonian exile. *The time of the kings of Assyria* include the aggressions of at least six Assyrian leaders between 745 and 663 BC (see 2 Kings 18:9, 13; 1 Chronicles 5:26; Isaiah 20:1; and Ezra 4:2, 10).

Even after the days of those kings pass, foreign powers—namely, Babylon and Persia—continue to rule over God's people. Persian overlords are exacting heavy taxation (Nehemiah 9:37). Having the temple rebuilt and the walls of Jerusalem repaired do not reduce such hardships.

D. Right and Wrong (vv. 33-35)

33. Howbeit thou art just in all that is brought upon us; for thou hast done right, but we have done wickedly.

If God's people are to confess properly and adequately, they must confess that God is in the right and they themselves are in the wrong. This is confessing at a corporate level. This kind of confessing contrasts with that done at an individual level, illustrated by King David's confession "I have sinned against the Lord" (2 Samuel 12:13; see also Psalm 51:1-4).

34. Neither have our kings, our princes, our priests, nor our fathers, kept thy law, nor hearkened unto thy commandments and thy testimonies, wherewith thou didst testify against them.

Moses warned in Deuteronomy 30:15-20 that if the people did not obey the law, then God would not allow them to keep the land. That warning went unheeded, and God was true to His word. It is interesting that there is no mention of "our prophets" in this listing of the leaders of Israel in contrast with the similar listing of Nehemiah 9:32. The prophets were the ones who pointed out the sinfulness of the people, encouraging them to repent and turn back to God. Perhaps that is why the prophets are left out in this confessional list, which is concerned with assigning blame. The prophets were not to blame, although they suffered along with everyone else (the topic of v. 32, above).

35. For they have not served thee in their kingdom, and in thy great goodness that thou gavest them, and in the large and fat land which thou gavest before them, neither turned they from their wicked works.

One of the most insidious sins of God's people is that of ingratitude. To take for granted God's gift of a good land and all the accompanying blessings has led to pride, selfishness, and corruption (see Deuteronomy 8:10-18; 9:4-6). On a few occasions a king might turn to God for deliverance, and God would deliver (example: 2 Kings 19:14-37). But for the most part, Israel's leaders were wicked in their words and deeds and did not repent, leading the people astray by their bad example (compare Jeremiah 44:15-18).

E. Consequences and Status (v. 36)

36. Behold, we are servants this day, and for the land that thou gavest unto our fathers to eat the fruit thereof and the good thereof, behold, we are servants in it.

Even though a remnant has returned from exile, the people are still subject to the Persian king. They are, in effect, slaves in their own land. What the people need is a clean slate of forgiveness and rededication to the covenant. That's something we all need at some point!

❈ *SLAVES IN A FREE LAND* ❈

Nehemiah pointed out that God had given the land of Palestine to the Israelites' forefathers, but the descendants were servants, or slaves, in it. Something similar could be said of many peoples and countries today, particularly of America. Americans pride themselves on their heritage of freedom. We tell of the daring resistance of our forefathers in the Revolutionary War and the bold pronouncements of the Declaration of Independence. We tell of the country's 400,000 deaths in World War II and sacrifices on the home front that helped defeat tyranny.

Americans glory in their freedoms, but often such self-congratulations ring hollow. Millions of Americans are slaves to addictions—whether of alcohol, drugs, or pornography. Other millions are slaves of materialism, constantly wanting more and more possessions, but feeling less and less satisfied with their acquisitions.

We are truly free only when we are faithful to God and His Christ. Only then will we experience the liberating freedom of His provision and His care for us. As Paul says, we were once "the servants of sin," but we are now "free from sin, . . . the servants of righteousness" (Romans 6:17, 18). Make sure you don't go back to the old slavery!

—J. B. N.

Conclusion

A. A Call to Confess

There is a little congregation near my home where I often serve as the "supply" preacher. The congregation has a liturgy each Sunday where sins

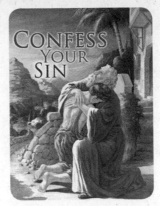

Visual for
Lesson 11

Point to this visual as you discuss how confession of sin looks both down in sorrow and up to God.

are confessed corporately. After the congregation repeats the confession, the worship leader recognizes forgiveness and acceptance of the promised grace of God. The congregation responds with a hearty "Amen!" There is something good and real about that liturgy. By contrast, the church where I am a member seldom confesses sins corporately. We hardly even talk about sin.

A problem in many cultures today is the highly individualistic and narcissistic attitudes that prevent people from identifying with the sins of their ancestors, much less their own personal sins. Many seem to have a difficult time criticizing their own country for social and economic injustices of the past and present. Perhaps it is time to admit corporate guilt for the sins committed by our culture and country, for social and economic wrongs in the past and present. Admitting personal sins on a daily basis is also very appropriate. Today's lesson is a call to confess.

B. Prayer

Father, we confess our sins, knowing that both our deeds and our thoughts have not been what You want. As a church, we are not the witness to our Lord Jesus that we should be. Forgive us and renew us in the power of Your Holy Spirit. In Jesus' name, amen.

C. Thought to Remember

Second chances come *after* confession.

INVOLVEMENT LEARNING

Some of the activities below are also found in the helpful student book, Adult Bible Class.
Don't forget to download the free reproducible page from www.standardlesson.com to enhance your lesson!

Into the Lesson

Have on display as learners arrive the word *SIN* in 10-inch letters; leave a small gap between the *I* and *N*. As class begins, say, "This is not a lesson about sin!" Hesitate, then add, in 6-inch letters the series *CONFES* before the *SI*; also add an *O* of that size between the *I* and *N*. Say, "This is a lesson about what sin necessitates, what sin—for an intellectually honest person—demands."

Into the Word

Give each learner a handout titled *Confession Elements of Worship,* which you have prepared in advance. List the following three statements down the left side, leaving plenty of blank space on the right for writing: 1. Confession of who God is. 2. Confession of current and past sin. 3. Confession of a need for God's grace.

Say, "As I read today's text aloud, jot down quickly the verse numbers beside these three elements where you see them. Then we'll go back over them more thoroughly." As you read the lesson text aloud, verbalize the verse numbers as you cross from one verse to the next.

After this initial run through, ask, "In which verses do you see confession of who God is?" As learners offer suggestions, ask, "What phrase or description in that verse makes you think so?" Expect learners to note God as sovereign Creator (v. 6), discerner of hearts (v. 7), compassionate (v. 9), able to perform miracles (v. 10), patient (v. 30), gracious (v. 31), merciful (vv. 31, 32), great (v. 32), mighty (v. 32), able to incite terror (v. 32), keeper of covenants (v. 32), just (v. 33).

Then ask, "In which verses do you see confession of current and past sin?" As learners offer suggestions, ask, "What phrase or description in that verse makes you think so?" Expect learners to note both confessions in the description of the people doing just that (v. 2). Confession of current sin is seen in the phrase "we have done wickedly" (v. 33), depending on whether the we is intended to refer only to those speaking it at the time or collectively to those of the current and past generations. Confession of past sin (sins of forefathers) is evident by "would they not give ear" (v. 30) in referring to the disobedience of kings, princes, priests, and fathers who "have not served thee" (vv. 34, 35).

Then ask, "In which verses do you see confession of a need for God's grace?" As learners offer suggestions, ask, "What phrase or description in that verse makes you think so?" Expect learners to note the confession of a need for God's grace in terms of "the affliction of our fathers" (v. 9), "let not all the trouble seem little" (v. 32) and "behold, we are servants" (twice in v. 36).

Have a good oral reader stand to read Luke 15:21, which is a confession of sin and unworthiness; then have another stand to read 1 John 3:2-10, which is a statement of our privileged position as forgiven children of God. Say, "Confession always changes relationships. Our confession of the lordship of Christ and our submission to His plan of salvation have made us His sons and daughters! Confession is good for the soul!"

Into Life

Divide the class into three "subcommittees for planning a confessional worship." Give these directions: *Subcommittee A*—Select three or four hymns or songs of praise that reflect praise similar to today's text; *Subcommittee B*—Select three or four hymns or songs that reflect confession similar to today's text; *Subcommittee C*—Select two shorter and two longer Scripture passages that parallel the ideas of today's text." Provide hymnals, songbooks, and Bible concordances to groups as appropriate. Discuss results as a class.

Option. Personalize the lesson by having learners complete either the "Since God Is . . . , Then I Must . . ." or "Separated" activities (or both) from the reproducible page, which you can download.

DEDICATION OF THE WALL

DEVOTIONAL READING: Psalm 96

BACKGROUND SCRIPTURE: Nehemiah 12:27-43

NEHEMIAH 12:27-38, 43

27 And at the dedication of the wall of Jerusalem they sought the Levites out of all their places, to bring them to Jerusalem, to keep the dedication with gladness, both with thanksgivings, and with singing, with cymbals, psalteries, and with harps.

28 And the sons of the singers gathered themselves together, both out of the plain country round about Jerusalem, and from the villages of Netophathi;

29 Also from the house of Gilgal, and out of the fields of Geba and Azmaveth: for the singers had builded them villages round about Jerusalem.

30 And the priests and the Levites purified themselves, and purified the people, and the gates, and the wall.

31 Then I brought up the princes of Judah upon the wall, and appointed two great companies of them that gave thanks, whereof one went on the right hand upon the wall toward the dung gate:

32 And after them went Hoshaiah, and half of the princes of Judah,

33 And Azariah, Ezra, and Meshullam,

34 Judah, and Benjamin, and Shemaiah, and Jeremiah,

35 And certain of the priests' sons with trumpets; namely, Zechariah the son of Jonathan, the son of Shemaiah, the son of Mattaniah, the son of Michaiah, the son of Zaccur, the son of Asaph:

36 And his brethren, Shemaiah, and Azarael, Milalai, Gilalai, Maai, Nethaneel, and Judah, Hanani, with the musical instruments of David the man of God, and Ezra the scribe before them.

37 And at the fountain gate, which was over against them, they went up by the stairs of the city of David, at the going up of the wall, above the house of David, even unto the water gate eastward.

38 And the other company of them that gave thanks went over against them, and I after them, and the half of the people upon the wall, from beyond the tower of the furnaces even unto the broad wall.

. . . .

43 Also that day they offered great sacrifices, and rejoiced: for God had made them rejoice with great joy: the wives also and the children rejoiced: so that the joy of Jerusalem was heard even afar off.

KEY VERSE

Also that day they offered great sacrifices, and rejoiced: for God had made them rejoice with great joy: the wives also and the children rejoiced: so that the joy of Jerusalem was heard even afar off. —Nehemiah 12:43

GOD'S PEOPLE WORSHIP

Unit 3: Worshipping in Jerusalem Again (Nehemiah)

LESSONS 10–13

LESSON AIMS

After participating in this lesson, each student will be able to:

1. Describe how ancient Israel gave thanks for a great accomplishment through a joyous but formal praise service.

2. Explain how the celebration and worship in the text can be a model for a proper celebration of any ministry task successfully completed.

3. Plan a detailed celebration for the church of a past or possible future great accomplishment.

LESSON OUTLINE

Introduction

A. Joyful Celebration

I teach a certain overview study of the Bible in the local church. The uniqueness of this particular study is in its use of symbolic pictures. To learn this system, teacher trainees commit themselves to an intensive study of two and half hours each week for two nine-month periods. After two years, the teacher trainees are ready to teach, but not until they celebrate their accomplishment at a graduation banquet. I plan every detail.

First, I set the theme of the banquet. My wife and I create a three-dimensional scene that illustrates the theme, and we place it in the center of the banquet area. Proper lighting heightens the impact.

The best cooks in the church prepare the meal; others serve with a touch of class. In addition to the graduates, we invite their spouses and the leaders of the church along with their spouses.

The dress is formal. We have a guest speaker who addresses our theme. A string ensemble plays throughout the banquet. Each graduate is called up to receive a personalized certificate inscribed by a professional calligraphist. A gold pin or pendant symbolizing this particular study also is awarded to each graduate.

There is special joy expressed, with hugs and picture-taking. The evening concludes with the feeling that we have celebrated a great accomplishment properly. Then the real work begins as the new graduates take on the task of teaching this particular overview study of the Bible.

I do everything I can to make this celebration meaningful, formal, and joyous. Today's lesson offers us something of a biblical precedent for celebrations conducted this way.

B. Lesson Background: Geography

The topic that dominates the first half of the book of Nehemiah is the rebuilding of Jerusalem's walls and gates. That task was completed in 445 BC, and it was an exceptional accomplishment. Nehemiah 12 (today's text) takes us to the dedication ceremony of those rebuilt walls.

The biblical writer is highly selective in his use of information to tell the story of the celebration, and piecing it together is not easy. Much information that we may wish to have is not included. For example, today's lesson is about two processionals that march around the rebuilt walls, but the starting point for these processionals is not stated.

An educated guess is that the starting place is the Valley Gate. This gate faced west, overlooking the Central Valley adjacent to the narrow City of David (the oldest section of Jerusalem). This is the gate where Nehemiah began and ended his nocturnal inspection after arriving in Jerusalem (Nehemiah 2:11-16). We will have more educated guesses to make regarding the locations of other named gates that the processionals crossed.

C. Lesson Background: Levites

Immediately preceding today's lesson text is an extended listing of the names and duties of priests and Levites who had returned to Jerusalem from exile. Levites play a vital role in today's lesson, so a refresher on their origin and functions is in order.

The designation *Levites* refers to descendants of the man Levi (Genesis 29:34; 35:23). All priests of Israel came from the tribe of Levi, although not all male Levites ended up becoming priests (Deuteronomy 17:9, 18; etc.; contrast 1 Kings 12:31).

The overarching task of the Levites was "to wait on the sons of Aaron [that is, the priests] for the service of the house of the Lord, in the courts, and in the chambers, and in the purifying of all holy things, and the work of the service of the house of God" (1 Chronicles 23:28; see extended

HOW TO SAY IT

Azarael	*Az*-air-el or Ah-*zay*-ree-ul.
Azariah	Az-uh-*rye*-uh.
Gilalai	*Gill*-ah-lie (*G* as in *get*).
Hanani	Huh-*nay*-nye.
Hoshaiah	Hoe-*shay*-yuh.
Maai	May-*a*-eye.
Mattaniah	Mat-uh-*nye*-uh.
Michaiah	My-*kay*-uh.
Milalai	Mih-ah-*lay*-eye.
Nethaneel	Nih-*than*-e-el (*th* as in *thin*).
Netophathi	Nee-*toe*-fuh-thi (*i* as in *eye*).
Shemaiah	She-*may*-yuh or Shee-*my*-uh.

description in vv. 29-32). A key levitical function under this umbrella was that of *musician,* which is an important part of today's study. Precedent for this function stretches back many centuries (see 1 Chronicles 6:1-31; 15:16-22; 23:1-5; 25:1-6; 2 Chronicles 5:12; 7:6). Levites were still musicians in the days of Ezra and Nehemiah (see Ezra 2:40, 41; 3:10, 11; Nehemiah 7:43, 44).

I. Dedication Preparation
(NEHEMIAH 12:27-30)
A. Musicians (v. 27)

27. And at the dedication of the wall of Jerusalem they sought the Levites out of all their places, to bring them to Jerusalem, to keep the dedication with gladness, both with thanksgivings, and with singing, with cymbals, psalteries, and with harps.

In ancient times as in modern, music is part of many great celebrations. The joyful expressions of thanksgiving planned by Nehemiah for *the dedication of the wall of Jerusalem* are to be accompanied by instrumental and vocal music. Because of the Levites' skills as musicians (see the Lesson Background), they are a necessary part of this celebration. The need to seek *the Levites out of all their places* should be understood in light of Nehemiah 11:20: "The residue of Israel, of the priests, and the Levites, were in all the cities of Judah, every one in his inheritance." Since not all Levites live in Jerusalem, it takes a lot of planning to ensure their presence at the ceremony to come.

> *What Do You Think?*
> What makes a celebration of thanksgiving memorable and meaningful to you? Why is that?
> *Talking Points for Your Discussion*
> - Thoroughness of the planning
> - Nature of the event being celebrated
> - Personal participation
> - Other

Three types of instruments are mentioned, and they match exactly the three noted in 1 Chronicles 15:16 and 25:1 regarding the days of King David. *Cymbals* are metal percussive instruments that are struck against one another (see 1 Chronicles 13:8; 15:16, 19, 28; Psalm 150:5). The *psalteries* are known from ancient drawings to be stringed instruments. They have a curved yoke and a sounding box shaped like a jar (see Psalms 57:8; 71:22; 150:3). The *harps* are a kind of lyre having a rounded bottom and yoke-arms curved only slightly (see Psalm 137:2).

This is not a complete listing of the musical instruments to be used (see Nehemiah 12:35, 36, below). The main idea is that all these instruments are portable—they can be held and played as the people march on the walls. Some large psalteries have as many as 10 strings (see Psalm 33:2), and these may not be included here.

B. Singers (vv. 28, 29)

28, 29. And the sons of the singers gathered themselves together, both out of the plain country round about Jerusalem, and from the villages of Netophathi; also from the house of Gilgal, and out of the fields of Geba and Azmaveth: for the singers had builded them villages round about Jerusalem.

Besides those Levites who can play musical instruments, singers from throughout the districts surrounding Jerusalem are called on to join the celebration. Good singers are always appreciated!

What Do You Think?

How can churches improve the contribution of singing to the worship experience? How do we avoid merely stating personal preferences in answering this?

Talking Points for Your Discussion

- Matching style to purpose and/or participants
- Use of variety or thematic selections
- Teaching music to worshippers
- Adding a music minister to the staff
- Other

The places where the singers live are mentioned. Notice that the phrase *round about Jerusalem* occurs twice. These two uses serve as bookends for the four location-names between them. This indicates that these four locations are fairly close to Jerusalem.

The villages of Netophathi draw their designation from the family name *Netopha;* these settlements are about 3.5 miles to the southeast of Bethlehem (compare Nehemiah 7:26), or about 6 miles from Jerusalem. This seems to be an ancestral home of the Levites, and some choose to resettle here after their return from exile (1 Chronicles 2:54; 9:2, 14-16; Ezra 2:22). *The house of Gilgal* is probably the traditional village of Gilgal near Jericho, where the Israelites renewed their covenant with God in the days of Joshua (see Joshua 4:19, 20; 5:9, 10). This is about 15 miles northeast of Jerusalem. *Geba and Azmaveth* are Benjamite villages about 6 miles north/northeast of Jerusalem (1 Chronicles 6:60; Ezra 2:24, 26; Nehemiah 7:28; 11:31).

This scattering of homes of the Levite singers may indicate how difficult it is to scratch out a living by dwelling any closer to Jerusalem. Nehemiah 11:1, 2 seems to indicate that the city of Jerusalem itself is not a desirable place to live.

C. Purifications (v. 30)

30. And the priests and the Levites purified themselves, and purified the people, and the gates, and the wall.

Before the proceedings can get underway, all participants are purified. Our text does not tell us what this involves. On other occasions, purification entails changing or washing one's clothing (see Genesis 35:2, 3; Numbers 8:21), bathing or participating in a ritual pouring of water over the body (Exodus 19:10, 14; Numbers 8:5-7; 19:12, 19; Ezekiel 36:25), and sexual abstinence (Exodus 19:15). See the extended discussion in Numbers 19.

How *the priests and the Levites* purify *the gates, and the wall* is not stated either. This purification may be similar to the cleansing of the temple during Hezekiah's reforms (2 Chronicles 29:15-19). The procedure involved in the cleansing of houses may also be used (Leviticus 14:49-53). The gates and walls are considered unclean because of human contamination in general and all the blood that was shed when the Babylonians destroyed the city. The people need to regard Jerusalem as "the holy city" (Nehemiah 11:1). Therefore, the priests, Levites, people, gates, and walls all have to be purified before the dedication can begin.

II. Dedication Participation
(NEHEMIAH 12:31-38)
A. Directives (v. 31)

31. Then I brought up the princes of Judah upon the wall, and appointed two great companies of them that gave thanks, whereof one went on the right hand upon the wall toward the dung gate.

Nehemiah launches the celebration by forming many of the purified participants into *two great companies* or processionals. The direction one group will take is noted here and in verse 37 (below); the direction of the other group is described in verses 38, 39 (below).

The unstated starting point of the two groups is probably the Valley Gate (see the Lesson Background). This possibility fits well with one group's counterclockwise direction of travel, since to go to *the right hand upon the wall toward the dung gate* is to go south from that gate if starting from outside the city (see further discussion in v. 37, below).

> **What Do You Think?**
> What have you seen worship planners and leaders do to enhance the worship experience?
> *Talking Points for Your Discussion*
> ▪ Use of visual media
> ▪ Use of drama
> ▪ Mixing various "moods" of music
> ▪ Incorporation of silence
> ▪ Other

B. Names (vv. 32-36)

32, 33. And after them went Hoshaiah, and half of the princes of Judah, and Azariah, Ezra, and Meshullam,

What an honor to have one's name recorded as a participant in this celebration! The name *Hoshaiah* means "Yahweh has saved," but other than that we know nothing about this man. The name *Azariah* means "Yahweh has helped," and there are numerous men with this name in the Old Testament. The *Ezra* mentioned here is not the well-known priest and scribe of this time, since that Ezra is mentioned three verses later as the one leading this

procession. The name *Meshullam* means "reconciled"; it is a common name (note two men with this name in Nehemiah 12:13, 16).

34. Judah, and Benjamin, and Shemaiah, and Jeremiah,

Judah and *Benjamin* are the well-known names of two of the tribes of Israel. But these are also the names of various individuals (see Ezra 10:23, 32; Nehemiah 11:9; 12:8). The name *Shemaiah* means "the Lord has heard," and roughly two dozen men have this name in the Old Testament (compare Ezra 8:13, 16; 10:21, 31; Nehemiah 3:29; 6:10; 10:8; 12:6). The *Jeremiah* noted here is not, of course, the famous prophet of that name.

> **What Do You Think?**
> What are some good ways to honor those who devote much time to enhancing our worship experience?
> *Talking Points for Your Discussion*
> ▪ Public expressions of recognition
> ▪ Private expressions of recognition

35. And certain of the priests' sons with trumpets; namely, Zechariah the son of Jonathan, the son of Shemaiah, the son of Mattaniah, the son of Michaiah, the son of Zaccur, the son of Asaph:

Numbers 10:8; 31:6 and 1 Chronicles 15:24 establish that priests blow trumpets. That pattern seems to be followed here as it is in Ezra 3:10.

The *King James Version* has the word *namely* italicized, meaning that this word does not occur in the original language; it has been added by the translators for smooth reading. Thus there is a bit of uncertainty whether this *Zechariah* is one of *the priests' sons with trumpets*. Some think that Nehemiah 12:41 establishes that he is a priest; others think that he is a Levite, not a priest, since his lineage goes back to Asaph (1 Chronicles 25:1, 2).

36a. And his brethren, Shemaiah, and Azarael, Milalai, Gilalai, Maai, Nethaneel, and Judah, Hanani, with the musical instruments of David the man of God,

The avalanche of names continues! *Shemaiah,* a common name, means "the Lord has heard." *Azarael* means "God is helper"; six men have this

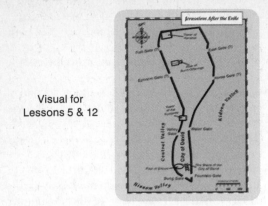

Visual for
Lessons 5 & 12

Use this visual to help your learners trace the routes of the two processionals in today's study.

name (with variant spellings) in the Old Testament. The names *Milalai, Gilalai,* and *Maai* occur only here. *Nethaneel,* a fairly common name, means "God has given." Regarding *Judah,* see comments on verse 34 (above). Nehemiah has a brother named *Hanani* (see Nehemiah 1:2; 7:2), but this is not the same person; the meaning is "gracious."

The phrase *the musical instruments of David* may indicate the use of instruments in addition to those listed in Nehemiah 12:27 (above). One such possibility is pipes (that is, flutes; compare 1 Kings 1:40; Isaiah 30:29). The timbrel (that is, the tambourine; compare Psalms 81:2; 149:3; 150:4) is another possibility.

36b. And Ezra the scribe before them.

Ezra leads the processional group that goes south (to the "right," v. 31, above). Nehemiah, for his part, accompanies the processional group that goes north (v. 38, below).

C. Processionals (vv. 37, 38)

37. And at the fountain gate, which was over against them, they went up by the stairs of the city of David, at the going up of the wall, above the house of David, even unto the water gate eastward.

The group that goes to the right (south), led by Ezra, first reaches the Dung Gate (not listed here, but see v. 31, above). That gate is near the southernmost point of the wall. This is a walk of about 1,000 cubits, or 500 yards (Nehemiah 3:13). In

this area, the group makes a sharp turn to the north, toward *the fountain gate.* This is located close to the Pool of Siloah (or Siloam; compare Nehemiah 3:15; John 9:7, 11).

Walking along the top of the wall apparently is interrupted as the group goes *up by the stairs of the city of David.* Perhaps the wall is not suitable to walk upon in this area. Farther north, the group seems to ascend the wall again as it makes its way to *the water gate* (compare Nehemiah 3:26; 8:1-3, 16). This gate is on the east side of the city, overlooking the Kidron Valley. Not much is known about this part of the procession.

❧ THE WATER GATE ❧

To those of my generation, it is hard to hear the phrase *the water gate* without thinking of the infamous burglary of 1972. In this notorious event, political operatives broke into offices of the Democratic National Committee at the Watergate office complex in Washington, D.C. Apparently, they were looking for evidence to discredit the opposition and thus help reelect the incumbent president.

We know the aftermath: several men went to prison, and President Nixon resigned in 1974 to avoid impeachment. What an ironic clash of images: the Water Gate of Nehemiah's day was the place where "the ears of all the people were attentive unto the book of the law" (Nehemiah 8:1-3; see lesson 10); the Watergate of Nixon's day was the place where individuals acted as if they were above the law!

When one of Nehemiah's processionals arrived "unto the water gate eastward," the recent reading of God's law there undoubtedly came to mind for many. Mention of *Watergate* today can serve to remind us of the necessity of obeying the laws of both God and man (Romans 13:1-5).   —J. B. N.

38. And the other company of them that gave thanks went over against them, and I after them, and the half of the people upon the wall, from beyond the tower of the furnaces even unto the broad wall.

Nehemiah himself accompanies the second processional. The phrase *I after them* indicates that he follows rather than leads this group.

Dedication of the Wall

If the starting point is the Valley Gate, then the direction of march of *the other company* is clockwise since *the tower of the furnaces* is to the north (compare Nehemiah 3:11). The distance from the Valley Gate to this tower is about 200 yards. The word *furnaces* refers to ovens used for baking.

The broad wall beyond the tower is noted also in Nehemiah 3:8. Nehemiah 12:39 (not in today's text) mentions additional landmarks crossed, in reverse order from Nehemiah 3:1-11.

III. Dedication Praise
(Nehemiah 12:43)

43. Also that day they offered great sacrifices, and rejoiced: for God had made them rejoice with great joy: the wives also and the children rejoiced: so that the joy of Jerusalem was heard even afar off.

Nehemiah 12:40-42 (not in today's text) notes the gathering of the two processionals at the temple for singing after each completes its half-circuit of the city. Sacrifices are not required at this ceremony, but they are freely and joyfully given nonetheless. Indeed, the emphasis in the verse before us is *joy*, with forms of the words *rejoice* and *joy* used five times. The picture is one of religious exultation accompanied by trumpets (v. 41). Passages such as Psalm 48:12, 13 may reflect such processional celebrations (compare Psalm 68:24-27).

This celebration seems to surpass the earlier ones for the temple (Ezra 3:13; 6:16) and the reading of the law (Nehemiah 8:12, 17). The people have had several weeks to rest from their wall-building labor (compare Nehemiah 6:15 with 7:73b and 9:1). There is nothing to hinder those present from praising God at the top of their lungs!

> *What Do You Think?*
> Should our worship be loud enough to be heard literally "afar off"? Why, or why not?
> *Talking Points for Your Discussion*
> - Appropriate witness
> - Zoning restrictions
> - Danger of high decibel levels (hearing loss)
> - Other

❧ *Where Is Our Joy Heard?* ❧

Nehemiah records that the celebration of dedication was so exuberant that it "was heard even afar off." Exactly how far away was it heard? We aren't told, but historical counterparts provide some clues. During the great frontier revivals of the early 1800s, the sound of the religious "exercises" was noted as being heard some miles distant. The same was recorded of the revival meetings during the Great Awakening of the 1740s.

In his "Concord Hymn" of 1837, Ralph Waldo Emerson referred to the first military engagement of the American Revolution as the "shot heard round the world." This is literary license, of course, but the significance clear. Modern zoning restrictions and ordinances against "noise pollution" may restrict the volume levels of our worship services or even that of church bells. But any restriction regarding our joy being heard in the sense of a "shot heard round the world" is self-imposed. May people everywhere hear our joy!   —J. B. N.

Conclusion
A. Celebrations, Then and Now

The ancient Hebrews knew how to celebrate! Today, we have more reason to do so, since Jesus has been raised from the dead and is now reigning at God's right hand. The Jews of Nehemiah's day celebrated a rebuilt wall; we can celebrate the fact that Jesus tore down a wall (Ephesians 2:14-18).

We should look for ways to celebrate in Christ. New buildings can be dedicated, milestones acknowledged, and teachers honored. Earthly celebrations in Christ can spur us to greater tasks of faith as we look forward to the great celebration by God of the new Jerusalem (Revelation 21:2, 9). That celebration will never end.

B. Prayer

Father, teach us to rejoice! May the Holy Spirit inspire us to great tasks of faith that call for great rejoicing when completed. In the name of our Lord Jesus, whom we celebrate always, amen.

C. Thought to Remember

Great accomplishments call for celebration.

INVOLVEMENT LEARNING

Some of the activities below are also found in the helpful student book, Adult Bible Class.
Don't forget to download the free reproducible page from www.standardlesson.com to enhance your lesson!

Into the Lesson

Alternative 1. Place celebratory balloons around your classroom and have some confetti ready to toss as you begin (assuming you don't mind sweeping up after class). Blow a simple noisemaker and/or have volunteers ready to do so. Say excitedly, "It's time to celebrate! This is quite an accomplishment!" After allowing learners to react a bit, say, "Our study today takes us to an ancient celebration. It's party time!"

Alternative 2. Instead of the above, place in chairs copies of the "Celebrate Accomplishment" activity from the reproducible page, which you can download. This will help your learners get into the celebration mind-set of today's lesson.

Alternative 3. Give poles with colorful streamers attached to the top to two volunteers, one pole each. Ask these two to walk ceremoniously around the perimeter of your learning space in opposite directions; have ceremonial music playing. When the two volunteers meet, say, "This appears to be what our text describes: two groups marching along the walls of Jerusalem until they met at the temple (Nehemiah 12:40). Let's take a look."

Into the Word

Have ready 10 inflated (non-helium) balloons within which you have inserted the following 10 slips of paper, 1 each. (*Option:* Include a few pieces of confetti.) 1. Joyful music is appropriate for times of celebration. 2. Special music by skilled singers can be part of celebrations. 3. Those who lead or participate in worship need to think about personal purity. 4. Setting apart certain physical things as holy to the Lord can be a good idea. 5. Drawing attention to the names of some of God's people in a public assembly can be appropriate. 6. A formal ceremony can be a focusing element in times of corporate worship. 7. Consulting Scripture to discern requirements and precedent is always right. 8. Bringing sacrificial gifts on special

days of the Lord's people is a good thing. 9. Loudness in worship can be an acceptable form of witness. 10. Joy should characterize celebrations of significant accomplishment.

Say, "Today's text reveals a number of principles for expressing joy in worship." Ask a volunteer to take a balloon, burst it, and read the message inside. As the statement is read, ask the class, "Where in today's text do you see this idea?" Repeat this procedure until all 10 statements are read and discussed. The statements as numbered follow the verse order of today's text. Random popping will alter that order, so be prepared to confirm responses in that light. (You can add other truths or principles you see in the text.)

Into Life

Ask learners to help you brainstorm how you can plan and implement a special celebration for a significant accomplishment or milestone concerning your church. Some possibilities: recognition of your minister's service to the congregation (five-year anniversary, etc.), a thank-you dinner for those who have been a part of your church's life for a long time, a teacher-appreciation banquet, an anniversary celebration for the existence of the church itself, a behind-the-scenes service accomplishment (one-time or continuous) that calls for recognition.

If your class chooses to plan such an event, be sure to emphasize in the program the element of thanks to God for enabling the one(s) being recognized; that element will help your celebration parallel the one in today's text. The celebration your group chooses to plan and implement can be large or small, but any choice the class makes can reinforce the truths of today's study.

Option. Distribute copies of the "Let Your Joy Be Known" activity from the reproducible page. Encourage learners to pair off to discuss the questions together.

Dedication of the Wall

SABBATH
REFORMS

DEVOTIONAL READING: Mark 2:23-27
BACKGROUND SCRIPTURE: Nehemiah 13:4-31

NEHEMIAH 13:10-12, 15-22

10 And I perceived that the portions of the Levites had not been given them: for the Levites and the singers, that did the work, were fled every one to his field.

11 Then contended I with the rulers, and said, Why is the house of God forsaken? And I gathered them together, and set them in their place.

12 Then brought all Judah the tithe of the corn and the new wine and the oil unto the treasuries.

· ·

15 In those days saw I in Judah some treading wine presses on the sabbath, and bringing in sheaves, and lading asses; as also wine, grapes, and figs, and all manner of burdens, which they brought into Jerusalem on the sabbath day: and I testified against them in the day wherein they sold victuals.

16 There dwelt men of Tyre also therein, which brought fish, and all manner of ware, and sold on the sabbath unto the children of Judah, and in Jerusalem.

17 Then I contended with the nobles of Judah, and said unto them, What evil thing is this that ye do, and profane the sabbath day?

18 Did not your fathers thus, and did not our God bring all this evil upon us, and upon this city? yet ye bring more wrath upon Israel by profaning the sabbath.

19 And it came to pass, that when the gates of Jerusalem began to be dark before the sabbath, I commanded that the gates should be shut, and charged that they should not be opened till after the sabbath: and some of my servants set I at the gates, that there should no burden be brought in on the sabbath day.

20 So the merchants and sellers of all kind of ware lodged without Jerusalem once or twice.

21 Then I testified against them, and said unto them, Why lodge ye about the wall? if ye do so again, I will lay hands on you. From that time forth came they no more on the sabbath.

22 And I commanded the Levites that they should cleanse themselves, and that they should come and keep the gates, to sanctify the sabbath day. Remember me, O my God, concerning this also, and spare me according to the greatness of thy mercy.

KEY VERSE

I commanded the Levites that they should cleanse themselves, and that they should come and keep the gates, to sanctify the sabbath day. —**Nehemiah 13:22a**

GOD'S PEOPLE WORSHIP

LESSON AIMS

After participating in this lesson, each student will be able to:

1. Summarize how Nehemiah corrected the neglect of the temple and the abuses of the Sabbath day.

2. Explain how the Sabbath rules have significance for Christians.

3. Commit himself or herself to living a holy life by eliminating bad spiritual habits.

LESSON OUTLINE

Introduction

A. A Look Back

I am old enough to remember "blue laws," which restricted commerce on Sundays. Most businesses in my hometown did not open on that day so employees and patrons would be free to attend worship services and otherwise have a day of rest. Some adults in my small church spoke of the need to honor Sunday as "the Christian Sabbath." Others argued that the biblical Sabbath had nothing to do with the Christian's day of worship, Sunday (the Lord's Day). This difference in interpretation confused some of us.

Fifty years after my time as a teenager, most "blue laws" have been repealed or simply ignored. Sunday has become just another strong commercial day in the life of the average American. Many Christians think nothing of eating at a restaurant after worship on Sunday morning. Many of us find Sunday afternoon to be a convenient time to shop. With few exceptions, stores will be open for business on the Sundays of the year 2013.

Were "blue laws" ever appropriate? Is Sunday really "the Christian Sabbath"? Is the Jewish Sabbath still in force for Christians in some way? Such questions are important. But before they can be answered, we must understand the significance of the Sabbath as originally intended and ideally practiced in Old Testament times. That is one focus of today's lesson.

B. Lesson Background: Late Fifth-century BC

Nehemiah 12:44–13:31 is a unit devoted to telling how Nehemiah dealt with various problems among postexilic Jews after the dedication of Jerusalem's rebuilt walls (last week's lesson). First, Nehemiah 12:44-47 notes that provisions for priests and Levites had been put in place. The resources to do so came from the tithes, redemption of the firstborn, and firstfruits of the people (see Nehemiah 10:35-39; compare 2 Chronicles 31:19). Providing such support was not a new thing to the postexilic Jews; the reestablishment of such provisioning dated back to "the days of Zerubbabel" (Nehemiah 12:47), when the rebuilt temple was dedicated in 515 BC (Ezra 6:15-18).

Second, the people had been convicted by the Law of Moses regarding the need to separate themselves from foreigners. Ammonites and Moabites were of particular concern in this regard (Nehemiah 13:1-3; compare Deuteronomy 23:3-5).

But then Nehemiah took a leave of absence from Jerusalem to report back personally to King Artaxerxes in Babylon. The time indicators in Nehemiah 13:6 compute to about 433 BC as the year of Nehemiah's return to Jerusalem after 12 years away (compare Nehemiah 2:1; 5:14). On his return, he did not find things as he had left them!

C. Lesson Background: The Sabbath

The issue of Sabbath-keeping is an important issue in today's text, so a bit of background on this issue is called for. The word *Sabbath* means "ceasing," and the first references to this day as a day of rest (ceasing from labor) for the people are in Exodus 16:23-30. The basis for this "cease day" is Genesis 1:1–2:3. In imitation of their Creator, the ancient Israelites were to work six days but cease from their labors on the seventh day (Exodus 20:8-11). This requirement extended to foreigners residing among God's people and even to animals. This was part of a covenant sign (Exodus 31:13-17; Ezekiel 20:12).

Deuteronomy 5:12-14 repeats this requirement but adds another rationale: Israel's deliverance from the slavery of Egypt by the mighty hand of God (5:15). The people were no longer to work as they had in slavery; rather, they were to work only six days and cease all labor on the seventh day as a free people. Violating this law carried dire consequences (see Exodus 31:14, 15; Leviticus 26:2, 14-35; Ezekiel 20:13-24). Nehemiah knew all this.

HOW TO SAY IT

Ammonites	*Am*-un-ites.
Artaxerxes	Are-tuh-*zerk*-seez.
Moabites	*Mo*-ub-ites.
Phoenician	Fuh-*nish*-un.
Tobiah	Toe-*bye*-uh.
Tyre	Tire.
victuals	*vih*-tulz.
Zerubbabel	Zeh-*rub*-uh-bul.

I. Support Neglected
(NEHEMIAH 13:10-12)

A. Worship Deteriorates (v. 10)

10. And I perceived that the portions of the Levites had not been given them: for the Levites and the singers, that did the work, were fled every one to his field.

Nehemiah discovers a sad state of affairs on returning to Jerusalem after an absence of 12 years (see the Lesson Background). Without his strong oversight, the local leaders have allowed (or caused) support *for the Levites and the singers* to drop off. Nehemiah 13:5 indicates that the porters and the priests also go unsupported. This lack of support violates previous commitments (see Nehemiah 10:35-39; 12:44-47).

The two phrases *that did the work* and *were fled every one to his field* reveal the consequences of this failure to provide support. The Levites are responsible for the functioning of the temple (1 Chronicles 23:28-32). In anticipation of the construction of the temple by his son Solomon, the elderly King David had established that the duties of eligible Levites were to be divided this way: (1) about 63 percent "were to set forward the work of the house of the Lord," (2) about 16 percent "were officers and judges," (3) about 10.5 percent "were porters," and (4) about 10.5 percent "praised the Lord with the instruments" (23:3-5).

At least some of the tasks of the "officers and judges" of the second category involved duties outside Jerusalem (see 1 Chronicles 26:29). The "porters" of the third category were gatekeepers (26:13); their duties involved ministry "in the house of the Lord" (26:12). Supervision of singers apparently was included in the fourth category (see 15:22, 27).

Without this kind of temple leadership readily available, worship practices have deteriorated or disappeared altogether in Nehemiah's absence. Failure to support the worship leaders means that those leaders have to scramble about to provide for their livelihood—they are no longer able to attend to their temple duties as expected. This lack of support points to unbelief and selfishness as root causes.

❧ *A Modern Fable* ❧

Everyone knows that many stories told by preachers are fictional. Here is one I remember from my early days.

A church in a farming community was having great difficulty paying its bills. As a result, no one wanted to be the church treasurer. Finally, church leaders asked the manager of the local grain elevator to take the job. He did so on one condition: no one was allowed to ask him any questions for a whole year. The desperate church members agreed.

Before long the church's bills were current; then the church began to run a surplus. Everyone wondered how the treasurer did it, but they could ask no questions until the year was up. When that time came, he explained that whenever a church member who was a farmer brought grain to his elevator to sell, he withheld 10 percent of the proceeds for the church; he then paid the farmer the rest. They never knew the difference.

Some churches now allow (or encourage) members to use automatic debits to have their offerings transferred electronically to the church's account on a regular basis. This somewhat matches the above fable in that the giving occurs before the giver has a chance to spend the money elsewhere. Whether or not it's a good idea to put one's giving on "automatic pilot" like this is debatable. What is not debatable is the fact that many ministries and missions today are not adequately supported. How will you help correct this problem?   —J. B. N.

B. Leaders Confronted (v. 11a)

11a. Then contended I with the rulers, and said, Why is the house of God forsaken?

Nehemiah is not one to avoid needed confrontation (see Nehemiah 13:17, 21, 25), and he does not hesitate to confront those responsible for the deplorable situation: the rulers of Jerusalem. The implication of their failure is clear in Nehemiah's question *"Why is the house of God forsaken?"* The ultimate issue is deterioration or abandonment of worship practices as prescribed by God.

C. Situation Corrected (vv. 11b, 12)

11b. And I gathered them together, and set them in their place.

This statement refers to the Levites and singers of verse 10. Nehemiah brings them back to Jerusalem from their farms to resume their proper tasks (compare Nehemiah 7:1). This is the initial stage for keeping the Sabbath day properly—having the necessary worship leaders attending to their work.

12. Then brought all Judah the tithe of the corn and the new wine and the oil unto the treasuries.

Nehemiah must be a powerful personality to be able to move the Judeans to bring in *the tithe of the corn and the new wine and the oil*! This response implies repentance. At one time, my church challenged its members to tithe, not on the basis of law, but out of Christian love. We did well for a while, but soon we lapsed back into previous giving patterns. One would think that Christians would be motivated to give far more than a tithe (10 percent) on the basis of grace rather than a legalistic requirement. But as a whole, Christians can't seem to rise above a giving rate of 3 or 4 percent!

Nehemiah 13:13 (not in today's text) lists some names of those placed in charge of *the treasuries* that Nehemiah reestablishes for the assets (compare 1 Chronicles 26:20). To get these treasuries back to their proper functioning, Nehemiah 13:4-8 reveals that he first has to do some "housecleaning."

II. Sabbath Violated
(Nehemiah 13:15-22a)
A. Problem Noted (vv. 15, 16)

15. In those days saw I in Judah some treading wine presses on the sabbath, and bring-

Sabbath Reforms

ing in sheaves, and lading asses; as also wine, grapes, and figs, and all manner of burdens, which they brought into Jerusalem on the sabbath day: and I testified against them in the day wherein they sold victuals.

Nehemiah also observes a general disregard for the requirement to do no work on the Sabbath. Instead of resting, people are going about their daily routines of making wine, harvesting, packaging figs, etc. Some goods are loaded on donkeys for bringing into Jerusalem's market; this violates the requirement that animals also are to have a day of rest (Exodus 20:10; Deuteronomy 5:14).

Keeping the Sabbath as a day of rest acknowledges God as the Creator, who also rested on the seventh day (Exodus 20:11). When the Judeans act like all other nations by working on the Sabbath, they fail to acknowledge God as Creator and giver of all good things. The people are forgetting the prophetic warning given before the Babylonian exile: "If ye will not . . . hallow the sabbath day, and not to bear a burden, even entering in at the gates of Jerusalem on the sabbath day; then will I kindle a fire in the gates thereof, and it shall devour the palaces of Jerusalem" (Jeremiah 17:27).

16. There dwelt men of Tyre also therein, which brought fish, and all manner of ware, and sold on the sabbath unto the children of Judah, and in Jerusalem.

The *men of Tyre* are Phoenician merchants famous for their trading skills (see Isaiah 23:8; Ezekiel 27:3-9, 12-25; 28:4, 5). They establish merchant colonies in every possible area of economic advantage. The prophets saw Tyre negatively in relation to Israel (examples: Isaiah 23:17; Ezekiel 26:2). In the case at hand, the corrupting influence is the temptation to transact business on the Sabbath, a problem that hardly touches the conscience of a foreign merchant. Knowing the content of their merchandise from the verse before us, the transactions probably take place at the Fish Gate, located northwest of the temple mount.

B. Leaders Warned (vv. 17, 18)

17. Then I contended with the nobles of Judah, and said unto them, What evil thing is this that ye do, and profane the sabbath day?

Visual for Lesson 13. *Use these two statements to discuss the difference between* leadership *and* management *in the church today.*

Nehemiah goes straight to the source of the problem: *the nobles of Judah* (see Jeremiah 27:20; 39:6). These leaders had not been entirely supportive of Nehemiah's previous leadership in rebuilding Jerusalem's walls (see Nehemiah 6:17-19). They probably are profiting from the illicit trading that is being conducted. Nehemiah doesn't mince words: what they are doing is evil, and they are profaning the Sabbath.

A key theme in the Old Testament is God's desire that His people recognize and maintain the distinction between the holy and the unholy (Leviticus 10:10; Ezekiel 22:26; 44:23). The nobles of Judah aren't doing that. Their example will lead the people astray. Nehemiah, an extremely conscientious man, has to admonish men who are insensitive to the things of God. Sometimes people sin grievously without having even a twinge of a conscience (compare 1 Timothy 4:2).

> *What Do You Think?*
> In what ways is the Lord's Day profaned today? Or is the issue of profaning a certain day only an issue of the Old Testament era? Explain.
> *Talking Points for Your Discussion*
> - Romans 14:5
> - 1 Corinthians 11:17-22
> - Hebrews 10:25
> - James 2:1-4
> - Other

18. Did not your fathers thus, and did not our God bring all this evil upon us, and upon this city? yet ye bring more wrath upon Israel by profaning the sabbath.

Nehemiah's rebuke of the nobles of Judah includes a history lesson: past leaders of Jerusalem had neglected the Sabbath and had suffered the wrath of God as a result. Prophets had issued warnings concerning the profaning of the Sabbath (see Jeremiah 17:19-27; Ezekiel 20:13; 23:38). The Babylonian exile is "Exhibit A" in testifying to Judah's punishment in this regard.

Since the Sabbath is a sign of the covenant (Exodus 31:13), then keeping the Sabbath holy (Deuteronomy 5:12) is equivalent to keeping the covenant (see Isaiah 56:1-8). Those who have returned from exile are in danger of experiencing God's wrath anew for the very same offense of their ancestors: violating the Sabbath day.

C. Procedures Altered (v. 19)

19. And it came to pass, that when the gates of Jerusalem began to be dark before the sabbath, I commanded that the gates should be shut, and charged that they should not be opened till after the sabbath: and some of my servants set I at the gates, that there should no burden be brought in on the sabbath day.

Nehemiah takes action to ensure proper Sabbath observance: he uses his personal guards *(some of my servants)* to make certain that *the gates of Jerusalem* are shut at sundown on Fridays, since that is when the Sabbath begins. These gates remain shut throughout the Sabbath to prevent merchants with laden animals from entering the city.

> **What Do You Think?**
>
> What "gates" do you need to shut in some ways and open in other ways to serve and worship the Lord acceptably? How will you do that?
>
> *Talking Points for Your Discussion*
> - Gates of your eyes and ears (Acts 28:26-28)
> - Gate of your tongue (James 3:1-12)
> - Gate of your house (2 John 10; 3 John 8)
> - Gate of your bank account (2 Corinthians 9:6-15)
> - Other

Apparently, some gates of the city are more profitable for commercial enterprise than others (Fish Gate, etc.), and these may receive special attention. The gates of ancient cities are built with rooms opening up to plazas so that plenty of traffic can go in and out daily. The plazas serve as marketplaces. A good example of this today is the Damascus Gate of the Old City of Jerusalem. Any tourist having been there can confirm this.

D. Resolve Tested (vv. 20-22a)

20. So the merchants and sellers of all kind of ware lodged without Jerusalem once or twice.

The merchants and sellers who camp just outside the city are probably foreigners. If Jews are involved, they definitely are desecrating the Sabbath by doing this. To make sense of this verse requires that we understand that individuals are still able to come and go through the gates (since smaller doors are provided), but not beasts of burdens. The vendors are trying to entice people to come outside to trade in spite of the closed gates. They do this only a couple of times before Nehemiah warns them (next verse).

21. Then I testified against them, and said unto them, Why lodge ye about the wall? if ye do so again, I will lay hands on you. From that time forth came they no more on the sabbath.

Again we see the confrontational part of Nehemiah's personality as he poses a rhetorical question: *"Why lodge ye about the wall?"* The phrase *lay hands on* means that Nehemiah threatens the merchants with arrest by his authority as governor. He has the authority to deal with them as he did with Tobiah in Nehemiah 13:4-8. Perhaps the memory of that action is why the merchants desist.

22a. And I commanded the Levites that they should cleanse themselves, and that they should come and keep the gates, to sanctify the sabbath day.

Nehemiah now applies a permanent solution to "the merchant problem": he orders the Levites to *cleanse themselves* in order to guard the city gates on the Sabbath (compare 1 Chronicles 26:12-19). Jerusalem is "the holy city" (see Nehemiah 11:18; Isaiah 52:1). From this point on, no one will sell or buy on the Sabbath. Nehemiah is determined that the remnant of exiles become God's renewed people and that the Sabbath be sanctified as a sign of the covenant. Otherwise, history will repeat itself!

What Do You Think?

What challenges will you have to overcome to protect one day each week as "a personal Sabbath" for rest and renewal?

Talking Points for Your Discussion

- "He who cannot rest, cannot work."
    —Harry Emerson Fosdick (1878–1969)
- "True silence is the rest of the mind."
    —William Penn (1644–1718)

❧ OUR CONTINUING CHALLENGE ❧

Several years ago, a friend who was a union carpenter told me of an interesting experience she had had (yes, this carpenter was female). Union rules stipulated that carpenters did not have to work in the rain. But what exactly constitutes rain? And how could that be determined easily on a work site?

The decision was that the presence of rain could be verified with a book of paper matches. If 10 drops fell on an open book of matches within a minute, that was rain. Otherwise, the carpenters had to keep working. Wherever there is a legal system, there will always be legalistic definitions!

Nehemiah's concern was to maintain the holiness of the Sabbath day, in keeping with the Fourth Commandment. Jesus shared the same concern in His disputes with the Pharisees. It was never the Fourth Commandment itself that Jesus objected to, but the legalistic interpretations that the Pharisees had added (Mark 2:23-28). The point of the Fourth Commandment is not to set up a legalistic system, but to help the people remember God and keep holy what He had made holy. That challenge continues to confront us.   —J. B. N.

III. Petition Made

(NEHEMIAH 13:22b)

22b. Remember me, O my God, concerning this also, and spare me according to the greatness of thy mercy.

This is the ninth of 11 prayers mentioned in this book; the other 10 are noted in Nehemiah 1:5-11; 2:4b; 4:4, 5; 4:9; 5:19; 6:9b; 6:14; 13:14; 13:29; and 13:31b. *Remember* is a key word in several of these prayers. Nehemiah may be thinking of a "book of remembrance" such as we see mentioned in Malachi 3:16 (compare Exodus 32:32; Psalm 139:16). This idea is strengthened by Nehemiah's request that God "remember me . . . and wipe not out my good deeds" in Nehemiah 13:14.

What Do You Think?

How would you complete a prayer that begins "Remember me, O my God, concerning ____"?

Talking Points for Your Discussion

- Regarding something completed
- Regarding something yet to be completed

Conclusion

A. Past, Present, Future

Nehemiah's reforms honored the Sabbath as a sign of the covenant with God. What about today? The basis of Sabbath-keeping is that God rested on the seventh day of creation. Today we celebrate the new creation in Christ (2 Corinthians 5:17). We "serve in newness of spirit, and not in the oldness of the letter" (Romans 7:6); those in Christ "are not under the law, but under grace" (6:14).

To be under grace is not a license for lawlessness (Romans 6:1, 2; 2 Peter 3:17; Jude 4), but certain requirements of the Old Testament law no longer apply. These include Sabbath-keeping (see Colossians 2:16). Even so, the principle of resting at least one day a week is good and humanitarian. Also, our Christian liberty requires that we be tolerant of those who honor certain days above others (see Romans 14:5, 6). We also keep in mind that the ultimate Sabbath-rest awaits us at Jesus' return.

B. Prayer

O God, may we honor You daily! As we labor, help us anticipate that great day when we will rest with You eternally. In Jesus' name, amen.

C. Thought to Remember

Honor God in days of work and rest.

INVOLVEMENT LEARNING

Some of the activities below are also found in the helpful student book, Adult Bible Class.
Don't forget to download the free reproducible page from www.standardlesson.com to enhance your lesson!

Into the Lesson

Have the word *Stewardship* displayed prominently on the board as learners arrive. Below it have the question, "What does this involve?" As each learner enters the room, ask him or her to jot a quick response below the question (have extra markers available, all black in color).

When all have had a chance to write an answer, use a marker in a color other than black to circle all those dealing with management of time. Then use a marker of a different color to circle answers dealing with use of talent or spiritual gifts. Finally, use a marker of yet another color to circle answers dealing with money. Say, "Today, we're going to see all three categories discussed—*time* in terms of the Sabbath day, *talent* in terms of worship leadership, and *money* in relation to the other two."

Into the Word

Display this question: "Why is the house of God _____?" Ask learners to suggest words to complete the question. This question is asked in Nehemiah 13:11, and learners familiar with it may voice the scriptural answer *forsaken;* other responses may include *empty, shabby,* and *disrespected.* Let learners react briefly to suggestions. After you affirm the scriptural answer, note Nehemiah's concern in asking the question: those who were to lead worship were unable to do so because they lacked financial support (Nehemiah 13:10, 11).

Read aloud today's text. Use the following question pairs to elicit answers from the text and to suggest solutions to parallel problems of today.

1. How was the lack of financial support for the worship leaders affecting their ability to do their duties in Nehemiah's day (vv. 10, 11)? How does the lack of similar support hinder the kingdom of Christ today?

2. How did "all Judah" respond to Nehemiah's appeal (v. 12)? In your church experience, when have you seen a similar response?

3. What wrong behaviors were the people engaged in on the Sabbath (vv. 15, 16)? Should commerce on the Lord's Day, Sunday, bother us?

4. How were non-Jews contributing to the sin (vv. 16, 20)? How do the ungodly of our culture tempt us to forsake worship on the Lord's Day?

5. What steps did Nehemiah take to reinstitute proper observance of the Sabbath (vv. 17-21)? How can we make sure to honor the Lord on His day, Sunday?

6. What did Nehemiah require of the worship leaders (v. 22a)? What parallel expectations should we have for worship leaders of our day?

7. What were the two requests that Nehemiah made in his prayer to God (v. 22b)? How can you make Nehemiah's prayer your own?

Alternative. Instead of the above discussion-question activity, distribute copies of the "Sanctified Sabbath, Sanctified Life" activity from the reproducible page, which you can download. Learners can complete this in small groups.

Into Life

Say, "Sabbath observance is not a requirement today (Colossians 2:16; etc.). Even so, the Sabbath principle of *rest* still has great value for several reasons." Distribute handouts that looks like this:

Remember _____!
Experience _____!
See _____!
Turn from _____!

Continue: "Complete this handout in terms of what rest helps you *remember, experience, see,* and *turn from* in your service to God." Allow time for sharing results.

Give each learner a copy of the "Checkup on Spiritual Habits" activity from the reproducible page. Since the responses this activity calls for are very personal in nature, you can use it as a silent meditative exercise just before the closing prayer.